Consciousness and Loneliness: Theoria and Praxis

# Value Inquiry Book Series

*Founding Editor*

Robert Ginsberg

*Executive Editor*

Leonidas Donskis†

*Managing Editor*

J.D. Mininger

VOLUME 327

---

# Cognitive Science

*Edited by*

Francesc Forn i Argimon

The titles published in this series are listed at *brill.com/vibs* and *brill.com/cosc*

# Consciousness and Loneliness:
# Theoria and Praxis

*By*

Ben Lazare Mijuskovic

BRILL

RODOPI

LEIDEN | BOSTON

Cover illustration: *Melancholy* (1893). Oil on canvas. Painted by Edvard Munch. Photographed by Athenium Commons. Retrieved by Edvard Munch Museet, Oslo, Norway. The illustration is in the Public Domain.

Library of Congress Cataloging-in-Publication Data

Names: Mijuskovic, Ben Lazare, author.
Title: Consciousness and loneliness : theoria and praxis / by Ben Mijuskovic.
Description: Leiden ; Boston : Brill Rodopi, [2019] | Series: Value inquiry book series, ISSN 0929-8436 ; VOLUME 327 | Series: Cognitive science | Includes bibliographical references and index.
Identifiers: LCCN 2018047331 (print) | LCCN 2018049634 (ebook) | ISBN 9789004385979 (E-book) | ISBN 9789004375642 (pbk. : alk. paper)
Subjects: LCSH: Loneliness--Philosophy. | Consciousness.
Classification: LCC B105.L65 (ebook) | LCC B105.L65 M53 2019 (print) | DDC 155.9/2--dc23
LC record available at https://lccn.loc.gov/2018047331

Typeface for the Latin, Greek, and Cyrillic scripts: "Brill". See and download: brill.com/brill-typeface.

ISSN 0929-8436
ISBN 978-90-04-37564-2 (paperback)
ISBN 978-90-04-38597-9 (e-book)

Copyright 2019 by Koninklijke Brill NV, Leiden, The Netherlands.
Koninklijke Brill NV incorporates the imprints Brill, Brill Hes & De Graaf, Brill Nijhoff, Brill Rodopi, Brill Sense, Hotei Publishing, mentis Verlag, Verlag Ferdinand Schöningh and Wilhelm Fink Verlag.
All rights reserved. No part of this publication may be reproduced, translated, stored in a retrieval system, or transmitted in any form or by any means, electronic, mechanical, photocopying, recording or otherwise, without prior written permission from the publisher.
Authorization to photocopy items for internal or personal use is granted by Koninklijke Brill NV provided that the appropriate fees are paid directly to The Copyright Clearance Center, 222 Rosewood Drive, Suite 910, Danvers, MA 01923, USA. Fees are subject to change.

This book is printed on acid-free paper and produced in a sustainable manner.

I would rather be in Hell with Ruth than in Heaven without her.

What has been will be again, what has been done will be done again, there is nothing new under the sun,
> *Ecclesiastes,* 1:9

# Contents

By Way of a Prologue     XI

### PART 1

1    Introduction to the Simplicity Argument and its Relation to Previous Studies    3

2    The Simplicity Argument: Meanings, Relations, and Space    64

3    The Simplicity Argument and the Freedom of Consciousness    137

4    The Simplicity Argument and Immanent Time-Consciousness    203

5    The Simplicity Argument and the Quality of Consciousness    245

6    Neuromania and Neo-Phrenology versus Consciousness    287

### PART 2

7    The Simplicity Argument versus a Materialist Theory of Mind    323

### PART 3

8    The Bicameral Mind, the Abyss, and Underworlds    365

9    Loneliness: In Harm's Way    403

10    Metaphysical Dualism, Subjective Idealism, and Existentialism    431

By Way of an Epilogue    445

Bibliography    446
Name Index    459
Subject Index    476

# By Way of a Prologue

*Into the mists of time, the reveries come drifting and sifting back through consciousness enhanced by old, faded photographs and filtered through the decaying memories of a slight boy of two-years sitting with a girl of similar age in a pony cart at the Budapest zoo; of two older children at the Russian Embassy mocking him from their balcony as he bids goodbye to his "Maman"; of his mother driving her convertible into the back of a hay wagon; of a larger than life portrait of King Alexander of Yugoslavia on the second-floor landing of the Embassy; of a German governess named Bette caring for him; and it was 1939; of a descent into the cavernous Catacombs in Jerusalem, where his mother bought a tin icon with little doors that opened displaying a coin of Mary the Mother of Jesus; of a seaplane skimming the shiny, sun-lit surface of the Dead Sea as it lands on the placid waters; of the strange sensation of bathing in its briny element; and it was 1940; of living with both his parents for a short while at the Gabalaya House, a British military residence in Cairo; of the officers eating alone in the large dining hall while reading a book and silently spooning their soup; of a photograph of him sitting with his mother on a camel while his father held the reins with a pyramid and the Sphinx couchant framing the background; of his father in a military uniform at the Gezira Country Club with its luxurious swimming pools, racetrack, polo and cricket fields, tennis courts, and the seemingly endless myriads of Egyptian servants constantly milling about prepared to be of immediate service; of moving into an apartment in a very tall building with his mother; of his father's absence for extended periods of time; of his mother's anxiety and frequent migraines; of the shrill, angry sounds of sirens signaling nightly bombing raids that never materialized; of passengers hurriedly abandoning streetcars in the dark; of frightened scurrying figures running toward underground shelters; of clutching his teddy bear and crowding with his mother into an elevator and descending into the bowels of the building; of being jostled and pushed and reaching out in the darkness for his mother's absent hand; of not understanding the language or gestures of other children or his cultural surroundings; and it was 1941; of the kindly Egyptian janitor who gifted him a child's fez and a little prayer rug for his personal use; of attending a French school and being too shy and embarrassed to ask the teacher to be excused so he could go to the bathroom and later walking miserably home along the Nile with the soiled contents clinging to his short pants; of disjointed images and photographs of him and his parents on the deck of a large ship sailing on the Black Sea en route to Odessa; of picking fruit from a fig tree on a second-floor balcony in Beirut; of visiting the medieval citadel in Damascus where the Moslem defenders poured boiling oil on the Christian invaders as they tried to scale the walls on tall ladders; and it was Cairo 1943 with its frightening, permeating atmosphere of the Second World War coloring all aspects of his existence as his imagination was invaded with spectral fears; of the anguish and the isolating strangeness of his conscious being; and it was still Cairo 1944; and then unexpectedly leaving the city for the Embassy in Ankara as the war was winding down; of attending an international school for French-speaking foreign children; of suddenly departing from the city and flying to Washington on an American B-49 military bomber; and it was the winter of 1944 and Germany was losing and hearing the words, "It is finished" echoing in his thoughts.*

*A dozen years later, as an undergraduate student at the University of Chicago, while rummaging aimlessly in Harper Library, he found a novel and became fascinated with its story about young Eugene Gant in Thomas Wolfe's* Look Homeward, Angel. *He was enrolled in an English composition course and doing rather poorly but the book suggested a unique theme—loneliness—and he composed the next week's essay assignment along its outlines. At the end of the next class session, the teacher asked if he would see her for a moment before leaving and when the room was emptied of all its students, she asked him if he would consider seeing someone at Student Health.*

# PART 1

CHAPTER 1

# Introduction to the Simplicity Argument and its Relation to Previous Studies

> The safest characterization of the European philosophical tradition is that it consists of a series of footnotes to Plato.
> ALFRED NORTH WHITEHEAD

∴

The following treatise concerns a special theory of consciousness and its application to human loneliness. In terms of a methodology, it follows along the lines of the History of Ideas discipline, which was originally instituted in the early part of the twentieth century under the aegis of Johns Hopkins University by A.O. Lovejoy and George Boas. In the ensuing years, it was emulated by other institutions of higher learning, including the Ideas and Methods and the Committee on Social Thought programs at the University of Chicago, the History of Ideas at Brandeis University, and the History of Consciousness at the University of California at Santa Cruz as well as various other universities all implementing different combinations, concentrations, and approaches between the disciplines.

It consists in an attempt to implement an interdisciplinary perspective by emphasizing certain strains of metaphysical dualism and subjective idealism and then applying these tenets to a substantive theory of the self and the innate quality of human loneliness. It concentrates on a historically important paradigm of the mind, grounded in a premise asserting that consciousness is *both* immaterial *and* active and more specifically that it exhibits a reflexive form of self-consciousness as well as the transcendent features of a purposive intentionality. It is a sequel to four previous efforts by the author, *The Achilles of Rationalist Arguments: The Simplicity, Unity, and Identity of Thought and Soul from the Cambridge Platonists to Kant; Loneliness in Philosophy, Psychology, and Literature; Contingent Immaterialism: Meaning, Freedom, Time, and Mind;* and *Feeling Lonesome: The Philosophy and Psychology of Loneliness,* with all four studies designed to coalesce in supporting a theory of consciousness in relation to human loneliness.

By their very nature interdisciplinary studies assume that there are certain principles and paradigms that are so central in Western thought that their themes are best explored in unison with other related disciplines thereby enhancing the possibility of comprehensive insights within the participating inter-related fields.

Against the combination of reductive materialism and naïve empiricism, the present study contends that these dual perspectives are unable to account adequately for the activity of human consciousness, the reality of the self, and its inescapable sense of an enclosed subjective isolation. It further seeks to coherently integrate the various intertwined filaments of dualism, rationalism, and idealism, which are threaded throughout the many historical conceptions of the self found in the Greek psyche, the Christian soul, the Cartesian cogito, the Leibnizian monad, German idealism, Husserlian phenomenology, and Sartrean existentialism, which mutually conclude in portraying human consciousness as inevitably lonely. The work defends a substantive concept of the self, while offering a theory of cognitive consciousness coupled with a psychology of motivational drives animated by the fear of loneliness and the consequent desire for shared intimacy. While defending this view, it criticizes and rejects the underlying assumptions in regard to the alternate model of the "self" presented in the related movements of materialism, mechanism, determinism, empiricism, phenomenalism, behaviorism, and the current vogue of reductivism and ethical relativism so evident in the neurosciences.

But first let me begin by addressing a distinction suggested by Kant between the *Critique of Pure Reason* employing the synthetic or progressive method of proof, as opposed to the *Prolegomena to Any Future Metaphysics,* which rather summons the analytic or regressive approach (Sections 263–64, 274–75, 278–79, 283–284) by recruiting his distinction for my own purposes. The difference is highlighted by a passage in Kemp Smith.

> The synthetic method would start from given, ordinary experience (in its simplest form, as consciousness of time), to discover its conditions, and from them to prove the validity of knowledge that is *a priori*. The analytic method would start "from the sought as if it were given," that is, from the existence of *a priori* synthetic judgments, and, assuming them as valid, would determine the conditions under which alone such validity can be possible.[1]

Thus there are two ways to address the problem of cognition. We can simply start with human consciousness—"in its simplest form, as consciousness of

---

1  Norman Kemp Smith, *A Commentary to Kant's 'Critique of Pure Reason'* (New York: Humanities Press, 1962), 43 ff.; hereafter cited as Kemp Smith, *Commentary.*

time"—and then proceed by amplifying on the *a priori* synthetic judgments that form the base. Or we can begin with the validity of scientific knowledge and mathematics and then move regressively backward by explicating the conditions under which alone such validity is possible. In other words, in the *Critique* Kant seeks to show how human consciousness is not only possible but necessary by exploring its transcendental conditions, whereas in the *Prolegomena,* he assumes the genuineness of certain *a priori* knowledge in mathematics and physics and proceeds accordingly. A further distinction can be made. In the First Preface to the *Critique,* Kant promises to outline the *conditions* under which ordinary experience and science can be objectively validated but he also suggests that there is an even more fundamental issue: How is consciousness itself possible? It is this second consideration that will consume our attention.

In my first studies on loneliness, I simply *assumed* its universality as a negative psychological first principle, something to be avoided, and then went on to argue for self-consciousness as its primary constitutive condition, while in the present work, I intend *to begin* with the earliest and most primitive forms of consciousness and then proceed to the conclusion that humans are innately and inevitably lonely. In brief, there are two very different ways to prove something. Either one can travel backward from an assumed conclusion to its premises, the explicative method; or one can move forward from an indisputable starting point in consciousness—time-consciousness—in order to arrive at a conclusion, the ampliative method. In the present text, I have chosen the latter and more difficult path but hopefully it will prove to be the more rewarding option.

In prior publications, including articles and books, I sought both historically and conceptually to trace the prevalence and influence of a single philosophical premise, or if one prefers, an assumption, namely that the mind is *both* immaterial *and* active, in order to document its frequent use as it appears throughout the conceptual history of Western philosophy in a set of four distinct arguments ending in an equal number of different conclusions. These combined invocations are found in Kant's first edition *Critique of Pure Reason,* in the Paralogisms of Pure Reason section of the Transcendental Dialectic (1781). Interestingly and significantly enough, the four arguments, all based on a single premise, are deleted and completely recast anew in the second edition (1787). The term "pure" in the title signifies their grounding in non-sensuous, non-empirical *acts* of consciousness culminating in four separate conclusions. The quartet of proofs is regarded by Kant as illusory metaphysical fallacies generated when reason is left unrestricted by the bounds of sensuous experience. The Second Paralogism, which is especially important and controversial, Kant christens the "Achilles," the most powerful of all rationalist doctrines pertaining to the activities of the soul. Historically, since the time of Plato and Neo-Platonism, these four demonstrations have served dualist, rationalist, and idealist philosophers as a formidable arsenal against materialism and empiricism. Nevertheless, for all four Paralogisms Kant systematically shows how reason, without adequate empirical criteria or supports, fails in its attempt to generate metaphysical truths that transcend human experience and what can be legitimately scientifically confirmed. Although the Paralogisms present *meaningful* theses, they illegitimately go beyond the possibility of any *empirical* confirmation or verification. Thus they stand self-condemned by their inability to furnish empirical criteria or proofs for their assertions. It is important to note in this context, however, that Kant's criticisms are different from those of the logical positivists and analytic philosophers, who reject these metaphysical proofs as inherently *meaningless* and in principle unverifiable because they cannot be tested empirically. By contrast, Kant believes they are *meaningful* assertions but nevertheless disprovable, although he continues to entertain the *conceivability* that they still may be true in a noumenal realm of "things-in-themselves," in some unspecified transcendent reality. Later Kant, in the *Critique of Practical Reason,* bases his ethical philosophy on the *conceivability* of the existence of God; the freedom of the will; and the immortality of the soul as articles of faith. But in any case, the four Paralogisms stand completely empty of any sensuous content and therefore they cannot be tested nor can they provide any scientific information. Kant thus distinguishes *transcendent* metaphysical propositions or judgments, which cannot be empirically confirmed, from *transcendental* epistemic knowledge, which legitimately lies at the base of all human experience thus supporting both our ordinary and scientific consciousness and human experience in general.

The Second Paralogism, *Of Simplicity,* is especially subjected to damning criticism by Kant.

> This is the Achilles of all dialectical [i.e., fallacious] inferences in the pure [rational, non-empirical] doctrine of the soul. It is no mere sophistical play contrived by a dogmatist [i.e., rationalist] in order to impart to his assertions a superficial plausibility, but an inference which appears to withstand even the keenest scrutiny and the most scrupulously exact investigation. It is as follows. Every *composite* [material] substance is an aggregate of several substances, and the action of a composite, or whatever inheres in it as thus composite, is an aggregate of several actions or accidents distributed among the plurality of the substances. Now an effect which arises from the concurrence of many acting substances is indeed possible, namely, when this effect is external only (as, for instance, the motion of a body is the combined motion of all its [physical] parts).

But with thoughts, as internal accidents belonging to a thinking being, it is different. For suppose it be the composite that thinks; then every part of it would be a part of the thought, and all of them taken together would contain the whole thought. But this cannot consistently be maintained. For [immaterial] representations (for instance, the single words of a verse), distributed among different beings, never make up a whole thought (a verse), and it is therefore impossible that a thought should inhere in what is essentially composite. It is therefore possible only in a *single* [i.e., simple, immaterial] substance, which, not being an aggregate of many, is absolutely simple.[2]

The controlling premise is that what is simple is immaterial and hence a unity. It is also important to notice that the argument doubles as both an argument against "dogmatic" or Leibnizian rationalism as well as indirectly against classical materialism and the "modern Epicureans," whose movement was gaining increasing prominence in the scientific world of the seventeenth- and eighteenth-centuries.

Prior to Kant, the "Achilles" argument had been consistently recruited by rationalist philosophers from Plato and Plotinus to the Cambridge Platonists and Leibniz in order to conclude that the "unity of self-consciousness" is only possible on the condition that the soul is *both* immaterial *and* active. While Plato's Forms are taken to be immaterial and unchanging, the soul was not only conceived as immaterial but also actively *self*-moving as well. In Platonic thought, it is this *dynamis,* this activity, which allows the soul to seek and attain a cognitive unification with a transcendent realm of realities predicated on the basis that *both* the soul *and* the Forms share in an attribute that is essential to each as well as common to both, namely immateriality. Metaphysically, however, the critical question revolves around a single question: *"Can senseless matter think?"* This issue will be the primary focus of my concern throughout all that follows.

---

2 Immanuel Kant, *Critique of Pure Reason,* translated by Norman Kemp Smith (London: Macmillan & Co., 1962), Second Paralogism, *Of Simplicity,* A 351–352; hereafter cited as Kant, CPR. The Second Paralogism is in turn related to the Second Antinomy, which dialectically argues pro and contra whether the universe is composed of immaterial simple monads (basically Leibniz's "spiritual atoms") or whether it consists of material compounds (Locke's Epicurean insensible particles). In the article on Kant, the *Stanford Encyclopedia of Philosophy* relates the simplicity versus compound issue to the opposing views of Plato and Epicurus as well as to refer to Leibniz and Locke. Further it is to be noted that the "internal accidents" referred to above are assumed to be both immaterial and active by the "rational psychologists" Kant is criticizing.

The First Paralogism argues for the soul as an independent substance, roughly Descartes position; the Second Paralogism, strongly reminiscent of Leibniz, infers the soul's unity of consciousness as deriving from its immaterial nature in the A edition, as in the quotation indicated above (1781), and in behalf of the soul's immortality in the substituted B edition (1787); the Third Paralogism similarly addresses Leibniz's conception regarding the continuous temporal identity of the self thus offering a criterion for personal, i.e., moral identity; and the Fourth Paralogism essentially provides a proof for the *apparent* ideal nature of an "external reality," of "outer things" as generated by the illusory *appearance* of spatial objects existing independently of the mind. Kant's "critical" transcendental and positive answer to the Fourth Paralogism actually depends on his celebrated Copernican Revolution, which contends that the noumenal realm of "things-in-themselves" must "conform" to the ideal structures, the *a priori* synthetic categories "spontaneously" generated by the activities of the mind (Kant, *Critique,* B xxiii).

All four Paralogisms are predicated on the premise that the soul is both immaterial and active, which is essentially a Platonic and neo-Platonic theory but nevertheless shares a critical feature with Aristotle's *reflexive* conception of the Unmoved Mover—the activity of thought thinking itself (*Meta.*, 1075a). This principle and paradigm will follows us throughout the text as well.

Once more, Kant rejects all four demonstrations, despite their seductiveness, as fallacies on the ground of their shared belief that rational, i.e., non-empirical or *a priori* knowledge is attainable concerning a metaphysical self and its relation to a transcendent realm of noumenal "things-in-themselves."

The immateriality premise, with its four separate conclusions, has historically exerted and continues to influence thinkers beyond Kant in Western thought. The assumption, which ultimately derives from Plato's *Phaedo* (78b ff.), continues to shape certain critical philosophical discussions ever since the Hellenic Age. The form of the argument is fairly straightforward. The essential nature of the soul consists in its ability to think; consciousness, or thought, being immaterial is unextended, i.e., simple, without parts; and what is both *simple* and *active* is intrinsically (a) a substance; (b) a unity; (c) a continuous (personal or moral) identity; and therefore (d) it constitutes the soul's *ideal* relation to an "external" realm of seemingly "spatial" and "material" existences. Such are the strengths imputed to the soul by the dualist, rationalist, and idealist traditions prior to Kant. In general, Kant's criticism of the Paralogisms is primarily directed at Leibniz's monadological metaphysics representing the culmination of rationalist thought in the West (*Monadology,* Sections 1–21).

However, in Plato's version of metaphysical dualism, which is offered in the *Phaedo* and the *Republic,* although humans possess both a physical body and an immaterial soul, it is the soul as a "pure," non-empirical entity that alone guarantees its substantial reality, continuity, and eventual immortality. Against this Platonic doctrine of an immaterial soul, the atomistic materialism of Leucippus and Democritus stand in opposition. The metaphysical disagreement between the two schools of thought leads Plato to comment on the much larger context of the controversy by referring to it as the Battle between the Gods and the Giants, between the Idealists and the Materialists as expressed in Plato's *Sophist* (245e-246e). Basically Plato's description of the conflict between the two camps characterizes the entire on-going struggle in Western thought between religion and humanism, on the one side, and science on the other.[3]

The controversy over "whether senseless matter can think?" is one of the most ancient and important arguments in the History of Ideas, as it concentrates on the nature of human consciousness and continues into our present Age. It is a struggle between two prevailing constellations of thought: dualism, rationalism, idealism, phenomenology, and existentialism versus materialism, mechanism, determinism, empiricism, phenomenalism, behaviorism, and our current neurosciences. It pits Plato against Democritus; Plotinus against Epicurus; Augustine and Aquinas against Skeptics and Atheists; Ficino against Valla; Descartes against Hobbes; Leibniz against Locke; Kant against Hume; Hegel against Marx; F.H. Bradley against J.S. Mill; Husserl and Sartre against D.M. Armstrong and Gilbert Ryle; and H.D. Lewis and Richard Swinburne against B.F. Skinner and Daniel Dennett. Whereas the Gods assert the reality of the self, reflexive self-consciousness, and transcendent intentionality, the Giants on their side defend the primacy of the brain and the assorted mechanisms of the central nervous system. As the counter-dialogues continue to unfold, it will pit the spontaneity of consciousness against the determinism of science.

It is possible, of course, to add other philosophical dimensions beyond the dualistic schema I am proposing. For example, Wilhelm Dilthey distinguishes three fundamental types of world views (*Weltanschauungen*): materialism (Hobbes); subjective idealism (Kant); and objective idealism (Hegel), each offering a different perspective on consciousness, reality, and values. The first consists of naturalism or materialism, which interprets the world as logically unified through a system of cause and effect relationships. The second is connected to subjective idealism, or the philosophy of freedom, which comprehends the world as unified by the imposition of an order forced upon it

---

[3] (Plato, *Sophist,* 245e-246e). Cf. Francis Macdonald Cornford, *Plato's Theory of Knowledge* (London: Routledge & Kegan Paul, 1964). See pages 228–232 for Cornford's comments on the eternal Battle between the Gods and the Giants as essentially consisting in the conflict between the idealists and the materialists.

through the moral strivings of the human will. And the third, that of objective idealism, springs from an intuition of an underlying cosmic harmony in which the apparent antinomies, contradictions, and conflicts are ultimately reconciled and resolved.

There is also Spinoza's "double aspect" theory, which proposes to solve the mind-body problem by interpreting the body and the mind as two sides of the same "coin" (substance) and the closely related later theories of neutral monism propounded by William James, Bertrand Russell, and A.J. Ayer, admittedly neither of which readily fits my dualistic schematic.

I have charted the course and force of all four paralogistic arguments from their initial uses in ancient Greek and Roman philosophy and then later on into Christian theology, the Italian and English Renaissances, and ending in the seventeenth- and eighteenth-centuries and more specifically from the Cambridge Platonists to Kant, a period during which the proofs become vitally important in the metaphysical, epistemological, religious, and ethical controversies of the time as they involve such issues as (1) the immortality of the human soul; (2) the "transcendental" conditions necessary for the unity of consciousness (or the rationalist premise that the soul *essentially* expresses a unifying immaterial activity in order for consciousness to exist and function as a unity); (3) the necessary and sufficient criterion for the establishment of personal or moral identity; and (4) its use as *the* major premise for metaphysical dualism and epistemological and ontological idealism. Thus if one assumes that active souls and thoughts are immaterial and directly, immediately *present* "to" or "within" consciousness, then it becomes problematic how an unextended soul, self, mind, or ego could conceivably "know" or "interact" with a material, extended, "external world" existing independently and separately from consciousness; or how the soul can have any possible commerce or interaction with the world or any knowledge of other minds. If the two realms—mind and matter, soul and body—share no common property, attribute, or predicate in common, it *necessarily* follows that any direct knowledge and/or interaction between the self, the world, and other selves becomes not only problematic but indeed inconceivable.

Welcome confirmation of the plausibility of my historical and conceptual thesis has appeared in the form of scholarly evaluations regarding my work. The legitimacy of the conclusions I reached in *The Achilles of Rationalist Arguments* are critical in serving as the common background for the historical, conceptual, and theoretical treatments I will be offering in the present work as I continue to explore the ramifications of Plato's perennial conflict between the Gods and the Giants.

A work that touches on the same issues [concerning materialism] as are discussed here is Ben Lazare Mijuskovic's *The Achilles of Rationalist Arguments: The Simplicity, Unity, and Identity of Thought and Soul from the Cambridge Platonists to Kant* (Nijhoff, 1974). Mijuskovic recognizes the central role played by Cudworth's formulation of doctrines in the eighteenth-century about the soul, the person, and the nature of thought.[4]

In the following discussion on the relationship between immaterial substances and personal identity, I am indebted to two studies: Ben Lazare Mijuskovic's *The Achilles of Rationalist Arguments* and John Yolton's *Thinking Matter.* Mijuskovic shows how the argument about immaterial substances and the grounding of personal identity developed independently in England prior to Descartes as a reaction to the perceived threat of the rise of Epicurean and newer forms of materialism. Mijuskovic details the intense sensitivity of orthodox thinkers to the threat of materialism posed by immaterial substance and documents their defenses against the threat.[5]

In and after the seventeenth century, consciousness figured in a central role in at least four fairly distinct themes: personal identity; immortality of the soul; epistemic certainty; and the transcendental conditions of experience, as in Ben Mijuskovic's discussion in *The Achilles of Rationalist Arguments* (Nijhoff, 1974), which touches on all four thematics.[6]

And:

What remains surprising, however, is that so little work has been done before on the Achilles argument. Ben Lazare Mijuskovic's pioneering work was the first in modern times to draw attention to the importance

---

4 John Yolton, *Thinking Matter: Materialism in Eighteenth-Century Britain* (Minneapolis: University of Minnesota Press, 1983), xiii. Cf. also John Yolton's book review of Ben Mijuskovic, *The Achilles of Rationalist Arguments: The Simplicity, Unity and Identity of Thought and Soul from the Cambridge Platonists to Kant: A Study in the History of an Argument* (The Hague: Martinus Nijhoff, 1974) in *Philosophical Books*, 16:2 (1975), 17–19; hereafter cited as Mijuskovic, ARA.
5 Dennis Todd, *Imagining Monsters: Miscreations of the Self in Eighteenth-Century England* (Chicago: University of Chicago Press, 1995), 304; cf. also Raymond Martin and John Barresi, *The Rise and Fall of Soul and Self: An Intellectual History of Personal Identity* (New York: Columbia University Press, 1995), 6.
6 *Consciousness: From Perception to Reflection in the History of Philosophy*, edited by Sara Heinamaa, Vili Lahteenmaki, & Paulina Remes (New York: Springer, 2007) 7.

of the argument, but aside from the subsequent work he has done, there is little else in print.[7]

Importantly, the four conclusions do not have to remain distinct from each other. Various philosophers combine two, three, or even appeal to all four enlistments, e.g., Cudworth and Leibniz. And still, in other cases, progressive conclusions are recruited and supportively interwoven. Thus, for instance, it is argued that (a) *if* the soul is immaterial and unextended; and it has no parts; then it cannot be destroyed; ergo it is immortal, since destruction is defined as the dissembling of a compound; further (b) *if* consciousness is constituted as a unity binding sensations, feelings, and thoughts together within the *same* consciousness, into *a single,* substantial self; and further (c) *if* the self *continues* as the *same* identical substance throughout its existence as a temporally-constituted awareness; *then* it necessarily follows that (d) the soul must always *continually* think at *some* level even when it is not consciously, explicitly aware of its own thoughts. By unifying these several major and minor premises together, the theory of the unconscious can be derived as a final consequence, a conclusion explicitly reached by Plotinus, Cudworth, Leibniz, and Kant (with his concept of the "productive imagination"), Schopenhauer (with his noumenal Will), and Hegel (even during sleep). This is a good example of how metaphysical premises can "seep" into epistemological conclusions.[8]

---

7   *The Achilles of Rationalist Psychology,* edited by Thomas Lennon and Edward Stainton (New York: Springer, 2008), 2. Their study is predicated on my discussion of the unity of consciousness in Kant in the *Achilles of Rationalist Arguments,* which concentrates solely on Kant's Second Paralogism in the first edition *Critique of Pure Reason.* Unfortunately, the editors fail to appreciate the larger scope of the simplicity premise as it functions in the context of immortality, the unity of consciousness, personal identity, and subjective and objective idealism. Cf. Charles T. Wolfe, "Elements for a Materialist Theory of the Self," 3: "Few of the commentators saw a continuity in what we here call 'internalization,' from Cudworth to Kant, with the exception of Ben Lazare Mijuskovic in *The Achilles of Rationalist Arguments; The Simplicity of Thought and Soul from the Cambridge Platonists to Kant* (The Hague: Martinus Nijhoff, 1974), published December 4, 2015; the text is both in French and English. https://hal.archives-ouverte.fr/hal-01238149

8   Ben Mijuskovic, "The Simplicity Argument and the Unconscious: Plotinus, Cudworth, Leibniz, and Kant," *Philosophy and Theology,* 20:1&2 (2008–09), 53–83; and "Kant's Reflections on the Unity of Consciousness, Time-Consciousness, and the Unconscious," *Kritike,* 4:2 (2010), 105–132. Hegel similarly states in the *Anthropology:* "[I]t is also inadequate to fix the distinction between [waking and sleeping] by saying vaguely that it is only in the waking state that man *thinks.* For thought *in general* is so much inherent in the nature of man that he is always thinking even in sleep," G.W. F Hegel, *Hegel's Philosophy of Mind, Being Part Three of the Encyclopedia of the Philosophical Sciences,* translated by William Wallace and A.V. Miller and Foreward by J.N. Findlay (Oxford: Clarendon Press, 1971), 69; hereafter cited as Hegel, POM.

Due to the simplicity principle, and implicit within the doctrine of *rationalism,* is the contention that the mind always thinks at some level. If it did not, then it could not continue to be the same self. For Descartes, for instance, once created by God, the soul, as an active immaterial simplicity, is permanent and indestructible. The power of thinking is its defining attribute and therefore it follows that it must *continually* think and hence exist forever, even during sleep, *"l'ame pense toujours"* (Descartes Reply to the Fourth *Objections*). Antoine Arnauld, however, in the "Fourth Set of Objections" to the *Meditations* criticizes Descartes on this point arguing that even if Descartes were to succeed in demonstrating that soul and body are *distinct,* it does not preclude the possibility that the Deity could *simultaneously* cease their connection at death and therefore he has not proved the soul's immortality. In response, Descartes added the Synopsis to the *Meditations,* written a year later, in which he appeals to a "purer" form of the simplicity argument in order to argue his case for immortality and Arnauld declares himself to be satisfied.

As we proceed we shall see that the possibility of an *implicit* uninterrupted consciousness *beneath* our *explicit* states of self-consciousness will soon lead us to considerations regarding Kant's spontaneous subterranean "productive imagination" and Hegel's "feeling soul."

But when we consider the opposing *empirical* paradigm regarding the discontinuity involved in interrupted *perceptions*, which is presented in Locke and Hume's contrasting position, namely that all states of consciousness can *only* be based in disappearing and evanescent sensory perceptions (Locke's sensations, Hume's impressions and/or ideas), it then follows that during deep sleep and fainting spells the soul ceases to think altogether and therefore for certain periods of time—basically every night—it would cease to exist. Even worse, if consciousness is not continuous, it then follows that "one" may be a different "self" at each unit of time. For strict empiricism, personal continuity cannot be secured.

---

Intrinsic to the doctrine of rationalism is the principle that the mind *always thinks at some level.* If it did not, then it could not continue to be the *same* self. The issue obviously involves the problem of *continuous* personal, i.e., moral identity. The self must be the same self who both committed the act and is the one who is being held responsible. As far as the issue of the self as *always* thinking and its relation to the immortality of the soul is concerned, my guess is that Hegel's position is the same as Spinoza's, namely that we are finite beings. Nevertheless, the dependence on the simplicity *premise* has always been and continues to be a substantive principle both in religion and spirituality. G.E. Moore, in his essay, "The Refutation of Idealism," defines idealism as the thesis that all reality is mental, mind-dependent or spiritual. According to this principle, a substantial part of the human universe has persisted in subscribing not only to idealism but spiritualism as well.

> When my perceptions [i.e., impressions and ideas] are remov'd for any time, as by sound sleep; so long am I insensible of *myself*, and may truly be said not to exist.[9]

Not only would we intermittently cease to exist and re-exist but then it is theoretically possible that each time we awoke, we could be a *different* person. Similarly, Locke had speculated that if reflective (as opposed to *reflexive*) mnemonic consciousness of the "self" supposedly establishes the criterion of personal identity, then in sound sleep, when we cease to think "doubts are raised whether we remain truly the same substance" or self. Indeed, this is also why Locke is able to speculate about a prince waking up with his own memory but transposed into the body of a cobbler.[10] The entire discussion in Locke occurs in the context of seventeenth-century speculations regarding the possibility of the soul's transmigration and its possible reincarnation.

Hence, Locke and Hume's strong empiricist positions are in marked contrast to the dualist, rationalist, and idealist traditions going all the way back to Platonism and Neo-Platonism, which holds that the soul (or self) continues to experience not only conscious thoughts but *unconscious* ones as well throughout its entire existence in this world (and presumably into the next as well). If one is restricted to considering empirical perceptions alone, i.e., Lockean sensations or Humean impressions and ideas as the *only* legitimate contents of consciousness, then not only are unconscious thoughts obviously excluded but even the reality of the "self" becomes problematic. Significantly this strict empirical train of argumentation would also disallow the Freudian unconscious as we shall see. But interestingly, it will open the door in Kant to the much deeper and irretrievable sphere of the subconscious mind.

Historically, the theory of the unconscious finds its first gestations in Plato's doctrine of innate ideas and reminiscence (*Meno*); Aristotle's "dispositional" distinction between knowing something *potentially* in our dormant states of consciousness as opposed to *actually* putting it into play when we are awakened (*De Anima,* 412a, 22–26); and Plotinus' principle that the soul *always*

---

9   David Hume, *A Treatise of Human Nature* (Oxford: Clarendon Press, 1955), I, iv, vi (page 252); hereafter cited as Hume, *Treatise;* page references will be provided from this standard text. Here again the term perception means mental, ideal, immaterial. Sensations are (presumably) *occasionally* "caused" or "attended by" by physical motions but *qua* impressions and ideas they are not themselves physical entities. Hume's point is that they are *mental* re-presentations but that is very different from claiming that they consist of physical entities. Cf. John Laird, *Philosophy of Nature* (New York: Methuen, 1967), 26–27.

10  John Locke, *An Essay Concerning Human Understanding*, II, xxvii, 6 ff. Cf. Ben Mijuskovic, "Locke and Leibniz on Personal Identity," *Southern Journal of Philosophy*, XIII:2 (1975), 205–214.

thinks (*The Enneads,* IV.3.30. 1–17; V.12, 1–15; V.3.2., 1–26). Hence, the theory of the unconscious derives from these inferentially connected premises regarding the immaterial nature of consciousness and its implicit *hierarchy* of thoughts. Again, I am not concerned to argue that the soul is immortal (possibly that is a matter of faith alone) but rather to suggest that there are *both* (a) unconscious thoughts which are grounded in *empirical* memories, as in Plotinus, Cudworth, and Leibniz—and later Freud—but more importantly and significantly that *beneath* the unconscious there is also (b) a much deeper "layer" of *spontaneous subconscious* activities and contents that lie much deeper and powerfully as endorsed by Kant, Schopenhauer, and Hegel as we shall see.

Plato's Divided Line passage in the *Republic* (VI. 509 D-511 B) distinguishes five levels of existence and five corresponding states of consciousness and cognition: (a) images and echoes leading to *eikasia* or the imagination; (b) physical objects leading to *pistis* or belief; (c) "pure" mathematical and geometrical concepts leading to *dianoia* or discursive understanding; (d) Universals or Forms leading to *episteme* or immediate intuitive knowledge; and (e) the Good leading to *noesis* or comprehensive knowledge. These *qualitative* differences are summarily and consistently denied by the empiricist tradition, which reduces consciousness to the immediacy of sensory or phenomenal appearances alone. Plato's Divided Line section thus represents a cognitive classification of lower and higher forms of consciousness as they progressively ascend toward an inclusionary coherence of *qualitative*—as opposed to quantitative— differences within consciousness. The Allegory of the Cave reinforces and illustrates the journey of the soul from its lowest subterranean depths to its highest attainment, from the obscurity of a shadowy darkness to the illuminated brilliance of the Good. There is a critical dualism lying between a realm of independent objects and corresponding levels of cognition that I propose to navigate: from (a) prisoners in a cave passively watching vagrant shadows and hearing echoes against a wall; (b) their unchainment allowing them to see visible objects; (c) their ascent and exit from the cave to view a diurnal landscape outside; (d) their nocturnal observation of the celestial order of the stars; and (e) finally their grasp of the sun as both the source and provider of existence and life as well as light and knowledge (*Republic,* VII, 514a–521b). The entire journey of the soul is intended to signify a series of metaphors representing the principle of *qualitative* distinctions *within* consciousness, a movement and a progression from passive sensory imagery to actively grasping pure, non-sensory concepts, imageless Forms, and intuited Intelligibles. It is a continuum of consciousness ranging from a state of relative darkness and confusion to the highest intensity and brightness of an immutable Goodness (Plato) or Oneness (Plotinus). All this, of course, is a Platonic vision but the principle of *qualitative* distinctions and levels of consciousness will play itself out against the reductive *quantitative* materialism of science as we continue, which only admits of a single, homogeneous substance reducing both reality and consciousness to mere matter, motion, and physical sensations. This is one of the great divides between humanism and religion on the one side and the empirical sciences on the other side. All dualists, rationalists, and idealists assume an extensive variety of *active qualitative* distinctions and levels within human consciousness, while the materialists and empiricists deny them and assert *quantitative* differences alone. Further, we will see that empiricism remains mired in the correspondence theory of belief, according to which in some unspecified sense mental ideas "correspond" to physical objects, whereas idealism reaches toward an increasingly graduated, comprehensive, integrated, and coherent system of knowledge. It is important to note that empiricism is ultimately grounded in physical sensations alone, whereas dualism and idealism both seek to stress various *qualitative* differences and levels, including distinctions between cognition and ethical and aesthetic values. This Platonic paradigm will be later reflected in Hegel's dialectical levels and structures of consciousness spanning from the prenatal, natal, psychotic, sensory, perceptual, conscious, and self-conscious to the rational and spiritual.

As we survey the depths and complexities of consciousness, we realize there is an incredible span of qualitative levels from shallow to deep and from superficial to intricate. Before us lies a panoramic hierarchy of sensory, affective, cognitive, and creative states of the mind, from the vegetative, prenatal, subconscious, unconscious, and conscious and spilling into an active reflexive self-consciousness and a transcendent intentionality, all of which leaves us quite uncertain about who we are, how we know, what we can know, and what we are capable of doing. But at the very fount of this hierarchical consciousness, there lies a creative, powerful, and mysterious subconscious that ultimately defies our ability to fully penetrate reality, human nature, and even our own psychological motives. Thus a question remains unanswered: Does man ever escape the original dark forces of primordial consciousness; or do these powers follow him like a tenebrous shadow as long as consciousness persists? None of these states, stages, or levels of consciousness is ever left behind. The evolution of human consciousness is not like a snake shedding its skin. It carries all its past within itself.

What exists? What can we really know? Is reality physical, mental, mystical, or all three? Does realism, conceptualism, or nominalism rule? Is consciousness spontaneous or determined; evolving or stationary; active or passive; reflexive or intentional or both? What is the relation, if any, between reason, experience, and faith; between sensations, feelings, meanings, intuitions, inductions, and inferences; are there imageless concepts or thoughts; is the imagination, reason, or language supreme; are analytic, synthetic, and/or *a priori* synthetic propositions the touchstones of truth or merely its vehicles? How do transcendent concepts, fantasies, dreams, hallucinations, delusions, and ineffable visions play into what we think and believe? In short, consciousness displays a startling fluidity as it meanders without secure barriers within the labyrinthine and expansive channels of the mind. Powerful passions and sustained thoughts flow and intermingle through the subterranean streamlets of the soul. But as we move forward, we will learn that beyond—or beneath—all this lies an unfathomable dark and *irretrievable* subconscious: a spontaneous fount of creative energy.[11]

Against all these protean permutations of consciousness is set forth the impoverished and restrictive catalogue of Hume's empirical impressions tied to the five senses and the constraining principle of the "association of ideas" mechanism most notably founded upon his notions of "resemblance," "contiguity" and the anticipatory psychological *feeling* or *sentiment* of expectations and "constant conjunctions," and all this generated by the accidental, fortuitous, and transient couplings of the imagination; mere *beliefs* in the existence of an external world; the doubtful security of the causal maxim; the contingent assurance of a fictional "self," and the uncertain companionship of other "selves." But Hume is unable to adequately account for his key epistemic elements. There is no *impression* of "contiguity," "identity," and/or "resemblance" as there is an impression of yellow or blue. Relations are not accounted for by Hume. They "derive" or "arise" from the *activities* of the mind and not from Hume's whirl and flux of passive impressions and their fainter ideal copies both superabundantly displayed under his general notion of mental "perceptions."

How deeply or how well have we penetrated reality? What are the limits of knowledge? Indeed how well do we even know ourselves? Consider the Hellenistic Skeptics and Sextus Empiricus, who point out that whether we appeal to the criterion of sensation or reason both merely lead to an infinite regress or circularity but never to any certainty. In his turn, Montaigne even more insistently questions the cognitive limitations of human sensation, let alone reason, which confines us to only five senses.

> The first consideration that I offer on the subject of the senses is that I have my doubts whether man is provided with all the senses of nature. I see many animals that live a complete and perfect life, some without sight, others without hearing; who knows whether we too do not

---

11   Ben Mijuskovic, *Feeling Lonesome: The Philosophy and Psychology of Loneliness* (Santa Barbara, CA: Praeger, 2015), Chapter 7, "The Subconscious and the Unconscious," 149–172.

still lack one, two, three, or many other senses? For if any one is lacking, our reason cannot discover its absence ... We have formed a truth by the consultation and concurrence of our five senses; but perhaps we needed the agreement of eight or ten senses, and their contribution, to perceive it [i.e., truth] certainly and in its essence.[12]

As Montaigne queries, "What do I know?" Man may be more of a question than an answer. And Pascal describes man as merely a "thinking reed" at the mercy of every wind that blows his way. Consider further Spinoza's "rationalism," which posits a single Substance he indifferently calls Nature or God, expressing an *infinite* number of attributes *but* that we—*qua* "rational" beings—are only conscious of two, namely, thought and extension. Recall Leibniz's

---

12   Michel de Montaigne, *The Complete Essays of Montaigne,* translated by Donald Frame (Stanford, CA: Stanford University Press, 1968), 454; italics mine; cf. also 444, 446. We notice that the restriction to the "way of ideas" impasse, namely that all our sensations, ideas, and conceptions can only serve as our *sole* modes of consciousness in Montaigne, will also carry forward and later dominate the cognitive theories of Descartes and Locke. Cf. Richard Popkin, *The History of Scepticism: From Erasmus to Descartes* (New York: Harper & Row, 1964), Chapter 3, "Michel de Montaigne and the 'Nouveau Pyrrhonienes.'" Both Descartes and Locke become entrapped by the "way of ideas" fly-bottle; Descartes in the first two Meditations and Locke when he announces that all our ideas are restricted to *immediate* modes of consciousness in *An Essay Concerning Human Understanding,* II, viii, 8; and II, viii, 11). Notice also the critical application of the italicized term "quality"—as opposed to the term quantity—the latter implying essential spatial extensity to the foreign object, while the mind because of its utter immateriality and simplicity is restricted to qualitative intensities alone; italic mine. In the History of Ideas, the critical issue of dualism arises acutely and continues chronically in Descartes. Once trapped within his own mind, Descartes' escape can only rely in the goodness of God not being a deceiver (Meditation V); in Malebranche's doctrine of "occasionalism" and God's continuous miraculous interventions; in Leibniz on God's pre-established harmony; and in Berkeley on God's immaterialization of the laws of nature. We shall continue to address the problem of solipsism and dualism throughout the text.

   "Mind is the existent truth of matter—matter has no truth. A cognate question is that of the *community of soul and body.* This community (interdependence) was assumed as a *fact,* and the only problem was how to *comprehend* it. The usual answer, perhaps, was to call it an *incomprehensible* mystery; and, indeed, if we take them to be absolutely antithetical and absolutely independent, they are impenetrable to each other ... Descartes, Malebranche, Spinoza, and Leibniz have all indicated God as this *nexus*. They meant that the finitude of soul and matter were only ideal and unreal distinctions; and, so holding, philosophers took God not only as incomprehensible but rather as the sole true identity of finite mind and matter" (Hegel, POM, Section 389).

   Hegel's solution is that both matter and mind are conceptual and mind-dependent and therefore ideal existents.

speculation that God has chosen only *one,* allegedly the "best of all possible worlds," from an *infinite* set of compossible universes thus implying that there may be many other possibilities and modes of consciousness as well as being(s) in the universe. And Kant confines human knowledge to phenomenal appearances provided by our *subjective* (a) intuitive forms of space and time and (b) the mediate categories of the Understanding, while making allowances for an absolutely unknowable reality, a noumenal, transcendent world of "things-in-themselves" ineluctably inaccessible to any ultimate knowledge of our own self, reality, or other selves.

A few others, however, are fully prepared to acknowledge the many paradoxes displayed by the physical universe and the natural sciences.

> The stable foundations of physics have broken up ... The old foundations of scientific thought are becoming unintelligible. Time, space, matter, material, ether, electricity, mechanism, organism, configuration, structure, pattern, function, all require reinterpretation. What is the sense of talking about mechanical explanation when you don't know what you mean by mechanics?... If science is not to degenerate into a medley of ad hoc hypotheses, it must become philosophical and must enter upon a thorough criticism of its own foundations.[13]

And yet, materialism, empiricism, behaviorism, and the current battalions of the neurosciences all fly under the same banner of observational science, while remaining confidently entrenched that we have nothing *qualitatively* new to learn but merely to add more upon more sophisticated and minute *quantitative* measures to our present store of "scientific knowledge." Armed with the single-minded epistemological principle, which holds that *all* our ideas are simply derived from *particular* precedent sensations; that there can be *no* idea in the mind, which is not first given in sensation; it follows that the possibility of a subconscious source of generative activity, of spontaneous energy is perfunctorily and summarily dismissed. In our present age, this is what passes for science—reductive materialism, lifeless mechanism, inexact determinism, superficial behaviorism, and the Faustian conceit of the neurosciences that we already know everything of value. As we proceed, we will discover that the rules and laws that appear to govern the natural world may not always apply

---

13  Alfred North Whitehead, *Science and the Modern World* (New York: Macmillan, 1926), 24–25. Cf. Herbert Spiegelberg, *The Phenomenological Argument: A Historical Introduction* (The Hague: Martinus Nijhoff, 1965), I, 78.

to the human realm; that psychological predictions will ever remain quixotic aspirations when consistently applied to human consciousness.

*And Kant's four discredited Paralogistic "fallacies" may yet portend of realities both below and beyond human accessibility.*

As H.J. Paton intimates:

> It is not unreasonable to suppose that Kant under the influence of Leibniz continued to regard [metaphysical] reality as composed of monads, although he became convinced that the proofs advanced by Leibniz were fallacious and that knowledge of reality is unobtainable by man. If we assume some such belief to be at the back of Kant's mind, it must be remembered that for Kant the conception of the monad has altered. His monads are not self-sufficient, and there is some sort of contact between the knower and the known.[14]

The allusion to "some sort of contact [or relation] between the knower and the known" remains unaccounted for and forever indeterminable by Paton as well it should, since presumably it "involves" an unknown reality, a noumenal realm. The *known* in the above context is the *conceptual* "object" and the *phenomenal* world but *qua* empirical it is still an *ideal* product of the human mind and vulnerable to all sorts of possible distortions. Reality itself, however, remains impenetrable. In short, it is quite possible that there are intrinsic and insurmountable limits to knowing our world, other selves, or even our own self.

One of the most far-reaching metaphysical implications of the four-fold employment of the simplicity argument is the last, Kant's presumably errant Fourth Paralogism, *Of Ideality,* which he also rejects, although ironically enough he assumes it throughout the *Critique* as the ruling premise for his entire doctrine of subjective idealism in the light of his version of the Copernican Revolution—namely that the unknown noumenal realm must *conform* to our subjective and ideal forms of intuition, space and time, and the equally ideal categories of the Understanding. For Kant, whatever reality is "in itself," it is the active structures of the human mind that organizes and orders our empirical experiences. The choice is simple: either concepts conform to objects or objects conform to concepts. He has chosen the latter solution.

---

14  H.J. Paton, *Kant's Metaphysic of Experience: A Commentary on the First Half of the 'Kritik der reinen Vernunft'* (London: George Allen & Unwin, 1965), I, 183; hereafter cited as Paton, KME. One cannot say that noumena *cause* phenomena because causality is a phenomenal category within human experience and therefore it cannot apply to things-in-themselves.

The Fourth Paralogism seeks to establish, on the basis of an immaterialist foundation of consciousness, that our awareness of the "reality," the ideality of an "external world" must always remain as a doubtful and even an illicit inference because the mind is immaterial and unextended and the external world is (presumably) material and extended. Since the two substances share no common property, predicate, or attribute, and we are *only* in immediate and direct contact with our own mind—and therefore *only* indirectly with an independent realm of an existence beyond our mind—it follows that we are completely confined to a form of metaphysical and epistemological idealism characteristic of the earlier idealist philosophies of Descartes, Malebranche, Leibniz, and Berkeley. (Kant attempts to refute these possibilities in his "Refutation of Idealism" (B 274–279) primarily on the grounds of empirical change).

And although Kant rejects the Fourth Paralogism, as a metaphysical illusion, nevertheless it continues to exert a determinative influence on his thought just as it had on past thinkers and promises to continue doing so on future thinkers as well by promoting an idealist interpretation of consciousness. Accordingly, the proponents of metaphysical dualism and subjective and objective idealism contend that *if* both the self and its activity of thinking are immaterial, *then it necessarily follows* that any real—or even adequate—form of (a) knowledge and/or (b) interaction concerning the *independent* existence of an "external world" as distinct from the mind becomes highly problematic.

> The view that consciousness (or, in general the mind) and its physical basis (or, in general the body) seem so essentially different from one another that they must have distinct existences is based on a deep-rooted idea in the history of philosophy. This idea and its variants were constitutive of arguments for the metaphysical independence of mind and body throughout early modern philosophy of the seventeenth and eighteenth centuries, perhaps most notably exemplified in the work of Descartes [and Leibniz]. The essential and complete nature of the mind, generally speaking, seems to consist solely in thinking, and, as such it must be unextended, simple (with no parts), and essentially different from the body and therefore immaterial. This was Descartes's idea in a nutshell, ultimately drawing a strong ontological conclusion (regarding the distinctness of mind and body) from a starting point constituted by epistemic considerations (regarding the distinctness of their appearances). As Ben Mijuskovic (1974, Chapter 5) observes, in this type of argumentation, "the sword that severs the Gordian knot is the principle that what is conceptually distinct is ontologically separable and therefore independent" (p.123). Mijuskovic, in locating this form of reasoning in its historical

context, also notes the presence of the converse of its inference: "If one begins with the notion, implicit or explicit, that thoughts or minds are simple, unextended, indivisible, then it seems to be an inevitable step before thinkers connect the principle of an unextended, immaterial soul with the impossibility of any knowledge of an extended, material, external world and consequently of the relation between them" (p. 121). That is, this time an epistemological conclusion regarding an epistemic gap (between mind and body) is reached from a starting point constituted by ontological considerations (regarding the distinctness of their natures).[15]

To drive the matter home: *if* we contend that the *only* instrument or means of contact open to us that we possess, in relation to our efforts to reach an independently existing external world, is *restricted* within our own subjective sensory *mental* sphere of the soul, that we are confined within our own immaterial mind, which includes Locke's *mental* ideas as "immediate modes of consciousness" and Hume's immediate impressions and ideas as *mental* "perceptions," *then* any possible "access," "contact," or "interaction" *beyond* our immaterial self-conscious existence is in principle impossible and contradictory. On these terms, the mind is *in principle* unable either to cognitively know or to physically interact directly with "outer objects" or "other selves" because it is trapped within its own "veil of perception," its own "way of ideas," and thus within its own solipsistic limitations. As Berkeley rhetorically inquired: "What can be like an idea but another idea"?

Obviously also precluded is the possibility of penetrating or knowing another's mind. Under these conditions, we are restricted to Descartes *inferential* guesses about what other minds are sensing, feeling, thinking, or experiencing

---

15   *The Nature of Consciousness: Philosophical Debates,* edited by Ned Block, Owen Flanagan, & Guven Guzeldere (Cambridge, MA: MIT Press, 2007), 10–11; see also: Mijuskovic *ARA,* Chapter 5, "The Simplicity Argument and Its Role in the History of Idealism," 117–142. In the chapter, I discuss Simon Foucher, a seventeenth-century French skeptic, who proposes reducing the primary (objective) qualities of extension, solidity, and motion to the secondary (subjective) qualities of color and touch thus collapsing the entire external world into the province of the mind alone. Foucher further argues that unextended ideas cannot *represent* extended material objects because ideas are mental modifications of the mind and therefore cannot *resemble* or *correspond* to physical substances. In Chapter 2, we shall examine the doctrine of the *minima sensibilia* in relation to space and the external world. Cf. Ben Mijuskovic, "The Simplicity Argument: A Study in the History of an Argument," *Philotheos,* 9 (2009), 228–252. Similarly, Berkeley's immaterialism transforms Locke's primary and objective "qualities," actually *quantities,* e.g., extension and solidity into secondary and subjective qualities of color and touch.

and in general whether they even exist at all. And does not all this doom us to an insoluble solipsism and loneliness?

Many historians of philosophy are mesmerized by Locke's empiricism and Hume's phenomenalism and therefore neglect to realize that both thinkers actually betray strong dualistic metaphysical tendencies. Locke's *tabula rasa* and sensory inputs and Hume's perceptual impressions and ideas are likewise mental existents, ideal constructs.

> Locke regards the mind as a substance, but a substance that is immaterial. He accepts the usual dualism, 'the two parts of nature,' active immaterial substance and passive material substance ... It is a fundamental point with him that the universe cannot be explained in terms of either matter alone or mind alone. The one cannot be reduced to the other. Of the two, perhaps, mind is the more indispensable; for mind is the active, productive principle. Matter produces nothing.[16]

Students and scholars have to realize that when an author transitions from matter to physical sensations and then to phenomenal, i.e., *mental* images, they have "imperceptibly" moved from a material realm to the psychic immaterial sphere of the soul or mind. This is an absolute act of trespassing.

But since Locke's strictly perceptual theory of consciousness is confined to simple, distinct, and immediate sensations, it follows that the *same* self cannot endure beyond the immediacy of the present moment; its only empirical reality is reduced to instantaneous sensations or to Hume's fleeting impressions: "Whatsoever the mind perceives in itself, or is the *immediate* object of perception, thought, or understanding, that I call an *idea*" (*An Essay Concerning Human Understanding*, II, viii, 8; italics mine). As we shall see, the empirical theory of a perceptual self will fail to account for both (a) the immanent temporality of consciousness and (b) the unity of consciousness and therefore a substantial self.

Consonant with our interpretation of Locke as a dualist, he goes on to problematically declare, "The next thing to be considered is how *bodies* produce [i.e., cause] *ideas* in us; and that is manifestly by [material] *impulse*, the only

---

[16] Richard Aaron, *John Locke* (Oxford: Clarendon Press, 1955), 142 and 147; cf. J.L. Bermudez, "Locke, Metaphysical Dualism and Property Dualism," *British Journal for the History of Philosophy*, 4:2 (1996), 223; Douglas Odegard, "Locke and Mind-Body Dualism," *Philosophy*, 45:172 (1970), 87–105; and John Gibson, *Locke's Theory of Knowledge and Its Historical Relations* (Cambridge: Cambridge University Press, 1968), 104. For Locke's "Representative Theory of Perception," confer J.L. Mackie, *Problems from Locke* (Oxford: Clarendon Press, 1976), 37–38.

way which we can conceive bodies operate in" (*Essay*, II, vii, 11). But how can that be if the two substances share nothing in common?

Hume's metaphysical dualism is much less obvious primarily because commentators concentrate on his phenomenalist rejection of the "self" as a substance. However, in the section in the *Treatise* titled *Of the immateriality of the soul,* he declares the following principle:

> This maxim is *that an object may exist, and yet be nowhere;* and I assert, that this is not only possible, but that the greatest part of beings do and must exist after this manner. An object may be said to be no where, when its parts are not so situated with respect with each other, as to form any [material] figure or quantity; nor the whole with respect to other bodies so as to answer to our notions of contiguity or distance ... Now this is evidently the case with all our perceptions and objects, except those [caused by the physical sensations] of the sight and feeling [i.e., touch]. A moral reflection cannot be plac'd on the right or the left hand of a passion nor can a [perceptual] sound or smell be of a circular or square figure. These [mental] objects and perceptions, so far from requiring any particular place, are absolutely incompatible with it, and even by imagination cannot attribute it to them (Hume, *Treatise,* 235–236; italics his).

The "*object exists*" in our perception but not in extra-mental reality. Clearly for Hume perceptions are immaterial, they exist *"no where,"* they are situated in no place. And yet he is not a metaphysical dualist precisely because *there is no real self* for Hume. There are only mental impressions and ideas, i.e., perceptions. Consequently in Hume's discussion of the Achilles argument, the following answer is proposed to the question, "Are there any immaterial beings?" and his answer is "yes," there are, namely impressions and ideas, i.e., *perceptions.*

> Hume argues that only impressions of color and solidity and the extended objects they compose can stand in spatial relationships. Only they, among our objects of experience, are capable of local conjunction. No other impressions, be they impressions of sensation or impressions of reflection, are extended or spatial. These non-spatial impressions confirm the maxim *"an object may yet exist and be nowhere"* (T, I iv 5, 235).
>
> One could hardly have a more fundamental distinction. Since extension was meant to be the essence of the material by many philosophers of the seventeenth and eighteenth centuries ... it is not far-fetched to claim that Hume is implicitly here developing a fundamental and irreducible distinction between mental and physical entities.... Hume

offers an argument which parallels the Achilles argument in many respects. He expressly condemns the materialists, "who conjoin all thought with extension."[17]

What this means is that for Hume perceptions are mental and immaterial and by explicit contrast both matter and motion are extended and material. In this respect Hume is categorized as a "Minimal Mental/Physical Dualist." He is not, however, a dualist in the strong and "proper" Cartesian sense of the term because he denies the reality of the self as an independent substance. His position is that there are *both* (a) extended material objects and motion in the world *and* also (b) immaterial perceptions *but* (c) there is no immaterial *soul* or *self.* Think of it this way. Perceptions are what we usually call thoughts. Here the term perception obviously means mental, mind-dependent, ideal and therefore *immaterial.* Confusion arises when one mixes the term sensation, because of the physical association of the word with material objects, and then concludes that physical objects *cause* mental perceptions. But Hume was perfectly aware that *qua* perceptions, his impressions and ideas are not physical as testified in his previous remarks (above). They are properties of the mind (absent a self) and not the body. Hume was influenced in this regard by both Malebranche and Berkeley: "Officially [Hume] renounced all the physical implications of 'impressions' just as Berkeley meant to do when he spoke (*Principles,* Section 5) of sensations as impressions in the sense of 'imprinting an idea on the mind" (Cummins, ibid., Section 19). Hume thus clearly elects to replace Locke's term "sensation" because of its material associations with his own mental terms of "impressions," "ideas," and "perceptions" as having ideal connotations alone. So to the critical question whether perceptions are physical or mental, Hume unequivocally answers they are mental and mind-dependent.

Are one's thoughts in space? Normally we do not think of a thought as having a spatial existence or of existing independently of our minds. But consider this. I have just experienced a fleeting thought. Try to catch it and paint it green.

Returning to Kant, he deletes the entire first edition Paralogism section, including the Second Paralogism, which deals with the unity of consciousness and basically replaces it with a philosophically irrelevant and uninteresting criticism of Moses Mendelssohn's proof for the immortality of the soul based on the latter's version of Plato's *Phaedon.* Gone also is the Fourth Paralogism

---

17    Phillip Cummins, "Hume as Dualist and Anti-Dualist, *Hume Studies,* XXI:1 (1995), 47–56; cf. also John Laird, *Hume's Philosophy of Human Nature* (New York: Methuen, 1967), 26–27; and B.M. Laing (New York: Russell and Russell, 1968), 143–144, who introduces Sextus Empiricus and Montaigne into his discussion of perceptions as well.

*Of Ideality,* which treats the relation of the self to "outer objects," which in actuality underpins Kant's Copernican Revolution (B xvi) and is intended to undercut metaphysical dualism.

I have suggested, in other writings and *Feeling Lonesome,* that Kant felt forced into these deletions and emendations in the second edition because his *positive* account of the unity of self-consciousness (apperception), offered in the second edition Deduction (1787, B 131–132), was compromisingly similar to his *negative* criticism of the metaphysical Achilles argument, which he presented in the first edition Second Paralogism (1781, A 351–352), and which he previously disavowed as a dogmatic error, a philosophical illusion, and a noumenal extravagance. But if the Achilles is a fallacy, according to Kant, then it would appear that the B 131–132 version, which posits the transcendental unity of apperception, should be as well.

To anticipate, essentially there are two Ariadne guiding threads leading us through the maze of the *Critique.* First is the question whether the ultimate premise is the transcendental unity of apperception as nestled in the following critical phrase:

> For [immaterial] representations (for instance, the single words of a verse), distributed among different beings, never make up a whole thought (a verse), and it is therefore impossible that a thought should inhere in what is essentially composite. It is therefore possible only in a *single* [i.e., simple immaterial] substance, which not being a [material] aggregate of many, is absolutely simple.
> *Critique,* A 352

Or as Kemp Smith, quoting William James' *The Principles of Psychology,* states:

> Take a sentence of a dozen words, and take twelve men and tell to each one word. Then stand the men in a row or jam them in a bunch, and let each man think of his word as intently as he will, nowhere will there be a consciousness of the whole sentence.
> KEMP SMITH, *Commentary,* 459, note 4

The alternative to the "unity of consciousness" premise is instead grounded in the "spontaneity" of internal time-consciousness (A 97 ff.) as I shall go on to argue.

The second critical thread is concerned with unraveling Kant's own *deeper* version of "transcendental idealism," which is heavily infected with his earlier criticism and rejection of the Fourth Paralogism, *Of Ideality,* and can only be salvaged, as we shall learn, by realizing that his "objective deduction" is actually grounded in his abbreviated discussion of the underlying psychological "subjective deduction," which is once more dependent on (1) the "spontaneity" of the creative "productive imagination" and (2) the issue of *how consciousness itself is possible?* (A xvi-xvii). In a later chapter we shall see more precisely *how* these two questions and issues are related to the subjective and objective deductions; and *why* Kant excised the first edition Paralogisms; and whether it is simply a coincidence that he rewrote the entire second edition Deduction while deleting the first edition Paralogisms?

In any case, all four Paralogisms are directly and positively dependent on the Achilles premise and the accompanying paradigm of an active mind.

Most commentators generally choose the second edition Transcendental Deduction version over the first edition because Kant himself clearly wishes his work to be judged by his later account. Schopenhauer, however, is a notable exception as he favors the premise of immanent time-consciousness emphasized in the first edition Deduction (A 99 ff.) over the unity of consciousness in the second edition (B 131–132) as being the stronger candidate for the *Critique's grounding* premise. As these issues and questions unfold throughout what follows, we will discover an intrinsic relationship between immanent time-consciousness, the reflexive unity of self-consciousness, and subjective loneliness, which can only proceed forward on the condition that *active* internal time-consciousness is the correct premise for the *Critique*. If I am correct in this interpretation, then obviously the consequent abandonment of time as merely a *passive* form of intuition proposed by Kant in the Aesthetic will have to be put aside.

My interest in the twin aspects of consciousness—reflexivity and intentionality—and their relation to loneliness began with several published articles I wrote during my early graduate studies and teaching career. The first paper deals with Plato's conception of synthetic *a priori* relations formulated in his dialogue, *Meno,* 75b, where he seeks to provide an insight into the inseparable *relation* between the Forms of Virtue, on the one hand, and Knowledge on the other—"Virtue is Knowledge [of the Good]"—as analogous to the proposition that "All colors are extended." To say that the relation is both necessary and universal is to say it is *a priori*.[18]

---

18  Ben Mijuskovic, "The Synthetic *A Priori* in Plato," *Dialogue,* 12:1 (1970), 13–23. Whereas Plato's synthetic *a priori* analogizes the relations between the sensations of color and surface extension to pure universal concepts, i.e., the Forms of Virtue and Knowledge as intrinsically connected to each other, Kant's synthetic *a priori* is confined to pure relational categories alone, e.g., cause and effect. Consequently, Plato's proposition, "All colors are extended," would not be accepted by Kant because of their "material," i.e., sen-

The critical point is that color and extension, although they are *qualitatively* and quantitatively distinct, are always found together. It tells us something about the world that is both necessary and universal; the two elements are *existentially* implicative. If one were to assert, "All colors are colors," obviously such a proposition would be tautologous and therefore analytically and trivially "true" (or valid) by the law of identity. But the statement, "All colors are extended" is synthetically true, meaningful, and informative (ampliative); it unifies two different concepts, which together form an intrinsic relation expressing an existential co-dependency, and it also offers something *informative* about the world and human experience *independently* of both.

The revolutionary nature of this Platonic synthetic *a priori* relation is later fruitfully exploited first by Kant and then by both Husserl and Sartre but for all three in very different ways and for quite different purposes. In Kant, it consists in positing a synthetic *a priori* connection unifying two distinct *concepts* (subject-rx-object); *relation* (cause-rx-effect); as well as *principles* (quantity-rx-quality). These synthetic *a priori* categorial relations function as sets of rules and judgments as they constitute the conditions for the possibility of human consciousness. In Husserl, the synthetic *a priori* provides the key to how phenomenological *eidetic* meanings are related to each other. And in Sartre, it constitutes the ontological, i.e., existential relation between "Nothingness" or Consciousness and the reality of Being.

I would further suggest that Hegel's categories in the *Phenomenology of Spirit* and the *Science of Logic*, which we will address in later chapters, as they unfold dialectically or emanate organically into his metaphor of the bud, blossom, and fruit (*Phenomenology*), also exhibit what basically amounts to synthetic *a priori* relations and processes. Hegel's dialectical "movements" are synthetically injected with the organicity of life, growth, and development as emanating from the inside of consciousness. Kant's categories, by contrast, are instead "statically" relational, while Hegel's are dialectical. But both Kant's transcendental categories and Hegel's dialectical categories or pure *structures* function *from the inside out*. This was Leibniz's transfiguring insight. Indeed, from where else could they possibly "arise"? The important consideration is that both for Kant's categories and Hegel's dialectical moments, stages, or

---

sory implications. By contrast, Husserl will use color (quality) and extension (quantity) to provide epistemological insight into phenomenological meanings and Sartre will similarly enlist it to offer ontological insight into the relation between Consciousness and Being. Significantly enough then as we shall see, a *material* synthetic *a priori* will be validated by Husserl on both *eidetic* and *experiential* grounds and also by Sartre on an ontological foundation in *Being and Nothingness*. Cf. Jacob Klein, *A Commentary on Plato's Meno* (Chapel Hill, NC: University of North Carolina Press, 1965), 59–60.

levels of consciousness, they are the result of interior activities native to the mind and the real issue is whether Kant's twelve relations are sufficient to account for human experience (Kant) or should they progressively emanate and grow in order to envelope all reality (Hegel).

The ultimate question between the Gods and the Giants is whether the solution to the "problem of consciousness," and more specifically to the question "whether matter can think?" is to be discovered as arising from "spontaneous acts" from within consciousness; or whether consciousness is instead empirically, passively, and contingently caused by and dependent upon physical external forces—i.e., physiological stimulus-response patterns?

These issues encouraged me to inquire more deeply into the possibility of a wider application for other synthetic *a priori* relations, judgments, and principles with the goal of deploying them and further assigning them to play a commanding role in advocating for a "coherence system of truth." I believe this possibility is already implicit in Plato's pregnant intimations describing the relation of his ethical Forms to each other, as for example the four cardinal Forms, Justice, Moderation, Wisdom, Courage, etc., as subsumed and unified *within* the ultra-Form of the Good; that the Forms of Virtue are all unified by, in, and through synthetic *a priori* relations resulting in Plato's intuitive principle that the multiple virtues are intrinsically bound and tied through knowledge of the Good. If we concentrate on Plato's Divided Line passage in the *Republic* (509d-511e), we note once more that the individual Forms are all comprehensively unified by the Form of the Good. Philosophically, as the soul dialectically, systematically ascends toward higher and higher stages of sensory, discursive, and intuitive knowledge, it realizes that knowledge of the Good is increasingly achieved and secured through the synthesizing and binding activity of conceptual unification. In effect, Plato's comprehensive ideal of the Good promotes an early version of the coherence theory of truth. In Plato as well as Spinoza, Leibniz, Kant, Hegel, and Blanshard there are identical qualitatively graded steps of ascension toward increasing levels of cognition, knowledge, and reality. As a goal in Kant, this would roughly correspond to his ideal Regulative Principle of seeking the Unconditioned but at the same time distrusting it (*Critique,* A 509=B 537 ff.). Correspondingly, as Kemp Smith has cogently and persuasively argued at length throughout his *Commentary,* Kant's transcendental system, with its virtues of synthetic *a priori* relations in the *Critique,* programmatically leads to a coherence theory of truth.[19] Thus

---

19  Norman Kemp Smith, *Commentary,* xxxvi–xxxix, 36 ff., and passim. Cf. Harry Austryn Wolfson, who credits Spinoza as well in having earlier expressed a coherence theory in *The Philosophy of Spinoza* (New York: Meridian, 1958), II, 99 ff. But a case can also be

one does not have to be committed to a transcendent reality in order to seek comprehension and coherence in this world.

Similarly, Hegel's dialectical use of a developmental synthetic *a priori* in the *Phenomenology of Spirit* and the *Science of Logic* also allows him to progressively evolve his system through continuously enriched circles of rational thought; circles within larger circles. And, in the next chapter, I intend to show that Husserl's phenomenological method also results in a web of synthetic *a priori* relations or structures providing him as well with his own possible account of a coherent system of *eidetic* meanings and rational truths replete with internal connections displayed within an infinite field of cognitive insights and intuitive possibilities. What I am contending is that once one is committed to heuristically emphasizing synthetic *a priori* relations, doing so discloses an incredibly wide cognitive portal well beyond Hume's restrictive twofold classification holding between his tautologous analytic "relations of ideas" and his contingent synthetic "matters of fact." In contrast, both Hegel's "dialectical phenomenology" and Husserl's very different *eidetic* phenomenological version, consisting of active synthetic *a priori* relations, both reach out *beyond* themselves; they are inherently intentional and transcendent; qualitatively they have somewhere to go, to develop from within their own internal resources as they are spontaneously generated. Intrinsically connected synthetic *a priori* meanings and relations are more than a mere accumulation of disconnected empirical facts, more than the sum of mere groupings of contingent parts. By contrast, in empiricism objects are fortuitous "aggregations," accidental collections of sensory "parts." Another disadvantageous feature of such empirical combinations is that the component parts are qualitatively homogeneous, which is to say that a heap of sand retains the same quality regardless of its size with the consequence that science is limited to quantities alone. This is a topic we will address further beginning in Chapter 3 and continuing.

---

made for Leibniz's form of idealism as supporting a coherence theory, since everything develops from within the monad and it is systematically confined and retained therein. Cf. A.O. Lovejoy, *The Great Chain of Being* (New York: Harper Torchbooks, 1962), chapter 5; hereafter cited as Lovejoy, GCB. Hegel, who is generally acknowledged without challenge as a strong exponent of the coherence theory, of course, held Spinoza in high esteem. In any case, my point is that the coherence theory was "in the air" during the age and found favor in several of the great "system builders." By and large rationalists naturally respect the completeness of mathematical and geometric systems and so it is an easy transition to extend and attach the ideal of a comprehensive and internally coherent system to their epistemological convictions. Again, the ideal derives from Plato's Divided Line with its interlocking levels of ascending knowledge.

There is, however, another very important set of cognitive distinctions concerning Plato's division, which arises in the Divided Line passage. Already in Plato, we discover a difference between *the immediacy of sensory givens versus discursive judgments,* between sensation and thought, as we shall see play out as we proceed. One of the complications will be that both *passive* sensations, on the one hand, and *active* intuitions, on the other, are "immediate," a problem because sensations are (presumably) physical, passively "given," while by definition intuitions are "pure" or immaterial and actively thought. The viability of this distinction will be tested when we deal with immanent time-consciousness in Chapter 4.

The second article I wish to enlist focuses on the issue of solipsism in Descartes' discussion concerning the problematic relation of the self to the external world, as well as to other selves, by maintaining that although the cogito—"I think=I am"—presents an *intuitive, immediate,* and *direct path to the truth,* it cannot similarly function as the "bridge" to the external world and/or to other selves. The "stretch" beyond the self to a world existing as distinct, separate, and apart from the reach of the self can only be vainly *attempted* based on the fallible power of thought *to make inferences beyond the bounds of the self, transcendent to the self* in regard to an independently existing external world and the existence of other selves. Contrary to the indubitable nature of intuitive knowledge in regard to our own self, mediate inferences are always dubitable as Descartes contends in his First and Second Meditations: *"Of the things which may be brought within the sphere of the doubtful"* and *"Of the Nature of the Human Mind; and that it is more easily known than the body."* This is the *locus classicus* of the self's own entrapment within the prison of solipsism.

In the article, I argue that the epistemic problem of the *identity* of the piece of wax (Meditation II), whether in terms of its *substantial* identity it remains the *same* after it has been removed from a heated oven, despite all the changes in its primary and objective *quantities* (e.g., its measurable extensity, shape, solidity, weight, etc.), as well as its secondary and subjective *qualities* (e.g., color, smell, touch, etc.) only allows *for a non-intuitive, inferential* act of thought; for a mediate judgment; and therefore restricts us to a dubitable inference concerning its continuous identity thereby limiting us to a mere belief as opposed to certain knowledge. Consequently, these *inferential* judgments are very different from the "clear" (immediate) and "distinct" (definable), universal, and necessary (*a priori*) acts of *intuitive* consciousness exemplified in the case of the cogito. (Physical pains are clear and immediate, e.g., a toothache, but not distinct and definable.)

Similarly, in Descartes' example of the passing hats and coats, which he perceives traversing by his window, he can only infer, judge, believe, or guess—but he cannot intuitively or directly *know*—that they are men with minds like his own and not instead automatons or robots. Their very existence, as well as their humanity, remains a doubtful inference at best; it can never reach the status of an infallible intuition and secure knowledge in the manner of the cogito. The conclusion thus follows that the "I think" entails a unique intuitive *act* emanating from an insular, hermitic substance, which is distinct from all other substances, assuming there are any such. (Aristotle defines a substance as that which can exist independently of everything else.) But in that case, all other existents beyond or transcendent to one's own mind must remain forever separate and/or unknowable and continue so. Nevertheless, the important conclusion for idealists and their advocacy in behalf of a self-conscious mind—as opposed to the passive Humean paradigm of the "mind" exhibited in empiricism—is that consciousness displays two distinguishable features. First there are passively given sensations and secondly there are acts of intuition, which both serve to confirm the existence of the self and provide a criterion for the truth: whatever is *both* clear (immediate) *and* distinct (definable) is intuitively true. The conclusion then follows that there is a threefold classification between elements within consciousness: (a) immediate passive sensations; (b) infallible immediate, intuitive acts as in the cogito; and (c) fallible mediate inferential acts concerning the external world and other minds. It follows that the soul or mind possesses the ability to perform both (b) and (c), namely *acts* of self-cognitive intuition *and* the *active* ability of inferring connective relations as well as conducting discursive judgments. But *if* one is confined to the intuitive certainty of one's own existence through direct acts of reflexive self-consciousness in the manner of Descartes, *then* one can *only* dubitably *believe* in the existence of an external world and other selves; in which case both solipsism and loneliness inevitably follow.

In addition, for Descartes a second problem arises in that the self is conceived, described as "pure," i.e., vacuously empty; it has no content; only reflexive, circular activity. In this respect, it is not unlike Aristotle's Unmoved Mover that only thinks about Its own pure contentless thought; it is a purely non-sensuous activity. So at this point at the start of my philosophical journey, I could only be certain of two things: *I* alone exist (an intuition) and I dubitably judge or infer that there *may* exist, i.e., there *may* be an existence "beyond" my self but I cannot be sure of the latter judgment or belief.[20]

---

20   Ben Mijuskovic, "Descartes's Bridge to the External World: The Piece of Wax," *Studi Internazionali di Filosofia,* III:3 (1971), 65–81; reprinted in *Rene Descartes: Critical Assessments,* edited by Georges Moyal (London: Routledge, 1996), II, 312–328. Cf. A.M. Gomez, "Descartes on the Intellectual Nature of Human Perception: From the Innermost Self to

Worse yet! When I next turned to Hume, there was a plenum of sensory impressions pervading my sphere of an indeterminate consciousness but no self. Hume's empiricism reduces consciousness to the immediacy of *mental "perceptions,"* which he further resolves into *simple, single* impressions and their fainter copies, i.e., ideas and then he contingently appends them (the impressions) to an untethered *natural feeling of belief concerning an imagined fictitious "self,"* which he describes as transacted by the force of the imagination. Hume's "self" consists of a randomly dispersed flux of vanishing impressions, tiny droplets of consciousness, with each simple, self-sufficient drop consisting of single separable impressions, and further each dot appearing momentarily as a fleeting, transient *substance*. Each single impression *is* a substance in its own right. In his famous section, *Of personal identity* in the *Treatise,* Hume reduces the "self" to a disunified aggregate or "bundle" of distinct instantaneous impressions (his "atomistic psychology") consisting solely of isolated disunited units (his impressions). His fictional "self" represents "something" other than a substantial *personal* self. Hume's "self" is merely a phenomenal, an artificial "construction" made from replaceable mental *sense-data* or *sense-qualia* (in the current empirical vernacular) fortuitously, accidentally, contingently patched together by an absent and undetermined agency (the elusive non-existent "self") and subject to the whim of a floating imagination. All that remains in "consciousness" are tiny rapidly disappearing spots of color, intermittent squeaks of sound, and pangs of hunger that somehow manage temporally to *succeed* each other "with inconceivable rapidity." As each unique impression passes by a *presumed*

---

the Material World," *Analisis. Revista de investigación filosófica,* 2:3 (2015), 185. Descartes in the Second Meditation forces the issue of solipsism to come directly to the fore where it has remained ever since inception. For *if* one can *only* be intuitively certain of one's own existence because of the innate insularity of a consciousness, which is restricted to the immediacy of its acts of reflexive self-consciousness; and further *if* one can *only* inferentially (and therefore dubitably) be conscious of other selves; *then* irredeemable aloneness results. Fortunately Descartes is saved from this absolute loneliness by his two proofs for God's existence (the cosmological argument in the Third Meditation and the ontological "intuition" in the Fifth) as well as his Christian faith. And even in order to be more certain, he is discreetly prompt to declare that although in the order of *knowing* his own existence precedes God's (Second Meditation) yet in the order of *being* the idea of God comes first (Third Meditation). Additionally, God's perfect goodness prevents deception. The tension between solipsism and subjective idealism will continually engage us throughout the course of the present study. In Husserl's *Cartesian Meditations,* he is forced to address the issue of solipsism head on and in the larger *Crisis,* he revisits it while attempting to transform Descartes' mediate forms of judgment into intentional and immediate "objectivities" concerning the *Umwelt* and *Lebenswelt;* cf. *The Crisis of the European Sciences and Transcendental Phenomenology* (Evanston, IL: Northwestern University Press, 1970), Sections 20, 68.

undefined "observational medium"—but not a self—which is, by his own account, entirely devoid of any connective attachments to an observing mind or self. The perceptions appear and disappear in a Heraclitean rate of flux. There is no real or substantial self; the "self" completely dissolves with each moment of time. In effect, according to Hume, the alleged substantiality and continuity of the "self" simply consists in a psychological *belief* produced by an anticipatory imagination of succeeding perceptions temporally *passing* beyond the present moment; what he nevertheless importantly describes *as a succession*.

> For my part, when I enter most intimately into what I call *myself*, I always stumble on some *particular perception* [i.e., impression] or other, of heat or cold, light or shade, love or hatred, pain or pleasure. I never can catch *myself* at any time without a perception, and can never *observe* any thing but the perception ... If any one upon serious and unprejudic'd relfexion, thinks he has a different notion of *himself*, I must confess I can reason no longer with him ... But setting aside some metaphysicians of this kind, I may venture to affirm of the rest of mankind, that they are nothing but a *bundle* or collection of different perceptions, which *succeed* each other with inconceivable rapidity, and are in a perpetual flux and movement (*Treatise*, I, iv, vi, (pages 252–253), italics mine).[21]

First it is critical to realize that Hume's "observation" of perceptions that are *other* than the "self" are diametrically opposed to Descartes's cogito, which is reflexively self-conscious of *the self itself*. Further, it is also important to note here that sensations as well as feelings are definable in terms of simple, single impressions. The mosaic portrait of the mind Hume offers paints each particular impression in the same style as Seurat's punctilistic painting, *A Sunday at la Grande Jatte*. Each dot is isolated and separate from every other, a disunified aggregate of atomistic sensory points. Thus the question naturally arises, is there even a "bundle"? For how do I *know*—or do I?—that the bundle *belongs* to me and not to you; how can I be sure they are *my* impressions and not *yours*?

Against Hume's celebrated "bundle theory" of the self, I argue that once Hume admits to a *temporal succession* of impressions, a flow, a stream of impressions, he has essentially forfeited his entire argument because one cannot be aware of a temporal flow, a *succession* of impressions without presupposing

---

21   Cf. Ben Mijuskovic, "Hume and Shaftesbury on the Self," *The Philosophical Quarterly*, 21:85 (1971), 324–336; see also: ARA, Chapter 4, "The Simplicity Argument and Personal Identity in the Seventeenth- and Eighteenth-Centuries," 93–118.

a permanent, underlying self connecting, synthesizing, binding, and thus unifying past-present-future-time in the *same* temporally extended consciousness. In effect, we cannot simply reduce human consciousness—and thereby individual existence, if indeed that has any meaning without a unified temporal structure—into unrelated, discrete instants; into disconnected moments. In order to be actively self-conscious, to be a *continuously* self-unified consciousness, there must be a secure repetitively re-cognized unification of a temporal flow *as belonging to me and to no one else*. This is Kant's point in his foundational description of the constitutive and temporal *a priori* syntheses of apprehension in sensory intuition, spontaneous production in the imagination, and the temporal retainment in conceptual cognition as all three moments contribute and are held together *in the same consciousness*.

> Whatever the origin of our representations, whether they are due to the [empirical] influence of [material] outer things, or, are produced [i.e., created] through [spontaneous and autonomous] inner causes, whether they arise *a priori* or being appearances have an empirical origin, they must all as modifications of the mind, belong to [a temporal] inner sense. All our knowledge is thus subject to time, the formal condition of inner sense. In it they must all be ordered, connected, and brought into relation [i.e., unified]. This is a general observation, which throughout what follows, must be borne in mind as being quite fundamental.
> KANT, *CPR*, A 99

It is critical to notice here that however skeptical we may be concerning the existence of an external world, the reality of other selves, and even of our own self as a continuous substance, we cannot under any circumstances or in any manner deny the existence of a (*self-*)conscious *temporal* presence or the inner flow of temporality. As Paton explains in behalf of Kant:

> Our minds seem to last though time, as they do not seem to extend through space. We are immediately aware only of colours or other sensa, and perhaps of bodies, as in space. If we think of minds as being in space, we do so because we ascribe to them the space occupied by the body with which they seem to be connected. On the other hand, we seem to be immediately aware of our minds as living through time, or at least to be immediately aware of the stream of our ideas as continuing through time.
> PATON, *KME*, 100–101, cf. 148; cf. KEMP-SMITH, *Commentary*, 241–242

The empirical "spatialization" of time is very important because it suggests that space is more fundamental than time; that time is subservient to space and thus space is promoted to the foundational status of an objective "science," whereas the *subjective* temporal nature of consciousness is demoted to an ephemeral *appearance,* as we shall see in Chapter 4. The opposing counter suggestion made by Kant, Bergson, Husserl, and others will be twofold: (1) time-consciousness is primary and original; and (2) space is secondary and derivative. Further, time is "expressed" qualitatively whereas space is "expressed" quantitatively.

Two articles address the ultimate premise of Kant's transcendental Analytic by discussing the importance of the Leibnizian themes of the *unity* and *continuity* of consciousness in Kant. Indeed, the origin of both principles—the unity of consciousness and its continuity—are basically Leibnizian (ultimately Plotinian) in origin and both are intended as counter-theses to the principles of materialism and empiricism. Kant, in his speculations about the self, is primarily following Leibniz's concerns. When in the *Monadology,* Leibniz defines and describes the activity of the soul as a unity, identity, and continuity (Sections 1–21), as well as when he declares that "nature makes no leaps" (*New Essays,* IV, 16), he is arguing for the innate powers of the mind. It is not nature that refuses to entertain gaps and discontinuities but rather it is consciousness itself that is constituted as *both* a unified *and* a continuous substance. As thinking beings, we could not be self-conscious if things appeared and disappeared randomly and without warning; or if we were deprived of *constant, continual* temporal re-cognitions and pervasive repetitions within our minds. Lovejoy's conception of Nature's "great chain of Being" is not situated "somewhere out there" in the cosmos but instead it resides in the mind.[22]

What again guarantees Kant's trust in the mind's ability to continuously unify and identify our human experiences as our own is once more the viability of his Copernican Revolution, which dictates that the "noumenal world" must conform to the mind's cognitive activities and structures; "reality itself" must surrender to Kant's "transcendental" conformative principles, imposed rules, and unifying relations, which are *already* lying in wait within the human mind (*Critique,* B xvi-xvii, B xxiii, note a). Consequently, "reality" must conform to the mind's innate and active patterns or structures rather than having consciousness be forced to "correspond" to the independent existence of objects external to the mind. It is the mind that secures the unity, identity, and continuity, which otherwise would be randomly scattered who knows where. In the coherence theory, it is the mind that does the work; in the

---

22  Cf. Ben Mijuskovic, "The Premise of Kant's Transcendental Analytic," *The Philosophical Quarterly,* 23:91 (1973), 155–161; and "The General Structure of Kant's Argument in the Analytic," *The Southern Journal of Philosophy,* XII:3 (1974), 357–365.

correspondence theory, the work is done for the mind by the external world. In the rationalist tradition of Western thought, ever since Plato and Aristotle, forms and concepts are intrinsically active. Actually even Kant's "given *forms* of sensibility," the "intuitions" of space and time suggest activity as opposed to passivity, as we shall discuss in the next chapter.

In any event, in order to make a case for the self's sense of subjective isolation and hermitic integrity, it is necessary to determine that there *is* a self and that it is unified, self-aware, and "substantial." It is both (a) the acts and (b) the structures of consciousness that actively coordinate sensory data within each of us that provides for the unity, identity, and continuity of the *same* self-consciousness, of an intransigent substance.

But how did all this begin, these endless questions, confusions, and uncertainties surrounding the issue whether our thoughts are completely reducible to the brain, its sensations, and its *re*-active responses; or whether consciousness is immaterial and its unity is attributable to the active ordering structures of the soul, mind, self, or ego? Why is it so complicated? Was it always so confusing from the very start of Western philosophical speculations about the soul, its thoughts, human consciousness, and the nature of man? This is precisely what David Chalmers has called "the hard problem of philosophy": the true nature of human consciousness.

Perhaps it is best to start all over again from the very beginning and hopefully disentangle the interwoven conceptual threads in order to eventually tie them together correctly and properly.

It seems patently obvious that certain distinguishable principles are critical in understanding our selves, our surroundings, and our connection to other selves. These premises have retained their conceptual identity and integrity throughout the history of Western ideas and consciousness, although quite often students and even teachers of philosophy are unaware of their many intrinsic implications. Because of this uncertainty, it is worth taking a more careful look at Plato's concept of self-consciousness as an active, self-contained, internal dialogue, which he briefly but succinctly summarizes in two important dialogues, the *Theaetetus* and the *Sophist*.

> Socr: And do you accept my description of the process of thinking?
> Theaet: How do you describe it?
> Socr: As a discourse that the mind carries on with itself about any subject it is considering ... I have a notion that, when the mind is thinking, it is simply talking to itself, asking questions and answering them, and saying Yes or No. When it reaches a decision—which may come slowly or in a sudden rush—when doubt is over and the two voices affirm the same thing, then we call that its 'judgment.' So I should describe thinking as [an

internal] discourse, and judgment as a statement pronounced, not aloud to someone else, but silently to oneself.

Theaet: I agree (*Theaetetus,*189e–190a).

In this description, the soul or mind is both immaterial and active. The "two voices" indicates reflexive self-consciousness; it is able to be self-aware of thinking its own thoughts in a decidedly *two-fold* manner. And the *purpose* of its thinking is intentionally directed to reach a decision, a judgment.

Again:

> Str: And next, what of thinking and judgment and appearing? Is it now not clear that all these things occur in our minds both as false and as true?
> Theaet: How so?
> Str: You will see more easily if you begin by letting me give you an account of their nature and how each differs from the other.
> Theaet: Let me have it.
> Str: Well, thinking and discourse are the same thing, except that what we call thinking is, precisely, the inward dialogue carried on by the mind with itself without spoken sound.
> Theaet: Certainly.
> Str: Whereas the [temporal] stream which flows from the mind through the lips with sound is called discourse (*Sophist,* 263D-E).

Clearly in this passage thought or consciousness is described as an internal temporal flow or stream.

In addition, there are two other passages in the *Theaetetus,* that provide foundational insights into the issues surrounding both (a) the activity of thought and (b) its passive contents. The first metaphor analogizes the mind or consciousness to a "good thick slab of wax" upon which sensory impressions imprint their likenesses, like a signet ring upon wax (*Theaetetus,* 194b-195b). This metaphor is similar in all major respects to Aristotle's later paradigm of the soul or mind as a blank tablet upon which sensory experiences "write" (*De Anima,* 430a). However, according to Plato, if this is our operational cognitive model, then it fails to explain how *errors* can occur, since the first and now weakened, passively given sensory "wax impressions" would be superseded, repressed, or even effaced by the more recent and stronger wax imprints=sensations =perceptions. If this is the case, then how are we to account for mistakes? What is lacking, what remains unaccounted for in this materialist and empiricist attempt to solve the "problem of error" is the *activity* of the mind both *to relate,* and *to compare,* and *to contrast* distinct judgments with and against each other *in the mind, in consciousness* in order (a) to deliberate on the differences; (b) to reflexively consider the options; and only then (c) to decide, to choose between them which wax-sensations or wax-impressions are "true" or closer to the mark. Such a power or capacity can only reside in the *transcending* ability of thought to overcome the immediacy of sensations, a temporal activity, which is able to reach *beyond* the merely immediate and passive sensations and to reflexively consider the several alternatives and then intentionally, purposively choose.

Later in the dialogue, Socrates analogizes memory to an aviary in which the owner has secured in his possession a number of birds each *representing* individual pieces of tentatively assumed "knowledge." When the possessor needs to "know" something, then he can *actively* catch, inspect, and select, i.e., judge each of the birds as the most appropriate or likely candidate and then hopefully select the correct one (*Theaetetus,* 197b-199b). In Plato's analogy, the owner may still be mistaken, but clearly in such cases the soul is an *active* participant and by comparing this paradigm with the prior empiricist *passive* model of consciousness, the *tabula rasa* model, we can see that the latter is unable to account for either knowledge or errors, the first because without a temporal consciousness the incoming sensations are immediately obliterated and replaced by the new ones; there is only a *present;* and therefore nothing to compare; and the second obstacle persists because the *option* of choosing certainty from error is non-existent; there is only a *now* and a pervasive absence of any evaluative mediating judgments capable of passing between truth and falsity, yea or nay.

The critical problem in philosophy is not so much how can we grasp what is real—insects do it instinctively—but how it is possible to make mistakes if the mind is passive and at the complete mercy of the incoming stimuli; if we are only capable of passively recording sensory inputs; if we are merely responsive and reactive, how can we ever be mistaken? Lower organisms, insects for example, simply react instinctively to stimuli; they cannot make mistakes, they cannot make judgments; they are unable to select one option over another or to make assessments concerning danger or taking chances, nor do they need to do so in order to survive. They do not exhibit levels of consciousness. But humans are primarily creative beings and certainly not simply instinctive creatures. The ability to make mistakes and to improve on them is the defining characteristic of higher order animals.

Two millennia after Plato, we might remember that Descartes invokes not only doubt and deliberation in the context of judgments concerning truth and error (Meditations I and II) but he also caps them both with "free will" precisely in order to "account" for the precipitous tendency of humans to rush to conclusions and therefore commit errors (Meditation IV, *Of the True and the False*). I am not so much anxious to endorse and attach the Cartesian "solution" of free will to the problem of error, of course, but I am determined to be critical of the severe limitations of naïve empiricism and the reduction of the "mind" to the brain and its attendant sensations. How do we make mistakes in empiricism? Is it really the case that we can leave the matter in the hands of passive and immediate sensations?

In response I wish instead to promote a viable alternative, namely by summoning the reflexive nature self-consciousness; its active ability to deliberate by forming relations of comparison and contrast; and also its transcendent power of *intentionally, purposefully* allowing the mind to select and choose between alternatives, thus enabling the self to draw both "true" and "false" conclusions.

There are four issues in regard to what the Platonic dialogues can teach us and what they cannot in going forward. The first is that Plato, as a metaphysical dualist, is unable to bridge the divide between (a) physical things; (b) active immaterial souls; and (c) unchanging eternal Forms. In the *Parmenides*, which presents a youthful Socrates conversing with the elderly philosopher, it quickly becomes clear that insurmountable difficulties lie before Socrates' effort to account for the proposed "interaction" of particular physical things to partake, share, or merge with the *essences* of the eternal Forms because of their radical differences as substances. Similarly, in the *Timaeus*, Plato's cosmological myth, he attempts to use Space (*chora*) as a *mediating, transitional link*, a *tertium quid* between a world of physical objects and the immaterial Forms. As such, Space is described as an existent reality, the "nurse or womb of all Becoming," an empty receptacle, a pure matrix of possibilities *in* which objects appear (while Time is described as "the moving image of Eternity" *during* which transient events take place). As such Space is without qualities. It represents a pure objectless extension. But the problem is that as an intermediary "substance" connecting things and Universals, although (a) Space in Itself as a "bastard" Form shares with the immutable Essences the *quality* of immateriality and likewise shares (b) with things the attribute of extension, nevertheless physical objects cannot "partake" (*metechein*) in the reality of the Forms because Forms and *material* objects share no attribute in common. Thus, Plato's vain hope "in like knowing like" is laid to rest and there is no path or bridge that can be established in order to overcome the "problem" of metaphysical dualism.

Matters appear more hopeful, however, in the middle dialogues, in terms of "like knowing like" by virtue that both active immaterial souls and the unchanging immaterial Forms share a common quality (*Phaedo*, 79b-80e). We know from Plato's middle dialogues, e.g., the *Phaedo* and *Republic* that the soul is able to partake in pure, imageless, non-empirical *meanings*. We know that in metaphysical idealism the "external world" is transformed into a *system* of mental, ideal concepts and structures. In the next chapter, we shall consider three philosophers who promote a version of ethical idealism through meanings and relations without any reference to *transcendent* Platonic Forms.

Thus a secondary issue that arises is whether there are imageless, non-sensory concepts at all. For instance, Plato considers that in the world of nature, no two things, for example two sticks, are ever "absolutely equal" and yet we possess the concept of perfect equality or conceptual identity and that the mind is able to formulate the *meaning* and *relation* of *absolute equality* as produced by the internal resources of the mind itself (*Phaedo*, 74b-74d). In any event, as we continue we shall see that there are both imageless meanings and relations as well. These are all issues we shall have to consider.

For Kant, of course, imageless categories serve as relational activities constituting the faculty of the Understanding. They are *indirectly* validated, justified, or "deduced"; they are deemed to be *a priori,* i.e., necessary and universal active forms of thought precisely because they are *conditions, presuppositions, assumptions* for the very possibility—and therefore actuality—of human self-consciousness and experience. They are described as constitutive, connective acts of self-consciousness precisely because of their capacity of providing active relational structures within consciousness. The problem then is to defend cognitive relations as *ideal forms or structures* of thought without having (a) to appeal to an independent or transcendent realm of pre-existing universal forms in the manner of Plato; or (b) to appeal to empirical sensations in the fashion of Locke and Hume. This can only be done if the ideal meanings and relations are generated from *within* the mind itself. In short, meanings and relations do not exist independently of minds and they are not "given" by sensory experience. In what follows, we shall compare and contrast these metaphysical and epistemological options in order to determine their respective plausibilities.

Second, the Platonic soul is *self-conscious, apperceptive,* and metaphorically *actively circular;* it initiates its own activity from *within* its self and reflexively returns those thoughts back to its self as their source; it thinks about its own thoughts and knows what it is thinking about. In the context of the history of ideas and consciousness, the principle and model of *reflexive* self-consciousness is shared by *all* dualists, rationalists, and subjective and objective idealists from Plato through Aristotle, Plotinus, Augustine, Descartes, Cudworth, Leibniz, Kant, Fichte, Hegel, Royce, and as we shall see even Husserl and others as well. Its clear formulation and intrinsic implications are expressed in the following illuminating quotation from J.N. Findlay's introductory essay to *Hegel's Philosophy of Mind.*

> The notion of *Geist* (Mind or Spirit) is of course central in Hegel. It is the descendant of the Kantian Unity of Self-Consciousness and of the Absolute Ego of Fichte and Schelling. It also claims a collateral source in the Aristotelian *nous* which, in knowing the [conceptual] form of an object, thereby knows itself [*Meta.,* 1075a] and which, in its highest phases, may be described as a pure [immaterial] thinking upon thinking. The Greek influence on Hegel's thought is all-important from the beginning but the roots of that thought remain Kantian and Fichtean. Kant had made plain that we require mind [i.e., conceptual] *objects,* unities which proceed according to a rule [according to the categories and principles] and which can be reidentified on many occasions, in order to have that unity in our conscious minding which makes us enduring conscious selves, and which enables us to be conscious of ourselves as self-conscious. In the conscious *constitution* of objects, athwart the flux of time, we have the necessary foundation for the latterly and hammered home by Husserl.[23]

It is important to note that Professor Findlay is underlining the universal co-relational connection between the conceptual subject and its object. It is a fundamental relation that is as crucial for Kant as it will be for Freud, as important for epistemology as it will be for psychology. It is critical that consciousness is *constituted* from *within* rather than being *caused* from without and the

---

23  G.W.F. Hegel, *Hegel's Philosophy of Mind: Being Part Three of the Encyclopaedia of the Philosophical Sciences,* translated by William Wallace and the *Zusatz* by A.V. Miller and Introduction by J.N. Findlay (Oxford: Clarendon, Press, 1971), vii-viii. To the best of my knowledge, Leibniz is the first to use the term "spontaneity" in a technical cognitive (as opposed to ethical) context and thus in a highly novel sense. Others are generally satisfied to simply contrast the activity of self-consciousness with the inertness and passivity of matter. But with Leibniz, it means something very special, a *sui generis act.* Because Leibniz's monads are absolutely self-enclosed and windowless, once more it necessarily follows that any activity can only start and issue from within consciousness. Gottfried Wilhelm Leibniz, *The Monadology and Other Philosophical Writings,* translated and Introduction by Robert Latta (Oxford: Oxford University Press, 1968), 145. According to Professor Latta, Leibniz, following Aristotle, connects spontaneity with intelligence, possibly through the concept of self-conscious "freedom." Cf. also Bertrand Russell, *A Critical Exposition of the Philosophy of Leibniz* (London: George Allen & Unwin, 1958), 193. *Bluntly put, idealism cannot go forward without spontaneity!* This is the grounding principle of idealism in contrast to physical causality as the critical assumption in determinism.

reference to "the flux of time" and Husserl is another connection we will pursue with profit.

Also significant is that the rationalist use of the terms self-consciousness and "reflexion," as opposed to the *empiricist* employment of the terms perception and "reflection," are very different and must be carefully distinguished from each other. For Locke, both outer and inner "reflections" are *always materially* and *causally* initiated by external sensory experiences, e.g., physically seeing a tree (an "outer" perception) or feeling hungry (an "inner" perception) and they are always contingently dependent on sensory stimuli involving receptive bodily organs. Thus, outer visual sightings and inner depletions of nourishment are merely *passive observations* of "objects," "events," or previous "states of affairs," e.g., memories present to consciousness. Seeing trees and feeling pangs of hunger are both *perceptions,* passive observational experiences of physical states of affairs attributed to the body. For Locke and Hume as well, "sensations," "ideas" or "impressions," *qua* immediate modes of consciousness, *cannot* refer either directly or indirectly *back* to the self in order to form a self-conscious *principle of unity*. I cannot *reflexively* think *about* what I am thinking. The self can only experience its sensations but never its self. Perceptions and reflections are caused by and directed at specific observations, either external or internal but both "reference" the body. They are caused by *experiencing* particular precedent physical objects or feelings that *cannot* be in any manner *self*-referential; *experience* is an empirical *observation; a response* to externally caused sense data passively registered, experienced—as opposed to an actively constituted relation—and it is always *restricted* to *prior* sensory experiences, which can never "go beyond" their circumscribed immediacy; it is a *perception* of externally produced sensations (Locke) or impressions (Hume). If one has never experienced the taste of a pineapple, it cannot be *conceptually* communicated to them. The sensation or impression *always precedes* the "thought" or idea. Consciousness can experience seeing a tree or being hungry *during* the occurring sensations; or *later* having *the mnemonic reflection of, the memory of* the sensations having occurred. Sensation and impressions are, of course, the "contents," "ingredients," or "elements" in conscious thinking. But the critical point is that the materialist and empiricist paradigm of consciousness completely negates any possibility of a *self*-conscious reflexive activity. Perceptions refer to sensations; reflexions refer to the self; reflections mirror, correspond, copy and re-present impressions; but reflexion is self-referential. In the materialist dictionary of Hobbes, for example, a "phantasm," is a bodily sensation, an appearance caused by a physical object impinging on the body's sense organs and imagined images are decaying sensations; there are physical events at both ends. Again, in the vocabulary of Locke and Hume, perceptions are *mental* entities. In Chapter 7, we shall confront more directly the "paradox of the unobserved observer."

It follows that in the empiricist paradigm, the concentration is on the impressions at the total *exclusion* of the self; all that is perceived are impressions, which are collectively uniquely various in terms of time, space, shape, strength, and circumstance; separable, distinct, and non-repeatable at each moment of time. Particular sensations momentarily exist and vanish. Impressions are essentially discontinuous, whereas the activity of the self is essentially continuous; impressions are non-temporal, i.e., instantaneous, while the self is temporally sustained. In strict empiricism, the "self" is irrelevant, non-existent. In Hume's analysis, consciousness is a dream without a dreamer. *But if there is no self, there can be no loneliness.*

The empiricist paradigm is basically *linear* and externally determined from the outside by physical motions striking the body and transmitting impulses to the brain resulting in *re*-actions like tiny billiard balls bouncing off cushions. The entire force of the interaction can be *quantitatively* measured and described as an external spatial occurrence even when the model is applied to events "inside" the human body, to feelings such as anger and fear. This is the same scientific paradigm employed by the ancient Epicurean adherents and continues today in our contemporary neurosciences. In mechanistic terms, it is no different than the atomism of Leucippus and Democritus. On the physicalist paradigm, without external stimuli, the brain lies dormant, in relative repose, the jagged lines of the encephalograph machine mutely repeating monotonously and meaninglessly the rhythm of the heart and the sleeping repository stirrings of the brain.

By contrast, self-consciousness in the dualist/rationalist/idealist traditions is active and circular. It is *spontaneously* generated from the mind's own internal resources. The synthetic *a priori* relations, Kant's categories, create a structured ordering, which is superimposed on the incoming "sensory" data. The relations in turn form recognizable patterns; but they are not the products of sensations, although they work upon and "apply" to sensations in the sense that the sensory "material," i.e., the mental contents or elements are forced to conform to an active epistemic order imposed on the "material" present to the mind. Again, consciousness is *constituted* from within the mind rather than *caused—and determined—*from without the mind.

As Professor Findlay underscores (above), at its most basic and essential level in Kant, the concept of the "self" is mutually *related to* and *distinguished from* the concept of an "object"; it is *self*-related, *self*-mediated (cf. *Critique*, A 107–110). Sensations are the "content" of consciousness and not its activity. Sensations alone cannot be self-aware *but* unlike particles of matter, which are gravitationally attracted to each other, *phenomenal* sensations are not. Their activity is chemical, electrical, and synaptic as opposed to gravitational. Further, relations are not sensations. Blue and loud are sensations but not relations. And there is no *sensation* of the causal relation itself. Relations are *spontaneous* products, creations of the mind. (We shall have quite a bit more to say about the word "spontaneity" throughout the text.) The conceptual *relation* of causality derives from the mind, not from nature. The empiricists, following, Hume substitute the imagination for reason and belief for knowledge. But there is no sensation of resemblance or contiguity. They are relations. Although the mind *requires* the existence of an external world, it is not identical or even compatible with the external world. The first is physical and the second is mental. Interestingly, Hume declares that the real nature of the human body is unknown and the brain is left unmentioned throughout the *Treatise*.

Third, according to the Platonic model, human consciousness is *intentional, transcendent, decisional, purposeful,* and *judgmental* as Plato intimates in the quotations selected above. It deliberates with an "end in view," while engaged in the active process of eventually plumping down for a resolution, a decision; it is teleological in intent; it points toward resolving issues and initiating an action *beyond* the deliberative process of considering options. Self-consciousness is one "aspect" of consciousness and intentionality is another but both are synthetically and *a priori* actively anchored in the same self. In opposition, the materialist and empiricist model is limited to a stimulus-response model of behavior. Physical sensations merely cause re-actions, unthinking responses in snails as well as in man.

As we shall see, both self-consciousness (Kant) and intentionality (Husserl) are active. In terms of metaphors, the first is circular and the second is unidirectional; the first activity *turns* inwardly and the second *points* outwardly. The difference is that although both sources emanate, erupt, or spontaneously arise from within the soul, they travel in different directions. In terms of Plato's description of the activity of thought and thinking *as* decisional and Aristotle's *as* deliberative both acts are incorporated in the following succinct Peripatetic dictum: "The intellect by itself, however, moves nothing; but only the intellect which aims at an end and is practical" (Aristotle, *Nicomachean Ethics*, VI, Ch. 3, 35–37). In effect, Aristotle's notion of choice includes *desire* first and deliberation second, both wanting and thinking in order to act. For Aristotle, consciousness is both motivational and cognitive, both practical and theoretical. It is structured, as W.D. Ross describes it, as a two-fold activity. It can be characterized either as desiderative reasoning or rational deliberation. The "means" are reflexively considered but the end, the goal is always intentional.

The *purpose* of thinking is either: (a) *to know* what is true; or (b) *to do* what is wise or good, or *to make* what is beautiful or useful. In short, consciousness is always purposeful, i.e., intentional, as opposed to outwardly mechanical as in empiricism. In Plato, ultimately the end consists in the soul's desired unity with the supra-Form of the Good. In Aristotle's case, the goal is always human well-being or happiness. In this manner, Aristotle seconds Plato's suggestion in the *Theaetetus* by linking thoughts that are intentionally aimed at arriving at a decision and discharged into actions. When combined these "rationalist" descriptions are diametrically opposed to the passive *tabula rasa* paradigm of classical empiricism (although originally derived from Aristotle, *De Anima*, 430a) and the Epicurean mechanistic model of behaviorism currently championed by the "cognitive behavioral" sciences and the neurosciences of our own day.

Fourth, Plato's view on language as expressed by Socrates in the *Cratylus* is basically that no safe conclusions can be reached from a study of the etymology of the name to the nature of the thing for which the name stands. Consequently, Plato's attitude toward language and linguistics is rather unfavorable and little can be learned from their study. For Plato active thoughts, imageless concepts, and intuitive insights are very different from the artificiality of languages and the conventional use of speech, which fail in conveying the elaborate and intricate modes of consciousness upon which we have been commenting. Concepts and meanings will always outrun both words and language. The highest form of knowledge for Plato is universal, rational, necessary, conceptual, and intuitive as opposed to particular, empirical, contingent, sensory, and transient. Verbal expressions are always handicapped by their indirect modes of representation. Initially there is the material object; then the visual representation; then the conceptual meaning; then the written symbol or nominal term applied, which is long-removed from the original object or reality and virtually "lost in translation." There is a world of difference between a meaning versus a symbolic sign and its indirectly mediated relation to the meaning's innermost reality. Thus, although in the *Theaetetus* and *Sophist* passages I cited above, Plato connects thoughts and discourse, consciousness and language, we know from the corpus of his work that consciousness and language are essentially opposites. Language at best serves as an artificial tool designed for pragmatic and classificatory uses as it is applied to the lower orders of reality diagrammed in the Divided Line passage. As opposed to the discursive conceptual mediacy of mathematical and geometric knowledge (third level), for example, language is first applied to sensations and limited to opinion (*doxa*). Second it describes tangible, physical objects, which lead to belief (*pistis*), both of which deal with the particular and the sensory. Thus, the implementation of languages is basically practical and technical. Languages in general simply serve as instruments of communication in order to *do* things as the ancient Epicureans long ago maintained (Lucretius, *De Rerum Natura,* V, 1028–90). Various languages are basically conventional tools artificially invented for useful purposes. The value of different languages is always pragmatic; they serve to get things done. Compare Wittgenstein's *Philosophical Investigations,* Sections 1–5. As we proceed, we shall see that linguistically oriented philosophers will fail to account adequately for the primacy and interiority of reflexive consciousness. For example, for both Bergson and Hussserl the use of language will be undercut by the fundamental *qualitative immediacy of intuitions and eidetic insights.* For both, consciousness is primary and original and language is secondary and derivative. Accordingly, words are viewed as limited and imprecise instruments, clumsy vehicles of communication used to distinguish things from each other only to be set apart and left hanging disconnectedly, separated from each other. The permutations and vagaries of language are *learned* behaviors; the words are mere nominal symbols and signs and accordingly their "nuanced meanings" vary from society to society and even from person to person as any competent anthropologist will be pleased to tell us. They are relative to various environments and specific situations. In short, language is a poor handmaiden to consciousness, thought, conceptualization, and the richness of intuitive insights. Today, in the Anglo-speaking world, the armies of linguistic analysts and analytic philosophers hold the field, but we shall soon see their hegemony challenged.

In terms of the history of ideas and consciousness, an important paradigm shift occurs in the seventeenth-century as Hobbes, Locke, Berkeley, and Hume embark on an empirical strategy to define the essence of man in terms of his use of language as opposed to reason, to discredit the definition of man as "the rational animal." Accordingly, the Battle between the Giants and the Gods turns on the pivotal question whether the empiricists or the rationalists are more capable of capturing "the truth of consciousness" and one of the important issues revolves around the question, which is more primary: consciousness or language?[24] As we proceed, we will address this critical issue in different chapters when we discuss at greater length the philosophies of Henri

---

24   Cf. Ben Mijuskovic, "The Simplicity Argument and Meaning in Wittgenstein and Russell," *Critica,* VIII:4 (1976), 85–103; "Loneliness and the Possibility of a 'Private Language,'" *Journal of Thought,* 13:1 (1978), 14–22: and *Feeling Lonesome: The Philosophy and Psychology of Loneliness* (Santa Barbara: Praeger, 2015), Chapter 6, "Consciousness and Language," 129–148.

Bergson and Edmund Husserl. For the time being, let us leave the issue in the subtle minds of the Platonists and the capable hands of the Epicureans.

Finally, let us turn now to Plato's dualist metaphysics, for an obvious difficulty looms before us in the form of the classic "problem of metaphysical dualism." If one defines (1) the mind as an immaterial, active substance and (2) the material world as an extended and inert physical entity (Descartes), then it follows that the first cannot possibly (a) know of the existence of the second or (b) interact, since they share no attribute, accident, property, or predicate in common. Rousseau regards this paradox as a testimony to the inexplicable mystery of God's Power and Will, which can only be appreciated through Christian fideism (*The Faith of a Savoyard Vicar*). But that is Rousseau.

By contrast, in what follows I wish to agree with David Hume that the (seeming) paradox, the inexplicable dilemma of how immaterial perceptions and the material world can be connected, is best addressed as one of the unfathomable mysteries of Nature—rather than religion and faith. In light of Hume's principle of radical empirical contingency—that "anything can produce anything"—he is able to draw a distinction between on the one hand (1) an extended material world of objects and motion and, on the other hand (2) the presence of immaterial mental impressions and ideas, in a word, perceptions in the mind. Thus he declares that as far as "matters of fact" are concerned, "any thing can produce anything." As he expresses it, "reason as distinguished from experience can never make us conclude that a cause or productive quality is requisite to every beginning of existence" (Hume, *Treatise* I, iii, xiv; page 157). Notice his problematic use of the concept of *quality* as opposed to *quantity*. Perceptions are qualities, not quantities. Causes, as material, are always expressed in quantitative terms but not perceptions. Further he declares that "Any thing can produce anything. Creation, annihilation, motion, reason, volition; all these may arise from one another, or from any other [material] object we can imagine" (Hume, *Treatise*, 173). Hume is here suggesting that matter under certain circumstances can spontaneously "produce" or result in perceptions.

> [T]o consider the matter *a priori,* any thing may produce any thing, and that we shall never discover a reason, why any object may or may not be the cause of any other, however great, or however little the resemblance may be betwixt them.
> HUME, *Treatise.* 247

Further, Hume goes on to assert that "there is no absolute or metaphysical necessity, that every beginning of existence should be attended with an object [as cause]." So it is conceivable, according to Hume, that particular *physical* causes may have very different and distinct *mental* effects. Thus not only are effects without causes possible, or that "nothing" may produce "something," but also various causes may "produce" very different effects, effects that are completely dissimilar in nature from their antecedent "causes" or better expressed "attendant circumstances." Hume's theory of the radical contingency holding between ideas and things was heavily influenced by Malebranche's "occasionalist" doctrine. Malebranche argues that the "interaction" between the *thought* of my moving my arm and the actuality of my arm physically moving is contingent on God coordinating the intervention. (Basically, this argument derives from Descartes' contention that God continually preserves, i.e., re-creates the entire universe and every event in it.) Accordingly, every empirical "connection" is radically contingent. For aught I know a thrown pebble could extinguish the sun; a bitten apple could turn into a puff of smoke. Hume's ruling metaphysical principle in these arguments and contentions is that, within the world of Nature, in terms of "matters of fact," whatever does not imply a logical or metaphysical contradiction is imaginable, possible, and conceivable. These three descriptive terms are essentially synonymous. Accordingly, one can *imagine* conditions or situations in which (1) *mental* impressions, ideas, and perceptions are *contingently* present along with and/or associated with (2) certain *physical* conditions or circumstances. Indeed for Hume the *contingent* possibility of immaterial states of consciousness, i.e., mental *perceptions* existing "beside," "along with," or "accompanied by" material causes is not only conceivable but actual. Simply put, certain material combinations can produce immaterial, mental perceptions. And later, in the *Enquiry*, Hume continues to insist "That the contrary of every [empirical] matter of fact is still possible; because it can never imply a contradiction."[25] Since (a) the cause and (b) the effect are distinct and contingent existences, it follows that something material can cause, produce, result, or condition an immaterial entity; that there is *no* necessary "relation" between a cause and what may conceivably follow; and that—under certain circumstances—material conditions can contingently

---

25  David Hume, *An Enquiry Concerning Human Understanding* (Oxford: Clarendon Press, 1972), Section 21; "The contrary of every matter of fact is still possible; because it can never imply a contradiction"; "nor is anything beyond the power of thought, except what implies a contradiction"; and further "that reason, as distinguish'd from experience, can never make us conclude, that a cause or productive quality is absolutely requisite to every beginning of existence" (*Treatise*, I, iii, xvi, page 157). What is extraordinary in Hume's assertions is that he is explicitly insisting that conceivably *nature* can be spontaneously creative and its products inexplicable.

evolve or eventuate to produce immaterial existences. Accordingly, Hume advises us that

> we must separate the question concerning the [material] substance of the mind [presumably the brain] from that concerning its thought; and that confining ourselves to the latter question we find by the comparing of their ideas, that thought and [material] motion are different from each other, and by experience, that they are constantly united; which being all the circumstances, that enter into the idea of cause and effect, when apply'd to the operations of matter, we may certainly conclude, that [matter and] motion may be, and actually is the cause of thought and [mental] perception
> 
>     *Treatise.*, I, iv, v; page 248[26]

Hume's radical separation between (a) matter and mind; the physical body and its mental perceptions; causes and effects is heavily influenced by Malebranche's "occasionalist" principle, namely that there is no possible rational or empirical connection between the two sets of occurrences. By the same token, Schopenhauer will similarly follow Malebranche's *Eclaircissement* and Hume as well in exploiting this principle of distinction in the *World as Will and Representation* and Bergson will follow suit in *Time and Free Will*.

Again, students of Hume are often misled by his empiricism to "connect" it, i.e., misinterpret it as materialism. But the first is an epistemic principle and the other a metaphysical one. They do not have to be mutually implicative or even dependent on each other as Hume demonstrates. Again, materialism is a metaphysical theory that reduces all reality to matter and motion. On the other hand, phenomenalism is an epistemological principle, which states that "the external world," "the causal maxim," and "other selves" are merely constructions of mental sense data and there is no problem in asserting that both exist.

The dualism illustrated above in Hume is between matter and motion on the one side and passive mental perceptions (impressions and ideas) on the other. Perhaps for Hume rather than saying that extended matter is the "product" of thought, it would be more precise to say that it is the "accompaniment"

---

26  Ben Mijuskovic, "The Simplicity Argument versus a Materialist Theory of Mind," *Philosophy Today*, xx:4 (1976), 292–306; *Contingent Immaterialism* (Amsterdam: Gruner, 1984), 97–98, note 12; and cf. Norman Kemp Smith, *The Philosophy of David Hume* (London: Macmillan, 1964), 393–394. In other words, we cannot infer from the properties of matter that it cannot produce or result in immaterial thoughts.

of thought. Similarly, H.D. Lewis essentially agrees with Hume's conditional dualistic principle, although he does not cite Hume.

> There seems, therefore, to be no limit to the disparities we may find between causes and effects, and there is no reason at all to rule out *ab initio* the possibility of interaction between mind and body when these are affirmed to be radically different in nature ... We find that certain sorts of things happen, others not; and it seems perversely conceited on our part to deny the facts as we seem patently to find them, namely that mind is distinct from body and that these do affect one another, simply because we are unable to say how this comes about or is possible.[27]

But as we proceed, we shall see that the problem of the "coupling" of (a) an extended material realm of physical objects and (b) an unextended mental sphere of the mind is the problem of *how* to "connect" (a) passive re-active brains versus (b) the spontaneity of consciousness "to" or "with" each other; *how* the two can be *meaningfully* related to each other. Doesn't matter get "in the way" of mind?

More recently, Noam Chomsky in his article citing my *Achilles of Rationalist Arguments*, which discusses Bishop Stillingfleet's disputation with Locke on whether God could have conceivably "created thinking matter," argues the same conclusion I had reached three-and-a-half decades ago in companionship with Hume.

> In Hume's judgment, Newton's greatest achievement was that while he "seemed to draw the veil from some of the mysteries of nature, he shewed at the same time the imperfections of the mechanical [materialist] philosophy; and thereby restored nature's ultimate secrets to that obscurity, in which they ever did and ever will remain." On different grounds, others

---

27   H.D. Lewis, *The Elusive Mind* (London: George Allen & Unwin, 1969), 173 and *passim*. We will return to a discussion of Lewis' views in Chapter 7. After Descartes, Malebranche appeals to God as the miraculous "occasional cause" of apparent human interaction between body and soul; Leibniz summons God's pre-established harmony; and Berkeley invokes God's divine ordering of the uniform laws of nature in order to account for the concordance between the soul of man and the laws of nature. Hume was familiar with the writings of Malebranche and it appears he fully subscribed at least to the conceivability of the "occasionalist" argument but obviously discarded its religious implications. Both material and mental elements clearly are represented in this world and they frequently display a pattern of co-occurrence. Beyond this knowledge any deeper insight seems futile and speculative. In this regard, I agree with Hume.

reached similar conclusions. Locke, for example, had observed that motion has effects "which we can in no way conceive motion able to produce"—as Newton had in fact demonstrated shortly before. Since we remain in "incurable ignorance of what we desire to know" about matter and its effects, Locke concluded, no "science of bodies [is] within our reach" and we can only appeal to "the arbitrary determination of that All-wise Agent who has made them to be, and to operate as they do, in a way wholly above our weak understanding to conceive."... [Similarly] Descartes claimed to have explained the phenomena of the material world in mechanistic terms, while also demonstrating that the mechanical philosophy is not all-encompassing, not reaching to the domain of mind—again pretty much in accordance with the common-sense dualistic interpretation of oneself and the world around us 167–168).[28]

We may therefore legitimately, or at least plausibly, conclude that there are certain (and possibly many) metaphysical issues that by their very nature absolutely defy strictly rational or empirical solutions. Why is there something rather than nothing, as Parmenides, Leibniz, Fichte, Schopenhauer, and William James inquire? Is not the existence of this world as possible as its nonexistence? As James remarks, "the unrest which keeps the never stopping clock of metaphysics going is the thought that the non-existence of this world is just as possible as its existence." Consider also Heidegger's formulation of the same sentiment in the opening paragraph to his *Introduction to Metaphysics,* which begins with "The Fundamental Question of Metaphysics."

> Why are there beings rather than nothing? That is the question. 'Why are there beings at all instead of nothing?' Many never run into this question at all, if running into the question means not only hearing it and reading the interrogative sentence as uttered, but asking the question; that is taking a stand on it, posing it, compelling oneself into the state of this question.[29]

---

28   Noam Chomsky, "The Mysteries of Nature: How Well Hidden?" *The Journal of Philosophy,* CVI:4 (2009), 167–200; he cites my *Achilles of Rationalist Arguments* on page 169 in regard to my discussion of Locke's controversy with Bishop Edward Stillingfleet over the issue whether God could have created thinking matter and whether senseless matter can think? Chomsky also cites my *Achilles* in his *New Horizons in the Study of Mind and Language* (2000), *Chomsky Notebooks* (2007), and "What Kind of Animals Are We?" (2013).

29   Martin Heidegger, *An Introduction to Metaphysics,* translated by Ralph Manheim (New Haven, CT: Yale University Press, 1959), 1. Locke conceived the contingent possibility of God creating "thinking matter." Hume simply substituted Nature for God.

To this question, no reliable or satisfying answer can be given, not by science, not by reason, and not by blind faith. And chance is hardly a compelling or even a satisfying philosophical answer—although perhaps it is a good guess.

The doctrine of materialism is a *metaphysical* "worldview"; it is not a science. By its very essence, the assertion that the nine (or eight or ten) planets would continue to revolve around the sun in the absence of any sentient life in the universe is an *unverifiable* proposition *in principle;* by its very terms it cannot be tested, confirmed, or verified. It is well beyond the protection of positivism. What sense would it make to declare that if all living organisms (including plants and sea urchins) in the universe were extinguished, the sun would still shine and the days would be warmer than the nights? In principle, there is no rational or empirical way to confirm or disconfirm these assertions. They are each and every one of them absolutely unverifiable. And so are the ultimate metaphysical principles of dualism and idealism. Both are underived premises, or "first principles." According to Pascal, "The heart has its reasons, which the head (reason) does not know" (*Pensées*). For Fichte, ultimate assumptions are spontaneous acts of volition determined by our subjective "interests and inclinations" (*Science of Knowledge*). And for William James, they are decisional convictions decided by our "passional natures" ("The Will To Believe").

There is no answer to the question *why* something exists rather than nothing any more than there is a solution to *how* our minds and matter interact, if they share nothing in common. It seems manifestly clear *that* both matter *and* mind, under certain obviously compatible conditions and circumstances within our commonly shared world, not only can be but actually are found "paired" together, alongside one another, and seemingly acting in "consonance" with each other just as sight and sound can act in concert despite their *qualitatively* functional differences and diversities. One cannot produce colors from sounds or sounds from colors, although both clearly serve the human body and the human mind. No matter how or by what manipulative adjustments we try to alchemically quantitatively maneuver sounds we cannot produce sights; and sights cannot cause sounds. As Hume perspicaciously points out, there is no causal explanation of *how,* nor any metaphysical reason *why,* when material objects strike each other there is both a physical reaction and a psychic awareness "within" our mind. Why is there motion at all? And there is no reason or explanation *why* the thought of volitionally moving my arm ends in my arm mechanically moving. Apart from Malebranche's occasionalism, Leibniz's preestablished harmony, and Berkeley's immaterialism and his plea that "we see all things in God," all these *ad hoc* explanations, adjustments, and accommodations are all fideistically and desperately predicated on the imposition of divine interventions or more literally intrusions. But in the end, we are simply left with either a supernatural or a natural mystery.

Finally, there is one vital activity of consciousness that we cannot ascribe to Plato but nevertheless it is critical to all that follows: the concept of spontaneity. In Chapter 3, which treats the freedom of self-consciousness, we will learn that Leibniz is the first to use the term "spontaneity" explicitly in conjunction with consciousness and in turn connects it and attributes it to Aristotle's notion of intelligence thereby recruiting it in a highly important and technical philosophical sense. Others simply assume that self-consciousness is in general active and that it stands diametrically opposed to the inertness of matter. But with Leibniz, spontaneity assumes a critical meaning; it intends something very special; a *sui generis act*. Because Leibniz's monads, as soul substances, are absolutely self-enclosed and windowless, they are logically and metaphysically forced to exclude any conceivable contact or interaction from outside or beyond themselves. It therefore *necessarily* follows that any activity of the psyche/soul/mind/cogito/monad/ego can only be initiated from *within* consciousness. In what follows, we shall document the manner in which Leibniz, Kant, Fichte, Hegel, Bergson, Husserl, Royce, and Sartre will enlist this critical concept in their philosophies.

In brief, then, I propose that the metaphysical—as opposed to the religious—philosophies of dualism and subjective idealism perform a more credible job of providing insight into the intricacies of human consciousness as opposed to the reductivist strategies and methodologies of materialism, mechanism, determinism, empiricism, phenomenalism, behaviorism, and the neurosciences.

Apart from the foregoing considerations, and they are admittedly speculations albeit incredibly important ones, there will always remain an unfathomable and impermeable factor underlying the hidden and often alienating powers of human emotions and cognitions. Kant was right. The metaphysical nature of man is such that he will always search in vain and never reach the unknown origins of our feelings and thoughts and values. But the endless seduction to seek both below and beyond in order to unravel, and understand human consciousness and reality in our search for answers and solutions will continue to defy empirical, rational, mystical, and fideistic penetration.

After completing the *Achilles* study and mapping the progress of the simplicity argument in its four traditional guises, I was surprised to discover four new applications for its immaterialist principle. The new contexts concern an establishment for: (5a) a doctrine of "absolute" meanings and relations in consciousness, with a special application to epistemological and moral idealism; and (5b) a foundation for both an idealist and phenomenalist interpretation of space; (6) the freedom or transcendence of consciousness; (7) the establishment of immanent time-consciousness (in contrast to the Aristotelian and Newtonian conception of time as an objective measurement of material objects traveling through space); and (8) the drawing of a critical distinction within consciousness between its *qualitative* and *intensive* features versus its *quantitative* and *extensive* features.

Accordingly, I propose to continue my historical and conceptual tracing of these newly discovered affiliations. By "trace," I also intend to indicate their intricate conceptual developments and consequences. Nevertheless, it is important to note that the immaterialist *premise*—although now recruited for a novel set of distinguishable conclusions—essentially remains what A.O. Lovejoy designates as a "unit-idea."[30] In other words, the "idea," or in the present context, the *principle* that the human mind is both (a) immaterial and (b) active remains the same and retains the same meaning. The *premise* cannot change, although to be sure, there are significant variations between the quartet of inferences we will now examine and their conclusions. All eight versions—the previous four as well the quartet of new ones—are developed in conjunction with the same identical premise. In terms of the History of Ideas discipline, as Lovejoy observes, the concept of God in Western thought is not a stable "unit idea," since it conceptually shifts from theism in St. Augustine, to pantheism in Spinoza, and deism in Lord Herbert of Cherbury, with each author manifesting very different conceptions and definitions of the Deity. But what is so unique and permanent about the Achilles premise-arguments-conclusions is first that its major assumption—that human consciousness is both immaterial and active—remains unchanging; and second that like a giant cosmic octopus its tentacles consisting of no less than eight distinct conclusions grip both man and reality. In addition, what is equally and doubly important is that all eight conclusions agree in demonstrating a single *universal* conclusion, namely, that *senseless matter cannot think!*

The goal of the present study, then, is to show that there is a conceptual constellation of intrinsically related problems and proposed solutions, which all stem from the same premise, but at the same time each conclusion is distinguished and stands alone from the seven other proofs.

One must appreciate the far-reaching influence of these eight arguments in order to achieve an adequate understanding of the ancient, modern, and contemporary periods in Western philosophical thought and its developmental trends toward dualism, rationalism, idealism, phenomenology, and existentialism. A primary value of this study, then, is to distinguish and disentangle

---

30  A.O. Lovejoy, *The Great Chain of Being: A Study of the History of an Idea* (New York: Harper & Row, 1953), Introduction, 21; hereafter cited as GCB.

separate lines of thought, aspects of argumentation that have been heretofore confounded and confused—if even recognized. Hence, I propose to treat these novel demonstrations in separate chapters although frequently the arguments overlap and interweave with each other. Thus an author may present a combination of Achilles proofs in the same work or even in the same passage. However, my justification for separating the arguments into their multiple uses is to clarify the issues involved. The fact that historically particular authors have enlisted the premise for one thesis but not for another, whereas other writers have recruited it for several conclusions, clearly testifies to the separateness of its employments. In this respect, the present exploration into the discipline of the history of ideas and consciousness is intended to assume an "analytic" and clarifying function.

A couple of qualifying comments are in order. First, historically quite often the immaterialist thesis has been summoned in order to argue in behalf of the immortality of the human soul. Although this does not happen to be my own inclination, nevertheless it is an undeniable consideration that innumerable numbers of human beings in history and contemporaneously have been and are committed to the soul's immaterial or spiritual immortality and that it is based on the Achilles principle, as in the case of H.D. Lewis above (*EM*, 324). Personally, in agreement with the emphases on "dualistic" metaphysical strains readily apparent in Aristotle, Hume, and Sartre, I believe consciousness is immaterial but once its contingent, physical conditions are neutralized and dispersed at death, so are human sensations, feelings, and thoughts and along with them any possibility of a continued conscious existence or an afterlife.

Second, I will go on to argue that the present combination of the natural, behavioral, as well as our current neurosciences together simply avoid out of hand the activities of self-consciousness and intentionality; spontaneity; the existence of the subconscious; and collectively deny the *qualitative* values of ethics and aesthetics by simply substituting crude *quantitative* molecular motions in the brain.

The edifice of human knowledge contains a number of metaphysical, epistemological, and ethical floors that are further subdivided into different corridors throughout the entire residence. Some tenants labor in the humanities or the social sciences while others are engaged in the natural or mathematical sciences and still others in the arts. Thus, once in the corridor, there are doors opening to rooms that are uniquely furnished and decorated. Each chamber serves as a sanctuary for its occupants. The simplicity premise possesses a passkey for a large number of corridors and many rooms. And sometimes there are even evictions.

To ask why the history of ideas and consciousness is valuable is somewhat like inquiring what benefit is it to unify such diverse phenomena as the falling of objects toward the earth, the ebb and rise of the tides, and the elliptical orbit of the planets with all three subsumed under the single comprehensive law of gravity. As an interdisciplinary methodology, the history of ideas and consciousness exhibits an intrinsically unifying and synthesizing force. The conception that the mind is immaterial, active, self-conscious, and intentional has had—and continues to have—a formidable impact on Western thought in general. Thus to question why it is important to highlight certain first principles, basic premises, or assumptions is to fail to recognize that there is a finite set of fundamental presuppositions, which either continue uninterruptedly and/or resurface time and again in the millennial annals of Western thought. The commitment to dualism, rationalism, and idealism, as opposed to materialism, empiricism, and behaviorism—and now the threat of the neurosciences—will always remain an option for the human mind. The idealist principle that "senseless matter cannot think" will perpetually be present with its contradictory thesis that "thinking" can be reduced to the material cellular motions in the skull and brain. But regardless how opposed someone may be to the immaterialist thesis, nevertheless it is worth studying if for no other reason than as Cicero advised, one should know his opponents arguments better than his own.

In what follows, I enlist the Achilles thesis in order to make the best case I can for (1) a version of metaphysical substance dualism; (b) epistemological subjective idealism; and (c) an existential description of the human condition by engaging in a historical and conceptual journey through the lengthy odyssey of the human spirit. The purpose of the current inquiry is to resist reducing the self solely to its material conditions. Ultimately I wish to connect a theory of consciousness to the inevitability of human loneliness.

A principle, as I understand it, is an underived, assumed starting point. A paradigm is the ensuing model, picture, or system derived from the principle. Individuals come and go and each of us dies in our own time but principles have the possibility of subsisting forever, as eternal options equally present to our intellectual capacities and existential choices.

The most dangerous limitation of the neurosciences is embedded in its implicit and explicit assault on the reality of qualitative differences between the sciences, which they pit against the valuative theories of philosophy as embodied in art, ethics, religion, and humanism.

Further, the history of ideas and consciousness seeks to break through the barriers between different disciplines. It is interdisciplinary in its approach, scope, and methods. And if there is any value in goals, which strive to remove obstacles between not only different disciplines or fields within the humanities, but also between the social and natural sciences as well, then this sort of inquiry I believe is worthwhile. What is critically at stake in the present study is the question "whether senseless matter can think?" It is as much the concern of the materialist, empiricist, physiologist, psychologist, behaviorist, sociologist, and neuroscientist as it is of the dualist, idealist, phenomenologist, and existentialist.

Before continuing, however, I need to discuss a serious criticism leveled at the History of Ideas discipline. It is put forth in a book review, which many years ago appeared in the Marxist New Left journal, *Telos*, authored by David Gross. It concerns George Boas' *The History of Ideas*. As the critic humorously but disparagingly points out, since, according to the historian of ideas, virtually all important ideas begin with Plato, it is not unexpected to discover that this is also the case with Professor Boas' erudite study. Only in this case, Professor Boas succeeds not only in locating the idea's birth but its death as well.

> The notion of a "microcosm" is a case in point. The concept first appears, not surprisingly, in Plato's Philebus, but the word [or idea] itself is not actually used until Aristotle coins it in his Politics. From that date on, the word jumps across centuries and millennia until it finally collapses from fatigue in the sixteenth century. The place de la mort has in fact been located by Boas. It is in Padua, in Northern Italy, where a commemorative stone exists to this day. In the meantime, the idea had entered the minds of a number of people along the way; there is evidence, for instance, that Philo Judaens, Seneca, Porphyry, Godefroy of St. Victor, and Agrippa of Nettesheim, among others, were at one time or another intimates of the idea. Finally, we are told, the notion of a microcosm began to vanish at the beginning of the modern period with the rise of empirical science.[31]

The preceding is obviously a strong indictment of the entire History of Ideas program, hardly tempered by its wittiness. Indeed, Gross expands the criticism and applies it to Lovejoy's classic, *The Great Chain of Being,* as well as to Boas' study, since Lovejoy himself confesses that the idea of a "Chain of Being" disappears, virtually expiring in the nineteenth-century. But truly seminal ideas are undeniably permanent, persistent, and intrinsically valuable and I would argue there are many seminal concepts and principles, which function like seeds

---

31    David Gross, book review of George Boas' *The History of Ideas* in *Telos,* Number 6 (1970), 211–212.

continually germinating ever anew throughout the intellectual soil of Western thought.

Gross' objection to the History of Ideas methodology is basically the same one which Karl Marx directs against Hegel in *The German Ideology,* namely, that "life determines consciousness" and not, as (allegedly) Hegel would have it, "consciousness determines life"; that our material economic conditions determine our social ideas and not the other way around. Indeed, Marx specifically refers to Hegel as a "historian of ideas" in *The German Ideology*. According to Marx, the capitalist economic system has resulted in necessitating the exploitation of masses of alienated workers, separating them from the fruits of their labor; the ownership of their own products; and by pitting them against their fellow men by competition. Unfortunately, Gross continues, philosophers like Hegel have merely sought to understand the world rather than improve it: "Philosophers have only *interpreted* the world in different ways; the point is to *change* it" (*Theses on Feuerbach,* Thesis 11). But Gross fails to acknowledge Marx's significant debt to Hegel because unless *self-conscious reflexive ideas*—in the guise of *class*-consciousness—intervene, man's lot would continue to get worse and worse without any hope of transcending the situation. Thus Marx actually appeals to a transcending dialectical *class*-consciousness in order to overcome the alienating situation of proletariat exploitation, a fact to which Gross is obviously unaware. Plus Marx's strategy for his world revolution is gleaned from Hegel's Lordship and Bondage dialectic because he realizes, as Gross obviously does not, that unless the proletariat *self-consciously, reflexively* realize what is happening to them, they could never overcome, transcend their enslaved conditions. The master, as Hegel is well aware, has nowhere to go, whereas the slave alone has the opportunity to develop, to transcend his alienated situation.[32]

Further, Gross' review condemns the discipline of the History of Ideas as valueless and unjustified because "For the Ideen-historiker it is essentially a concept in a vacuum, i.e., a notion which somehow floats above time and space, and therefore above history [and independently of men]." Consequently, according to Gross:

> The greatest weakness of intellectual historians like Boas or Arthur Lovejoy is their inability to understand how ideas are generated out of society—how they (figuratively) grow and expand in response to [economic] problems within a specific social milieu. Ideas don't "happen"

---

[32] Ben Mijuskovic, "Marx and Engels on Materialism and Idealism," *Journal of Thought,* 9:3 (1974), 157–168.

> because the Weltgeist decides to objectify itself through the minds of philosophers. This is what Boas seems to suggest when he announces that ideas "shape human thought and action." The inference here is that the energizing agents of thought are ideas themselves, and that intellectual concepts increase and multiply by virtue of their own inherent dispositions. As a methodology this is a patent absurdity. Ideas are effusions that arise out of life, which is to say, out of the particular social and personal *Lebenswelt* of the thinkers involved ... To crystallize a moment of transcendence and to hypostatize that a particle of thought (i.e., "idea") apart from its necessary interconnection with practice, and apart from its essential nature as activity, is to fundamentally misrepresent The Nature of Thought itself. And yet this is substantially what the historian of ideas sets out to do. His job is to transmute intellection into "ideas," and thinking into "thoughts" (i.e., reified categories which appear to have a separate existence divorced from history). These fossilized forms, these "ideas," are then studied for themselves.
> 
> Gross, BR, 212

Here a number of things must be said. In one sense, Gross is partly right. Factually, the History of Ideas is repeatedly accused of irrelevancy and abstractness. It is criticized for treating ideas as if they were Platonic essences, completely independent of the world and its problems, while "subsisting" apart from living men and human concerns. However, I would rather agree with Etienne Gilson that great ideas, principles, and arguments "never die; they are ageless and always ready to revive in the minds which need them, just as ancient seeds can germinate again when they find fertile soil."[33]

This does not mean, however, that the value of important principles and arguments can exist apart from men, but rather, quite the opposite; they will always survive within human minds, human surroundings, special contexts, and revive whenever they are needed and the occasion demands. This is also the reason why we are able today to uncover living continuities between our own period and that of former times enabling us not only to understand but also to empathize with former ages. For example, our forensic notion of voluntary and involuntary choice, personal imputability, and moral responsibility is strongly indebted to Aristotle's *Nicomachean Ethics*. The alternative politics of Hobbes, Locke, and Rousseau guide us today as forcefully as they have in their own age painted as they are with the wide brush strokes of Plato's Ring of Gyges myth

---

33  Etienne Gilson, *History of Christian Philosophy in the Middle Ages* (New York: Random House, 1955), 540.

in the *Republic* and its conceptual exploration of the dynamical relations between the State of Nature, Human Nature, and the Social Contract.

But Gross is fundamentally wrong. It is clear he has a specific and unfortunately narrow definition as to what counts as a philosopher and philosophical issues. For Gross, it is confined to a person who understands "how ideas are generated *out of* society—how they grow and expand in response to problems within a specific social *milieu*." Gross is here obviously influenced by Marx's notion, expressed in the *Theses on Feuerbach* quoted above. This suggests that ideas—he is obviously restricting himself to economic, political, and social ideas—are the only relevant ones. But this would confine philosophical ideas to specific *relative* and *particular* contexts by restricting them to fundamentally economic situations alone. This would be an unfortunate violation of philosophy's liberating interdisciplinary mandate. The *Republic* of Plato alone offers an entry into an incredible wealth of metaphysical, epistemological, ethical, psychological, aesthetic, and educational subjects and approaches. Rousseau in *Emile* called it the greatest work on education ever written. The individualized treatises of Aristotle deal with metaphysics, physics, logic, psychology, ethics, politics, aesthetics, rhetoric, the heavens, and so on. What in this universe is Gross thinking? Although Marx argues that the economic base may be the reality, nevertheless even he clearly recognizes the inestimable value of the ethical and aesthetic superstructure, which guides man in producing according to higher and nobler laws. When man's alienated labor is freed and performed with the unbounded energy of unalienated labor, "man then constructs in accordance with the laws of beauty" (*Economic and Philosophic Manuscripts of 1844*). In what follows, we shall learn that the strict economic approach alone, much like the neuroscientific approach, makes no allowance for the humanistic values of ethics and aesthetics. Economics is fundamentally quantitative; not evaluative.

The simplicity premise already has an entrenched impressive and long-standing presence in the disciplines of philosophy, psychology, ethics, religion, art, sociology but most especially in the powerful literary expressions of man's innate loneliness spanning the time from the Greek myths and dramas to our current existentialist writings. The present work serves to extend that literary presence and also to serve as a plea to promote the History of Ideas as an architectonic discipline precisely because it has a great deal to do with us, our world, our values, our time, and our ideals. Great ideas exhibit an overpowering and forceful integrity of their own. That does not mean, of course, that they are independent of human beings but rather that we must think in terms of universal principles, arguments, and strategies common to all mankind. The History of Ideas is an intrinsically synthetic, unifying, and coherent enterprise.

Finally, it seems appropriate to caution the reader about certain inherent weaknesses in the study of the history of ideas and consciousness. The discipline is by its very nature both extremely broad and, at times, admittedly quite vague, even in its general outlines concerning the fields which may be said to comprise it. This latter consideration makes it difficult to achieve the desired thoroughness in regard to the "completeness" of any particular study. There will always remain a sentiment that more works or authors should have been consulted, more hidden sources and relationships uncovered, as well as the frequent and normal pitfalls of interpretation. These difficulties are obviously discouraging but unavoidable, since unlike those academic colleagues, who only concentrate and confine their research on a single author, period, or discipline. By contrast, interdisciplinary historians range deep and wide in their nomadic quests and journeys. In the course of pursuing his or her task, historians of ideas treat many authors, often too many. If they are honest and cautious, they will not pretend to a greater competence than their abilities dictate and they themselves possess. But even within these recognized scholarly limitations, the philosophical historian is more vulnerable to hasty generalizations, to being influenced by Bacon's idiosyncratic "idols of the cave"; and to being unduly impressed by passages and arguments taken out of context from the many diverse authors and numerous works she or he consults. The result is that there is too much material to master and the lone scholar cannot always hope to be an authority on all she or he treats. Obviously, one will be more familiar about some authors rather than others, but even so there simply cannot be the expertise one expects in commentaries that are confined to a single author, discipline, or historical period. In confessing this weakness, I take a certain degree of comfort in the fact that others have felt it as acutely as myself but yet had the resolve to continue despite the risks. I cannot help but gather a considerable degree of encouragement from Professor Lovejoy's concluding comment.

> The study of the history of ideas is full of dangers and pitfalls; it has its characteristic excess. Precisely because it aims at interpretation and unification and seeks to correlate things which are not on the surface connected, it may easily degenerate into a species of merely imaginative historical generalization and because the historian of an idea is compelled by the nature of his enterprise to gather material from several fields of knowledge, he is inevitably, in at least some parts of his synthesis, liable to the errors which lie in wait for the non-specialist. I can only say I am not unmindful of these dangers and have done what I could to avoid them; it would be too sanguine to suppose that I have in all cases

succeeded in doing so. In spite of the probability, or perhaps the certainty, of partial failure, the enterprise seems worth attempting.
  LOVEJOY, *GCB*, 21

The present study is integrally connected to my four previous studies, *The Achilles of Rationalist Arguments: The Simplicity, Unity, and Identity of Thought and Soul from the Cambridge Platonists to Kant* (1974); *Loneliness in Philosophy, Psychology, and Literature* (1979; 2012); *Contingent Immaterialism: Meaning, Freedom, Time and Mind* (1984); and *Feeling Lonesome: The Philosophy and Psychology of Loneliness* (2015), as well as related articles. But unlike Professors Boas' and Lovejoy's defining works, the Achilles premise with its diverse eight demonstrations and conclusions continues to endure since Plato's time and accordingly reaches out today with an invitation for collaborative studies by other scholars representing various disciplines.

In the present chapter, I have tried to show that in terms of the history of consciousness and ideas several key ideas and principles have withstood the neglect of time and the assaults of critics. In the text that follows, however, I intend to explore a variety of distinctions between the subconscious, unconscious, and self-conscious; sensations and relations; immediacy and mediacy; intuition and inference; determinism and spontaneity and freedom; scientific and objective time as opposed to personal and subjective time-consciousness; a *posteriori* propositions and *a priori* synthetic judgments; quantitative extensities and qualitative intensities; consciousness and language; the correspondence theory of truth and the coherence theory; and loneliness and intimacy among others.

In any event, I feel much as Hume did—although unable to express myself with his wonderful eloquence—constrained to embark upon uncharted seas, in a fragile intellectual vessel, which I can only hope will sustain me through difficult journeys and unfamiliar visitations. My thesis is a sail, at times strong, at other times quite ineffectual, and even on occasion a cumbersome hindrance; my scholarly abilities are but slender and brittle oars, which momentarily aid me but remain clumsy implements as I struggle to successfully navigate my explorations. Will I founder on "Doubt's Boundless Sea"; will I completely lose my bearings before the obscurity of endless ideas and timeless ages; or will I perhaps reach a pleasant shore and in retrospect view my travels as a worthwhile passage?

CHAPTER 2

# The Simplicity Argument: Meanings, Relations, and Space

> Every man is born either a Platonist or an Aristotelian.
> SAMUEL TAYLOR COLERIDGE

∴

Man is infinitely complex, eternally creative, and absolutely alone. In all that follows, we shall have the opportunity to test these claims. My overriding goal remains to defend a form of substance dualism based on the simplicity premise and its singular distinction—no matter how outmoded this may appear—and correspondingly to promote Kant's version of subjective idealism, which is equally grounded in his conception of the immaterial and active nature of the mind beginning with immanent time-consciousness and the unity of consciousness, while coupling both with Husserl's principle of transcendent intentionality.

After having completed my former studies, I discovered yet another cluster of four distinct uses for the simplicity premise and the initial one I shall introduce I find instructive and relevant in the context of the immaterialist paradigm of consciousness I am concerned to trace and defend.

Two very different applications of the Achilles premise resurface prominently in the modern period and play out in two very different contexts. First it appears in arguments intended to establish an ideal and absolute theory of ethics couched in a comprehensive system of unified meanings and relations with thinkers contending that because of the unique immaterial and active nature of consciousness, immutable moral meanings, traditionally called Forms, Ideas, Essences, Universals, or "Intelligibles," in deference to their Platonic heritage, are implemented in order to represent values that are attainable by pure, non-sensory intuition and/or reason. This is true of Ralph Cudworth's *immediate* intuitionist ethical criterion as well as Immanuel Kant's *discursive* synthetic *a priori* categorical imperative.

Secondly, and in a very different manner, the simplicity premise can also be shown to ground an idealist (Leibniz) as well as a phenomenalist (Hume) "idea" of space, which is required as a critical underpinning for the Scientific

Revolution. The complex metaphysical and epistemological aspects of space and the problem of the *scientific* status of space will occupy us in the second half of the chapter. Thus in addition to inducting the immaterialist premise for the purpose of establishing an ethical base, it is *also* pressed into service as a theoretical foundation for the *idea* of space and the *appearance* of an "external world" chock full of inanimate material objects and sentient creatures. Because there is both an objective and a subjective time, I will treat internal time-consciousness as a special category in Chapter 4.

But returning to the original theme of the study, the Battle between the Giants and the Gods, a contemporaneous critical distinction can be found between the primary single *quality* of matter and the multiple tertiary *qualities* of consciousness, namely ethical (and aesthetic) valuations. Thus for example, both Freud's empirical and phenomenalist psychoanalytic principles directly lead to a form of *psychological* determinism while the materialism of the neurosciences culminate in a version of *physical* determinism and moral relativism in behalf of the Giants. By contrast, the dualists and idealists appeal to immaterial active concepts and laws in support of the Gods and a universal moral system. (This quantity-quality distinction will be the main focus in Chapter 5.)

But historically prior to the seventeenth-century and before the advent of the Scientific Revolution, it seemed quite natural for both metaphysicians and theologians to posit the possibility of a realm of Platonic realities overseen by a theistic God ministering to a population of immortal souls. Universal ethical concepts and commands served as guiding principles for human conduct, which in turn, if negotiated successfully, would grant certain obedient souls with the eligibility for a rewarding afterlife.

Again historically metaphysical speculations concerning materialism were usually—but not always—connected to atheism and the denial of the immortality of the soul. Tertullian would be an exception: "I believe because it is absurd." But generally speaking, human mortality was explicit within the philosophical heritages of Leucippus, Democritus, Epicurus, and Lucretius and their followers both ancient and modern. Hobbes, will claim to be an exception to the rule.

In the atomic theory, the universe is conceived as eternal and human entities are regarded as material mortal compositions and therefore subject to decomposition and death. In classical materialism, a theistic God was considered as both an implausible and an unnecessary hypothesis. The doctrine of materialism was *relatively* infrequent during the Middle Ages and generally only surfaced sporadically during the lengthy span of time extending from the great Hellenic and Hellenistic thinkers through the millennium of Christian dominance. Saint Augustine successfully replied to the Academic and Pyrhonnien

Skeptics by anticipating the Cartesian cogito and Thomas Aquinas refuted the atheists in his five proofs for the existence of God and his rejection of the prevalence of evil used by the non-believers in their denial of God's existence. But during the period of the Italian and English Renaissances, all that changed and a refreshing wave of humanism and skepticism began to re-emerge anew. And although Marsilio Ficino continued to promote a form of Christian Neo-Platonism, Pietro Pomponazzi turned to the scientific system of Aristotle, and Lorenzo Valla favored Epicureanism, as a more scientific attitude was steadily gaining ground and influence, especially through the increasing ascendance of Epicureanism during the modern period as it was more forcibly ushered in through the writings of Pierre Gassendi and the works of Thomas Hobbes. This resulted in a counter-movement promoted by a group of thinkers generally known as the Cambridge Platonists, who promptly rallied their spiritual and intellectual forces against Descartes' mechanistic tendencies but especially against Hobbes' materialism in their defense of orthodox Christian theism buttressed by Platonic and Neo-Platonic ethical doctrines as they committed to a dualistic metaphysic and an absolute moral idealism.

Prior to Hume's famous distinction between the Is and the Ought, assertions of Fact versus judgments of Value, and the interests of Science versus those of Ethics, differences were readily blurred, and both theologians, moralists, and philosophers moved smoothly and unhindered back and forth among metaphysical, epistemological, and ethical theories and claims. This mode of argumentation was characteristic and congenial to the cohesive group of Cambridge theologians and their brand of rational intuitionism. It is against this line of thought that Hume offers his celebrated and famous critical distinction.

> In every system of morality, which I have hitherto met with, I have always remark'd, that the author proceeds for some time in the ordinary way of reasoning, and establishes the being of God, or makes observations, concerning human affairs; when of a sudden I am surpris'd to find, that instead of the usual copulations of propositions, is and is not, I meet with no proposition that is not connected with an ought or ought not. This change is imperceptible; but is, however, of the last consequence. For as this ought, or ought not, expresses some new relation or affirmation, 'tis necessary that it should be observ'd and explain'd; and at the same time that a reason should be given, for what seems altogether inconceivable, how this new relation can be a deduction from others, which are entirely different from it.[1]

---

1 David Hume, *A Treatise of Human Nature* (Oxford: Clarendon Press, 1973), II, i, 1, page 469; hereafter cited as Hume, *Treatise;* the page numbers will be cited from this standard edition.

To place the ethical issue in the larger context of Platonism versus Aristotelianism, or rationalism versus empiricism, Hume's own ethics appeals to both the *immediacy* of an empirical sentiment, an *immediate* feeling of approbation or censure, while also offering an early form of calculative utilitarianism benefiting society at large and dependent upon the artifice of a generalized sympathy engendering a sense of social justice (*An Enquiry Concerning the Principles of Morals*). In fundamental agreement with Francis Hutcheson's moral sense theory, he appeals to an empirical criterion, a moral sentiment grounded in universal human nature and contends that our *feeling* natures exhibit an ability to pronounce *immediately* upon certain species of actions as either praiseworthy or blameworthy. When we "disinterestedly" observe the moral actions of others in which our personal interests are suspended, our moral sense is naturally endowed with a capacity to judge directly in distinguishing the *quality* of ethical actions. Our "uninvolved" evaluation naturally determines virtue from vice as we "objectively" observe human conduct. Thus, by contrast, while Hume offers the criterion of a *moral sense,* the Cambridge thinkers propose rational *intuition* as the alternative standard. This difference within an ethical context represents the contrast between rationalism and empiricism we need to keep in mind as we proceed.

Later Kant will also endorse the same distinction between the Ought and the Is, between ethical and empirical judgments, but in his case his moral criterion will be based on the mediacy of a relational synthetic *a priori* "categorical imperative." In doing so, Kant will metaphysically separate an empirical world of science from a (conceivable) noumenal realm of ethical realities; a phenomenal world of causal determinism as distinct from a transcendent realm of freedom. But the important point is that in the context of the history of consciousness and ideas, prior to both Hume and Kant, speculations concerning ethical subjects essentially disregarded the distinction between empirical facts and ethical values. It simply went unnoticed and consequently philosophers, theologians, and moralists moved "imperceptibly," as Hume remarks, between the two realms, but whereas the Cambridge ethicists appealed to a transcendent universe of immutable Platonic Forms and Kant to a noumenal reality of things-in-themselves and freedom of the will, Hume

---

It is the Cambridge men Hume has in mind when he refers to "Those who affirm that virtue is nothing but a conformity to reason and that there are eternal fitnesses and unfitnesses of things, which are the same to every rational being that considers them; that the immutable measures of right and wrong impose an obligation not only on human creatures, but also on the deity himself. All these systems concur in the opinion that morality, like truth, is discern'd merely by ideas, by their juxtaposition and their comparison" (Hume, *Treatise,* 456–457). This declaration is intended as a rejection of William of Ockham's voluntarist tradition in Christianity and also Calvinism.

turned to empirical sentiments grounded in human nature. These are the dual arenas of our ensuing discussion of rationalism versus empiricism.

But both the Cambridge men and Hume, although basing their arguments on different ethical principles, were devoted opponents of Hobbes' species of moral relativism and self-interested egoistic motivations.

My purpose in what follows is to show how the Achilles premise serves as a bridge connecting the ancient Platonic world of metaphysical, epistemological, and ethical concepts with both our modern and contemporary principles and our current speculations about the nature of human consciousness. My conviction is that philosophical continuities can be established connecting the philosophical past in a way that both illuminates and ties us to the present. I also believe there is a connecting identity between ancient modes of Epicurean materialism and our current neurosciences of today as anticipated in Plato's prescient warning regarding the Battle between the Gods and Giants as it continues to persist.

I have selected three figures, Ralph Cudworth, Ralph Waldo Emerson, and Edmund Husserl as representing rationalism, idealism, and phenomenology, respectively, in order to show how the argument from the immaterial nature of consciousness functions in their religious and ethical speculations. But, in light of the current interest in Husserl, I offer a more elaborate discussion of his "idealist" sympathies by presenting how an ethical theory might be based on particular tendencies in his thought. After concluding these discussion, I go on to treat how the immaterialist principle is also pressed into service in order to establish either an idealist or a phenomenalist interpretation of space, an issue which is obviously critical in the context of determining a firm foundation for the Scientific Revolution of the seventeenth and following centuries to the present.

Ralph Cudworth (1617–1688), the leading figure in the Cambridge Platonist movement, discusses the simplicity argument in connection with all four uses cited in the first chapter of the present work: the immortality of the soul; the unity of consciousness; personal or moral identity; and metaphysical, epistemological, and ethical idealism in his monumental study, *The True Intellectual System of the Universe* (1678), in which he discusses the works of the ancient Greek philosophers with the end in view of criticizing the atomic theory of Democritus, Leucippus, and Epicurus; ancient and contemporary materialism; determinism; Calvinist predestination; atheism; and ethical relativism from the time of Protagoras to Hobbes, as well as "hylozoism" or the doctrine of "thinking matter," while defending free will, Pelagianism, and a system of absolute morality. In what follows, I shall concentrate on Cudworth's ethical thought as he presents it in *A Treatise Concerning Eternal and Immutable Morality* (1678), while prescribing his brand of moral intuitionism.[2]

As Cudworth conceives it, his system refutes a constellation of related views grounded in metaphysical materialism, including Socinianism, or the "mortalist heresy," demonstrating that man is "naturally," i.e., rationally mortal and after he expires he will await his ultimate destiny during some unspecified dormant state until which time he will be physically resurrected by God and his body restored to him on the Day of Judgment. This view was championed in England by George Withers, Richard Overton, Thomas Hobbes, John Milton, and later John Locke. Indeed Locke maintains that in order to suffer pains and punishments, or the reverse to enjoy pleasures and rewards in the afterlife, the possession of a body is a prerequisite.[3] Cudworth thus criticizes the contentions of the "modern Epicureans," who maintain that matter alone can think as well as Hobbes' ethical relativism, which reduces all moral terms to convention, custom, or *nomos*. Against these combined materialist principles, Cudworth puts forth his challenge of an "eternal and immutable morality." The idealist ground for his doing so, and his interweaving of moral arguments within the context of the simplicity argument's previous four uses, is the subject of the ensuing analysis of Cudworth's ethical thought. In addition, Cudworth,

---

2   Ralph Cudworth, *A Treatise concerning Eternal and Immutable Morality* (Cambridge: Cambridge University Press, 1996; first published in 1731); hereafter cited as *EIM*. Cf., Ben Mijuskovic, *The Achilles of Rationalist Arguments: The Simplicity, Unity and Identity of Thought and Soul from the Cambridge Platonists to Kant; A Study in the History of an Argument* (The Hague: Martinus Nijhoff, 1974); hereafter cited as Mijuskovic, *ARA*. For Cudworth's dependence on the argument for immortality, see 35–37; for the unity of consciousness see 67–70; for personal identity see 93–96; and compare *The True Intellectual System of the Universe* (Stuttgart-Bad Canstatt, 1964; four volumes), first published in 1678 although probably completed by 1671) and consult I, 130, 147, 150–173, 222, 259–261 299 ff.; see also 111–125 for Cudworth's rationalism and ontological "idealism." Rationalism basically consists in a method for *discovering* a pre-existing truth whereas idealism by contrast consists in a process of *creating* or *making* the truth. In that strong sense, Cudworth is a dualist but he also exhibits idealist and spiritualist "tendencies" when he refers to non-conscious "spiritual plastic powers" as effecting purposes in nature. Subjective idealism relates the concept of the self and the concept of the object to each other within consciousness (Kant), whereas by contrast objective idealism identifies Being and Knowing, the known and the knower (Hegel). For confirmation of Cudworth's idealism, see Tom Rockmore, *Kant and Idealism* (New Haven, CT: Yale University Press, 2007), 20. Cf. also Ben Mijuskovic, "The Simplicity Argument and Absolute Morality," *Journal of Thought*, 10:2 (1975), 123–135; and "The Argument from Simplicity: A Study in the History of an Idea and Consciousness," *Philotheos*, 9 (2009), 228–252.

3   Cf. Mijuskovic, *ARA*, Chapter 1, "The Simplicity Argument and the Immortality of the Soul," 19–57 for a fuller account. The original source for the "mortalist heresy" is Faustus Socinus' *Operibus Omnibus* (Irenopoli, 1656).

in concert with his colleague, Henry More, endorsed More's rather unorthodox assertion that although the soul is immaterial nevertheless it is *spatially extended*. This qualification seems to have been a concession to his friend's influence and a relatively rare exception in the annals of Western philosophy but it also offered certain theological advantages to the two Cambridge men in terms of an *active* "spiritualist" perspective endowing the immaterial soul with a certain extensity and dimensionality providing for the possibility of an individualized "specificity" to the soul, namely it retained the capacity to display identifiable visual qualities after death, i.e., souls could be recognized. As a parenthetical note, we recall that in Homer's *Odyssey*, the "Shades" in the Underworld similarly exhibit a non-physical but recognizable visual and spatial form and the ghostly apparitions even have voices suitable for communication as in the case of Odysseus' visit with Achilles in Hades.

More importantly, scholars like Alexandre Koyre have gone on to connect More's conception of an extended soul to Newton's theory that absolute space and time are the *sensoria* of God, Newton going so far as to maintain that the Deity Himself is literally present spatially everywhere and temporally forever, i.e., infinitely and eternally. Newton's quasi-theological attribution of *absolute* space and time to God will play out later in Kant's subjective version of intuitional space and time. Despite this issue, however, Cudworth and More both agree that unlike matter, which is essentially divisible, the soul is "indiscernible," i.e., simple, indivisible, and hence indestructible and therefore immortal by virtue of its essential *quality* of immateriality despite its "extensity." An oddity of this notion of extended immaterial entities is that the soul is penetrable whereas matter is not, a theory which encourages a belief in ghosts. By contrast, matter is both extended and "impenetrable."[4]

Correspondingly for Cudworth moral ideals, values, or meanings—*qua* essences—are also immaterial realities and hence unchanging (cf., Plato, *Rep.* II, 380d), for what is incorporeal, having no parts, cannot possibly change; consequently ethical Forms and mathematical concepts are immutable, imageless, and eternal due to their intrinsic simplicity, i.e., immateriality.[5] Thus, the *active* soul is able through its conduit of immaterial ideas to cognitively share and participate (*metechein*) in an eternal moral order; to be engaged in a realm of transcendent, universal ethical meanings, which form an ideal *system*. Accordingly, these "Intelligibles" are accessible to intuition. As one commentator succinctly states it:

---

4  Alexandre Koyre, *From the Closed World to the Infinite Universe* (Baltimore: Johns Hopkins University Press, 1968) 125–129; hereafter cited as Koyre, *CWIU*; and John Gibson, *Locke's Theory of Knowledge and Its Historical Relations* (Cambridge: Cambridge University Press, 1968), 247.

5  Robert L. Nettleship, *Lectures on the Republic of Plato* (St. Martin's, 1967), 89.

> Whereas the objects of sense are particular and changing corporeal things the objects of intellection are the intelligible 'rationes' ... and are themselves nothing else than modifications of the knowing mind. Such are concepts like justice, duty, truth ... *Of these things no image or [Hobbesian] phantasm can be formed;* they cannot be derived from sense-perception ... Only the intelligible natures or essences [the rationes] of things are objects of certain knowledge. *Considered formally, they exist only in the mind,* but yet they have an immutable nature of their own.[6]

The claim that there are imageless, non-sensory concepts, of course, runs completely counter to all empirical principles. It is prominently found not only in German idealism but also in philosophers like Husserl and Brand Blanshard, as we shall see. By contrast, according to Hobbes' nominalist thesis, the notion of an imageless thought is no less of a contradiction in terms than the conception of an immaterial substance. Again, according to Hobbes, sensations are caused by the motions inherent in bodies while images and phantasms are "decaying sensations." Hobbes' version of metaphysical materialism is reflected today in our contemporary neurosciences.

During the seventeenth-century, Plato's cosmic Battle of the Giants and the Gods continues to play out between the materialism of Hobbes against the idealism of the Cambridge Platonists. Despite Hobbes' many avowals of traditional Christian commitments in the *Leviathan,* the Cambridge men remain unconvinced of his religious beliefs because of his (a) materialism, which they regarded as intrinsically atheistic but also because of his (b) moral relativism and (c) commitment to Calvinistic predestinarianism with its denial of free will. In Calvinism, following St. Augustine, an omniscient God foreordains whether we will go to hell or heaven. Consistently, their unnamed enemy remains Hobbes, an adversary so disliked by his contemporaries that his very name was often avoided by them. Thus despite his many Christian claims, he remains disliked by his adversaries as insincere. His materialism condemns him as an atheist in their eyes and his moral relativism proves him to be a religious hypocrite. Additionally, the mechanical materialism they attribute to both Descartes and Hobbes is collectively regarded by them as dangerous threats to their defense of man's freedom of the will as well as their dedication

---

6 W.R. Sorley, *A History of British Philosophy to 1900* (Cambridge University Press, 1965), 94; italics mine. Cudworth insists that even the *meanings* of ordinary terms like "whiteness" or "triangularity" are unchanging because meanings, qua *universal* ideas, are not composed of body, figure, site, or motion as the modern Epicureans maintained. Note the reference to imageless concepts in the quotation; this is a critical difference in rationalism as opposed to empiricism; cf. Cudworth, *EIM*, 11–12, 34–35, 111, 113–114. The point is that universal essences are ideal existences.

to an "immutable and eternal morality." According to Cudworth, the view of those thinkers, like Descartes and Hobbes, who believe that God can voluntarily, by His arbitrary Will, i.e., Power determine the values of good and evil is actually grounded in materialism precisely because it is based on the voluntarist claim that God's Will is above Reason, that He can *freely, i.e., contingently*—independently of reason—reorder the material atoms in human nature as well as in the individual soul differently, if He so willed. This position, of course, is reflected in the long-standing controversy between the voluntarist and the rationalist traditions in Christian theology receding historically back in time to William of Ockham and the issue whether God is constrained by reason or whether He is absolutely free, i.e., independent of the law of non-contradiction and its dictates. After all, God's power to create the universe *ex nihilo* in itself testifies to His ability to overturn a "rational" contradiction and bring forth an absolutely creative *act* inconceivable to human reason. This intrinsic power of absolute willing in God will later translate into an *epistemic*—as opposed to ethical—force, a *quality* of "spontaneity" animating human consciousness in Leibniz.

On this account, matter intrinsically implies the possibility of change, impermanence, and mutability precisely because it consists of parts that are separate from each other and therefore vulnerable to chance or arbitrary redistributions, whereas immaterial existences—*qua* essences—necessarily entail an immutable and unchanging ideal world of eternal moral concepts guided by God's rational commands.

For the Cambridge philosophers, by contrast, ethical concepts and truths are intrinsically rational as opposed to being divinely volitional. We also recall that in Plato's dialogue, the *Euthyphro,* the question arises whether the *quality* of goodness is good in-itself—intrinsically—or whether it is worthy merely because it pleases the gods; whether morality is absolute or relative (Cudworth, *EIM,* 19, note 33). Consequently, what is immaterial—and eternal meanings or essences meet that condition—cannot change or be altered. Only what has parts is liable to change and redistribution. Cudworth consistently criticizes Hobbes' position for holding that "good" and "evil" depend on the absolute Power or Will of God, Who can, if He so chooses, enforce very different moral values and indeed fashion a very different human nature.

Interestingly Hobbes' nominalist theological claims parallel our own contemporary scientific and positivist principle that the contradictory of any empirical fact is always conceivable (credit Hume); that the entire realm of human experience is radically contingent; and that the various spheres of morality (really our conventions and customs) can be shown to vary from society to society as well as from person to person. Accordingly, Cudworth's Platonic response is directed against a triad of longstanding ancient principles advocated by (1) Democritean and Epicurean atomic materialism and mechanistic determinism; (2) Protagorean skepticism and subjective relativism itself grounded in his principle that "[Individual] man is the measure of all things; of what exists that it exists; and of what exists not that it exists not"; and (3) Heraclitus' metaphysical flux theory of universal and continual change (Cudworth, *EIM*, 43–57). The incessant change evident in matter along with the intrinsic possibility of endless varying compositions follows from its essential divisibility and its consequent volatile disunity. Again, for Cudworth absolute truths, by contrast, are identified as both (a) immutable because of their utter simplicity and indivisibility as well as (b) their consequent essential unity. In sum, there can be neither knowledge nor morality if everything is subject to constant flux and change. In all this he is closely following Plato (Cudworth, *EIM*, 54–56).

In addressing the problem how an idea or meaning in human consciousness is nevertheless able to participate and share in eternal and immutable essences, Cudworth offers the familiar Plotinian analogy of self-consciousness as a circle. The center of the circle is "Simple Goodness." It is an immaterial, indivisible unity and as the rays radiating from the center of the circle are said to "partake" or "share" from *within* and *through* the center, and in a sense to *be* the center, just so the various rays of virtue together constitute the central concept of Goodness within human consciousness. Ultimately the rays radiate from and converge back, "double back" to the unity of "goodness in-itself" (Cudworth, *EIM*, 54, 56, 75–76). Conversely, the soul's sensuous descent into matter means a regressive disunity and self-isolation.[7]

---

[7] For Cudworth, it is because meanings are immaterial that diverse human minds and consciousnesses can share "in" the same universal and immutable essences in virtue of their innateness. Sensations by their very nature cannot be shared. Mine are mine and yours are yours. The foregoing is, of course, a Platonic thesis; the soul and the Forms, both being incorporeal, it follows that they are akin and hence "like can know like." Again, it is important to notice in these passages the conviction that there are pure imageless concepts. This is a frontal assault on the very principle of empiricism, which reduces all thinking to particular fleeting sensations. Meanings cannot be reduced to Hobbesian phantasms or sensory images. Cudworth is here following Plotinus, *The Enneads*, Fourth Ennead, Seventh Tractate, which offers the metaphor of the circle, its radii, and an immaterial center to account for (1) the unity of consciousness and (2) the accessibility of human consciousnesses to penetrate eternal meanings (cf. *ARA*, 8–10, 67–70); the terms "unity of consciousness" and "self-consciousness" are taken to be synonymous. Cudworth's views often parallel those of his friend, John Smith (1618–1652); cf., for example, Smith's *Select Discourses* (1660) and especially the "Discourse concerning the True Way or Method of Attaining Divine Knowledge"; see *ARA*, 62–66.

The terms "unity of consciousness" and "self-consciousness" are intended to be synonymous and derive from Plato's reflexive paradigm of consciousness discussed in Chapter 1 but it is most definitively expressed by Aristotle in his *Metaphysics* where the highest level of reflexive consciousness is conceived as a perfect unity of the active subject grasping itself as the conceptual "object" of its own thought. It is essentially and effectively an active unity of subject and an ideal object.

> Since, then, thought and the object of thought are not different in the case of things that have not matter, the divine thought and its [conceptual] object will be the same, i.e., the thinking will be one with the object of its thought. A further question is left—whether the object of the divine thought is composite [and made of physical parts external and separate to each other]; for if it were, thought would change in passing from part to part of the whole. We answer that everything which has not matter is indivisible [and therefore a unity]—as human thought, or rather the thought of composite beings, is in a certain period of time, so throughout eternity is the thought that has *itself* for its [conceptual] object.
> *Metaphysics,* 1075a

This is one of the most important passages in Western philosophy. It assumes both the immaterial nature of the mind and its activity; it defines the essence of self-consciousness as the unity of a reflexive self-awareness; "All things which have no matter are essentially unities" (*Meta.,* 1045b, 23–24); it forms the defining property of reason; the designation of man as a rational animal; and most importantly the explicit rejection of reductive materialism. To conceive of the mind and its thoughts as immaterial and active *is* the defining characteristic of the simplicity principle. We will see it recruited in the next chapter in Hegel's argument for the freedom of self-consciousness.

Inactive matter has no such power of unification, and Cudworth rhetorically inquires whether the index of a watch can tell the time; a mirror perceive what it reflects; or a pair of glasses what it sees. These are commonplaces in the writings of the British Platonists. As always, the premise and the conclusion are the same: *Senseless matter cannot think.*

There are two kinds of perceptions for Cudworth. First, sensory consciousness, which he illustrates by appealing to the model of physical objects moving along straight lines extending from the external world of things, traveling toward the cognitive soul, and then striking the five senses. These given sensations, he also calls them *passions,* are "passive and inferior." Secondly there are active and "superior" self-conscious thoughts. Whereas sensory objects projected from the external world are inherently incapable of "intellection," of reflexively returning to the initial source from whence they first originated *and* in the same moment reflexively acknowledging the origin from which they emanated or arose, these higher thoughts are alone free and privileged to grasp innate and intelligible ideas (Cudworth, *EIM*, 113–114). As opposed to the Cartesian mind-matter dualism, Cudworth rather prefers to concentrate on a passive-active dualism *within the mind* as opposed to separating them dualistically in terms of distinct opposing substances.

> If intellection and knowledge were mere passion [i.e., sensation] from without, or, the bare reception of extraneous and adventitious [externally caused] forms, then no reason could be given at all why a mirror or a looking glass should not understand, whereas it cannot so much as [passively] sensibly perceive those images which it receives and reflects to us.
> CUDWORTH, *EIM*, 75

Again, the controlling metaphor for self-consciousness is circularity; it is both a necessary requirement for unity as well as the defining characteristic of man as a rational animal. Indeed, the Aristotelian syllogism is its most exquisite expression. But whereas intuition grasps pure ideas immediately, inference moves from premises to a conclusion and in doing so it displays an active *process* that knows itself; the *self* reflexively both knows *that* it knows and *what* it knows. This can only be accomplished if the soul is active and consciousness is metaphorically circular; it turns upon itself. Matter is neither.

> Having hitherto showed that sense or passion from corporeal things existent without [or external to] the soul is not intellection or knowledge, so that bodies themselves are not known or understood by sense, it must needs follow from hence that knowledge is an inward and active energy of the mind itself, and the displaying of its own innate vigour from within, whereby it doth conquer, master, and command its objects, and so begets a clear serene, victorious, and satisfactory sense within itself.
> CUDWORTH, *EIM*, 73

It is this ill-defined "inward and active energy," this "innate vigour" that is the crux of the distinction between active mind and passive and inert matter. In Descartes, matter is inherently passive, inert. Its movement is instituted by God (*Principles*, II, xxxvi). Thus Cudworth alludes to the mind as the source of "spiritual plastic powers." This indeterminate "plasticity" *does* something; it is energetic. But he goes no further. As we go forward, however, we will explore what the German idealists accomplish starting with Leibniz, which is to ground consciousness in a specialized form of a creative "spontaneity." For Cudworth, this initial pregnant assumption is that in some unspecified sense, the mind is "innately vigorous," whereas matter and sensation are passive. But what is missing from his description and remains still-born is what this "vigour" *does* and *how*. To anticipate, as it will turn out, in Leibniz and Kant, *it will be endowed with the ability to create, to give birth to the structures of consciousness.*

According to Cudworth the Plotinian metaphor of the center of a circle symbolizes self-consciousness as a self-contained and self-sufficient unity (recall Plato's *Theaetetus* and *Sophist* passages in Chapter 1). Again, since the soul is active and it is not composed of parts, it is able to collect and unify various "pieces" of knowledge within itself. Agreeing with the Platonic tradition and against the Epicurean modernists, Cudworth contends that even *if* one were able to *causally* account for sensation and perception on the mechanistic model of physical sensory reactions to external stimuli, nevertheless one could never explain the reflexive and unified character of self-awareness by an appeal to such a paradigm because the reflexive activity of consciousness, which must be "transcendentally constituted" (in the Kantian sense) by immaterial *acts* of consciousness, is left unaccounted for (Cudworth, *EIM*, 75 ff., 94 ff.). On the assumption that matter is inherently "senseless," "lifeless," "inert," and motionless, it follows that the aggregation of material parts cannot, as Plotinus argues, "knit itself into a unity," i.e., be self-conscious. We also need to remember that according to the tradition following from Aristotle, nature is an inherent principle of motion or rest *with the emphasis on rest, on inertness, on passivity.* This determinative assumption, namely that matter is inherently at rest is to be found in Descartes (see above). In the atomistic Epicureanism of Hobbes, however, motion is inherent in matter (*Anti-White*, 148; *De Corpore*, 8.10).

Pre-Newton, in the dualist tradition—as opposed to Epicureanism—material objects and the entire universe are put in motion by God. Aristotle's Unmoved Mover as an "object of desire" is both the efficient and final cause of motion for the heavenly bodies and the sublunar sphere as well. But metaphysically the crucial point for the Cambridge thinkers is that matter is *passive, inert*. This is also why Descartes identifies matter, space, and extension as equally inert and then credits the Deity with continually re-creating, conserving, and sustaining the entire universe, including each individual soul, at each instant of time. The premise that matter is essentially motionless is metaphysically critical for the philosophies of dualism, rationalism, and idealism *of the time*. Only the mind is active and reflexive. We shall see in the next chapter, however, that both Hegel and Schopenhauer realize that because gravitational and electrical forces are at work in nature, we cannot simply leave the discussion to rest on those antiquated terms alone. Certain physical phenomena are clearly and obviously active. The introduction of an *active* matter and not only in terms of physical motion but also in terms of Anton Mesmer's animal magnetic forces and the combination resulting from chemical compounds as well will elevate the Battle between the Gods and Giants to a much higher level. But these transformations will only appear later.

Whereas the modern Epicureans argue that all knowledge reduces to particular images, which in turn represent copies or resemblances of things, Cudworth instead contends that universal meanings and knowledge, as Platonic essences, are imageless.

> The mind can clearly understand a triangle in general without determining its thought to any particular species, and yet there can be no distinct phantasm of any such thing. For every distinct phantasm or sensible picture of a triangle must of necessity be either equilateral or equicrular or scalene, etc. And so as we can in like manner clearly understand in our minds a thing with a thousand corners or ten thousand corners though we cannot possibly have a distinct phantasm of either of them.
> CUDWORTH, *EIM*, 110; so Sorley above

Not long after Cudworth's stated position, Locke's empiricism stumbles in his own account of "abstract" or universal ideas.

> For when we nicely reflect upon them, we shall find that *general ideas* are fictions and contrivances of the mind that carry difficulty with them. For example, does it not require some pains to form the general idea of a triangle (which yet is one of the most, comprehensive, and difficult) for it must be neither oblique, nor rectangle, neither equilateral, nor scalene; but all and none of these at once.
> LOCKE, *Essay*, IV, vii, 9

It is most likely that Locke borrowed the example of the triangle from Lady Masham, Cudworth's daughter, since Cudworth's treatise only appeared in 1731. They were good friends. But the point is that *the meaning, the concept of a triangle cannot be reduced to sensations*. For the rationalist and idealist traditions, meanings and universals are "intelligible" apart from *particular* sensations or instantiations. Not so for Locke and the empiricist tradition. He argues that general and abstract ideas (or "words") are directly derived from particular sensations: "Universality belongs not to things themselves, which are all of them particular in their existence, even including those words and ideas which in their signification are general. When therefore we quit particulars, the generals that are left are only creatures of our own making" (Locke, *Essay,* iii, 11). But then a major problem arises because it turns out we are unable to invest our abstract or general ideas, i.e., his fictions with *any* meanings. The idea of a triangle is all and none of these at once. It is both none and every particular image. The conclusion therefore follows that one cannot manufacture meanings or knowledge from passive and particular sensations alone.

For Cudworth the inference follows that ethical truths can only be discovered by an immediate intuitive grasp, by a direct *apprehension* as opposed to a discursive *comprehension,* thus mirroring the medieval distinction between the two ways of attaining knowledge.

Cudworth's ethical philosophy is generally characterized as belonging to the Intuitionist School and he is grouped, along with Henry More, Samuel Clarke, John Balguy, and Richard Price as holding that moral distinctions are demonstrable by a power of "intellection," which ultimately *conceptually* depends on Platonic intuitions (Cudworth, *EIM,* 128). By contrast, as we shall see, Kant's categorical imperative criterion is discursively rational.

Cudworth's theory is considerably more complicated and sophisticated than histories of ethics have presented it and his intuitionist insights suggest a strong comparative affinity and consonance to the later thought of Husserl because of their shared idealism. My guess is that if Cudworth had continued to extend his moral reflections further in pursuing a more comprehensive Platonic and Plotinian perspective, he would have discovered—as Plato long ago suggested—that ethical meanings manifest synthetic *a priori* relationships *to each other* thus forming a coherent ethical system unified by knowledge of the Good. Perhaps by taking a Kantian "transcendental clue" from the *Republic,* Cudworth might have gone on to synthesize, bind, or unify the individual Forms of virtue to each other as Plato had intimated within the ultra-Form of the Good; or for Cudworth, God (Cudworth, *EIM,* 83–84). As we shall see, it is just these synthetic *a priori* connections that Husserl will go on to emphasize in our re-construction of his ethical philosophy. Whereas Cudworth is committed to a pre-existing realm of transcendent Platonic *essences,* by contrast Husserl will ground and couch his universal eidetic *meanings* in subjective consciousness. In both cases, however, essences and meanings are simple, immaterial, and shine by their own illuminated light.

In his contribution to a commemorative anthology of essays in behalf of William James, A.O. Lovejoy uncompromisingly asserts that Cudworth and the English Platonist movement in general anticipated Kant's first *Critique* at every major turn, including his transcendental idealism. And he even goes so far as to argue that not only did Cudworth foresee Kant's Copernican Revolution but that he directly influenced it.

> [W]hat I also believe to be a precisely verifiable fact is that the Kantian doctrine was destitute of any radical originality; that none of the more general and fundamental contentions of the "Kritik der reinen Vernunft" were particularly novel or revolutionary at the time of their original promulgation; and that the principal developments of post-Kantian philosophy were not dependent upon the historic interposition of the ingenious complexities of the critical system, but were clearly present in germ, sometimes in fairly full-blown form, in the writings of Kant's predecessors or contemporaries, out of which they would in time inevitably come to fruition (page 266).[8]

Further he suggests that Kant's formulation of the transcendental categories is also anticipated by Cudworth when he asserts that *"sensible things themselves* (as, for example, light and colors) *are not known and understood by either the passion* [sensation] *or the fancy of sense, nor by anything merely foreign and adventitious, but by intelligible ideas* [i.e., the categories] *exerted from the mind itself, that is, by something native* [innate] *and domestic to it"* (ibid., 273–74; italics and parentheses his). In addition, according to Lovejoy, Kant's Aesthetic, which deals with the intuitions of space and time, as well as his mathematical Antinomies in the *Critique* are already prefigured by Cudworth and his British colleagues in their writings. Basically Lovejoy views the relation between Hobbes to Cudworth as analogous to the relation between Hume to Kant. Lovejoy accordingly concludes that only "If [Kant] had read and remembered Cudworth, or any other writer of the same school, he could have hardly flattered himself so complacently as he did upon the entire novelty of his Copernican Revolution" (ibid., 280).

My interest in Lovejoy's interpretational conjecture is not so much whether he is historically accurate in his "transcendental" attribution to Cudworth (although he may well be when we consider the entirety of his full documentation) but rather that Kant's strategy of compelling noumenal "things-in-themselves" to conform to the active categories and structures of the mind was already

---

8  A.O. Lovejoy, in *Essays Philosophical and Psychological in Honor of William James by His Colleagues at Columbia University,* edited by "His Colleagues at Columbia University" (New York: Longmans, Green, 1909), "Kant and the English Platonists," 263–302. On the influence of idealism during this time, cf. John Yolton, *John Locke and the Way of Ideas* (Oxford: Clarendon Press, 1968), 98–113.

"in the air" because of the aggressive revival of the Achilles premise beginning with Leibniz's monadological paradigm of the mind. In other words, if one begins with (a) the premise that the mind is immaterial and active; and (b) absolutely self-enclosed; then it follows that (c) either the appearance of an "independent world" is spontaneously created from within the mind as Leibniz argues; or, if Kant is right, then consciousness is *already* prepared and constituted by *a priori* structures formed by the innate activities of the mind and then superimposed upon the "presented" noumenal "data," which is Lovejoy's point about Kant's Copernican Revolution.

Crucial philosophical principles and themes often serve as journeying vessels that visit and anchor in many ports thus encouraging their passengers to disembark and share similar intellectual concerns and solutions with others. This sort of "meeting of the minds" is a feature that is readily accounted for when one considers that key principles and ideas, which in Etienne Gilson's sense have "a life of their own," frequently display the virtue of allowing for ready interchanges between contending arguments among different thinkers of like minds and talents, as happened when Leibniz and Newton mutually discovered the infinitesimal calculus. Revolutionary discoveries also readily occur when a newcomer visits a new port or a foreign clime and suddenly experiences a fortuitous "paradigm shift" in his outlook (Thomas Kuhn, *The Structure of Scientific Revolutions*). During the seventeenth-century, The "Republic of Letters" enjoyed a steady commerce between thinkers, who, although not published or professional philosophers, nevertheless were able to carry on spirited intellectual discussions with others often facilitated by personal emissaries. Father Mersenne, for instance, collected no less than six informal sets of Objections to Descartes' *Meditations,* including those of Hobbes and Arnauld. Basically, Kant was the first "professional" philosopher. Neither Descartes, Spinoza, and Leibniz nor Hobbes, Locke, and Hume were institutional philosophers. Before that, unpublished philosophical treatises were readily circulated among the learned.

We have already considered the future impact envisioned by Platonism's architectonic gradations and exemplified in Plato's Divided Line and its imposing cognitive hierarchy with its ascension to higher and more complex qualitative levels of consciousness, knowledge, comprehensiveness, and unity as it was organically incorporated within German idealism by Kant and Hegel. And when we compare this with Locke's and Hume's impoverished guiding epistemological premise that all our knowledge and all our sciences can be reduced to (a) *quantitatively* simple and compound sensations (Locke) and impressions (Hume) as determined by our five senses along with (b) our imaginatively-anchored "association of ideas principle" as coincidental conjunctions, we realize how limited intellectually all this would be. For one thing, it would be difficult to account adequately for new discoveries and free creations. Insight into intellectual, ethical, and artistic creations would be confined and reduced to "explanations" proposed in terms of sensations alone. Hobbes and Locke are stuck in Aristotle's *tabula rasa* paradigm, like flies on wallpaper, which may be adequate for explaining lower animal *behavior* but it is hardly sufficient in accounting for human creativity. As we proceed, we shall learn that below the surface of consciousness, below the empirical grounding of Kant's reproductive imagination lays the spontaneous productive imagination leading to a subconscious sphere of mental activity.

Empiricism is even more conceptually impoverishing when we turn from idealist meanings and consider relations. For Kant, there exist certain *transcendent* pure concepts like God, the soul, and freedom of the will, which are imageless but remain "meaningful," although empirically inaccessible, i.e., untestable. *But* in addition there are also *transcendental,* i.e., constitutive active forms, *categories of relation,* e.g., substance and accident, cause and effect, etc.; *pure imageless relations,* which constitute the necessary conditions for the possibility of human experience, as a foundation for a seamless *coherent system of principles and laws,* all ultimately based in the Achilles premise of immaterial activity.

Whereas empiricism is restricted by its commitment to singular propositions serving as detachable parts for its scientific edifice, idealism is rather invested in forming self-sustaining organic wholes. What is significant—from a History of Ideas perspective—is that Plato's Divided Line intellectually arises from immediate sensory images, physical objects, discursive mathematical concepts, intuitive imageless definitions, and finally reaches an ultimate comprehensive unity. Simply put, idealism offers an access to a doctrine of self-sustaining "internal relations," which allows for connective intellectual insights, while materialism and empiricism force us to hunt for scattered factual pieces and then puzzles how they might fit together.

The difficulty is that empiricism in conjunction with phenomenalism is only able to impart "significance" to external part-to-part contingent connections, whereas internal relations, especially of the synthetic *a priori* kind, are able to internally develop and expand toward increasingly coherent heuristic systems. It is more plausible to connect imageless meanings and relations with sensations than to deal with sensations alone if one intends to create a system of *principles* and *laws* as active modes of consciousness in the manner of Kant and Hegel. Consider for example Newton's "law of gravity." For an empiricist or phenomenalist, the "law" is indirectly "represented" in consciousness as a "construction," a manufactured composition of *particular* visual or tactile sensory images, sense-data, or sense qualia. But what would that "look" or "feel" like? Let us try to translate it into *specific* images, such as (a) imaging *simultaneously or* (b) imaging very quickly a *series* of fluctuating sensory images, like an apple falling from a tree; the ebb and rise of the tide at the seashore; and envisioning a map of the oval elliptical orbits of the planets on an astronomical chart; either *instantaneously* "at once" or as a really fast series of *sequential* images. Does that fulfill what we *mean*, what we *intend* by the "law of gravity"? Or try to imagine what visual images would adequately fulfill Einstein's E=MC2 formula? Perhaps visualizing the equation written in white chalk on a blackboard might be effective? Would any of these *imaged* experiences accomplish the necessary and sufficient requirements for "conceptualizing" the "law of gravity" or E=MC2? Would they be *adequate* in capturing the *meaning, the significance,* and/or the *relation* of gravity to the entirety of the universe? I think not. But why not? It is because sensations, concepts, meanings, relations, laws, and principles are qualitatively different sorts of cognitive "things." They form a conceptual hierarchy. As we proceed in examining the thought of thinkers like Kant, Fichte, Hegel, Schopenhauer, Bergson, Royce, and Husserl, we will come to realize that meanings, relations, laws—and above all principles—cannot be reduced to Hobbesean "phantasms" and nominal definitions.

Ralph Waldo Emerson (1803–1882) is interesting because he is generally not regarded as a "philosopher" in the usual sense of the term. But since he depends on the simplicity argument in his varied writings, his work testifies to the broad appeal and interdisciplinary tenor of the Achilles argument. There is no question that Emerson is as influenced by the Cambridge brand of British neo-Platonism and idealism as he is by its German counterpart. He is familiar with Cudworth's *True Intellectual System of the Universe* (he owned the 1820 edition consisting of four volumes); and there is strong evidence that he studied Cudworth's *A Treatise Concerning Eternal and Immutable Morality*.[9] Similarly, he is impressed by the works of other English Platonists, including John Smith, Henry More, and John Norris, and by the epistemological and ontological idealism of Bishop Berkeley. Weaving all these diverse strands together, Emerson composes a short, actually incomplete piece, titled "Ideal Theory"

---

9   In regard to the British Platonist, Emerson states, "Cudworth was excited by the evil tendency of the writings of Hobbes to compose the Immutable Morality, and the Intellectual System a vast storehouse of wisdom," *The Early Lectures of Ralph Waldo Emerson,* 1833–1836 (Cambridge, MA: Harvard, 1959), I, 356, note 16. On the possibility of an indirect knowledge of *Eternal and Immutable Morality,* see *The Journals of Ralph Waldo Emerson, 1819–1822* (Belknap, 1960), I, 253, note 6; cf., John Yolton, *John Locke and the Way of Ideas* (Oxford: Clarendon Press, 1968), 98–113 and especially for a helpful discussion concerning the conflict between materialism and idealism during the period.

(Undated *Prose Fragment*). It is hardly two pages long but in it he offers three distinct arguments in behalf of epistemological idealism. (1) Perhaps the "external world is but a dream, since I can dream of objects without those objects being physically present; maybe I do it all the time." This argument has a rich history and is offered by Berkeley in the *Principles*. Its ultimate origin goes back to the Skeptics, Pyrrho of Elis, Sextus Empiricus, Pierre Bayle, and of course it reappears in Descartes' First Meditation. (2) But *if* the mind can *only* know its own ideas, then it follows that *mental* ideas are in principle incapable of apprehending an external world beyond the self, beyond its own intimate sphere of consciousness. As early as Plotinus, he states, "it may be well doubted concerning sensible things themselves, that we seem to have the greatest assurance of, whether they really exist in the objects without us, or whether they be passions in us" (*Enneads,* v. 5. I, 13–16). And (3) Emerson explicitly invokes the simplicity argument in his reflections when he suggests in a monadic context that "Perhaps the mind is at rest in an immaterial point of infinite space ... Perhaps space is peopled with these little assemblies of disembodied dreamers" (*Letters,* vi, 337–338). But he hastens to add that even if this should be the case, "I do not know that it sets aside any system of morals, any one bond of moral obligation" (ibid.). And why not? It is because an ideal moral system exists as absolutely as the incorporeal minds which experience these immaterial ideas within their own respective spheres of monadic consciousnesses. The physical world may or may not exist, but certainly human consciousness, with its attendant moral meanings and distinctions, remains real and ethically obligatory. In the above quotation, we notice the reference to space and its problematic status, an issue we will soon address head on.[10]

Again as we noticed already in the first chapter and as Hegel indicates, once trapped within the "way of ideas" argument, the only assurance dualist and idealist philosophers have of reaching an independent world beyond themselves depends on God's interventions. For Descartes it is grounded in the goodness of God not being a deceiver (Fifth Meditation); for Malebranche it rests on God's miraculous continuous co-ordinations of mind and body; for Leibniz on His apparent pre-established harmony between self-enclosed monads; and for Berkeley on God's ordering of the laws of nature in such a fashion that "We see all things in God."

---

10   *The Letters of Ralph Waldo Emerson,* edited by R.L. Rusk (Columbia, 1939), VI, 337–338. Emerson was strongly attracted to Victor Cousin's work, in which a form of idealism is expressed congenial to Emerson's. Cf. *Introduction to the History of Philosophy* (Boston, 1832), 21–22, 65, 129–134; and *The Complete Works of Ralph Waldo Emerson,* edited by E.W. Emerson, 12 vols. (Boston: Houghton Mifflin, 1903–1904), I, 334; II, 282–283; IV, 40.

In his essay, "The Transcendentalist" (1842), Emerson further elaborates on his commitment to the simplicity principle. Kantian transcendentalism *is* idealism and the sort of idealism that has battled gross metaphysical and evaluative materialism since the dawn of thought. "As thinkers mankind have ever divided into sects, Materialists and Idealists; the first class founding on experience, the second on consciousness and thought." Consequently, according to Emerson, it is because the "idealist takes his departure from consciousness" that

> He can behold the procession of facts you call the world, as flowing perpetually outward from an invisible [i.e., immaterial] unsounded centre in himself, centre alike of him and of them, and necessitating him to regard all things as having a subjective or relative existence, relative to that aforesaid Unknown Centre of him. From this transfer of the world into consciousness, this belonging of all things in the mind, follow easily his whole ethics.
> *CW*, I, 34

That at least universal ideas are essences is explicitly declared in his essay, "Nominalist and Realist in Plato" (III, 231). Reminiscent of Cudworth, Emerson invokes St. Augustine in "Circles," when he says of God that "He is like a circle whose center is everywhere and His circumference nowhere" (II, 301). The concept of unity is critical not only in terms of unifying consciousness but also in comprehensively unifying all of reality and ethics and of identifying all eternal knowledge with goodness.

Following Kant, he maintains that the sheer *activity* of consciousness can create and generate both (a) the *appearance* of an "external world" and (b) the *existence* of moral values and meanings. This is what Emerson means by his "spiritual doctrine." It is, when unpacked, a thoroughgoing epistemological, ontological, and moral idealism. For Emerson, Kant is the philosopher who has most clearly and ably defended idealism. Thus, Kant's *"transcendentalism"* heralds the advent of "a very important class of ideas and imperative forms" and these forms condition both the possibility of empirical knowledge (the categories of the Understanding) as well as the possibility of a noumenal freedom supporting an ethical criterion (the Categorical Imperative). Emerson puts it all in concise Platonic metaphors when he refers to truth and values as "the eternal trinity of Truth, Goodness, and Beauty"; and perhaps it is with Cudworth's latitudinarian views and his *Eternal and Immutable Morality* in mind that Emerson concludes his essay by appealing for men to "tolerate one or two solitary voices in the land, speaking for thoughts and principles not marketable or perishable," advocating for values, as he puts it, "that are not based on experience, custom, or convention but rather on something innate, ideal, and eternal."

How are we to know or recognize these values? By "sentiment" Emerson informs us. And what does he mean by sentiment? Certainly not what the empirical psychologists of human nature, the moral sense theorists Shaftesbury, Hutcheson, and Hume mean by it. Rather what he intends is in essential agreement with an expression John Smith, the Cambridge Platonist, summons when he suggests that "the immaterial soul itself hath its sense by which it knows immaterial natures" (Smith, *op. cit.*, 11; cf., Emerson, *Works*, IV, 40, II, 282–283.). This intuitive "sense" is incorporeal and active.

In his Neo-Platonic essay, "The Over-Soul," Emerson seeks to describe "the one universal Spirit or Consciousness, that Unity, that Over-Soul," as the unique and eternal One or God. In traditional Plotinian fashion, he emphasizes that the One is ineffable and thus beyond description, i.e., beyond the capacity of human language to describe, but nevertheless he wishes "to report what hints I have collected of the transcendent simplicity and energy of the Highest Law."

> The nature of these revelations are the same, they are perceptions [i.e., conceptions] of the absolute law ... To truth, justice, love, the attributes of the soul, the idea of immutableness is essentially associated.
> *Works*, II, 282–283

In this manner, Emerson forges a familiar necessary and universal (*a priori*) connection between the immaterial simplicity, unity, and identity of the soul with the continuity of human consciousness and absolute truths. In "Plato; or, the Philosopher," he quotes with obvious approval that "the essence or peculiarity of man is to comprehend a whole; or that which in the diversity of generations can be comprised under a rational unity," i.e., a cosmic "multiplicity in unity" (IV, 63). It is this unity, I submit, which can only take place for these thinkers on the condition that the soul is incorporeal and as such empowered to collect, synthesize, and unify diverse sensations and concepts in the same consciousness. Once more, this "moral sense" is a rational intuition. In "The Transcendentalist," he insists that the ancient formulation of the materialist position is inherently unstable because it is forced to degenerate into phenomenalism, itself merely a self-defeating and crude species of idealism, which attempts to construct "the real" upon a foundation of mental impressions and appearances. Accordingly, he maintains that under the historical exigencies of prolonged and severe criticism, most notably at the hands of Kant, materialism and empiricism subsequently passed into phenomenalism and then subsequently into true idealism, for which "the mind is the only reality ... [and] Nature, literature, history are only subjective [ideal] phenomena." This theme is repeated in "The Over-Soul" when Emerson maintains that "Before the great revelations of the soul, Time, Space and Nature shrink away." What remains are eternal and immutable moral meanings. In Kant's Aesthetic in the first *Critique*, of course, space and time are intuitions, "ideal forms of sensibility."

As a point of historical fact, idealism and phenomenalism are closely related through their common commitment to a mentalist presupposition as well as their twin reliance on *perceptions* leading to Montaigne's "way of ideas" argument. Thus, idealism and empiricism can be readily connected through phenomenalism, as in Locke's immediate modes of consciousness; Berkeley's rhetorical query: "What can be like an idea but another idea?" and Hume's conflation of mental perceptions as consisting solely of vivid and forceful impressions and ideas.

In sum, according to Emerson, ethical meanings are eternally present for all men to share for, as he puts it in "Spiritual Laws," in referring to Plato, "A man cannot bury his meanings so deep in his book but time and like-minded men will find them." And why? Because meanings not only exist in individual minds but also in eternal, simple, immaterial, immutable ideas perpetually generated and shared by many consciousnesses at different times and in diverse places.

I have not tried to make Emerson appear as a consistent thinker, for I believe few think that he is. Rather I have sought to show how certain Platonic, Neo-Platonic, and Kantian themes—undoubtedly reinforced by his sympathies with currents of thought prevalent in the Cambridge Platonist and German idealist movements—are clearly expressed in his work and contribute to his broad system of intuitive and rationalist ethics. The inconsistencies in Emerson derive not from the ideas or themes themselves but from the fact that he expressed conflicting tendencies as well throughout his many essays and writings. But, of course, with these inconsistencies I am not concerned. Obviously, for both Cudworth and Emerson there is an emphasis on moral Forms as existing *independently* of human minds, a commitment to Platonic "realism," to a pre-existent transcendent realm of Forms, which will not be shared by Edmund Husserl as we go forward. But my interest in the foregoing is focused on the influence and force of the simplicity premise and its positive exploitation during a period in philosophy when strong interests were committed to expressing both the powers as well as the limitations of human consciousness; a time when ethical idealists were dedicated in supporting intuitionism and rationalism, whether of the Platonic or Kantian persuasion. What I believe to have shown is that a considerable segment of mankind found it *necessary* to ground their philosophical thinking on the immaterialist paradigm of consciousness and its activities in order to account for the nature of meanings and relations. And further that a central issue raised by the idealists concerned the *genuine* conceivability of imageless concepts, which can only be entertained and established if one assumes that the mind is immaterial and active. This stream of thought can now be extended to more contemporary times.

Although my own position leans heavily on humanism, it is still the case that historically and conceptually an overwhelming segment of mankind has committed to expressing themselves in veins of thought that are mystical, spiritual, and religious as well as in both transcendent and transcendental modes of expression. At either end of the spectrum of consciousness, from its spontaneous beginning as well as its continuous power of transcendence beyond itself, the "issue" is not so much about "truth" but rather about the creativity and freedom of consciousness. "Truth" is conditional, ephemeral, and transient; freedom is concrete. The very fact that humans can create such a diversified span and range of principles, structures, and values testifies to the freedom of consciousness and the impossibility of ultimate predictions about what humans can feel, think, and do. What is important to realize in the Platonic tradition as highlighted by Cudworth and Emerson is that (1) there are meanings and concepts that cannot be reduced to sensory images and that (2) they are dependent on the reflexive nature of the mind.

The two philosophers we have considered rely on meanings both within the mind as well as extra-mentally. With Husserl, we shall more properly "internalize" meanings and relations *within* consciousness but at the same time carry forward a common Platonic perspective by examining how he might have progressed from a mathematical model of Platonic meanings or essences to other non-mathematical essences as well by insisting all the while that the *eidos* are constituted *intentionally* in subjective consciousness. Husserl is not appealing to meanings as Platonic transcendent Universals but rather to *eidos* and *essences* while adapting Plato's sense that they are *ideal* entities but rejecting Platonic realism as I understand him.

But before turning to Husserl, it is important to confirm a vital assumption he shares with other rationalist thinkers regarding the status of imageless concepts or meanings. It is provided in a work by a more contemporary author.

> Ideas are not to be reduced to images for the further reason that we can think of things of which no image or copy is possible (1, 264) ... No less signal was the collapse of the [empiricist] image theory in its attempt to deal with relations. This attempt was most notable in Hume, whose struggle to reconcile the view that perception is nothing but sensation

and thought nothing but imagery, with the fact that we somehow grasp the relations of identity and causality, is one of the decisive battles of philosophic history ... But is there any *sensation* or *image* [of the relation] of identity. Hume saw that there was not. But instead of revising his theory of knowledge to fit the fact, he denied the fact in order to save his theory of knowledge. He denied that there was any such thing as identity and held that our supposed thought of it was an illusion ... And not less so the idea of causality, which Hume did his best to explain away. When we see a hammer about to descend on a nail, and say it will cause the nail to sink in, we seem to be thinking not merely of hammer and nail, but of something distinct from either, a peculiar connection [i.e., relation] between them. Hume saw with perfect clearness that if there were such a connection we could certainly form no image of it. But he was so confident that if we could not imagine it we could not think it, that he held that we did not have the idea of it at all, but only a habit produced by experience of expecting [i.e., a psychological feeling of anticipating] one thing upon the occurrence of another.[11]

There is no way to account for the *relation* of equality, identity, resemblance, to the left of, to the right of, below, above, greater than, less than, etc., by an appeal or a reduction to sensations or images. Any attempt to do so would simply lose the meaning of the relational element(s).

With this pivotal principle in mind, I now want to explore how Husserl might have unfolded a comparable idealist ethical system by extending and building on the simplicity argument. More has been done for Wittgenstein with far less available material. So let us turn now to Edmund Husserl (1859–1938).

It is interesting to consider if Husserl would respect Hume and Kant's distinction between the Ought and the Is, since he is (primarily) committed to phenomenology as a *methodology* as opposed to a philosophical doctrine or system. If so, then we would expect that he would not separate the cognitive and ethical realms from each other in the manner of Hume and Kant by splicing them in terms of their different subject matters.

Like Wittgenstein, Husserl did not expound a full-blown ethical theory, although I believe there are sufficient indications to imagine at least its guiding principle and rough outlines and how he might have unfolded one. Consequently, I will begin with his theory of meaning and relations and claim that it is entailed by his adoption of the simplicity paradigm of consciousness.

---

11    Brand Blanshard, *The Nature of Thought* (George Allen & Unwin, 1969), I, 266–267; cf. I, 471; cf. II 554, 559, 565.

According to Husserl, ideas, meanings, and intentionalities are not in space; they are not presented as material or extended presences in the brain; and hence they are not reducible to the behavioral and mechanistic model of the brain as a complex set of electrochemical reactions occurring among cerebral cells.[12] But that ideas, as unextended, are not in space is a direct implication of the simplicity thesis. Husserl's position that consciousness and its meanings are non-extended is indebted to Kant's conception of the transcendental unity of apperception. Thus, in the *Cartesian Meditations,* for instance, in his discussions of the unity and identity of meanings found in all acts of consciousness, Husserl holds that it is constitutive, structural syntheses that make possible the unification of ideal multiplicities into unified meanings and relations. Originally, this unity, as all unities, is grounded in the transcendental ego, the source of all intentional constitution.[13] The unity of consciousness

---

12   Probably Husserl's most explicit acknowledgment that meanings and ideas are essentially non-spatial occurs in a lecture given on May 7, 1935, at the University of Prague. In the presentation, Husserl announces the goal of European man consists in an infinite striving toward rationality and idealism. He declares: "Ideas, within individual persons as sense-(meaning) structures that in a wonderfully new manner secrete within themselves intentional infinities, are not in space like real things, which latter, entering as they do into the field of human experiences, do not by that very fact as yet signify anything for the human being as a person"; "Philosophy and the Crisis of European Man," in *Phenomenology and the Crisis of Philosophy* (New York: Harper Torchbook, 1965), 160, italics mine; see also 182–183. And consult *Formal and Transcendental Logic,* translated by Dorion Cairns (The Hague: Martinus Nijhoff, 1969), §57b; *Ideas: General Introduction to Pure Phenomenology,* translated by W.R. Boyce Gibson (New York: Collier, 1962), §49; and *The Paris Lectures,* translated by Peter Koestenbaum (The Hague: Martinus Nijhoff, 1964), 8, 17–18, 32. In the larger *Crisis,* Husserl generally avoids allusions concerning the immateriality of souls, although there is a hint of it even there; cf. *The Crisis of European Sciences and Transcendental Phenomenology* (Evanston, IL: Northwestern University, 1970), 222. See also: Franz Brentano, *Psychologie vom empirischen Standpunkt* (Hamburg, 1955), I, Bk. II, Ch. 1, §§iv-ix. Husserl's involvement with the simplicity argument was probably initiated by Brentano, who follows Kant's version of it. See Ben Mijuskovic, "Brentano's Theory of Consciousness," *Philosophy and Phenomenological Research,* XXXVIII:3 (1978), 315–325. For further support of my interpretation that Husserl's ideas or meanings are unextended and immaterial, cf. E. Parl Welsh, *The Philosophy of Edmond Husserl* (New York: Octagon Press, 1965), 164, 178, 188–189, 249, 252, 254, 283, 285; Joseph Kockelmanns, *Edmund Husserl's Phenomenological Psychology* (Pittsburgh: Duquesne University Press, 1967), 175, 288–290; and Paul Ricouer, *Husserl: An Analysis of His Phenomenology* (Evanston, IL: Northwestern University Press, 1970), 42, 54, and Note 17.

13   Quentin Lauer, *Phenomenology: Its Genesis and Prospect* (New York: Harper Torchbook, 1965), 138–139, 196; hereafter cited, Lauer *PG*. Simply put Kant's unity of consciousness becomes transformed into a unity of meaning. See especially *Cartesian Meditations,* Second Meditation, Section 22; hereafter cited as Husserl *CM*.; *Ideas,* Part 2, "The Fundamental Phenomenological Outlook"; *Formal and Transcendental Logic,* Sections 94–95.

now becomes a unity of intention, of meaning, and of identity, for both unity and identity are intentional, as Husserl advises in the *Cartesian Meditations*. For Descartes, the cogito is a unity, an identity of *both* thought *and* existence. For Kant, the constitutive syntheses of subject *and* object, cause *and* effect are rule-directed relations, although immediately "seeable" for Husserl but not so for Kant, depending for the latter on mediate or relational syntheses generated through the spontaneous structures of consciousness.[14] All this follows from Kant's position that the transcendental self, along with its categories and activities, is not in space, space being merely a *form* of mental intuition, a pure form of sensibility. Neither is Husserl's ego in space, the independent existence of the "external" world having been bracketed, "put out of gear," suspended by the device of his celebrated *epoche*. What remains is the absolutely immanent and infinitely rich field of phenomenological consciousness; and the task of the phenomenologist is to *describe* the eternal and immutable meanings present in this plenum of ideal possibilities.

On this model of consciousness, what would intentionalities "look" like? Well, they definitely would involve *a priori* synthetic relations, such as those found in the judgment "All colors are extended" or "All sounds have pitch and timbre."[15] Consciousness is intentional; it constitutes meanings; it is meaning-intending.

---

As Husserl admits, in the *Cartesian Meditations*, his conception of the ego is modeled on Leibniz's theory of the monad and Kant's unity of apperception. In the *The Paris Lectures*, Husserl even describes the ego in terms reminiscent of Plotinus' circle-consciousness analogy, in which concepts and judgments "radiate" from a center or ego-point (pages 26–28). See also Lauer, page 97; and "Philosophy as Rigorous Science," in *Phenomenology and the Crisis of Philosophy,* 107–108. For Kant's "I think," Husserl would substitute "I mean" or better still "I intentionally mean a transcendent object." The object-meaning within consciousness has its own integration as a unity and an identity that is inviolable. Although nuances can be added to it, the nucleus, the ego-center remains constant. On this interpretation, Husserl never really overcomes the monadic model of consciousness and despite his attempts to describe the ego-pole and the object-pole, both appear given in immanent consciousness and mimic the traditional rationalist concept of consciousness.

14  Edmund Husserl, *Ideas: General Introduction to Phenomenology,* translated by W.R. Boyce Gibson (New York: Collier Books, 1962), Part 2, "The Fundamental Phenomenological Outlook"; and *Formal and Transcendental Logic,* translated by Dorion Cairns (The Hague: Martinus Nijhoff, 1969), and more specifically the famous solipsism passage; Sections 94–95; and Lauer, *PG,* 138–139, 196.

15  Husserl is here following Carl Stumpf; see Gaston Berger, *The Cogito in Husserl's Philosophy* (Evanston, IL: Northwestern University Press, 1972), 25–26. Plato first invokes the synthetic *a priori* relation between color and extension in the *Meno.* Although Kant grounds his transcendental philosophy on the validity of synthetic judgments *a priori,* he would reject this example for its sensory, i.e., "material" implications. Max Scheler, however, following Husserl, discusses a "material," factual synthetic *a priori* relation between goods and values; see *Formalism in Ethics and Non-Formal Ethics of Values* (Evanston, IL:

While Kant is concerned with the temporal unity of consciousness over time and the identity of the self, by contrast Husserl is concerned initially to focus more on the immediate, non-temporal, *eidetic,* unity of meaning. (I wish to postpone until Chapter 4 Husserl's important discussion of immanent time-consciousness in his *Phenomenology of Internal Time-Consciousness.*)

To begin, there are three idealist themes that need to be identified before proceeding. First there is Husserl's doctrine of ideal "Platonic" *essences,* eidetic *meanings* in consciousness. Second there are his many references to the Leibnizian ego or monad as a center of consciousness. And third there is the transformation of the Kantian unity of consciousness into a unity of meaning. And despite the fact that he wishes to "bracket" metaphysical presuppositions, I would argue that his form of "idealism" is inextricably committed to the simplicity premise as he develops his thought along the same ethical roots we previously uncovered and brought into prominence in our investigations of Cudworth and Emerson. In short, I submit that Husserl's ethical intuitions will turn out to be congruent with those of Cudworth and Emerson. That is not to suggest that Cudworth and Emerson anticipated the act of intentionality but rather that all three express a principle of idealism in their outlooks.

The reason I wish to pursue this line of thought is because I believe there is a conceptual continuity consonant with my overall commitment to a History of Ideas perspective and I expect to show that it is entailed and justified by Husserl's adoption, implicitly or explicitly, of the simplicity premise of consciousness. Admittedly my interpretation of Husserl lies on the idealist and rationalist side, especially as displayed in his *Cartesian Meditations* (1931), which clashes with the later *Crisis of European Man and Transcendental Phenomenology* (1935). In the former work, he was convinced he had solved the problem of solipsism by offering a fuller description for the meaning of "empathy," which was predicated on Theodor Lipps' earlier concept of *aesthetic empathy (einfuhlung).* I criticized Husserl's version not only as incomplete but indeed as a failed venture. Nevertheless, he continued to appeal to empathy in the larger *Crisis,* which is significantly influenced by Heidegger's descriptions of *Da-sein/Mit-sein* as being-in-the-world-*with*-others. But unless Husserl can successfully solve the problem of solipsism, which he addresses in his Fifth Meditation, he is not justified in simply assuming we share a "lived world," a "surrounding world," an *Umwelt* with other sentient beings. The result is that I welcome his earlier direction in the *Cartesian Meditations,* which are

---

Northwestern University Press, 1973), 12, 21; and confer, Herbert Spiegelberg, *The Phenomenological Movement* (The Hague: Martinus Nijhoff, 1965), I, 253.

fundamentally Leibnizian, Kantian, and "subjectively idealist" in tone, whereas the larger *Crisis* is clearly Heideggerian in its emphasis.[16] Basically this is also Paul Ricoeur's interpretation of Husserl.

As Husserl admits in the *Cartesian Meditations,* as well as elsewhere, his conception of the ego is patterned after Leibniz's theory of the monad and Kant's conception of the unity of apperception as evidenced in his intentionality formula of ego>noetic act>noema=idea-meaning. In the *Paris Lectures* and *Cartesian Meditations,* he describes the ego in terms highly reminiscent of Plotinus' circle-consciousness analogy, where concepts and judgments "radiate" from a center or ego-point. For Kant's relation, "I think—synthetic unifying relation—object," Husserl substitutes the structure of "I">>>intentionally mean>>>a transcendent *eidetic*-object. The object-meaning or "object-intended" *within* consciousness has its own integrity as a unity and identity, which is paralleled by the unity and identity of the ego. On this interpretation, he never overcame the monadic Leibnizian model. Nor should he have.[17]

Husserl's commitment to essences is heavily influenced and indebted to his early studies of the ancient rationalist ideals promoted by Plato and Aristotle.[18] Like our previous ethical theoreticians, Husserl is fully capable of validating imageless meanings and even ascribing "meaningfulness" to such non-*hyletic* essences as square-circles and circular decahedrons, which cannot possibly be exhibited as images nor be presented in any imaginable sensory content and yet they are authentic *intentional* meanings that can be investigated *qua* meaningfulness. This would also include *irreal* meanings or entities, such as unicorns and goblings, which present the *eidetic* property of fictionality. All this testifies to his liberal and ecumenical attitude toward essences. How else could he invite a community of phenomenologists to commit themselves to

---

16  For my criticism of Husserl's *version* of empathy, see Ben Mijuskovic, *Feeling Lonesome: The Philosophy and Psychology of Loneliness* (Santa Barbara, CA: 2015), 185–191. And for Husserl's inextricable entanglement in solipsism, see pages 88, 96–98.

17  Cf. Paul Ricoeur, *Husserl: An Analysis of His Phenomenology,* translated by G.E. Ballard (Evanston, IL: Northwestern University Press, 1967), 78; hereafter cited as Ricoeur, *AHP*. For Husserl's idealism and Ricoeur's assertion that Husserl is pursuing an "egology" as opposed to an "ontology," see pages *xviii–xix*, 24, 83–84, 106–107, 122, 128, 131–133, and 174. Much of Ricoeur's interpretational emphasis is on Descartes, especially the *Cartesian Meditations* (passim) and on Kant's influence on Husserl (3, 68, 79, 80–81, 109, 111, 152–153, 157, and an entire chapter on their comparison, 175–201.

18  David Woodruff Smith, *Husserl* (New York: Routledge, 2013), 135, 267; hereafter cited as Smith, *Husserl*; cf. Burt Hopkins, *The Philosophy of Husserl* (McGill-Queens University Press, 2010), *passim*; and J.N. Mohanty, *Edmund Husserl's Theory of Meaning* (The Hague: Martinus Nijhoff, 1969), 74–76.

working together in exploring and searching for an *infinite* field of *rational* essences unless the possibilities were themselves infinite, mutually connective, and inclusionary, i.e., synthetically *a priori* related and all intentionally pointing toward a coherent phenomenological system. For instance, certain axioms in geometry, such as the proposition "The shortest distance between two points is a straight line" constitutes a synthetic *a priori* principle connecting the quantitative feature of shortness with the qualitative feature of straightness.

For Husserl, all meanings are directly constituted within the subject. Therefore, although they exhibit Platonic essences they do not refer to a Platonic ontology. Nor are they "caused" by the motion of material particles in the brain that become inexplicably transformed into mental sensations, ideas, and perceptions as featured in Locke's brand of empiricism; or passively and imaginatively "constructed" and patched together from mental atomistic sense impressions in the manner of Hume's phenomenalism. Neither are Husserl's essences dependent on the mediate nature of the categories of the Understanding in the fashion of Kant, who requires that consciousness is empowered to go *beyond* the immediacy of the present moment and the sensorily given. (We recall the oddity that both sensations and rational intuitions are "immediate.") But in agreement, both Kant's sensations and Husserl's *hyletic* data and feelings—in and of themselves—are meaningless alone. However, by contrast to Kant, for Husserl, since essences or meanings are *directly* constituted in consciousness, it follows that they can be *immediately, eidetically, intuitively* "seen." As intentional acts, they are open to intuitive insights. Husserl's intuition then is not dependent on the intervention of Kantian mediating, categorial structures. For Husserl, we might recall Plato's metaphorical suggestion that the soul is the mind's "eye"; the soul directly "sees" the truth. Hence Husserl's command: "To the things themselves." Husserl's model of the intuitive act is predicated on Descartes' ideal of *immediately* intuiting, grasping, and apprehending the cogito *directly* as a unity and identity of *both* thinking *and* existing: the self cannot exist without thinking and it cannot think without existing. Husserl's mission is to intuitively access "the things themselves," to intentionally drive forward to "the things themselves," and to phenomelogically *describe* them. His rationalism essentially conforms in all major respects to the by now familiar Platonic model much in the manners of Cudworth and Emerson by capturing, grasping, and apprehending ideal meanings. As Platonic essences *within consciousness,* they are (a) universal, i.e., absolutely true in any conceivable universe; and (b) necessary, i.e., the opposite assertion implies a logical (or metaphysical) contradiction. In short, they are *a priori.* Their fulfilled meanings can be continually enriched and expanded by his method of "free imaginative variation" forging increasing comprehensive synthetic *a priori* connections as outlined in Husserl's *Experience and Judgment.*[19] These progressively developing and expanding internal relations between intrinsically related essences and meanings can be confirmed by *eidetic* intuition—much in the same manner as Cudworth and Emerson—in order to constitute for Husserl a system of *coherent* synthetic *a priori* meanings, relations, and judgments (Kant).

Although the traditional definition of rationalism—the mind's active "discovery" of pre-existent truths—is insufficient to establish the coherence theory of truth, certainly rationalism in conjunction with its expansion to include synthetic *a priori* relations and judgments would suffice.

We remember that the empiricist position asserts that there are only two forms of *meaningful* statements, meaningful in the sense that they can be confirmed or disconfirmed by the laws of logic or by experience. First, there are *a priori* analytic, formal, or tautologous propositions, which conform to the law of identity, wherein the predicate term is already contained within the subject concept, e.g., a=a; and mathematical identities or equations. They are merely "explicative." The criterion of validity is purely "internal." Secondly, however, in *a posteriori* synthetic propositions, the predicate concept *adds, contributes* something significantly different to the subject concept, e.g., a + b; as in the proposition "There are mountains on the other side of the moon" (Ayer). These statements are "ampliative"; they extend our knowledge. Their confirming criterion is external; it is grounded in experience. The latter are regarded as contingent propositions based solely on experience; they exemplify the principle of *possible* confirmation. And, following Hume's distinction between "relations of ideas" and "matters of fact," the distinction is generally credited as forming the foundational support for the empirical sciences in general.

What both Kant and Husserl share in common is the conviction that there are spontaneous constitutive synthetic *a priori* acts which lie at the very foundation of human consciousness.

According to Plato and Kant, however, there is also a third class of relations and judgments, technically synthetic judgments *a priori,* which intrinsically entail mutually implicative *sets* of categories, judgments, and principles of connection, in a word *systems of relations* (Kant's Categories and Principles). For Kant not only is all consciousness *self*-conscious, *apperceptive* but it is also both *relational* and *judgmental* as well; it binds two (or more) concepts within a single judgment and two or more judgments within a principle according to

---

19 Edmund Husserl, *Experience and Judgment: Investigations in the Genealogy of Logic*, (Evanston, IL: Northwestern University Press, 1973), translated by James Churchill and Karl Ameriks, "Free Imaginative Variation," Section 87.

synthetic *a priori* rules and laws as regulated by the faculty of the Understanding. The categories themselves are non-empirical, formal, structural, and *actively* relational; and yet they have the ability to be "imposed" upon or "applied" to all given or "incoming" sensory data and thus creatively productive of all the configurations manifest throughout the natural world at large. When the categories are "impregnated" with sensuous content, they result in constitutive cognitive acts leading to the possibility of (a) ordinary human experience and (b) Newtonian science. Kant also insists, as we have seen in Chapter 1, that synthetic *a priori* categories are *conceivably* meaningful independently of any sensory content. For example, the Paralogisms are *meaningful* metaphysical arguments but completely non-empirical and thus unverifiable. Synthetic *a priori* judgments, of course, stand in direct opposition to the restrictive tenets of the logical positivists, logical atomists as well as analytic and linguistic philosophers, etc., all of whom condemn Kant's *pure* concepts as meaningless and empty. For Kant, we remember, not all meanings, however, are susceptible to empirical verification. The categories, however, are eligible for "transcendental," i.e., *indirect* confirmations, "deductions." They can be demonstratively justified in regard to their underlying synthetic *a priori* principles as *conditions* for the possibility of human experience; and when they are invested with sensory content, they become fully constitutive of human experience. But again, assertions regarding the existence of God, the freedom of the will, or the immortality of the soul are meaningful although unverifiable metaphysical propositions according to Kant. Similarly for Husserl, they would be meaningful and open to eidetic insight.

For Husserl, all moral meanings obviously lend themselves to phenomenological investigation and therefore descriptions. The critical difference between Kant and Husserl, in contradistinction to the empiricists, is that both Kant and Husserl have the advantage of discussing and investigating *imageless* meanings and relations as we have observed in Cudworth and Emerson as well.

According to Kant, these categorial presuppositions, *qua* pure relations, actively form, i.e., *constitute*—rather than *cause*—the transcendental conditions for the possibility of human consciousness and hence experience. Kantian examples of such relations are "substance and accident," "cause and effect," etc. Further, according to Kant, they would also apply to other rational beings in the universe that might not share our human "forms of sensibility" or intuition. In addition, we remember that Kant's Copernican Revolution dictates that the noumenal world—"in a manner contradictory to the senses" (*Critique,* B xxiii)—must *conform* to the active structures of the mind (*Critique,* B xvi). This means we can know something incredibly important *a priori*, "independently" of the external world and our "outer" experiences because the source of that formal knowledge is *already* within us. The upshot of all this is that once more Kant's categories can be meaningfully "contemplated" apart from any and all sensory content. They are meaningful as pure imageless active relations. Similarly, this also means that Husserl can investigate *irreal* or purely imaginary essences whether or not they involve *hyletic* material. Imaginary *intentional* meanings are every bit as revealing as actual *intentional hyletic* ones. The meaning of "horse" or "horseness" is as meaningful as the idea of "unicorn." Even puzzling paradoxical judgments, such as "Simonides the Cretan says 'All Cretans are liars'" is a meaningful proposition.

Spontaneous relational *acts* constitute the ground from which all consciousness and experience arises; while sensations randomly disperse themselves, relations collect and unify. In effect, there are meanings in which the sensory image is incidental to the nucleus of the meaning, which remains universal and necessary. Consider, for example, Kant's meaning of the Unconditioned as an *ideal* that is responsible for the *rational* distinction between "appearance" and "reality." Its meaning is not applicable to either realm alone (Schopenhauer). Our awareness of the phenomenally conditioned being *limited* presupposes beyond the categories and principles, a *transcendent* conception of an Ideal of Reason pointing toward an *infinite* systematic unity (Schopenhauer). As Hegel holds, to reach a limit is *already* to be beyond a limit. The limited can only be defined in opposition to the limitless, the unlimited. Empiricism, by contrast, is limited by the five senses.

For Husserl and Sartre, however, such synthetic *a priori* judgments as "All colors are extended" and "All sounds display pitch and timbre," are not only meaningful but they cognitively inform us about the relational structures of consciousness itself precisely because they are the products of an active consciousness. This radically extends the boundaries and horizons of our investigations. It means in effect that the synthetic *a priori* can be expanded to include a "material" *a priori;* it means that judgments can be *content*-full and exhibit ideal but sensuously given *a priori hyletic* contents. Accordingly, it turns out that the phenomenological method is quite suited to serve in uncovering relations that although ideal can also be discovered to be present within consciousness and at the same time underlie our natural naive attitudes and our ordinary human experiences in general. Far from applying only to the relatively narrow field, which Kant grants them, there is an enormous range over which such judgments are possible, i.e., are applicable. It is only because Kant misunderstood the full nature and scope of the synthetic *a priori* that he failed to appreciate this. Indeed this was the conviction of Husserl himself and it was echoed by many of his disciples and collaborators, especially among the earlier phenomenologists. Consequently it can be shown that Husserl is actually arguing for a necessity and universality, which, although grounded in *eidetic* insights, intuitions, and relations between ideal contents of consciousness, between intrinsically related meanings are nevertheless *also* present in our daily experiences, *in our commonly shared phenomenal world*. In other words, he is denying the Kantian position that necessity and universality cannot (a) be discovered in human experiences and (b) at the same time display *ideal* possibilities, meanings, and relations that are at once universal, necessary, and synthetic.

> Among the most important challenges to Kant's interpretation of the synthetic *a priori* has been that issuing from the camp of Husserl and the phenomenologists. Their case is especially interesting because unlike the empiricists, who deny the occurrence of synthetic *a priori* judgments altogether, they contend that Kant has unduly *restricted* the range of such judgments. Far from applying only to the field which he granted them, there is an enormous range over which such judgments are possible; only because Kant misunderstood the nature of the synthetic *a priori* did he fail to grasp this. This was the conviction of Husserl himself, and it was echoed by many of his disciples and collaborators, especially among the earlier phenomenologists.[20]

Again:

> What Husserl is holding for is a necessity [and universality] which is based upon insight into essential connections between the *content* of subject and predicate. In this sense, the insight of necessity, far from being a formal condition for the experience of objects, is rendered possible *through* the experience of certain objects. He is, therefore, simply rejecting the Kantian view that necessity and universality cannot be founded on experience. When one judges, for example, that "Everything colored is extended," "Every tone has a pitch," or "Nothing that is red is green," he is not uttering an analytic statement, and yet he is uttering a necessary truth. No formalization could ever reveal that the predicate is contained in the subject, and yet we know that these statements must be true, that they are without exceptions and strictly [necessary and] universal. Our knowing in this case is not based on anything formal, but upon a grasp of the meaning-content of the subject and predicate and of the essential connection [i.e., relation] between these meaning-contents. If we wish

---

20   Kenneth Gallagher, "Kant on the Synthetic A Priori," *Kant-Studien*, 63:3 (1972), 341–342.

to use the word a priori to apply to this necessity, we must realize that we are speaking of a material a priori, a necessity based upon [experienced] content, not a formal a priori (ibid., 343–344).

By invoking this wider meaning, we can now speculate how Husserl might have gone on to formulate an ethical position along the lines of the synthetic *a priori*, which would be compatible with an idealist philosophy. As previously mentioned, like Wittgenstein, Husserl did not expound a full-blown ethical theory, although it is not difficult to imagine at least its possible rough outlines based on hints he provides in his writings. In pursuing this path, I believe it can be shown how it is possible to move from concepts endemic to idealism, emphasizing terms like essences, meanings, *eidetic* intuitions, and even relations and then allow them to temporally flow from epistemological contexts into ethical ones. Then the question becomes whether it is possible to combine *both* epistemological *and* ethical relations into a single seamless system, a coherent systematic whole? Whether or not this is a violation of Hume and Kant's distinction between the Ought and the Is remains an interesting question. For Husserl, however, it seems possible to avoid the Humean and Kantian trespassing prohibition, since the phenomenological *method*—as opposed to the empirical—serves as a secure bridge expansively connecting all aspects of consciousness and disciplines. Because of his bracketing "device," it appears open to Husserl to override Hume's epistemic-ethical distinction and treat both as a unified field for an open phenomenological investigation.

According to Husserl, the intentional *act* of consciousness is always *about* an ideal object or *directed at* some meaning (presumably) *other* than "the self"; it is uni-directional and "vectorial."[21] It transcends itself; it is beyond itself. Hegel and Husserl, in their very different ways, are dedicated to establishing a "presuppositionless" philosophy. For Hegel it is established through an enriched *circularity* that continually returns upon itself carrying what went before it within itself. For Husserl, however, his system will be based on the principle of immediate and direct intuitional "seeings" identical to the one envisioned in the Cartesian cogito. In Descartes, it is the criterion of clarity and distinctness, which guarantees the validity of his insights (*Rules for the Direction of the Mind*). Likewise for Husserl, the criterion is *self*-validating; it is the intuitive

---

21  Husserl, *Ideas*, Sections 57 and 84; and *The Crisis of European Sciences and Transcendental Phenomenology: An Introduction to Phenomenological Philosophy*, translated by David Carr (Evanston, IL: Northwestern University Press, 1970), Sections 20, 21, and 68.

insight itself; it does not depend or assume an external or independent criterion as in either rationalism and empiricism.

Various meanings obviously display different intentional acts and structures resulting in various *eidetic,* intuitive "seeings" but they can all be described apart from any reference to the natural and naïve world of ordinary experience or science, which has been bracketed, "put aside." For instance, in terms of intentionality I can *see* a goat; *imagine* a goat; *fear* a goat; *feed* a goat; *avoid* a goat; *sell* a goat; etc. The structure of the act will vary but the meaning of "goatness" will persist and remain. Ideas as meanings can also be *irreal* and completely imaginary, and yet they are all immanently present within consciousness and fully open for phenomenological investigation. Thus exposed to direct "seeing" and inspection from a first-person point of view, the phenomena can be described *eidetically*. In turn, the essences exhibit an ideal "multiplicity in unity"; the ideality of meaning being understood as referring to essences, which remain unitary, identical, and continuous. And yet, although unity and identity are grounded in intuitive insights, Husserl also contends that there is a *process* of "uncovering" (Heidegger's *aletheia;* truth revealing, disclosing itself) thereby acknowledging the underlying *temporal* activity that occurs as the phenomenological investigator searches for the *eidos* by revisiting and revising the original, constitutive, intentional acts. In this regard, he is similar to Kant with both thinkers requiring an underlying immanent temporal context, a *subjective* time-consciousness. For Husserl, all intentional acts transpire through a temporal "stream of consciousness." Again, we need to postpone this critical implication until we are in a position to address it i.e., address it more fully when we treat Husserl's *Phenomenology of Internal Time-Consciousness* in Chapter 4.

But for the purposes of this chapter, we need to compare Kant's description of "inner sense" as a threefold-synthesis of immanent time-consciousness, as a flow, a stream of *continuous* syntheses through the temporal phases of an *original* apprehension in intuition; creative "production" in the imagination (versus a re-production); and *continuous* recognition in a unified conception (Kant, *Critique,* A 97 and A 99 ff.). With a closer reading we can determine that Kant is here introducing a pure and spontaneous creative imagination as opposed to an *empirical, associative* imagination. This is a subjective immanent time-consciousness in contra-distinction to objective scientific time, which is the external measure of physical objects moving in and through space.

Although Kant and Husserl's phraseology differs, both share the same ruling principle of an internal time-consciousness bonding the two philosophers together. The fact that this subjective, temporal *activity spontaneously* transpires *entirely* within consciousness is of the utmost importance (*Ideas,* Sections 28, 122). Internal time-consciousness betrays no dependency on the *physical* external movement of matter in space. Immanent temporality in Kant is underscored by a principle we have already quoted from Paton but it is well worth repeating because it captures the very nature of human consciousness: "our minds seem to last through time, as they do not seem to extend through space" (Paton, I, 100–101, 148). We exist with others in space but we dwell alone in time. This is the province of subjective idealism, solipsism, and negative solitude.

Husserl's intentionalities are *acts,* which, by their very nature signify, point to, indicate, and target meanings beyond and transcendent to the self (*Ideas,* Section 57). This is one of the critical differences between Husserl's concept of rationalism and that of traditional rationalism. In classical rationalism, cognition is always circular, self-conscious; this remains one of the hallmarks of rationalism and it is an essential feature that persists from the dialogues of Plato and the treatises of Aristotle and proceeds to the transcendentalism of Kant and the dialectic of Hegel. Classical rationalism discovers pre-existing "truths," e.g., the causal maxim. Idealism creates it but it cannot do so without intentionality.

However, *if* we draw together these critical elements in Kant and Husserl, while dwelling at the same time on the key concepts of reflexivity, intentionality, synthetic *a priori* relations, time-consciousness, and the unity of consciousness, *then* we will be able to form a unified coherent idealism as it constitutes a phenomenological *and* a purely "material" ethical system.

Having laid this mutually supportive groundwork bare, we are now in a position to undertake its implementation in regard to a *system* of ethics in behalf of Husserl. But first we must grant that moral meanings can exist epistemically in normal, everyday consciousness, in the world with and among other selves, and this contention nevertheless depends on an idealist paradigm. Moral principles cannot be derived indirectly; they must be non-inductive, non-inferential; they need to be immediately, intuitively grasped. Second, morality or ethical values intrinsically *require* the presence of other selves (Fichte). Third, the principle must be rational, i.e., both universal and necessary, in short *a priori*. Fourth, if we respect what Mandelbaum calls "the immediate data of moral consciousness" as our ruling principle, we will discover certain ideas whose ethical values strictly derive from their intuitive presence in consciousness.[22] According to Mandelbaum, the mistake made by previous methods seeking to establish an ethical principle and system lies in the fact

---

22  Maurice Mandelbaum, *The Phenomenology of Moral Experience* (Baltimore: Johns Hopkins University, 1969), 25, 30. Unlike Plato's criterion of the Good, which exists independently of the human mind, Aristotle's sense of duty, like Kant's, is readily accessible to the common man, and it is embedded in the human mind as he makes clear in the *Nicomachean Ethics.*

that the *indirect* or mediate-deductive approach is employed. For example, both act and rule utilitarianism are founded on the *empirical* claim that there is a calculative procedure required in adding and subtracting *quantitative* consequences in terms of physical pleasure and pain (Bentham); or intellectual "happiness" and "unhappiness" (Mill). These calculative measures first must be conducted in order to implement the utilitarian criterion. These mediate procedures, of course, may be exposed to the challenges of both subjectivity and mismeasurement. Consequently Mandelbaum advocates for a *direct* approach or, as Husserl would term it, a method of *eidetic* "seeing." What one observes in such ethical "seeings" are synthetic *a priori* interconnected relationships constituting moral meanings as unified thus enabling the ethicist to develop a full-blown idealist system of intentionally structured moral essences; in effect, a coherent ethical system. If this is the case—or better yet since it *is* the case—then we can see a connection between the "intuitive" methods of Cudworth, Emerson, and Husserl.

This is the exact point where Kant's concept of freedom and the categorical imperative can guide us as a synthetic *a priori* relation: "I as subject will the objective moral law"; my subjective will is *synthetically* related to an objective law. In the *Critique of Practical Reason,* according to Lewis White Beck, Kant's conception of morality requires a synthetic judgment *a priori,* a moral principle grounded in a positive, i.e., an *actual* existing concept of freedom. Unlike the Categories of the Understanding, which are transcendentally presupposed, assumed in the first *Critique,* by contrast freedom must exhibit a *real,* an *actual,* an *experiential* value, i.e., an *experienced* presence in consciousness, one which is acknowledged by the common man in regard to his sense of *duty.* This duty can only be fulfilled on the condition that the will is free. This would serve as an actual synthetic *a priori* relation connecting freedom and duty. Freedom implies the ability to do otherwise.

> There must be some realm of experience which, upon analysis, shows the necessity of some *a priori* synthetic judgment which is possible only if free causes are asserted actually to exist ... The moral law is an *a priori* practical [moral] proposition, and these two works [the first and second *Critiques*] show that it is possible [i.e., not only conceivable but *actual*]. It is possible only if the will is a free cause. "There really is freedom and this freedom is revealed by the moral law" [which commands certain duties].[23]

---

23  Lewis White Beck, *A Commentary to Kant's Critique of Practical Reason* (Chicago: University of Chicago Press, 1960), 27; hereafter cited as Beck, *Commentary.* Recall Kant's dependence on the pure activity of *spontaneity* in the *Critique of Pure Reason;* cf., Beck,

Spontaneity is completely presuppositionless. Synonyms for spontaneity are absolute freedom and creativity. We create "reality" just as many of us are convinced that God created the world *ex nihilo* we are free to create meanings and structures for our selves alone. For Kant, the act of spontaneity assumes a critical role in all three of his *Critiques*.

We, as empirically determined selves, of course, do not have phenomenal "knowledge" of a freedom of the "supersensible" kind, and yet according to Beck a form of noumenal "causality" can be applied to a phenomenal subject, viz., ourselves as noumenal beings: "We think ourselves free, though in another context (nature) we know ourselves as phenomena under the law of nature" (Beck, *Commentary,* 27). In other words, we can *conceive* ourselves as free without contradiction and that is sufficient for both Kant and presumably it would be for Husserl as well, i.e., we know, we are conscious of the synthetic *meanings* of *both* freedom *and* duty as ideal *a priori* intentional essences. The conclusion follows that "Practical concepts *a priori* are direct cognitions of what *ought* to be, because they are consequences of a primal fact, the law of pure practical reason that a rational being as such necessarily wills to act in such and such ways" (Beck, *Commentary*, 141). Although for Kant in the phenomenal realm, we are both physically and psychologically determined, nevertheless, in order for moral intentions, duties, commands, and ethical actions to be possible and actual, we *must* and *do* begin with the synthetic *relational* meanings of freedom and duty. Ought implies can.

A similar interpretation to that of Mandelbaum (above) is accorded to both Kant and Husserl in an article by Paul Ricoeur, "Kant and Husserl," who begins by declaring that "behind the Kantian epistemology there lays an *implicit phenomenology,* of which Husserl will be in some sense the revealer." According to Ricoeur, to his "embarrassment Husserl fails to solve the problem of transcendental solipsism in the *Cartesian Meditations*" and thus he is forced to turn to a Leibnizian solution.[24] And it is through the transcending ethical relation

---

184, 194–195. In the *Critique of Judgment,* Kant's treatise on aesthetics, he endows creative genius with the power of the "productive imagination," i.e., the "creative imagination" with a freedom from the "empirical association of ideas," which allows the imagination "to give the rule to art," Sections 46, 48, and 49.

24  Paul Ricoeur, "Kant and Husserl," *Philosophy Today,* 10:3 (1966), 147; hereafter cited as Ricoeur, *KH*. In the article, both spontaneity and temporality assume leading roles (see esp. page 154). Cf. also Ricouer, *AHP*, 11, 84, 93, and 122. The entire article is well worth reading (pages 147–168). Cf. Herbert Spiegelberg, *The Phenomenological Movement: A Historical Introduction* (The Hague: Martinus Nijhoff, 1965): "Husserl insists that other egos thus constituted are themselves transcendental and that these egos form a community of 'monads,' as he calls them with deliberate allusion to Leibniz's Monadology" (I, 159). Indeed, Leibniz envisions a spiritual "kingdom of rational beings," a kingdom of mutually

of intentionality that he seeks to solve the issue of solipsism. Thus according to Ricoeur, the most manifest overall intention of the *Cartesian Meditations* is to lead phenomenology toward a true phenomenological egology without an ontology, while avoiding the paradox of solipsism (Ricoeur, 162). This can only be done by shifting from a Cartesian form of language, which invokes an *ego-cogito-cogitata* relational structure, to Leibnizian (and Kantian) forms of expression.

> What is the significance of this passage from Cartesian language to Leibnizian language? It marks the total triumph of interiority over exteriority, of the transcendental over the transcendent. Every thing which exists for me is constituted in me and this constitution is my concrete life ... Phenomenology will attempt to cross the desert of solipsism by right of philosophical ascesis ... Phenomenology is the science of the sole ego of which I have original evidence—mine. The deontologization of the object in Husserl virtually implies that of other bodies and of other persons. Thus the description of the concrete subject, placed under the sign of idealism, leads to this metaphysical solitude which Husserl has assumed with an exemplary honesty in spite of the consequences. This is why the constitution of others, which assures the passage to intersubjectivity, is the touchstone of defeat or success, not only of phenomenology but of the implicit philosophy of phenomenology (Ricoeur, 163) ... Has Husserl succeeded in the Fifth Meditation in constituting the stranger as a stranger in the sphere of experience itself? Has he succeeded in overcoming solipsism without sacrificing egology?
> 
> RICOEUR, *KH*, 164

It is here that Ricoeur in answering his own query summons Kant's *Foundation of the Metaphysics of Morals* and more specifically the second formulation of the categorical imperative: "Act in such a way that you treat humanity as well as in your own person as in the person of others and always at the same time as an end in himself and never as a means to your own [egoistic or utilitarian] ends." In other words, Husserl is relying on Kant's conviction that the very *meaning* of an "ethical command" in and of itself *intends* the presence of other egos toward whom we acknowledge synthetic *a priori* moral duties ("perfect duties to other selves"). Actually Kant extols the virtue of sacrifice, even if it is unsuccessful. His moral command is considerably higher than

---

reciprocating ends by virtue of their intrinsic moral worth and dignity. In this vision he is following Kant.

the "Golden Rule," which merely requests that we treat others as we treat ourselves—a frightening prospect in my own case! In any event, this reference to a kingdom of ends is clearly influenced by Leibniz. For Kant, the consciousness of freedom and its practical expression is a synthetic *a priori* imperative, a command that *unites* my will with the welfare of another rational being as a duty; and it also *relates* and *unifies* my subjective will to the objective moral law. For Ricoeur, this is the best "solution" Husserl is able to muster in his failed attempt to respond to the dilemma of solipsism. In other words, although Husserl's interpretation of empathy misfires in the Fifth Meditation, a more hopeful approach lies along the path of Kant's second formulation of the categorical imperative. *Our freedom and our moral duty to others are only conceivable if and only if there are other egos.* Nevertheless, Ricoeur concludes with this cautionary declaration: "Husserl does phenomenology. But Kant limits it."

In this context, it is important to recognize the difference between Kant's two *Critique* titles. The first cites a "critique of *pure* reason"; the second is significantly different and is simply titled the "critique of practical reason." It is not pure; instead it is both experiential and practical, in other words ethical. I might also add that if we consider Aristotle's *Nicomachean Ethics* it is also grounded in the common man, in his natural sense of social obligation.

Later we shall examine Fichte's spontaneous creative positing of the ethical Ego. But without positing the non-Ego of the other self, ethical acts are meaningless. Kant instead believed that we had "imperfect duties" to our selves, for Fichte this would be meaningless.

So far in the chapter, I have stressed that there is a striking similarity of thought to be found in the writings of Cudworth, Emerson, and Husserl, a consonance, which has resulted in a common "philosophy of meaning" despite their radically divergent backgrounds. In great part, their mutual faith in—or dependence on—idealism, I believe, is due to the fact that their works obviously reflect a reliance on the simplicity or immateriality premise of consciousness and, in turn, it inevitably confirms their idealist tendencies. In Cudworth, the simplicity principle leads to an epistemological and moral Platonism. For Emerson, it supports his dedication to Kantian "transcendentalism" as well as to an ontological and ethical idealism. And in Husserl, it leads to an idealist theory of consciousness that emphasizes connective intentional acts of synthetic *a priori* meanings and relations. Essences and relations are based on the principle that both ideas and consciousnesses are immaterial and therefore essentially unities and identities in terms of intuitionist thought. In conclusion, I would include Cudworth, Emerson, and Husserl as Ethical Intuitionists.

Since according to Husserl, ideas and meanings are not in space, they cannot manifest actual *physical* properties or predicates and therefore they are not reducible to the behavioral or mechanical model of the brain as a complex set of electrochemical reactions occurring among cerebral cells. That "ideas," *qua* meanings, are immune from physical and spatial predicates or metaphors is a direct implication of the simplicity or immateriality thesis. And although idealism itself is admittedly a metaphysical principle—and therefore presumably programmatically avoided by Husserl—nevertheless his description of the intentional nature of consciousness and its attendant meanings, while eliminating, bracketing, and putting in abeyance the external, natural world, the common world we all share together in some unspecified sense, nevertheless leads him inevitably to a form of metaphysical idealism. So Ricoeur (*AHP*, 24, 28, 84, 89, 112, 131, 133, and *passim*). Further, Husserl's emphasis on essences as a "multiplicity in unity" is, if not consciously borrowed from Leibniz's concept of the monadic unity of consciousness and Kant's unity of apperception paradigms at least very similar to them in major respects. In the *Cartesian Meditations,* it is clearly expressed in his promotion of the unity and continuous identity of meaning involved in all acts of *cognitive* consciousness as intentional or meaning-intending; consciousness *essentially* expresses the twin attributes of unity and identity and consequently continuity. The motions of quantum particles in the brain offer no such virtue. Furthermore Husserl holds that it is the constitutive structural syntheses that make possible the unification of multiplicities of sensory, *hyletic* data into *unified* meanings. Originally, this unity, as all unity, is grounded in the transcendental ego, the center and source of any and all intentional constitutive acts. In addition, the structure of consciousness (intermittently) assumes the tripartite *active* form of intentionality: ego>>>spontaneous noetic act>>>transcendent object-*meant*=noema. Once more, this is a direct consequence of the simplicity principle. The unity of thought now becomes a unity of intention, of meaning, for both unity and identity are intentional. As for Kant, so for Husserl, the constitutive *a priori* syntheses are rule-directed, i.e., strict structural activities, although (presumably) *immediately* "seeable" for Husserl but not so for Kant, depending as they do for the latter on relational structures generated through the twelve mediating categories of the Understanding, which once more *spontaneously* "emanate" or "arise" and are thus "generated" from within the ego to form human consciousness. These spontaneous acts are also prominently evident in Kant as well as in Husserl (*Ideas,* Sections 28, 121). The term "spontaneous" occurs no less than a dozen times in the *Critique*. But for Husserl, similar to William James' doctrine of radical empiricism in his essay "A World of Pure Experience" relations can be phenomenologically experienced *directly, immediately* and therefore they are open to intuitional insight in Husserl. For Kant, of course, relations are always mediate, formal, and discursive.

Whether ideas are ultimately dependent on the brain is one question; but whether consciousness and its attendant meanings are simply reducible to, identical with, or caused by physiological processes is a completely different claim, one which Husserl consistently denies after 1900. In short, he had disengaged from his earlier "psychologistic" phase most notably exemplified in John Stuart Mill's empirically oriented *System of Logic*. In fact, Mill had even argued that in sidereal space, the numbers 2+3 might not equal 5.

For Husserl, the "objective," "scientific," external world of matter and motion—allegedly an existent separate and independent from human consciousness—is irrelevant; it is not part of the phenomenological equation. What remains after the bracketing procedure is the absolutely immanent field of consciousness and the task of the phenomenologist consists in exploring and describing the eternal, immutable meanings or essences—the Platonic "Intelligibles"—present "within" this infinitely rich sphere of awareness and cognition. In light of the above contentions and findings, we can expect that synthetic *a priori* meanings in relational couplings will be absolute, eternal, and immutable. We can also anticipate that the investigation of new meanings and relations will be *constituted from within* as opposed to being passively discovered externally, empirically, and contingently *caused from without*. *Eidetic* meanings will be uncovered by the phenomenological explorations of immanent structural activities as they remain available and potentially "open" to on-going excavations and confirmations leading to further *eidetic* "seeings" and intuitions.

It is important to realize that Husserl's *descriptive* science is radically different from the empirical "sciences" of psychoanalysis and the neurosciences both of which rely on the *causal principle* and are allegedly capable of *predicting* human feelings, thoughts, and behaviors. In fact, description and prediction represent opposing concepts. Predictive pronouncements are not Husserl's goal; this would simply be a return to experimental psychologism. In fact, the term "prediction" seems to be singularly absent from Husserl's vocabulary. The goal is internal insight.

Prediction is not something selves can impose either on themselves or on alien selves. It would be rather odd for someone to predict what s/he was going to do next. It is not a transitive verb, and if I can't do it on myself or for myself or to myself certainly no one else can do it for me or to me. That is precisely why selves are free. Prediction is always instituted, implemented from the *outside, externally*. I can't "predict" what I am going to do next; I either do it or I don't.

For an external agent to claim to predict what I am going to do next would mean that s/he is able to enter my field of reflexive self-consciousness; that s/he is me. If I can't predict what *I* am going to do to or for myself, I certainly can't predict what *you* are going to do for your self. I can guess from your habits but habits are intrinsically such that at one time in the past they were not a habit at all.

A thought is not like a chair nor is an idea measurable in terms of weight or length. If I entertain an idea of *this* room in my mind, or I intend *this* room-meaning, it is obviously not the case that its concrete physical expanse is thereby situated within my skull. Long ago, Plotinus expressed the incomprehensible dynamic of the eye being able to compress an entire visual field within the pupil of the eye and then further compress it within the simplicity and unity of the soul. And, although an electroencephalograph may determine *that* a brain is thinking or dreaming, it nevertheless cannot inform us of *what* it is reflexively or intentionally thinking *about* or *of.* A physiologist may "define" or identify the emotion of fear with certain chemical and physiological responses, visceral reactions, sweating palms, heart palpitations, dilated pupils, and so forth, but it is eminently clear that such a description completely fails to take into account what Husserl calls the intentionality, the meaning-intending act, and the structure of what the fear is *about* or *of.* My fear when I am being robbed is drastically different than my fear when I have been told I have terminal cancer. I am afraid of some definite meaning-object or meaning-situation or meaning-event; my fear is *about* or *of* something which I myself have actively constituted. My fear has meaning and I am the source, the origin of its meaning as well as its recipient. An electroencephalograph can *quantitatively* record the spikes on a machine, the "intensity" of my *bodily* fear on a gyrating graph but not its *quality*. Consequently, my frightened state is not reducible to a set of physiological interactions between brain cells, which are in turn triggered by certain external stimuli. Simply put, to be present to wavelengths of light or to be bombarded by photons of energy is not to see, intend, or be conscious of a color. I do not "see" wave-lengths; I see a *particular* red and I am aware of it as a relational member *of* redness on a spectrum of hues; I am aware of the *essence* of redness and not photons of electrical energy; "my" red is constituted as a meaning along a range of varying colors. If everything were red, nothing could be red. Every concept must have a significant *meaningful* opposite. That means that during intentional acts I am not only aware of what is red but also of what is not red (Spinoza, Hegel). Determination is negation. Distinctions and opposites do not arrange themselves *for* me in experience but rather *by* my mind. Minds order; sensations do not.

One last comment before we go on to our next topic—space. Whereas rationalism discovers truth idealism creates it. Newton did *not* discover gravity; he *created* it; gravity did not exist before him. To be sure, apples continued to fall to the ground from trees; the tides continued to ebb and rise at the seashore; and the moon continued to appear in the nightly sky once a month; but they were simply unrelated natural occurrences until Newton conceptualized and formulated their richer *meanings and relations,* and unified them under a single *universal law.*

We can now turn to the problematic problem of space and recall our earlier summons by considering Plato's *Sophist* and his characterization of the Battle between the Gods and the Giants. This conflict is readily replayed even more forcibly during the period of the Scientific Revolution. On the side of the Gods are those who believe that (a) there are at least *some* immaterial and active realities "alongside" material ones; and/or that (b) "realty" is fundamentally mental, mind dependent, or spiritual. On the side of the Giants stand those who assume that the real is nothing else but matter and body, material things, which can be touched and handled and are forever in motion. Let us listen and heed once again to the words of Plato:

> Str: What we shall see is something like a Battle of Gods and Giants going on between them over their quarrel about reality.
> Theaet: How so?
> Str: One party is trying to drag everything down to earth out of heaven and the unseen, literally grasping rocks and trees in their hands; for they hold upon every rock and stone and strenuously affirm that real existence belongs only to that which can be handled and offers resistance to the touch. They define reality as the same thing as body, and as soon as one of the opposite party asserts that anything without a body is real, they are utterly contemptuous and will not listen to another word.
> Theaet: The people you describe are certainly a formidable crew. I have met quite a number of them before.
> Str: Yes and accordingly their adversaries are very wary in defending their position somewhere in the heights of the unseen, maintaining with all their force that true reality consists in certain intelligible bodiless Forms. In the clash of the argument they shatter and pulverize those bodies which their opponents wield, and what those others allege to be true reality they call, not being, but a sort of moving process of becoming. On this issue an interminable battle is always going on between the two camps (246a-246c).

In the seventeenth- and eighteenth-centuries, the battleground for this conflict is the open fields of Space and Time. However, we soon notice that one of the complications is that the metaphysical and epistemological status of space is essentially represented only through external manifestations (Descartes), whereas time in relation to consciousness exhibits two very different manifestations to consciousness, both an external as well as an immanent nature.

During the period of the Scientific Revolution, the ontological and epistemological status of space (and time), become "viewed" through both idealist and phenomenalist lenses, It is much easier, of course, philosophically to discuss and argue in behalf of an absolute and immutable sphere of moral meanings, either as transcendent (Plato) or immanent within consciousness (Cudworth, Kant, Husserl), as opposed to accounting for (a) the independent existence of an extended space and material objects (Cartesian dualism); (b) its self-sufficient relational creation within the monadic soul (Leibnizian idealism); or (c) its subjective perception as an appearance given to human consciousness (Humean phenomenalism). Plus in this context it is important to notice that although for Descartes, space, extension, and matter are identical, others distinguish physical objects from space.

For materialism and empiricism, both space and physical objects are simply there. Both are "given" to us in sensation. It seems an obvious and unavoidable empirical *fact* that a spatial world teeming with material objects and motions is *already* there before us; that it is real beyond any doubt; that it is directly presented to our bodily senses; and that it has always existed in its present form and will forever continue so. This fact is readily confirmed by a simple appeal to sensory contacts, by what Husserl criticizes as the natural, naive attitude. Common folk, who do not think of describing themselves as materialists or idealists or phenomenalists, nevertheless simply take it for granted that there is a separate and distinct world of things beyond their souls and that it will go on without them when they are gone but as long as they are alive they are physically embedded in that world along with others of their kind.

We recall that in the first chapter, A.N. Whitehead in 1926 questioned the very foundations of physics and science. His catalogue of problems begins with the words "Time, space, matter...." We flatter ourselves that it is merely a matter of deciding whether it is either relative or absolute while simply ignoring the whole problem of its relation to the activity of consciousness unattended.

Originally Cartesian dualism considered space=extension=matter as synonymous and as an independent, homogeneous, and monolithic substance alongside a separate plurality of immaterial monadic souls. By a dramatic contrast, Kant assigned a co-equal status to both space and time as "given" intuitions, as immediate pure forms of sensibility in the Aesthetic, but didn't simply leave it at that; instead, he qualified his prior definitions when he proceeded to undercut his own contentions by promoting "inner sense" as foundationally *underlying* space.

> Time is nothing but the form of inner sense, that is, of the intuition of ourselves and of our inner state. It cannot be a determination of outer [spatial] appearances; it has to do neither with [Epicurean] shape nor position, but with the *relation* of representations in our [self-conscious] inner state... Time is the formal *a priori* condition of *all* appearances whatsoever. Space, as the pure form of all *outer* intuition, is so far limited; it serves as the *a priori* condition *only* of outer appearances; ... time is an *a priori* condition of *all* appearances whatsoever. It is the *immediate* condition of all inner appearances (of our souls), and thereby the *mediate* condition of outer appearances (*Critique*, A 34=B 51; italics mine).

This last phrase suggests an important distinction. It clearly indicates that in terms of consciousness, Kant's position in the A edition is that time is in some significant sense more primary than space. And yet in the Aesthetic he presents both space and time as co-equal forms of pure sensibility. Notice also that in the above citation that in some *insufficiently* specified manner time is both immmediate and mediate. This suggestion that time can be "spatialized" will generate a host of problematic relations as we go forward. We err when we attempt to "represent the time-sequence by a line progressing to infinity."

It seems then that in terms of metaphysics there is (a) one continuous space we all share in common; but both (b) an objective, scientific "outer time," a time of clocks and calendars; nights and days and years; but also (c) a subjective, intimate "inner time" that is unshareable and personal. If that is the case, then it follows that space and time do not run on all fours and that "ontologically," "experientially," and metaphysically they are quite different. It is to Kant's great credit that he more than any other thinker before him placed the temporal nature of consciousness in the forefront.

But now we are poised to question and inspect the nature of that seemingly "obvious" spatial and physical world through a mixture of historical and conceptual approaches. My goal in the ensuing is not so much to "prove" what space *is* but rather to show that what appears as (a) space-in-itself; and (b) an extended world of distinct objects "in space" cannot just *simply be there*. That space and objects cannot be there without some sort of mental activity being "involved" and that this activity will depend on a doctrine of relations.

The possibility, indeed the necessity of an eternal Aristotelian formless prime matter, I would not deny. In fact I have already endorsed a version of it in the first chapter as an essential feature of reality in light of my commitment to substance dualism. Speculatively I would venture to hazard that perhaps extended matter is "something" *de trop,* something analogous to Sartre's blobby, viscous, sticky, and undulating stuff; something akin to his nauseating roots of the chestnut tree (*Nausea*). Possibly also the Stoic and Nietzschean doctrine of the "eternal recurrence" is also true and the material universe has undergone numerous rebirths and repetitive resurgences because of an endless string of Big Bang explosions. But before we can speculate about these astronomical possibilities, we first need to address the "conceptual" status of both (a) space and (b) matter and (c) their relation to each other. Can there be space without material objects? Can there be time without movement?

First it is important to remind ourselves of the three metaphysical options we have outlined above. Materialism contends that all reality is reducible to matter and motion. It assumes that the physical world has always existed and will continue to do so uninterruptedly even if there were no sentient creatures left in existence. Supposedly the nine (or eight or more or less) planets and our earth will go on revolving around the sun while unobserved by sentient beings; and the temperatures will be warmer in the day than at night. Therefore both materialism and the empirical sciences assume the spatial universe and physical objects will unceasingly continue to exist *apart from minds*. To deny that assumption and to assert the opposite is to fall into the arms of idealism.

During the period of the Scientific Revolution, the guiding thought within the multiple and various outlets of science was to conceive the physical universe as operating in accordance with *quantitative,* causal, mechanical, determinist, and predictive laws. Science assumed the independent reality of both space and material objects and accounted for time in terms of measuring the movement of objects through space. Again, this made space more "substantial" than time. This also explains why Descartes relegates temporal "succession" to God's continual creative conservation of the universe. As a consequence, science tended to "objectively" view space first and then time as dependent on the movement of objects in and through a pre-existent space. Metaphorically time was perceived as the movement of points along a line. Newton actually conceived of both space and time as infinite and eternal containers conceivably "empty" of material objects as well as of temporal events. Further, in the seventeenth-century, philosophers elaborately conceived of God as a mathematician and the Laws of Nature as written in the quantitative language of mathematics. In all these assumptions, science essentially took space and time for granted and unproblematic and virtually as quasi-substantial realities as opposed to physical objects as defined by Aristotle's ten categories. The important consideration was that space, matter, motion, and time could all be described in *quantitative* terms and in strict accordance with mathematical units. The laws of physics could all be mathematically expressed. *It is important to note in this context that the system of mathematics is separate from the things and events that are being "described," i.e., counted.*

That the actual *qualities* of the objects are distinct from the application of the *quantities* measured. This is one of the great divides in consciousness as well as science: the quality versus quantity distinction.

Descartes' dualism and his radical epistemic doubt that perhaps the external world and other selves do not exist essentially implies a position tantamount to solipsism. Except for some anecdotal information concerning Pyrrho of Elis, whose friends had to rescue him from the paths of oncoming horses because he wasn't sure if they existed (Hegel) and Berkeley's extreme immaterialism that only souls and ideas exist, to the best of my knowledge no Western thinker has seriously denied the existence of space and the external world altogether. As Hume remarked of Berkeley's theory, "it admits of no answer but produces no conviction." Dualism assumes there are two irreducibly distinct and mutually *independent* substances: matter and mind; body and soul; material extended *quantities* and mental immaterial *qualities*. Descartes identifies space with matter, extension, infinite divisibility, and Aristotelian inertness, while still others, like Henry More the British Platonist and Schopenhauer will distinguish space from physical objects by adding the predicate of impermeability or impenetrability.

Idealism, by contrast, maintains that "space," "the external world," "material objects," and "time are essentially *known* through the monadic relational mediation of our *"confused concepts"* (Leibniz); *ideas rather than simple impressions* (Hume); or *intuitions as pure forms of sensibility* (Kant). Hence all three thinkers translate time into ideal or insubstantial mental entities. For idealists, space and matter exist only insofar as the mind is able to conceive the *concept of* space, the *concept of matter,* and so on. Nevertheless, these considerations once more alert us to the issue of solipsism, which, as we have seen, Husserl felt so constrained to address in the *Cartesian Meditations*. Thus the difficulty of the relation between the external world and a solipsistic soul or the subjective mind are inextricably compounded and intertwined. What exactly is the relation between the independent existence of an external world and *each* of our minds?

In the following I intend to examine Leibniz's position of subjective idealism, Hume's phenomenalism, Kant's transcendentalism, and Husserl's phenomenological perspective on the nature of space, matter, and the external world of "objects" with all four challenging the common man's naïve assumption that space is simply given as unproblematic. Roughly Leibniz interprets space as a relational ordering of simple sensory monads (perceptions) *within consciousness*; Hume as a relational ordering of simple empirical impressions given to consciousness and forming the *idea* of space; Kant as a pure form of intuitional sensibility (setting aside any discussion of immanent time-consciousness for the time being) as native or innate to human consciousness; and Husserl as "intuitively seen" through intentional perspectival views of *hyletic* objects.

So the problem is: how to make sense of the *meaning* of space and matter without sacrificing the existence of the material world. In order to do this, we have to start from consciousness, either with Leibniz's "confused conceptions,"; Hume's mental perceptions; Kant's intuitional form of sensibility; and Husserl's intentional meaning of "objects" as essentially "perspectival." It will turn out that space can only be known and experienced *after* certain structural *activities* are performed by the mind; that the mind must in some fashion *actively relationally* "extend" the appearances and *order* the qualitative features in relation to each other. All four philosophers we will consider are convinced that space and matter are not simply "there" and do not have to be in some manner accounted for. *Once more, the critical issue between materialism and idealism thus turns on (1) the epistemological status of space, the external world, and material objects; and (2) the underlying issue whether senseless matter can think?*

That is why everything hinges on the following discussion. Is space distinct or separate from mind? What is the relation of space to the mind? Currently, I think it is fair to say that the Giants, the materialists, empiricists, behaviorists, linguists, and neuroscientists in the English-speaking world hold the field and exert the more powerful sway. Space and matter are simply taken for granted. But it was not always so. And in the following discussion, I shall try to make a case why, beginning with the Scientific Revolution, many philosophers believed otherwise, and that the "problem of space" had to be directly addressed before science could credibly proceed forward. And again it all has to do with the persuasive force of the simplicity premise and its constant companion, the Achilles argument.

As early as Democritus, who posits the notion of an empty space (the void) through which atoms move relentlessly, restlessly, and eternally, philosophers began to speculate how space and physical matter and motion may be different from human minds. We recall that in the *Timaeus,* Plato refers to Space as the "womb or nurse of all becoming," a medium interposed between extended things and the unextended Forms, while unsuccessfully suggesting that Space may mediate between the Forms and material objects and he fails. And he refers to Time as the "moving image of eternity." Both are absolute existences. Aristotle connects time with physical motion and change and Augustine rejects the notion that time is related to motion and declares that if no one asks him what time is, he knows; but when he is asked then he no longer knows. According to Descartes, space, matter, and extension are synonymous. And when Princess Elizabeth presses him to explain *if* they are the same, *then* how can motion be possible, for without empty space for objects to move into, nothing can move. And Descartes replies that the universe is a plenum akin to a fishpond and as the fish swim the space they vacate is immediately filled by water and other fish. Time is basically unreal for Descartes because it continually requires God's active intervention *to conserve, to re-create* the entire universe at each moment of time as well as to preserve each soul throughout its temporal visit on this earth. Newton, however, following Henry More's contention that souls are immaterial *but extended,* maintains that space and time are both absolute existences; they are God's infinite and eternal "sensoria," literally God's sense organs, both infinitely and eternally extended and therefore absolute.

But with the advent of the Scientific Revolution all these vague metaphors and puzzling answers no longer suffice. In the context of the Scientific Revolution, the discussions surrounding the ontological and epistemological status of space, the controversies and terms all become crystallized in the famous *Leibniz-Clarke Correspondence* with Samuel Clarke representing Newton.

This brings us directly to the idealist and phenomenalist interpretations of space, objects, and motion. Because there are strong ontological and epistemological differences between space and time, we shall address their issues separately. But basically the argument may be reduced to the question whether space (and time) are external and absolute (Newton) or internal and relative (Leibniz).

Very roughly, for Leibniz as a subjective idealist, the argument rests on the principle that essentially the existence of "space," "matter," and "motion" only exist to the extent that they are perceived, that they *appear* or are "known" *within* the minds of conscious beings. According to Leibniz, space is a *confused concept* created by the relational ordering of perceived simple monads, perceptions *within* consciousness. Because the soul is entirely self-enclosed but active, it follows that the *appearance* of space must be generated from *within* the mind. This thesis is supported by the contention that the mind actively structures and orders its "monadic," i.e., simple, unextended perceptions in relation to each other, relative to each other *within* consciousness. Space thus becomes a relational ordering constituted by the active mind. In the Leibnizian vocabulary, single perceptions are described as simple "monadic" ideal elements and the "whole" soul represents the dominant soul as an organizing monadic *substance*. For Leibniz, there is an infinite gradation of self-enclosed monads from the lowest to the highest with each representing the universe from its own particular "point of view."

Hume studied the *Leibniz-Clarke Correspondence*. For Hume, as a phenomenalist, space is likewise a form of *mental* perception; it is an *"idea"* that results from the relational ordering of *given* perceived *simple* impressions. Indeed, in the *Treatise,* one notes that Hume, in his discussion of "extension," titles the relevant section *Of the* ideas *of space and time.* This is especially important because it signifies that the "presence" of "space" and the "external world" are not only attributable to but indeed completely dependent on human consciousness, on mental perceptions, *on ideas* for Hume.

Kant also studied the *Correspondence* but in his case, he assumed a mediating position. In deference to Newton, he posited space as "absolute" but as subjective—and frankly innate—and placed within the mind as a pure form of sensibility, a human intuition in the Aesthetic; but because it was universal and necessary (*a priori*) in consciousness, it fulfilled the requirements for scientific empirical knowledge. Since it was *inter-subjectively* shared by *all* human consciousnesses, it was "objective" and therefore "scientific." (Again, bear in mind that for Kant extra-terrestrial *rational* beings may exist elsewhere in the universe but nevertheless experience different forms of intuition.)

All three philosophers are operating with a model predicated on the immaterial nature of consciousness and restricted within the confines and framework of the simplicity premise. Again, if the mind is unextended, then whatever *appears* to the mind must be unextended despite its appearance (Chapter 1). Accordingly, *because of the simplicity argument,* a paradigm shift occurs, which turns away from the Cartesian dualist position—that posits *both* an independent extended, material world *and* the immaterial nature of the mind—and it turns instead to an idealist and phenomenalist account of space by accommodating it *within* human consciousness. Ontological dualism is challenged on epistemic grounds. Both matter and mind are idealized.

Meanwhile, multiple questions arise: Does space have relational components? Is it grounded in idealism or phenomenalism? Is it a form of transcendental intuition native to the human mind? Is it actively synthesized? Is it given whole or in parts? Is it a confused conception or does it depend on a cluster of phenomenal impressions? Or is it an intentional meaning? These are the manifold critical issues regarding the "nature," the "essence," the "meaning," and the ontological "existence" of space, which all need to be addressed: what precisely is it; what are its constitutive elements and its "contents"; and is it passively given or does it require conscious acts for its "appearance"? All these questions surface during the Scientific Revolution *and today they continue as unanswered.*

It is at this point that the peculiar doctrine of the *minima sensibilia* first surfaces, whether in reference to Leibniz's monads; Berkeley's immaterialism; Hume's phenomenal impressions; or Kant's passive forms of sensibility. The *minima sensibilia* suddenly appear against the background of Kant's pure forms of intuition. And the considerations now regarding the *minima sensibilia,* which represent the *qualitative* contents permeating our confused concepts

(Leibniz); our immaterial souls (Berkeley); our ideas (Hume); or our intuitions (Kant) of space are directly related to the Achilles premise. While *quantitative* material elements are naively assumed to be extended and causally related; mental *qualitative* states of consciousness—sensations and feelings—are not. The result is an idealist and phenomenalist account of both space and its contents for Leibniz as a subjective idealist; Berkeley as an immaterialist; Hume as a phenomenalist; Kant as a transcendental idealist; and Husserl as a phenomenologist. Each is in agreement that space can only be interpreted as *mental* rather than "real" and therefore it cannot "exist" as an independent substance apart from the mind.

Starting from the premise that sensations and perceptions *qua* mental are unextended (Chapter 1), it appears manifestly obvious that in order to account for either the direct presentation or the indirect *re*-presentation of space in human consciousness, we must operate with *minima sensibilia,* which generically includes both the *minima visibilia* (the sense of sight) and the *minima tangibilia* (the sense of touch), i.e., *dimensionless* points of color and touch.[25]

By drawing on Kemp Smith's *Commentary,* we learn that in regard to space, "Kant's statements are precise and definite—the view, for instance, of sensations as non-spatial" (NKS, *Commentary,* 51); "sensations have no spatial attributes of any kind" (ibid., 86); "sensations are non-spatial, purely qualitative. Though this is an assumption of which Kant nowhere attempts to give proof, it serves none the less as an unquestioned premise from which he draws all-important conclusions. The first argument on space derives its force entirely from it" (ibid., 101); and "[Kant] is maintaining that no space relation can be revealed in sensation"; "sensation as such is non-spatial."

This assumption is as true of Hume as it is of Kant.[26] The presence of *minima sensibilia* in consciousness clearly derives directly from the simplicity premise and it now promises to guide us throughout what follows.

One only needs to consult the famous debate between Clarke and Leibniz in order to appreciate just how important the concepts of space and time are in eighteenth-century scientific discussions because unless some plausible account can be made of them, the physical sciences would tumble into an

---

25 Norman Kemp Smith, *A Commentary to Kant's 'Critique of Pure Reason'* (New York: Humanities Press, 1962), 51, 86, 101, 103, 105); cf. also: 275, 279, and see pages 460–461 for his interpretation of the mind as immaterial; hereafter cited as NKS, *Commentary;* and cf. Paton, *KME,* 138–139.

26 Norman Kemp Smith, *The Philosophy of David Hume* (London: Macmillan & Co., 1964), 276 ff. hereafter cited as Kemp Smith, *PDH.* Cf. John Laird, *Hume's Philosophy of Nature* (Archon, 1967), 68–69; and B.M. Laing, *David Hume* (New York: Russell & Russell, 1968), 143–144.

abyss of epistemological skepticism. Both Hume and Kant studied the Leibniz-Clarke debate and both crafted responses they believed to be compatible with its conflicting Leibnizian versus Newtonian assumptions. Accordingly, Leibniz, Hume, and Kant are all constrained to develop a theory of space within their own self-imposed conceptual restrictions that the mind, i.e., consciousness is essentially mental, immaterial, and unextended; that the "external world" is in some fashion mind-dependent; and consequently that whatever *appears* to the mind ultimately must be simple and unextended despite its representational appearances of spatiality, extension, or "spread-out-ness." Basically there are only two candidates in accounting for the ontological existence of space: either it exists independently of the mind or it its presence in consciousness depends on the essential *nature* of the mind, i.e., its immaterial activity. In the famous controversy over the status of space (and time), Leibniz (and later Hume) advocates for a relational theory in opposition to Newton and his defender, Samuel Clarke, who adopts an absolutist position.[27] (As a parenthetical note, Newton declined to directly debate Leibniz because he believed Leibniz had plagiarized his discovery of the infinitesimal calculus during a personal visit.)

According to the Newtonians, space and time are absolute, infinite containers or receptacles (reminiscent of the role they assume in Plato's *Timaeus*), both existing independently of human minds and physical objects, although not independently of God of course. They are things-in-themselves, virtually quasi-substances. Consequently, space and time can exist apart from human perception. Furthermore, theoretically space can be completely empty of objects and time can be perfectly devoid of events. Differently stated, the assumption is that space and time can be conceived (imagined) independently of objects and events (a position denied by contemporary psychologists). Nevertheless, there are absolute positions in space and time, an absolute left and right; an absolute before and after. (For a relational theorist, this would make no sense.) As mentioned previously, Newton, in apparent agreement with Henry More, the Cambridge Platonist, envisioned space and time as God's sense organs; God was literally present everywhere and always. Several interpreters of eighteenth-century thought, including Ivor Leclerc, A.O. Lovejoy, and Alexander Koyre, for example, have stressed the affinity between the views of Newton and those of Henry More, the Cambridge Platonist. More clearly

---

27   *The Leibniz-Clarke Correspondence,* edited by H.G. Alexander (Manchester University Press, 1965); first published by Samuel Clarke himself (1717) and then by Pierre Desmaizeauz (1720). Cf. Robert Paul Wolff, *Kant's Theory of Mental Activity; A Commentary on the Transcendental Analytic of the Critique of Pure Reason* (Cambridge, MA: Harvard University Press, 1963), 2–8.

they would have been influenced by Plato's *Timaeus*. Basically, the Cambridge men simply substituted Plato's supra-form of the Good for the Christian God.

> There are not, as Descartes asserts, two types of substances, the extended and the unextended. There is only one type: all substance, spiritual as well as material, is extended. Descartes, according to More, fails to recognize the specific character both of matter and of space, and therefore misses their essential distinctions as well as their fundamental relation. Matter is mobile *in* space and by its impenetrability *occupies* space; space is not mobile and is unaffected by the presence, or absence, of matter in it. Thus matter without space is unthinkable, whereas space without matter, Descartes not withstanding, is not only an easy, but even a necessary idea of our mind.
> KOYRE, *CWIU*, 127

Newton, who was highly religious, seems to have picked up on More's emphasis on the possible "spiritual" (malleable and "plastic") qualities of space and simply accommodated it by analogizing it to God's *sensoria*. But the salient distinction More makes is between space, objects, and mobility, which introduces the concept of motion and hence objective time. Souls being spiritual but extended are fluidly penetrable while inert matter is impenetrable.

Against Newton, Leibniz conceives space and time as a result of a relational ordering between first perceptions, then visible points (sensations as "confused conceptions"), and finally non-extended and immaterial monads. The internal structures of space are mind-dependent. Space is not a substance, not a thing-in-itself but rather a well-grounded phenomenon, a *phenomena bene fundata*, an appearance, and actually a form or type of imperfect *conception*. Space is ideal, mental, and dependent on minds, on states of consciousness; it is the *active* product or result of the arrangement, manner, or order of *appearances* between perceived punctual distances or successive moments when time is concerned. Ultimately, the visible points are simple but when they occur within a contextual framework of subjective *relational* possibilities, i.e., mental perceptual monads or points or dots, then the relational (but confused) concept of space is generated. These points within consciousness are *minima sensibilia*; they are unextended, immaterial, and therefore simple entities, i.e., they have no parts and consequently they are indivisible; in short, they partake of the immaterial essence of consciousness. Leibniz even refers to them as "spiritual atoms."[28] Since space depends on *conceptual* relations; more properly, it

---

28   Ivor Leclerc, *The Philosophy of Nature* (New York: Humanities, 1971), 243–272.

*is* relations, it *is* an ordering; it *requires* ordering. It follows that the origin of space is mental and ideal and depends on the *active* capacity of the mind to form relational orders. Matter is unable to order itself. Hence Leibniz invokes the rationalist premise that order and relation come from the *active* powers of the mind. Now an implication of this theory is that if there were only a single point in the universe, while eliminating all others as well as one's own perceptual self as a point of reference (Berkeley), one could experience neither the appearance of space nor of time, time being defined in terms of apperceptual monadic motion through space. Leibniz accordingly concludes that space and time are "the order of co-existing things" i.e., perceived *minima visibilia* or *tangibilia* and their relations. The appearance of space itself occurs within the self-conscious (apperceptive) domain of the single, unified monad. There is, strictly speaking, no physical, extended, material world "out there," external to the mind with which the substantial monadic soul interacts. (Monads in Greek implies oneness and unity.) The dominant soul-monad is perfectly self-contained, insular, and "windowless" (*The Monadology,* Section 7). Consequently, Leibniz is able to develop his entire epistemological theory of knowledge while "logically" and metaphysically restricting himself to the principle that only unextended, immaterial monadal/points/perceptions plus unifying *dominant* monadic souls exist. The infinite range of active souls throughout the great expanses of the universe are the only true substances; and any apparent interaction between various monads and different orders and degrees of monadical consciousness can only be accounted for by an appeal to the pre-established harmony instituted by God. The foregoing quite obviously is a thorough exploitation of various aspects of the simplicity premise/argument in regard to the *minima sensibilia* and the attribution of monadic apperception to rational souls.

Nevertheless, once again it must be remembered that according to Leibniz, sensations are "confused conceptions," whereas for Kant passive sensations and active conceptions are generically distinct. For Kant, sensations are *given* immediately, passively as spatial because of our intuitive representational *form* of sensibility. Space is not thought, not conceived; it is passively given; but concepts are mediately, relationally thought and actively connected to other sensory contents or to pure concepts in order to actively form connections between spatial objects and judgments *in consciousness.*

But if sensations are in some significant sense conceptions, then it follows they must incorporate *relational* implications for Leibniz. In short, Leibniz is not merely positing immaterial points but going beyond them by conceiving points as *relationally, mediately* distributed and ordered in order to produce recognizable patterns and thus *to create the appearance* of spatial extension, a *phenomenon bene fundata.* Finally, for Leibniz, God is infinite, i.e., not spatially extended and eternal, i.e., not temporally extended. For both Descartes and Leibniz infinity is the negation of space and eternity is the negation of time. This implication of course means that space and time must be subjective human modes of thought or creations.

Kant's criticism concerning Leibniz's position is well-known.[29] But for the purposes of our discussion, the objection that requires our attention occurs in the First Argument of the Metaphysical Exposition of Space (Kant, *Critique*, A 23=B 38). Kant's point is that Leibniz, or more properly the "metaphysical students of nature," have assumed the very existence of space, while paradoxically claiming to explain its origin and derivation. Kant's challenge accordingly insists that before we can place points or monads (A 438=B 466 ff.) "beside," "alongside," "next to," or "outside of" each other, we must *already presuppose* a representation of space; we must *already* have the pure intuitive form of sensibility "within" us or "before" us in order to "see" and intuit the points as distributed and ordered. It follows for Kant, then, that space is not generated *after* we have placed points at distances from each other, or in relation to other points, but rather that the pure representation of space is itself a condition, which *precedes* (and must) the placing of the points relative to each other. The intuition of space is therefore *passively* given as a pure form of human sensibility. Simply put, for Kant, the intuited form of space precedes both the positing and the positioning of the points. Further, according to Kant, we can "think," or more properly *imagine,* space as empty of points or objects as the mathematically oriented Newtonian proponents of nature contend, whereas for the Leibnizian "metaphysical students of nature," the points must precede space. On this latter view, space is *actively* generated from points and their relational ordering. (According to Kant, pure empty space is "imaginable." To repeat, his assertion has been challenged as a psychological impossibility.)

Kant's alleged criticism of Leibniz is plausible only if one assumes Leibniz to have actually held the identical position, which Kant sets forth as the one advocated by the metaphysical students of nature. But now I want to consider another possible interpretation of the relational theory and (1) see how it differs from the first position, which Kant rejects; and (2) examine if the second view

---

29   Kant studied the Leibniz-Clarke debate and forged his own theory in response to the views of his two great predecessors. In point of fact, Kant goes out of his way *not* to cite Leibniz by name in these sections of the Aesthetic, which deal with space. The avoidance, I believe, may be due to the fact that it is not really Leibniz's view that Kant is presenting for attack but rather something suggested by Leibniz's theory. See NKS, *Commentary*, 140, note 6. Cf., Sadik Al-Azm, *The Origins of Kant's Arguments in the Antinomies* (London: Oxford University Press, 1972), 5–9.

is immune to Kant's criticism. In doing so I shall suggest a different interpretation, one which concludes that, in spite of himself, Kant, as well as Leibniz and Hume, are all enmeshed in a relational *conception* of space and that the controversy over whether points precede space or space precedes punctual distribution is secondary to the contention on which all three theorists agree, namely that the mind has the capacity to *actively* perform relational operations. Consequently, Kant's "forms of intuition" are not as passive as he intimates.

Hume had earlier, like Kant, modeled his views on space and time while under the influence of the *Leibniz-Clarke Correspondence*. According to Hume, the *minima tangibilia* and *visibilia* comprising or composing the "material"—actually the mentally perceived, imaged contents populating our idea of space—are not themselves extended. As Kemp Smith, John Laird, B.M. Laing, and others have emphasized, the points of color are unextended *sensibilia* (later termed sense-qualia or sense-data by our contemporary positivists). Consequently, Hume's *idea*—but certainly not the impression—of space (and time) are "founded on that simple principle, that our ideas of them are compounded of parts, which are indivisible" (Hume, *Treatise,* 38); of "indivisible points or atoms" (ibid., 42, 58). Hume's phenomenalist conclusion, then, is that "extension ... is nothing but a composition of visible or tangible parts [i.e. *minima sensibilia*] dispos'd [i.e., perceived as distributed] in a certain order" (ibid.,62). In addition:

> There is another very decisive argument, which establishes the present doctrine concerning our ideas of space and time, and is founded only on that simple principle, *that our ideas of space and time are compounded of parts that are indivisible.*
> ibid., 38; italics his

Notice that the title to the section refers to the *qualities* of our *ideas* of space and time. And thus Hume concludes that "we have no idea of any real [i.e., independently existing] extension without filling it with sensible objects [i.e., simple mental impressions, perceptions], and conceiving its parts [the simple, unextended points] as visible or tangible" (ibid., 64). Further, since, according to Hume, points and impressions precede space, it follows that space depends on pre-existing points; and Hume is thereby led to claim that unextended impressions, when they are placed adjacently, contiguously to each other, actually result in extended ones (ibid.,19, 41). It is here that commentators like Kemp Smith finally give up trying to understand Hume and regard the whole issue as a howler: "In other words, two unextended sensibles, if contiguous, will generate what is genuinely extended" (Kemp Smith, *PDH,* 300). Obviously, for Kemp Smith, if the points did not have extension originally, no grouping, jamming, or bunching of unextended points together could possibly produce an extended quantity. It is in the context of this criticism that I wish to defend Hume's view by showing that Kemp Smith may have misunderstood it; that Hume's position, as well as that of Leibniz, implies *active* relational presuppositions, which are not dependent on the passive visual distribution of points but rather on the *innate* and *active* "propensities" and "dispositions" of the mind. How this different view is immune to Kant's attack on the relational theory of space; and that in fact Leibniz's, Hume's, and Kant's theories are not at all as dissimilar to each other as it might seem at first sight to appear. In effect, I am claiming that (1) Leibniz held a relational theory similar to that of Hume; and Kant was aware of this and therefore Kant was either attacking someone other than Leibniz in the Aesthetic; or (2) he misunderstood the great rationalist and his challenge fell wide of the mark.[30] It is within this larger context that Hume's principle of the *minima sensibilia,* which he shares with Leibniz, Berkeley, and Kant and, as in all their cases, derives from their commitments (a) to the simplicity premise with its accompanying argument; and (b) whatever appears to the mind must be simple surfaces. It may also be recalled that Berkeley had previously held, in *A New Theory of Vision,* that the third dimension of space, namely depth, is *mediately inferred* and not directly given. In short, it depends on a further *active* and "extra-relational" factor (*Principles,* §§ I ff.). Therefore, a man born blind, whose eyesight was suddenly restored, could not at first judge distances (§ XLI). All these philosophical maneuvers are forced by two ruling underlying principles: (1) the mind's *immaterial* simplicity; and (2) its *active structuralizing* nature.

But going forward, the issue between Kant and Leibniz-Hume is the following: (a) Kant holds that the innate intuition of space precedes punctual location whereas (b) Leibniz and Hume *seem* to insist that points and their arrangement precede space and only then actively generate (the possibility of) spatial appearances. For Leibniz, the points are confused conceptions; for Hume, the points are (presumably) given as perceptual (empirical) points, impressions. But view (b) is open to two very different interpretations. The first

---

30   Cf., Ben Mijuskovic, "Hume on Space (and Time)," *Journal of the History of Philosophy,* XV:4, 387–394 (1977); reprinted in *David Hume: Critical Assessments,* edited by Stanley Tweyman (London: Routledge & Kegan Paul, 1994). In the article, I contend that Hume's principle of the *minima sensibilia,* which he shares with Leibniz, Berkeley, and Kant, derives, as in their cases, from their adoption of the simplicity argument. It may be recalled that Berkeley had previously argued, in *A New Theory of Vision,* that the experience of a three-dimensional space is mediately inferred rather than directly given (Sections I ff.). It follows that a man born blind, whose eyesight is suddenly restored, cannot at first judge distances (Section XLI).

doctrine (b1) presupposes that the points are "spread out," at distances from each other throughout an already given space. Thus, regarding points x y z, we could say that the extension between x and y is greater than between y and z; or that x is to the left of y and to the right of z assuming, in Berkeleyan fashion, our own "point" of view as another relational perspective. Now interpretation (1a) is clearly vulnerable to Kant's objection, namely, that the existence of points has been presupposed. Notice that in this discussion, the interjection of relational factors is paramount.

The (possible) solution to the "problem of space"—what is it; how do we know it?—will be found somewhere among and along the foregoing philosophical reflections; and also that the previous considerations need be taken into account before we simply assume that space is merely *given* without question, unproblematically as being "out there" in the manner assumed by naïve materialism and its later attendant neuroscientific doctrines. But it is extremely shortsighted to simply assume that space is as obvious as a newborn's first visual experience. Relatively speaking, very little has been done in the philosophical literature on Hume's "ideas" of space and time. But it only takes a glance at the Table of Contents of the *Treatise* to realize that the entire subject matter of consciousness begins first with Hume's title, *Of ideas* and then moves to the section titled *Of the ideas of space and time*. And why? Simply because without a viable "explanation" for space science is mere guesswork. If science cannot account for space but only assume it, everything else remains merely an assumption.

In any case, how important and complex these reflections by eighteenth-century and early nineteenth-century philosophers is can be judged by considering the following passage from Kemp Smith. Of special significance, notice below that again *"sensations are non-spatial and differ only qualitatively."* Sensations are simple and therefore non-quantitative. This assumption will figure prominently in the next three chapters.

> The proof that sensations are non-empirical may be stated as follows. As sensations are non-spatial and differ only qualitatively, the representation of space must have been added to them. And not being supplied by the given sensations, it must, as the only alternative, have been contributed by the mind. The representation of space, so far from being derived from external experience, is what must render it possible. As a subjective form that lies ready in the mind, it precedes experience and co-operates in generating it. This proof of the apriority of space is thus proof of the priority of the *representation* of space to every empirical perception.
> NKS, *Commentary*, 101

In addition:

> Kant proceeds to argue: (a) that the distinction is between two elements of fundamentally different nature and origin. The "matter" is given *a posteriori* in sensation; the form, as distinct from all sensation, must lie ready *a priori* in the mind. (b) Kant also argues that form, because of its separate origin, is capable of being contemplated apart from all sensation. The above statements rest upon the unexpressed assumption that sensations have no spatial attributes of any kind. In themselves, they have only intensive, not extensive magnitudes. Kant assumes this without question, and without the least attempt at proof .... Herbart's doctrine of space, Lotze's local sign theory, also the empiricist theories of the Mills and Bain, all rest on the same assumption. It was first effectively called into question by William James. Cf., Bergson, *Les données immédiates*. The solution given by Kant does not seem to have been seriously disputed since his time; indeed it has forced itself, sometimes without their knowledge, on the majority of those who have approached the problem anew, whether nativist [i.e., innatist] or empiricist. Psychologists agree in assigning a Kantian origin to the nativistic explanation of Johann Muller; but Lotze's hypothesis of local signs, Bain's theory, and the more comprehensive explanation suggested by Wundt, may seem at first sight quite independent of the *Transcendental Aesthetic*. The authors of these theories seem to have put aside the problem of the nature of space, in order to investigate simply by what process our sensations come to be situated in space and to be set, so to speak, alongside one another: but this very question shows that they regard sensations as inextensive, and make a radical distinction, just as Kant did, between the matter of representation and its form. The conclusion to be drawn from the theories of Lotze and Bain, and from Wundt's attempt to reconcile them, is that sensations by means of which we come to form the notion of space are themselves *unextended and simply qualitative: extensity is supposed to result from their synthesis, as water from the combination of two gases*. The empirical or genetic explanations have thus taken the problem of space at the very point where Kant left it. Kant separated space from its contents: the empiricists ask how these contents, which are taken out of space by our thought, manage to get back in again (NKS, *Commentary*, 85–86; brackets mine).

For further on Kant's doctrine of the *minima sensibila*, cf. Paton, KME, I, 138–139. The *minima sensibilia* portrayed in the passage above are "unxtended and qualitative." The empirical explanation for "extensity is supposed to result from their synthesis, as water from the combination of two gases." Two comments are in order. First, it was a commonplace of the time for philosophers, like Bertrand Russell, to claim in their "critical naturalism" phase that consciousness is analogous to the formation of two chemical elements forming something new, e.g., hydrogen and oxygen turning into water. But the problem is that in this analogy both of the elements are *material,* whereas in dualism and idealism, the contention is that at least one of the elements is *immaterial* and it exhibits a very different essential property: an *unxtended quality.* Thus the materialist's analogical explanation fails. Today, neuroscientists simply elect to avoid and disregard all these questions and issues as metaphysical and confine themselves to what they can see, touch, and measure and simply avoid the entire problem of the origin of space in relation to the human mind. They are Plato's contemporary Giants. That may be fine but then to pronounce their "findings" as "scientific truths" is both pretentious and misleading. Their maneuvers are mere misguided attempts to transform subjective qualities into objective quantities: to materialize the immaterial. For the neuroscientist, all qualities—secondary and tertiary—are reductively physical. There is only one reality: matter. But the problem persists: if only matter exists, what is space? Can there be space without material objects? And aren't Hume's impressions, ideas, and perceptions equatable to mental objects? Descartes identified space as equal and synonymous to matter. Are we then compelled to return back to Descartes' fishpond universe?

From the idealist perspective, clearly the doctrine of the *minima sensibilia* fulfill the requirements for the necessary *content* of our experiences of space but I have also tried to propose how an active relational component is required as well. We have already discussed Kant's implementation of synthetic *a priori* spontaneous acts in the constitution of internal time-consciousness. Why wouldn't space similarly require active relational features as well?

In the following chapters we will adopt the principle that the *qualitative* elements or contents of consciousness are composed of these immaterial *minima sensibilia.* But beyond that, both self-consciousness and intentionality require the agency of spontaneous acts to relationally unify the contents within a substantial self.

But there still remains a further consideration and it involves another possibility in the conceptualization and formation of space. In order to explore this possibility, let us return to Hume and try to imagine his "idea" of space as consisting of three unextended, simple, indivisible *visibilia* lying "contiguously" (let us avoid defining "contiguity" for the moment) to each other. Each dot is colored differently, say R Y B, red, yellow and blue. Now Hume (and perhaps Leibniz) is not saying that the collection is extended because it is a "contiguous" group of *minima visibilia*. Rather what is being proposed is that space is the *relation* of red to blue; red is to the left of blue; blue lies "farther" away from red than yellow; red is separated from blue by yellow; or yellow is between blue and red; etc. And the phrases "left of," "front of," "between," "behind," "separated from," etc., surely are not points or simple impressions. Indeed, they seem to be *relations*. And our postponed definition of Humean contiguity, then, can be expressed as follows: contiguity means a manifold of simple points, which imply visual separations, distinctness, *and relations* but not necessarily different spatial locations. I believe this interpretation is supported by the following passage in Hume:

> But my senses convey to me only the impressions of color'd points, dispos'd [i.e., related] in a certain manner ... we may conclude with certainty, that the idea of extension is nothing but a copy of these color'd points and their [relational] manner of appearance.
> HUME, *Treatise*, 34

In a different context, Hume suggests, for example, that by a scholastic "distinction of reason," if interpreted correctly, we may make sense of how we can meaningfully distinguish various "elements" of perception, which nevertheless constitute a relational unity. Thus although Hume wishes to reject *abstract* ideas and the validity of scholastic "distinctions of reason," he nevertheless sometimes betrays himself into the arms of rationalism by appealing to relational factors, which are not completely reducible to impressions. On Hume's own principle, what is distinct is separable and what is separable can exist apart. But it does not follow that distinct qualities cannot *also* be related to each other and thus unified in one consciousness. Thus, according to Hume

> 'Tis certain that the mind wou'd never have dream'd of distinguishing a figure from the body figur'd, as being neither distinguishable, nor different, nor separable; did it not observe, that even in this simplicity there might be contain'd many different *resemblances* and *relations*. Thus when a globe of white marble is presented, we receive only the impression of a white colour dispos'd in a certain form, nor are we able to separate and distinguish the colour from the form. But observing afterwards a globe of black marble and a cube of white, and *comparing* them with our former object, we find two separate *resemblances*, in what formerly seem'd, and really is inseparable. After a little more *practice* of this kind, we begin *to distinguish* the figure from the colour by a *distinction of reason;* that is, we consider the figure and

colour together, since they are in effect the same and undistinguishable; but we still view them in different aspects [i.e., relations], according to the *resemblances* of which they are susceptible ... By this means we accompany our ideas with a kind of [rational] *reflexion* of which custom renders us, in great measure, insensible (*Treatise*, 24–25).

In this passage, we find Hume, while in the process of trying to explain away abstract ideas actually affirming relational *activities* as he appeals to the relation of "resemblance," the relation of "comparing" (and contrasting), and even "reflexion," i.e., self-conscious unification. This, or something like it, I believe, is what Hume has in mind when he holds that our *idea* of space is a relational, an active ordering; an arrangement of existing points or impressions. On this interpretation, points precede space only in the sense of serving as possible material for an even more fundamental relational power. In other words, the mind displays *active* "propensities" and "dispositions," as Hume expresses it. Extension or space thus becomes "dependent" on *relational acts,* which are essentially formal, immaterial, and unextended. This I take it is what is implicit in Hume's later enigmatic passage:

> I ask any one, if he sees a necessity, that a colour'd or tangible point would be annihilated upon the approach of another colour'd or tangible point? On the contrary, does he not evidently perceive, that from the union of these points there results an object, which is compounded and divisible, and may be distinguish'd into two parts, of which each preserves its existence distinct and separate, notwithstanding its contiguity to the other: Let him aid his fancy by [actively] conceiving these points to be of different colours, the better to prevent their coalition and confusion. A blue and a red point may surely lie contiguous without any penetration or annihilation. For if they cannot, what possibly can become of them? Whether shall the red or the blue be annihilated? Or if these colours unite into one, what new colour will they produce by their union?
> HUME, *Treatise,* 41

Again, whatever "union" and "contiguity" are for Hume, they are not themselves points or impressions but rather, in some significant sense, *relations*. The interpretation I have offered above, I believe, is what Hume has in mind in the citation. And it seems to me that the advantages of this exegetical account are important for it allows us to make sense of the relational theory of space with some degree of consistency, e.g., it is not liable to Kemp Smith's "howler" (Kemp Smith, *PDH,* 300–303). For if I am correct in my interpretation of Hume, then he is a convincing and persuasive advocate for the relational theory of space. The ultimate origin of these relations for Hume seem to lie in some unspecified *active* powers of the mind, propensities, and dispositions, which the mind enjoys, enabling it to relate, connect, and synthesize separate impressions into a single unified idea of space. In an article, Robert Paul Wolff, concludes that Hume actually attributes a relational *activity* to the mind, which is comparable to Kant's transcendental activities performed by the categories, and I am very sympathetic to his thesis. The basis of Wolff's claim lies in the following distinction in Hume *between* the contents of the mind, on the one hand, *and* its activities on the other hand.

> Hume began the *Treatise* with the assumption that empirical knowledge could be explained by reference to the contents of the mind alone, and then made the profound discovery that it was the activity of the mind, rather than the nature of its contents, which accounted for all the puzzling features of empirical knowledge.[31]

As Wolff pursues his interpretation, he makes it clear that Hume's "associationist psychology" actually becomes compromised by his admission that some impressions "will return upon the soul," thereby strongly suggesting that Hume is prepared to appeal to *self*-consciousness in the Kantian sense of the term and that he is entirely capable of venturing well beyond his merely passive "reflections."

> [Hume] very quickly came to see that knowledge and belief [i.e., both forms of immediate consciousness as feelings] result from what the mind does with its contents rather than simply from the [passive] nature of those contents. Hence, most of Book I is devoted to a discussion of the activities of the mind ... The central thesis is that there is a "uniting principle" among ideas which can be regarded as a "gentle force," influencing the imagination in its arrangements and rearrangements of perceptions.
> WOLFF, *HTMA*, 292

As another confirmation of Wolff's thesis, I would refer the reader to Hume's discussion of *personal identity* in the Appendix (Hume, *Treatise*, 633–636) in regard to the problem of the unity of consciousness, wherein he frankly confesses his confusion and testifies to the paradox of consciousness, namely

---

31   Robert Paul Wolff, "Hume's Theory of Mental Activity," *The Philosophical Review*, 69:3 (1960), 289–310.

that consciousness is both a disunity and a unity, a Leibnizian "multiplicity in unity."

> But having thus loosen'd all our particular perceptions, when I proceed to explain the principle of connexion, which binds [i.e., synthesizes] them together, and makes us attribute to them a real simplicity and identity; I am sensible that my account is very defective, and that nothing but the seeming evidence of the precedent reasonings cou'd have induc'd me to receive it.

Further:

> In short, there are two principles, which I cannot render consistent; nor is it in my power to renounce either of them, viz. *that all our distinct perceptions are distinct existences* and *that the mind never perceives any real connexion among distinct existences*. Did our perceptions inhere in something simple and individual, or did the mind perceive some real connexion among them, there would be no difficulty in the case. For my part, I must plead the privilege of a sceptic, and confess that this difficulty is too hard for my understanding.

Further, according to Wolff, Hume's paradigm of the mind "has a small number of innate propensities and dispositions," which are imbued with an active power to constitute the necessary and universal conditions for the possibility of the unity of consciousness (ibid., 295). According to Wolff:

> Hume developed a theory of mental activity in which the key elements are certain innate propensities, and the dispositions which result when those propensities are "activated" by sensations. I think it is now clear that the various "principles" invoked by Hume do have the characteristics of dispositions and propensities ... When he comes to describe the "transitions" and "principles of union," however, he makes it clear that the transition is a transition *of the mind* from one perception to another; that the principle of union is a principle by which the imagination recalls a set of perceptions; and in general that the [active] propensities which precede experience and the dispositions which result are mental pronenesses [i.e., dispositional *activities*] to reproduce the perceptions in imagination.
> WOLFF, *HTMA*, 307–308

And finally Wolff concludes his interpretation by a positive comparison of Hume's propensities and dispositions with Kant's "Table of the Categories" in the *Critique of Pure Reason*. All this may seem as if I have converted Hume into some sort of proto-Kantian. I confess I was myself startled at first by this sort of reading of Hume but its acceptance was made easier by Wolff's forceful suggestion that Hume's "principle of the association of ideas" can only derive from certain *innate* and active propensities, i.e., relational activities performed by the mind.

What impresses me about all this is that I am convinced Wolff is substantially correct in terms of Hume's "idea" of space. Hume's theory of mental activity is the very reverse of passivity and in a number of passages he lays aside his empirical armor and unsheathes his forceful discerning sword. That is why he battles so mightily to bring space around because it is not simply "given." Consciousness of space depends on the impregnating activities of the mind, whether we can adequately describe them or not. But whatever space is it is certainly not something passively given to us in impressions but instead something actively thought through relational ideas.

In the final analysis, Kant's theory of space, shaped by the demands of the simplicity argument and the doctrine of the *minima sensibilia*, likewise convinced him to accept an active, synthetic, and relational theory of space, while according to commentators Kemp Smith and Paton, Kant's Metaphysical Exposition of space, in the first edition *Critique,* tries to show that our intuition of space is *a priori* alone. Thus, for example, Paton insists that "For Kant sensibility is essentially passive" (Paton, *KME*, I, 94); passive intuitions "are not created by us but simply received"; given to us and not produced or generated synthetically (Paton, *KME*, I, 94 ff.). Also arguments 1, 2, 4, and 5, in the A edition, demonstrate that spatial intuition is: (1) *a priori* and (2) distinct, in kind from empirical concepts and the pure, formal relational categories. Argument 3, however, is more properly a "transcendental" argument and therefore it was shifted in the second edition. It argues as follows: assuming the validity of geometry as a science, and given that the judgment, for example, "the shortest *distance* (relation of quantity) between two points is a *straight* line (relation of quality)" is a synthetic *a priori* judgment, such a proposition is only possible if space is given to human beings as both *a priori* and synthetic as well. The difficulty is presented to perfection by the following passage from Paton:

> A *metaphysical* exposition of an idea analyses the idea *by itself,* and analysis shows it to be given *a priori.* A *transcendental* exposition of an idea exhibits it as a principle in the light of which the possibility of *other* synthetic *a priori* cognitions can be understood. It shows (1) that

> other synthetic *a priori* knowledge is derived from the idea, and (2) that such knowledge is possible only if the idea is explained in a particular way (namely as given *a priori*). In the present case synthetic *a priori* propositions (especially those of mathematics) are shown to be possible only if space and time are explained to be *a priori* intuitions.
> PATON, I, 108; italics his

But if intuitions are *a priori* and formal only, how can they result in the (alleged) synthetic propositions of arithmetic? Would they not simply result in *a priori* analytic judgments? Kant as we know believes he is able to provide for synthetic judgments that apply to mathematics and geometry and thus consist in synthetic *a priori* knowledge. (Schopenhauer concurs in this conviction while the empiricists deny it.) But if so, such knowledge is only possible if intuition *already* contains and manifests a content or manifold; and further it must be either immediately or mediately relational in the manner I have suggested for Hume. In certain passages, Kant certainly argues for the former thesis. The second point is more troublesome because generally he holds that relations are mediate, discursive, not passively given but rather actively thought into our experiences. For Kant the source of all relational principles is the twelve categories, which spontaneously provide for the relational structures of unity.

Now of course, commentators have recognized that in the Analytic Kant states that space is synthetically derived by an addition of "parts" to each other, whereas in the Aesthetic he had argued that the whole of space precedes the synthesis of the parts. What troubles Kemp Smith and Ewing, for example, is that "It is not clear how this contradiction can be resolved." Paton, however, "solves" the difficulty by simply saying that Kant cannot deal with everything at once and that, by and large, he concentrates on immediacy in the Aesthetic by placing relational issues in abeyance for the moment. Perhaps. But Paton's own uncertainty is betrayed when he refers to presumably immediate intuitions as "systems of relation." (On the contention that Kantian intuitions are really "systems of [immediate] relations," see Paton, *KME*, I, 103.) But the difficulty is: How can relations be passive? Paton maintains that Kant "proves" our intuitions are *a priori* and, therefore, may produce synthetic judgments in mathematics. But that is just the problem: Where does the synthetic "element," i.e., activity come from? Certainly not from the *a priori* character of an intuition, which is both pure but passive (ibid., I, 108).[32]

---

32   A. C. Ewing, *A Short Commentary on Kant's Critique of Pure Reason* (Chicago: University of Chicago Press, 1967), 65; and in a companion study of idealism, Ewing says that Kant insists space is synthetic in character because it is sensuous, *A Critical Survey* (Methuen,

But I do not think this is correct. Thus, for instance (a) the pure categories are synthetic but not sensible. If, on the other hand, the implication intended by Ewing is that (b) space is sensuous because it intrinsically involves a manifold, a plurality, a variety of givens (qualitatively or quantitatively?), this cannot be right either since Kant himself argues that we could be aware of a perfectly single, simple quality—totally unrelated to any other given—and indeed that even this simple entity could gradually diminish and vanish beneath awareness "by elanguescence" (*Critique,* B 414; NKS, *Commentary,* 85).

Given these conflicting interpretations, what I wish to claim is that for Kant (1) a mediate (or immediate) relational element certainly plays a part in our experience of space in the Analytic; but (2) he also implicitly (or unconsciously) presupposes an *immediate* relational factor, a *direct* synthesis to operate, or at least to be present, in pure intuition (in the manner of Hume) in the Aesthetic. Again, there is no question that Kant's 5 (A edition) or his 4 (B edition) transcendental "arguments" for space in the Aesthetic are intended to show that our intuition of space is immediately given; and that it is an *a priori* (universal, necessary) form of apprehension. What is not clear, however, is whether Kant also wants to claim that intuition has certain synthetic powers within its *activities,* in the manner of Wolff's endowment presented in behalf of Hume, if that is not a contradiction in terms for Kant. On Kant's view, empirical concepts, having as transcendental conditions of their possibility pure concepts, which are in turn unified by the unity of apperception, are described as a "multiplicity in unity," thus following Leibniz's model of monadic self-consciousness. But the question remains: since consciousness is "a multiplicity in unity," is it then dependent on a synthesis of distinguishable "spaces" within the one given whole of space; or is it simply a pure matrix of relational *possibilities* "into" which incoming sensations are "plugged" and ordered? Argument 3, in the A edition, is shifted to the Transcendental Exposition in the B edition. There it is made clear that the *a priori* (and implicitly connective?) character of space alone makes possible "geometry as a body of *a priori* synthetic knowledge" (Kant, *Critique,* B 41), since now geometric figures can be "constructed"—this is the critical term, *synthetically* constructed. But how? Is it because space is not only *a priori* but intrinsically synthetic, relational, and hence active and non-passive as well? Is this a hidden assumption in the Metaphysical Exposition? If, e.g., geometry is actually to result in synthetic *a priori* knowledge, is it because the form of spatial intuition is itself *both a priori and* synthetic? Does

---

1974, 68. Cf., Ben Mijuskovic, "Kant's Reflections on the Unity of Consciousness, Time-Consciousness, and the Unconscious," *Kritike,* 4:2 (2010), 105–132; the opening section of the article addresses the complexities of space in relation to the synthetic *a priori*.

it help to amplify the synthetic *a priori* to cover math and geometry as well as empirical judgments? Once more, a remark by Husserl may lend some insights here. He points out that the meaning of a straight line as the shortest distance between two points is both *a priori* and synthetic, since the notion of "straight" implies quality and the concept of "short" entails quantity, two very different intentional meanings. If so, then the proposition, "A straight line is the shortest distance between two points," is not an analytic or tautologous statement.

When Kant insists both in the Introduction to the *Critique* and in the *Prolegomena* that 7 + 5 equals 12 is a synthetic *a priori* judgment, presumably it is because the number 12 is further generated and constructed and depends on an *additional act* of thought (versus an intuition) by the mind. At that point, he appears to be appealing to an act of synthesis. For example, suppose a primitive tribe had developed a system of mathematics in which 7 was the highest number they had attained. They would also have the number 5 as well. But if they needed to synthetically extend their mathematical system to include the number 12, then this would involve an additional counting activity in intuition (as well as in conception). In addition, the concept of infinity, as a *pure* mathematical concept, certainly suggests synthesis. My further guess is that Kant believes there are immediate, intuitive "syntheses" as well as conceptual ones grounded in the categories. But there is a huge difference in the example of geometric figures and the 7 + 5=12 example. The latter clearly requires additional *ampliative* acts, namely the addition of extra units in time, whereas the former leans more toward an explicative, analytic interpretation. In any case, it is possible to read Hume's and Kant's theories of space (and time) as inclusive of or dependent upon both mediate and immediate relational acts and powers inherent in the mind. And if our consciousnesses were void of these *potential* pure active relations, then we could not be aware of space; or differently put, space would be meaningless for us. I am aware that this interpretation may be somewhat controversial but I am convinced that Kant managed—either wittingly or unwittingly—to smuggle in a species of *immediate* relations under the guise of intuitions that are not only *a priori* but synthetic structures/relations as well.

Furthermore, Kant, in certain passages, suggests we could be (*self-*)conscious through intuitions alone, without the activity of the categories operating (A 48, A 77, A 90, A 91, B 103). Does he say this because all along he assumes that intuition is not merely passive? Remember, in Aristotle, a form is always active—and immaterial. And the purest form—the Unmoved Mover—is in the highest degree both active and immaterial. Finally, is it possible that Kant's "pure *forms* of sensibility" could potentially include acts of spontaneity? Indeed, since Kant alludes to a pure manifold of intuition, presumably this could serve as a "mental content," which could operate in further syntheses and relational orders within the representational matrix of space (see Paton, *KME*, I, 105, 466; Kemp Smith, *Commentary*, 88–89, 92 ff., 95–97, 134).

Lastly, Kant contends that pure intuition "allows of being ordered in certain relations" (A 20=B 34). But how if it is merely passive or contentless? Has Kant smuggled in relations in his doctrine of space? Has he, in some significant and important sense, an *immediate* relational theory of space? The conclusion then would be that intuition is both (a) *a priori* and (b) immediately synthetic. Remember also that the "features" of the *productive imagination* are spontaneous acts, free, and yet sensuous.

Having stressed the differences between Hume and Kant, concerning their respective views on space, it seems appropriate now, in order to balance the picture from a History of Ideas perspective, to emphasize the more important similarities. In Hume, the ability to connect or relate points, which results in producing *the appearance, the phenomena, the idea* of space depends on certain inherent active structures within consciousness, space not being simply or directly given in the manner of *sensuous* impressions for Hume. For Kant, although space is described as given as a pure, i.e., passive form of sensibility, of "receptivity" nevertheless as he amplifies his discussion it appears there are synthetic forces at work as well.

> Time and space are, therefore, two sources of knowledge, from which bodies of *a priori* synthetic knowledge can be derived. (Pure mathematics is a brilliant example of such knowledge, especially as regards space and its relations.) Time and space, taken together are the pure forms of all sensible intuition, and so are what *make a priori* synthetic propositions possible (*CPR*, A 39 = A 56; italics mine).

In sum, I have tried to show how Hume's own claim that we have no direct or immediate impression of space (we have no "sensation" or impression of space) but rather only an *idea* of it—and not merely as a fainter copy of an impression—is generated by the order, manner, or arrangement of points situated in relation to each other leads the Scottish philosopher to posit certain relational activities as intrinsic to the mind. These propensities, as Wolff suggests, are in turn credited with the power of relating, ordering, synthesizing, and binding impressions so that they result in our awareness of a unified spatial world.

Thus, it seems to me that for Kant there is either a mediate or an immediate relational activity operating within the pure form of space, which entails that Kant is able to conceive of space as a synthetic *a priori* form of cognitive awareness (see especially *Critique*, B 40, B 44). Sometimes Kant suggests that there is a pure manifold, a pure content given to intuition, whereby mathematical judgments could be generated and we could be conscious of pure intuitions alone. At other times, however, he expresses a contradictory view. But in either case it appears that Kant's theory of space depends on certain *active a priori* relational structures immanent to human consciousness.

Interestingly Husserl has very little to say about the *meaning* of space "in itself"; its *eidos;* but quite a bit to say about the meaning or essence of physical objects *in* space as essentially given perspectivally, through various dimensional aspects and through alternating views. For example, when we experience an object, we can never see both the front and the back at once. Later, in the larger *Crisis,* he provides numerous descriptions of how we experience inanimate and lived bodies as situated or moving *in* the lived world, in the surrounding world of things and selves. But again he has very little to say about space in-itself as an independent "reality" in terms of science. Apparently all that is put in brackets. Obviously, the *meaning* of space is not itself extended. However, Husserl considers it an *a priori* insight that all spatial or external objects must be presented *perspectivally, in profiles (Abschatungen)*; it is a necessary structure or ingredient of their meaning. What he does say and how he illuminates the distinction between consciousness as opposed to physical objects is that thoughts are given completely and whole when they are given at all, whereas material objects are eidetically confined to always being experienced perspectivally through various aspects. But whereas the "scientific" problem of space is addressed directly by Leibniz, Newton, Hume, and Kant, Husserl rather diplomatically circumvents it by approaching it from behind, so to speak. He assumes that objects are spatially presented by and through various angles but on space itself he has little or nothing to say (Smith, *Husserl,* 208–217, 451).

I have embarked on this perhaps unduly long exegesis because I want to persuade the reader that something that appears on the face of it as straightforward as our "experience" of space is not so simple after all and that it cannot be *explained* empirically and accounted for in mechanistic terms alone. Whether the subjective idealist approach to space is a promising one or not still it has the advantage of portraying the mind as active as opposed to unreflectively believing that the "existence" of space is there for all to see and touch and that it would still continue to exist in the absence of all sentient life. What *meaning* would there be to claim that the planet Mercury (?) would circle (?) the sun (?) in the absence of any and all sentient forms of life?

Finally, let me address the modern scientific, materialist, and our current contemporaneously neuroscientific theory and allow me to redirect them to their fellow metaphysician and progenitor Thomas Hobbes and his notion of space.

> According to the doctrine of [Hobbes'] *De Corpore, space (spatium)* is simply the phantasm (that is, the image) of a body absent its other properties, that has an existence outside of the mind: "space is the phantasm of a thing existing without the mind simply; that is to say, that phantasm, in which we consider no other accident, but only that it *appears* without us" (*De Corpore,* 7.2). Since every body exists outside the mind, space is *imagined* as being external to the mind. But in fact space is only in the mind. Bodies are not literally in space.[33]

On my account, space is not given; it has to be earned.

I have not been concerned in the present discussion with the question whether Kant's conflicting utterances are real or only apparent. In this respect, it does not matter in the least whether Hans Vaihinger and Kemp Smith are right in holding that the *Critique* is a "patch-work" written over an extensive period of time and whether Kant's claim that we may be conscious of intuitions alone is merely a pre-critical and immature remnant of Kant's more mature theory. Rather, what I wish to contend is that whether or not we can be conscious of intuitions alone, it is still appears to be the case that Kant subscribes to a doctrine of space, which emphasizes an immediate relational element.

In summary, the present chapter concentrates on some key meanings and relations, which vary rather wildly as we veer from a subject as different as ethics is from science and we try to show how ultimately they both derive from the active, spontaneous powers of the mind. Many of us would consider it odd to think of an idea as having length or weight, or as Cudworth asks, "whoever heard of an idea a foot long and a yard thick?" But because of their incorporeal nature, meanings and relations are able to "account" for immanent time-consciousness, the unity of consciousness, and I would say even space. Long ago, Plato theorized that color and extension "always accompany each other," although they are not identical concepts and he further implied that this sort of relation should function as a model for other conceptual knowledge (*Meno*).

The history of ideas and consciousness has the ability to trace the continuity of certain key concepts that unfortunately have often been obscured by time and neglect. The simplicity premise with its many implications of an active reflexive self-consciousness, transcendent intentionality, immanent time-consciousness, and synthetic *a priori* relations I believe offers an important alternative to materialism, mechanism, determinism, empiricism, phenomenalism, behaviorism, and the impoverished neurosciences.

---

33   A.P. Martinich, *A Hobbes Dictionary* (Cambridge, MA: Blackwell, 1995), 287.

CHAPTER 3

# The Simplicity Argument and the Freedom of Consciousness

> Man is condemned to be free.
> JEAN-PAUL SARTRE, "Existentialism Is a Humanism"

∴

Historically mankind has always been fascinated with the issue of freedom versus determinism ever since the dawn of philosophical thought. Some scholars contend that the ancient Greek concept of Destiny or Fate (*moira*) is a precursor to our scientific paradigm of determinism. But Fate is different. It foretells a particular event but not the specific and intermediate chain of connecting causes leading to the final conclusion. For instance, Oedipus is predestined to kill his father, Laius, but we do not know when, where, or how the event will occur. On the other hand, there is an intriguing passage in the *Iliad* of Homer where the poet describes an argument between the Olympian deities and Zeus over the fate of his favorite mortal son, Sarpedon, implying that Zeus is able to save him from his appointed death. But when Hera expresses her strong disapproval concerning his possible intervention, Zeus relents. In this situation, however, it appears Zeus' decision could have circumvented the decrees of Fate (*Iliad,* 16.431–462). Perhaps this is the first recorded conflict between will and reason. Plato's Myth of Er recounts the choosing of lots in Hades in preparation for the soul's reincarnation. The individual souls are portrayed as possessing the freedom to choose their own future destiny based on the knowledge they attained in their previous life on earth (*Republic* x, 617d–618b). And Aristotle's concept of *choice* offers a sophisticated analysis balancing the dynamics of desire against rational deliberation as the soul reflexively considers both the good and the bad, the wise and the foolish, and all that lies in between in order to choose the best plan of action before making a voluntary choice (*Nicomachean Ethics* VI, 1139a). According to St. Augustine, God has gifted man with free will in order to enable him to proceed along the path to eternal salvation—provided, of course, that God has also bestowed His special *grace* on the sinner—since as far as the good Saint is concerned the outcome is already predestined. Meanwhile Jean Buridan contends that a donkey, positioned equidistant between two bales of hay, would expire because it does not have the gift of free will enabling it to choose between options.

Opposed to the foregoing instances of freedom, the ancient Greek atomists, Leucippus and Democritus, propose an inflexible mechanical worldview in regard to both the laws of nature and those of man. Determinism rests on two assertions: the validity of both (1) universal physical and/or psychological causality; and (b) complete *theoretical* predictability. Empirical science is defined by its strict commitment to both causality and predictability.

Further, according to the atomic model, reality is composed of an infinite number of solid particles, which move through an endless spatial void. The atoms, although physically indivisible, nevertheless exhibit at least some minimal *extensive, quantitative* attributes. They also display various hooks and barbs that allow them to attach together by forming into different physical compounds and shapes resulting in various objects as they naturally "fall" through empty space. This "fall" or motion although physical and "causal," it is to be noted, is conceived independently of the Newtonian law of gravity. Further, for the atomists, not only is matter eternal but so is motion as well.[1]

Later, during the Hellenistic period, Epicurus posits a "random swerve" to the atoms as they fall through space, which, to a certain extent, allows for an element of *chance,* thus allowing for the possibility for an unspecified sort of human "freedom" for moral purposes. In the 1930's, the Vienna Circle of philosophers, including Otto Neurath, Moritz Schlick, and Rudolph Carnap, similarly advocated for an element of "indeterminism," of "randomness" in human conduct predicated on Heisenberg's principle of uncertainty in quantum physics as applying to the human brain. Needless to point out, even if one assumes they are correct, in such cases the "agency of the brain" would be completely unaware of what it might do next; hardly a basis for moral responsibility.

For Plato, one cannot "willfully" act against one's own knowledge of what is best, for then one would be acting against one's own interest and no one

---

[1] Article on "Leucippus and Democritus," *The Encyclopedia of Philosophy* (London: Collier Macmillan, 1967), IV, 448; and article on "Determinism," *Dictionary of the History of Ideas* (New York: Charles Scribner's, 1973), II, 18. The atomic theory is the lifeless womb of the neurosciences. The opposing metaphysical theory is represented by the simplicity principle (Plato, *Phaedo,* 78 b), which holds that the soul is both immaterial and active. Cf. *The Oxford Handbook of Hegel,* edited by Dean Moyar (Oxford: Oxford University Press, 2017), article by Andrea Novakovic (Chapter 18), who defines the simple and simplicity in Hegel by stating "that the soul is, unlike the body, immaterial. Hegel is hoping to preserve the important aspects of the soul (its immateriality and simplicity) as it was traditionally conceived. In particular he wants to reject the picture of the soul in rational psychology [Kant's Second Paralogism] in which the soul is a *thing,*" i.e., an immaterial inactive substance, 18:2, 410.

knowingly intends to harm himself; virtue is knowledge and vice is ignorance of the Good. For Aristotle, although one can be "weak willed" or incontinent, still it is because of poor training and the formation of ineffective habits but certainly not because of a "free will" in the Christian sense.

In traditional Christian doctrine, in contrast to the philosophical thought of the ancient Greeks, two closely related principles are powerfully put into play. First, God is conceived as *spontaneously* creating not only the world but each individual human soul as well "out of nothing," *ex nihilo,* by His absolute and infinite Power, i.e., Will. The same volitional power is also accorded to mankind but not, of course, the power of creating material existences or neighboring human souls. But like the Deity, man's freedom of the will is potentially infinite in power; it *transcends* human reason (St. Augustine, Descartes). In other words, although man's knowledge is finite and limited, his power of willing is boundless. Significantly rational beings are endowed with the ability to "create," i.e., to choose between good and evil; either to increase or decrease the amount of a moral *substance* in the universe. God's knowledge is *transcendent,* it is beyond all human reason or comprehension but man's will, like God's, is potentially infinite in power. Thus, the conception of the "freedom of the will" serves as a means to account for man's ability to sin, to be morally responsible for both his *intentions* as well as his *acts*. For example, a person can *know* that adultery is wrong and yet *will* it and therefore be as guilty as if they had committed the act itself. But philosophically, the critical issue is that Christian free will—simply *qua* will—acts spontaneously; like God's Will it is *causa sui, sui generis*.[2]

One of the strengths implicit in the Christian conception of free will is that it separates the faculty of reason from the will and in effect the faculty of feeling from thinking. None of the ancient Greek philosophers, not the Pre-Socratics, Plato, Aristotle, Stoics, or Epicureans conceived of the possibility of a distinct

---

2  Interestingly, in the context of contemporary existential thought the controversy surrounding the "problem of evil" surfaces in Paneloux's second sermon in Albert Camus' novel, *The Plague* when the Augustinian priest challenges the parishioners to *will* the agonizing death of an innocent child. Granted that it transcends human understanding, the issue is whether we can *will* it. God's knowledge is beyond reason but the dilemma concerns not His knowledge but *volition.* In his "defense" of evil, St. Augustine approaches it in two quite incompatible ways. First man is born in original sin due to his free act of disobedience leading to his Fall from God's grace and therefore he requires God's explicit *grace* in order to be saved. Second, following Neo-Platonic thought, "evil" is merely a negation, an absence of goodness, it is not a substance, nothing in itself, just as darkness is the negation of light. By contrast goodness is a positive substance. The vital issue between freedom and necessity is inseparable from the question of good and evil as well as moral responsibility. Cf. Ben Mijuskovic, "The Problem of Evil in Camus' *The Plague,*" *Sophia,* 15:1 (1976), 11–19.

faculty of willing separate from reason. This opens the possibility that in its new guise of *spontaneity* it is transformed into a *sui generis* power, a *causa sui* completely independent of ethical entanglements. Thus the question arises whether there is such a power. Is there a species of spontaneity, an uncaused cause *within* consciousness that is *not* solely exploited within a moral context but rather assumes a critical function in an epistemological role as well? And I believe there is. It is to be found in Leibniz's concept of a primitive power within consciousness that provides an indeterminate but powerful force. In brief, the Christian doctrine of free will is reconstituted in terms of the spontaneity of consciousness. This notion of Leibnizian spontaneity will assume a commanding role in Kant's conception of the "productive imagination" and Fichte's unconditioned "act of self-creation."

In the first chapter, I alerted the reader that not infrequently the simplicity premise throughout its various arguments allows for interspersions between its various conclusions. This was certainly true of Cudworth and it will be true of Bergson as well. His *Essai sur les données immédiates de la conscience* makes clear that both the freedom of consciousness and time-consciousness are able to interweave with each other because they are given immediately, intuitively in consciousness; they are fluidly and indelibly intermixed, like a blue dye in a soluble liquid. We shall see this "fusion" in other writers as well. And once more it all depends on the simplicity premise.

The natural sciences are basically committed to the correspondence theory of truth, which is primarily concerned with itemizing and classifying sensations, facts, and propositions. That is why Hume distinguishes empirical objects and their correspondent statements as "matters of fact" thus separating *particular impressions, statements,* and *events* from each other. Along with the suffusing force of the empirical imagination soldering his psychological "association of ideas" principle, it forms our belief in *distinct* propositions and *specific* causal events. In turn, the twin bulwarks of simple impressions and their associated ideas together combine to form our contemporary notion of the empirical sciences. Each impression, object, and event can be isolated from the rest. Presented in this fashion human experience consists of particular facts and events that can be separately catalogued, tested, and confirmed. Nevertheless, Hume also offers a lengthy disquisition in Book I of the *Treatise* on both the contingent vagaries of chance as well as the frequent accompaniment of causal probabilities, which together produce psychological beliefs through custom and habit concerning our shared world of nature. Science is founded upon the conviction that every proposition is distinct and disconnected from all the others, if by nothing else at least by time; and that we must separately test each statement as verifiable apart from others in order to piecemeal an aggregate of parts together in establishing *general* probabilities (Hume, Russell, Ayer). And he clinches his argument that the "uniformity of nature" principle is not beyond doubting and challenging. Accordingly, we have no certainty that the future will relentlessly and always resemble the past. Even greater inconsistencies appear in the social sciences. Although human habits are usually dependable gauges of conduct, they hardly make for secure predictions. Sociology takes those uncertainties for granted and essentially sticks to rough statistical generalizations and vague "predictions." Thus the epistemic attitude leading to the correspondence theory of "truth" means that each fact must be confirmed separately. The relation of facts and propositions to each other are external and contingently adjoined from without.

The opposite of the correspondence theory of truth is the coherence theory. Certain key premises intrinsically lend themselves to richer complexities and intricacies than others. They build on each other. And there are lower and higher levels of truth. Truth also grows and develops. It harbors a doctrine of internal relations. Truths are judged in relation to each other as opposed to something external. In opposition to the current model of the natural and social sciences, which heavily advertise their predictive virtues, while operating observationally as they apply their criteria from the outside, by contrast phenomenology in both the Hegelian as well as the Husserlian sense are descriptive, interior-laden "sciences" and "arts." The owl of Minerva only flies at dusk when a form of life has already grown cold. In Hegel truths are uncovered retrospectively; in Husserl they are insightful. They provide understanding and insight from the inside rather than trumpeting public pronouncements and declarations based on the robotic and mechanistic "findings" of the neurosciences and the presumably instinctive sexual fumbling of desire studied by psychoanalysis. Thus, in the last analysis, there is a critical difference between what both the neurosciences and psychoanalysis attempt to tell us, to predict, and to cure versus the internal reality that idealism, phenomenology, and existentialism show us and describe as the human situation and condition. Within the capacities of human intelligence, truth is made and not found; created not discovered. What now follows demonstrates that the simplicity premise will find its expression through various forms of freedom.

One of the advantages of the history of ideas and consciousness discipline is that it is sacred to the Roman god, Janus, whose dual visages are turned to view both the past and the future.

This is a legacy the god has bestowed on Plato as he surveys the Battle of the Gods and the Giants. Thus before moving forward, it behooves us to pause for a moment to reflect from whence we have come, where we presently stand, and even to whither we are going.

Prior to Newton, the dualist and rationalist factions traditionally juxtaposed the mind as intrinsically active and argued that *inert* matter, despite its superabundant physical permutations and configurations, would forever remain impotent to give birth to thought. Thus there was an unbridgeable chasm lying before any adventuresome trespasser, who might seek to cross the forbidding maw between inanimate matter and animate thought, between matter and mind, and body and soul.

We shall now examine how, after Newton, Hegel as well as others felt compelled to devise fresh grounds of attack against the bastions of materialism and more specifically in opposition to the *universal* laws of gravitational motion that seemed to endow matter itself with activity and the promise of the endowment of future generations with animal magnetism and electromagnetic forces empowered to *explain* the workings of the brain. No longer was matter to be merely regarded as inactive, passive, and inert as the tenets of classical dualism and Descartes proposed. In these suddenly more expansive naturalistic environments, Hegel, Schopenhauer, Schiller, and Bergson each sought to turn their singular defensive and offensive strategies against imperial materialism and empiricism, while marching under the banner of the Achilles argument. We shall discover the various strategies they recruit in their refurbished attacks by deploying the weaponry of spontaneous and transcendent acts of freedom in their counter-attacks. In the idealist literature, spontaneous acts are by their very nature essentially self-caused and therefore capable of adding a special dimension to self-consciousness and intentionality as they assume an increasingly critical role in German idealism, phenomenology, and existentialism. Unlike the ethical notion of Christian "free will," spontaneity becomes a resurrected *epistemological* weapon. The titanic conflict between Giants and Gods now advances from pitting certain material, natural *forces*, like Newtonian gravity, electricity, Mesmer's magnetism, and chemical combustions on the one side, and spontaneity and self-conscious reflexivity on the other side (Leibniz, Kant, and Hegel). As we shall see, this spontaneity is conceptually related to Malebranche's "occasional causes" (without God's intervention); Hume's principle that in nature, "anything can create anything"; and Schopenhauer's *"causa occultae"* sprinkled throughout his voluminous texts.[3]

---

[3] Jean Hyppolite, *Genesis and Structure of Hegel's Phenomenology of Spirit* (Evanston: IL: Northwestern University Press, 1974), 121 ff.; Jacob Loewenberg, *Hegel's Phenomenology: Dialogues on the Life of Mind* (La Salle, IL: Open Court, 1965), 61, 64, 69; and cf. Henri Ellenberger, *The Discovery of the Unconscious: The History and Evolution of Dynamic Psychiatry* (New York: Basic Books, 1970), 62–63. Schopenhauer throughout *The World as Will and Representation* makes numerous references to electricity, magnetism, chemistry, etc., and according to him, while at the same time closely following Malebranche and Hume, he holds that there are

That there are novel conceptions of matter presents a new challenge for dualism, rationalism, and idealism. Descartes maintained that matter displayed three aspects: extension; divisibility; and inertness. But the new conception replaces the old notion with force and energy as exemplified in the phenomena of gravitation, magnetic, and electrical forces. This is the new challenge. It is no longer sufficient to say that matter is inert and cannot result in thought for now matter is endowed with energy, with force. Accordingly, Hegel will be compelled to pit reflexive self-consciousness not only against inert matter but against gravitational forces as well.

The thesis I am concerned to defend is that because consciousness (intermittently) displays acts of spontaneity, transcendence, and freedom, it is *theoretically* not possible to consistently predict human passions, thoughts, and actions in many situations. It is not because of insufficient factual information but rather because of the inherent nature of human consciousness and specifically its *mode* of spontaneity. The consequence of this freedom or transcendence is that in a variety of contexts, including intellectual formulations, aesthetic expressions, and emotional conduct creative acts lead to truly novel consequences good, bad, and indifferent. Assuming this is the case, it follows that the pseudo-sciences of psychoanalysis and the currently flourishing neurosciences are not only suspect but actually, in the last analysis, ineffective. Although both psychoanalysis and the neurosciences are relatively adept at "diagnosing," for example, psychiatric aberrations and mental disorders, nevertheless they often stumble badly when the issue is concerned with *predicting* human behavior and/or curing it. This often leads to mistakes in the prescription of psychiatric medications, failure to anticipate human violence, and/or to control human aggression to say nothing of the pretentious claims of therapeutic "cures."

Both the principles of the reflexivity and the intentionality of consciousness involve mercurial acts of spontaneity, which in turn directly imply the innate freedom of consciousness. With Leibniz, a very different scene of thought emerges promising a fresh theoretical infusion within German idealism as it enlists the possibility of *spontaneous* acts of freedom and indeterminacy in response to the mechanistic determinism of materialism and empiricism. For instance in Fichte, the spontaneity of the Ego is characterized as absolutely

---

many situations in nature in which phenomena result in producing *qualitates occultae:* "For everything in nature there is something for which no ground can ever be assigned, for which no explanation is possible, and no further cause is to be sought" (I, 124). This possibility directly leads back to our discussion in the first chapter regarding Hume's suggestion that matter and motion can "produce" *immaterial* thought, i.e., perceptions. Again, Hume is not a metaphysical substance dualist but he is a dualist.

creative; in Hegel it appears as the underlying transcendent force animating the dialectic of consciousness.

Thus the situation changes dramatically during the period of the Scientific Revolution as the introduction of Newtonian *forces* of gravity first come to be recognized, although concurrently the traditional conceptions of matter and motion continue to operate mechanically and causally, both in nature and in man for Hobbes in England and La Mettrie in France. But the new scientific vista means that it is no longer credible for dualists and idealists to simply argue that souls and minds are active and that matter is not. The addition of somehow inherent physical forces, including Mesmer's "animal magnetism," gravity, and electricity presents new possibilities of investigation. Now it becomes possible for physicists, chemists, biologists, and physiologists to apply the laws of physical and electromagnetic forces to "explain" the human brain and predict its behavior. We also need to remember that Schopenhauer was trained as a physician as he appeals to electric, magnetic, and gravitational forces as well as *causa occultae* and inexplicable causal outcomes.

But the salient point is that implicit in the Christian concept of man's absolute freedom is an ethical seed that when sown elsewhere in consciousness unexpectedly germinates into the possibility of *spontaneous acts* before, beneath, and beyond its original ethical context, while offering the conceivability to create, to fashion, and to structure something novel purely from within the self; purely from the soul's internal resources. In the case of Descartes, Leibniz, Kant, Fichte, and Hegel, we can see how the Christian concept of the freedom of the will actually becomes transformed from an ethical context into acts of spontaneity both affective and theoretical. All five philosophers, of course, are immersed within Christian backgrounds. In Schopenhauer, the spontaneity will be transformed into the irrational acts of the metaphysical Will, a *willing, creative noumenal force*. And even in Husserl it will generate constitutive acts of meaning, and in Sartre it will be expressed in his evocative phrase that *each* of us—absolutely *alone*—is sentenced to the spontaneity of a *personal* ethical freedom, to create meanings and values for our selves alone.

Descartes importance in the history of ideas and consciousness is at least three-fold. (1) He single-handedly effects the transition from the metaphysical age with its discussion of substances by ushering in the epistemological age; the questions no longer address what exists but how we know; we move from ontological substances to human consciousness; (2) he introduces the egocentric predicament and the dilemma of solipsism; and (3) he initiates a shift from invoking freedom solely in an ethical context to expanding it into an *epistemological* one as well. Thus although the will continues to serve within its traditional moral functions, now it begins to assume an important *epistemic* role as well in order to account for the possibility of human error when the self precipitously engages in hasty inferences leading to erroneous judgments (Meditation IV, *"Of the True and the False"*). Conceptually this involvement of spontaneity in relation to intelligence within consciousness also directly influences Leibniz "to conceive of freedom as consisting essentially in spontaneity and intelligence ... And as all Monads alike have spontaneity (for they unfold the whole of their existence from within themselves), the degree of freedom belonging to any Monad depends on the degree of its intelligence."[4] A defining thesis in Leibniz's metaphysics is that every soul-substance or monad is itself the spontaneous source of all the changes that occur within its states of consciousness as he writes in his *Theodicy*.

> [W]hen it is a question of explaining oneself precisely, I maintain that our spontaneity suffers no exception and that external things have no physical influences on us speaking with philosophical rigor. In order to better understand this point, we must realize that a genuine spontaneity is common to us and all [enclosed] simple [monadic] substances [i.e., souls].
> *Theodicy*, 290–291; cf. 400

This momentous and revolutionary shift leads directly to Leibniz's version of subjective idealism as it moves from simply characterizing consciousness as active to defining it as creative. And what it creates are *structures* of order. In Kant spontaneous structures are involved in all three of his *Critiques* and in Hegel they underlie the dialectical "movements" in the *Phenomenology* and *Logic*.

---

4 Gottfried Wilhelm Leibniz, *The Monadology and Other Philosophic Writings*, translated and with an Introduction by Robert Latta (Oxford: Oxford University Press, 1968), 145. Interestingly, Professor Latta credits Aristotle as being Leibniz's source for the concept of coupling spontaneity with intelligence, 145. Cf. Bertrand Russell, *A Critical Exposition of the Philosophy of Leibniz* (London: George Allen & Unwin, 1958), 193–194; and "Compulsion is an influence that comes from the outside. When such influences are entirely absent, there can be nothing but spontaneous activity. In that sense the monad is therefore free"; C.A. van Peursen, *Leibniz: A Guide to his Philosophy* (New York: Dutton, 1970), 69; cf. also: Donald Rutherford, "Laws and Power in Leibniz," in *God, Man and the Order of Nature: Historical Perspectives* edited by Eric Watkins (Oxford University Press, forthcoming), 15–16. Cf. Robert Pippin, "Kant on the Spontaneity of the Mind," *Canadian Journal of Philosophy* 17:2 (1987), 449–475. But neither of the last two commentators goes nearly far enough.

In *Hegel's Lectures on the History of Philosophy,* in his section on Leibniz, he defines the monad as *"pure activity."* In his *Philosophy of Mind,* he connects spontaneity with pictorial intelligence, i.e., imagery (Sections 456, 457). All this permits us to establish a direct line of influence concerning the possibility of a spontaneous force operating solely from within consciousness as it increasingly begins to be drawn into philosophical discussions concerning epistemic contexts. First in Descartes in order to account for the possibility of error; in Leibniz in connecting spontaneity with intelligence and structured order; in Kant by empowering spontaneity in the generation of synthetic acts as well as the categories of the Understanding, time-consciousness, and the "productive or creative imagination"; in Fichte by endowing it with the responsibility for the creation of the Absolute Ego and the Non-Ego; and in Hegel by attributing to it a formative power of dialectical movement (ibid., Sections 456–457). Accordingly, spontaneity is actually the true source fueling Hegel's concept of dialectical transcendence, *the carrying forward of qualitative categories.* Consequently, after the Christian Middle Ages, the conception of purely spontaneous acts begins to evolve away from its original religious and ethical uses toward more epistemic and positive exploitations. But it is also important to anticipate that Schopenhauer will transform it into a subconscious irrational Will as it underlies our phenomenal consciousness in the guise of an insidious affective, passional force.

In other words, I am suggesting we can trace a clear conceptual path forward from the Augustinian concept of free will, with its principle of absolute volition, and continue on through Descartes (who belonged to the Augustinian Oratory), and from there through Leibniz and into the German idealist traditions of the eighteenth- and nineteenth-centuries.

The ultimate source of this spontaneity lies in the subconscious—below the Freudian unconscious. For instance, genealogically spontaneity rules as our common heritage in various contexts, including *intellectual creations, ethical standards, artistic expressions as well as our affective impulses.* In the latter case, although *ad hoc* "causes," "motivations," and "justifications" are always subsequently available to be imputed, superimposed, and/or rationalized in terms of human behavior, the underlying ground, the true origin of many of our darkest feelings, thoughts, motivations, fantasies, and actions ultimately emanate, arise, or erupt from a spontaneous subconscious origin. Both powerful emotions and irrational thoughts can arise without any external causes or determining factors solely from the agent's own *internal* acts; from one's desires, emotions, fears, angers, hatreds, and even from simmering dark moods—as well as from cognitive, ethical, and artistic impulses.

All these ultimately derive from the spontaneity of the creative imagination. And why? Because if all there is *at the start* of consciousness is a Leibnizian, monadic soul, cogito, self, or ego, then whatever begins *must* begin spontaneously from *within* consciousness. From where else? It is Kant who first and foremost deserves the credit for elaborating on this newfound creative force and providing it with the full power to generate pure meanings, relations, time-consciousness, and unity *from within the mind's own internal resources,* from the very bowels of a pure productive imagination (A 118, A 123). As we have noted, the imagination has the advantage of being both free and sensuous. But although he discovered the subconscious as potentially "a new faculty," he failed to adequately—let alone fully and fruitfully—exploit its power.[5]

With this general background before us, we are now in a position to start with the first of our four arguments for the freedom of consciousness based in the simplicity argument, while always remembering that freedom is a double-edged sword; we can enlist it to do as we please or to do as we should. Spontaneity only dictates that the act is free but it is not responsible for its structural directions or results.

---

5  Norman Kemp Smith, *A Commentary to Kant's 'Critique of Pure Reason'* (New York: Humanities Press, 1962): Now Kant seems to have been unwilling to regard the 'understanding' as ever unconscious of its activities. Why he was unwilling, it does not seem possible to explain; ... To the end he continued to speak of the understanding as the faculty whereby the *a priori* is brought to consciousness. In order to develop the distinctions demanded by the new Critical attitude, he had therefore to introduce a new faculty, capable of taking over the activities which have to be recognized as non-conscious. For this purpose he selected the imagination, giving to it the special title, *productive* imagination. The empirical reproductive processes hitherto alone recognized by psychologists are not exhaustive of the nature of the imagination. It is also capable of *transcendental* activity, and upon this the "objective affinity" of appearances and the resulting possibility of their empirical apprehension is made to rest. The productive imagination is also viewed as rendering possible the understanding, that is, the conscious apprehension of the *a priori* as an element embedded in objective experience. Such apprehension is possible because in the pre-conscious elaboration of the given manifold the productive imagination has conformed to those *a priori* principles which the understanding demands of the possibility of its own exercise in conscious apprehension. Productive imagination acts in the manner required to yield experiences which are capable of and conformity to the unity of the categories and self-consciousness. Why it should act in this manner cannot be explained; but it is none the less, on critical principles, a legitimate assumption, since experience can only be possible and exist. The existence of such an unconscious faculty is a legitimate [hypothetical] inference from the results of the transcendental deduction (Kemp Smith, *Commentary,* 264; cf. Kant, *Critique,* A xvi–xvii).

Despite Kant's deep seated respect for moral autonomy and the freedom of the will, he "formally" relegates the freedom of the will to the noumenal sphere. Fichte, however, virtually commandeers it and returns it to a pure world of volitional idealism. In the *Science of Knowledge,* we find him appealing to the simplicity argument while insisting that the sensory *qualities* immanently given to the mind are unextended and he concludes, as others had before him, that the source for the *appearance* of an external world is actually the product of an internal creation fostered by the productive ego.[6] Correspondingly he endows consciousness, the Ego, with the same spontaneous power to posit not only Itself but also the entire ethical world of other souls as its private domain in order for the Ego to pursue its ethical goals. The moral world is created *ex nihilo* as an open field to pursue its moral purposes. Its teleological principle is its sole justification.

> The self's own positing of itself is thus its own pure activity. The *self posits itself,* and by virtue of this mere self-assertion it *exists;* and conversely, the self *exists* and *posits* its own existence by virtue of merely existing. It is at once the agent and the product of action; the active, and what the activity brings about; action and deed are one and the same, and hence the 'I am' expresses an Act, and the only one possible.
> FICHTE, *SK,* 97; italics his; cf. page 93

Interestingly, when the book was first published, it was believed to have issued from the pen of Kant. Obviously as described, the act is an act of pure immediacy. For Fichte, as opposed to Kant, immediacy rules alone independently of mediate categories and inferences. This primordial act, this *causa sui,* he informs us, is an absolutely *original* synthetic act and self-sufficient unto itself. What is important to notice in this context is the difference between Kant and Fichte on this issue of the self. In the *Critique,* Kant actually seeks for an answer to the question: How is self-consciousness itself possible (subjective Deduction)? And what are its epistemic conditions (objective Deduction)? Fichte undercuts these questions by an absolute act of spontaneity that makes creativity original and primary and self-consciousness derivative and secondary. Accordingly, Fichte distinguishes two-self-initiated activities of the mind: "An act of the mind, of which we are [self-]conscious as such, is called freedom. An act without consciousness of it is called spontaneity." Obviously, in this formulation it is clear that non-reflexive spontaneity is the ultimate ground for

---

[6] Johann Gottlieb Fichte, *Science of Knowledge* (New York: Appleton-Century-Crofts.1970), 49; hereafter cited as Fichte, *SK.*

self-conscious freedom.[7] Again, the active creation of both the essence and the being of consciousness emanates from the spontaneity of a consciousness, which is independent of external matter and passive sensations. "This act of the mind is called thought ... and it is said thought takes place with spontaneity, in opposition to sensation, which is mere receptivity" (Fichte, *VOM*, 7). Before *self*-consciousness, the act of spontaneity creates itself, posits itself. Citing Kant's first *Critique*, B 132, he says, "But this representation ('I think') is an act of *spontaneity*, that is, it cannot be regarded as belonging to sensibility."

Nevertheless, the essence of these acts of the soul depends on the *creativity* of thought, which is independent of external and bodily, material sensations. However, whereas Kant sought both to establish *how* human consciousness is possible *and* its transcendental *constitutive* conditions—and he starts with "positing" "inner sense" in the first edition *Critique* (A 99 ff.) and the unity of apperception in the second edition (B 131–132), respectively—*spontaneity courses throughout both versions*. Fichte completely undercuts both of these premised starting points as illicit assumptions or presuppositions and starts with spontaneity as the identical ground for both (a) freedom and (b) self-conscious reflexion (Fichte, *SK*, 49). But this "absolute spontaneity" is not only the source for reflexion, it is also the essential contributing factor in "the original synthetic act of the self" (*SK*, 135). Spontaneity is the immediate, intuitive, and conceptual opposite of causal determinacy. It is the unconditioned *act* of spontaneity that precedes and constitutes the "active self," that makes thought possible (Fichte, *SK*, 190, 196). It is also the absolutely free act, which brings before itself not only the *self* but—at the same moment—the "object" of reflexion:

> It was the spontaneity of the human mind which brought forth, not only the object of reflexion—those very possibilities of thought, though according to the rules of an exhaustive, synthetic system—but also the form [i.e., structure] of reflexion, the act of reflexion itself.
> FICHTE, *SK*, 198; cf. 49, 82–83, 135

For Fichte spontaneity brings forth not only (a) the original act; (b) the synthetic unity of Ego and Non-Ego; but also (c) the entire system as well. It follows that this absolute spontaneity is an *intuitive*, immediate, direct act of consciousness "for the self must posit itself as intuiting, simply because it is a self" (ibid., 205).

---

7 Johann Gottlieb Fichte, *Vocation of Man* (La Salle, IL: Open Court, 1955), 57; hereafter cited as *VOM*; cf., *Hegel's Lectures on the History of Philosophy* (London; Routledge and Kegan Paul, 1968), III, 481–484; hereafter cited as Hegel, *HLHP*.

The significance of all this is that although Fichte is obviously concerned with the establishment of cognitive knowledge for the purposes of ethical action, his spontaneity—stating it as nakedly as he does—also opens wide a door to an *affective* unbridled freedom that can just as readily lead to acts of goodness as well as evil, acts of altruism as well as egoism. It is this absolute license that also impressed the later thought of Schopenhauer, Nietzsche, and Sartre as well as entombing the human soul within itself through an extreme subjective idealism.

In addition, Fichte's debt to the simplicity argument is also notable in the *Vocation of Man* where he rejects the existence of an independent external spatial world and offers his own version of the *minima sensibilia* doctrine by describing them in terms of simple, unextended "mathematical points." As such, sensations are unextended *qualities*.

> *Spirit.* Thou shouldst therefore see the red in itself as simple, as a mathematical point, and thou dost see it only as such. In *thee* at least, as an [internal] affection of thyself, it is obviously a simple, determinate [qualitative] state, without connexion with anything else—which we can only describe as a mathematical point.
> FICHTE, *VOM,* 43; cf. 44–50 and *passim*

Indeed, for Fichte, we create the appearance of space from points extended on a line from within our self.

> *Spirit:* Now then, it will be entirely clear to thee, how that, which really proceeds from thyself, may nevertheless appear to thee as an existence external to thyself—nay, must necessarily appear so.
> ibid., 69; cf. 81–82

Following up on Fichte's conception of a necessary connection between spontaneity and self-consciousness we can now proceed to document Hegel's contribution to the argument for freedom through the agency of self-consciousness. Consequently the second variation on the simplicity proof and theme in behalf of freedom belongs to Hegel. The general structure of the demonstration commences once again with the premise that minds and states of consciousness, ideas, and thoughts are immaterial and active, hence self-contained, self-sufficient, i.e., free. The conclusion then follows: *only* self-consciousness is free. Basically, it is a conflation of themes found in Aristotle and Plotinus, in passages, which originally offered to the Western philosophic establishment, a base for both the unity and the freedom of consciousness. But before turning to Hegel, it is worth recalling from Chapter 2 Aristotle's reflexive principle describing the mind's ability to perform "pure" acts of thought; to conceive of thought as perfectly *self-contained* and *unified* within itself; by characterizing consciousness as a "thinking on thinking"; when the *act* of thinking and the *conceptual* object of its own thought are the same (Aristotle, *Meta.*, 1075a). Hegel appeals to this same peripatetic principle in support of his twin theses, positively that only the reflexive mind is free and negatively that matter and gravity are inherently self-destructive; not merely inert but actively self-destructive. Indeed Hegel's entire philosophical system is essentially Aristotle's reflexive principle writ cosmically large and all-inclusive.

According to Hegel, the thinking *self* and the *conceptual object* of its thought are both mental; consequently they can be "merged," "fused" or unified because they share in the *same* essence, the *identical* attribute of immaterial thought. Physical objects, however, cannot be merged or fused because they consist of impenetrable parts. Separate parts can always be removed or added. In the case of the act of thinking, however, the *conceptual object* cannot be removed precisely because there is no thought without an object; self and object relationally, reciprocally, and meaningfully constitute each other (so Kant). The unity and identity of the act of thinking with the content of its own thought, of subject and object, of knower and known is best represented by the metaphor of a circle, which returns upon its self. As such it is symbolized by both circularity and infinity; a circle has no beginning and no end; its essential immaterial activity is eternal, since it is "endless." In Hegel's grand version of objective idealism, the dialectic continually creates larger and more intricate and complex circles *within* the larger circles. Truth develops from within and expansively develops, grows with each circle as it self-coheres with all of the other circles inside itself. This is the essence of the coherence theory of truth. There are levels, a hierarchy of inclusive circular self-expansions. For example, while Tycho Brahe charted the nocturnal positions of the planets, and Kepler spontaneously formulated their elliptical orbits, it was Newton who created the "law" of gravity by synthetically incorporating the previous conceptual elements.

Material gravitational forces, however, belong to the world of science and therefore challenge the Hegelian sphere of the freedom of Spirit. The form of Hegel's proof begins once again with the principle that the mind and its *reflexive* activities are (1) immaterial; (2) reflexively active; and (3) therefore self-contained, self-sufficient, independent, i.e., free.

> The nature of Spirit may be understood by a glance at its direct opposite—Matter [or force as external and quantitatively extended]. As the essence of Matter is [Newtonian] Gravity, so on the other hand, we may

affirm that the substance, the essence of Spirit is Freedom. All will readily assent to the doctrine that Spirit, among other properties, is also endowed with Freedom; but philosophy teaches that *all qualities of Spirit* exist only through Freedom; that all are but means for attaining Freedom; that all seek and produce this and this alone. It is a result of Speculative Philosophy [as opposed to Kant's Critical Philosophy and his criticism of freedom in the Third Antinomy] that Freedom is the sole truth of Spirit. Matter possesses gravity in virtue of its tendency [i.e., motion] toward a central point. It is essentially composite, consisting of parts that exclude each other. It seeks its Unity; and therefore exhibits itself as self-destructive, as verging toward its opposite (an indivisible [simple, immaterial] point). If it could attain this, it would be Matter no longer, it would have perished. It strives after the realization of its Idea; *for in unity it exists ideally.* Spirit, on the contrary, *may be defined as that which has its centre in itself.* It has not a unity outside itself, but has already found it; it exists in and with itself. Matter has its essence out of itself [in extension]; *Spirit is self-contained existence.* Now this is Freedom, exactly. For if I am dependent, my being is referred to something else which I am not; I cannot exist independently of something external. I am free, on the contrary, when my existence depends on myself. This self-contained existence of Spirit is none other than self-consciousness—consciousness of one's own being. Two things must be distinguished in consciousness; first, the fact *that I know;* secondly, *what I know.* In self consciousness these are merged in one; for Spirit knows itself (italics his).[8]

---

8   G.W.F. Hegel, *The Philosophy of History,* translated by. J. Sibree (New York: Dover, 1956), 17; and cf., Hegel, *Philosophy of Mind,* translated by A.V. Miller (Oxford: Clarendon Press, 1971), Sections 388, 389, and Note. For Aristotle's influence on Hegel in terms of "spontaneity" (*energeia, dynamis*), consult HLHP, II, 138–139. But most important is Hegel's realization that after Newton, the *essence* of matter is not only expressed through extension but also by the *force* of Gravity. Previously philosophers could simply argue that matter was passive, inert (Descartes) and therefore incapable of producing thought. But after Newton, that was no longer a viable option. This is why Hegel does not simply deny the existence of matter (as Leibniz and Fichte do) but rather goes on to argue that gravity—as a force, as an activity—is intrinsically self-destructive and therefore cannot possibly serve as a principle of reflexive unity. (We will return to this issue later.) Consistently, Hegel equates self-consciousness and freedom. Actually rationalism connects the three concepts: self-consciousness>reason>freedom. In the *Philosophy of Mind,* Hegel states that "In man's case ... his truth and reality is the free mind itself, and it comes to existence in his self-consciousness. This absolute nucleus of mind—mind intrinsically concrete—is just this—to have the form (to have thinking) itself for a content. To the height of the thinking consciousness of this principle Aristotle ascended in his notion of the entelechy [fulfillment] of thought" (§ 552). Hegel's summaries of Plotinus and Proclus in the *Lectures* are helpful as well. The passages from Plotinus are too lengthy to cite, but consult *The Enneads,* IV, 7, 6; see also: Hegel, HLHP, II, 411–412, 418–419; III, 402; *The*

Spirit transcendently, i.e., spontaneously moves Itself; its dialectical movement synthetically unifies and identifies Freedom with Self-Consciousness into Spirit.

Because gravity is able to "express" a natural force, it follows that it is not inert. Nevertheless, it is unable to be self-sufficient, i.e., *self*-conscious. Only active reflexivity is self-contained and therefore free, independent. Matter because it is extended and composed *of quantities, of parts* external to each other, is merely a transient, contingent, and dependent existent and therefore unfree. Only *qualities* that form and constitute the self-enclosed unity of reflexive self-consciousness can exhibit freedom and independence. It is important to notice that Spirit is *essentially* "qualitative being," whereas Matter is "quantitative being," extended being. Therefore the motions of physical bodies are predetermined. The introduction of this critical quantity-quality distinction will follow us throughout the remainder of the study.

The second prong of Hegel's argument above lies in combining the separated italicized phrases so that they read: (a) *"all qualities of Spirit"* ... *"in unity exist ideally,"* which means that (b) *"Spirit...may be defined as that which has its centre in itself."* This last phrase is a definite reference to Kant's unity of apperception, the unity of a synthesized multiplicity. Its original derivation is once more Plotinus and its later adoption is to be found in Leibniz. The conclusion thus follows: Only unextended *qualities*—as opposed to quantitative, separate, and extended parts—can form a multiplicity in unity and thus constitute a reflexive sense of freedom.

Hegel further emulates Kant by exploiting the two senses of "synthetic." A judgment is synthetic when it universally and necessarily, i.e., *a priori* connects two (or more) distinct concepts to each other. Thus, in the above citation, Hegel relates the notions of unity and freedom as a self-contained existing reality. But more specifically, the synthesis arises from a three-fold relation between the judgment's (a) immaterial nature; (b) its spontaneity; and (c) its reflexivity. But there is also another sense of synthetic, which Hegel borrows from his predecessor. A judgment is synthetic when it tells us something about what human experience (Kant) or reality (Hegel) *must* be like independently of experience because the forms, the structures come from the spontaneity of consciousness and so the judgment that freedom and self-consciousness are inseparable tells us something about the world independently of the world; it is informative, ampliative. In this second sense of synthetic, the simplicity proof applies directly to realty itself. Indeed, all Hegel's categories are *a priori*

---

*Logic of Hegel* (London: Oxford, 1959), 118; and W.T. Stace, *The Philosophy of Hegel* (New York: Dover, 1955), 373, 441. Cf., Ben Mijuskovic, "The Simplicity Argument and the Freedom of Self-Consciousness," *Idealistic Studies*, VIII:1 (1978), 62–74.

and synthetic in this latter sense. This is true of the *Phenomenology* but even more studiously elaborated in the *Science of Logic*. Simply put: the Hegelian categories internally *constitute* reality from *within* consciousness as opposed to being causally *conditioned* from without as in the empirical sciences. *The Science of Logic* is Leibniz's *Monadology* and Spinoza's *Ethics* (or *vice versa*) writ large; it is Isaiah Berlin's *The Hedgehog and the Fox* combined: "The fox knows many things but the hedgehog knows one big thing" (or vice versa) writ large; it is both Hegel's *Phenomenology* and *Science of Logic* (or vice versa) writ monumentally large; a cosmic synthesis of concrete Universality, Particularity, and Individuality wherein "only the whole is rational and real."

Unlike matter, which moves as a collective aggregation of separate and therefore disunified material particles, it must always remain restrained, unfree, and (allegedly) determined by the mechanistic Newtonian force of gravitational pushes and pulls, actions and reactions. However, collections of material parts are forever unable to provide for the unity required for human consciousness. By contrast, the soul, spirit, mind, self, or ego acts spontaneously and reflexively *from within itself.*

Correspondingly, the activity of the dialectic in the *Phenomenology* similarly moves in a threefold manner: consciously, self-consciously, and rationally. By contrast, whereas Kant's categories remain essentially dyadic, Hegel's are triadic; Kant's categories reverberate statically back and forth while Hegel's progressively move forward.

> In thinking an object, I make it into thought and deprive it of its sensuous aspect; I make it into something which is directly and essentially mine. Since it is in thought that I am first by myself, I do not penetrate an object until I understand it; it then ceases to stand over against me and I have taken from it the character of its own which it had in opposition to me.... An idea is always a generalization, a concept, a universal, and generalization is a property of thinking. To generalize means to think. The ego is thought and so the universal. [The ego is universally present as a subject to all particular acts of cognition.] When I say "I," I *eo ipso* abandon all particular characteristics, my disposition, natural endowment, knowledge, and age. *The ego is quite empty, a mere point, simple, yet active in this simplicity.* The variegated canvas of the world is before me; I stand over against it; by my theoretical attitude to it I overcome its opposition to me and make its content my own, I am at home in the world when I know it, still more so when I have self-consciously recreated and understood it.[9]

---

9 G.W.F. Hegel, *The Philosophy of Right,* translated by T.M. Knox (London: Oxford University Press, 1969), 226. Leibniz, as we have seen, defines the monad as a simple substance, without

What is critical in Hegel's account is that *after* Newton, it was no longer possible for philosophers—specifically dualists, rationalists, and idealists—to claim that matter is *inert* and *inactive*. That is why Hegel is pressed to provide a different answer and a different defense to the materialists. Accordingly, Hegel must show that gravity is not only opposed to consciousness but indeed that it is "self-destructive," actively sterile and impotent as it destroys the very possibility of freedom and transcendence. What is material, external, and composed of parts is *self*-destructive. Think of erecting a building with more and more floors. At a certain point, from the quantitative force of gravity alone, it will either collapse on itself or topple over. By contrast, consciousness can absorb innumerable qualitative levels as well as elements without imploding because they are non-physical. Two or more ideas do not weigh more than one.

The preceding citation from the *Philosophy of History* is an argument both *for* idealism and a demonstration *against* materialism, the latter in the guise of gravity. Obviously, this specific proof could not have been recruited before Newton. The atoms of Leucippus and Democritus are described as haphazardly "falling" through the voids of space; they are compounded fortuitously; they gather and part, endlessly regrouping, and often by chance but always in a contingent and disunified fashion. Thus Hegel's ultimate point is threefold: (a) consciousness is spontaneous and free of material affiliations; (b) matter and gravity can never result in a unity of reflexive *self*-consciousness; and

---

parts, indivisible, non-extended, and therefore a unity. Again, self-consciousness is essentially a multiplicity (a manifold of images and conceptions) in unity. Leibniz, like Plotinus, appeals to the analogy of the circle in order to express this unity; see *The Achilles of Rationalist Arguments,* Chapter 3, "The Unity of Consciousness in the 17th- and 18th-centuries," 58–92. Furthermore, the monad cannot be influenced "from without" and consequently its entire activity is internal. In this respect, it is free from external determinative causes or influences. Although the monad itself is not in any sense a "quantity," it nevertheless enjoys an awareness of qualities within itself. In relation to its qualitative content, the monad relates these elements spontaneously, actively, i.e., freely. This entire idealist tradition spanning the period from Plotinus to Hegel, rejects the possibility of matter and mechanical motion accounting for the unity of consciousness. See Leibniz, *The Monadology and Other Philosophical Writings,* translated by Robert Latta (London: Oxford University Press, 1968), § § 1–14, 16–17; *The Principles of Nature and Grace,* §§ 1–2 ff.; cf. HLHP, III, 331–337, 345. Similarly, Fichte appeals to the simplicity argument while holding that the qualities immanently present to the mind are all non-extended; cf., *The Vocation of Man* (La Salle, IL: Open Court, 1955), 43, 44, 47, 50, 68–69, 81, and he concludes that the source of the appearance of an external world is in actuality merely the internal creation of the productive ego. Again, the essence of both these acts of the soul is a freedom of thought, which is independent of external matter and passive sensations: "This act of the mind is called thought ... and it is said thought takes place with spontaneity, in opposition to sensation, which is mere receptivity" (ibid.). See also: HLHP, III, 481 ff.

(c) matter always "expresses" itself unfreely because it is constrained by an external force: gravity.

As early as Descartes in Meditation VI and the *Passions of the Soul,* Hobbes in the *Leviathan,* Spinoza in the *Ethics,* and Hume in Part III of the *Treatise,* philosophers have regarded the passions as the causes, as the "springs of conduct" for human behavior and have invested in scientifically cataloguing the emotions. Indeed, Hume goes so far as to apply Newton's mechanical and determinist principle and paradigm in the natural sciences to the arena of human action (*Treatise, Of Liberty and Necessity,* 400 ff.). As Newtonian gravity rules in the world of nature, Hume's psychological principle of the "association of ideas" operates as a "gentle force" directing and connecting our impressions and ideas to each other in the perceptual universe of the mind. In addition, the animating passions of desire and aversion, pleasure and pain have a determinative power because, as Hume explains, "by the *will,* I mean nothing but *the internal impression we feel and are conscious of, when we knowingly give rise to any new motive of our body or perception of our mind*" (*Treatise,* 399, italics his). This italicized phrase serves as the common manifesto of the Scientific Revolution in forwarding its agenda of relegating all human behavior to the intransigent laws of physical and psychological determinism. The same programmatic goals can be found as the desideratum of our contemporary neurosciences, except for the critical distinction that Hume expresses dualistic tendencies and concessions while our neuroscientists are commited materialists.

For Hegel, the physical "sciences" of physiognomy and phrenology in his own day were similarly mired in materialism as are our neurosciences of today; and neither then or now are they able to account for immanent time-consciousness, the unity of consciousness, and self-consciousness (Hegel, *Phenomenology,* Sections 185–210). Matter, because of its inherent divisibility, its parts intrinsically excluding each other, is inherently self-destructive. Indeed, even organic compounds are vulnerable to disintegration and disease. Matter alone can never constitute a necessary mental unity. But without its inherent unity, consciousness cannot exist. Only immaterial, i.e., *simple* elements and thoughts can be unified within an immaterial substance and a self-conscious self.

And finally, it is critical to remember that Spirit is defined by its *qualities*—in contradistinction to *material, extended quantities, such as cells, neurons, and little bits of brain matter.* Because of their intrinsic immaterial nature, *qualities* are and can be uniquely *related sui generis to each other,* and thus they stand fully capable of *inter-*penetration, a fusion *within* consciousness itself. The critical difference is that material or quantitative parts exclude each other whereas qualitative elements are fully capable of mutually coalescing "to" and "within" each other "in" the mind. A thought has no inside or outside; only a metaphoric center, a dimensionless point. Thoughts are completely given when they are given at all; even when they are interrupted, there is nothing left out or unattended to. It simply *is* itself.

But the critical point in all this is that whether one begins with the *Phenomenology* or the *Logic*, one can *only* start with Consciousness and it can never begin with Matter or external Nature. In idealism, whether of the subjective or objective variety, matter can only be known *through the concept of matter*. There is no such substance or reality as matter in-itself *alone*, not even in Sartre. That would be a contradiction in terms. A universe of stones and lightning alone could neither express self-consciousness or intentionality.

Further, according to Hegel, one must also *initiate* all discussions concerning philosophic thought with the Category of Quality *before* moving to Quantity, i.e., science. It is impossible to start metaphysically and epistemologically with matter and conclude later with idealism. The beginning must be *both* rooted in consciousness (as opposed to Matter and Nature) *and* also end with Spirit in order to fulfill the requirements of a presuppositionless ontology. Mind can *conceptually* know both itself and matter; but matter alone cannot know mind.

We can now turn to Schopenhauer, who was a stern critique of Hegel but an admirer of Kant. Kant influenced him in four fundamental respects. They both shared a commitment to a doctrine concerning an unknown metaphysical reality, a noumenal realm. But while Kant's version was relegated to a strictly unknowable realm beyond human experience, Schopenhauer sought to endow his with an *indirect* efficacy on mankind, which "influenced" human consciousness in powerful but indeterminable, i.e., non-causal ways. Second, Schopenhauer also favored the so-called first edition Subjective Deduction (*Critique*, A xvii) over the second edition, which promised to explore "how the faculty of thought is itself possible?" This pledge was never fulfilled by Kant, but Schopenhauer inducted it within his irrational Will underlying all human experience and indeed the realm of nature itself. Third, like Kant, he believed time-consciousness prevailed over the unity of consciousness. This afforded him an opportunity to "intermingle" phenomenal time-consciousness with a noumenal eternity. And lastly, Schopenhauer's conception of the Will is grounded in Kant's assumption of spontaneous acts concerning the creative "productive" imagination and his *unresolved* hints regarding the Subjective Deduction (Kemp Smith, *Commentary*, 264 ff.). These are hallmarks of Kant's deepest thinking, which Schopenhauer exploits through his doctrine of the irrational and uncontrollable metaphysical Will, the ultimate source of all phenomenal appearances.

Before discussing Schopenhauer's involvement in the simplicity argument, let me clarify my position in regard to my interpretation of his version of subjective idealism. First, there is the controversy whether Schopenhauer can be viewed as a "double aspect theorist," much in the vein of Spinoza. However,

Spinoza's version basically cites two *knowable* "parallel" aspects of the same substance, extension and thought. This is not what Schopenhauer is suggesting. He is contending that there is a noumenal reality (in the manner of Kant), i.e., the Will, and that phenomenal representations, i.e., *appearances* are dependent upon an unspecified relation to a Will-in-Itself; that the representations are in some indeterminate manner an "outcome" of a *real* or *metaphysical* Will. This Will not only inexplicably "affects" the natural world, including gravity but human consciousness as well. So just as in Kant, there are two worlds: noumenal and phenomenal. This is why I feel confident in interpreting Schopenhauer as an idealist. A relevant question one might ask of Schopenhauer is the following: What if the entire universe were bereft of all sentient life, would he still affirm the existence of the noumenal Will? I think he would not and therefore I believe it means that his fundamental position is *subjectively* idealistic. On the other hand, if he would still insist that the Will exists apart from human and all sentient consciousness, then he would be in a very odd and contradictory position in relation to his representational theory of consciousness. In the absolute absence of any consciousness whatsoever, an eternal Will is utterly meaningless. As Fredrick Copleston argues, the conceptual distinction between noumenal reality and phenomenal representations can only be drawn if there are minds distinguishing the two.

In Schopenhauer the spontaneity of the *metaphysical* Will courses like a liberated plague let loose among an unsuspecting mankind. Schopenhauer's notion of the freedom of consciousness is very different from Hegel, who associates Freedom with both reflexive Self-Consciousness and Reason. By contrast, according to the great pessimist, it is not phenomenal man who is free (except subconsciously and unknowingly) but rather it is the *noumenal,* irrational, boundless, eternal Will, while man remains determined by the empirical laws of science and his motives and behaviors are all predictable—and determined psychologically and physically—in the phenomenal plane. Nevertheless, since the "subterranean" Will continues to "work" through man—at a level deeper than the Freudian unconscious—it is capable of overflowing into an abundance of expressions signaling spontaneous passions, thoughts, and actions.

However, Schopenhauer nevertheless also wishes to have it that in some unspecified manner or fashion, man's active self-consciousness is able to partake, share, or intersect with the metaphysical Will, the thing-in-itself during certain privileged moments when phenomenal time-consciousness and eternity overlap or intersect. It would be meaningless to introduce a noumenal Willing reality in his system unless it had *some* ascertainable effect or influence "in" or "on" our lives and "within" our shared phenomenal world. A distinction without a difference is meaningless. Thus there must be a juncture of interaction between the phenomenal world of human thoughts, behaviors, and events and the eternal realm of the Will; between man's subjective self-consciousness and the reality of an omnipresent, ubiquitous Will; *some* contact, however minimal or transient, between phenomenal appearances and noumenal reality. In forging this connection, Schopenhauer needs to make the Will accessible or knowable, not in-itself necessarily but at least in *some* form of human "acknowledgment." Or else how can he claim it exists? He is, of course, strictly precluded from saying the Will *causes* phenomena precisely because his Kantian "causes" are only perceptible structures as given through human appearances. In place of Kant's twelve phenomenal categories, he reduces them to a single one; the causal relation.

Schopenhauer describes the Will-in-itself as an immaterial, simple, irrational, surging force; a striving, volatile *noumenal* existence or presence underlying human consciousness, while distorting how we experience not only others but even how we understand ourselves. Motives that we ascribe to ourselves and to others are in actuality at best rationalizations and at worst genuinely psychotic outbursts. The Will dwells and manifests itself unpredictably in and through us by impelling us to act according to forces over which we have no control, understanding, or insight. The Will is a seething cauldron in which the human self is at times precipitously dipped in its turbulent waters. At other times, we are submerged in its deepest waters for extended periods of time in hallucinatory and delusional episodes and states of madness and disorientation. In-itself the Will is absolutely lawless, unpredictable, and purposeless. The result is that man *appears* determined on the surface, but deep-down, beneath the surface, his actions are uncaused and unpredictable. At the lowest most primitive grade of consciousness, the passions manifest themselves as blind impulses, as dull obscure urges completely remote from any direct "knowableness" by the human mind, which consists of a tissue of secret desires; a striving devoid of knowledge; a swarm of impulses without rational aims or ends; and a swirling plethora of sexual lusts.

> In general, the thought-process within us is in reality not so simple as its theory…To make the matter clear, let us compare our consciousness to a sheet of water of some depth. The distinctly conscious ideas are merely the surface; on the other hand, the mass of the water is the indistinct, the feelings, the after-sensation of perceptions and intuitions [of space and time] and what is experienced in general and mingled with the disposition of our will that is only the kernel of our inner nature.[10]

---

10  Arthur Schopenhauer, *The World as Will and Representation*, translated by E.F.J. Payne (New York: Dover, 1969), II, 135; hereafter cited as Schopenhauer, *WWR*. Cf. also: I, 285–290, 351, 402, 501–503; II, 173–174, 318, 530. Indeed, as Schopenhauer informs us, perhaps with

Phenomenally, from the human standpoint of empirical "reflective" consciousness, we see everything from the "outside," "externally," and "objectively," so to speak. The external world conforms to the Kantian intuitions of space and time and the overarching principle of causality. *But* beneath the watery film of our surface consciousness, reality consists of unexposed powerful subterranean currents, a turbulent flowing Will seeping through the uncharted and protean channels of the conscious mind. Whereas Kant posited an inaccessible noumenal reality, Schopenhauer assumes an unrestrained noumenal Will. Although human beings are *in reality* irrationally free and at the mercy of the noumenal Will, at the same time they *appear* phenomenally determined both physically and psychologically and thus predictable in the disguised world we humans mistakenly call our own. In effect, man's freedom is a purloined, a second-order "freedom," unacknowledged and unknowingly borrowed by and indebted to a hidden source throughout our lives. Obviously on these terms, *true* self-knowledge or human predictions are impossible. It is like a congenitally blind man struggling to listen to colors.

> Kant, whose merit in this regard is especially great, was the first to demonstrate the coexistence of this [causal] necessity with the freedom of the Will in itself, i.e., outside the phenomenon, for he established the difference between the intelligible and empirical characters. I wholly support this distinction, for the former is the Will as thing-in-itself, in so far as it appears in a definite individual in a definite degree, while the latter is this phenomenon itself as it manifests itself in the mode of action according to time and in the physical structure according to space. To make the relation between the two clear, the best expression is that already used in the introductory essay [on free will], namely that the intelligible character of every man is to be regarded as a [spontaneous] act

---

Buddhism in mind, the sheer and absolute freedom of the will extends so far as to be capable of self-extinction (I, 116, 285, 391); ibid., I, 308. The active striving which characterizes the universal, eternal Will is aimless, futile, and blind (I, 163, 275, 321). According to Schopenhauer, madness and genius share a common root. On Schopenhauer's subjective idealism, see Georg Lukács, "The Bourgeois Irrationalism of Schopenhauer's Metaphysics," in *Schopenhauer: His Philosophical Achievement,* edited by Michael Fox (Sussex: Harvester Press, 1980): "Schopenhauer supported unreservedly Berkeley's subjective idealism; it was wholly alien to him to mask his idealism as a 'third road' between idealism and materialism, as an 'elevation' above this antithesis...He therefore identifies himself with the Berkeleyan *Esse est percipi* (185–186). On Schopenhauer's position on the unconscious, cf. Roderick Nichols, "Schopenhauer's Analysis of Character," 123–125; and Henri Ellenberger, *The Discovery of the Unconscious: The History and Evolution of Dynamic Psychiatry* (New York: Basic Books, 1970), 208.

of will outside of time, and thus indivisible [i.e., simple, immaterial] and unalterable.
*WWR*, I, 289

The psychic distance between the phenomenal passions and the thoughts of man and the reality of the Will is profound and the consequence is that the thousands of behaviors that social scientists, psychologists, psychoanalysts, and neuroscientists claim to predict—control and cure—are merely the superficial surface of an unknown reality.

But Schopenhauer's "mystical" strain, like all those before him, demands that at a certain juncture during *human* time, individual consciousness and the Will—or Reality—must "touch," "intersect," or momentarily "trespass" each other. Worthless is any mystical or transcendent allusion if it does not at some point "connect" with the Absolute. William James, in his essay on "Mysticism," offers four defining characteristics concerning mystical qualities: (1) ineffability, a state of consciousness that is beyond any possible expression or description in words or language; (2) a *feeling* that results in a special *quality* of incommunicable knowledge; (3) transiency, a state of consciousness that cannot be sustained for long; and (4) passivity, the experience that our own will is placed in abeyance and inoperable, that something is happening *to us* rather than by us. Notice that the mystical interlude is a *qualitative* state of consciousness as defined by James and thus not a state that can be quantitatively, communally, objectively, or intersubjectively shared with others or described and measured scientifically. Presumably then man is self-aware of *what* he feels, imagines, or intuits but not *why*.

Whereas Hegel's state of self-consciousness is imbued with rationality, Schopenhauer's on the contrary is susceptible to the unknown and irrational forces of the Will. Therefore often our outward human manifestations and expressions are intrinsically unpredictable to others and even opaque to one's own self-conscious efforts at penetration because the subconscious force of the Will is operating "within" us and we are completely unaware. We are free but condemned not to know either how or why.

In Hegel, there is a clear dichotomy and antipathy between self-consciousness and gravity, freedom and self-destruction, Spirit and Matter. In Schopenhauer instead there is ambivalence and confusion. Reminiscent of Hegel's argument contrasting self-consciousness and matter, Schopenhauer credits the Will as the final ground underlying not only Newtonian gravitational phenomena but indeed all natural and causal appearances as well. Thus for Schopenhauer, the Will is the ultimate source for the phenomenal appearances of gravity, universal causal mechanism, and therefore determinism. There is no difficulty in incorporating even gravitational forces as manifestations of the Will. Whereas Hegel sees an opposition between self-consciousness and material gravity, Schopenhauer *appears* to accommodate it as a creation of the metaphysical Will. For Schopenhauer, matter presents two universal features: impenetrability and gravitational force. These twin aspects are in turn the basis for mechanical causality and determinism. Beyond that, we can go no farther: they are *qualitas occultae* (WWR, I, 80, 122, 125, 127, 131, 137, 140; II, 14, 249, 314, 317). The conceptual source for this "irrational" separation between causes and their effects is attributable to Malebranche and Hume. Their notion of force is manifested in physical motions but the hidden source of their "expression" remains an eternal secret, an implacable mystery, something strange and entirely unknown defying any and all explanations to the question: *Why* (WWR, 80, 97). For everything in nature, there is something for which no ground can ever be assigned, no ultimate explanation ever given.

> In fact, absence of all aim, of all limits, belongs to the essential nature of the Will in itself, which is an endless striving. It also reveals itself in the simplest form of the lowest grade of the Will's objectivity, namely gravitation, the constant striving of which we see, although a final goal for it is obviously impossible. For if, according to its Will, all existing matter were united in a lump, then within this lump, gravity, ever striving towards the centre, would still always struggle with impenetrability as rigidity or elasticity. Therefore the striving matter can always be impeded only, never fulfilled or satisfied.
> 
> WWR, I, 164

In this passage, the Will, *qua* matter, is obviously the occult source of nature itself whereas in Hegel's idealism both matter and gravity are conceptual constructs. In addition, the metaphysical Will is also "behind" or "beneath" *all* phenomena, not only our human desires, sexual lusts, and illicit impulses but also the very activity of all the natural phenomena that appear causally determined and ruled by universal gravitational forces. Once more no longer can dualists, rationalists, and idealists claim that matter, gravity, magnetism, and electricity are inert, lifeless, and passive realities in their essential natures (Schopenhauer, I, 124–126).

But it is important to notice that nevertheless Schopenhauer draws a critical distinction between matter, whose essence is *impenetrability*, and the appearance of spatial extension as opposed to consciousness, which latter presents the ability to exhibit the *a priori* forms of intuition (space and time) and the "faculty of reason" (*WWR*, 1, 50). It follows that although all is mere phenomenal representation, there are two radically different and opposing *kinds* of "representations," since phenomenal consciousness is not "impenetrable." Unlike matter, it exhibits reflexive acts of self-consciousness and it does not intrinsically self-destruct when it retreats within itself. In a second passage on gravity some of his ambivalence readily surfaces.

> The Will dispenses entirely with an ultimate aim and object. It always strives, because striving is its sole nature, to which no attained goal can put an end. Such striving is therefore incapable of final satisfaction; it can be checked only by hindrance [i.e., physical impediments], but in itself it goes on forever. We saw this in the simplest of all natural phenomena, namely gravity, which does not cease to strive and press towards an extensionless central point, whose attainment would be the annihilation of itself and of matter; it would not cease, even if the whole universe were already rolled into a ball
> *WWR*, 1, 308

Here there appears to be more of a concession to the "dualistic" thought of Hegel—there is both gravity and self-conscious freedom. In any case, his underlying point is the same as Malebranche and Hume's.

> Every explanation of natural science must stop at such a *qualitas occultae,* and thus at something wholly obscure. It must therefore have the inner nature of a stone [e.g., gravity] just as unexplained as that of a human being [and self-consciousness].
> *WWR*, 1, 80

What is important in these revealing passages from Hegel and Schopenhauer is that we are seeing the Battle between the Giants and the Gods, between science and idealism playing out with both thinkers trying to avoid the strict metaphysical dualism of past ages, of Plato, Christianity, and Descartes, by advancing to a position wherein matter, space, and objects are conceptualized and idealized.

The gravitational force underlying matter would assuredly self-destruct were it to reach the center of the universe—perhaps in the manner of the Big Bang—but representations, unlike matter, are "inter-penetrable" and "interfusional" even though they cannot exist without a brain; there is a qualitative difference between quantitative brains and qualitative thoughts.

Matter because of its extended parts is self-exclusionary, while the Will, invulnerable and eternal subsists as an ultimate immaterial reality; it is inclusionary—as opposed to exclusionary—and therefore metaphysically able to permeate; to indiscriminately interpenetrate; and to unify all phenomenal manifestations within the self. Now, again, although initially the proof commences by contrasting mind and matter, spirit and body, and Will and gravity, the crux of the demonstration depends on Schopenhauer's ability to transform gravitational energy into the *causal appearance* issuing from an underlying noumenal Will. Thus the Will becomes the final source of extended gravitational *appearances* and indeed of all phenomena. And he is able to manage this union because the complete skeleton of the demonstration, not finalized until the second volume (II, xxiv), proceeds as follows. Matter, with its phenomenal *aspects* of extension and causality, serves as a gravitational force lying at one extreme, while the Will, as the noumenal thing-in-itself, lies at the other extreme. Combining three elements, namely (a) matter as Newtonian gravitational extension, as the simplest, most primitive manifestation of nature's power; (b) human perception as man's mediate phenomenal representation of his self, the world, and other selves; and (c) the surging, unknowable, irrational Will as Reality operating within man's self-consciousness, all three become forged together as the essential elements of Schopenhauer's metaphysics. Schopenhauer is thus able to bring his tripartite elements together: matter; perception; and Will (*WWR*, II, 305 ff.): "and this is why we cannot give up the idea that anything can come out of anything" (*WWR*, II, 304). Recall Hume: "to consider the matter *a priori*, any thing can produce any thing, and that we shall never discover a reason why any object may or may not be the cause of any other." Schopenhauer knew English well and frequently refers to Hume throughout his major work and he is similarly convinced that in the natural world, "anything can produce anything." And of course, he is aware that Kant credits Hume for having awakened him from his "dogmatic," i.e., rationalist slumber.

On the surface, everything runs smoothly and predictably but below the seemingly placid waters of consciousness there are intimations of violent eruptions. The active striving, which characterizes the universal and eternal Will, is aimless, irrational, futile, purposeless, blind to all values and completely mysterious. Human beings tend to think that their intentions and purposes are transparent to at least themselves and usually to others as well not realizing that the real subconscious forces are the hidden ground swell of an impersonal, transcendent, and inaccessible Will. No doubt to a great extent Schopenhauer's pessimistic vision is indebted to his oriental studies of Hinduism and Buddhism, namely, that existence is a struggle and all life is suffering (WWR, I, 163, 275, 321). Avowed human "intentions," "purposes," and "goals" are in actuality artificial, fictional constructs and rationalizations deceptively superimposed on our thinking by the distorting faculty of the imagination (WWR, I, 186–187, II, 73, 135, 379). In this manner, the imagination fosters illicit desires, forbidden lusts, and feigned motives as they become inextricably intertwined without any possibility of anticipating the paths our human passions, thoughts, and conduct will take (WWR, I, 113–114, 163, 327). Schopenhauer, more than any other thinker before Freud, is impressed and understands the intensity of human sexuality. Often the accumulation of pent up feelings and passions over time will suddenly explode without warning. Human egoism and narcissism are the only constants (WWR, I, 334). And if the Will is irrational, then it follows that in many instances our human desires, motives, and actions will take equally irrational paths in search of their their fulfillment as well (WWR, I, 163, 275, 321). Man's "rationality" is a complete illusion. Throughout all this man's motives and actions are unpredictably free in spite of himself. The subconscious is the true realm of an uncontrollable human freedom. We are metaphysically free and mercifully completely unaware of it; and if we did know it, it would be terrifying.

Again, the "forms" through which we are conscious of phenomena—space, time, and causality—are purely formal and unextended although they project the illusion (*Maya*) of spatial and temporal extensity.

No one doubts we need a brain in order to think; but it does not thereby follow that the mental representations are identical with and reducible to little bits of brain matter. The Will, which is Itself immaterial, simple, and indivisible creates the phenomenal appearances of the self, the world, and other selves. And this is why man can partake and share in the uncontrollable adumbrations. In this fashion, Schopenhauer wishes to convey that man's lusts, desires, and his imagined schemes of dominating others are immaterial, even when it manifests itself through its bodily appearances, through the phenomenal "aspects" of space, time, and causality. In the end, at best all a human being can aspire to in the face of human suffering is to practice asceticism and contemplate a realm of Platonic aesthetic Forms.

Schopenhauer exposes his underlying immaterialist assumption in at least two important passages. The first virtually initiates his major work and significantly colors everything which follows in his philosophy. His theory of self-consciousness is directly indebted to the simplicity principle.

> Therefore the world as representation...has two essential, necessary, and inseparable halves. The one half is the *object*, whose forms are space and

> time, and through these plurality. But the other half, *the subject, does not lie in space and time, for it is whole and undivided* [i.e., simple] *in every represented* [self-conscious] *being*....Therefore these halves are inseparable even in thought, for each of the two has meaning and existence only through and for the other; each exists with the other and vanishes with it. They limit each other immediately, where the object begins, the subject ceases. The common or reciprocal nature of this limitation is seen in the very fact that the essential, and hence universal, forms of every object, namely space, time, and causality, can be found and fully known, starting from the subject, even without knowledge of the object itself, that is to say, in Kant's language, they reside [synthetically] *a priori* in our [self-]consciousness.
>
> WWR, I, 5

As in Kant, subject and object mutually condition each other. However the contention that there is two distinct halves entails a non-traditional form of "dualism." Space, time, and causality provide the illusion of plurality, the separation of objects and events. But the self remains an immaterial unity. The two halves—the reflexive self and the Will—are "inseparable," which is to say they are *a priori* synthetically related. This union is not dissimilar to Sartre's synthetic *a priori* relation holding and binding Consciousness and Being to each other.

The external world is always quantitatively manifold, a multiplicity, while the Will on the contrary is pure qualitative simplicity and oneness. Both the Will and phenomenal self-consciousness, however, partake of an active immateriality. Consciousness needs the body to exist and the body needs consciousness to be known. Together they constitute a synthetic *a priori* relation. This reciprocal relation in turn exemplifies Schopenhauer's "double aspect" metaphysical vision of body and thought, which is more properly a metaphysical dualism in the manner of Kant's noumenal-phenomenal distinction.

In developing his immaterialist premise, both for the Will and for self-consciousness, Schopenhauer suggests that the latter, through its essential underlying activity of willing, is more fundamental and primordial than "objective" knowledge, for it is directly apprehended in a fashion in which the world of objects is not and never can be.

> Everyone knows only *one* being quite immediately, namely his own will in self-consciousness. He knows everything else only mediately, and then judges it by analogy [i.e., inferentially] with that one being; according to the degree of his power of [self-conscious] reflexion, this analogy is

carried further. Even this springs ultimately and fundamentally from the fact that there is *only one being;* the illusion of plurality (*Maya*), resulting from the forms of external, objective apprehension, could not penetrate right into the inner, simple consciousness; hence this always meets with only one being.
>> *WWR,* II, 321, italics his

As Schopenhauer envisions it, the noumenal Will can be experienced, at least partially, inadequately (II, 196–197), as inner being, although not through the form of phenomenal time, which is Kantian and consciously representational. *But* at the same time, in another manner, the self is grasped inwardly and immediately by self-consciousness:

> In the will, therefore, we recognize the thing-in-itself in so far as it no longer has space, but time for its form; consequently, we really know it only in the most immediate manifestation, and thus with the reservation that this knowledge of it is still not exhaustive and entirely adequate.
>> *WWR,* II, 494–495

But self-consciousness is, at the same moment, nevertheless *directed* outwardly through the vehicle of phenomenal *intentional* motivations; it transcends itself by reaching toward objects (and other selves) and thereby forms the various impulses through which the empirical world is constituted and structured. In this fashion, it is comparable to Fichte's Ego "positing" the Non-Ego. Meaningless sensations are transformed into "human" projections beyond the *a priori* structures of consciousness and into the practical, phenomenal world of common sense and science (*WWR,* 12). Here we begin to see a spontaneous transcending force moving from self-consciousness toward *intentionality,* the involvement of consciousness in creating the structures that will carry the conceptual burden of "the external world" forward. In this dynamic description, we also notice that *phenomenal* motivations have the capacity to transcend the confines of reflexive consciousness.

> While inwardly obscure, our consciousness is oriented, with all its objective cognitive powers, entirely outward. All of its completely assured, that is, *a priori* certain cognitions concern only the external world, and in that area it can judge with assurance, in accordance with certain general laws which are rooted in itself, what in that outside world is possible, impossible, and necessary; and in this way it brings into being [Kantian] *a priori* pure mathematics, pure logic, indeed pure basic natural science.

Accordingly, the application of its *a priori* conscious forms to the [intrinsically meaningless] data given in sensation provides the perceptible, real external world and therewith experience; further, when to this external world logic is applied and the faculty of thought which underlies logic, we get concepts of the world of ideas, and these again yield the sciences, their achievements, etc. Thus it is there, on the outside; great clarity and illumination spread themselves [through the *a priori* forms] before the gaze of the consciousness. But on the inside it is dark like a thoroughly blackened telescope. No *a priori* intuition illuminates the night of its interior; these lighthouses shine only toward the outside...to the so-called inner sense [of time-consciousness] nothing is present except our own [simple, non-extended] Will, and properly all so-called inner feelings must be traced back to its movements. But...everything that produces this inner perception of the Will reverts to willing and not willing, accompanied by the commanded certainty "what I Will, that I can do," which really means: "I see every act of my Will present itself to me immediately (in a way which is quite inexplicable to me) as an action of my body," and which, strictly speaking, is a proposition of experience for the knowing subject. More than that nothing can be found here.[11]

In the phenomenal sphere, all human action is determined. The metaphysical Will, of course, is not in time. Nevertheless, Schopenhauer is impressed by Kant's first edition *Critique* argument in support of subjective time-consciousness and accordingly it follows that there exists for him a natural affinity—indeed a crossing-over—between eternity and the intimate immediacy of personal time, a topic we will address more fully in the next chapter.

If the preceding descriptions of consciousness—however we categorize them—are persuasive and insightful, then it clearly precludes any ascription of psychological or neurological predictions in regard to *ultimate* human feelings, passions, and motives. Causal structures are mere phenomenal appearances. Further, if we apply this dark and foreboding description—"on the inside it is dark like a thoroughly blackened telescope"—to human consciousness, to this subterranean, unfathomable nether sphere of the mind, then we must also realize the limits of self-knowledge, the ineluctable boundaries not only of knowing other selves but even of knowing our own self. We will revisit this tenebrous subconscious terrain more thoroughly in the next chapter as well.

---

11   Arthur Schopenhauer, *Essays on the Freedom of the Will*, translated by K. Kolenda (Indianapolis, IN: Bobbs-Merrill, 1960), 22–23.

Schopenhauer has a deep interest in the historic problem of the freedom of the will and its relation to evil and he has many interesting things to say about the Pelagian heresy and St. Augustine's conception of original sin. Schopenhauer even intimates that to be born a human being is mankind's original and unpardonable sin (*WWR*, I, 405–406, II, 603 ff.).

Hence we are all innocent to begin with, and this merely means that neither we nor others know the evil of our own nature. This only appears in our motives, and only in the course of time do the motives appear in knowledge. Ultimately we become acquainted with ourselves as quite different from what *a priori* we considered ourselves to be; and then we are alarmed at ourselves (*WWR*, I, 296).

Again:

> It is quite superfluous to dispute whether there is more good than evil in the world for the mere existence of evil decides the matter, since the evil can never be wiped off, and consequently can never be balanced, by the good that exists along with it or after it.
> *WWR*, II, 576

And further on.

> But against the palpably sophistical proofs of Leibniz that this is the best of all possible worlds, we may even oppose seriously and honestly the proof that it is the *worst* of all possible worlds...Consequently, since a worst world could not continue to exist, it is absolutely impossible; and so this world itself is the worst of all possible worlds.
> *WWR*, II, 583

Despite his qualified respect for the morally neutral pantheism of Spinoza and the unrealistic optimism of Leibniz, in the end he is more than content to reject both as serious misconceptions regarding human nature (II, 643 ff.). There is evil in the world, indeed a great deal of it. He also sees fit to remark on the universality of egoism and selfishness regarding every human being as one who "only wants everything for himself, wants to possess, or at least control, everything, and would like to destroy, whatever opposes him" (*WWR*, I, 333 ff.), while underscoring how we are infallibly able "first of all to trace to its source egoism as the starting-point of all conflict" (*WWR*, I, 312). It is an egoism born of an incurable narcissism and he cites the natural inclination in mankind for retaliation and revenge, for "paying evil for evil" (*WWR*, I, 364), as well as man's inherent maliciousness in general.

Contemporaneously, Dostoyevsky in *Crime and Punishment* describes some boys maliciously—i.e., committing evil for its own sake—feeding a hungry dog a crust of bread embedded with needles and a peasant whipping an old fallen carthorse across the eyes in order to force it to rise. If God does not exist, everything is permitted. In *The Brothers Karamazov* he narrates the exchange between Alyosha and Ivan with Ivan taking the dominant role as he declares, "I think the devil doesn't exist, but man created him in his own image and likeness." He also elaborates on the sadism of Turks in their effort to quell a rebellion of Slavs.

> They burn villages, murder, rape women and children, they nail their prisoners to the fences by their ears, leave them so till morning, and in the morning hang them—all sorts of things you can't imagine. People talk sometimes of bestial cruelty, but that's a great injustice and insult to the beast; a beast can never be so cruel as a man, so artistically cruel... These Turks took a pleasure in torturing children, too; cutting the unborn child from the mother's womb, and tossing babies up in the air and catching them on the points of their bayonets before their mother's eyes. Doing it before the mother's eyes was what gave zest to the amusement.

The horrors conclude with the following image.

> Imagine a trembling mother with her baby in her arms, a circle of invading Turks around her. They've planned a diversion; they pet the baby, laugh to make it laugh. They succeed, the baby laughs. At that moment a Turk points a pistol four inches from the baby's face. The baby laughs with glee, holds out his little hands to the pistol, and he pulls the trigger in the baby's face and blows out his brains. Artistic, wasn't it? By the way, Turks are particularly fond of sweet things, they say (*Rebellion*).

Even God cannot atone for this victimization of the innocent, cannot compensate for an evil that was once done. The death of an innocent child can never be assuaged or extirpated even by God. It exists eternally as an unpardonable wrong and God cannot change the past. And Ivan concludes, "What good can hell do, since those children have already been tortured?" "If God doesn't exist everything is permitted."

Although Schopenhauer in numerous passages coaxes us toward a path of contemplative tranquility, nevertheless there is also before us the well-worn hidden track leading to a precipice of self-destruction. There is always the danger, the looming *possibility* of evil, which arises and abounds whenever the self stands outside and beyond phenomenal time and the causal nexus, when the Will rules and the self is totally free of phenomenal encumbrances, perfectly undetermined, and endowed with an absolute power to express man's true nature.

Schopenhauer's philosophy is incredibly intricate and complex and every bit as daunting as Kant's. But whereas Kant pondered the *Critique* for a dozen years before putting pen to paper and then waited yet another half a dozen more before completely rewriting both the Second Deduction and the compromising Paralogisms, amazingly enough Schopenhauer committed his entire dissertation at once and never looked back.

My interest in Schopenhauer derives from my agreeing with him about what he says concerning the noumenal Will but not because I believe such a Will exists independently of human beings but because as depressing as it is, I am convinced that Schopenhauer's insights into human nature with its darker aspects are fundamentally correct. But rather than attribute these intimate "motivations" to an other-worldly existence or reality altogether, I wish to place these feelings and thoughts squarely in the heart of man himself, in the same sort of themes that one recognizes in Conrad's *Heart of Darkness* and Golding's *Lord of the Flies*.

Henri Bergson's arguments in behalf of the freedom of consciousness are quite different from Fichte's, Hegel's, and Schopenhauer's, but he shares with his predecessors the simplicity premise. He begins by interpreting the outwardly directed, spatializing, causally structuring activity of the intellect as a practical, instrumental function in which concepts serve as tools for the analytic understanding as they aid us in controlling the natural world (and presumably other men). In this respect, he shares strong affinities with his forerunners in regard to an instrumental and pragmatic conceptual usage of the mind in a world so heavily dominated by a reliance on scientific determinism and technological advances. But apart from addressing the world scientifically, there is another sphere of existence where intuitions rule and a plenitude of *sui generis* feelings, emotions, and intuitions dominate over the intellect. Concepts are mediate, detached, abstract, and useful; they essentially display a pragmatic role, while intuitions are direct, engaged, concrete, and living. The first realm is the external world of science and determinism and the second is the immanent sphere of self-consciousness and the home of spontaneity and freedom.

Whereas Sartre emphasizes a singular source of freedom as issuing from the intentionality mode of consciousness and agrees with Schopenhauer that man stands in a dark confrontation against the background of a meaningless universe with its radical purposelessness, which can only be escaped temporarily by bad faith, but whose prison is human existence itself, Bergson instead discovers freedom as grounded within the immediacy of consciousness.

Thus Bergson begins by drawing a distinction between sensory and affective *qualities* as essentially non-extended spatially and temporally and intimately personal as opposed to our scientific concepts as *quantitative,* extended, and shareable. The first set of qualitative factors properly belongs to the faculty of intuition and the second set of quantitative elements attaches to the faculty of the intellect and understanding. Further he concludes that the "real" and "whole self" is independent of all causal, mechanical, and determinist structures. As he conceives it, pure consciousness consists in an awareness of unextended *qualities*—*les donées immédiate de la conscience*—as opposed to extended *quantities*.[12] The sensory data directly present to the mind are "purely," instantly apprehended during certain acts of privileged *duration* and grasped by intuitive reflexion within the deep, the "true self," *le mois profonde,* as it experiences an absolutely compressed and fused non-spatial but special and unique *qualitatively* temporal "stream" of consciousness. Sensations and feelings, as pure qualities, by virtue of their intrinsic *subjective* nature as immaterial and unextended existences, cannot be formed into extended, quantified, mathematical measurements, or analytic causal relations. And *if* the "contents" or "elements" of self-consciousness were discreetly and distinctly quantifiable, *then* they could not form or be structured, stretched into a temporal unity of immanent time-consciousness because empirical time—in opposition to intuited time—is separated by the essential discontinuity of its abstract moments and spatial cause-effect motions. Think of of it this way. The qualitative primary colors of red and blue can be fused together into purple, which as a new color is qualitative dissimilar to the original two hues. But if a scientist abstractly analyzes it back to its elements, he has destroyed the qualitative meaning of "purpleness." Analysis severs; synthesis unifies.

For Bergson, *pure* intuited time is an *immediate* "flow," an unextended "stream" of uninterrupted consciousness, as opposed to objective external time, which restrictively moves through a one-dimensional linear space.

---

12   Henri Bergson, *Time and Free Will: An Essay on the Immediate Data of Consciousness,* translated by F.L. Pogson (1910); reprinted by Harper-Row, 1960; hereafter cited as Bergson, TFW. Recall our discussion of the *minima sensibilia* in Chapter 2. Bergson's writings were extremely popular and impactful in his time. They displayed a wonderful novelty and freshness the public not realizing that his work was steeped in the history of philosophy and Neo-Platonism. For example, Inge comments on the similarity between Bergson's and Plotinus' theories. Cf. William Inge, *The Philosophy of Plotinus* (New York Greenwood Press, 1968), I, 173–180. In *Creative Evolution,* he absorbs the thought of Plato, Aristotle, Galileo, Descartes, Spinoza, Leibniz, Kant, Fichte, as well as others.

Des états "purement interne" sont opposés à des états "purement externe," une "région des faits "subjectifs" est considérée comme inverse de la région des faits "objectifs," l'inétendu est pur de toute étendu, ...ils sont purement spirituel...Cas des états simple. Mais il serait contradictoire avec l'hypothèse dualiste des constanter une causalité directe entre des natures différentes, entre des ébranlements matériels inconscients, et des événements spirituels distincts. D'où un occasionalisme de fait; il n'y a "rien de commun" entre des vibrations superposable et quantifiable et des sensation qui n'occupent aucun espace. Par consequent, du côté du senti, on ne peux réellement observer que des données qualitative, purement spirituelles [et simple].[13]

Two comments are in order. First, regarding the term "occasionalism." It's an oblique reference once again to Malebranche's occasionalist causes, namely that body and soul as well as quantity and quality are completely distinct and their dual appearance and relation is absolutely incomprehensible. Second, even colors, as pure presences appearing within and to consciousness are nondimensional, *minima sensibilia* (TFW, 70–71, 92–93). And when we attempt to compare different shades of color against each other and try to apply the *device,* the *tool* of computing "degrees" of dimness and brightness as an objective criterion, we are unable to do so because each sensation, each color is unique and *qualitatively* self-sufficient. It is simply what it is and not another thing and therefore it is completely distinct from any other hue or thing. Just as hearing and seeing are different, just so are qualities and quantities, although obviously both are present within consciousness. Although we all share in a common humanity, each person is uniquely different from every other and thus our own inner experiences are different from everyone else's. And why? Because once again (1) the mind is unextended and therefore (2) its residing qualities do *not* lend themselves to any descriptions in terms of *shareable* objective, quantitative, measurable, magnitudes, or dimensions *in terms of extensity*. Pragmatically we can both agree that the room we are occupying measures a ten-foot square but whether or not it *looks* dark or *feels* comfortable

---

13   Andre Robinet, *Bergson et les métamorphose de la durée* (Paris: Seghers, 1965), 40, 42. In this passage, Bergson successfully responds to the criticism that his *durée* is simply a version of Heraclitus' temporal flux; cf. 40, 42; hereafter cited as Robinet. See Bergson, *TFW,* 6, 31–32, 90, 112, 130, 213. The *qualitative* simplicity of sensations once more directly derives from their mental, i.e., non-physical, nature. Notice the reference to Malebranche's "occasionalism," which highlights the essential discontinuity between the causal extensions of science and the simple or "pure" qualitative elements of consciousness.

(secondary qualities), or aesthetically attractive or plain (tertiary qualities) to each occupant is quite another matter. When we apply this monadic principle of uniqueness to the mind as well as to its interior qualitative "presences," it follows not only that all the contents of separate minds are heterogeneously unified and perfectly "enclosed within each unique self," and therefore cannot be duplicated, but also that each soul, person, or ego is absolutely singular, which is to say that no two people are exactly alike and beyond that no two experiences of the same person will ever be exactly alike. Each conscious experience is unrepeatable. It is Leibniz's "principle of individuation" writ both large and small; small since each experience is unique and large because the whole person contains them all within himself and is absolutely different from every other person (Bergson, *TFW*, 213). Thus, human experiences are qualitatively unique and unrepeatable. Imagine, for example, revisiting a former childhood home. It can never be the same experience; the quality of the experience will be very different. (Interestingly Marcel Proust, the novelist of *À la recherche du temps perdu*, was the nephew of Bergson by marriage.)

By contrast, in empiricism the elements within consciousness are treated as distinct separate *quantities,* e.g., Locke's simple sensations and Hume's simple impressions; *but* then they are artificially patched, compounded together, i.e., constructed and manufactured in order to form homogenous, spatial, measurable, extended experiences; all the parts, *qua* quantities, are homogeneously the same, identical with all the other parts, and thus *abstractly* indistinguishable from each other. For *practical* purposes, quantitatively a red expanse is no different than a green one with both measuring six inches square. Thus quantities can be duplicated, reproduced, magnified, minimized, added, subtracted, and separated for the express purpose of pursuing practical goals or conducting scientific experiments. But the qualitative states of consciousness cannot be duplicated because in this case the primary and sole mode of their *presence* in consciousness is *subjectively* immediate, non-repeatable, self-contained, and non-shareable. Imagine, for example, the infinite evocative range of qualitative differences experienced when admiring the *expressive* features of an oil painting as opposed to measuring its frame. The first experience will evoke different "durational" pleasures with each subject's viewing, while the second behavior will merely repeat the same mathematical dimensions of the frame by all the different observers. And, just as importantly, the *temporal* inner quality can never be repeated twice in the same subject as we shall see in the next chapter. The result is that we are able to compare, contrast, and measure various quantities from the *outside* because they share a common attribute, property, or predicate, namely spatial or temporal extension. In those instances there is a common public criterion or standard available to all of us. But with qualities, we must get *inside* the experience, the expression, the meaning.

Consider for a moment the emotions of pity, sympathy, and grief experienced by a mourner during a funeral. Could an outside observer imagine what the mourner is "going through"? Although the external behavior of the bereaved will appear the same to various spectators, the quality of the internal feelings in the griever will be immensely different during the funeral's span of time. Imagine further that a reporter asked observers to *adequately* describe their observational descriptions verbally. They will fail. Each human being is unique and cannot be compared and contrasted with any other self, since each sphere of consciousness is insularly permeated by unrepeatable qualitative "contents," by unique sensations, passions, and thoughts. It also means that the same subject at different times is uniquely different from every other moment. This is also why it is frequently impossible for outside observers in their capacity as spectators to predict the feelings or the behaviors of others. We are each of us only bystanders in relation to the other selves and often even in relation to our own self.

But once more, the very concept of prediction in the human sciences—psychology, psychoanalysis, sociology, and the neurosciences—sounds peculiarly hollow and odd if I try to apply it to my own *self*-consciousness. I "know" what I am going to do next (or do I?); but to say I can predict what I will do sounds quite strange. It sounds as if I am observing myself at a distance; as if I am an "objective entity" preparing causally to go into motion. Causality is always external; motives are internal. There is a seismic difference between how I regard my own consciousness and how external observers from their perspective try to "get inside," to penetrate *my* self-consciousness. Thus when others claim to predict what *I* am going to do, they are actually claiming they can place their consciousness within mine, basically an existential contradiction. Others have their own feelings, thoughts, and wills but they cannot have mine. I can predict what billiard balls will do when struck but not what the players will do. Thus although the human sciences valiantly indulge in predictive adventures in their applications to the minds of other selves, it seems manifestly peculiar because prediction is an "external" enterprise and freedom by contrast emanates from within the self. And although the self reflexively knows what it knows and what it wills, that does not mean that it can infallibly predict what it will do in either present or future situations and under different circumstances. I may imagine myself a perfect hero until I am placed before a firing squad (Sartre's *The Wall*).

The entire problem of free will versus determinism arises when we try to quantify and "measure" our purely mental and qualitatively inner, i.e., "durational" states of consciousness. But as Bergson warns, there is always an ensuing distortion engendered whenever we confuse pure, immediate, inner phenomena, which do not occupy space, with those that are *represented as* spatially objective and measurable. But to conceive subjective sensations and feelings (secondary qualities) as spatial and objective is as misleading as to describe atoms as blue or red. Rather when we operate with abstract spatial and measurable predicates, we are simply imposing *ad hoc* practical or scientific *timeless, immobile* concepts on lived experiences. It is an accommodation in behalf of our utilitarian, pragmatic, analytic, and scientific interests. It is the difference between painting a house and admiring a painting. Qualities cannot be measured; quantities can. Qualities are intimate; quantities are public. Something very important is lost in the attempted translation from facts to values; from descriptions to expressions; and from quantities to qualities. Words and languages are always an imprecise and clumsy way of communicating and sharing sensations, feelings, meanings, motives, and values. Descriptions and expressions are very different orders, different levels of thought and consciousness. Intuitions and meanings, unlike words, have nuances. Worse yet. Words are circumscribed, defined, and static; meanings are expressive, flowing, nuanced; they instantiate temporal fluidity. A facial expression can be nuanced but not defined.

Accordingly, in the transition from the intuitive to the practical, a schism intervenes between the real and the artificial; quality and quantity; intuition and conception; heterogeneity and homogeneity; pure duration and chronological time; inner and outer; the unique and the repeatable.

Even the designation of "degrees of intensity," as we have seen, which we falsely attribute to certain feelings and psychic states, is an artificial construct perpetuated by the dominating practical faculty of the understanding. The practical and the useful always imply *mediacy:* future goals, planning, means available, and an external direction. It is diametrically opposed to the self-sufficient *immediacy* of duration and the *directness* of intuition, which is to "live within the moment," to be imbued (existentially) in the immediacy of *becoming,* to be perched on a sheer brink, on the absolute precipice of freedom, while surveying infinite possibilities before and transcendent to one's self (Kierkegaard).

> Pure duration, that which consciousness perceives, must thus be reckoned among the so-called intensive magnitudes, if intensities can be called magnitudes: Strictly speaking, however, it is not a quantity, and as soon as we try to measure it, we unwittingly replace it by space.
> TFW, 106

For the analytic concepts of the understanding, time "means" the measure of motion across spatial points of determination; objective time is fundamentally a spatial, visual picture; inter-subjective time traverses a common space. Hence time presupposes space; but for intuition, there is a pure duration independent of space given directly to consciousness. Bergson opposes intelligence and intuition. Once more, the assignment of quantifiable measurements as applicable to the "real" material world is the result of the analytic intellect, which distorts our inner reality by imposing artificial spatial, measurable, and mathematical structures upon it. To try to quantify sensations and feelings as "more" or "less" intense, to assign numerical "degrees" to emotions is to deny their intrinsic quality; their uniqueness; they simply are what they are. The anxiety of fear cannot be compared to the violence of anger; and a child's anguish cannot be contrasted with an adult's despair. They lack a *common, i.e., identical* qualitative feature. They are unique on to themselves.

Bergson thus expounds a theory of consciousness, which he shares with others that matter alone cannot think; that the materialist principle, which transforms consciousness into electro-chemical motions and impulses in the brain *alone*, is misplaced and wrong-headed (*TFW*, 86–87, 205). The vain attempt to turn freedom into determinism is grounded in a quixotic effort by the materialists to translate spatialized, extended time into strictly cause-effect events. Against this alleged scientific program, Bergson posits a "pure duration" in which sensations and desires are "melded," "amalgamated," and "fused" not only "through" each other but also "into" indivisible, indissoluble, and impregnable *unities* of consciousness. This radical divergence from the scientific methodologies of materialism and empiricism prohibits any theoretical possibility of forming a functional determinism for human consciousness. Bergson's paradigm of consciousness consisting of qualitative "elements," *les donées immédiates de la conscience,* cannot by definition be sequentially ordered into an extended temporal line of contiguous external, spatial causes and effects because they are perfectly self-sustaining, self-sufficient, i.e., free; they transpire *within* "the moment of duration"; duration cannot *reach* beyond itself to something else; *it is already beyond itself.* To reach "different times" is to *spatialize* it by connecting time through external spaces. But *durational* time is not a line; it is not a linear extension of punctual moments or dots that can be diagrammed on a line. It is a non-extensive "flow"—metaphorically an immediate internal "stream of consciousness," which is not situated in space. If it were, it could not be free; it would be determined along a spatial timeline. We might recall, that dualists and idealists strongly tend to describe consciousness in terms of metaphors, such as a dimensionless point or as the unextended center of a circle both designed to impart a sense of spacelessness. Imagine the drama of an outfielder pursuing a fly ball. Each moment is dramatic; will he get to it? and he gets to it; WOW! Climax! But drops it.

Furthermore, the artificial and distorting nature of language effectively shields us from our four levels of consciousness, from its "interiority." First there is the reality of an *actual* material universe existing independently of us. Second, there is the level of *immediate* meaningless sensations and feelings, which intervenes between the physical world and our subjective "appearances" of it. Third, there are *mediate* conceptual thoughts further separating us from the physical world. And fourth there is the immediate intuitional "duration" of uniquely lived temporal flows. Generally, we assume that we exist in three dimensions of space as well as an elongated single extension of time, time as motion. But Bergson is inviting us to acknowledge a special fourth dimension, one which *collapses* the three dimensions of past-present-future into a simple and single one: duration. Without connection to the past, completely sustained by the present, and perfectly oblivious to the future, it is absolutely free. Whereas causality is restricted to the past, chained to the present, and expectant of the future, duration is absolutely free.

Linguistic and analytic philosophers conveniently avoid the "issue" of consciousness by substituting nouns as symbols for objects and verbs as the connecting causal links for thoughts.

> We should see that if these past [immediate] states [of consciousness] cannot be adequately expressed in words or artificially reconstructed by a juxtaposition of simpler states, it is because in their dynamic unity and wholly qualitative multiplicity they are phases of our real and concrete duration, a heterogeneous duration and a living one.
> BERGSON, *TFW*, 239

An important qualifying comment needs to be made here. For Bergson and Husserl there is a crucial distinction between words versus meanings. Words are *static*, they are definitional; dictionaries confine words within strict barriers and if they violate these boundaries they become vague and ambiguous. By contrast, meanings inherently display the *nuances* of consciousness. They are much closer to the "flow" of temporal consciousness. They are chock-full of *double entendres*. Meanings have fringes and horizons. If I am in the throes of a unique fear, I cannot describe it in words. Nevertheless, my fear is violently *meaningful*. In this regard, both Bergson and Husserl agree that consciousness is primary and original and language is secondary and derivative—if not actually consisting of a third and even more removed order of reality: abstraction. Human infants master and recognize feelings and thoughts long before they learn the use of language. Words confine, separate, and distort. Words do not flow or "durate." A "caution" traffic sign does not go anywhere. It remains immobile and static. Long ago the Epicureans were the first to maintain that the source for the implementation of human language springs from its pragmatic use and not from any direct grasp of reality itself. Hobbes is right; languages and words are nominal and relative. Their import depends on their use. Indeed Locke himself regards language as conventional, artificial, arbitrary and primarily invented for communicative purposes. Language is dependent on the prior establishment of thinking rather than the other way around. Infants feel and think and know that they are doing so long before they learn to talk.

Bergson's model for the unity of consciousness ultimately grounds his argument for the freedom of self-consciousness in the *immediate* durational "flow" or "stream" as *singularly* self-sufficient. Thus isolated in a "succession" of *present* durations, consciousness cannot be connected to anything past or future. The durational present alone *is*. Free of past alliances and future obligations, consciousness is poised on the brink of a steep precipice over which it must choose to plunge or stay. We frequently experience these "dilemmas," these decisional crises, these momentous choices throughout our lives.

Intuitions cannot be connected as links in an unbreakable chain precisely because each "link" is a chain within itself; it is its own chain, so to speak; and therefore it cannot be interlocked with any other precedent or consequent links. Physical objects displaying mechanical parts, motions, and causes may be described in terms of spatial extensions and temporal events but they cannot be causally projected along a line leading to motives and ending in a decision. And then there is this remarkable phrase: "Duration is what occurs when we completely telescope the past into the present, and make our life a fiery point eating like an acetylene flame into the future." For Bergson, the future is always only a possibility, a becoming. The past is closed but the future is open, free, and unpredictable. There are countless instances in life when I do not know what I am going to do next. Just because I do something or nothing, it does not mean that I was determined to do what I did or did not do. If this were not the case, the concept of "regret" could not exist.

Consequently, there are discrete moments in life when our habits are put aside or fail us; when our routines are interrupted and we intuitively know that causal explanations and motivational narratives are not only irrelevant but they are not even possible. We are confronted by all sorts of decisions. They are Kierkegaardian either/or dilemmas. Hegel was convinced the actual was real but for Kierkegaard and Bergson possibility and freedom are what is real. Whether to marry or not? Who to marry? Where to live? This profession or another? Join the Resistance or Collaborate (Sartre)? Commit suicide or not (Camus, *The Myth of Sisyphus*)? Betray a friend, myself, or a value (Graham Greene)? Commit adultery? Abandon my children? But if each moment of pure duration is disconnected from every other, it follows that prediction is impossible and freedom frighteningly inevitable. André Gide, in *Les Caves du Vatican,* tells the tale of a young man traveling on a train, who decides to commit an absolutely free—purely gratuitous, motiveless—act by killing a stranger. And although the act may have consequences, this is totally irrelevant to the free act itself. It is the act that is free, not the consequences. This is the sort of situational act that underlies many suicidal thoughts, gestures, attempts, failures, and successes. There is no past and no future: only the present. In Albert Camus *The Stranger,* Merseault "with no reason" kills an Arab. Nevertheless, at his trial, he is portrayed *by others* as the sort of man who is a "murderer"; he is insensitive at his mother's funeral because he is smoking; hence he is the "sort" of person who is capable of murdering someone.

The question naturally arises whether in retrospect we ourselves can have any insight into our previous lives and decisions. Consider attempting to *qualitatively* "understand" something one had decided and done decades ago or as a child. One's circumstances, memories, and attitudes were very different then. What sense does it make to ask one's self what happened and why? One merely superimposes present feelings and thoughts on the past; one rationalizes, suppresses, represses, interprets, atones, excuses, and interjects present fears and hopes into the child who once was "you" but is no longer the "same" person. Memory alone is an insufficient criterion for selfhood. We constantly re-write our autobiographical histories. They are more fictional than historical (Sartre's *Nausea*).

Bergson argues in numerous passages that freedom can be directly apprehended by intuition. But in other key sections, he offers a more discursive philosophical argument for the freedom of consciousness, one which, as indicated above, also rests on the simplicity argument. Thus he insists that we are free during those special, privileged moments when the "whole self" decides: "It is the whole soul, in fact, which gives rise to the free decision." By the "whole soul," he means the temporally unextended soul. And he appeals to the Plotinian metaphor of emanation. As we plunge into the deepest waters of consciousness, we find our selves completely submerged within the *true* self as opposed to the artificial ego.

> As we descend further into the depths of consciousness: the deep-seated self which ponders and decides, which heats and blazes up, is a [true] self whose states and changes permeate one another but they undergo a deep alteration as soon as we separate them from one another in order to set them out in space [as in the case of the artificial ego].
> *TFW,* 125; cf. 165, 170–172, 219, 224

Accordingly:

> Chaque sentiment contenant en lui "l'âme tout entière," "exprimant le moi tout entière," car "c'est de l'âme entière que la décision libre émane." Bref, nous somme libre quand nos actes émanent de notre personalité entière.[14]

The term "free emanation" breathes with the liveliness of spontaneity. In the text, Bergson appeals to spontaneity, as opposed to inertia (the ancient conception of a passive "matter"), referring to it as an unextended active simplicity (Bergson, TFW, 141, 217, 219–220). In the dualist and idealist literature, we find a variety of terms *metaphorically* recruited to define—or better still to *identify*—this spontaneous act of *immediate* consciousness as *creative, sui generis, causa sui, causa occultae,* and *transcendent*. Actually, the Plotinian term "overflowing" (as from a fountain) or emanational (above) is not the best (although it later shows up in Bergson's *Creative Evolution* as well) because it generally connotes a "process" but Bergson clearly wishes to use a term that is free of causal or procedural temporal implications. Spontaneity is more like a flash of lightning rather than rolling claps of thunder. Accordingly, Bergson concludes that the whole self lives immediately and completely in the present durational moment of a perfectly unified and free self.

> Hence there are finally two different selves, one of which is, as it were, the external projection of the other, its spatial and, so to speak, social representation. We reach the former by deep introspection [i.e., immediate self-conscious reflexion], which leads us to [directly] grasp our inner states as living, constantly *becoming,* as states not amenable to measure, which permeate one another and of which the succession in duration has nothing in common with juxtaposition in homogeneous space.
> BERGSON, TFW, 231

Both Kiekegaard and Bergson counterpose possibility against Hegel's actuality. Consistently the problem of determinism arises when immanent time-consciousness is distorted, spatialized, and extended because objective time is infected with causality and explanatory motives.

Perhaps the distinction between the activity of an elongated concentration versus being consumed by a single durational moment might help. There is

---

14 Robinet, 33.

an extended temporal element when I concentrate; I am thinking through a number of interconnected thoughts, a math problem for example. But when I am consumed by and within the immediacy of the moment and there is nothing beyond it, within the durational flow, my whole self is immersed and oblivious to how long the clock is ticking and I do not separate my self from my thought.

In any case, Bergson intends by "emanation" an act that issues from the *interiority* of the self. It is consistently intended, meant by him to oppose the determinist and causal versions offered by the opponents of freedom, the associationist and behavioral psychologists (and later the neuroscientists), who fundamentally *explain* everything in causal and mechanical terms. The common error of these psychological theories is that collectively they end up reducing consciousness to the contingently associational theory adopted by the English empiricist tradition of Hobbes, Locke, Hume, Priestley, Taine, the Mills, and Bain, among others; or to its attendant behavioral stimulus-response physiological accompaniments in the brain. Historically, both these movements have much in common with the "psychologism," which Husserl no less than Bergson criticizes.

Basically these experimentally-oriented schools of psychology imagine the brain to be analogous to a billiard table upon which physical stimuli (the balls) strike sensory organs and are transmitted off the rails of the table to the brain thus causing behavioral responses. The emotions then become the secondary triggering causes, the assumed "springs of human conduct." The foregoing naive psychological theory merely serves to translate the misnamed "mental" aspects into physiological motions; to misidentify the mind with the brain; and then to give causal explanations couched against the background of minute atomic particles physically interacting with biological cells, brains, neurons, and cellular synapses. Bergson's paradigm of creative life and the non-spatial qualitative intensity of consciousness stands opposed to all these crude, reductivist, and allegedly "scientific" accounts of the "mind"=brain.

But whether it is termed *freedom, spontaneity, transcendence, emanation, etc.,* it all means a first beginning from *within* consciousness, an initiation without prior antecedents or causes. All these meanings signify the same activity as self-caused, *sui generis;* a primary, original *existential* act without material or sensuous preconditions or dependencies. Indeed, without initial acts of spontaneity, "sensations" would amount to no more then the reactive instincts of a fly. In certain philosophical systems of the West, in dualism and idealism, *spontaneity* has come to mean "independent of material and sensuous conditions."

There are two ways in which we can present Bergson's argument for freedom. They are found to consist in two different ways of expressing the same premise and an identical conclusion. Again, both depend on the simplicity argument. According to Bergson, since qualities are simple and without extensive features, they cannot be spatially disposed in relation to each other and thus they cannot reciprocally cause, interact, or determine each other. They are absolutely unrelated. Since they are uncaused by virtue of their essential self-sufficiency, it means they exist independently of *external* causes; they are instead self-caused and, thereby, once more *spontaneous* (Bergson, TFW, 140) and thus "spontaneity is simpler than inertia" and what is simpler is always more primary; cf. 141–142, 217, 220). Secondly, and alternatively, Bergson contends that pure time, real duration manifests itself in consciousness as an unextended *flux* of "successive" immediacies (TFW, 99–103). To say they are "successive immediacies" means that *although* temporally *each* moment is blended, fused "into" another, it does not mean they are connected or related to each other in a temporal *ex*-tension. Again, each moment is unique unto itself. This is not simply a verbal quibble. It is to say that in the context of human consciousness the *moment* of the actual *decision* is perfectly enclosed and unique within itself, since a moment *before* the *choice,* the *decision* had not been made; the decision simply did not exist in any fashion, since it had not been executed. So the two moments are absolutely separate, distinct. Obviously the free act is qualitatively different from what preceded it; it is made, done decided, while the previous moment was left unmnade, and undone. And just as clearly, the act is different than what will follow because it is past and the unique act cannot be redone or undone. For example, consider a person contemplating suicide for many years and he has the ready means to do it. Until he actually does it, each immediate moment is separate from the actual final act and an observer—as well as he himself—cannot "predict" the actual moment when he will end his life. Then on a certain day, at a certain hour, at a certain minute, and at a certain second, in a single moment, the deed is consummated. The last act is an absolutely unique "durational" moment distinct from all the other moments of his life. It could also be described—not understood—as a Schopenhauerian irrational impulse. Each day and each moment is a choice: now or later, today or tomorrow; now or never? But the spontaneous act of suicide is both momentary and momentous.

> We here put our finger on the mistake of those who regard pure duration as something similar to space...But if our consciousness *does not*

> *yet possess the idea of space*—and this is the hypothesis which we have agreed to adopt—the succession of states through which it passes cannot assume for it the form of a line; but its sensations will add themselves dynamically [spontaneously] to one another and will organize themselves, like the successive notes of a tune...In a word, pure duration might well be nothing but a succession of qualitative changes, which melt into and permeate one another.
>
> TFW, 103–104; italics mine

In Chapter 4, dedicated to time-consciousness, we will explore more fully how Bergson's free durational intuition is related to the immediacy of a fused melting of time-consciousness. But in the present chapter we are primarily concerned with his qualitative *value* of freedom

But notice in the passage above, Bergson is intimating that there can be a time, a "pure duration" apart from any "concept of space." This obviously difficult quotation needs some commentary. In certain respects, Bergson wants it both ways. Many of these difficulties can be laid at the doorstep of the ongoing confusion between Bergson's temporal *immediacy* as "pure duration" as opposed for instance to Kant's synthetic temporal *mediacy* (*Critique,* A 99 ff.). Bergson wishes to deny the conception and involvement of internal time with a "spatial" succession but still wishes to induct a form of temporal succession that is given *intuitively, immediately;* a duration that "melts," "fuses," "interpenetrates," "amalgamates" the various qualities into each other and therefore into a single, simple, unique moment, a durational instant. The difficulty is that "normally" we conceive of the self *through* different times if not also *in* spatial time. Memory thus deceives us.

Again, in the following chapter on time-consciousness, we shall examine the metaphoric comparison of consciousness with a song, the latter consisting of two distinguishable elements; (a) the separate notes representing sensations; and (b) the melody representing the "flow," the "stream of consciousness." Although the notes, *qua* sensations are discrete, distinct, and separate, nevertheless we "hear" the melodious thread of the song as a meaningful whole and not only the notes; we are conscious of the entire tune *as a unity* at *that* moment; we hold, bind, and synthesize the melody without "carrying" the notes as separate divisible sounds. If there is only the one note, then there could be no melody; if we are conscious only of the single note in and through time, there could be no song. This is the paradox of self-consciousness: it is *both* immediate *and* mediate in the same moment and at the same time.

When it is freedom that is at stake, it is the "durational momentary act" of decision that is purely immediate. By contrast, when we consider the corresponding consciousness of the "musical flow," the paradox is that it is *both* immediate *and* mediate *at once.*

Although both freedom and internal time-consciousness are grounded in the Achilles premise, namely that they are constituted as twin immaterial-active modes of consciousness, there is something quite exceptional about immanent time-consciousness. Imagine that human consciousness has only one form of Kantian intuition—temporality; that as cognitive creatures, we exist in time but not in space. Then consciousness could not possibly spatialize or conceptualize time as the movement of objects traveling through space. But the mind could still be conscious of immediate intuitions as well as temporal extensions of before and after but not of near or far. In such a case, the mind could still enjoy music and communicate with other minds, perhaps telepathically, but not visually or audibly. Whether this answer is sufficient to untangle the knot of "immediate mediacies," it remains the case that we can entertain a universe that denies spatial dimensions but nevertheless is able to account for communication with other creatures apart from the existence of space. Obviously, however, it could not be by sound, since sound *means* a communicative passage through space with another physically distant pole. Again, recall that Kant claims it is possible that rational extra-terrestrial beings could exhibit different forms of intuition that are neither spatial nor temporal. Spatially it could be like those blind cave fish that dwell in complete darkness.

Pure qualities, as intuitively, immediately present to or apprehended by consciousness are *given*, i.e., directly accessed. Since pure time is spatially non-dimensional—it cannot be expressed as a single dimension, which could be represented as a (straight) line between points/instants. It therefore follows that it cannot be causally connected, related, or synthesized to other points, "times," or events on the line in any external or mechanical fashion. Time is not a line. If this is correct, if pure time cannot be determined or spatially represented, then it must be, by a process of simple elimination, the true and real source of freedom (*TFW,* 208). For the scientific interpretation of space, as we have shown, time is the measure of motion through space; but for Bergson's intuition, there is a pure duration independent of space, a pure unextended time given directly within and to consciousness.

> But the principle of causality, in so far as it is supposed to bind the future to the present, could never take the form of a necessary principle; for the successive moments of real time [i.e., duration] are not bound up with

one another; and no effort of logic will succeed in proving that what has been or will continue to be, that the same antecedents will always give rise to identical consequents.

BERGSON, *TFW*, 208

Again, what Bergson seems to be suggesting is that if we were to *reverse* time and proceed backward to the "past," then the sequence of "events" might not—could not—repeat itself.

I apologize for conflating the above discussion of freedom and time together but obviously Bergson, as the English title to his work testifies, regards the two themes as inextricably intertwined.

Basically what Bergson has set out for himself is to solve the perennial problem of free will versus determinism as he announces in his Introductory declaration:

> The problem I have chosen is one which is common to metaphysics and psychology, the problem of free will. What I attempt to prove is that all discussion between the determinists and their opponents implies a previous confusion of duration with extensity, of succession with simultaneity, of quality with quantity; this confusion once dispelled, we may perhaps witness the disappearance of the objections raised against free will, of the definitions given of it, and, in a certain sense, of the problem of free will itself.
>
> BERGSON, *TFW*, ix–x

By the same token, Bergson is convinced that the self cannot be "constructed" from an empirical composition of simple or compound sensory phenomenal contents or from a random collection of partial memories. Nevertheless, he maintains that there is a "whole," a unified self. And so we may inquire in what sense he intends to speak of a "deep self" as opposed to an artificial or conventional "ego" (*TFW*, 125). His meaning very importantly is this. Bergson asserts that numerous qualities are in fact present within momentary states of awareness at the same time. He insists on the intrinsically heterogeneous aspect of a consciousness perfectly self-aware within its interior chambers of various qualities as *immaterially, non-spatially* compressed in an immediate "durational flux." This seems to make our psychic states, if anything, complex rather than simple and unextended. But this is the point in the discussion where Bergson introduces the metaphors of "melting," "fusion," and "inter-penetration." Pure time—duration—and pure qualities are simple, quantitavely unextended;

what is not spatial can "successively" co-exist together at the same moment, since the "elements" do not occupy space; the "parts" are not in space in the manner of physical parts that essentially exclude each other because of their *impenetrable* nature. Notice here the radical difference with the neuroscientific paradigm, which is constrained to spatially locate neuronal responses in specific locations in the brain.

By contrast, duration is the *immediate* successive *flux* we intuit, not the mediate sequence. Thus the constitutive qualities do not, in principle, exclude each other from being present in a unified center, *le moi profonde*. Basically it sounds as if Bergson's melting, fusing, interpenetration amounts to an *immediate synthesis, an ideal temporal unity.* Recall, however, in Kant syntheses are (supposedly) always relational, mediate.

> Duration, thus restored to its original purity, will appear as a wholly qualitative [i.e., unextended] multiplicity, an absolute heterogeneity of elements which pass over into one another without any connection to the prior moment.
> 
> TFW, 229

Once more, I am not concerned to reconcile Kant and Bergson but rather to emphasize that the paradoxes of consciousness do not lend themselves to any possible neuro scientific resolution.

Bergson is convinced that the opposition between free will and determinism is solved by grounding consciousness in his theory of pure duration—the principle that each moment is absolutely self-contained and yet each moment exists as a successive *now*. Once more, because it is self-contained, self-sufficient, and reflexive, it is free. Since materialism, empiricism, and determinism are committed to conceiving human decisions and actions as conditioned by a prior extended chain of inflexibly spatialized causes—and pure duration is not—it follows that freedom can only exist in and through pure duration.

By contrast, the associationist theory of psychology views the causes as physically following each other in linear fashion. Once the metaphor of the line disappears and the links are perfectly separated from each other, so does the possibility of determinism and prediction. For Bergson, as the qualitative moments "pass" within the "flow" of the *immediacy* of duration, the true self is created ever anew. Nothing is transported from the past; nothing is carried into the future.

In an interesting passage toward the end of the book, Bergson refers to Descartes conception of God as re-creating the entire universe at each uniquely singular moment of time; "an instantaneous physics, intended for a universe the whole duration of which might as well be confined to the present moment." In God, of course, pure duration is called eternity. Similarly he provides further insight by alluding to Spinoza's contention that

> the indefinite series of phenomena, which takes for us the form of succession in time, was equivalent, in the absolute [i.e., in Spinoza's monistic substance], to the divine unity; [Spinoza] thus assumed, on the one hand, that the relation of apparent causality, between phenomena melted away into the relation of identity in the absolute, and, on the other, that the indefinite duration of things was all contained in a single moment, which is eternity.
> BERGSON, *TFW*, 208

Both intuition and eternity are apprehended as simple immaterial timelessnesses. They are not trapped in the inflexible objectivity of a past-present-future extension or in endless cause-effect-cause-effect-and-so-on relations, connections, and extensions. Bergson's notion of melting and fusing consists in a positive collapsing of qualities into a single, simple immaterial duration. This consideration along with his illuminating comparison with Spinoza (Bergson, *TFW*, 147 and *passim*) calls to mind the classic "problem of divine attributes" and its reconciliation with the absolute simplicity, unity, and identity of God's essence in Medieval philosophy, namely that in God, *all* the manifold attributes, all His infinite number of perfections, e.g., omnipotence, omniscience, omnibenevolence, etc., are identical due to the absolute *simplicity* of His divine nature. To the theological question, *if* God possesses infinite attributes, *then* how can He be a *simple* unified Substance? And the solution is *because He is Pure Quality without extensity.* Qualities, being unextended, they can be fused into a single perfect unity; quantities cannot.[15]

These helpful analogies to which Bergson alludes allows us to gain an insight into precisely how he conceives consciousness to be able to "squeeze" numerous qualities into one moment by compressing them all into a single durational unity and identity as constituted within the flux of human consciousness. This spontaneous accomplishment, this act of unification would then be similar to the Deity's "compression" of all His attributes and each of His acts in a single eternal *now*. It would be comparable (even identical?) to what Descartes and Spinoza conceive to be manifested only in God. In short,

---

15 Harry Austryn Wolfson, *The Philosophy of Spinoza* (Cambridge, MA: Harvard, 1934), Chapter 5, "Simplicity of Substance and Attributes," I, 112–157.

Bergson has transferred within the individual human soul the divine power of fusing and compressing the heterogeneity of qualities present to consciousness within the single, monadic self; his concept of the "whole self" is positively "collapsed" within a single moment. And when this moment of unity and identity is achieved, the whole self is attained and it is *poised* to step toward the future; at that moment, man is free and knows himself to be free.

Similarly, he credits Leibniz with having recognized that "these qualities must be regarded as simple conscious states or perceptions, and the substance which supports them as an unextended monad analogous to our soul" (TFW, 213). Recall that for Leibniz, the dominant soul monad is perfectly self-enclosed, "windowless," and active. It therefore follows that its *acts,* its activity must and can only self-sufficiently spontaneously generate from *within.*

As Bergson puts it in his summation, "Every demand for explanation in regard to freedom comes back, without our suggesting it, to the following question: Can time be adequately represented by space?" And Bergson's unequivocal answer is that real time, the flux, the stream of consciousness, i.e., duration cannot be spatialized and it is only accessible as an intuitional flow immediately present to and within consciousness (TFW, 229).

> We should therefore distinguish two forms of multiplicity, two very different ways of regarding duration, two aspects of conscious life. Below homogeneous duration, which is the extensive symbol of true duration, a close psychological analysis distinguishes a duration whose heterogeneous moments permeate one another; below the numerical multiplicity of conscious states, a qualitative multiplicity; below the self with well-defined states, a self in which *succeeding each other means melting into one another* and forming an organic whole.
> 
> BERGSON, TFW, 128; italics his

Compare this passage with Kant's suggestion, in the Dialectic that *pure* reason can *conceive* the possibility that the immaterial self may be unextended in time, instantaneous; and that at every single moment each of us is completely self-contained and unrelated to every external thing, time, event, or any prior sense of individual self identity (Third Paralogism). Also recall that all four demonstrations in the Paralogisms are equally grounded in the simplicity premise. And compare William James, who declares:

> Each pulse of cognitive consciousness, each Thought, dies away and is replaced by another....Each later Thought, knowing and including thus the Thoughts which went before, is the final receptacle—and appropriating

> them is the final owner—of all that they contain and own. Each Thought is thus born an owner, and dies owned, transmitting whatever it realized as its Self to its own later proprietor. As Kant says, 'It is as if elastic balls were to have not only motion but knowledge of it, and a first ball were to transmit both its motion and its consciousness to a second, which took both up into its consciousness and passed them to a third, until the last ball held all that the other balls held; and realized it as its own'.
>
> Kant, *Critique*, A 364, note a[16]

Assuming this is possible, conceivable—and why should it not be? —when it happens, it demonstrates that the pure qualities present within awareness are compressed into a non-extended, a whole self, which is free because it has no past to determine it and as yet an absolutely open future before it as an indeterminate field of pure possibilities, of pure potential becomings, a state of untainted, undetermined freedom. Elsewhere, Bergson criticizes James for representing consciousness not as an immediate flow or stream but as a series of interrupted flights and perchings, an obviously spatial metaphor.

In *Creative Evolution* Bergson directly involves the factor of indeterminacy and unpredictabilty:

> Thus our personality shoots, grows and ripens without ceasing. Each of its moments is something new added to what was before. We may go further: it is not only something new, but something *unforeseeable* [i.e., unpredictable]. Doubtless, my present state is *"explained"* by what was in me and by what was acting on me a moment ago. In analyzing it I should find no other elements. But even a superhuman intelligence would not have been able to foresee *the simple indivisible form* which gives to these purely abstract elements their concrete organization. For to foresee consists of projecting into the future what has been perceived in the past, or of imagining for a later time a new grouping, in a new order, of elements already perceived. But that which has never been perceived, and which is at the same time simple, is necessarily *unforeseeable.* Now such is the case with each of our states, regarded as a moment in history that is gradually unfolding: it is simple, and it cannot have been already perceived, since it concentrates in its indivisibility all that has been perceived and

---

16   William James, *Principles of Psychology* (New York: Dover, 1950), I, 339. The Third Paralogism is coordinated with The Third Antinomy, which deals with causality and determinism versus "spontaneity" and freedom (*Critique*, A 445-B 473). Cf. NKS, *Commentary,* 339–340 and 461–462.

what the present is adding to it beside. It is an original moment of a no less original history.[17]

Notice the positive appeal to the Achilles premise and the gibe at causal "explanations."

Differently put, the simple, not being complex, cannot be stretched out as a directional arrow pointing toward determinate future events. Rather the simple, the indivisible as concentrated or indissolubly compressed into a single and unique moment is actually an exploding point or center of conscious activity, which may take any direction, i.e., it is absolutely free and undetermined. Can the neuroscientist predict from the brain of the infant who and what s/he will develop to be? Can the astronomer predict which stars will implode? Can I even tell what will become of me?

In the Introduction to *Matter and Memory,* Bergson admits that his study is "frankly dualistic" and in considering the representational images of memory, he believes he is able to account for the interaction between consciousness and the brain.[18] But with this later "solution," I am not concerned, since I have previously offered my own preferred defense of metaphysical dualism in the company of Hume before me and Noam Chomsky after me.

Bergson, of course, holds that "nothingness" is inconceivable, since consciousness is a Leibnizian plenum of qualities (*Creative Evolution,* IV) and Sartre in turn rejects Bergson's analysis of the qualitative fullness of freedom, while endorsing his own version of "spontaneity" or "ek-stasis" as a freedom

---

17  Henri Bergson, *Creative Evolution* (New York: Holt, 1928), 6; italics mine. Critics also charged that Bergson's durational flow was comparable to a Heraclitean flux, but Bergson's unity of consciousness, like Kant's in the first edition Deduction—as opposed to the Aesthetic—is a temporal unity. See Robinet, *op. cit.,* 30–31. Nevertheless, Bergson is more likely influenced in his view by Plotinus' conception of the unity of consciousness. Once more, according to Plotinus—as well as Leibniz, Kant, and Hegel—space or matter intrinsically implies *partes ex partes*; and, therefore, matter is intrinsically opposed to unification. Bergson accepts this criticism of materialism but, as opposed to Plotinus, Leibniz, and Kant (in the B Deduction), Bergson "locates" the unity in self-consciousness in sheer immediacy, in the intuition of duration rather than in a monadic or transcendental unity of consciousness. Cf., I.W. Alexander, *Bergson* (Bowes and Bowes, 1957), pp. 73–74.

18  In a later work, Bergson seeks to interpose memory through perception in order to link mind and matter; *Matter and Memory* (London: George Allen & Unwin, 1970), xx–xxi; see especially 31 ff., 292 ff.). Bergson struggled with the issue of dualism throughout his career. In an article by Andrew Bjelland, "Bergson's Dualism in *Time and Free Will,*" *Process Studies,* 4:2 (1974), 83–106, the author connects him to Cartesian Dualism. We have seen that at other times, Bergson appeals to the doctrine of emanation, an exploitation, an accommodation between creation *ex nihilo* and Greek atomism.

of consciousness beyond and transcendent to the for-itself.[19] Nevertheless, Sartre's own definition of consciousness as an "existential nothingness," as a Cartesian and immaterial translucent medium depends on the simplicity argument. But Sartre's concept of freedom is actively intentional as opposed to Bergson's reflexive state of the "whole self," as it struggles to escape its inner loneliness. Indeed, for Sartre, man is free precisely because he is absolutely alone and lonely; each human consciousness owes nothing to anyone else and is indebted to no one but its own "self." "Freedom is the human being putting his past out of play by secreting his own nothingness" (*TOE*, 38; cf. *B&N*, 34, 46). The *only* "obligation" is to the self—not to others. Moral responsibility is a purely internal intentional relation.

According to Sartre, consciousness is the "for its-self" *but* it is a nonpositional, a non-thetic awareness of its "self." In the *Transcendence of the Ego*, he disavows equally the Kantian as well as the Husserlian constitutive *structures* of consciousness as merely adding to the opacity of awareness and thus ruining its clarity and in effect destroying its absolute freedom to act in an unhindered and unrestricted fashion. He strains mightily to avoid the prevailing Kantian ego with its encumbering structures as so prominently found in Kant's transcendental unity of apperception and Husserl's *"ego-cogito-cogitatum"* structure presented in the *Cartesian Meditations*. Indeed, for Sartre the "self" is like any other transcendent object—opaque—and it can only be perceived perspectively through its varying incomplete aspects, whereas consciousness must be clear and translucent if there is to be the transparency of an undisturbed apprehension of the thing-in-itself. While the material presence of an object given to awareness is extended, by contrast the "for-its-self" is a simple, immaterial nothingness and yet somehow intentionally free. Sartre

---

19   Jean-Paul Sartre, *The Transcendence of the Ego: An Existentialist Theory of Consciousness*, translated by Forrest Williams and Robert Kirkpatrick (New York: Noonday, 1962), 80; hereafter cited as Sartre, *TOE*. Consciousness is empty because it is an immaterial existing "nothingness." Cf. *Being and Nothingness: An Essay on Phenomenological Ontology*, translated by Hazel Barnes (New York: Washington Square Press, 1966) 13, 42, 51–52, 54; 218–219; "As for the for-itself, if it is not in space, this is because it apprehends itself precisely as not being being-in-itself in so far as the in-itself is revealed to it in the mode of exteriority which we call extension. It is precisely by denying exteriority in itself and apprehending itself as ek-static that the For-itself spatializes space," (page 225). Fichte had previously insisted that the Ego, by virtue of its intrinsic power of negativity, projected "negation," multiplicity, divisibility into extension; hereafter cited as *B & N*; cf., J. Catalano, *A Commentary on Jean-Paul Sartre's Being and Nothingness* (New York: Harper & Row, 1974), 13–14; and Wilfrid Desan, *The Tragic Finale* (New York: Harper Torchbook, 1960), 19–20, 23; Sartre, *TOE*, 91, 93. Consciousness is clear, translucent, lucid and empty because it is a "nothingness," i.e., an immaterial simplicity. Cf. translator's comments, 1, 21, 22.

consequently manages paradoxically to deny self-consciousness, while yet at the same time asserting its freedom.

> The revelation of the spatiality of being is one with the non-positional [i.e., the non-thetic] apprehension by the for-it-self of itself as unextended. And the unextended character of the-for-itself is not a positive, mysterious virtue of spirituality, which is hiding under a negative denomination, it is a natural ecstatic [a transcendence beyond itself] relation, for it is by and in the extension of the transcendent in-itself that the for-itself makes itself known to itself and realizes its own non-extension. The for-itself cannot be first unextended in order later to enter into relation with an extended being, for no matter how we consider it, the concept of the unextended makes no sense by itself; it is nothing but the negation of the extended.... In this sense extension is transcendent determination which the for-itself has to apprehend to the exact degree that it denies itself as extended.
> 
> *B & N*, 218–219

Thus, the for-itself exists as an unextended, indivisible, presence. It exists and thrusts itself outwardly—ek-statically, spontaneously, transcendently, standing out from itself—toward Being, from its own "nothingness" whose concrete existence is supported by its own activity of negation ("determination is negation," Spinoza, Hegel). Moreover, the for-itself exists in an *a priori* synthetic relation with the in-itself. Sartre's ontological *ek-stasis* corresponds to the idealists' spontaneity (Sartre, *TOE*, 79, 80, 91, 92, 96).[20]

> As for the For-itself, if it is not in space, this is because it apprehends itself precisely as not being being-in-itself in so far as the in-itself is revealed to it in the mode of exteriority which we call extension. It is precisely by denying exteriority in itself and apprehending itself as ek-static that the For-itself spatializes space.
> 
> Sartre, *B & N*, 225; *TOE*, 91, 93

As he makes clear in the Conclusion of his major work, the for-its-self (Consciousness) and the in-itself (Being) constitute a synthetic *a priori* relation.

---

20   Sartre, *TOE*, 91–93. Consciousness is clear and translucent, it is immaterial and empty; this is a requirement, for if it had Kantian categories obstructing its vision, it would be opaque. Cf. J. Catalano, *A Commentary on Jean-Paul Sartre's Being and Nothingness* (New York: Harper & Row, 1974), 13–14; and Wilfrid Desan, *The Tragic Finale* (New York: Harper Torchbook, 1960), 19–20, 23; hereafter cited as Desan, *TF*.

Consciousness exists as a vacuous "hole in Being" toward which it irrationally, i.e., without Kantian or Husserlian structures of consciousness, explodes ekstatically despite its immaterial existence. It is a substance dualism predicated on the Spinozist and Hegelian ontological principle that negation is determination.

> If the in-itself and the for-itself are two modalities of *being,* is there not a hiatus at the very core of the idea of being? And is its comprehension not severed into two incommunicable parts by the very fact that its extension is constituted by two radically heterogeneous classes? What is there in common between the being which is what it is, and the being which is what it is not and which is not what it is?...[But] we have just shown in fact that the in-itself and the for-itself are not [ontologically] juxtaposed. Quite the contrary, the for-itself without the in-itself is a kind of abstraction, *it could not exist any more than a color could exist without form or a sound without pitch and without timbre.* A consciousness which would be consciousness of nothing would be an absolute nothing [i.e., an existential impossibility]. But if consciousness is bound [i.e., unified synthetically] to the in-itself by an internal relation, doesn't this mean that it is articulated with the in-itself so as to constitute a totality, and is not this totality which would be given the name being or reality? Doubtless the for-itself is a nihilation [a "nothingness"], but as a nihilation it is; and it is in *a priori* [synthetic] unity with the in-itself.
>
> B&N, 760–761; italics mine

Note well the allusion to Plato's and Husserl's synthetic *a priori* relation. Also another way of putting the same existential point is that Consciousness could not exist without Being and Being could not be known without Consciousness.

Based on the foregoing analysis, Sartre concludes that the totality of Being is constituted "by the synthetic organization of the in-itself as well as the for-itself" (Sartre, *B&N,* 761), by a dual diversity whose relation nevertheless is held, or bound together, "within a unitary synthesis" (ibid.). To be sure, generally speaking, Sartre's syntheses are existential or ontological relational unities independent of *a priori* structures, since, unlike Husserl, Sartre is not committed to accepting what is immanently and immediately present in consciousness *after* the application of Husserl's bracketing procedure. Sartre, in fact, denies the possibility of the *epoche.* But in any event, it is still the case that, according to Sartre, Being, or the in-itself, is material, spatial, perspectively presented, opaque; a blobby viscous, sticky, overwhelming, *de trop,* and *contingently,* i.e., existentially given without rhyme or reason. Being is extended, murky, and divisible (at least by the negative determinations of the for-itself), while consciousness by comparison is unextended, clear, and indivisible because it is an immaterial, active, translucent "nothingness." Nevertheless, it is an *existing* "nothingness"; undeniably it exists; it is. It is immersed "in" being but not *part* of Being; again existing "out of itself," "transcendent to itself," and existing *ek-statically* in time, struggling to free "itself," to go "beyond" its "self" toward objects that stand against it. We are thrown meaninglessly and contingently into the world. For Sartre, to exist through *ek-stases* means to be beyond one's "self," beyond one's own givenness; and in a sense not to be one's "self," which is a requisite in order to create one's self ever anew. Basically, what Sartre has done is exploited Husserl's concept of intentionality and transformed it into a spontaneous consciousness of freedom. "This transcendental sphere of consciousness is a sphere of *absolute* existence, that it to say, a sphere of pure spontaneities, which are never objects and which determine our own existence" (Sartre, *TOE,* 96).

But although consciousness can be described as an existential nothingness, it is permeated by a volitional *desire,* an overpowering motivation to escape from its self. Differently put, it is by the sheer possibility of a pure intentionality unrestricted by Freudian determinism or neurological mechanisms that freedom can be secured: "consciousness is defined by intentionality. By intentionality consciousness transcends itself. It unifies itself in a projected choice, escaping from itself." Because neither God, nature, nor mankind is able to provide an *essential* meaning for human existence, it is only by man's transcendent intentionality, his irrational freedom that he is able to escape the prison of his meaningless confinement, his self-enforced solipsism. *Man's existence is meaningless; that is the only absolute truth.* Once this is recognized, "all bets are off"; "les jeux sont fait." Only if consciousness is absolutely free can, it create "ethical" meanings for its self *alone,* and for which it is singularly responsible.

There is a striking description of freedom, emanating from the nothingness of consciousness in Sartre's *The Age of Reason.* It begins with Mathieu as a seven-year-old child, who one day, in a mood of utter boredom, "played at ceasing to exist." In fact, he quite succeeded at "completely emptying his head," his consciousness. Thus empty, his consciousness nevertheless exploded in the direction of the external world, a world which the small boy realized was one in which he could act absolutely free, without care or responsibility, if he so willed.

> On the table there were some tattered magazines, and a handsome Chinese vase, green and grey, with handles like parrots' claws. [His uncle] Jules had told him that the vase was three thousand years old. Mathieu

had gone up to the vase, his hands behind his back, and stood, nervously a-tip-toe, looking at it: how frightening it was to be a little ball of breadcrumb in this ancient fire-browned world, confronted by an impassive vase three thousand years old. He had turned his back on it, and stood grimacing and snuffling at the mirror without managing to divert his thoughts; then he had suddenly gone back to the table, picked up the vase, which was a heavy one, and dashed it to the floor—it had happened just like that, after which he had felt as light as gossamer. He had eyed the porcelain fragments in amazement: something had happened to that three-thousand-year-old vase within those fifty-year-old walls, under the ancient light of summer, something very disrespectful that was not unlike the air of morning. He had thought to himself: 'I did it,' and felt quite proud, freed from the world, without ties or kin or origins, a stubborn little excrescence that had burst the terrestrial crust.[21]

And again later toward the conclusion of the novel:

[H]e was free, free in every way, free to behave like a fool or a machine, free to accept, free to refuse, free to equivocate: to marry, to give up the game, to drag this dead weight about him for years to come. He could do what he liked, no one had the right to advise him, there would be for him no good or evil unless he brought them into being and endowed them freely with meaning. All around him things were gathered in a circle, expectant, impassive, and indicative of nothing. He was alone, enveloped

---

21   Jean-Paul Sartre, *The Age of Reason,* translated by E. Sutton (Hamilton, 1947), 58–59; hereafter cited as Sartre, *AR.* "Consciousness is frightened by its own spontaneity because it senses this spontaneity as *beyond* freedom. This is clearly seen in an example from [Jean] Genet. A young bride was in terror, when her husband left her alone, of sitting at the window and summoning the passer bys like a prostitute. Nothing in her education, in her past or in her character, could serve as an explanation of such a vertigo of fear. She found herself monstrously free, and this vertiginous freedom appeared to her *at the opportunity* for this action which she was afraid of doing. But this vertigo is comprehensible only if consciousness suddenly appeared to itself as infinitely overflowing in possibilities" (Sartre, *TOE,* 100; italics his). "Freedom is the human being putting his past out of play by secreting his own nothingness" (20, 38; Sartre, *AR,* 289–290); these twin passages from Sartre are cited by Desan, *The Tragic Finale,* 99–100. Thematic freedom is also at the core of Sartre's play, *The Flies.* Cf. Ben Mijuskovic, "Loneliness and a Theory of Consciousness," *Review of Existential Psychiatry and Psychology,* XV:1 (1977), 19–31; and Ben Mijuskovic, *Contingent Immaterialism: Meaning, Freedom, Time, and Mind* (Amsterdam: Gruner, 1984), 63–64.

in this monstrous silence, free and alone, without assistance and without excuse, condemned to decide without support from any quarter, condemned forever to be free (ibid.).

This is metaphysically *why* man both requires freedom and cannot escape it. He must assume responsibility for his values, for the meaning of his life, just as Sartre's anti-hero Jean Genet did. Freedom, for Sartre, is a direct consequence of being absolutely alone, of loneliness. We are free precisely because we are alone. The very existence of our being overwhelms us as each of us separately realizes that we are finite, transient beings and that someday we will each leave this shifting earth only to be buried and forgotten from all traces of human memory forever. The unconcerned world will continue perfectly well without us. One owes nothing to anyone else because one is completely unconnected to everyone else.

In Dostoyevsky's Grand Inquisitor passage, man is burdened by his freedom; it is the source of his existential anxiety, his *angst*. He much prefers his happiness over freedom and the forgiveness of the confessional for his sins.

In his 1949 essay, "Existentialism Is a Humanism," Sartre suggests that when each one chooses his or her values, one chooses for all. That is impossible according to Sartre's own ethical principle. Kant can say that, but certainly not Sartre. For Kant, indeed, the principle of autonomy requires us to universally choose for all. But that is Kant, not Sartre. Rather, according to his own strict existential principle, each creates values for herself or himself completely alone. But despite that glaring ethical inconsistency, his description of the human condition is both powerful and convincing. We are in *despair* because human existence is profoundly meaningless. We are *anxious* because we are radically free and alone responsible for what we choose. And we are *forlorn* because we are absolutely alone. In response to Kant's epistemological categories, these are descriptive existential categories of the human condition. Thus freedom is a direct consequence of our loneliness; we could not be absolutely free unless we were completely alone.

Sartre, no less than Hegel, Fichte, Schopenhauer, and Bergson before him, employs the simplicity argument as an ultimate ground for their own conceptions of freedom. But in denying reflexion, he denies the reality of the self. Without the self ethical responsibility is a vacuous concept. He has secured freedom, but it is a freedom purchased at the cost of losing the self and without the tether to an imputable self there can be no conceivable moral responsibility.

Individual consciousness exists and it manifests both the power to assert as well as to negate, to create as well as to destroy; to reflexively think as well as to intentionally act; and to live as well as to die. Thus, although we are able to grasp and recognize ourselves as substantial beings by our own "reflexive thought," it is nevertheless through the spontaneity, the intentionality, the freedom of consciousness that we are able to liberate ourselves; to transcend our selves for better or for worse. We create the world that we inhabit and to the degree that we are its origin and recognize our own product, we are the masters of it and thereby free. The concepts of *spontaneous* or *sui generis acts* is a critical assumption, an assumed first principle in the various forms of idealism, phenomenology, and existentialism we have discussed in this chapter as it dominates the thought of Leibniz, Kant, Fichte, Hegel, Schopenhauer, Bergson, Husserl, and Sartre. It originally shares a genealogy with the Christian ethical doctrine of the freedom of the will. But its role in the modern and contemporary period is primarily epistemological and essentially ontological as opposed to religious and ethical. It begins with Leibniz because the monads are "windowless," which can only mean that all activity must necessarily, *a priori* initiate from inside the soul rather than from anything external to the self. Existential freedom, whether from the standpoint of Kierkegaardian subjectivity, the Nietzschean will to power, or Sartrean intentionality all mutually start *with the spontaneous essence of human consciousness.*

Both psychoanalysis and the neurosciences deny the freedom of consciousness and advocate for determinism by couching their explanations in terms of objective causal sequences. In Chapter 6, I intend to offer a sustained criticism of the materialist thesis inherent in the current neurosciences of the day. But since the present chapter is about the battle between freedom and determinism, I wish to take this opportunity to address what I regard to be serious limitations to the aspirations of psychoanalysis. (I shall address the inadequacies of the neurosciences in Chapter 6.)

There is a current controversy in philosophy between "hard" and "soft" determinism and so let us ask if psychoanalysis is compatible with either. Hard determinism disallows the possibility of ethical responsibility while soft determinism allows for it. But for our purposes, the psychological question is not about moral responsibility but rather about the possibility of therapeutic insight. (Freud aspired to be a scientist, not a moralist.) Both versions, however, hard and soft, rest on the ability to measure *quantitatively* the factors of mental pain and pleasure, anxiety and tranquility and then use these objective measurements as criteria in order to test the efficacy of the treatment. Hard determinism, basically adopts Freud's position, holding that human anxieties are determined by past *external* causes, often conflicts that are maternal in origin. When this occurs the anxiety is initially intra-psychic. In other instances, the pressures are interpersonal, as in the cases of childhood bullying by peers. When these happen, the distress is interpersonal.

Soft determinism, by contrast, asserts that our desires and motives exhibit an *internal* origin—since they are conceived as issuing from "within" our (allegedly) stable character; and although we are able to predict human behavior, nevertheless we can assign a certain degree of "self-determination" to our conduct thus allowing for a dimension of "moral responsibility." (Both Locke and Hume have been interpreted as soft determinists.) Now the question is not about moral imputability but about reflexive insight. The strict or hard determinist responds that these alleged "internal causes," desires and motives are themselves in turn strictly dependent on *external* factors beyond the subject's control, namely heredity, environment, and more specifically in Freud's case, parental or custodial "molding" or "imprinting." Now if we interpret Freud as a hard determinist (above) and assume that the painful emotions related to the past are repressed and forced into the unconscious, they are nevertheless uninterruptedly connected with the subject's present conscious states of anxiety. It then follows that the traumatic event represents the psychic "cause" and the neurotic symptom reflects the "effect." Repression conceals the relation but cannot disconnect or extinguish it. We recall that Freud began his career as a neurologist and envisioned a rather mechanical, physiological model of the mind. In *Civilization and Its Discontents,* Freud analogizes the unconscious to the submerged and dangerous part of an iceberg. He also compares it to all the past and current cities of Rome co-existing simultaneously, while the patient awaits his therapeutic relief from the liberating diggings, excavations, and uncoverings aided by the psychoanalyst. For Freud both the unconscious memories and the conscious anxieties are qualitatively the same; they are emotionally versus intellectually homogeneous. On this reconstruction of Freud's theory, it follows that he is a hard determinist and there is no possibility of breaking the chain of causes and effects. In short, the soft determinist position allowing for therapeutic insight is not even a possibility.

> The deed may be planned, it may be acted out in cold calculation, it may spring from the agent's character and be continuous with the rest of his behavior, and it may be perfectly true that he could have done differently *if* he had wanted to; nonetheless his behavior was brought about by unconscious conflicts developed in infancy, over which he had no control and of which he has no knowledge. He may even *think* he knows why he acted as he did, he may even *think* he has some conscious control over his actions, he may even *think* he is fully responsible for them; but he

is not….How can anyone be responsible for his actions, since they grow out of his character, which is shaped and molded and made what it is by influences—some hereditary, but most of them stemming from early parental environment—that were not of his own making and choosing?[22]

So here is the problem. Freud's therapeutic goal is to secure "rational" *insights* into these formerly destructive *causal* connections thereby freeing patients from their unreasoned, "irrational" anxieties. Thus, according to Freud, every repressed emotionally-laden *painful, distressful* event is in principle *completely* recoverable. It is simply a forgotten memory. This is a requirement for therapy to be successful. But the paradox is that while Freud is committed to a psychological determinism, he also wants at the same time quite inconsistently to posit a *self*-conscious reflexive "loop," an *insight*, which allegedly frees the self to *reflexively* liberate its self. But Freud cannot have it both ways: either we are determined or we are not. If one is strictly the product of one's parental upbringing, intra-psychic, and interpersonal conflicts throughout life and therefore "locked in" to the entire generational caretaking heritage of one's familial predecessors, including parents, grandparents, and on and on, then the entire hereditary lineage of dysfunctional ancestors are all likewise determined by their collective upbringings. So no one is free and insight is impossible because there is no possibility of breaking the chain of causes for better or for worse. All that could occur in therapy sessions is a repetitive re-enactment of past traumas.

As Hospers proceeds to argue, one's ability to "reverse" the determinist process of heredity, parental missteps, and stressful environments can only be "a matter of luck" and not insight, the possibility of the latter being in principle excluded (Hospers, 326). Any reversal of direction in determinism, going backward, can only occur as a unidirectional return from the present to the forgotten past or from the past to the present but nothing can change and nothing new or insightful will appear. It is simply a railroad track that goes back and forth north and south. We can go from effects to causes or from causes to effects but it is not open to any insertions of *qualitative* changes precisely *because* insight is a reflexive mode of self-consciousness; it is circular and not unidirectional. We may pronounce this internal contradiction in determinism as "the paradox of predictability." But this unflinching caricature of an absolute predictability is endemic within psychoanalysis. If one is a scientist in the usual sense of the term conducting a physical experiment, it would be surprising to be asked

---

22  John Hospers, "The Range of Human Freedom," in *Problems of Moral Philosophy*, edited by Paul Taylor (Belmont, CA: Wadsworth, 1978), 318.

what "insight" was obtained. Each experiment merely provides *quantitavely* the same answer: the repetitious validity of the causal maxim but never any *new* "insights." Reflexive insight rests on freedom; science depends on causality. Insight is a reflexive meaning. Causality is a mechanistic description.

If we review what we have surveyed so far, it follows that both hard and soft determinism are based on the assumption of causes that are *quantitatively* homogeneous (Bergson). That is to say, they all exhibit the same *measurable* psychic causal energy of pleasure and pain or anxiety and distress. Pleasure means therapeutic success and pain therapeutic failure. In effect, Freud is an Epicurean. There is nothing different in Freud that could not already be found in Epicurus. For both the goal was human happiness, pleasure certainly but not reflexive insight.

Finally, Freud's Id is not comparable to Schopenhauer's irrational Will. Schopenhauer's Will is intrinsically unpredictable and will remain so. It is not amenable to rational structures or insights. Schopenhauer's Will may *appear* in phenomenal terms as causally structured but it is in noumenal reality in principle *subconscious:* it is both unknown and unpredictable. In short, if Freud is committed to determinism, insight is impossible. If, on the other hand, he wants to endow the Id with an intrinsic and unknowable Schopenhauerian irrationality, then he must abandon predictability and science.

I can think of no better way to end this chapter on freedom and determinism than with the following citation. There is a wonderful passage in Kemp Smith's *Commentary* on Kant's *Critique* where he extols the creative and transfiguring virtues of self-consciousness.

> When Voltaire in his *Ignorant Philosopher* remarks "that it would be very singular that all nature, all the planets, should obey eternal laws, and that there should be a little animal, five feet high, who, in contempt of these laws, could act as he pleased, solely in accord with his caprice," he is forgetting that this same animal of five feet can contain the stellar universe in his thought within himself...and has therefore a dignity, which is not expressible in terms as his size may seem, for vulgar estimation to imply. Man, though dependent upon the body and confined to one planet, has the sun and the planets as the playthings of his mind. Though finite in his mortal conditions, he is divinely infinite in his powers.
> 
> KEMP SMITH, *Commentary,* xxxi

It is Leibniz he has in mind.

One of the advantages of the History of Ideas methodology is that it strongly encourages and facilitates the dialogue between the past with the present. It also assists in the argument between religion and humanism on the one side—both of which posit freedom but with different goals—against science, which espouses a physical and a psychological determinism. But if humans are existentially free, then neither psychoanalysis nor the neurosciences can possibly be sciences in the strong *predictive* sense of the term.

CHAPTER 4

# The Simplicity Argument and Immanent Time-Consciousness

> Heraclitus says that all things are in process and nothing stays still, and by likening existing things to the stream of a river he says that you could not step twice into the same river.
> PLATO, *Cratylus*

⋯

> Cratylus criticized Heraclitus for saying that that it is impossible to step twice into the same river; for he thought one could not do it even once.
> ARISTOTLE, *Metaphysics*

∴

Generally speaking, the philosophers I am discussing in the text I believe it is fair to say can be described as system-builders, whereas the current "coin of the realm" in philosophy favors the "analytic" thinkers, the conceptual and linguistic analysts, whose favorite methodological principle consists in dividing and conquering, in compartmentalizing; in simplifying and reducing the subject matter to its component parts and consequently, in a decidedly piecemeal fashion, to get at the empirical and linguistic "truths." This entire approach harkens back to what John Gibson has characterized as the "compositional" theory of knowledge classically pursued in the fashion of Locke and Hume, who sought to resolve compounds into their simple elements.

> For thinkers of the seventeenth century, to whom all ideas of development were entirely foreign, the place which is now filled by the conception of evolution was occupied by the idea of composition, with the implied distinction between the simple and the complex. A complex whole being regarded as the mere sum of its constituent parts, these latter were not thought to undergo any modification as a result of their combination; similarly, the whole was supposed to be directly resolvable into its parts

without remainder. The whole temporal process containing nothing but different combinations of the same simples, out of which nothing genuinely new could emerge, the historical point of view from which we trace development in time and seek to comprehend the new determinations which arise in its course, was without significance. To comprehend a complex whole, all that was required was a process of direct analysis by which the simples in it were distinguished. Then starting with the simples, thought could retrace with perfect adequacy the process by which the whole had been originally constituted.[1]

Obviously, this methodological principle is a complete repudiation of synthetic *a priori* relations. The purpose of these relations is precisely to connect concepts and judgments into wholes, to unify.

According to Locke and Hume, knowledge is gained by emphasizing that what is distinct is separate—and what is separate can exist apart—severing the whole into its constituent parts, its simple sensations or impressions; or by analyzing "truth" into single factual propositions. By contrast, the system-builders I have concentrated upon mainly rely on a decidedly comprehensive methodology and their conviction that the unity of the whole is greater than the sum of its parts; that there is a qualitative difference between simples and wholes. It is founded on a perspective that mixes and blends themes and arguments in such a manner that they can best be described as both organic and interdependent, which means that the intellectual nourishment provided to the body of the text is promoted by the efforts of the inquiring scholar in assimilating multiple sources in a mutually supportive fashion. Hence it is hoped the reader will find that the themes I have sought to commit to the varied limbs of the present corpus—the subject matter of meanings, relations, space, the unity of consciousness, time-consciousness, and so on will be assimilated in the same way as the richness of life itself, which is to say that s/he will be persuaded to appreciate how the simplicity premise serves as the heart and the life blood for all that has preceded and for all that promises to follow.

Before plunging into the main topic for this chapter, I need to alert the reader to a special problem concerning consciousness of time. First of all, there are two times, objective and subjective, scientific and intimate, but we have already addressed that. What I am referring to is the puzzling distinction between immediate and mediate temporal consciousness; between immediate sensations and feelings as opposed to the discursive mediacy of thought; and between intuitions and relations. How are present, past, and future time

---

[1] John Gibson, *Locke's Theory of Knowledge and Its Historical Relations* (Cambridge: Cambridge University Press, 1968), 47–48.

related? Is time simultaneous or successive or both? Can there be such a thing as immediate succession? But how can that be? The earliest acknowledgment that there is something very mysterious about time is to be found in St. Augustine's *Confessions.* What is troubling St. Augustine is the dubitable relation of time to space and consequently indirectly to motion. "I have learned from a certain learned man that the movements of the sun, moon and the stars constitute time but I did not agree with him."

> But how is the future, which as yet does not exist, diminished or consumed, or how does the past, which no longer exists, increase, unless there are three things in the mind, which does all this? It looks forward, it considers, and remembers, so that the reality to which it looks forward passes through what it considers into what it remembers. Who then denies, that future things are not yet existent? Yet there is already in the mind an expectation of things to come. Who then denies that past things no longer exist? Yet there is still in the soul the memory of past things. *Who denies that present time lacks spatial extent, since it passes away in an instant?* Yet attention abides, and through it what shall be present proceeds to become something absent.
> Chapter 28, *The Mental Synthesis*[2]

In this passage we already sense again that consciousness of time involves a puzzling relation between time and space and the interplay of the retained past, the immediate present, and the anticipated future. In addition we notice the unfolding of two species of time: external and internal; time as related to motion and time as related to consciousness. The first "solution" to the problem of time focuses on the exterior world of science and the second on the interior sphere of consciousness. Two considerations will be especially troublesome and challenging in our following discussion: is time instantaneous or elongated; and how is it related to space, if at all? Can space and time be separated? Is one primary and other secondary? Are they independent or are they interdependent?

In the ensuing discussion, I wish to maintain that the simplicity argument also found its way into a species of what, for want of a better description, might be characterized as a "temporal" or "mystical" romanticism. The same immaterialist premise that has provided us in the prior chapter for the freedom of consciousness can also be revived in order to establish the

---

[2] St. Augustine, *The Confessions of St. Augustine* (New York: Doubleday, 1960), Chapters 23 and 28, "The Mental Synthesis," 301. The phrase separating time *from* space is significant, as we shall see as we proceed.

immanent activity of a temporal consciousness manifesting itself as an indwelling "life force." As previously cautioned, it is not unusual for thinkers who are committed to defending the essential immaterial nature of the mind to blend and mix arguments demonstrating different conclusions as derived from the same premise. Nevertheless, it is my belief that the eight uses are both distinctive and yet collectively combine to offer eight distinguishable conclusions.

Once again, guided by the interests of the Scientific Revolution Kant begins in the Aesthetic with a pressing concern to establish the epistemological foundations of space and time and he contends they are *immediate* forms of sensibility passively *given* rather than actively *thought*. The difficulty is that on this view sensibility is merely receptive. In the Analytic, however, time is accorded a higher status than space and it is actively constituted, i.e., synthesized by *spontaneous acts* of consciousness.

In what follows, I will concentrate primarily on Kant, Schopenhauer, and Bergson's views emphasizing the special *quality* of internal—as opposed to external—temporal consciousness as they develop their arguments. As before, the general structure of the proof in support of immanent time-consciousness is ushered in by the principle that consciousnesses and minds, ideas and thoughts are immaterial and active. Furthermore, consciousness of subjective time is dominated by an awareness of pure inextensive *qualities* (as opposed to extensive quantities), whether these qualities are directly given as (a) sensations and/or (b) feelings. The consequence is that we live communally and together in space but insularly and alone within immanent time-consciousness.

In Kant's Analytic of Principles, he distinguishes awareness of quantities as extensive, "elongated" appearances versus qualities as unextended "intensive" presences in consciousness. This is to say that the Axioms of Intuition are perceived, experienced, and consciously *thought* as spatially and temporally extended, measurable magnitudes. By contrast, the qualities described in the Anticipations of Perception are consciously *thought* as *intensive, unextended* presences. Thus Kant's qualities are given as pure *intensive* "magnitudes" or more properly as he corrects himself, as intensive, i.e., simple, unextended "degrees." The awareness of color, for example, as a *pure* quality, is unextended as we have already seen in our discussion of the *minima sensibilia* in Leibniz, Berkeley, Hume, Kant, Fichte, and a host of other thinkers cited by Kemp Smith. Additionally for Kant, the *appearance* of extension is constituted through the *form* of spatial intuition, which, of course, as a *pure* form of sensibility, is not itself spatially or materially extended, since he is not speaking about the brain or the eye as contributing physiological organs. Correspondingly, inner sense, time-consciousness also rest on an ontological model of non-spatial consciousness. This idealist paradigm is endorsed by Schopenhauer, Schelling, and Bergson. It is also championed by other metaphysical writers as well, including Jacobi, Coleridge, Emerson, and Novalis and later by Joseph Segond and Edouard Le Roy in France. In what follows, we shall see a shift in importance away from the consciousness of space to the advantage of time.[3]

With Descartes, Hobbes, Locke, and the spirit of the Scientific Revolution in general, the ontological pre-eminence of space gains considerably in status in the seventeenth- and eighteenth-centuries, whereas time, by contrast, assumes a much more subservient and one might even say a dependent role. Descartes dualism, for example, identifies the predicates of extension, space, and matter as a monolithic *substance,* although divisible into separate parts by the mind. And pre-Newton basically matter is conceived as inert, inactive, or passive, which in turn can be expressed in terms of objective, measurable, and mathematical magnitudes. Thus for Descartes, space consists of a ubiquitous plenum of possible measurements, whose "reality" is conceived as existing independently of the thinking subject. The original first cause of motion according to Descartes as we have seen is God. Motion to be sure Descartes sometimes regards as a primary "quality," i.e., an independent existence apart from the mind; but it is clear that motion, as pertaining to the observation of the movement of an object's trajectory through space (time as the measure of physical motion through space) assumes both that time is metaphysically *dependent* on space and/or matter; and also that space is *already* there, which therefore presupposes that it is possible to experience space without motion but not motion without space. Further, one space, with its homogeneous but *divisible* "spaces" or "parts," appears to co-exist simultaneously and although it is infinitely divisible (conceptually and/or by the imagination), nevertheless it is "given as a whole," as a quantitative, continuous reality "all at once." Time, on the other hand, with its discrete instants, is relatively unreal; and the successive movement of objects from moment to moment, their transition from point to point, according to Cartesian metaphysics, is ultimately conceived to depend on an act of "conservation," i.e., the continual miraculous *re*-creation of the entire universe at each dimensionless instant of time by God (Descartes, *Principles,* II, xxxvi). Quite likely this appeal to divine intervention led to Malebranche's later "occasionalist" theory, namely that God perpetually coordinates the separate movements of the soul and the body in man.

As a parenthetical comment, it seems more natural to objectively couple space and mathematics together as opposed to time possibly because of its subjective aura. Recall that in the period, God was conceived as having penned the laws of the universe in mathematical terms.

---

[3] Ben Mijuskovic, "The Simplicity Argument and Time in Schopenhauer and Bergson," *Schopenhauer Jahrbuch,* 58 (1977), 43–58.

It is not until Kant and especially in the first edition Deduction that a doctrine of immanent time-consciousness philosophically receives its due. Kant's treatment of time as a passive form of intuition in the Aesthetic is very different from his dynamic description of it as resulting from synthetic *a priori* constitutive acts, the threefold transcendental syntheses in the first Deduction. "Synthesis" is the result of "spontaneous creative *acts*" whereas the empirical "reproductive representations" are not (A 97). What Kant offers in the A and B Deductions in the *Critique* are two very different ultimate first premises as candidates for an undeniable foundation for his theory of consciousness: (1) "All consciousness, i.e., human experience is grounded in immanent time-consciousness" (First Deduction, A 99–104, dated 1781) as opposed to (2) "All self-consciousness is a unity"—his famous transcendental unity of apperception—(Second Deduction, B 131–132, dated 1787). The two premises, of course, are not mutually exclusive. Thus, for example, one could argue that the unity of consciousness is essentially and fundamentally a temporal one. *But* as they stand, separated by half a dozen years by Kant, they need to be addressed as distinct premises/inferences/conclusions because they have different implications, namely the A premise version is experiential, while the B treatment is more properly "logical" or "transcendental"; it is an (allegedly) presupposed "condition" for the possibility of human experience. But then there is also the compromising problem of Kant's criticism of the Second Paralogism version of the "unity of consciousness" as illicitly metaphysical. If so, why does the B Deduction work, while the Paralogism in the A edition fails? Interestingly, Robert Paul Wolff, actually inadvertently defends the Second Paralogism as a persuasive explication of the unity of consciousness in the B edition.[4]

No such shadow darkens the brow of immanent time-consciousness. And in any case, even so the unification of (a) time-consciousness with (b) the unity of consciousness in regard to their theoretical compatibility—their identity and unity—requires a further formal synthesis, which is promised in the first Preface but never delivered by Kant: How is consciousness possible? Thus the subjective Deduction "seeks to investigate the pure understanding itself, its possibility and cognitive faculties upon which it rests; and so deals with it in its subjective [psychological] aspect" (*Critique,* A xvi–xvii). As he goes on to declare:

---

4  Robert Paul Wolff, *Kant's Theory of Mental Activity: A Commentary on the Transcendental Analytic of the Critique of Pure Reason* (Cambridge, MA: Harvard University Press, 1963), 105–106; hereafter cited as Wolff, *KTMA*; cf. Ben Mijuskovic, "The Premise of the Transcendental Analytic," *The Philosophical Quarterly,* 23:91 (1973), 155–161.

> Although this [subjective] exposition is of great importance for my chief purpose, it does not form an essential part of it. For the chief question is always simply this:—what and how much can the understanding and reason know apart from all experience? not—how is the faculty of thought itself possible? (A xvii).

But this is precisely the issue: How is consciousness itself possible? How is immanent time-consciousness possible? And this inquiry directly leads us to *acts of spontaneity*—and not to pure receptive forms—and the activities of the subconscious mind.

> Now Kant appears to have been unwilling to regard the [faculty of the] 'understanding' as ever unconscious of its activities. Why he was unwilling, it does not seem possible to explain…In order to develop the distinctions demanded by the new Critical attitude, he had therefore to introduce a new faculty capable of taking over the activities which have been recognized as non-conscious. For this purpose he selected the imagination giving to it the special title, the *productive* imagination.[5]

Nevertheless, according to Kemp Smith, "The teaching of the subjective deduction is, however, preserved in almost unmodified form throughout the *Critique* as a whole and its 'transcendental psychology' forms an essential part of Kant's central teaching" (ibid., xliii-xliv). As we proceed, we shall learn that Schopenhauer's noumenal Will is indebted to this subconscious force presaged by Kant.

Robert Paul Wolff, however, similarly accounts for how Kant's synthetic activities are made possible by turning to the Subjective Deduction and more specifically to the constitution of internal time-consciousness (Wolff, *KTMA*, 100–102, 128, 189–208). Interestingly, neither Kemp Smith nor Wolff nor for that matter Paton mention spontaneity in their commentaries but it is the *act of spontaneity* that is the trigger which is essential to activating the "productive imagination."

That there is a *real* difference between time-consciousness and the unity of consciousness is an assertion forcefully defended by Kemp Smith's *Commentary*. And I agree. But that is not to say that they can be separated from each other. Mother and child are separated by body but not by blood. Rather spontaneity

---

[5] Norman Kemp Smith, *A Commentary to Kant's 'Critique of Pure Reason'* (New York: Humanities Press, 1962), 241–242, 264; hereafter cited as Kemp Smith, *Commentary*. It is Kemp Smith who first underscores the critical qualitative difference and the defining distinction between Kant's subconscious and Freud's unconscious.

and time-consciousness display an *a priori* synthetic relation with each other. Kemp Smith clearly prefers time-consciousness as the critical *premise* for the entire *Critique of Pure Reason* (and again I agree), whereas the predominantly English-speaking "analytic" interpreters and linguistically oriented commentators on Kant clearly regard the second edition Deduction as the more persuasive allegedly on the basis of "logical" and "transcendental" grounds.

I have chosen to concentrate on Schopenhauer for three reasons. First, his conception of a possible intercession, a crossing-over of temporal self-consciousness with intuitional time as eternity is transacted through the simplicity premise. Secondly he demonstrates how an idealist theory of the noumenal Will can *indirectly* "influence" the complexities and intricacies of both human passion and thought. His theory of an irrational motivating force in consciousness emphasizes the nature of the subconscious as an unpredictable power animating *all* human feelings, thoughts, and actions. Thirdly and most importantly he fruitfully exploits the possibilities of Kant's spontaneous productive imagination within his conception of the noumenal Will by internalizing it within the subjective mind.

Before turning directly to Schopenhauer, I need to appeal to Frederick Copleston's study concerning the issue of Schopenhauer's "transcendental idealism" developed in his study, *Schopenhauer: Philosopher of Pessimism,* and more specifically to Chapter 3, "Life's a Dream," where importantly Schopenhauer undertakes to transcend the distinction between phenomena and noumena through idealism.

> One may not be able to discern the thing-in-itself through the veils of perception directly; yet everyone carries the thing in itself within himself and therefore everyone can penetrate thereto through self-consciousness, attaining the noumenon within himself. Thus the bridge by which metaphysics passes beyond experience is nothing else than that analysis of experience into phenomena and the thing-in-itself. For it contains the proof of a kernel of the phenomena different from the phenomenon itself.[6]

In other words, the ability to distinguish and also *at the same time* posit and grasp the existence of both worlds, *both* the phenomenal *and* the noumenal

---

6 Quoted in Frederick Copleston, *Arthur Schopenhauer: Philosopher of Pessimism* (Oxon, England: Heythrop College, 1947), 63; hereafter cited as ASPP. The chapter is well worth reading in its entirety. On Schopenhauer's subjective and transcendental idealism, cf. D. M Hamlin, "Schopenhauer: On the Principle of Sufficient Reason," 79–80, 85–86, 92–93, in *Schopenhauer: His Achievement* (Sussex, England: Harvester Press, 1970), edited by Michael Fox.

realms, can only be accomplished from an elevated *idealist* perspective; it's like getting above two things that initially seemed entirely different and then seeing them in an *a priori* relation to each other: *the distinction plus the relation constitutes the idealism; it* is *the idealism.* As Hegel critically argued against Kant, to *know* that there is a noumenal realm *beyond* the phenomenal is *already* to have transcended the phenomenal; it is to *know* both; in a very significant sense the "noumenal" is no longer unknowable; it is no longer a "limiting" concept. To reach a barrier is already to *know* something *beyond* it. It then follows that *both* the distinction *and* the relation are in the soul, in self-consciousness and therefore ideal.

In Chapter 3, we primarily—but not completely—concentrated on Schopenhauer's conception of freedom and its relation to evil. In the following we will focus on his conception of salvation in light of his commitment to the simplicity premise and argument.

Schopenhauer begins his monumental work with the assertion, "The world is my representation: this is a truth valid for every living being, although man alone can bring it into reflexive, abstract consciousness."[7] This declaration is soon followed by an equally important one. "That which knows all things and is known by none is the *subject.* It is accordingly the supporter of the world, the universal condition of all that appears, of all objects, and it is always presupposed; for whatever exists, exists only for a subject." Agreeing with Kant's epistemic commitment that there are two forms of pure, *a priori* intuition, namely space and time, he further radically reduces Kant's twelve categories of thought to only one: causality (*WWR,* 5). But whereas Kant posits an absolutely unknowable reality of "things-in-themselves," an undefined and indeterminate noumenal realm, Schopenhauer rather *claims* an equally unknowable, underlying, metaphysical reality—the Will—*but* nevertheless it is one that powerfully "forms" natural phenomena as well as subconsciously "influences" human motivations. The Will is the *underlying* substratum of all phenomenal appearances both natural and human. Hence although the Will is "unknowable," nevertheless it exerts a creative force upon this world as well as on human passion, thought, and conduct. This reading of "reality" is very different from Kant, who resists specifying any knowledge or relation between the noumenal realm and our human spheres of subjective consciousness for the obvious reason that for Kant all relations are phenomenal whereas Schopenhauer asserts an active involvement—indeterminate and unpredictable—between the Will and its phenomenal aspects both in nature and man.

---

7 Arthur Schopenhauer, *The World as Will and Representation,* translated by E.F.J. Payne (New York: Dover, 1969) I, 3; hereafter cited as *WWR.*

> Here we see at the very lowest grade the Will manifesting itself as a blind impulse, an obscure dull urge, remote from all *direct* knowableness [but not indirect]. It is the simplest and feeblest mode of its objectification. But it appears as such a blind urge and as a striving devoid of knowledge.
> WWR, I, 149

Schopenhauer's concept of the Will is a principle of self-preservation similar to Spinoza's notion of the *conatus* in man, a striving, desiring, and willing force; it is "the will to life." And it also anticipates Nietzsche's "will to power" principle, namely that all existence, inanimate as well as animate, seeks to preserve itself and above all to *express* itself.

Thus there is a very important difference between Kant and Schopenhauer on the ultimate "derivation" or "source" of empirical human consciousness and its consequent actions. For Kant, the unknown noumenal realm is epistemically forced to channel into, to "conform to," i.e., to be "structured by" the dictates of his Copernican Revolution as the noumena are "worked into" the phenomenal intuitions of space and time and the categories of the Understanding. *But* quite differently for Schopenhauer, the subconscious Will powerfully "influences"—not causes, not determines—man's desires. Kant is dealing with cognition; but Schopenhauer is dealing with emotions; Kant is concerned with philosophy; Schopenhauer is concerned with psychology.

Schopenhauer's promise of salvation from all the torments and miseries of life resides in a realization that in *some* unspecified manner self-consciousness is somehow connected to *eternity* and that this realization allows the soul to derive some element of tranquility as it reaches toward the contemplation of Platonic Forms and archetypes or an ascetic way of life. And although it is not a complete escape and even hardly a victory over life's sufferings, at least it is a neutralization of pain and anguish for a while. This is accomplished by a unifying identification between the immediacy of the self-conscious *present* with the timelessness of *eternity*.

> The thing in-itself [as the Will] remains untouched by [phenomenal] time and by that which is possible only through time, that is, by ARISING AND PASSING AWAY, and that the phenomena in time could not have even that restless, fleeting existence that stands next to nothingness, *unless there were in them a kernel of eternity*. It is true that *eternity* is a [pure] concept having no perception as its basis; for this reason, it is of a merely negative content, and thus implies a timeless existence. *Time,* however, is a mere image of eternity [Plato, *Timaeus*], as Plotinus has it; and in just

the same way, our temporal existence is the mere image of our true inner being. This must lie in eternity, just because time is only the form of our knowing; but by virtue of this form alone we know our own existence and that of all things as transitory, finite and subject to annihilation.
    *WWR*, II, 484, italics mine; cf., II, 325

First it is important to notice that Schopenhauer is not thinking of Kant's intuitional time but rather his time as inner sense, as self-consciousness, while eternity consists in a pure imageless conception. And secondly that if the goal of salvation is to be successfully accomplished, there must be *some* sort of contact, *some* sort of momentary unification between the phenomenal temporality of self-consciousness with a noumenal eternity; only if in *some* manner the self-conscious *present* is able to connect to an immutable *eternity;* that both can be *somehow* unified and shared; that they can *somehow* intersect and interact in order for a fleeting salvation to be secured.

For Kant, of course, immanent time-consciousness—as opposed to the intuition of time, the pure passive form of sensibility—is mediate, synthetic, and relational. In the Aesthetic, time merely lies in wait, potentially pregnant with sensuous possibilities, a matrix for the receptivity of "given" sensory placements. In the Analytic, however, inner sense, time-consciousness *does* something. We recall the threefold transcendental syntheses of spontaneous acts of apprehension through the portal of sensory immediacy; the creative retentive production of the imagination; and the reflexive self-conscious recognition of its own conceptions. Again, the synthesizing mediating link is the productive imagination, which is both sensuous and free. But as our immanent time-experiences meander throughout our lives sustaining the interwoven themes of our continued existence, it is existentially involved; it constitutes an existential *engagement* throughout the rich tapestries of our being; in the vicissitudes, the victories, and the tragedies of our lives. Time threads and interweaves all our conscious states; it is the fabric of our solitary existence; it is the continuous warp and woof of our very being.

Unlike Kant, Schopenhauer expresses a far different use for our temporal nature by anchoring and engaging it with eternity, if even only for a moment. It is the key to our transient salvation while we visit on this earth. In effect, Schopenhauer is seeking to couple (1) the *present* moment, the immediacy of self-consciousness with (2) the timelessness of eternity through their shared commitment to the simplicity argument.

It is here that Professor Copleston's interpretation can rejoin our conversation and I leave it to the judicious reader to adjudicate the issue.

> The will in itself, apart from all phenomenal appearance, may have ways of existing which to us are entirely unknown and incomprehensible. But it is really very difficult to see how, after laying down his theory of knowledge and his doctrine of the phenomenon, Schopenhauer can give any satisfactory formal justification for a metaphysic. Either all knowledge is knowledge of the phenomenal, in which case there can be no knowledge, at the very least no communicable knowledge, of the noumenal, or there can be knowledge of the noumenal, in which case knowledge is not essentially knowledge of the phenomenal.
>
> COPLESTON, *ASPP*, 64

Copleston's point is well taken, but Schopenhauer was impressed by Oriental thought, especially Indian philosophy, which evinces a strong strain of mysticism. There is a fine line between the metaphysical and the mystical (and for that matter the spiritual as well). We see this in the German Romantics, especially in Schelling, the intense searching desire to connect to something beyond both human knowledge and communicable language. But its yearning and the desperation that follows does not make it any the less real for the subjective mind. Whether we are discussing human time-consciousness or eternity, both are grounded in the Achilles premise, argument, and conclusion.

My goal throughout all these discussions is grounded in exhibiting the force of the simplicity premise in all of its many variations throughout Western philosophy as evidence in support of the thesis that consciousness is immaterial and active and that matter cannot think. "Reality" has the capacity to appear in many, many guises precisely because of its spontaneous ability to create and sustain a variety of principles and relations whether we wish to call them phenomenal or noumenal; mystical and spiritual; apparent or real; primary, secondary, or tertiary.

Actually Schopenhauer credits Plotinus as having been the first to hold to "the paradoxical assertion that matter has no extension, for extension is inseparable from the form, and that it is therefore *incorporeal*" (*WWR*, II, 45; *Enneads*, II, Bk. 4, c. 8 and 9) again, "Plotinus and Giordano Bruno were right when they made the paradoxical statement that matter itself is not extended, and consequently incorporeal" (*WWR*, II 308); and "Therefore Plotinus and Giordano Bruno could only be brought on the completely objective path to the assertion that matter in and by itself is without extension, consequently without spatiality, and hence without corporeality" (*WWR*, II 309). These three declarations are a clear confirmation of Schopenhauer's commitment to a subjective form of idealism. And further by describing it as a "paradox," this is a virtue rather than a deficiency. Consequently, the "brain" and its attendant "sense organs" are to be translated into the *concepts* or *ideas of* the brain and sense organs, since they are mere phenomenal appearances.

As for Kant, so for Schopenhauer the phenomenal *concept* of the self and the *concept* of the object mutually condition each other. Thus, not only the Will but self-conscious *reflexion* as well is immaterial even when it *appears* to be operating in *apparent* concurrence with the brain and the body (*WWR*, I, 119, 128; II, 196–197, 251, 277, 321, 325). Schopenhauer consequently draws a clear distinction between (a) sensory perceptions in contrast to (b) conceptions, abstractions, inferences, and reason. Theoretical knowledge is a higher form of "non-perceptive" or non-imaged consciousness and one *"which is entirely different from representations"* and "which can only be conceived and not perceived" (*WWR*, I, 36, 39). This once more conjures up the possibility of imageless thoughts. Throughout all this, Schopenhauer is able to relate, connect, bind, synthesize, and/or unify the immediacy of the temporal *present* in self-consciousness with *the eternal, surging, irrational, and eternal Will.*

> The present alone is that which always exists and stands firm and immovable. That which, empirically apprehended, is the most fleeting of all, manifests itself to the metaphysical glance that sees beyond the forms of empirical perception as that which alone endures, as the *nunc stans* of the scholastics. The source and supporter of its content is the will-to-live, or the thing-in-itself—which we are. That which constantly becomes and passes away, in that it either has been already or is still to come, belongs to the phenomenon as such by virtue of its forms, which render coming into being and passing away possible.... For life is [immediately] certain to the will and the present is certain to life. Therefore everyone can also say: "I am once and for all lord and master of the present, and through all eternity it will accompany me as my shadow; accordingly, I do not wonder where it comes from, and how it is that it is precisely now." We can compare time to an endlessly revolving sphere; the half that is always sinking would be the past, and the half that is always rising would be the future; but at the top, the [simple] indivisible point that touches the tangent would be the extensionless present. Just as the tangent does not continue rolling with the sphere, so also the present, the point of contact of the object whose form is time, does not roll on with the subject that has no form, since it does not belong to the knowable, but is the condition of all that is knowable.... The form of the present is essential to the objectification of the Will. As an extensionless point, it cuts [phenomenal] time which extends infinitely in both directions and stands firm and immovable.
> 
> *WWR*, I, 279–280

With all this imagery of unextended points, centers, and circles, with the heralded escape of the finite and temporal toward the real and eternal, one is naturally reminded of Plotinian modes of expression and especially of "the flight of the alone to the Alone" at the very close of *The Enneads*. It is Plotinus' tribute to the ego's lonely journey toward salvation and its escape from this earthly veil of tears (*WWR*, I, 267). Schopenhauer's attitude is sympathetic to this absorbing mode of thought. This is what he emotionally finds so appealing in Oriental thought; the escape to nowhere.

Beyond that, Schopenhauer's commitment to the immateriality argument also assists him in the contemplation of eternal Platonic Forms as well as promoting an ascetic attitude toward our phenomenal world of suffering and misery. In this manner, he seeks to assemble and comprehensively unify certain ideas about the noumenal Will, phenomenal self-consciousness, time-consciousness, and eternity together. His desire is to collapse all that went before within a single moment; the self's escape from the world within the timeless inner sanctum of eternity. Again, the connecting link is the simplicity premise. Given that the eternal Will as the thing-in-itself—as Reality-In-Itself—is inextensional and self-consciousness is equally immaterial and active, the latter is able to *somehow* transcend the entirety of its *representational* appearances. Man is privileged to summon, attain, and secure an immediate, mystical *point* of contact *with* or *to* eternity. In this perfect moment, the present self becomes animated, energized by the "will to live"; it realizes the opportunity of a transition from phenomenal time, which always signifies a past and a future, to an eternal timelessness with its consequent independence from causal determinative structures. On this account, eternity implies the loss of the empirical ego, always causally conditioned, and its immersion within a timeless Will. Thus, through the mediation of our reflexive awareness, we are in direct contact *with* and *to* a metaphysical present, i.e., eternity. At the juncture of a self-conscious present with an eternal timelessness, man is absolutely free from all his phenomenal, causal, and bodily chains, woes, and sufferings.

> [Human] time is merely the spread-out and piecemeal view that a human being has of the [Platonic] Ideas. These are outside time and consequently *eternal.* Therefore Plato says that time is the moving image of eternity.
> WWR, I, 176

During these temporal moments of contemplative reflexion, the human will is suspended. It functions as a renunciation of the "will to live" thereby fostering a secondary liberating attitude of asceticism and "disinterested" aestheticism (Shaftesbury and Kant).

For the moment, perhaps it is sufficient to say that Schopenhauer's vision of a temporal immediacy has achieved a considerable degree of insight into the problematic nature of our consciousness of time as *both* mediate *and* immediate, *both* phenomenal *and* eternal at once. Schopenhauer's insistence that there are moments when we dwell and desire "outside" and "beyond" human time leads to our efforts to neutralize the irrational imperatives of the Will. When this state of consciousness is achieved, the self attains a sense of resignation not unlike the one advocated by the Stoic attitude of tranquility, of *apatheia,* or Spinoza's third order of knowledge, an intuitive contemplation of the whole of reality ending in a state of ethical withdrawal, quiescence, and salvation (*WWR*, I, 152). For Schopenhauer, the goal is the loss of individuality as the soul immerses itself in a *universal* "knowing" thereby escaping the miseries of human life by achieving a quietude and a freedom from all its narcissistic, egoistic, wolfish drives and from all the vanities of life (*WWR*, I, 199).

> This *egoistic* conflict shows itself throughout all the grades of the Will's objectification, it shows itself most clearly and most poignantly in man—*homo homini lupus*. The individual is identical, in his inner nature, with Will and the Will's striving reflects itself in him as *egoism,* so that he regards himself as the centre of the world and has respect only for his own existence and well-being, not caring for the existence and welfare of others.
> COPLESTON, *ASPP,* 87; italics his

When we address the issue of the dynamics of loneliness more directly in a later chapter, we will see that narcissism and egoism form the very foundation of the self's base. It is our narcissism that serves as the flint that sparks the flame of entitlement, vanity, and pride; the desire to compete with others and destroy them.

In the previous chapter on freedom, I presented Schopenhauer's metaphysical Will as surreptitiously, indirectly, or subconsciously influencing the passions, thoughts, and actions of mankind. Although we phenomenally *appear* determined, nevertheless in reality we are "by proxy" free through the irrational forces of the Will. We are free whether we know it or not; like it or not. Theoretically it is open to us to creatively express ourselves aesthetically and he refers several times to artistic genius as a special mode of an ameliorating consciousness, as a form of sublimation and a search for tranquility in a disengaging asceticism. But there is also the powerful tendency to project our distress and disappointments through acts of violence on others and even ourselves. The creative spontaneity of the Will can result in goodness as well as evil; intelligence as well as banality; industry as well as sloth; and beauty as well as plainness.

Dostoyevsky, in *Crime and Punishment,* declares that psychology is a knife that cuts both ways. Analogously, the Will is a knife that cuts many, many ways. Spontaneously the soul is free of all determinative factors; man is free to plunge toward good or evil; salvation or destruction. When the self stands poised without a past behind it or a future before it, when it becomes completely free to act without boundaries or responsibilities, it has achieved a state of consciousness and transcendence without limitations. Between phenomenal self-consciousness and the eternal reality of the metaphysical Will, there exists a simple, indivisible point, a pure present when the temporal self and eternity "touch," "cross," and "intersect." When the Will as a thing-in-itself and the pure immediacy of reflexive self-consciousness are compressed and fused into a single moment and consumed by it (Bergson's "acetylene flame"); when the self *feels* but does not *know* itself, it is liberated from all the burdens of human existence. Dangerously poised and perched at the edge of a timeless precipice, the self hurls itself forward in a leap of blind passion recklessly verging toward creation or annihilation.

> It is also well known that we seldom find great genius united with preeminent reasonableness; on the contrary, men of genius are often subject to violent emotions and violent passions...It is often remarked that genius and madness have a side where they touch and even pass over into each other, and even poetic inspiration has been called a type of madness.
> WWR, I, 190; cf. I, 303; and cf. Plato's *Ion*

But these interludes of "violent emotions and violent passions" are not only found in the fertile soil of artistic geniuses but indeed in all men and women in all conditions of life and status and in diverse contexts.

> The Will which constitutes our being-in-itself, is of a simple nature; it merely wills and does not know....In self-consciousness, as that which alone knows, the subject of knowing stands facing the Will as a spectator, and although it has sprung from the Will, it knows that Will as something different from itself, something foreign to it, and thus only empirically, in time, piecemeal, in the successive [temporal] agitations and acts of the Will; only *a posteriori* and *often very indirectly does it come to know the Will's decisions.* This is why our own inner being is a riddle to us, in other

words, to our intellect, and why the individual regards himself as newly arisen and as perishable, although his inner being-in-itself [i.e., in its absolute simplicity] is something timeless and therefore eternal.
*WWR*, II, 499; italics mine

This is the same existential schism that Kierkegaard confronts when he describes himself standing on the edge and before a 60,000 fathoms deep chasm, and he is forced to decide what to do; stay or leap; or choose between an aesthetic, an ethical, or a religious life and its solitary lonely values. It is the same dilemma described by William James' when one is faced with a forced, living, and momentous option; when a climber is confronted in the Alps with the peril of a deadly leap; or to risk waiting and perhaps be rescued ("The Will To Believe").

The self has the power to act with boundless abandon as it feels itself absolutely severed from phenomenal time and causality and suspended in a momentous instant. There is a centerless point in time when the self completely annuls itself from any relation to other selves; in that moment, it is irresponsibly, absolutely, and metaphysically free. It is severed from all obligations. Underlying each life is the human reality that there are multiple situations nestled throughout our existence when self-consciousness realizes it has kicked itself loose from heaven and earth; when it is absolutely free to create or to destroy; to love or to hate; to live or to die. Accordingly, Schopenhauer's "extensionless point" is a non-conceptual, non-temporal state of consciousness. The self, confined to a single moment, instantaneously grasps freedom; choices without consequences; it has nothing behind or before itself. It is suspended in a timelessness without beginning or end; without antecedents or consequents; without the earth below or the sky above; without the fear of hell or the hope of heaven—it decides! And what transpires beyond that moment is absolutely unpredictable to others, to the self, or to the gods.

Below our ordinary unreflecting consciousness, below our Freudian unconscious, repressed anxieties and conflicts, there is a deeply submerged uncanny feeling of an unknown indecipherable presence in consciousness, a pervasive premonition, which whispers and disturbs the self that its human desires and acts may be *beyond* its conscious control. As evolved creatures, we sometimes uncomfortably sense that we are capable of doing unspeakable things; to commit acts that not only others cannot understand but indeed that even we ourselves are unable to comprehend; acts that defy any and all causal explanations and motivational justifications. During these potential acts of "pure," causeless willing, our own inner darkness obscures the light of consciousness from self-knowledge. Man is capable of loving life as well as death, good as well as evil through the same willing breaths. There is an entire spectrum of antithetical "motives" and choices lying in wait between our innumerable conflicting desires testifying to the paradox of human existence and all its strivings. In Dostoevsky's *Crime and Punishment,* Raskolnikov, a philosophy student, murders a miserly old pawnbroker and her impaired sister and yet he ultimately finds redemption, which expresses the infinite breadth between evil and salvation.

But it is desire above all that spurs man into action. We need to remember that when Kant opens the portal of consciousness to this subterranean realm with the key of spontaneity and enters within the obscure recesses of the soul, he has suddenly thrust himself into an enclosed chamber allowing him—like it or not—to address the ultimate questions. Not only how consciousness is possible but also how deeply and profoundly does consciousness descend. Which is the master—passion or intellect? He has inadvertently thrown open the door exposing us to the hidden and obscure regions, sources, and forces not only of the intellect but the passions as well. *If* indeed consciousness "perhaps springs from a common but unknown root" (A 15=B 29); *if* "the power of the imagination is a blind but indispensable function of the soul…but of which we are scarcely ever conscious" (A 78=B 104); *if* consciousness is "an art concealed in the depths of the human soul, whose real modes of activity nature is hardly likely ever to allow us to leave open to our gaze" (A 142=B 181); *then* this revealed path, for better or for worse, allows us an entry into the chambers of the subconscious Will with all its dark forbidden desires and disturbing hidden fantasies and lusts for power. Is there not then a terrifying second question: *what is man really capable of?* May not this secret entrance lead us into the deepest caverns of the soul to which Schopenhauer, Nietzsche, Conrad, Golding, and Jung have peered into before us? Is there an even darker Hades beneath Plato's cave?

The Christian and Kantian promise of salvation and immortality as a reward for goodness in this world only makes sense if one assumes that mankind is capable of deserving it. Schopenhauer is clearly free from any such illusions as we saw in the previous chapter. Although the Will is eternal, the soul quite likely is not. It merely occupies a contingent tenancy with the body. But when the house is raised, its tenant disappears.

Schopenhauer is well aware of the timeworn invocation of applying the simplicity argument to demonstrate the immortality of the soul and he pointedly ridicules and mocks it.

> From the time of Socrates down to our own, we find that a principal subject of the interminable disputations of philosophers is that *ens rationis* called soul. We see most of them assert its immortality, which means its

> metaphysical nature; yet we see others, supported by facts that incontestably show the intellect's complete dependence on bodily organs, unweariedly maintain the opposite. By all and above all, that soul was taken to be absolutely simple; for precisely from this were its metaphysical nature, its immateriality, and its immortality demonstrated, although these by no means necessarily follow from it. For although we can conceive the destruction of a formed body only through its decomposition into its parts, it does not follow from this that the destruction of a simple substance or entity, of which, moreover, we have no conception, may not be possible in some other way, perhaps by its gradually vanishing [a reference to Kant's doctrine of "elanguescence" in the Second Paralogism]. I, on the other hand, start by doing away with the presupposed simplicity of our subjectively conscious nature or of the ego, since I show that the manifestations from which this simplicity was inferred have two very different sources, and that in any case the intellect is physically conditioned, the function of a material organ, and therefore dependent on it.
> 
> WWR, II, 270

Schopenhauer's reference to the soul "gradually vanishing by elanguescence" is an obvious reference to Kant's own criticism in the second edition Second Paralogism, which is raised against Mendelssohn's proof for the immortality of the soul in his version of the *Phaedon*.

But it is important to distinguish the immateriality *principle* or *premise* from the Achilles *argument* or *demonstration*. Half of universal mankind believes that the soul, self, or mind is non-physical, while the second half is convinced that the body and brain rule. But what is important is to realize that one can reject the proof for human immortality based on the immateriality premise (as Schopenhauer obviously does above) and yet accept it in arguing for (a) the immaterial nature of self-consciousness; (b) a metaphysics of the Will; and (c) the noumenal status of eternity, as Schopenhauer clearly does. Immortality is one conclusion but at least there are seven others.

For Schopenhauer, Kant's version of self-consciousness is an unwarranted presupposition because Kant fails to recognize that it is grounded in the *prior* existence of an eternal Will although both continue to rely on the Achilles argument. And Schopenhauer proceeds to object that it is only because the Will—and not because of Kant's categories of the Understanding—that consciousness is capable of performing its required synthesizing, unifying, binding functions. Only the Will is simple, immaterial, spontaneous, and uncaused and therefore a true unity. Kantian empirical "unities" are merely modes of appearance, loose sensory associations whose phenomenal "unity" is gathered together by the intuitional *representational* forms of space and time and the causal relation. By contrast, Schopenhauer's Will is universally omnipresent and eternal, while it manifests Itself through an infinite variety of expressions in individuals and as It courses through the innumerable multitudes and complexities of human experience, one of which happens to be Kant's transcendental unity of apperception.

> Kant's proposition: "The I think must accompany all our representations," is insufficient; for *the 'I' is an unknown quality, in other words, it is itself a mystery and a secret [to itself]*. What gives unity and [temporal] sequence to consciousness, since, by pervading all the representations of consciousness, it is its substratum, its permanent supporter, cannot itself be conditioned by consciousness, and therefore cannot be a representation. On the contrary, it must be the *prius* of consciousness, and *the root of the tree of which consciousness is the fruit*. This, I say, is the Will; it alone is unalterable and absolutely identical and has brought forth consciousness for its own ends. It is therefore the Will that gives it unity and holds all its representations and ideas together, accompanying them, as it were, like a continuous ground-bass. Without it the intellect would have no more unity of consciousness than has a mirror, in which now one thing now another presents itself in succession, or at most only as much as a convex mirror has, whose rays converge at an imaginary point behind its surface. But it is the Will alone that is permanent and unchangeable in consciousness.
> 
> WWR, II, 139–140; italics mine

Both Fichte and Schopenhauer seek to discredit Kant's version of the unity of consciousness as a presupposition and in doing so they rely on their own interpretations and use of the simplicity premise. Schopenhauer's proof only makes sense if the Will is immaterial and active; only if it is a substantive and infinitely magnified version of the Achilles premise. This disagreement between Kant, Fichte, Schopenhauer, Hegel—and later Husserl—centers on each of their efforts to legitimize their own presuppositionless beginning. But in actuality in all of their cases the real premise remains the Achilles principle. Importantly, however, the italicized phrase above provides us with an insight on how Schopenhauer views his entire system. Metaphorically the Will "is the root of the tree of which consciousness is the fruit." Fleshed out, this suggests that the connecting trunk is the self; the branches are the relations; and the fruit and leaves are the changing phenomena. We will revisit this image momentarily.

For Schopenhauer, the dualism is not between matter and mind but between the World and the Will. Senseless matter cannot think because matter (including gravity) cannot will. It is the product, not the source. Only the Will is active and man is able to partake of it only in so far as he drinks from the trough of that eternal fountain. Matter is physical and extended and the Will is not and it cannot be if It is to fulfill its relentless modes of unencumbered expression, *which is to act without constraints.* Phenomenal consciousness is always tethered to the brain. The immaterial "I," however, is "an unknown *quality,*" a dangling puppet barely hanging on the frayed strings of a manipulative Puppeteer hidden behind a curtain. The self, intrinsically unknowable to itself and to others, is incapable of being intellectually penetrated or understood. To be sure, it is phenomenally, scientifically determined but these are merely distorting *appearances; they are not reality.* Man can always invent artificial natural causes and psychological motives for what he does. But at the deepest and darkest level of the Platonic cave, man is surrounded by shifting shadows and muted echoes and remains a mystery unto himself. Thus in the final analysis science is ultimately unable to predict human passions, thoughts, and actions, although we can always entertain and invent artificial causes and provide inaccurate predictions. The Will alone is free and mankind is simply a parrot perched on the shoulder of a drunken sailor.

But when his own turn for a positive account for the unity of consciousness is in order, Schopenhauer is unable to avoid his own criticism of Kant and instead surrenders before his utter dependence on the simplicity premise.

> Therefore such an intellect must first of all unite in *one point* all the impressions together with their elaboration through its [active] functions, whether for mere perceptions or for concepts. This point becomes, as it were, the focus of all its rays, so that there may arise that unity of consciousness which is the theoretical ego, the supporter of the whole consciousness. In this consciousness itself, the *theoretical ego* presents itself as identical with the *willing* ego of which it is the mere function of knowledge.
> 
> WWR, II, 251; cf., Plotinus, *The Enneads,* IV, 7, 6, and ARA, 8–10

Basically, this is a conflation of Kant's epistemic unity of consciousness with Fichte's actional ego. But is this "one point" noumenal or phenomenal? Apparently Schopenhauer wishes to have it both ways again. He confirms that phenomenally the ego is a principle of unity in *this* empirical world; and yet at the same time this same unity nevertheless, in some undefined fashion, also owes a deep allegiance or subjugation to the eternal immaterial Will.

Schopenhauer then goes on to compare the self to a magic lantern with each self displaying its own churning kaleidoscopic of mosaic images. Throughout our separate lives these monadic transmutations vary within the self and display no genuine correspondence with those of other selves. In reality, however, there is only the one *Will* that intrudes in each of us and everything else is merely an appearance, an "objectivity," while the Will Itself remains inviolable amidst all earthly changes. It alone is the thing-in-itself, while everything else is merely a phenomenal appearance (*WWR*, I, 153).

> From all this it is evident that human consciousness and thinking are by their very nature necessarily fragmentary...In this our thinking consciousness is like a magic lantern in the focus of which only one picture can appear at a time and every picture, even when it depicts the noblest thing, must nevertheless soon vanish to make way for the most different and even the most vulgar thing.
> *WWR*, II, 138

Although Schopenhauer was familiar with Hume's writings, he never questions the identity of the self. The lantern remains the same although the flame constantly flickers. It is the surreptitious Will that unifies consciousness and it is the Will that indiscriminately leads to either good or evil; intimacy or loneliness. In any case, for Schopenhauer, only the Absolute Will is in reality truly simple and indestructible, immune from the phenomenal decomposition of material parts, and therefore eternal. And no less is "eternity" simple. Schopenhauer is determined to point out that in his philosophy, as opposed to Kant's, "the *will* which appears as one of the last in all other systems...is with me the very first" (*WWR*, II, 270–271).

Often his various arguments in relation to the self are reminiscent of certain Hindu and Buddhist doctrines, which in concert question the reality of the empirical self. In Buddhism, for instance, all life is suffering; all suffering stems from desire; all desire is grounded in the atman or ego; if one extinguishes the self, then one will have eliminated desire, even the desire not to desire and "one" will have reached enlightenment and blessedness.

But just as often he emulates Plotinus by drawing on the great Neo-Platonist's familiar analogies and metaphors when he writes that

> immortality, by virtue of the eternity of the true inner being of the whole phenomenon, is comparable to the return of that point on the radius to the centre, whose mere extension is the surface. The Will as thing-in-itself is entire and undivided in every being, just as the centre is an integral part of every radius; whereas the peripheral end of this radius is in the most rapid revolution with the surface that represents time and its content,

> the other end of the centre where eternity lies, remains in profoundest peace, because the centre is the point whose rising half is no different from the sinking half.
> WWR, II, 325–326

In any case, Schopenhauer advises us that Death, the final visitor, is the most welcome of all guests, which may remind us of Socrates' last thoughts in the *Apology* where he suggests that Death may conclude our life's journey with the best night of all, an eternal dreamless sleep. Indeed, "True salvation, is a deliverance from life and suffering, which cannot be imagined without a complete denial of the Will" (WWR, I, 397). For Schopenhauer, having rejected the immortality of the soul for the nothingness of inexistence, death has opened its eternal maw and swallowed him whole.

After "death," the empirical ego disappears and the phenomenal will returns to the single all-encompassing reservoir of the noumenal Will. Immortality implies eternity, the conquest of time as appearance; and this victory can only be achieved when the human will becomes immersed within the utter immaterial simplicity of an immutable universal Will. Consequently, through the simplicity premise and argument, the transient self-conscious human will and the eternal Will become unified but only in the sense that the greater force both consumes and annihilates the lesser one forever.

Before leaving Schopenhauer, I need to append two important remarks. First, his irrational Will plays out both its destructive as well as its creative forces through man's impenetrable subconscious, in acts that defy understanding and human predictability. Second, interestingly enough, Schopenhauer, similar to Malebranche (and Hume) suggests that through the Will "anything can produce something or an other thing"; "This is why we cannot give up the idea that anything can come out of anything. For example, gold for lead. For *a priori*, we can never see why the same matter that is now the supporter of the quality of the lead might not one day become the supporter of the quality of the gold" (WWR, II, 306; 307, 309). It follows that the relation between body and soul, matter and mind is an inexplicable but natural "mystery."

> The Will in itself is absolutely free and entirely self-determining and for it there is no law (WWR, I, 285). We shall also recognize the perfect truth and deep meaning of Malebranche's doctrine of occasional causes [God's continuous miracle coordinating body and soul]. It is well worthwhile to compare this doctrine of his, as he explains it in the *Recherche de la Verite* ...and the *Eclaircissements*...with my present description and to observe the perfect agreement of the two doctrines.... Indeed I must admire how

> Malebranche...hit on the truth so happily, so correctly...Malebranche is right; every natural cause is only an occasional cause. It gives the opportunity, the occasion, for the phenomenon of that one and indivisible Will, which is the in-itself of all things, and whose graduated objectification is this whole visible world.
> WWR, I, 137–138

Schopenhauer thus substitutes the Will for Malebranche's God. We recall Hume was also familiar with Malebranche's "occasionalist" thesis and takes full advantage of it in his own solution to the problem of Cartesian dualism (Hume, *Treatise,* 249–250). In the empirical world, any thing is possible short of a logical or metaphysical contradiction. And there exists not only multiple levels of consciousness but also infinite expressions of reality as well as acts of will and passion.

Obviously, the relation between the sphere of the reflexive self, the phenomenal realm of the outer world, and the noumenal Will is highly problematic in Schopenhauer. There is, however, a second clue to the one previously tendered about Schopenhauer's system and its likeness to a tree. Toward the close of the second book when he returns to the image about the tree and its roots he states, "In the supplement to the second volume, the Will was compared to the root of the tree and the intellect to the crown; and so inwardly or psychologically it is" (*WWR,* II, 510). This connects with the earlier statement commented upon.

> Know your inner being as precisely that which is so filled with the thirst for existence; recognize it once more in the inner, mysterious sprouting force of the tree. This force is always *one* and the same in all the generations of leaves and it remains untouched by arising and passing away.
> WWR, II, 478

Imagine a hundred-year-old oak tree. The Will is represented by the underlying hidden contorted roots beneath the earth supporting the entire tree; consciousness of the self is like the connecting trunk of the tree; the branches are the sustaining physical, reflexive, and intentional tributaries; and the ever-changing leaves are like our sensations, feelings, and thoughts while silhouetted above everything is the arc of the canopy, the crown of the tree as a visible unified whole. The will to live is the thirst for existence. The trunk of the self connects the phenomenal realm to the subterranean roots of the subconscious. There is an inexplicable co-relation between the roots below and the branches above and it is one of mutual co-existence but not mutual knowability.

But however we choose to interpret Schopenhauer, the simplicity premise will confront us at every turn. If phenomena appear to be in some sense material and spatial, then certainly the active noumenal Will cannot be either.

What has Schopenhauer proved? If indeed the Will is a cauldron of irrationality tirelessly animating human desires, thoughts and actions, then Schopenhauer's metaphysical contentions prove that not only is man an irrational animal but even worse a remarkably dangerous one.

Having lived in Europe and North Africa as a child during the entirety of the Second World War and later growing up surrounded by events and stories about Buchenwald, Treblinka, Dachau, Auschwitz, and especially Jasenovac, and today being exposed to the current repetitious news stories about the gratuitous evil and the cruelties occurring in the Middle East, where I doubly spent my formative years, I find it even more frightening now because of the potential of the greater destructive power from all the novel armaments and their global proliferation. The ability of man to wreak greater harm today than before leads to a genuine possibility of the complete self-extermination of humanity and its total annihilation. The strange image of the final scene of the movie, *Planet of the Apes*, keeps recurring to me: the human hero stumbling along the shore and suddenly falling upon the half-buried Statue of Liberty. And the realization that we may have done all this to ourselves before is frightening. Perhaps the Eternal Recurrence of the Stoics and Nietzsche is the best we can expect from ourselves. An endless repetition of violence and self-immolation!

I have concentrated on Schopenhauer at considerable length because his concept of an irrational universal Will "operating within" or "influencing" us is congenial to my own psychological conviction that each of us—independently of Schopenhauer's metaphysical Will—is motivated by unpredictable subconscious impulses toward both good and evil and everything in between. The critical difference between Schopenhauer's position and my own is that I ground the predilection for evil in man's subconscious soul rather than in a metaphysical Will. Perhaps Schopenhauer would have been tempted to do the same had he lived in Germany during the two world conflicts. It's simply amazing how the highest intellectual accomplishments of Kant, Fichte, and Hegel could have turned into the Nazi atrocities perpetrated from 1933 until 1945. Even today we learn that nations with nuclear capabilities are threatening each other with complete annihilation. Madness!

Quite different is the attitude of the German Romantics, although once again Schelling begins his first phase of subjective idealism by positing the simplicity premise as the founding principle for his metaphysical outlook in regard to both freedom and eternity. For Schelling, the Ego's essence is freedom; that is the Ego cannot be conceived except in so far as it posits itself through its absolute power as pure Ego and never as any *thing*. This freedom may be positively ascribed directly to it and not to any external thing-in-itself but only to an Ego, which is pure, immaterial, autonomous, and self-conscious. Its defining characteristic is that the Ego is exclusively present to itself alone.

> In all of us there dwells a mysterious and wonderful power to withdraw into our selves from the changes of time into our innermost self, freed from all that comes to us from without and to intuit the eternal in us under the form of immutability. This intuition is the most inward and the most individual of experiences, upon which alone depends all that we know and believe in a supersensible world. This intellectual intuition appears then when we cease to be an *object* to our selves; when withdrawn into itself, the intuiting self is identical with the intuited. In this moment of intuition, time and duration vanish for us; we are no longer in time but time is in us—or rather *not* time but pure, absolute eternity.[8]

There is an absolute and pure time that is completely independent of space and the Ego when it is "experienced," intuited in its highest feeling state; when it has its whole unbounded activity concentrated in a single point. To think of time as extended along a line is to introduce it as dependent on space. Space is extensity; pure time is unextended intensity. Further according to Schelling, the true Ego can be directly known in intuition as a pure unity, one in which there are no parts external to each other. Given in this fashion, the pure Ego experiences itself as an unextended consciousness of time.

> Because the Ego is indivisible, it is likewise incapable of change. For it cannot be changed by anything external. But if it were self-changed, it would

---

8  Quoted in A.O. Lovejoy, *The Reason, the Understanding, and Time* (Baltimore: Johns Hopkins University Press, 1961), 78–79 and 81–82; cf. also Schopenhauer, *WWR*, I, 178–179, 198; the self entirely loses itself, immerses itself in being, in time. Schelling's Ego is exclusive simplicity, eliminating all multiplicity within itself, whereas Bergson's *durée* is a multiplicity in a unity. The *durée* does not "change" in any empirical sense but rather it "becomes," which is to say that its freedom emanates, arises dynamically from within, spontaneously. For a helpful and comprehensive historical discussion regarding the continuous unity of the soul or mind as a center of consciousness. See Professor Lewis E. Ford, "Boethius and Whitehead on Time and Eternity," *Philosophical Quarterly*, VII:1 (1968), 39–53, for the distinction between exclusive and inclusive simplicity. Cf. C.D. Broad, *The Mind and Its Place in Nature* (London: Routledge and Kegan Paul, 1925), Chapter 13. Nevertheless, for the purposes of this chapter, what commands our attention is not Schelling and Bergson's differences on this issue but their mutual debt to the Achilles argument; that the subject and the object, the knower and the known become indissolubly one, simple, unified, and indivisible.

> be necessary that one part of it should be determined by another, it would be divisible. The Ego, therefore, must always be the same, an absolute unity placed beyond the reach of all mutation...One cannot say of it: it was, it will be; but only *it is*...The form of the intellectual intuition of it is eternity.
> LOVEJOY, *RUT*, 77

The eternal time-transcending act of self-consciousness is that which gives existence to all things and therefore does not need any other being to support it. Thus the Ego is eternally the same and unchanging; it cannot even change itself from within. It is not in phenomenal time. We recall that Aristotle's Unmoved Mover is impermeable to change, since in order to suffer change a substance must first alter within itself; but if it is simple, it has no internal "parts"; it is Its own Self and therefore cannot change. If we request the argument upon which the preceding conclusion rests, we may turn to another passage from Schelling provided by Lovejoy.

> Of qualities as such we have no concepts, but only intuitions and feelings. Even of our own existence we have a feeling and no concept...When we say that we have explained a quality, we mean simply that we have reduced it to figure, number, position, and motion, have resolved it into those ideas—which is merely a way of saying that in the objective [external] world we have annulled quality altogether.
> LOVEJOY, *RUT*, 134–135

A critical distinction thus follows between time and space with pure time defined as the realm of *qualities* in contrast to space as absolutely homogeneous and therefore entirely destitute of qualitative differentiation: "What has magnitude in time only, we call quality. No one has ever supposed that color, taste, and smell are something in space" (Lovejoy, *RUT*, 135). This is important because it means that qualities—*qua sensations and feelings*—are pure inextensive realities. Remember our discussion of the *minima sensibilia* in Chapter 2.

In order to more fully understand the dynamics of internal time-consciousness, it is helpful to start with a fundamental distinction provided by C.S. Peirce, who was strongly influenced by Kant. The distinction centers on the immediate nature of sensations and the mediacy of thought. Both are required in order to account for the experience of time-consciousness as an *internal* flowing stream within subjective consciousness:

> We observe two sorts of elements of consciousness, the distinction between which may best be made clear by means of an illustration. In a

piece of music there are the separate notes and there is the air. A single tone may be prolonged for an hour or a day, and it exists as perfectly in each second of that time as in the whole taken together; so that, as long as it is sounding, it might be present to a sense from which everything in the past was completely absent as the future itself. But it is different with the air, the performance of which occupies a certain time, during the portions of which only portions of it are played. It consists in an orderliness in the succession of sounds which strike the ears at different times; and to perceive it there must be some continuity of consciousness which makes the events of a lapse of time present to us. We certainly only perceive the air by hearing the separate notes; yet we cannot be said to directly hear it, for we hear only what is present at the instant, and an orderliness of succession cannot exist in an instant. These two sorts of objects, what we are *immediately* conscious of and what we are *mediately* conscious of, are found in all consciousness. Some elements (the sensations) are completely present at every instant so long as they last, while others (thoughts) are actions having beginning, middle, and end, and consist in a congruence in the succession of sensations which flow through the mind. They cannot be immediately present to us, but must cover some portion of the past or future. Thought is the thread of melody running through the succession of our sensations.[9]

What is clear in Peirce's discussion of the nature of internal time-consciousness is that it addresses the issue from *within* consciousness and avoids trying to account for time in terms of the measure of motion in space, which explains time as the perception of objects moving in and through space. Peirce thus distinguishes two sorts of elements *within* consciousness, both immediate sensations and mediate thoughts. What he calls the "air" in a piece of music actually consists of *thoughts* that continuously unify and bind the sensory notes together, to each other. The notes alone would produce nothing. It is the air, the melody that temporally threads the musical strings throughout thus producing the *meaningful* experience of hearing the music. Neuroscientific neurons and synapses fail to adequately account for that sort of experience as well shall see in Chapter 6.

Husserl similarly avails himself of the same analogy in order to phenomenologically describe his notion of internal time-consciousness. Hearing sounds and listening to a melody are very different experiences. It is the *relational* identity, unity, and continuity of the tune that is at stake.

---

9  C.S. Peirce, "How To Make Our Ideas Clear," in *Essays in the Philosophy of Science*, edited by Vincent Tomas (New York: Liberal Arts Press, 1957), 37–38.

When, for example, a melody sounds the individual notes do not completely disappear when the stimulus or the action of the nerve excited by them comes to an end. When the new note sounds, the one just preceding it does not disappear without a trace; otherwise, we should be incapable of observing the *relations* between the notes, which follow one another. We should have a note at every instant, and possibly in the internal between the sounding of the next an empty phase, but never the *idea* [or intentional meaning] of a melody. On the other hand, it is not merely a matter of the presentations of the tones simply persisting in consciousness. Were they to remain unmodified, then instead of a melody we should have a chord of simultaneous notes or rather a disharmonious jumble of sounds such as we should obtain if we struck all the notes simultaneously that have already been sounded. Only in this way, namely, that the peculiar modification occurs, that every sensation, after the stimulus which begets it has disappeared, awakens from within itself a similar presentation provided with a *temporal* determination, and that this determination is *continually* varied, can we have the presentation of a melody in which the individual notes have their definite place and their definite measure of time.[10]

---

10   Edmund Husserl, *The Phenomenology of Internal Time-Consciousness* (Bloomington, IN: Indiana University Press, 1966), 23, 30–31. In the book, Husserl invokes the role of fantasy and imagination in securing the "stream of consciousness" (page 33); as "creative" as opposed to empirically repetitive once more feeding off Kant's "productive imagination" (pages 53–54, 60, 68, 73); and it is also coupled with Kant's "unity of consciousness" (page 145). Cf., Ben Mijuskovic, "Loneliness and Time-Consciousness," *Philosophy Today*, XXII:4 (1978), 276–286. Beyond the involvement of the simplicity argument in the service of the German Romantics, it also figured prominently in the more "psychologistically" oriented views on temporality of Herbart, Lotze, and Brentano. Thus, for instance, Husserl chides his former teacher for expressing the following argument:
"For the comprehension of a sequence of representations (A and B, for example) it is necessary that they be the absolutely simultaneous objects of a referential cognition which embraces them completely and indivisibly in a single unifying act. All representations of a direction, a passage, or a distance—in short, everything which includes the comparison of several elements and expresses the relation between them—can be conceived only as the product of a temporally comprehensive act of cognition. Such representations would all be impossible if the act of representation itself were completely merged in temporal succession. On this interpretation, the assumption that the intuition of a temporal interval takes place in a now, in a temporal point, appears to be self-evident and altogether inescapable. In general it appears as a matter of course that every consciousness which concerns any whole or any plurality of distinguishable [temporal] moments ... encompasses its object in an indivisible temporal point. Whenever consciousness is directed toward a whole whose parts are successive, there can be an intuitive consciousness of

For Husserl as well as Peirce, the melody consists in, is constituted by the *temporal relation*—the immediate/mediate syntheses between the separate notes while the intentional, transcending structure of the melody is actively synthesizing them. Single immediate sensations in and of themselves cannot be melodious.

Recall for Schelling, qualities are intensive magnitudes while space is homogeneous and extensive. Qualities as pure can be given immediately and inextensively in consciousness. Just so for Bergson, when we think of a melody, "the notes succeed one another, yet we perceive them *within* one another and their totality may be compared to a living being whose parts, although distinct, permeate one another just because they are so closely connected," i.e., they are temporally *fused* into and within each other.[11] In other words, unlike Peirce and Husserl, Bergson, similarly to Schelling, wishes to avoid temporal successions and emphasize instead an intuitive temporal unity—Husserl's duration. A musical composition is not extended in space (like a painting) but rather it is both a flowing collapse as well as a retention of past, present, and even future notes. Paintings are essentially spatial whereas melodies are by their very nature temporal. But what is so problematically puzzling in regard to the temporal nature of consciousness is exemplified in hearing the *immediate,* the *separate* notes in a piece of music, while in the *same* moment the activity of the mind mediately blends, fuses, and melts the notes into a single unified harmonious whole while *the simple, single* moments transcend each other in constituting and forming a *continuous* melody. There are the separate notes and there is the air. But how can something that is immediate be continuous? (Bergson, TFW, 103–104, 111, 162–163, 171, 231). All three philosophers, Peirce, Husserl, and Bergson appeal to both the notes and the melody in order to *describe*—not cause—the flow or stream of internal time-consciousness. In effect, the analogy between consciousness

---

this whole only if the parts combine in the form of representatives of the unity of the momentary intuition" (*Phenomenology of Internal Time-Consciousness,* §7).

To be sure, Brentano's conception of temporality is syllogistically argumentative, whereas Husserl's professes to be "immanently descriptive" and given intuitively, immediately; nevertheless, it remains to be seen whether Husserl's own account, with its collapsing of protentions and retentions into the "immediate flow" of subjective consciousness, is not also grounded in the very same paradigm of the indivisibility and unity of temporal consciousness as that of Brentano. Again, I regard this passage to be welcome confirmation of the continuing influence of the simplicity premise. Cf. Ben Mijuskovic, "Brentano's Theory of Consciousness," *Philosophy and Phenomenological Research,* XXXVIII:3 (1978), 315–375.

11   Henri Bergson, *Time and Free Will: An Essay on the Immediate Data of Consciousness,* translated by F.L. Pogson (New York: Harper & Row, 1960), 100; 110–111. Cf. C.E.M. Joad, *How Our Minds Work* (London: Westhouse, 1946), 65–66.

and listening to a song offers an important insight not only into the process by which the mind is able to think and function but also the realization that without the *quality* of time, there can be no consciousness at all. Listening to a "piece" of music is a *qualitative* experience and not a quantitative one. The written musical score is quantitative but not the harmony. It also highlights the fact that throughout the music playing (a) the immediate notes and (b) the activity of binding them together is required in order to form synthetic *a priori* temporal connections. In consciousness, the "element" of the sensations is passively and directly experienced, while the process of thinking is mediately activated from within to produce the structures of an immanent time-consciousness. All three philosophers, however, are collectively critical of "explaining" time in terms of the measure of moving objects traveling through space and reject the appeal to a spatial analysis of consciousness in terms of matter and motion. What is critical is that a melody is a synthetic and relational *meaning*. Dogs can hear sounds but they don't sing or dance. A howl is not a song.

For Bergson, we recall, *all* sensations—colors, sounds, and touches—as qualities—are likewise non-extended (*TFW,* pp. 31–32, 90, 92, 106, 130, 213). The intuitive awareness of true Being or Reality is in essence a subjective, qualitative, heterogeneous, concrete, and immediate "lived"—as opposed to mechanical—experience diametrically opposed to the mechanizing stimulus-response paradigm advocated in the neurosciences.

In more general terms, for the scientific mind, for someone who is empirically oriented, a "song" is merely a set of associated stimuli and responses. The notes can be objectively and uniformly measured by diverse observers in terms of pitch, tonality, number, and order. The whole operation is conducted from the outside, externally. But for Peirce, immediate sensations and mediate thoughts constitute the essence of the song's presentation. The approach is from within the subjective mind. For Husserl, a song carries a structural intentional meaning emanating from the composer's wish to please and the listener's with to be pleased. And for Bergson, each song presents unique qualities, of sound, sadness, joy, rhythm, harmony, beauty fused into a single moment throughout the performance.

Bergson's approach to the simplicity argument is two-fold. He recruits it in order to connect it to both the freedom as well as the temporal nature of consciousness. His views on time-consciousness are an attempt to unify intuitive consciousness *with* reality; and more specifically *with the freedom of the temporality of becoming*. In *Creative Evolution,* he holds that "the spontaneity of life is manifested by a continual creation of new forms succeeding each other," which he identifies with freedom. Thus freedom is applicable to the species as well as to the individual.

Starting with Leibniz, increasingly idealist thinkers appeal to spontaneity as an ultimate grounding principle in combating determinism as well as penetrating the inner recesses of time-consciousness. Qualities as presences in consciousness are (a) simple, indivisible (having no parts); (b) intrinsically unified (again, what has no parts cannot be a disunity); (c) *qualitatively* heterogeneous and uniquely varying; and (d) unrepeatable. Quantities, by contrast, *appear* as (a) extended, manifold, divisible; (b) inherently disunified (each component part excluding every other); (c) homogeneous (qualitatively the same); and (d) essentially reproducible, since in their nature of abstract conceptions they are entirely devoid of any *essential* distinguishable qualitative features. For Bergson, each experience is *existentially* unique. His goal is to distinguish the immediacy of intuition from the mediacy of the intellect. Thus he insists that we can apprehend ultimate reality only through certain qualitatively temporal moments that are given in pure intuition; through a specialized form of durational intuition. The artificial and analytic cognitive faculty of the understanding spatializes,, separates, quantifies, and "spreads out" our consciousness of the "world" for practical and scientific purposes. Bergson's premise is once again grounded in the contention that consciousness is not extended or physical.

> We generally say that a movement takes place *in* space, and when we assert that motion is homogeneous and divisible, it is the space traversed that we are thinking of, as if it were interchangeable with motion itself. Now, if we reflect further, we shall see that the successive positions of the moving body really do occupy space, but the process by which it passes from one position to the other, a process which occupies duration and which has no reality except for a conscious spectator, eludes space. We have to do here not with an *object* but with a *process;* motion [i.e., duration], in so far as it is a passage from one [indivisible] point to another, is a mental *synthesis,* a psychic and therefore unextended process...We are thus compelled to admit that we have here to do with a *synthesis,* which is, so to speak, qualitative, a gradual organization of our successive sensations, a unity resembling that of a phrase in a melody.
> BERGSON, *TFW,* 110–111

Further insight is provided by Ian Alexander's commentary.

> The time of consciousness, *temps vécu* [individually lived time] is something quite different from the time of the physicist and the clock-time of everyday use. Whereas the latter consists of discrete points juxtaposed in

a homogeneous medium, which has all the characteristics of space, the former is a *duration,* a fusion of heterogeneous instants, an indivisible flux and becoming: the one is a quantitative, numerical relation; the other a qualitative, internal relation. The first is the product of intelligence which, for the better handling of reality, analyses, disjoins, 'spatializes'; its instrument is analysis, its mode of progress is [analytic] discourse, and its materials are concepts. The second is the object of immediate experience, grasped in an intuition, when, by [reflexively] turning back upon itself, the mind seizes its own activity at the source in the full *spontaneity* of its becoming. Moreover, it is in every sense a reality, an 'absolute,' being the very substance of mind and consciousness which, ceasing to be temporal, would vanish.... Thus the mind can attain knowledge of the absolute by intuition, for 'an absolute can only be given in intuition.'[12]

Once more, the term spontaneity gets the entire enterprise going. Without spontaneity, there is no intuition and no reflexion. Interestingly, one of the consequences of Bergson's theory seems to be that *if* scientific, objective, and causal time were reversed, *then* its backward direction could not be repeated and the same events could not be reproduced in the same reverse order. This would demonstrate that external, objective, scientific time is not even uniform with itself. It would be like a sort of reverse entropy. Hume we recall questioned the assumption that nature is uniform, that the future will necessarily resemble the past. But on this account not even the past will resemble itself or be uniform with itself. Hume, however, was only speculating in one direction.

For Bergson it is because of the *qualitative,* subjective features of "lived time," *le temps vécu* (above), that each moment of consciousness is intrinsically unique—irreversibly backward and unpredictably forward—that the "sciences" of psychology and sociology are only capable of charting individual conduct and social movements in general and statistical terms. In reality, our wakeful fantasies are often as freely structured as our dreams. And there is no more of a "causal" order in our fantasies than in our dreams.

In summary objective time is the time of clocks and calendars, of train schedules and children's birthdays. We share it with our friends and no less with the world at large. But subjective time is intimately personal. I may share my objective time with my dentist but I do not share my time in the dental chair with him.

---

12  Ian Alexander, *Bergson: Philosopher of Reflection* (London: Bowes & Bowes, 1957), 8–10. Notice the term "spontaneity"; again, especially in the rationalist and idealist tradition, it signals a causeless creation, a beginning without a prior cause.

A dedicated opponent of Bergson, Wyndham Lewis, places full responsibility for the introduction of time, with all its "unfortunate" current prominence in Western thought, on Bergson.

> It is Bergson who put the hyphen between Space and Time. The at the time unborn hyphen is suggested by him when he is insisting on continuity [and unity], as against, in Descartes, the conceptualizing of time. "Evolution," he writes, "implies a real persistence of the past in the present, a duration which is, as it were, a hyphen, a connecting link." It is out of the Bergsonian "durée" that the hyphenated "space-time," in philosophy, was born. His doctrine of durée is personified; and he has an ecstatic feeling of veneration at the thought of the latter. But at the thought of Space he has nothing but a sensation of disdain and hatred. So to all the pagan, "spatializing" instincts he is hostile…the unfolding of the fan is the spatial image. The closing of it is the time image. They are, respectively, extension and intensity.[13]

Bergson thus concludes that although within our sensations, feelings, and even our values, the essential qualitative ingredients or contents of our consciousnesses are simple, nevertheless a multiplicity can be co-presently given at once in consciousness through the intuitional act of "durational" grasping.

---

13  Wyndham Lewis, *Time and Western Man* (Boston: Beacon Hill, 1957), 419; hereafter cited as *TWM*; originally published in 1927, the same year as Heidegger's *Being and Time* and Heisenberg's Principle of Uncertainty; the entire chapter is well worth reading. Thus, "duration only exists for us, because of the mutual inter-penetration of our [non-extended, simple] states of consciousness" (*TWM*, 422–423); further, "It is produced by the manipulation of Kant's idea of 'intensive quality,' which is at the bottom of Bergson's conception of time—a use, it is hardly necessary to say, to which Kant did not anticipate its being used" (425). Lewis thus lays the blame for Bergson's conception of quality as purely intensive at Kant's transcendental doorstep (425); cf., Ian Alexander, *Bergson* (Bowes, 1957), pp. 8–9, 22. See also A.O. Lovejoy, *The Reason, the Understanding and Time* (Baltimore: Johns Hopkins University Press, 1961), especially Lecture V and the Appendix, for an excellent and thorough discussion of Bergson's views on time; hereafter cited as *RUT*. Both Lewis and Lovejoy connect Bergson's theories with the British and German Romantic movements in philosophy, literature, and poetry. For a helpful comprehensive discussion regarding the *continuous* unity of the soul or mind as a center of consciousness; for an extended historical discussion, confer Lewis E. Ford, "Boethius and Whitehead on Time and Eternity," *Philosophical Quarterly*, VIII, 1 (1968), 39–42, 49–53; and consult C.D. Broad, *The Mind and Its Place in Nature* (London: Routledge and Kegan Paul, 1925), Chapter 13, which provides a thorough schematic analysis concerning the continuous unity of mind symbolized by the self as a unified metaphysical center.

This paradigm of temporal co-presence is thus the product of a spontaneous, creative *act*. Again, both freedom and time are inextricably bound.

> "Duration" is what occurs when we completely telescope the past into the present, and make our life a fiery point "eating" like an acetylene flame into the future. "Duration" is *inside us,* not outside. There is nothing but "mathematical [spatial and measurable] Time" outside us. "Duration" is the *succession* of our conscious states, but *all felt at once* and somehow, caught in the act of generating the "new" as "free"....It is the organization of the past into a moving and changing present, into an incessantly renewed intensive quality...Memory, on the other hand, unorganized, with its succession of extended units, is that degraded *spatial-time*.... "Duration" is all the past of an individual crammed into the present, and yet this present is not the bare present that forgets its past and is unconscious of its future. [Rather] the past is hauled in like a rope, and concentrated upon the present spot, gathered into unity by action.
> LEWIS, *TWM*, 422

Thus "duration only exists for us because of the mutual [inter-]penetration of our [non-extended] states of consciousness" (Lewis, *TWM*, 423).

Once more:

> Real time or duration is therefore what gives meaning and significance; it is the essence or 'sense' of things. And this is so because it is a structure or form. Pure change and heterogeneity it is, but the heterogeneity of organic [temporal] growth, which does not exclude continuity but indeed implies qualitative heterogeneity and unity within multiplicity...As for space, it is the representation of an infinitely divisible homogeneous medium wherein we can locate the isolated juxtaposed images which substitute for the mutual penetration of our states of consciousness, pure quantity without quality.
> ALEXANDER, *BPOR*, 22

What is so significant in this passage is that Alexander is maintaining that Bergson is arguing that duration *and* meaning are intrinsically related as a "continuous intuition" (perhaps similar to the Cartesian cogito, which is continuous as long as it is contemplated). This would mirror Husserl's struggle to connect *eidetic* meaning, intuition, time-consciousness, and unity all together at once; to seal an inseparable *conceptual* connection, a *meaningful* relation between time-consciousness and unity. Again, any effort in this direction, whether successful or not, can only rest on the Achilles argument. Try doing these unifications with brain neurons and synapses. Once more, it is Kant who is the most dominant figure in all this; it is Kant's luminous shadow that rises above all others.

We can now interject the Battle of the Giants and the Gods in Bergson's own words.

> The fact is that there is no point of contact between the unextended and extended, between quality and quantity. We can interpret the one by the other, set up the one as equivalent to the other; but sooner or later, at the beginning or at the end, we shall have to recognize the conventional character of our assimilation...And the more our knowledge increases, the more we perceive the extensive behind the intensive, quantity behind quality, the more also we tend to thrust the former into the latter, and to treat our sensations as [spatial] magnitudes. Physics, whose particular function it is to calculate [and predict] the external cause of our internal states, takes the least possible interest in these states themselves; constantly and deliberately it confuses them with their cause.
> *TFW*, 70–71

The important consideration is that whatever we decide about our sensory, affective, and thinking consciousnesses, a single truth remains.

> There is at least one reality which we all seize from within, by intuition and not by abstract conceptual analysis. It is our own person in its journey through time, the self which endures. With no other thing can we sympathize intellectually or spiritually. But one thing is sure, we sympathize with our selves.[14]

The existence of which we are most assured and which we know best is unquestionably our own, for of every other object we have notions, which may be considered external and superficial, whereas for ourselves, our perception is both internal and profound.

Concerning the critical issue of the unity of consciousness, Bergson writes the following:

> That the personality has unity is certain: but such an affirmation does not teach me anything about the extraordinary nature of this unity which is

---

14   Henri Bergson, *A Study in Metaphysics: The Creative Mind,* translated by Mabelle Andison (Totowa, NJ: Littlefield Adams, 1970), 162–163.

the person. That our self is multiple I further agree, but that there is in it a multiplicity which, it must be recognized, has nothing in common with any other. What really matters to philosophy is to know what unity, what multiplicity, what reality superior to the abstract one and the abstract multiple is the multiple unity of the person. And it will know this only if it once again grasps the simple intuition of the self [as object] by the self [as subject].[15]

The entire plausibility of these claims, however, depends on a single premise and two interrelated moves: (1) sensations are qualitatively simple; (2) feelings are likewise qualitatively simple; and (3) all awarenesses are given temporally in consciousness (Bergson, CM, 12–20). It follows that time and consciousness (or the "soul," "self," "mind," or "ego") are essentially identical and hence equated by Bergson.

Seven years later, Bergson modifies his views as he valiantly tries to offer a "frankly dualistic" philosophy.

> The problem is no less than that of the union of soul and body. It comes before us clearly and with an urgency because we make a profound distinction between matter and spirit. And we cannot regard it as insoluble since we define spirit and matter by positive characters, and not by negations. It is in every truth within matter that pure [sic] perception places us, and it is really into spirit that we penetrate by means of memory.[16]

Frequently anti-dualists criticize the definition of an immaterial mind by stating what it is not rather than assigning positive predicates to it. For example, dualists maintain that the mind is *not* material; it is *not* extended; it is *not* in space; it is not disunified; etc. But Bergson in this later work is trying to solve "the problem of dualism" by claiming that memory is the experiential bridge connecting "the extended and the unextended on the one side, between quality and quantity on the other side...between inextension and quality on the one side and extensity and quantity on the other side." And he finally concludes by confessing that it is only a hypothesis (Bergson, MM, 292, 293, 296–297, 331). Driven by the exigency of accounting for the union of body and soul, matter

---

15   Henri Bergson, *An Introduction to Metaphysics,* translated by T.E. Hulme (Indianapolis: Bobbs Merrill 1955), 37.
16   Henri Bergson, *Matter and Memory,* translated by N.M. Paul and S.W. Palmer (New York: Humanities, Press, 1962) xi, 234–235; hereafter cited as *MM.* It was originally published seven years after *Time and Free Will* in 1896 as *Matière et mémoire.*

and spirit, Bergson still continues to insist, as he had previously in *Time and Free Will,* on the non-spatial character of our sensations and he repeatedly appeals to various versions of the simplicity argument but now "extended images" intervene as mediating entities (*MM,* Chapter 3, see especially 33, 36, 43–77, 180–181, 235–237, 246, 267–268), and he now paradoxically insists that "*All* sensations partake of extensity" (*MM,* 288–289). What seems to have occurred between Bergson's earlier and later studies is that he became increasingly impressed by investigations in physiological psychology. He cites James Ward, for example, as holding that all sensations are extended. Consequently, he seems to have devised some ingenious, albeit doomed, means of attempting to reintegrate quality and quantity; time and space; the inextensive and the extended; freedom and necessity; and mind and matter, realities which he had originally completely severed. Thus, in *Matter and Memory,* Bergson tries to distinguish between (a) pure memory, as imageless, unextended, indivisible, simple, and immaterial; (b) memory-images, as a "materialized," extensively-presented data of consciousness; and (c) perception, as a physiological, bodily event occurring through the interaction of brain states in conjunction with the external, spatial world (Bergson, *MM,* 180–181). Upon this threefold differentiation, Bergson valiantly, although rather quixotically, strives to secure for his new philosophical undertaking a bridge which will account for what he regards as the real interaction between spirit and matter. Memory (both pure and impure) he is now convinced shall serve as the connecting medium. Memory seemingly has *extensive* causal implications. And he proceeds by seeking to unify the "immediate past" with an impending future unified by an "indivisible present," which together form an "undivided whole" (*MM,* Chapter 3, and especially 176–179, 232; Chapter 4, 235–236, 246 ff., 319–320). Through these later reflections, Bergson offers the bewildered reader some very strange moves in which he tries to give a physiological account of self-consciousness, (*MM,* 123, 127, 205); or worse yet, he seeks to establish a parallel between a physical and a mental model of the unity of consciousness (*MM,* 164–166, 170–171, 214–216). But into all this we need not concern ourselves. Suffice it to say, the entire affair collapses when Bergson tries to "materialize" pure memories, which remain in principle, simple, indivisible, immaterial, and non-extended. The whole bizarre affair appears to be brought about by his determination to reconcile principles that earlier he had so thoroughly opposed to each other in *Time and Free Will.* Finally, he tries to effect a partial accommodation between realism and idealism, which satisfies neither movement.

Despite Bergson's failed attempt, it leaves us in a position to observe how metaphysically difficult it is to mix opposing first principles, as Pascal, Fichte, and William James have warned. Contradictory first principles are just that:

irreconcilable. They cannot be synthesized. In the case of my principles of reflexive self-consciousness and transcendent intentionality, however, the ground for their synthetic *a priori* compatibility is that they are both grounded in spontaneous *acts* of consciousness (Kant and Husserl), in the *activities* of consciousness, and hence not only compatible but indeed universally and necessarily related to each other. The self exhibits the capacity to look inwardly as well as outwardly.

In this chapter, I have maintained that there is an essential affinity, which underlies the claims of certain philosophers, who subscribe to the principle that pure qualities are non-extended, simple, indivisible, and unified. Similarly, duration is not to be represented as consisting of unrelated points on a line or as the movement of a body through space. Quite the contrary, pure duration, says Bergson, is a perfectly compressed "flow," without dimensions and without a predisposed direction. Although it *consumes* a past and a future, it is not a combined past and a future of events causally extended in space. Rather it is a pulsating now, pregnant with the sublated germ of the past and throbbing with the spontaneous birth of possibilities, which are not as yet. Since consciousness is fundamentally temporal and its resident sensations and feelings as directly present to consciousness are simple, indivisible, and unified, it follows that emotions cannot function as the "causes" for our conduct. Subject and object are indissolubly fused into one metaphysical reality, which may be termed "Absolute Being." In turn, this reality can be immediately apprehended in a temporal grasp, as a "lived" intuition, an indivisible duration.

The immanent consciousness of time consists of an awareness of pure, non-extended qualities (as opposed to quantities), whether these qualities are directly given in awareness as (a) sensory *minima sensibilia* that are intrinsically non-extended, purely intensive; or as (b) feelings and desires. The upshot is that the proof from simplicity is exploited by Schopenhauer's theory of the self's transitory intercession with a noumenal eternal Will; by Schelling's unity and identity of self-consciousness with an absolute eternal reality; and by Bergson's intuition of a durational "whole self." The foundational source of agreement for all three thinkers centers on their shared conviction that consciousness of internal time is the central feature of human awareness and that in its most undeniable sense it is *subjectively* present. It follows that because both insular freedom as well as the uniqueness of the inner temporality of consciousness are independent of material and efficient causes, the prediction of human feelings, thoughts, and behaviors is strictly precluded.

In William Barrett's wonderful study of existentialism, he praises Bergson for so powerfully illuminating "the irreducible reality of time" and the immanent nature of consciousness.

Without Bergson the whole atmosphere in which Existentialists have philosophized would not have been what it was. He was the first to insist on the insufficiency of the abstract to grasp the richness of experience, on the urgent and irreducible reality of time, and—perhaps in the long run the most significant insight of all—on the inner depth of the psychic life which cannot be measured by the quantitative methods of the physical sciences.[17]

The impact of immanent time-consciousness is clearly manifest in the "stream of consciousness" narrative styles of James Joyce's *Ulysses,* Thomas Wolfe's *Look Homeward, Angel,* and William Faulkner's *The Sound and the Fury* and *As I Lay Dying.* Professor Barrett observes how in Faulkner's novels, "time, instead of space, is flattened out; past and present is presented as occurring simultaneously" (ibid., 50). Commenting more specifically on Faulkner's *Sound and the Fury,* he states:

> In the course of the last day of his life, Quentin Compson breaks the crystal of his watch. He twists off the two hands and thereafter throughout the day, the watch continues to tick loudly but cannot with its faceless dial, indicate the time...Real time, the time that makes up the dramatic substance of our life, is something deeper and more primordial than watches, clocks, and calendars.
>
> ibid., 53

In Joyce, the emphasis on the immaterial aspects of the temporal unity of consciousness is made evident in the final chapter of *Ulysses* when Molly Bloom divests herself in her uninterrupted soliloquy during the course of a sleepless night. All intimations of space or even objects are completely suspended in the darkness. Molly is alone in the pitch-black night with every suggestion of extended substances bracketed, put out-of-gear. All that exists is her monadic consciousness; a temporal awareness during which she remains entirely confined within her self. Her feelings and fantasies solely revolve around the acts that had transpired on that particular day, June 16, 1904. The utter darkness of her surroundings envelope her while enhancing her journey, her retreat toward the inner confines of the solitary inner chambers of her heart and mind. The temporal filament of her consciousness wanders aimlessly

---

[17] William Barrett, *Irrational Man: A Study in Existential Philosophy* (New York: Random House, 1990), 15; hereafter cited as Barrett, *IM.* Cf., Ben Mijuskovic, "Loneliness and Time-Consciousness," *Philosophy Today,* XXII:4 (1978), 276–286.

during her nocturnal reveries in a continuous stream of consciousness as the ebbs and flows of her desires search through the vagaries of her mind ceaselessly, continuously. Laying in the darkness, with space in abeyance, Molly is certain only of one existence: her own. The unraveling thread of consciousness becomes a temporal melody with intimate and repetitious themes and variations weaving through her consciousness. Through Joyce's narrative style, a single literary structure completely dominates the entire chapter, namely the temporal continuity and unity of her awarenesses. Through the longest unpunctuated sentence in the English language, Joyce seduces the reader to reflexively feel the sense of longing so common during our nocturnal visitations. But then sleep intervenes and consciousness passes its yearnings over to its dreams.

Similarly in Thomas Wolfe's novel, *Of Time and the River*, in a passage reminiscent of Molly Bloom's ruminations, he describes his sister Helen's thoughts of loneliness as she lies enclosed within her personal cocoon of internal time-consciousness.

> A thousand scenes from her past life flashed through her mind now, as she lay there in the darkness, and all of them seemed grotesque, accidental and mistaken, as reasonless as everything in life. And filled with a numb, speechless feeling of despair and nameless terror, she heard somewhere across the night the sound of a train again, and thought:
> 
> "My God! My God! What is life about? We are all lying here in darkness in ten thousand little towns—waiting, listening, hoping—for what?"
> 
> And suddenly with a feeling of terrible revelation, she saw the strangeness and mystery of man's life; she felt about her in the darkness the presence of ten thousand people, each lying in his bed naked and alone, united at the heart of night and darkness, and listening, as she, to the sounds of silence and sleep. And suddenly it seemed to her that she knew all these lonely, strange, unknown watchers of the night, that she was speaking to them, and they to her, across the fields of sleep, as they had never spoken before, that she knew men now in all their dark and naked loneliness, without falseness and pretense as she had never known them. And it seemed to her that if men would only listen in the darkness, and send the language of their naked lonely spirits across the silence of the night, all the error, falseness and confusion of their lives would vanish, they would no longer be strangers, and each would find the life he sought and never yet found.

"If we only could!" she thought. "If we only could!"

But the poignant glimmer of possible optimism, shining through the opaque obscurity of the night, is irrecoverably extinguished.

> What is wrong with people? Why do we never get to know one another? Why is it that we get born and live and die in this world without ever finding out what any one else is like?...We talk and talk in an effort to understand another person, and yet almost all we say is false; we hardly ever say what we mean or tell the truth—it all leads to greater misunderstanding and fear than before—it would be better if we said nothing.[18]

The train of course symbolizes objective time.

So far throughout the present text, I have sought to interweave the themes of metaphysical dualism and subjective idealism with the freedom of consciousness, and the immanent nature of time-consciousness. I submit that the richness and complexity of human consciousness requires nothing less than a frank acknowledgment and a concerted appraisal of the power of the Achilles argument in relation to these existentialist themes as they dominate the throes of human consciousness and loneliness.

---

[18] Thomas Wolfe, *Of Time and the River,* Chapter 25; see also *Look Homeward, Angel,* Preface, and *You Can't Go Home Again,* IV, 31. The sound of the train symbolizes time. Again, sounds are primarily temporal while colors are essentially spatial. Wolfe frequently appeals to metaphors of sounds, hearing, and particularly listening in order to convey the impression of loneliness; cf. C. Hugh Holman, *The Loneliness at the Core: Studies in Thomas Wolfe* (Baton Rouge, LA: Louisiana State University Press, 1975), 27–30, 52–53, 69–70, and 122 ff. for discussions of Wolfe's concept of temporal subjectivity.

CHAPTER 5

# The Simplicity Argument and the Quality of Consciousness

> Quality therefore is immediate determinateness, and as such is prior and must constitute the Beginning.
> HEGEL, *Science of Logic*

∴

## 1       Introduction to the Chapter

The simplicity argument plays a major role in both an *epistemological* as well as an *ontological* context. Since these two uses will be very different and distinct, they must be treated separately. Historically, the Achilles argument dominates the epistemic theories of consciousness in the subjective idealism of Kant and it also assumes a critical role in the objective idealism of Hegel (and later Sartre). More specifically, the issue turns on the difference between the functions the categories of Quality and Quantity serve for the two philosophers and the reasons for their divergence.

The thesis of the current chapter is that in individual consciousness qualities as simple, immaterial existents are *intrinsically* immediate, transient, and *inherently* incapable of being incorporated within strict determinist, i.e., causal structures. This essential limitation applies to both psychoanalysis and the current neurosciences as they pursue their different methods of gaining insight into human behavior, its prediction, and/or its control. Consciousness has two elements: passive contents and relational acts, and both have to be adequately accounted for.

In *Feeling Lonesome,* in the chapter titled "The Unconscious and the Subconscious," I discuss at length Kant's *creative* "productive imagination"—as distinguished from its *empirical* or "re-productive" counterpart, which is restricted to phenomenal sensations and the empirical "association of ideas" principle. The productive imagination is *spontaneous.* It is inherently generative and therefore responsible for the crea*tion* of immanent time-consciousness as well as the unity of apperception. I cannot emphasize enough that when I describe the mind as active or spontaneous, this is the most essential feature of consciousness. Leibniz, Kant, Fichte, Hegel, Schopenhauer and later Bergson, Husserl, Royce, and Sartre all invoke its centering virtues. Hegel is more subtle and circumspect as he disguises his notion of spontaneity within his dialectical method of progressively positing, negating, and unification but its powers are clearly implicit in the transcending features of the dialectic as we observed in his description of the passage from Sense-Certainty to Perception when he connects the subject to the object in the *Phenomenology* (Section 116) and in the *Philosophy of Mind* (Sections 456, 457).

For Schopenhauer, although he does not specifically mention spontaneity, it forms the basis for his transcendent metaphysical Will as it indirectly but "influentially" surfaces through phenomenal self-consciousness. In one fashion or another, however, each thinker—e.g., Kant, Hegel, and Schopenhauer—is careful in his own fashion to make a critical allowance for the active nature of consciousness. But if the activity of consciousness is initially spontaneous, its immaterial *contents* essentially consist of determinate but unextended qualities.[1] Accordingly, the initiating *formative* power of the mind has to be attributed to *acts* of spontaneity that are capable of generating relations as well as structures of connection that impregnate the soul with intentionality and meaning. But unlike Kant's overly restrictive rigorous principles that limits the relational categories to only twelve, as Husserl suggests, there are innumerable synthetic *a priori* possibilities of connection that are operative as long as they are logically compossible (Leibniz), as long as they avoid internal contradictions and ring true in *eidetic* intuition and insight.

Although Hume sought to emulate Newton's influence in the realm of the natural sciences with his own version of psychological gravitation through the "association of ideas" principle, his challenge was very different because Hume also quite deliberately turned loose the swarms of impressions and then it became impossible to rebundle them without an active force in consciousness to unify them, to knit them together. Following Francis Hutcheson, this led to Hume's "new scene of thought" (Kemp Smith, *Philosophy of David Hume*, 18–20). In effect, Hume collapsed the distinction between the immediacy of impressions and the mediacy of relations by reducing them to feelings, to sentiments of *belief* as opposed to a system of *knowledge*. With this strategy, Hume basically replaces reason with the imagination and relations with feelings.

---

[1] Ben Mijuskovic, "The Simplicity Argument and the Unconscious: Plotinus, Cudworth, Leibniz, and Kant," *Philosophy and Theology*, 20:1&2 (2008–09), 53–83; "Kant's Reflections on the Unity of Consciousness, Time-Consciousness, and the Unconscious," *Kritike*, 4:2 (2010), 105–132; *Feeling Lonesome: The Philosophy and Psychology of Loneliness* (Santa Barbara, CA: Praeger, 2015), Chapter 7, "The Unconscious and the Subconscious," 149–172; and "The Cognitive and Motivational Roots of Loneliness," *Addressing Loneliness; Coping, Prevention and Clinical Interventions* (London: Routledge, 2015), 20–33.

In many respects the eighteenth-century can be called the Age of the Imagination. Hume's impressions and ideas only differ in vivacity and faintness and he admits that upon occasion ideas may be more forceful and vivacious than impressions, e.g., a nightmare as opposed to walking in a fog. And Hume's demolishment of the reliability of the causal principle pretty much concludes that all that is left are impressions, ideas, and more or less forceful beliefs, i.e., feelings. This is what passes for knowledge: simple and compound impressions (currently termed sense qualia or sense data); their fainter ideas; associative feelings; and beliefs. Subsequently William James, in his essay, "A World of Pure Experience," while advocating for his doctrine of "radical empiricism," contends that "relations" are immediately, directly given in experience and thus he fares no better than Hume because the assertion completely breaks down the obvious distinction between sensation and thought, the difference between the immediacy of sensations and the mediacy of relational connections. It is this sort of denial of clear separations that result in Hume's inability to separate the self from the external world and in John Dewey's failure to separate man as the "problem solving organism" from his environment, to clearly distinguish the subject from the object, the dualism of the mind from what it knows. In order to legitimately dichotomize the knower from the known, one has to realize the difference between the qualitative from the quantitative, the intensive from the extensive, the immediately "given" from the mediately "active"; and most of all the contents, i.e., the elements, from their very different functions and roles. If one reduces cognition to the immediacy of impressions, its fainter copies, and feelings of belief, then one has failed to progress beyond the level of mere instincts. But even insects have instincts.

In what follows, we need to distinguish (a) immediate sensations and feelings from mediate thoughts and (b) unextended qualities from extended quantities *in consciousness*. And in order to anticipate future discussions related to human loneliness, I need to point out that humans are first and foremost sensing and feeling creatures and only later thinking beings. It therefore follows that *when—qua* human—we become dominated by compelling immediate *affective* factors, *then* behavioral explanations, psychoanalytic causality, and neuroscientific chartings will consistently go woefully astray. They may have a *surface,* an external objective "meaning" and application, but applied subjectively they are meaningless. Aristotle long ago reminded us that the intellect alone moves nothing: "Intellect itself, however, moves nothing, but only the intellect which aims at an end and is practical" (*Nicomachean Ethics,* VI, 2, 35–37), an intellect aimed at a purposeful, desired goal. It is only *desire* that impels us to imbibe from the trough of material existence. If the intellect is overwhelmed by irrational desires, then obviously the alleged science of prediction must falter and humans will act in radically unexpected ways.

Affects, emotions, and feelings are intrinsically *qualitative*. In connection with acts of spontaneity they frequently result in *affective* crises. When the ego is under full assault from its own subjective feelings and thoughts, then the subconscious manifests itself through destructive and *inexplicable* impulses that are very different from the sources offered by the Freudian unconscious, which assumes a series of causal structures determined by antecedent traumatic experiences, forbidden desires, and repressed memories. Fueled by spontaneity, the subconscious is very different from anything psychoanalysis is able to offer. It acts independently of psychoanalytic guidelines, which fail to account for the uncontrollable urges as the human mind first retreats back to the darker abyss of the subconscious and then lurches forward. Precisely because there are spontaneous elements within consciousness, our misshapen surface desires remain fundamentally unrecognizable and impenetrable. It follows that violent and powerful feelings arise *sui generis* and become expressed in our unregulated desires and fantasies, in our impulses, urges, and initiating acts that will always remain to a great extent inexplicable. Often in the parlance of mental health professionals these outbursts are called "acting out behaviors." These are mere superficial descriptions whose actual sources and roots lie deeply twisted within consciousness. The critical point, however, is that spontaneity can lead to a wide spectrum of thoughts and actions: from brilliant intellectual discoveries, wonderful aesthetic expressions, noble ethical principles to acts of sheer violence and self-destruction.

Habits are predictable. Spontaneity is not. For example, is it plausible to claim that one could have predicted Newton's discovery of the law of gravity if they knew his complete biographical history? John Stuart Mill held that if one knew the entire history of each grain of sand on a beach and each drop of water in a wave one could predict how each wave would break. But that model is impossible to apply to human consciousness, to emotions, and to cognition. Imagine telling a friend that you can predict what s/he will do. It then becomes a chess game. Perhaps this is why the *Diagnostic and Statistical Manual of Psychiatric Disorders* wisely restricts itself to simply providing nominal definitions for dysfunctional and affective mental aberrations and avoids all epidemiological theories. It sagely confines itself to merely classifying symptoms and personality disorders while avoiding to inform us on how they came to be or what we can do about them. Classification is the lifeless modality of science; spontaneity is the living expression of consciousness.

How often do we learn or hear about acts of violence perpetrated by individuals and the bewildered response of family members, intimate companions, and ubiquitous peers, who are caught unaware by these unexpected outbursts of aggression and cruelty by those whom they thought they knew so well.

Often we are at a complete loss to "explain" *why* it happened or the "motivation" for the act. The judgments and reactions of those closest to the assailants are frequently the most bewildered and mystified by these "meaningless" eruptions. There is no guarantee that a person's public "character" is a secure prelude to their future choices and behaviors. Despite all our assurances of a close acquaintanceship with the agent, we frequently fail to anticipate what human beings are capable of doing or not doing; or even what we ourselves might do in different circumstances. We can never be too confident in our assessments of what our solitary, hermitic passions might lead us to imagine, think, and commit. The weather of our moods and the tempests of our soul are every bit as unpredictable as the climate outside.

The many limitations of psychoanalysis as a "science" have increasingly become patently obvious. It assumes a strict causal determinism linking past experiences to present symptoms but all too frequently as a science it fails in accounting, predicting, controlling, or relieving the alleged disorders of "disturbed patients."

Assume that Schopenhauer is right about the Will "operating" within the context of an individual consciousness. If so, then it is clearly the case that psychoanalysis is incapable of addressing the much deeper acts and the possible outcome of one's subconscious Will, which he portrays as an irrational, seething, primary force below and independent of the Freudian unconscious. The difference between the subconscious and the unconscious is that the former surges from powerful indeterminate *affective* sources, from essentially *qualitative* origins, while psychoanalysis patiently focuses on excavating presumably determinate causes generally receding back to early childhood for its presumed "insights." Emotions and reasons both dwell within consciousness but they are as distinct and diverse as sound and sight or pain and pleasure.

And how would Schopenhauer portray the German nation from the early 1930s till the end of the Second World War? Who predicted that the most intellectually advanced and sophisticated nation the world had ever known would disintegrate into a systematic impulse to destroy half of humanity?

Legend has it that many years ago there was a famous survey asking psychoanalytic patients about the success of their therapies. A third reported improvements, a third reported setbacks, and a third reported no change. My guess is that if today a similar survey sought results regarding the efficacy of psychiatric medications, the same results would be reported.

The critical barrier to predicting human feelings and thoughts, as it applies to the pretentious claims of medical doctors, psychoanalysts, and behavioral therapists, is that they dismiss out of hand the unbridgeable divide that exists between the *qualitative* factors involved as opposed to the *quantitative* features of consciousness and thereby end up neglecting the most important "determiner" of human existence: its unique submerged affective forces. As Hegel will argue, quality is the *active, generative* source of "conscious movement."

Similarly neuroscience completely disregards the fact that *qualities,* as inextensive non-positional presences in the mind, cannot be in any way or manner "positioned" spatially or causally. In addition, there is no viable possibility of differentiating quantitative from qualitative brain neurons from each other. But without the structural ability to sequentially interconnect neurons with their synaptic causal associations, to secure quantities and qualities to each other, *strict* prediction is impossible. At best, the synaptic electrical impulse is just that, an unpredictable charge. Imagine trying to predict precisely where bolts of lightning will strike in an electrical storm. And the additional problem in the neurosciences is that primary, secondary, and tertiary qualities are all transformed into homogeneous quantitative neuronal factors.

Another major consideration against the possible predictive power of neuroscience is that it is compromisingly implicated in quantum theory, that its paradigm is actually built on shifting bits of sand, since we know that ultimately neurons are composed of minute *quanta,* which move and dart in "discontinuous" motions implying that at best neuroscience can only offer indefinite percentages, gross statistical outcomes for individual behavior much in the same way as sociologists do for large groups of humanity.

A current misconception is that psychology is now finally a science entering into its own, that it will soon be a discipline on all fours with physics, chemistry, biology, and physiology (Auguste Comte); that the neurosciences are already gifted with the ability both to predict and control human behavior. This new scientific perspective is now held hostage by our neuroscientists of today. Similarly, the American Psychiatric Association christened the 1990s as "the decade of the brain" declaring that *all* mental disorders, including depression, anxiety, bipolar disorders, psychosis, etc., are *caused, determined* by contingent hereditary, environmental, cultural, and situational conditions, including chemical imbalances in the brain. By causes and conditions which are transient, avoidable, and readily treated by cognitive behavioral therapy, psychoanalysis, and psychiatric medications. But the truth is that psychology has been around since the *Republic* of Plato and the *De Anima* of Aristotle, and we are no nearer to predicting human thought and behavior—or controlling it (Orwell's *1984*)—than we were two-and-a-half millennia ago. Actually Plato long ago speculated that the soul consisted of three parts: the appetitive, the spirited, and the rational (*Phaedrus*) much in the manner of Freud. But neither Plato nor Aristotle envisioned psychology as a science. Today, the American Psychiatric Association and the prevailing scientific community remain singularly committed to the doctrines of materialism, mechanism, determinism, empiricism, behaviorism ("evidence- based practices"), and the neurosciences. In effect, the behavioral and neuroscientific approaches propose eliminating the mind as a metaphysical fiction altogether. Indeed, Ryle's "ghost in the machine" is now transformed into the "the robot in the brain." The combined "scientific" tenets and goals of the materialists are popularly supported by the writings of neuroscientists and neo-phrenologists like John Cacioppo at the University of Chicago and Patricia and Paul Churchland at the University of California at San Diego (ironically enough two institutions where I spent my tenure of sixteen years as an undergraduate and graduate student respectively). Theoretically these researchers emphasize the application of strictly *causal* and *external*—allegedly "objective"—*quantitative* measurements to the study of human thought by eliminating consciousness and the mind as irrelevant, even non-existent, in favor of charting the electro-chemical reactions in the brain and their consequent publicly observable behaviors. They also strongly advocate for the application of psychiatric medication in the treatment of mental disorders.

Americans are slavishly devoted to the physical and biological sciences and all the latest technological advances, from cell phones to driverless cars to psychiatric medication, which basically leads them to consider not only other human beings as machines but even themselves as such. The paradigm of man as essentially a machine is a common philosophical theme as we previously cited in Leonora Cohen Rosenfield's study, *From Beast-Machine to Man-Machine*.

There are two rather conflicting paradigms of "humanity" that neuroscientists problematically and inconsistently draw upon and seek to exploit. The first is consistently materialistic and the second is basically biological. The first appeals to the metaphor of a machine and essentially regards the brain as a computer. And the second rests on Darwinian evolution. The problem, of course, is that computers do not evolve "from within"; animals and humans however do. In any case, this burgeoning trend toward seriously interpreting mankind as a "computer/animal" began in the seventeenth-century with Descartes view that animals were automatons without souls and feelings.

The Darwinian theory of evolution is obviously correct about the origin of animal species. There is no question we are evolving. But the computer metaphor is more problematic and as we shall see in the next chapter it is buttressed by a further claim that the brain has a power of "neuroplasticity," of "self-modification"; that it is able *to modify itself cellularly;* not only that it somehow "knows" what is "better" or "wiser" for its own cellular composition but that it can physically *alter* the brain and improve it. But "better" and "wiser" are *valuative*—and not chemical or biological—terms and judgments and if they are simply assumed and not proven, then the entire question is begged. Further, there is the chicken and the egg issue: Does the mind trigger the change, or does the brain mutate the mind. In any case, the important issue for both paradigms is that neither the biological nor the computer model are able to account for the *qualitative* elements, which are clearly present and involved in consciousness. This problem will be addressed at greater length in the following chapter.

Throughout the text, I have maintained that there are innate activities; spontaneous acts of reflexive self-consciousness (Kant) as well as acts of transcendent intentionality (Husserl) that are universal, permanent, and necessary features of human consciousness. These acts can only be "productive" by interacting with the qualitative as well as the quantitative factors operating in consciousness and present within consciousness. Materialism denies the *reality* of these qualitative features just as it denies any real distinction between primary, secondary, and tertiary qualities. Only material, measurable quantitative factors exist. That is why in what follows, a case must be made for precisely those determinately important qualitative features.

As mentioned, generally speaking, human beings feel, respond, and behave predictably from *habit.* Few of us indulge in existential *angst* prior to getting into our cars each morning and driving to work. But there are other times during our ordinary lives when we experience varying emotional stressors when the affective and troublesome forces of the mind dominate and overwhelm us by unstructured feelings and thoughts, which explosively burgeon into a spectrum of unresolved issues. These situations primarily have to do with the *quality* of the experiences as they are incubated in the individual mind and therefore they must be approached through a mental—versus a behavioral—perspective.

I remember many occasions when as a Child Protective Services worker I observed fathers, who were legally prevented from returning to their families by court order because of incidents of spousal and/or child abuse and the resulting unpredictable responses that followed. They were uniformally provided with a behavioral "family reunification contract" specifying various mandatory compliances as a condition of family reunification: random drug screenings; no parental visits or only supervised visits; individual or family therapy; mandatory employment searches; etc. Some simply just quit trying and gave themselves up to depression and went back to drinking and drugs; others complied with the treatment plan; and yet others lashed out with rage and threats. Their sense of sudden estrangement, their forced alienation from their families often resulted in retaliatory acts against all those they blamed for their misery and separation. Often dangerously unpredictable to the clinical observer and with situations frequently leading to confrontations as well, it was uncertain how these lonely and lost individuals would react. Often they felt the entire world had turned against them; feeling betrayed and abandoned, they would narcissistically rebel against those they held "accountable," including their own family members, the mothers, the children, and our agency. High security precautions were also instituted in the mental health offices. Lonely, disoriented, and feeling misunderstood, they often turned to violence and acts of retaliation and self-destruction. The point is that in order to try to "understand" their various reactions, one would have to approach them from "within" their feelings and address their experiences primarily in qualitative terms, not quantitative ones and that can only be done from a standpoint of separating the qualitative from the quantitative features, the meaningful from the causal. At best it was a game of chance whether therapeutic interventions "helped." Many times I "understood" their loneliness but never the intricacy of their subconscious feelings. Often I had "insight" into their solitary desperation but seldom knew how to "help" them.

For example, I recall a situation in which a father, who after his divorce was awarded joint physical (but not legal) custody of his teenage son and allowed biweekly overnight visits with him. During such a visit, while the boy was asleep, the father set him on fire in his bed with horrific results. In terms of quantitative or causal factors, no one could have predicted this outcome based on the father's past history. Obviously he had never done anything like this before. But that is just the point. Our lives are chock-full of "first times." Nor am I claiming that one could have predicted it qualitatively. But in order to *understand* the act, to have *insight* into the act, and admittedly *after the fact,* one could phenomenologically "see" the dynamics, the meanings involved; one could *describe* his act as a qualitative "expression" of subconscious animating forces, including issues of displacement, projection, the need to blame others, a desire for vengeance at any cost, the impulse to reassert lost power, the malicious obsession to punish those who had deprived him of his familial entitlements, his indulgence in overweening narcissistic fantasies, abandonment and betrayal issues, etc. In short, one could achieve some *insight* into the deep rage of his loneliness *in retrospect*. But in any case, the ability to consistently predict and successfully prevent dangerous human activity is often highly overrated. In the event I have described, I don't believe this act could have been "predicted"—if that term has a meaning—even by the father himself. But I remain convinced that in cases such as these there are spontaneous subconscious forces at work. Again, phenomenology is a descriptive "science" but not a predictive one and the "best" we can do is simply to look for insights and sacrifice the illusion of control.

Yesterday (October 3, 2017), as I was writing, CNN cable news reported Stephen Padock has just killed fifty-eight people and injured almost five-hundred in Las Vegas and six months later everyone is mystified about his "motives." *Why* did he do it? Not *how* did he do it. That's rather quantitavely clear. But *whys* are qualitative; hows are quantitative.

Imagine if neuroscience were truly a science with all its quantitative and causal tools, instruments, and batteries reliably at its disposal. Then every two years or so we could mandate universal brain scans and imprison or hospitalize individuals *prior* to their commission of violent acts. And even more, by using an individual's DNA as the criterion of a person's self-identity, we could predict how s/he would respond in certain environmental circumstances; we could provide percentages of dangers for violence and then track them throughout their lives.

On another occasion, I remember a long-term schizophrenic client coming late to our clinic for her medication appointment. In this particular case, the psychiatrist declined to see her and instead the patient was directed to reschedule a future appointment through her social worker, who tried to advocate in her behalf but to no avail. That night she killed both her parents and herself with her father's revolver. The psychiatrist resigned shortly thereafter.

The client was in her late forties, and she could have killed herself at anytime between her troubled adolescent years or never done it at all. The local newspaper carried the story about the double murder and suicide unaware that she had been under our "care." But again my point is that no one could have predicted her act including herself. And why? Precisely because of the very sort of *qualitative* considerations that Schopenhauer and Bergson propose. There was something qualitatively different on that *particular* day, in that *particular* visit, in that *particular* incident, on that *particular* night, and in that *particular* relation between her parents and herself and in that *moment* after she arrived home. What transpired involved the spontaneity of a subconscious willing and a heterogeneity of Bergsonian durational qualities.

Not infrequently, social workers are sued when they fail to protect a child, dependent adult, or elderly person, and there are often tragic consequences. I recall a number of workers who "lost a child" on their Child Protective Services caseloads. They left the agency within six months. Easy enough to see what went wrong *after* the tragedy and all the missed "red flags." But the sense of guilt, shame, and failure is overwhelming. It is very difficult to continue to work "professionally" when a child has been murdered, incestuously molested, or tortured, and when the worker has "failed" to remove the child from parental custody.

## 2 Part One: Kant's Transcendental Analytic and Hegel's *Phenomenology*

I now want to turn more directly to the philosophical status of the qualitative-quantitative distinction. In what follows, I intend to recruit an eighth use for the simplicity principle by arguing that the immaterial and active nature of consciousness initially begins with its *qualitative* primacy of subjective sensory and affective features, which often precludes predictability precisely because the qualitative elements cannot be reproduced or reconstructed in a chain of structural causes and events, and hence in many cases there is neither the ability nor the possibility to anticipate or predict what will happen or how to prevent it.

In order to gain a deeper understanding and insight into the subconscious mind, we must start with its subjective immediate *qualitative* features, the *active* factors that lie inherent within awareness, and more specifically with its foundational sensations and feelings of pleasure and pain, comfort and discomfort, excitement and boredom, anger and sadness, fear and resolve, love and hate, etc., as opposed to the later *cognitive* developments instituted by our mediate, relational, causal, and explanatory superstructures as they become activated within consciousness. The former manifest themselves as *intensive* elements in the mind, while the latter are the result of structured *subsequent* acts dependent upon *quantitative* distinctions achieved by the mind in response to external stimuli, e.g., conceptualized spatial, objective, measurable, and causal relations that are a later more advanced cognitive development. According to Hegel qualities are actively spontaneous as opposed to quantities that are *abstractly* descriptive and measurable.

In pursuing this line of thought, I shall however begin with Kant's views on the category of "extensive Quantity" in the *Critique of Pure Reason* (1781, 1787) and then contrast it with Hegel's category of Sense-Certainty with its emphasis on the immediacy of Quality as it initially pervades the subjective mind in the *Phenomenology of Spirit* (1807). Later we shall also find Hegel instituting Quality as his initiating foundation for the *Science of Logic* (1812–1816). Hegel will first treat Quality in relation to individual human consciousness and second in relation to metaphysical Being. The category of Quality will be primary and original and Quantity secondary and derivative in both his major works. By first concentrating on the primal moments of sensory and affective awareness prior to the more active cognitive states of consciousness and by focusing on the mind's most basic sensory and *affective* feelings, we will be able to appreciate the hidden origins of our aberrant emotions and thoughts and gain an appreciation into our limitations in gauging human desires, emotions, thoughts, actions, and consequences, which frequently erupt in acts of violence that are directed toward the self and others; acts that are commonly described and dismissed in our daily vernacular as seemingly "senseless," "meaningless," and "incomprehensible." These are the dangerous shoals of psychology. The impulse for aggression is embedded in our narcissistic and egoistic sense of entitlement issues and the consequent resentment of others. Additionally, when one feels lonely, alienated, or estranged, it breeds a desire for irrational retaliation and revenge; when one feels separated from family, friends, peers, or the social world in general, two momentous affective consequences are engendered: anger and anxiety. This is a natural but unfortunate result of our early psychological—as opposed to intellectual—solipsistic illusion of self-sufficiency and insularity (again Schopenhauer's egoism and narcissism).

At first, our sensory and affective qualities are *felt* rather than *known* as outlined in Hegel's description of the "feeling soul" explored in his *Anthropology*. As uniquely intimate constellations of feeling develop in the self, each shifting set of passions and motivations are dynamically expressed within the subjective mind; they are exclusively personal and non-shareable thus condemning each of us to *exist* qualitatively alone although we *appear* quantitatively to *subsist* together in a commonly shared spatial world. Schopenhauer describes consciousness as a "magic lantern" but under periods of great stress—or great boredom—the oil spills out from the lantern and the conflagration consumes even the lantern itself. At other times, consciousness is like a kaleidoscope that offers various mosaic vistas and with each revolution of the spyglass the self envisions an unpredictable world through refracting lenses. A mood can precipitously change in the blink of an eye or the rotation of the kaleidoscope; it can turn suddenly into anger, anxiety and inconsolable loneliness. Often our feelings of isolation account for why during intense or prolonged periods of loneliness, our sense of separation from others impels us to act impulsively, irrationally, and destructively against our own interests or the safety of others.

At the very dawn of amorphous human consciousness, there is both a sensory and an affective "pool" of sentience and feeling as well as an immediate presence of an indeterminate jumble of sensations and emotions, which animate the subjective mind in highly idiosyncratic and non-shareable ways. By turning to Kant and Hegel as foils, I intend to show the strengths of a qualitative approach to both consciousness and loneliness as opposed to the restrictive methods promoted by the pseudoscientific quantitative and causal approaches favored by psychoanalysis and the neurosciences.

The thesis I wish to pursue in the following discussion is twofold: (1) In order to adequately address the elements and acts of consciousness, one must include both its qualitative and quantitative factors; and (2) recognize that qualities are primary and original and quantities secondary and derivative.

My interest in the Kant-Hegel controversy is also two-fold. First it is based in the conviction that Hegel has something important to say about the subjective mind that resists reducing consciousness to the brain and its electrochemical responses. And second, by endorsing Hegel's criticisms pertaining to the current vogues of physiology and phrenology in his own age, which anticipates our own neuroscientific period, I hope to secure a different path for the study and understanding of man's existential situation of loneliness as it confronts each of us as individuals. In a significant sense, it can be said that *we experience qualities alone as individuals but quantities together as a species.*

Let me begin by exploring the reasons *why* Kant starts with the category of Quantity, whereas Hegel begins with Quality. In doing so, I wish to offer a number of important differences between them on the issue. Nevertheless, both philosophers maintain that the *higher* modes of cognitive consciousness are at least implicitly judgmental—all *self-*consciousnesss is judgmental, assertive—and our conceptions about the world, our self, and other selves only originate later through relational and structural activities native to the human mind. However, according to Hegel, the Kantian transcendent*al* categories, although admittedly *active* products of the mind—ultimately spontaneous creations of the "productive imagination"—nevertheless are merely *assumed* and artificially "superimposed" on Kant's problematic noumenal "presentations brought" to the mind from "without." Again, by virtue of Kant's Copernican Revolution, a realm of unknowable transcendent "presence(s)" is forced to *conform* to the relational structures of the active mind (*Critique*, B xvi–xvii). But Hegel rejects the asserted dualism between phenomena and noumena. According to Hegel, Kant's categories of the Understanding are simply naively assumed, presupposed without any true transcendental "justification" or epistemological "deduction." The result is that the Kantian structures of consciousness are not only "externally" spatially, temporally, i.e., artificially applied to what the noumenal realm "presents" in general, but they are static as well, both in terms of intuition and the categories; devoid of any possibility of immanent or progressive development *from within;* they are simply applied. Kant's categories, for example, merely reverberate *formally, vacuously* bouncing back and forth without any possible dialectical advancement between the cause and its effect and back again. There is no true development or evolvement. By contrast, Hegel's categories *dialectically evolve,* posit, "move," negate, carry, support, transcend, and advance as they progress continuously *forward*—logically and temporally—through fits and starts, ebbs and flows, exhaustion and replenishment from the in-itself (Being as Consciousness) to the for-itself (Self-Consciousness as Being), toward increasingly sophisticated progressions ending in Absolute Spirit, into Substance as Subject. Unlike Darwin's evolution of the species (1859), Hegel's philosophical evolution is dynamic, conceptual, social, historical, scientific, and cultural. *But* his categories begin from the earliest incipient "moment" of nascent infant consciousness. While Kant's categories are static, Hegel's are organic, developmental, and progressive. Although Hegel avoids referring to his categories as *a priori* synthetic relations, and prefers to describe them as dialectical, nevertheless like Kant's, they emanate, they arise *from within* consciousness; Hegel's are inherently ampliative and even more heuristically so as they "move" from immediacy to mediation to self-mediation and beyond. But for both the critical feature is basically Leibnizian: thought moves from within—spontaneously—whereas for empiricism the propulsion is from without.

The second difference is that Kant begins from the standpoint of a full-blown mature intellect, actually with a "Newtonian mind," while Hegel commences with the very first germinations of human awareness in his *Anthropology*. Significantly the *Phenomenology of Spirit* begins by ushering in the qualitative features of infant consciousness through the conscious portal of Sense-Certainty. And later in the *Science of Logic* he correspondingly starts with the infancy of philosophy and Parmenides' assertion concerning the metaphysical Quality of Being. Consequently, I shall emphasize Hegel's treatment of the category of Quality in both those contexts, while differentiating it from the category of perceptual Quantity, as it initially manifests itself in individual consciousness in the *Phenomenology of Spirit* (1807) and later in the *Science of Logic* (1812–1816). Quality is not only the essence of Consciousness but it constitutes the very nature of *active* Being. It is the category of Quality that *fist* moves both itself and Quantity. This pattern of development follows Hegel's desideratum that objective idealism should be conceived as a unity, an identity of Being and Consciousness and that Subject and Object are one. The constitutive acts and structures of both the mind and reality are deeply implicated in a system of synthetic *a priori* relations. Hegel is an objective idealist, while Leibniz, Kant, and Fichte may be more properly described as subjective idealists. Throughout the study, I have been concerned to defend my version of subjective idealism because of my basic Kantian position that *self*-consciousness begins with a distinction between self and objects rather than with Hegel's master-slave dialectic which is constituted by an inter-personal conflict between the self and other self, thus fostering a consequent sense of separation and loneliness that can only be assuaged by seeking intimacy with an other sentient being.

An anticipatory clarification concerning my ultimate goal in pursuing the distinction between the quality and quantity relation in consciousness will help define my position on loneliness. I will side with Hegel on his views on the primacy of sensory and affective qualitative features and his developmental description concerning the origin of consciousness in infancy, but I will also agree with Kant on his reflections concerning subjective self-consciousness by contending that the original source of loneliness is constituted by the subject-object dichotomy, i.e., the separation between self and a distinct world and other selves, as opposed to Hegel's self-other conflict described in the Lordship-Bondage dialectic, although notably that dynamic appears as early as the mother-infant relationship.

Recall that my initial purpose in writing the present study was (a) to begin with bare consciousness and then continue on to the inevitability of human loneliness, whereas my first study of loneliness (b) started with loneliness and then worked backward to its self-conscious base. In effect, I sought to demonstrate how the subjective idealist paradigm of the mind serves to provide insight and understanding into both loneliness and intimacy. So throughout the present text the question remains whether loneliness is externally and passively conditioned by hereditary, environmental, and situational *causes* and therefore transient and avoidable (the scientific and empirical perspective); or whether it is instead innately *constituted* by the very activities and structures of reflexive self-consciousness and transcendent intentionality and therefore permanent, universal, and unavoidable (the subjective idealist approach).

We previously alluded to Plato's prescient characterization of philosophy as a conflict between the Giants and the Gods, between materialism and idealism, and the role the simplicity premise and argument assume in the context of safeguarding proofs in support of a *conceptualizing* spontaneity, meanings, relations, unity, freedom, temporality and even the ideality of space during the period of the Scientific Revolution. The crux of the disagreement between the opposing factions lies in the fact that for the idealists and dualists *consciousness arises* from its spontaneous immaterial, sensory, and affective qualitative factors, while for the materialists *experience* is physically *caused* by quantitative material motions prevailing in the external world as they impinge upon the brain.

As previously outlined Kant's criticism of Hume's "bundle theory" of the self results in two conclusions. First, Kant points out that when Hume admits to a *succession* of impressions, he can only do so if there is a substantial present self available to bind, unify, and synthesize the successive moments within the same self-consciousness. Second, Kant's own description of "inner sense," of an immanent temporal consciousness in his threefold transcendental syntheses (*Critique,* A 99 ff.) offers a powerful argument for an unassailable reality, namely that consciousness is temporal, a flow that is self-aware of itself as a flow.

But Kant's second direction takes us very far afield and away from subjective idealism and instead leads us directly toward a Newtonian objective science. In what follows we will put aside Kant's deeper treatment of time-consciousness and instead concentrate on two sections in Kant's Analytic of Principles, as he institutes the Axioms of Intuition (invoking the Principle of Quantity) and the Anticipations of Perception (asserting the Principle of Quality) both serving as conditions for the possibility of our common human experience as well as Newtonian science. In doing so, Kant will assume a more decidedly "scientific" attitude. Basically what Kant offers is a *transcendental* defense of Newtonian science. Still constrained by the architectonic rigors of his Table of Judgments, he begins with the category of Quantity. Recall that the Scientific Revolution started with the Cartesian identification of a "space-matter-extension" and its defining feature of infinite divisibility and mathematical measurability. Hence Kant begins by instituting Newton's presuppositions concerning the pre-existence of both an "absolute" space and time as together *already* there in the mind prepared to "condition" human experience and available for objective quantitative measurements in his Axioms of Intuition. The Axioms represent spatial, i.e., *extensive magnitudes*, while, by contrast, sensations and feelings, as purely *qualitative* mental contents, are presented in the Anticipations of Perception as *intensive,* i.e., as non-spatial, *minima sensibilia;* as unextended sensations and feelings. In short, quantities are extended spatially and temporally in the Axioms; qualities are neither in the Anticipations. When combined with the *activity* of the relational, structuring categories of thought (as well as Kant's subsequent formulation of the Schemata) they result in human consciousness both of the ordinary and scientific variety. And it is the Axioms of Intuition, of both space and time that essentially symbolize Newtonian science, the science of causal mechanisms and mathematical measurements. In other words, Kant begins the Aesthetic with a conflation of Leibniz and Newton's scientific views on space and time; while by contrast Hegel starts from the very different perspective of the primitive "feeling soul," from nascent human consciousness in the *Phenomenology* and later in the *Philosophy of Mind.* The former will dictate his opening treatment of individual consciousness in his phenomenological description of Sense-Certainty in the *Phenomenology.* By contrast, it is not until Kant's Anticipations of Perception that the discussion will turn to the qualitative contents of consciousness.

The above dichotomy between the Axioms and the Anticipations accords with Kant's Table of Judgments, which is based on his "clue" provided by the Categories of Logical Judgments. This displays Quantity as *preceding* Quality; it shows the Axioms of Quantity and measurement *before* the Anticipations of Quality and perception; consciousness of extensity is *prior* to consciousness of *intensity*. Again, the essence of empirical science is objective quantification and causal predictions. Basically Kant institutes space over time. In fact, he is rather ambivalent about the ability to apply measurable quantities to qualitative intensities as signaled by his equivocal use of the term "degrees" as opposed to "extension" or "extensity" when discussing quality (below). We recall in this context that in the second edition Paralogism, he suggests that the "pure" or "simple," unextended, i.e., immaterial *qualitative* soul ("As regards its quality it is *simple*," A 344=B 402) could nevertheless disappear by "elanguescence," a possibility that seems conceptually and materially impossible for *extensive* and material magnitudes because of the assumed conservation of matter principle during the Scientific Revolution. We recall in Chapters 3 and 4 the emphasis on the philosophical separation between quantity and quality in the context of consciousness and reality.

By contrast, Hegel starts with the *qualitative* elements of consciousness in the section on Sense-Certainty in the *Phenomenology of Spirit*. He begins with the *immediate* primacy of sensations and feelings (the "feeling soul"); with the unextended "here" and "now"; with the relatively *passive* elements of consciousness—not yet acts—in terms of reconstructing a genetic, psychological, developmental history of consciousness as given *directly, immediately* to and within awareness. During this thoroughly primary and primitive juncture of consciousness as it surfaces from the depths of newborn life with its "own" defining appearances, there is a complete absence of synthesizing or dialectical relations *as yet*. Newborns sense and feel but they don't think *in relational terms*. Hegel's phenomenological descriptions of the earliest stages of consciousness are intrinsically subjective, private, and intimate; they are conscious but not yet self-conscious. Nevertheless, in experiencing the sensory and affective contents, they become *unconsciously* "personal"; the qualities *belong* to "something" conscious; and they are at this stage absolutely unshareable with other selves. Indeed, there are *no* other selves at this earliest level of awareness. Hegel's more mature active feeling state *as desire* will only come later when consciousness develops more fully and *after* the self becomes aware of the distinction between self versus object(s). The soul cannot "desire" before it is able to distinguish its self *as separate, as distinct* from a realm of opposing recalcitrant objects, which first initiates the self's primitive desiderative struggle and journey toward the "appropriation" of objects, the natural world, and a world of other selves (Marx).

In contrast to Hegel, Kant's objective, inter-subjective, and scientific *a priori* intuitions of space and time in the Aesthetic—as humans we collectively share them—and the Axioms in the Analytic are all publicly communicable; their combined meanings carry shareable, inter-subjective, i.e., scientific import. We share an objective and measurable space and time because of our (presumably) common intuitions of Newtonian space and time. They are transcendentally inter-subjective, i.e., objective and essentially inter-communicable precisely because they are mathematically measurable. The number 2 is universally meaningful as a relation between the numbers 1 and 3. In the world of mathematical systems, nothing is ever lost in "translation."

But for Hegel, we notice that the movement from Protagorean Sense-Certainty to Lockean Perception cannot even begin until the dialectic of consciousness can advance to focusing on external objects.

> The categories of Quality correspond to Sense-Certainty. Thus, the Sense-certainty section makes it clear that the category of Being is associated with Sense-certainty...The categories of Quantity correspond to Perception.[2]

As we proceed, we will take up in turn Hegel's treatments of the category of Quality in both the *Phenomenology* as well as the greater *Logic*.

By contrast, for Kant, the Anticipations of Perception, which apply to the sensory qualities of the sensations and feelings in relation to the mind are completely immune to quantification because of their inextensive essence. For instance, if one attempts to communicate, to conceptually convey to someone the taste of a fruit the other has never experienced, it cannot be done conceptually: "the real in sensation [is] merely a subjective representation, which gives us only consciousness that the subject is affected" (B 208). In other words both sensory and affective experiences, which include sensations as well as feelings, are intrinsically and intimately personal and non-communicable (Bergson). For instance, if you have never tasted pineapple, I cannot convey to you the quality of its taste but I can describe to you certain quantitative aspects in terms of weight, size, and density.

The difference in approach between Hegel and Kant occurs because Kant's interests are "scientific"; they are addressed in behalf of the natural sciences. In addition, Kant is also in terms of psychology a hard determinist. He is engaged in "transcendentally" defending Newtonian presuppositions pertaining to the mechanical, causal, and mathematical sciences, while Hegel's concerns by contrast are genetic, organic, developmental, and evolving. Beyond that, Hegel's categories are also social, historical, and finally cultural. Again, Hegel starts with qualities and by contrast Kant begins with quantities that can be

---

[2] Michael Forster, *Hegel's Idea of a Phenomenology of Spirit* (Chicago: University of Chicago Press, 1998), 524–525.

displayed in a causal framework and in line with strictly determinist sequences. Imagine gravity as an external natural force controlling the entire universe "at a distance" and yet it is all mathematically expressible. Kant is thus constituting the consciousness of a mature ego, while Hegel is conducting a genetic or developmental inquiry. Accordingly, Hegel is concerned to dialectically describe primordial awareness—Sense-Certainty—and the anticipatory burgeoning categories of Perception, Understanding, and Self-Consciousness. And Hegel is not a determinist; the dialectic does not predict; instead it offers insight, understanding, and rational penetration.

Hegel thus initiates his phenomenological description from within the first stirrings of a *singular* human consciousness, i.e., from within infancy. If this interpretation is correct, it follows that the initial starting point of Sense-Certainty in the *Phenomenology* (1807) will correspond in all important respects to the "infancy" of philosophical thought in the opening passage regarding the intensive Quality of Being in the *Science of Logic* (1812–16). Indeed, Hegel was engaged in revising the latter work when he died in 1831 thereby strongly suggesting that he remained dedicated to the priority of the category of Quality over Quantity and also regarded his "speculative" metaphysical philosophy, expressed in the *Science of Logic,* as more important than his historical allusions and social reflections in the *Phenomenology* (see especially the second Preface to the greater *Logic*). If this reading is correct, then it follows that in order to understand individual mind, one must first begin from the very inception of nascent consciousness and its attendant *qualities*. In sum, the category of Quality initiates both individual Consciousness in the *Phenomenology* and Being in the *Science of Logic*. In pursuing this reading, I will begin with the *Phenomenology* and postpone Hegel's discussion concerning the aspects of *qualitative* Being for later when we have the occasion to consider the *Science of Logic* more fully.

Despite Kant's "dynamic" descriptions of human consciousness, he remains committed in the phenomenal realm to both a physical and a psychological determinism. Freedom, of course, is relegated to the noumenal world, while paradoxically spontaneity actually still rules in the phenomenal realm (*Critique,* A 97) as well as in the production of the synthetic *a priori* categories constitutive of internal time-consciousness (A 98-A-104). Spontaneity is the pulsating heart and soul of the "productive imagination" as well as the activating source for the animating acts operating in the synthesis of inner sense.

It seems more than just a puzzling fact why none of the Kantian and Hegelian scholars even offer a comment let alone any discussion regarding the disagreement between Kant and Hegel on the Quality versus Quantity controversy as even worthy of consideration. For example, neither Kemp Smith in his comprehensive *Commentary* on Kant's *Critique* or Paton in *Kant's Metaphysic of Experience* addressing the first half correct this neglect and they are followed in similar omissions by a company of commentators, including A.C. Ewing in *A Short Commentary on Kant's Critique of Pure Reason* (1938); T.D. Weldon in *Kant's Critique of Pure Reason* (1958); Stephen Korner in *Kant* (1960); Fredrick Copleston in *A History of Philosophy* (1964, VI, 2); Jonathan Bennett in *Kant's Analytic* (1966); P.F. Strawson in *The Bounds of Sense* (1966); Roger Scruton, *Kant* (1982); G.R.G. Mure in *An Introduction to Hegel* (1940) and *The Philosophy of Hegel* (1965); W.T. Stace in *The Philosophy of Hegel* (1955); Stanley Rosen in *G.W.F. Hegel* (1974); Charles Taylor in *Hegel* (1977); and Robert Pippin in *Hegel's Idealism: The Satisfactions of Self-Consciousness* (1993). All these authors offer no discussion for this critical divergence at the very foundation of the Kantian and Hegelian idealist systems, although in an earlier work, G.R.G. Mure, in his *Introduction to Hegel* (1940), avoids the issue, in a later study he discusses Hegel's explicit dissatisfaction with Kant's formulation of the priority of Quantity over Quality, the latter being for Hegel "the undeveloped germ of all the categories" (29). In another passage discussing Quality, Mure also forges an essential connection between the unity of consciousness and the awareness of Quality.

> The unity of self-consciousness and Being is 'original' because first and last there is only active spirit. The Pure Being with which Hegel's Logic begins, die Kategorie [of Quality] in its utmost abstract phase, is just this 'original' unity; it is Descartes cogito and Kant's unity of apperception in their true meaning.[3]

In a previous chapter, we already enlisted the critical insight offered in J.N. Findlay's Foreword from *Hegel's Philosophy of Mind*. It is worth repeating it here.

> The notion of *Geist* (Mind or Spirit) is central in Hegel. It is the lineal descendant of the Kantian Transcendental Unity of Self-Consciousness and of the Absolute Ego of Fichte. It also claims a collateral source in the Aristotelian *nous* [*Meta.*, 1075a] which, in knowing the form of an object, thereby knows itself, and which in the highest phases may be described as a pure thinking upon thinking…The Greek influence upon Hegel's thought is all-important from the beginning of the Jena period but the roots of that thought remain Kantian and Fichtean. Kant had made plain

---

3   G.R.G. Mure, *A Study of Hegel's* Logic, (London: Oxford University Press, 1950), 30.

that we require to mind *objects*, unities which proceed according to rule [as guided by the categories and principles] and which can be reidentified on many occasions, in order to have that unity in our conscious minding which makes us enduring [self-]conscious selves, and which enable us to be conscious of ourselves as conscious. In the conscious constitution of objects, *athwart the flux of time,* we have the necessary foundation for the constitution of a consciousness of consciousness, *a point remade latterly and hammered home by Husserl.* Our subjective life may and must be in many ways arbitrary and inconsequent, but object- and rule-oriented it must also be if it is to have unity at all, if it is not to evaporate into a truly impossible [Humean] flux. The unity which informs, and which we recognize in our conscious life, is accordingly rational, whatever spice of the irrational it may also harbour.[4]

It is the energy and dynamic of spontaneity that initially creates the distinction between subject and object, self and other than self. Without the constant conceptual re-cognition of this difference, there is literally nowhere to go and nothing to desire.

What is important in Findlay's interpretation above is his highlighting of consciousness as (a) a mutual reciprocal relation between subject-object, a point on which both Kant and Hegel agree; (b) a continuity of immanent time-consciousness; (c) the dominance of the unity of consciousness (going as far back as Aristotle); (d) the distinction between subjective and objective consciousness; (e) the difference between irrational and rational consciousness; and (f) Kant and Husserl's universal adoption of temporal constitution. Beneath and supporting all this is *Kant's spontaneous "productive imagination," which remains the primary generative source for the consciousness of man as it is carried forward by Fichte, Hegel, Schopenhauer, Royce, Husserl, Bergson, and Sartre.*

For Hegel, the unity of consciousness first unifies a *qualitative* content *before* it has the ability—the opportunity—to assimilate and implement the more sophisticated quantitative structures. From the very beginning of incipient consciousness, Sense-Certainty already *unreflexively* constitutes a certain amorphous *unity* of immediate qualities, a *unity* of sensory/feeling contents albeit unconsciously, i.e., non-cognitively grouped in the *same* consciousness. Otherwise the compositional elements that must follow could not be constituted as *belonging* to the *same* consciousness and subsequently unified

---

[4] *Hegel's Philosophy of Mind,* translated by William Wallace and Introduction by J.N. Findlay (Oxford: Clarendon Press, 1971), vii–viii; hereafter cited as Hegel, *PM.*

at a higher level later. The qualities are sensed and felt but not conceptually re-cognized as belonging to the same self. At a certain later "terminal" juncture, however, they are experienced as temporal, changing, alternating, and no longer simply immediate. They become relationally mediated. The first inkling of self-awareness is transmitted by the experience of "change." Hegel's "here" and "now" become "there" and "when." There is a flux of *succession,* a flux of *qualitative* sensations and feelings. Consciousness of temporality thus becomes primary and original and spatial extensity secondary and derivative. The infant notices temporal *changes* as well as negations and differences. (This parallels Kant's notice of empirical change in the Refutation of Idealism, B 277–278.) The infant at first is unaware of an external world but it is (presumably) primitively aware of its own *changing* perceptions, in other words it *becomes* aware *of changes, of time-consciousness, of something* happening, transpiring. And it does not require an "external" world in order to form that experience. Consciousness is alone and self-sufficient. But it does not yet possess *self-*consciousness although it is aware of temporal changes; as something happening, of "eventualities." Only subsequently does spatial awareness appear as a further distinction between self and not-self.

The infant for an indefinite span of time is at first unable to synthesize, connect, or unify "his" sensations and feelings, to "appropriate" them, to *self-*consciously "own" them as his own. Nevertheless, these original affective roots will remain not so much accessible as influential throughout our lives and resurface both under severe duress and overpowering desires. Because of this deepest level of consciousness, at this *subconscious* depth—in contrast to the *unconscious* level—infants, children, adolescents, and adults will frequently revert back to these primitive disorganized feelings and emotional urges and they are fully capable of *acting* "out of character"—for better or for worse. This subconscious Hegelian "pit" or "mine" is frequently manifest in dreams, hallucinations, nightmares, and the evanescent tissues of madness.

Accordingly, if one compares Kant's Aesthetic and Analytic in the *Critique* with Hegel's opening section of Consciousness in the *Phenomenology,* beginning with the section on Sense-Certainty, one realizes how completely different they are. Kant's approach is formal, inflexibly structured, transcendental, and deterministic, while Hegel's phenomenological and slippery descriptions portray a shifting panoramic mentalscape accompanied by a disarray of sensations and feelings, an awareness *before* reflexive thinking intervenes. It virtually consists in "a solipsism of the present moment"; a fragment of consciousness completely restricted to the *mere* Here and Now of sensuousness and affectivity couched in a complete absence of relational connections until awakened by an internal temporal consciousness and a corresponding awareness of external change.

But initially at this most primitive of all levels of consciousness, only the qualitative persists. There are no measurable quantitative factors; quantity does not yet exist; quantity always means mediacy and measurement. As yet there is no *conceptual* extension; no inside and outside; before and after; and all the qualities are enclosed, imprisoned, contained within a subjectivity that has no prescience of anything beyond its determinate non-cognitive qualitative sensations and feelings. During these affective moments, desire has not yet appeared on the horizon of our perceptions or the fringes of self-consciousness because of the infant mind's inability to distinguish the self from objects=the non-self. As the self develops further, however, it learns to differentiate itself from the external world. This is the category of Perception, consciousness of the object, of the thing and its predicates. But it is not until the actual category of *Self*-Consciousness is reached that the *feeling* of Desire is attained. And in the Lordship and Bondage dialectic, *desire* becomes expressed as a desire to assert the freedom of one's self against the freedom of the other, a desire for Recognition even at the risk of one's own death. These are the seeds of narcissism and egoism, the desire to appropriate things, to control situations, as well as others (Marx, Kojeve).

Accordingly, Hegel begins by describing subjective consciousness purely from within rather than from without, internally as opposed to externally. Hegel's "science" can only "logically" grow and develop from within. But it is obviously difficult to "describe" the "interiority" of consciousness without lapsing into compromising spatial metaphors like "access to," "contact with," or in phrases like "in the mind," "within consciousness," etc. But since the mind is non-spatial, any terms suggesting quantification or spatial adjectives can only lead to distorting misconceptions.

The critical issue is: Dualism, rationalism, and idealism hold that there are *some* states of conscious *activity* that are "independent" of "externally caused" sensations and experiences. By independent, I mean the mind is focused on the activity and not the contents. It is the activity, *not the sensations that are active*. The activities are spontaneously, causelessly, creatively generated by the mind's internal resources. Furthermore, some of those active conceptions are imageless relations, not reducible to specific sensations, sense data, or sense qualia. What is being explicitly denied is that *all* of our ideas are dependent on, derived from, or caused by preceding spatial and material motions or causes. *Some are not.* The thesis of rationalism is that *some* of our concepts and acts are independent of external origins. The thesis of empiricism is that *all* of our sensations, impressions, and ideas are derived from the external world.

The *methods* of the empirical sciences are *in principle* presumptively restricted to various operations of *measuring* and *recording* alleged objective, physical, spatial, and motional *quantities* with the consequence that the rich mentalscape of secondary and tertiary qualitative features are summarily excluded and falsely relegated and condemned to the dungeons of matter. If empirical science *alone* is successful in dictating *all* future aspirations for human knowledge, then the absurdity of gaining insight into the psychological, intellectual, ethical, and aesthetic enterprises of humanity will be sentenced to the grotesque physicality of clusters of brain cells and synapses. Objective science vivisects the active soul or mind.

According to Paton's reading of Kant's Aesthetic, "An extensive quantity is made up of parts (or quantities) outside one another in space or time, while an intensive quality is given as a whole all at once."[5] The latter is given all at once precisely because it has no extensity, i.e., parts. In the Aesthetic, Kant presents us with an empty, i.e., a pure non-empirical canvas, which is nevertheless replete with *possibilities* of ordering the "incoming" sensations, of "spreading" a plenum of sensory qualities "within" consciousness. But once more, in Kant the spatially extensive quantitative factor *precedes* the qualitative one, which theoretically could be completely absent of any and all sensory or affective content. In effect, Kant believes we could psychologically *imagine* (and not simply conceive without contradiction) an empty space and/or a motionless time. Again, Kant's purpose in all this is grounded in his determination to secure a scientific, an objective, inter-subjective status for space and time in behalf of the Newtonian science of mechanics as further supplemented by the application of mathematical tools of measurement and analytic conceptual instruments in Bergson's terms.

But in examining Kant's Axioms of Intuition, which introduces the activity of thinking in conjunction with sensuous awareness, Kant now declares that the reigning premise attributed to the faculty of the Understanding is that "All appearances [involving space and time] are, in their intuition, extensive [continuous] magnitudes" (A edition); or "All intuitions [involving space and time] are extensive [continuous] magnitudes" (B edition). These magnitudes or extensities are for Kant spatially exemplified in the science of geometry and temporally instantiated in the science of mathematics, which latter is based in

---

5   H.J. Paton, *Kant's Metaphysics of Experience: A Commentary on the First Half of the Kritik der Vernunft* (London: George Allen & Unwin, 1965), II, 136, 142–143.

counting units in time. The underlying principle of continuity is due to Leibniz's lasting influence on Kant.

Of course one could argue that Kant is not saying that extensity *temporally* "precedes" intensity in the formation of consciousness; or that the quantitative features of consciousness come *before* the qualitative ones. The transcendent*al* (as opposed to the transcendent), epistemological, formal, or "logical" distinctions are not developmental ones for Kant as they are for Hegel. They are simply "logically given" to consciousness. Nevertheless they are *distinguished, separated* from each other by him presumably in terms of scientific priority. *First* the objective intuitive magnitudes of space and time; *second* the subjective sensuous contents; and *third* the structuring relations of causes and effects. These three modes of awareness are clearly distinguished, separated by their formal—as opposed to developmental—roles and functions.

By contrast, Hegel's phenomenological descriptions describe a developmental and dialectical "flowing" into each other with the later moments carrying the former attainments into the next stage. Sense-Certainty evolves *into* Perception and then *into* Understanding as each stage permeates consciousness with its special conquests of increasingly richer, concrete, and expansive "fields" and "horizons" of awareness and cognition. Evolution is always from within.

Still concentrating on Kant, we notice that the qualitative features of consciousness in the Anticipations of Perception are introduced next in the following manner: "The principle which anticipates all [sensuous and affective] perceptions, as such, is as follows: In all appearances sensation, and the *real* which corresponds to it in the object (*realitas phenomenon*) has an *intensive* [continuous] *magnitude,* that is, a [non-measurable] degree" (A edition); or "In all appearances, the real that is an object of sensation has intensive [continuous] magnitude" (B edition). These perceptions refer to sensory and (presumably affective) presences. But notice, when Kant is careful, he refers to extensities as exhibiting magnitudes whereas intensities display "degrees." This is reminiscent of Bergson's qualitative "degreeless" intensities, his assertion that there can be no quantitative difference among qualities, as for example between a dim versus a bright light. Since both are essentially sensory, they are on an *equal* qualitative and existential footing. By contrast, quantitative extensions can always be equal or unequal, larger or smaller.

But this is where Hegel dramatically reverses the order. The category of Quality in terms of growth and development clearly *precedes* Quantity and Measure. For Hegel, the category of Quality is identical to consciousness *per se; Quality is Consciousness* in the *Phenomenology*. And it forms the very essence of Being Itself in the *Science of Logic; Quality is Being*. The critical importance of this distinction is that it constitutes the ideal unity, identity, and continuity of Consciousness *qua* Being. This second development will occupy us in Part Two of the present chapter. But suffice it to say that materialism and the neurosciences explicitly deny qualitative distinctions; so-called secondary and tertiary qualities are simply eliminated and translated into physical causes and the collision of neurons within the brain.

According to Kant, again setting aside for the moment the complication of immanent time-consciousness, axiomatic, extensive descriptions cover both spatial and temporal dimensions and magnitudes and therefore all future ensuing phenomenal or empirical objects will be transcendentally represented in human experience as objective, i.e., scientifically measurable entities. This principle, however, as already mentioned, clashes with certain passages in the Aesthetic, where, as we have seen, Kant insists that space and time are "given whole"; as wholes they precede the parts; whereas he now contends that the parts must be successively synthesized.[6] Paton defends Kant on this issue by explaining that in this passage Kant has involved the faculty of thought, the Understanding, in the activity of phenomenal cognition. In any event, it is not my purpose to reconcile Kant with himself. Rather my goal is to highlight the critical differences in consciousness between qualitative intensities and quantitative extensities and to show how they relate to human emotions, cognitions, actions, and valuations. Clearly, intensive qualities owe their allegiance to the Achilles premise.

But the resulting problem is that Kant, by placing the quantitative and mathematical measures of space and time *in the forefront* is thereby committed (1) to situating our sensory, affective, desiderative, and evaluative experiences *before* and *in place of* our so-called secondary and tertiary qualities; (2) to assigning them to matrixes of physical and psychological determinism; and (3) to a conforming framework of inflexible spatial dimensions and temporal sequences, as if human motives could *always* be analogized along the lines of natural events and then structured according to *psychological* causal principles and laws. By *subjugating* qualitative intensity to quantitative extensity and magnitudes, Kant is effectively weakening the essential *spontaneity* of human consciousness, which he repeatedly previously cited not only in the Dialectic but more importantly in the Analytic. By eliminating the spontaneous primacy of qualitative forces, he has surrendered any *real* possibility for the existence of a genuine freedom. He has betrayed himself into the arms of Newtonian science and phenomenal determinism. Left disempowered are the multiple references to spontaneity scattered throughout his three critiques, the *Critique*

---

6  Norman Kemp Smith, *A Commentary to Kant's 'Critique of Pure Reason'* (New York: Humanities Press, 1962), 347–348, 353.

*of Pure Reason,* the *Critique of Practical Reason,* and the *Critique of Judgment.* Perhaps this is why he was unable to reconcile his promise to show how ultimately the Objective and Subjective Deductions are compatible (*Critique,* A xvii). Spontaneity expresses individual freedom while the categories require the restraints of universality and necessity. Perhaps the two Deductions are indeed irreconcilable. But my thesis is that subconscious spontaneity is primary and original and the categories of the Understanding are secondary and derivative (cf. A 50=B 74, A 51=B75, A 68=B 93, A 97, B 130, B 132). Later when Kant turns to the *Critique of Practical Reason* and the *Critique of Judgment,* he accords a much more positive and sustained role to spontaneity and freedom. Curiously absent are commentators' analyses regarding Kantian spontaneity.

Hegel's very different treatment regarding the primacy of qualitative intensities over quantitative extensities, offered in his section on Sense-Certainty rather describes the initial simple, determinate, and unbounded awareness of consciousness in terms of "a host of distinct qualities" (the phrase is repeated twice); a state of consciousness replete with "immediate" (as opposed to mediate), "receptive" (as opposed to active), "direct" (as opposed to indirect), and "apprehensive" (as opposed to comprehensive) presences in consciousness. All these descriptive terms *mean* the absence of relational, i.e., cognitively *conceptual* thought processes. As Hegel indicates in the Section, these conscious but non-reflexive "experiences," *prior to the subject-object relation,* are non-conceptual; "there is no imagining or thought" involved; consciousness (before self-consciousness) is "simple [i.e., immaterial] immediacy." Even the imagination implies a recognition of selfhood. Further, these indeterminate "groups" of amorphous "qualities" nevertheless constitute a *unity* of *non-*reflexive consciousness; they *belong* to the *same* consciousness. Sense-Certainty corresponds to the "feeling soul" in his *Anthropology* (*Philosophy of Mind*) where he also declares that "thought *in general* is so much inherent in the nature of man that he is always thinking even when he is asleep" (*Philosophy of Mind, Anthropology,* Section 398).

Like Kant, Hegel essentially describes perception as the result of two moments, which spontaneously "merely *occur* and come into being"; "one being the [intentional] movement of pointing-out or the *act of perceiving;* the other being the same [reflexive] movement as a simple event or the *object perceived*" (*Phenomenology,* Section 111). Three comments repay consideration in this context. The act of perception describes the two potential elements or as Husserl would say "poles"—a (subjective) act in relation to an object—specifying that the two terms are *mediately* related to each other; the *temporal* thought "movement" involved in connecting them; and the *intentional* nature of the pointing act. Now of course, each dialectical advance in the phenomenology of consciousness carries forward all the prior qualitative moments previously achieved. So the acts and elements of Sense-Certainty are synthesized in the richer act of perception. This analysis accordingly corresponds to Kant's *Critique*, A 107–110, which describes the dual synthetic *a priori* relation between self and object as a reflexive unity. Consciousness will be constituted as a *reflexive* self-conscious unity consisting of *mediated* syntheses binding together sensuous and affective contents with active thoughts; the subject related to and with the object. However this will be an advanced stage attributed to the further development of the original state, stage, or moment of Sense-Certainty as it *devolves* into Perception; as consciousness transcends immediacy and carries forward the sensory and affective data of consciousness into self-consciousness. Thus there is an instructive similarity between Hegel's Sense-Certainty Section and a corresponding passage treating incipient infant consciousness in William James' *Principles of Psychology*.

> The undeniable fact that *any number of impressions, from any number of sensory sources, falling simultaneously* [i.e., non-temporally] *on a mind* WHICH HAS NOT YET EXPERIENCED THEM SEPARATELY *will fuse into a single undivided object for that mind*...The baby, assailed by eyes, ears, nose, skin, and entrails at once, *feels* it all as one great blooming, buzzing confusion.[7]

During these first moments of rudimentary consciousness, there is neither space, nor time, nor a sense of measurement of near or far, or of slow or quick—just a *qualitative* splurge of colors, a cacophony of sounds, confused feelings as well as indistinct pleasures, pains, frustrations, anxieties, and anger—in short, an indiscriminate fusion of *determinate* sensory and affective qualities (so Hegel). Waking states, dreams, and fantasies all blend together, disappearing without warning, forgotten as quickly as they invade consciousness. There is only the amorphous immediacy of consciousness in the infant's sphere of "attention," if it can even be called that. There is no question of parts "outside" or "inside" each other; or "before" or "after" one another. There are no distinct objects, no self, no other selves; just variegated colors, murmuring

---

[7] William James, *Principles of Psychology* (New York: Dover, 1950), I, 488. I am not, of course, suggesting any direct influence of Hegel on James, although James took Kant seriously but had only disdain for Hegel. Nevertheless, the agreement between Hegel and James on what transpires at the earliest stages of infant consciousness seems highly significant. But the fact of their independent agreement testifies even more to an undeniable acknowledgment concerning what must transpire at the first stage of consciousness. James, however, was impressed by Kant and discusses him seriously in the *Principles of Psychology*.

sounds, pressured touches, and feelings of cold, warmth, hunger, satiety; alternating and undulating moods, vibrant emotions without any discernible relation to an object let alone a re-cognition of another "self" or a relation to an other sentient being. It is essentially a *hallucinatory* state of consciousness. At this earliest phase in the newborn's life, the child passively waits for what will come next. This psychological inheritance marks us as human and persists for the remainder of our existence. It is a prelude to our later feelings, thoughts, and actions. And still later during our nocturnal dreams and diurnal fantasies we frequently retreat to these subconscious dissociative feelings, impulses, and thoughts.

Similarly in Freud's description of the "oceanic feeling," there is an undifferentiated unbounded "oneness" at birth before the babe is able to distinguish its self from the "other." Both Kant and Freud agree that consciousness of self is mutually constituted (Kant) or experienced (Freud) by a *cognitive* relation between the self and an opposing independent realm of objects.

> [O]riginally the ego includes everything. Later it separates off an external world from itself. Our present ego-feeling is, therefore, a shrunken residue of a much more inclusive—indeed an all-embracing—feeling which corresponded to a more intimate bond between the ego and the world about it...[T]he ideational contents appropriate to it would be precisely those of limitlessness and of a bond with the universe...which my friend elucidated as the 'oceanic feeling.'[8]

For Hegel consciousness moves forward from Sense-Certainty to Perception while Kant and Freud move reciprocally between subject and object. Notice also especially the emphasis on feeling. As humans, feeling often supercedes cognition. We come into existence and the world with and through feelings rather than thought.

If we inquire into the dynamics of the separation between ego and other, self and world, we discover that it is founded in a desiderative relation between the infant's narcissistic ego and the mother's breast *as an inanimate object*. And that although it produces great pleasure it often comes at the cost of a considerable struggle.

---

8 Sigmund Freud, *Civilization and Its Discontents* (New York: W.W. Norton, 1961), 15; italics mine. Cf. Margaret Mahler, Fred Pine, and Anni Bergman, *The Psychological Birth of the Human Infant* (New York: Basic Books, 1975), "Separation Individuation," 3–8. The study focuses at length on such critical issues as separation anxiety, from the mother, the dynamics of individuation issues, narcissism, and aggression due to the "object loss" of the mother.

> Further reflection tells us that the adult's ego-feeling cannot have been the same from the beginning. It must have gone through a process of development, which cannot, of course, be demonstrated but which admits of being constructed with a fair degree of probability. An infant at the breast does not as yet distinguish his ego from the external world as the source of the sensations flowing in upon him. He gradually learns to do so in response to various promptings. He must be very strongly impressed by the fact that some sources of excitation, which he will later recognize as his own bodily organs, can provide him with sensations at any moment, whereas other [mediate, relational] sources evade him from time to time—among them what he desires most of all, his mother's breast—and only reappear as a result of his screaming for help. In this way there is for the first time set over against the ego an object in the form of something which exists outside and which is only forced to respond by a special action (ibid., 13–14).

First we should note that psychological "separation" *necessarily* connotes a state of opposition between the self and a realm of independent objects. Second, it indicates both a sense of anxiety and a sense of loss relative to a previous state. It also produces anger and frustration when the breast is unavailable. Third, Freud describes it originally as a feeling-state; not a cognitive-state indicating that unlike Kant's analysis, it requires doing something about it, or at the very least adjusting to the situation beyond simply "knowing" that a change is taking place. In other words, for Freud it is essentially an affective state whereas for Kant it is primarily a cognitive state. But for both Freud and Kant there occurs a momentous cognitive shift when the ego distinguishes itself from the amorphous "oceanic feeling" by realizing its separation from a realm of external objects. In brief, the child first becomes aware that the mother's breast is a *separate object* from its self; the breast represents an *object of desire* but initially the infant remains oblivious to the realization that it is attached, related to another self-conscious being. At this early stage, the child is self-conscious but not socially or inter-personally conscious. Nevertheless, a dynamic of narcissism and entitlement issues ensue, which generates feelings of conflict and a desire for domination and mastery over the mother. Throughout our lives this dynamic is constantly repeated.

In all three thinkers, Hegel, James, and Freud, however, this speculative description of our initial state of primordial awareness is "phenomenologically" intended to describe a purely qualitative state of conscious immediacy—but not *self*-consciousness as yet. That will be constituted as a later development of Hegelian moments, as "a work in progress." Within consciousness, sensations pertaining to a realm of colors, sounds, tastes, touches, and smells are dramatically coupled, associated, and permeated with and through feelings of pain, pleasure, anxiety, anger, discomfort, boredom, and isolation. As such, they are radically subjective and unique; they exist as slumbering unstructured presences before awareness is able to develop the capacity to fully open the doors of self-consciousness to a world, which is separate and appears strangely beyond and alien to the earlier primitive states and moments of selfhood, of self-consciousness. But after the initial phases of consciousness, dormant and encrusted passions coalesce like coral formations in the sea, repositories of accumulated layers of subconscious impulses, urges, and instincts as they progressively develop in the child. And even later in life, as the child grows toward adolescence, maturity, and old age, they will persist; no two experiences within this shadowy sphere of the self will ever be alike, congruent, or communicable to any other self. We breathe as we live, feel, think, and desire always alone. These sedimentary feelings are always ready to be revived by future circumstances. They are never left far behind, never extinguished entirely. Opaque and confused troublesome reminiscences are never exact copies. Nevertheless, they fuel submerged, powerful, unrestrained emotions; they are surreptitiously connected to various moods throughout our lives and we are—each of us—highly vulnerable to being irrationally and suddenly plunged into impulsive decisions and actions without rhyme or reason. Suppressed feelings can suddenly erupt uncontrollably and unexpectedly in violence toward the self and/or others; into emotional volcanic outbursts seething with malevolence through fissures of intensity as they emerge from unresolved emotions surrounding a sense of loneliness and isolation. In vain often to search for underlying "motives," "causes," "reasons," "excuses," and/or "justifications" for what we feel, think, and do. In bewildered exasperation, family, friends, peers, therapists, onlookers, and the media later simply describe these violent and destructive acts as "senseless" and "meaningless." Senseless they are not. In fact they are all too "senseful." They are virtually reptilian in nature as they reflect the instinctual, emergent impulses erupting from the depths of time, the human all-too-human repositories of the soul and the darkest side of human evolution.

It is important to emphasize and realize once more that Hegel, James,' and Freud's descriptions of infant consciousness amount to hallucinatory and delusional experiences. At this earliest of all levels of consciousness, there is no time; no space, no self, no external world, just sensations, feelings, and purely subjective valuative sentiments of comfort and discomfort, pleasure and pain, boredom and excitement. It is these narcissistic tendencies, obsessive preoccupations, and egoistic urges and fantasies that are readily put into play when self-consciousness painfully retreats within its interior domain and then explodes outwardly from the unmanageable pressures of acute and chronic loneliness as the ego is poised to destroy indiscriminately its self and/or others. "The mind of man is capable of anything—because everything is in it; all the past as well as the future" (Joseph Conrad, *Heart of Darkness*).

These long submerged and subterranean forces animating the first conscious manifestations of the soul remain hidden and resistant to our delayed reflexive gaze. Thus, Hegel's levels, stages, and moments of amorphous unity—prenatal, subconscious, unconscious, sensory, affective, psychotic, and hallucinatory expressions as described in his *Anthropology*—are all in their own fashion indicative of a "monadic," hermitic, insular, and irredeemably lonely soul. In Sections 402 and following, Hegel describes how *for us* as outside observers "the qualitatively determined soul" advances through its "monadic simplicity" (Hegel, *PM*, Sections 403, 405) and even from its symbiotic relation within the womb it verges toward mental illness (Section 406) leading to insanity and hallucinatory madness (Sections 406 and 408). This is the proper sphere of the subconscious mind. And yet, all these sensory and affective feelings *belong* to the *same* consciousness, although they lurk inaccessibly submerged well beneath the reach of the self-reflexive mind. "Man alone has the capacity of grasping himself in this complete *abstraction of the 'I'.* This is why he has, so to speak the privilege of folly and madness" (Hegel, *PM*, Section 408).

Freud's unconscious conflicts, which are repressions, i.e., basically forgotten memories caused by traumatic incidents, are in principle painfully but readily accessible through free association and the interpretation of dreams and if they were not, then psychoanalysis could not pretend to be a science in the proper meaning of the term, which, as a scientific discipline, requires the essential ability to predict human feelings, thoughts, and actions. Against Freud's relatively straightforward paradigm of the unconscious, consisting essentially of repressed mnemonic causal structures, lies the much deeper and inaccessible contortions of the subjective subconscious with its powerful, incendiary, and irretrievable forces (Hegel, Schopenhauer). Because of their essential spontaneity and opaqueness, these acts unpredictably seek and find fulfillment among a spectrum of expressions and existential choices. Unexpectedly, they fluctuate between pursuing intellectual creations; aesthetic expressions; hedonistic indulgences; ethical commitments; and religious convictions. And often, all-too often they are also poised in postures of sudden discharges, in explosive acts of violence or the subtle retaliations for slights both real and imagined. The existential leaps of Kierkegaard's *either/or* and Nietzsche's *will to power* rule and prevail over each of our lives.

Kant's analysis of the reflexive self is primarily *intra-psychic, intimate,* and *personal* and well within the traditions of Descartes cogito and especially Leibniz's monad, and even vaulting forward to Husserl's ego pole, whereas Hegel's treatment of the self by contrast is decidedly *inter-personal* and *social,* although clearly combative as described in the Lordship and Bondage dialectic. Thus, for Kant, self-consciousness is mediated by consciousness *of objects* whereas for Hegel the reflexivity of the self, of self-consciousness, and personal identity are dialectically mediated by and through the consciousnesses *of an other self.* This critical difference means that Kant's self is constituted *intra-*psychically within its self (self-rx-to-object) whereas Hegel's is reflected socially, *inter-*psychically, and inter-personally (self-rx-to-other-self).

This leads Hegel to emphasize an interpersonal conflict between the self and others, to describe hostile confrontations grounded in the *desire for recognition* at the expense of the other self, literally a battle to the death as we realize that Self-Consciousness and Desire are synthetically *a priori* related (Self-Consciousness: "Lordship and Bondage," *Phenomenology,* Sections, 186 ff.).[9] The desire for recognition can only arise in the context of a competitive struggle between opposing selves.

In this context, it is important to note that the category of Desire first appears in the section on Self-Consciousness. Not until then is Hegel ready to embark upon a path describing the individual soul's journey toward fuller selfhood. As he conceives it, the self demands *recognition* from the other self; to be recognized as a *free* agent *at the expense* of the other. For Hegel, the self asserts its demands, its freedom, its controlling desire *against* the other self's desires and the assertion of the other's freedom. This is not a relation between two selves seeking mutual recognition but rather the assertion of each self's own freedom at the expense of the other; it is a demand for *sole* recognition. But the phenomenon of *Desire* cannot appear within Self-Consciousness until *after* consciousness is able to distinguish its self from and against the *intentional* object of its desire and its mastery *over* the desires of the other self (Kojeve).

---

9 Jean Hyppolite, *Genesis and Structures of Hegel's Phenomenology of Spirit* (Evanston, IL: Northwestern University Press, 1974), 157–169. In general, commentators and scholars become so focused on cognitive and epistemological issues that they tend to neglect motivational drives such as Desire, which actually only first surfaces in the Self-Consciousness section of the *Phenomenology.* Cf. also, Alexandre Kojeve, *Introduction to the Reading of Hegel* (New York: Basic Books, 1969), 37–43. The study concentrates on promoting a heavily Marxist interpretation of the Lordship and Bondage theme, which fruitfully exploits the dynamics of self-consciousness, desire, and the intense struggle for recognition.

The Lordship and Bondage conflict *a priori* and synthetically can only define its own self in direct opposition to the other self's demand to be himself recognized by the other, who stands opposed to him. *This conflict between opposing desires is the natural and inevitable source of all human narcissism and entitlement issues.* Until the Lordship and Bondage stage, we were still engaged in describing individual consciousness. Now we have "progressed" to a more complex dynamic, one in which self-consciousness is mutually constituted by a conflict of desires between two mortally engaged selves. Each self exerts all his strength in order to turn the other into an object, into an unwilling object. Similarly, in Sartre's "The Look," he describes a man caught spying through a keyhole as he is presumably observing a lascivious scene within a room when suddenly he sees himself in turn observed by "the other." In this situation, the captured self is turned into an object, a voyeur, a despicable sort of person who secretively spies on others, one who is suddenly caught by the transfixing gaze of the other. He is robbed of his freedom to control the illicit nature of his desire.

Finally, we are left to choose between two critical issues concerning human self-consciousness. Is it constituted by a reciprocal *conceptual* relation between subject and object, as Kant and Freud assert; or is it instead formed by a conflict between opposing selves, as Hegel maintains? Kant's conviction is primarily *intra-psychic* and monadic while Hegel's is *inter-psychic, inter-personal,* and social. In this debate I have sided with Kant.

## 3  Part Two: The Quality of Being in the *Logic*

We have just finished exploring the epistemological role of the category of Quality assumes in the context of individual consciousness. Now in order to complete the picture, we need to take up how the category of ontological Quality fares under Hegel's treatment in regard to speculative Being-in-Itself. For Hegel, there is a similar progression, which identifies Quality with Being, with Reality in terms of dialectical sub-categories and moments as they develop in his *Science of Logic* (1812–1816; 1831), where he describes the primacy of the relation holding between Quality and Being as opposed to Quantity and the phenomenal sciences along with the latter's tools of objective measurement. In the most general terms, on the grand scale of philosophic thought, it all depends on the ability to dialectically penetrate, synthesize, and unify Leibniz's monadic Consciousness with Spinoza's monistic Substance.

Leibniz came closest to the solution. His monads are creative [i.e., spontaneous] centers of life, which, as external to each other, *appear* as phenomena and physical aggregates; he failed, however, to see, that the monads are not absolutely separated, but are actual individual modifications of one and the same life. To insist on this unity is the merit of Spinoza.[10]

In Spinoza, there is only one Substance, which is known through two attributes, thought and extension, and individual souls and objects are mere modifications of the one Substance. But given Hegel's idealist unification of Substance and Subject, our principal question is: how does Quality stand in relation to Being. Oddly enough, a convenient place to start is with Hegel's defense of the ontological "argument" for the existence of God against Kant's criticism of it as put forth in the Ideals of Pure Reason (*Critique,* A 592=B 620). Hegel mounts his alternative metaphysical vision by promoting his own version of pantheistic idealism with Substance becoming Subject (*Phenomenology,* Introduction). It is important to realize that for Hegel the consciousness of Being "spontaneously" generates its meaningful opposite: Nothing is subconsciously active.

> Consciousness, as manifested Spirit, which as it develops frees itself from immediacy and external concretions becomes Pure Knowing, which takes as object of its knowing those pure essentialities as they are in and for themselves. They are pure thought. Spirit thinking its own essence. Their *spontaneous* movement [of thinking] is their spiritual life: by this movement philosophy constitutes itself; and philosophy is just the exhibition of this movement.
> HEGEL, *SL,* I, 37, italics mine

Again:

> That activity of Thinking [or Consciousness], which works in all our ideas, purposes, interests, and deeds is *un-self-consciously active*; what is present to consciousness is the content, the objects of our ideas; that in which we are interested; in this connexion the determinations of Thought are

---

10  G.W.F. Hegel, *Science of Logic,* (London: George Allen & Unwin, 1951), 45; cf. especially the Doctrine of Essence, "The Philosophy of Spinoza and Leibniz," "The Absolute: Observation," II, 167–172.

> regarded as Forms, the earliest and "emptiest" which are not the content itself but only attached to the content.
> HEGEL, *SL*, I, 45; italics mine

In other words, at first we are only operating with pure immaterial Forms, the earliest, most general, and emptiest conceptual categories and structures of thought as they initiate the movement toward the *spontaneous* synthetic dialectical connections constituting Reality. These innate activities of the Mind or Spirit are also applicable to the earlier *Phenomenology*.

> It is after this fashion that I have tried to present consciousness in the *Phenomenology of Spirit*. Consciousness is Spirit as knowing which is concrete and engrossed in externality; but the *schema of movement* of this concrete knowing (like the development of all physical and intellectual life), depends entirely on the nature of the pure essentialities which make up the content of the Logic. Consciousness, as manifested Spirit, which as it develops frees itself from its immediacy and external concretions becomes Pure Knowing, which takes as the object of its knowing those pure essentialities as they are in and for themselves. They are pure thought, Spirit thinking its own essence. Their *spontaneous movement* is their spiritual life; by this movement philosophy constitutes itself; and philosophy is just the exhibition of this movement [of thought].
> HEGEL, *SL*, I, 108; italics mine

For Hegel as for Bergson, quality trumps quantity. It is the essence of reality. It dominates Consciousness and Being. Quality constitutes the beginning of Being.

The critical point in all this centers on the question whether one must start with Consciousness instead of Matter; and correspondingly whether one also needs to begin with the category or Quality rather than Quantity, i.e., Newtonian science. But if one commences with Quantity, with spatial material reality, with metaphysical materialism, then it is impossible to move forward to either a subjective or objective idealism because the precise advantage of idealism is that it can also "envelope" the *concept of, the meaning of* space, matter, and measurement *within* itself whereas, by contrast, materialism cannot accommodate the concept of an immaterial, unextended qualitative Being, which includes within its speculative domain secondary and tertiary qualities as well. Materialism simply denies the reality of secondary and tertiary realities. Matter has no *conceptual* or *creative* powers, in a word, no spontaneity just passive sensory ones buttressed by physical stimulus-response motions.

For Hegel, we must begin, proceed, and end with Consciousness. In short, Matter, Space, Time, and the world of Nature all *first* appear in Consciousness *as* qualitative categorial concepts.

Consequently, the *Science of Logic* must start with the Quality of Being. Being *is* Quality and Quality *is* Being. The *Logic* is Hegel's ontological work and it incorporates all his dialectical, logical, metaphysical, and epistemological structures of an enclosed Reality-within-Itself. In the *Phenomenology,* Quality initiates the identification of individual Consciousness with Being: "When I say 'quality,' I am saying simple determinateness; it is by quality that one existence is distinguished from another, or is an existence; it is for itself, or it subsists through this simple oneness with itself. But it is thereby essentially a *thought*" (*Phenomenology,* Preface, 33). It is the identity of thought and being. Like life itself, even in the most primitive manifestations or forms of the infant's initial fetal stirrings, there is prenatal restlessness and consciousness.

Similarly, in the *Science of Logic,* Hegel's goal is the identification of Being with Consciousness on the grandest scale. That is why he opens his defining treatise with the *a priori* synthetic dialectical triad of Being<>Nothing<>Becoming. For Hegel, it is the "movement" of thought, its transition from Being to Nothing that creates the temporality of Becoming. "What renders Space and Time, *a priori,* pregnant with Number and Measure and changes them into pure multiplicity; what causes a pure spontaneity (Ego) to oscillate?" It is the spontaneous activity of Consciousness (Hegel, *SL,* I, 108).[11] Above all, it is critical to realize that for Hegel, Being and Nothing are spontaneously activated, subconsciously, synthetically and *a priori* connected. Indeed, in the second edition of the *Science of Logic* (1831), Hegel cites Jacob Boehme by name and credits his mystical symbolism in having invested the essence of Quality with bodily "activity," with incarnate restlessness. This connection will gain in significance when we discuss Jon Mills' Hegelian *Abyss* and his *Underworlds* in Chapter 8.

Hegel's "defense" of the ontological "argument" is not theistically motivated but rather he wishes to reopen the door to legitimizing speculative metaphysics as a discipline in its own right, something that Kant had abandoned by relegating the "Queen of the Sciences" to an unknowable noumenal realm. Of the three rational arguments for God's existence, only the ontological "proof" is intuitive, direct, immediate, while the other two—the cosmological and the teleological—arguments are both partly empirical and partly *a priori.* The initiating premise of the cosmological argument either *assumes* that motion exists (Aristotle) or the world exists (Aquinas) and that *a priori* everything that

---

11   Ben Mijuskovic, "A Reinterpretation of Being in Hegel's *Science of Logic," Telos,* (1970), 6, 286–294; cf., "Spinoza's Version of the Ontological Argument," *Sophia,* 12:1 (1973), 16–24.

exists must have a cause. The teleological argument likewise reasons that there is order, purpose, and design in the universe and therefore there must be an intelligent cause for this virtue. But the ontological "proof" is an intuition; it immediately identifies the intuitional *qualities* of Essence and Existence as identical, inseparable, and unified, in God and God alone as necessary Being; these "two" essential attributes are identical in God. Again, this identification can only be accomplished if qualities are essentially simple, immaterial, and immediately "fused" and present in defining Hegel's pantheistic God. Being is Consciousness. This is Parmenides' philosophical intuitive insight (cf. the entry on Parmenides in *Hegel's Lectures on the History of Philosophy*).

The very opening of Hegel's triune identification of Being-Nothing-Becoming, in the *Lectures* constitutes *in germ* all of philosophical Reality as *already* there. It only has to be unfolded by thought. But unless the reader makes the effort to plow through the four Observational notes, which profusely elaborate upon the category of Being as it pertains to Quality by connecting it to the writings of the Eleatics; Plato's *Parmenides;* the nothingness of Buddhism; the void of Democritus, the flux of Herakleitos; the principle of *ex nihilo nihil fit;* the Christian rejection of Epicurus and the Stoics' principle "that nothing comes out of nothing"; "the creation of the world out of nothing"; Spinoza's pantheism; Kant's synthetic *a priori;* Fichte's self-positing A=A, and so on and on we won't be able to see how each philosopher ontologically summons the identical first principle, namely that qualitatively "Something exists"; "Something has determinate [qualitative] Being" (Hegel, *SL,* 113); that "Something" is Consciousness and from this purely elemental Consciousness philosophers and theologians have foreshadowed the advent of Hegel's version of absolute idealism; a Notion of God as Absolute Qualitative Being. The ontological argument reigns supreme because it is grounded in the qualitative immediacy of intuitive consciousness. This is where Hegel's presuppositionless beginning dwells and rules as it stands ready to dialectically transcend itself, unfold itself, and self-evolve (Hegel, *SL,* I, 95–118). The quartet of lengthy observations presages the entire attainment of organic development through and within the categories in the *Logic*.

This is also why in the first *Preface* to the *Science of Logic,* Hegel ushers in a discussion of metaphysics by situating it within his reflections on the "Immaterialism of the Soul" (Hegel, *SL,* I, 33), while lamenting the topic's neglect in contemporary philosophy. He then goes on to announce that following the bankruptcy of reason caused by Kant's attack on traditional metaphysics, he wants to inaugurate and revive the pressing demand for the "digestion and development of a new method to be applied to the subject of speculative metaphysics." The new method will begin with Quality before Quantity, with dynamic movement rather than Kant's static categories. Throughout the section, Hegel's metaphors remain organic, genetic, developmental, and above all evolutionary. While Darwin's notion of evolution is biological, Hegel's is social, cultural, and philosophical. But what is of paramount importance for him is that it is Quality that defines Life and Consciousness; Being and Knowing. Without quality, art, religion, ethics, and philosophy would all be meaningless.

Now we can understand why Hegel begins with asking the question: "With What Must Science Begin?" And he answers his own query in no uncertain voice by declaring that "Quality therefore is immediate determinateness, and as such is prior [to Quantity] and must constitute the Beginning." In direct opposition to Aristotle and Kant's assertive placement of Quantity before Quality in their Table of Categories, Hegel elects to begin with the most primitive and elemental manifestation of human consciousness in the *Phenomenology* and philosophical knowledge in the *Science of Logic*. Originally, the term category derives from Aristotle and indicates one of the ten universal attributes or predicates of Substance, of Being.

Hence Hegel chronicles a genetic and developmental account of key junctures pertaining to both (a) individual Consciousness as well as (b) metaphysical Being: "Determinateness, taken thus isolated and by itself as existent determinateness, is Quality—something quite simple and immediate...This simplicity makes it impossible to say anything further about Quality as such" (Hegel, *SL*, I, 123). Obviously, this statement only has plausibility and meaning in so far as one is committed to the simplicity principle, namely that consciousness is ideal, immaterial, and spontaneous.

A comparable metaphysical and epistemological ascription to Quality is similarly echoed in the lesser *Logic* as well.

> Quality is, in the first place, the character identical with being; so identical, that a thing ceases to be what it is, if it losses its quality. Quantity is the character external to being, it does not affect being at all.[12]

Whether we are considering the initiation of individual consciousness or the conceptual implementation of Being in general, they are both *essentially* what they are by virtue of their quality; their meanings are permeated through and through by quality. The quality yellow, for example, is just that whether the patch of color is large or small. Quantitatively adding or minimizing the expanse neither increases nor diminishes its "yellowness," its essence, its

---

12   G.W.F. Hegel, *The Logic of Hegel: The Encyclopedia of the Philosophical Sciences,* translated by William Wallace (Oxford: Oxford University Press, 1959), Section 86.

meaning, its universality. Quality defines Consciousness and Being. The same vein of life and development courses through both. Only later developmentally and cognitively can the quantitative measurements of empirical science be externally applied to an "objective" space and time, to objects and events. Numerical attributions are abstract and non-existential. One cannot change the essential quality of a thing by adding or subtracting numerically to it. Matter plus motion does not develop or evolve. But internal qualities live and breathe; they constitute the intrinsic essence of Spirit, of Consciousness itself *because* they develop *from within*. The very notion of development implies qualitative change from within. Even Darwin's theory of the origin of species depends on internal qualitative changes within the species. Growth is only meaningful in the context of qualities and their intrinsic relation to spontaneous dialectical activities; spiritual growth can only occur and transpire from the inside outwardly. A pile of stones can be altered externally but it would make no sense to claim that they were in some fashion qualitatively altered. This is where the paucity of materialism, empiricism, and the neurosciences betray their unimaginative lifelessness.

According to Ellis McTaggart, "It is at the point of Quality that we first get the real."[13] Hegel's Qualities are what differentiates and determines what a thing is and in the same moment what Being is. Qualities do not inhere in anything more substantial than themselves. Their immediacy is their reality. "Each Quality has Determinate Being and the entire universe is nothing but the aggregate of [intensive] Qualities...These may be called not inappropriately, Something."[14]

This is precisely what Hegel means when he states:

> Existence is Quality, self-identical determinateness, or determinate [immaterial, ideal] simplicity, determinate thought; this is the Understanding of existence. Hence it is *Nous,* as Anaxagoras first recognized the essence of things to be...Precisely because existence is defined as Species [or the Universal], it is a simple thought; *Nous,* simplicity, is substance. On account of its simplicity or self-identity it appears fixed and enduring. But this self-identity is no less negativity [since determinateness is a principle of distinction]...but having otherness within itself, and being self-motivating [and spontaneous], is just what is involved in the *simplicity* of

---

13  Ellis McTaggart, "Hegel's treatment of the categories of the mind," *Mind,* 11:44 (1902), 503–526.
14  John McTaggart and Ellis McTaggart, *A Commentary on Hegel's Logic* (New York: Russell and Russell, 1964), 22.

thinking itself; for this simple thinking is the self-moving and self-differentiating thought, it is its own inwardness.[15]

Materialism, mechanism, and empiricism eliminate the quality of life along with all its secondary sensory and affective immediacies as well as its tertiary aesthetic and ethical qualities, the very richness of life itself. Spirit is essentially life, spontaneous, restless, and developmentally creative, productive. Matter and motion are merely manipulable at best and inert and dead at worst.

One final word on the *Science of Logic,* I need to postpone until Chapter 8 a discussion in regard to Jacob Boehme's principle that it is Quality that is active, restless, productive, and struggling—that Quality is the principle of the *movement* of consciousness (Hegel, *SL,* 1, 127) where we will find that Hegel credits Boehme as initiating the entirety of modern philosophy.

In Summary, Kant's theory of self-consciousness is intra-psychic and pre-social. It cognitively separates the subject from the object. In Freud the separation is psychological Loneliness begins when the self's cognitive (Kant) or psychological desires (Freud) are forced to contend against a sphere of non-responding objects (Kant, Freud) or selves (Hegel). The self experiences the alienation of dealing with a realm of recalcitrant, non-responding objects, troublesome things. Very differently, Hegel addresses the issue of personal identity through a dynamic of narcissistic conflicts between separate selves, which is hardly an endorsement in behalf of natural sociability. The concept of *separation* however serves as a constant watchword for loneliness. Even in Hegel's Civil Society phase of mankind's political evolution the dominant impulse remains egoistic. As Stace describes it:

> Hence arises a multiplicity of independent persons, externally related to each other as so many independent social atoms. So long as they remained within the family they were not [egoistic] ends in themselves, but the family was their end—a higher end than the individual. Now, however, each independent atomic person becomes an end in himself and admits of no other end than himself. Each therefore is bent upon treating himself only as an end and treating all other persons as a means to his ends.[16]

---

15 G.W.F. Hegel, *Phenomenology of Spirit,* translated by A.V. Miller (Oxford, Clarendon Press, 1977), 34. If consciousness were not immaterial and active, this declaration would be absolutely meaningless.
16 W.T. Stace, *The Philosophy of Hegel: A Systematic Exposition* (New York: Dover, 1955), 412.

Basically it is and remains a Hobbesian "war of all against all" and human life is depicted "as solitary, poor, nasty, brutish and short" (*Leviathan*). Nevertheless, Hegel contributes a critical element within human consciousness by stressing the affective qualities, which Kant thoroughly neglects. The important issue concerning the quality versus quantity controversy is that it powerfully unfolds the hidden but essential dominance of emotional intensity—versus quantitative extensity—involved in human consciousness and action and thus it is directly involved in the possibility of a human unpredictable spontaneity, while spatial and temporal extensity remains mired in determinism. As the Hegelian dialectical process continues in the individual, one can no more separate the sensory and affective qualities from a person's life than one can sever the child from the adolescent and the adolescent from the adult. For Hegel, we carry those intensive subconscious emotional qualities throughout our lives as always ready to volcanically erupt against a dark sky and the consequent devastating lava of destruction.

Generally both students and professors of philosophy strongly tend to prefer studying the exciting passages of the *Phenomenology* rather than the ponderous movement of the categories in the *Science of Logic*. But in fact, Hegel himself regarded the *Logic* as more important because it conceptually "logically," rationally, and systematically outlines the entire system of his philosophy from the inside perspective of Spirit. Actually, he was editing it when he died in 1831.

CHAPTER 6

# Neuromania and Neo-Phrenology versus Consciousness

> We neither commit theft, murder, etc. with the skull-bone, nor does it in the least betray such deeds by a change of countenance, so that the skull-bone would become a speaking gesture.
> HEGEL, *Phenomenology of Spirit*

∴

Before plunging in, I need to offer a few preliminary comments. First, the word "phrenology" in the chapter heading is intended to signal the same negative attitude that Hegel expresses in the *Phenomenology of Spirit* when he criticizes the attempt to transform Spirit and Mind (*Geist*) into facial features, brain, bone, and skull in the physiognomical and psychological sciences of his time (Section on "Physiognomy and Phrenology"). Second, throughout this work, I have steadfastly rejected reductive materialism, naive empiricism, and crude behaviorism and instead defended dualism, subjective idealism, a form of *conditional* internally consistent rationalism (e.g., mathematical systems), synthetic *a priori* relations as well as an existential description of the human condition.

The American Psychiatric Association heralded the 1990s as "The Decade of the Brain." In an article in *Newsweek* magazine titled, "May I Take a Message, Please?" dated February 7, 1994, an illustration of the brain is sketched and it is intended to show *how* the brain operates (see Figure 1).

In by now increasingly familiar terminology, we are told that "In the brain, neurons *communicate* through chemicals called neurotransmitters." [Normally communication means the *intentional* transmission of information between two or more separate self-conscious selves as opposed to single bundles of cells colliding with each other in the brain. And the question arises does the first set of cells *remember* what it communicated?] "These molecules seep out of one neuron and *excite* another, triggering electrical *signals* that produce *thoughts, emotions, memories, and will*." [Generally excitement means a highly charged emotional state. Do single neurons get excited? Sentient creatures can become excited; but I don't know about molecules and neurons. Usually a "signal" *intends* a meaning other than itself'; it points to, it tells us something different from the signal, the symbol itself; it is not self-referential; a STOP sign is not a

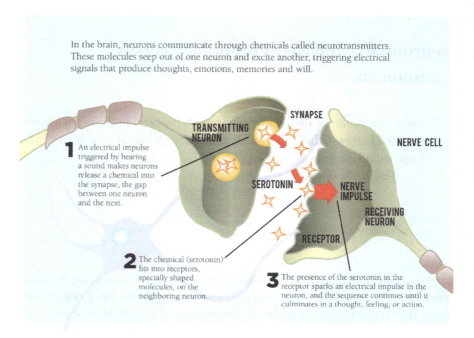

FIGURE 1    Newsweek diagram

meaning; rather it is an intentional *symbol* used for communicating and commanding a complex message for human consumption. But especially notice the sudden *physical* and *quantitative* jump from the mechanical motions of neurons to the *mental* and *qualitative* features of "thoughts, emotions, memories, and will" (free will?). And surely at least these *conceptual* "objects," "desires," "purposes," "goals," etc., are *intentionally* directed at something *beyond* cellular matter and electrical synapses in the brain. Worse yet, there is also a suggestion that *single* neurons are in some unspecified sense "self-aware"; and therefore that neurons *communicate* with each other; tell each other things. People do, of course, but neurons? Neurons may transmit electrical impulses through each other but not *with* and *to* each other. Communication is not only reflexively self-conscious but reciprocal with other self-conscious selves. When we turn on a switch and a light bulb ignites, does that qualify as a communicative relation? What kind of communication? When two billiard balls collide, is that a communicative exchange?]

The neuroscientific position presupposes the stimulation of the brain by *external* agencies, specifically matter and motion, causing electrical discharges in the brain. In the following discussion, I propose to criticize the assumptions surrounding the neuroscientific position from the "inside," from "within" the mind, so to speak, from the vantage point of consciousness itself by contrasting the passive reactions and responses of the brain against the activities of the mind. In criticizing the neuroscientific perspective, I shall combine the above *Newsweek* article with a more recent companion lecture promoting the neuroscientific position and then confront both of their extravagant assertions by proposing, defending, and contrasting them against an active mentalist paradigm of consciousness. In doing so, I shall rely heavily on passages that I believe show the neuroscientific system collapsing on itself from within by countering its series of unsubstantiated and extravagant endorsements beginning with a paper prepared for the Mount Perlin Society Conference in 2010 in Australia presented by Dr. Peter Whybrow from the Semel Institute for Neuroscience at UCLA titled "After Freud: What Do Neuroscience Advances Tell Us About Human Nature?" I wish to use Dr. Whybrow's talk as a convenient manifesto delineating the current basic principles, methods, goals, and the alleged accomplishments of neuroscience while at the same time responding to a number of his claims. He begins by stating:

> In my professional lifetime, something over three decades, we have learned more about the brain than the whole of human history. We know for example there are more than one hundred billion nerve cells in the brain and that each of these brain cells has many thousands of synaptic [causal] connections, portals of chemical *communication with its neighbors*. We know too an increasing amount about the anatomy of the different functional centers that make up the brain, what *responsibilities* they have, how they *execute their duties,* and *why* they have evolved. We have learned much about the *superhighways* that maintain *communication* among these centers and the physical and chemical processes that sustain that *communication*. We are beginning to understand how *memory,* which lies at the core of the *subjective self,* is dependent on the strength of the networks that are *forged* [i.e., causally connected; blacksmiths forge iron] among brain cells by what we *experience, think, and feel.* It is even becoming generally accepted that brain gives rise to *mind,* to the agency that supports the ability of each of us to act as a unique [moral] *person*.[1]

First it is important to note that a recognized classic distinction defining science from other disciplines, and especially from metaphysics, is that science seeks to describe and explain ***how*** things happen and ***not why***, whereas

---

1 Peter Whybrow, "After Freud, What Do Neuroscience Advances Have To Tell about Human Nature?"; italics mine; talk given at the Mount Perlin Society Annual Meeting in Sydney, Australia (2010); PDF available at https://elbertcounty.net/blog/wp-content/uploads/2010/11/after-freud-what-do-neuroscience-advances-tell-us-about-human-nature-dr-peter-whybrow.pdf.

Dr. Whybrow claims to explain *why* rather than simply describing *how* all this occurs. *Why* implies human purposes and independent justifications as opposed to mechanical and causal—versus motivational—explanations. Because Dr. Whybrow believes he is proposing "whys" and not "hows," he illicitly allows himself to "humanize," to anthropomorphize his essentially physiological sequences. Second, the phrase "that brain gives rise to *mind*" clearly begs the entire issue of substance dualism, of *personal* identity, and the difference between mind and matter and it implies that he believes there is some sort of easy transition between the two, as if both brains and minds were basically composed of the same *material* substance and "mind" simply being a more convenient term for more complicated or sophisticated physical systems of brain functions. As in the *Newsweek* article, we discover once again in Dr. Whybrow's use of the italicized terms above the similar but also more sustained anthropomorphizing we earlier viewed in the previous article and diagram. The identical mechanistic motions and electromagnetic couplings are accounted for by transforming them into human—as opposed to simply physiological—descriptions and by endowing physical, electrochemical, biological, and physiological events as if they were synonymous with *mental acts* and *activities*. Although Dr. Whybrow tells us that there are more than one hundred billion cells in the brain, the whole process can be reduced to three connecting terminals according to the *Newsweek* article and Dr. Whybrow's account, both of which concur in describing the following process: (1) "An electrical impulse triggered by *hearing* a sound makes [causes?] neurons to release a chemical into the synapses, the gap between one neuron and the next." [So presumably neurons *hear* sounds. I would rather have thought that they should be described in terms of physical vibrations in or upon the eardrums]; (2) "The chemical (serotonin) fits into receptors, specially shaped molecules, on the *neighboring* neuron." [Why *neighboring*? Why not adjacent or contiguous *a la* Hume? "Neighboring" is a human term. Cells don't have neighbors any more than they enjoy eating ice cream]; and (3), "The presence of the serotonin in the receptor sparks an electrical impulse in the neuron and the sequence continues until it *culminates* in a *thought, feeling, or action.*" [But *before* it "culminates," it was only a nerve cell or a nerve impulse! Culmination implies a purposeful goal, a teleological end. Material motions simply stop; human goals culminate in a final end either achieved or failed. Why not simply say neurons "cause" or "impact" or "result in?"] This anthropomorphizing of brain cells appears deceptively suggestive; it intimates that there is somehow a plausible *identity* between (a) cellular motions, neurons, and synapses and that these *quantitative, measurable* events can magically, suddenly, and inexplicably become *interchangeable* with (b) *qualitative, self-conscious, reflexive experiences,* while continuing to share or exhibit an essential commonality between "thought, feeling, or action"; with sensations, emotions, thoughts, the will, the self, and the person. It begs the very question at issue: how do physical neurons become mental thoughts? How do synapses equate to meanings, relations, time-consciousness, and/or the unity of self-consciousness? How is physical motion *per se, in itself* the same as, identical to or with the *self*-conscious awareness *of motion as continuously transpiring within self-consciousness?* (Interestingly, in *The True Intellectual System of the Universe* (1678), Cudworth successfully attacks the doctrines of *hylozoism, of living matter* head-on.)

Both Dr. Whybrow and the *Newsweek* article camouflage their arguments by masquerading them as *physical* descriptions as if they carried *mental* meanings and by disguising them in human metaphors; essentially by letting them "fly under false colors." Dr. Whybrow easily glides between terms that *causally explain and describe how* brain cells mechanically operate and yet at the same time seductively suggesting *why* they "communicate" with their "neighbors" while exhibiting "duties and responsibilities," when in fact the whole causal sequence of events is simply a physical, cerebral interaction between brain cells, which can be completely described in physiological terms apart from any reference to the mind, mental perceptions, or human purposes. This misleading and subtle shift virtually allows him to move imperceptibly from causal synapses and electrochemical discharges to human intentions, purposes, and goals. The neuro-scientist, he assures us, has the special ability to *directly* "scan"—with the aid of an electroencephalograph machine—the minute motions in the brain as a person thinks and then s/he is able to *identify* and *equate* the jagged convulsions of the needle on his mechanical device with human self-consciousness. But he fails to distinguish between two very important issues: (a) *that* a person is thinking from (b) *what* s/he is *reflexively, intentionally,* and *meaningfully thinking of or about.*

Dr. Whybrow naively goes on to appeal to *memory* as Locke's necessary and sufficient criterion for the establishment of personal identity perfectly oblivious to the fact that Locke in his famous passage on personal identity in the *Essay* introduces the problem of a transposed memory as he asks us to imagine "the soul of a prince, carrying with it the consciousness [and memory] of a prince's past life, entering and informing the body of a cobbler as soon as deserted by his own soul, everyone sees he would be the same person with the prince , accountable only for the prince's actions but who would say it was the same man?" (*Essay*, II, xxvii, 15). Thus Locke distinguishes the *soul* of the Prince from the *body* of the cobbler. But according to Locke, the Prince is no longer the *same* man because the body is different. In this transfer of memory, "the more than one hundred billion brain cells" would not be transported as well, since the body was left behind. Also remember that Locke is a dualist; Dr. Whybrow is not. And Locke confesses that we frequently forget many things in our lives and that memory is highly unstable (*Essay*, II, xxvii, 10). Further, as Leibniz proposes against Locke, there are also *unconscious* thoughts (*petit perceptions*), which Locke and Dr. Whybrow simply disregard. Thus in Locke's famous controversy with Bishop Edward Stillingfleet, he suggests that conceivably God could have created "thinking matter." Is Dr. Whybrow also assuming that God is intervening through the hundred billion brain cells? All these complications testify to the fact that it is not at all easy to interpret and cite Locke as having provided a definitive "solution" to the problem of the continuity of the self and personal identity simply by an appeal to memory.

And what about the relation between bodily identity and memory? Already in the eighteenth-century, anatomists are well aware that all the cells in the human body are completely replenished every seven years. How long do individual brain cells last? How quickly are they replaced? Are only certain cells memory cells? Which ones are they? Physiologically, then, in bodily neuroscientific terms, in what sense am I still the *same* person that I was seven years ago. If each of us is restricted to a seven year bodily tenancy, what does that imply according to the neuroscientific model of the "self"? Does that mean that I cannot be held morally accountable for what "I" did more than seven years ago because "I" am no longer the *same* person=body? And how are "my" memories to be transmitted beyond each and every seven year cycle? If all the seven-year cells are defunct, am I then restricted to only seven years' worth of memories? Are there special memory cells empowered to "carry" or "transmit" the memories to the next seven year generation of cells beyond the original seven years?

Previously we suggested that the only viable stable criterion for "personal identity" according to neuroscience consists in a person's DNA, in her or his molecular "identity." Is a person in a coma without a memory still the same person? And what does that really tell us about our "human nature" in general as Dr. Whybrow intimates in the title of his lecture?

Dr. Whybrow next expounds on the "creative" aspects of Locke's theory of the self once more oblivious to the fact that Locke is a metaphysical dualist.

> It is to Locke that we owe the modern concept of the self—"that conscious thinking thing [*sic*]"—and of the importance of experience in shaping individual identity. For Locke the mind [brain?] in the beginning is a blank slate, a [physical] *tabula rasa*. We *create* ourselves and in doing so, we draw upon the world around us: every step we take is connected to the past and to the future (3; italic his).

Any and all issues regarding the substantial reality of the self, the reflexive creativity of the self, and the immanent temporality of consciousness are simply assumed and remain unaddressed. Previously I indicated how in the oft-invoked empirical paradigm of the mind as a "slab of wax" upon which sensations imprint their impressions like signet rings on wax (Plato's *Sophist*); or as a *tabula rasa* upon which experience writes (Aristotle's *De Anima* and Locke's *Essay*) both models confine awareness to a passive *perceptual* receptivity that merely observes and records incoming, externally-generated sensory data. For the neuroscientist, the initiating causal physical motions resulting in the brain's *perceptions* are *always* materially set in motion from *outside* the brain rather than *spontaneously* generated from within the mind. But if the brain is a soft blob of wax or a blank stone slate, then sensations alone are incapable of "creating" anything. Completely incognizant of any problems in reconciling the metaphor of a *physical tablet*—*the brain*—as an extended physiological surface in order to explain *mental* perceptions, Dr. Whybrow insists that "we create ourselves"! How? If we are all merely cellularly-programmed machines in the manner of manufactured computers made from electrical wires and circuits, how do we "create" ourselves? From whence derives the reflexive *insight* for computers to improve themselves? Cameras do not see and tape recorders do not hear. They merely record. But minds do. Seeing, hearing, understanding, and creatively thinking ahead are very different acts from the brain registering colors or recording sounds.

Meanwhile Dr. Whybrow also seems unaware that Hume, to whom he also refers in connection with his own discussion of personal identity, actually reduces the "self" to a fleeting "bundle" of disconnected impressions, "which succeed each other with inconceivable rapidity," which metaphor readily translates into Dr. Whybrow's one hundred billion electrical firings among separate brain cells is insufficient to unify the self. The only difference between Dr. Whybrow's hundred *billion brain* cells is prefigured by Hume's trillions of simple *mental impressions*! But the problem for both is how is the "bundle tied?" If there is no *real* self for Hume (although again see his rethinking *Of personal identity* in the *Appendix* to the *Treatise*, 636), then how are Dr. Whybrow's distinct billions of brain cells unified? By the same token, it is difficult to understand how brain cells can be the locus of moral responsibility. What is the mechanism of transition from cells to synapses and from synapses to thoughts and from thoughts to self identity and from self identity to the morality of the person *and* to the persons of others? Electricity? Perhaps lightning bolts think and clouds cry.

Dr. Whybrow also praises Locke for his moral stance on the *liberty* of the individual, which he readily translates into the freedom of economic capitalism via Adam Smith's *laissez faire* doctrines expounded in *The Wealth of Nations*. But Marxist economists may have a rather different account of the salutary evolutionary paths traversed by William Vanderbilt and the other Robber Barons of Victorian America with their combined manifold of trillions of brain cells.

> In the natural struggle for survival [Adam] Smith asserted self-love—what we call self-interest today—was God's "incomprehensible remedy" through which human society could achieve a balanced order. Such self-interest, argued Smith, when *appropriately shaped* through the give and take of the [economic] market made possible a society where the products of individual labor are fairly traded placing a decent life within the reach of all (10).

"*Appropriately shaped*" indeed! Don't we wish! Nevertheless, Dr. Whybrow proceeds with a praiseworthy flourish that all of the foregoing explains why capitalism and competitive *laissez faire* economics of the Hobbesian and Smithian variety is so humanely beneficial and predispositionally cooperative. Incidentally all this smacks of Hobbes' egoism but Hobbes' God is material (page 10). Is Dr. Whybrow's? This may require further explanation.

It is difficult to read this optimistic conclusion without once again calling to mind Hobbes' motives of self-preservation and egoistic self-interest; or recalling Marx's concerns surrounding all the ills of the Industrial Revolution, especially in England, and the rapacious exploitation of the workers by the Captains of Industry and the Lords of the Manor, while at the same time the industrialists' and capitalists' brains lagged far behind in terms of beneficent neuronal "plasticity." Hobbes' views on human nature on the one side and Schopenhauer's insights into the deeper psychology of egoism on the other side seem much closer to the mark in describing the narcissistic character of capitalism than Locke's tendencies toward a soft liberalism. For all those who optimistically trumpet the coming age of our "brave new world" (Skinner, *Walden Two*), they should heed the warning that the brain may still harbor within its pulsating cells and reptilian entrails a warlike past as we travel toward an unknown future (10). Nevertheless, Dr. Whybrow stands magnificently firm in his determination to assure us of our secure moral evolution and advancement.

> Thus human behavior is best understood when brain anatomy is placed within an evolutionary context. A primitive "lizard" brain, designed millennia ago for survival, lies at the core of the human brain and cradles the roots of ancient dopamine reward pathways that are the superhighways

of pleasure, curiosity, and desire. When the dinosaurs still roamed around this reptilian pith there evolved the limbic cortex—literally the "border crust"—of the early mammalian brain. This is the root of kinship behavior and the nurturance of the young that is characteristic of all mammalian species and particularly evident in our own social behavior (5).

He seems to forget that dinosaurs and lizards and their larger alligator cousins all lay eggs, that their egg-laying mothers abandon their repositories to the warmth of the nurturing sun and that perhaps their reptilian brains also may have persevered and endured by penetrating into the higher forms of mammalian life. During Dr. Whybrow's wonderful age of higher economic evolution, all this was also transpiring while William Graham Sumner was trumpeting his version of Social Darwinism and the economic survival of the fittest.

Dr. Whybrow also goes on to applaud Locke's religious toleration conveniently neglecting Locke's opposition not only to atheism but to Catholicism as well.

Whether Dr. Whybrow recognizes it or not, his model of reality and man is much closer to Hobbes' materialism and self-interested (selfish? egoistic? narcissistic?) motives than it is to Locke's Latitudinarian moralism or Hume's beneficent sentiments embedded in universal human nature, which are both unchanging. Neither Locke nor Hume, of course, is a Darwinist. Biological evolution was not yet firmly on the intellectual horizon of thought. That is precisely why for Hume, in our capacity as human beings, we are able to *understand* and *sympathize* with the virtues of the past on its own terms. But that is important because neuroscientists appear to base so much optimism on evolution by assuming and claiming naively that human beings exhibit a continuous *progress* from the "lizard brain" to our present human state. But it isn't just our warlike tendencies that belie our "gentle natures" but also our ruthless economic and competitive practices as well. Whether in the name of tribalism, world conquest, religion, colonialism, nationalism, Nazism, Fascism, or Communism, the human race is more plausibly described as an appropriating, colonizing, and accumulating swarm. As Hobbes muses in the *Leviathan,* nations are ever in a posture and atmosphere of impending war against each other.

Consequently Dr. Whybrow is naively assuming that biological evolution is not only making humans smarter but also in some significant sense "morally" better as well. He claims that as human beings evolve intellectually, we are at the same time progressing ethically; that the smarter we are, the nicer we are becoming. This is reminiscent of Stephen Pinker's thesis in his influential book, *The Better Nature of Our Angels.* Nice thought! But one could argue just as convincingly that as humans become smarter our intelligence is turning to even more powerful and efficient means of exterminating each other. When we observe the fascination with the violence so overwhelmingly manifest and prevalent in our sports, entertainment, movies, video games, television shows, and all this under the misleading banner of exciting pastimes, we begin to realize just how seductively these vicarious fantasies play upon our need to imagine and identify ourselves with anger and aggressors under the illusion that we are on the heroic side. Historically when we ponder the military engagements of America along with the "evolution" and "refinement" of more destructive means used during the Revolutionary War, the Civil War, the First and Second World Wars, the Korean War, the Viet Nam War, the Afghan War, the Iraqi War, and now the War against ISIS, and we remember we were the first to drop two atomic bombs—evolutionary precursors to the hydrogen bomb—and there seems to be an impending promise that we may not be the last to do so, it seems appropriate to reflect on exactly how we are becoming kinder and better. And when we view our global surroundings and the current dangerous proliferation of atomic and nuclear weapons among multiple nations, it appears more likely that the dark pessimisms of Hobbes and Schopenhauer shine much brighter than the dim light projected by Leibniz's optimism and Hume's gentleness.

Dr. Whybrow's metaphysical and epistemological stance is much closer to Hobbes whether he knows it or not. It is Hobbes, who like Dr. Whybrow, also seeks to show that things that appear to be very different from each other, as for example mind and matter, are at bottom really the same; that all existence can be reduced to matter plus motion; that subjective qualities are reducible to physical quantities; that things that have been categorized as non-physical or immaterial are in fact physical and bodily. In fact, Hobbes' consistent project is being systematically pursued today by biochemists, brain physiologists, neuroscientists, and neo-phrenologists, who merely replace his general materialistic theories with interactive electrochemical ones.

> Hobbes wants to show that things that appear to be very different from each other are at bottom very similar; and that things that look as if they must have been categorized as non-physical or non-material in fact are physical and bodily. Hobbes' project is being pursued today by biochemists and brain physiologists. They replace psychological concepts with chemical and physical ones. Hunger is a certain state of brain cells and certain chemicals in the blood stream.[2]

---

2  A.P. Martinich, *Hobbes: A Biography* (Cambridge: Cambridge University Press, 1999), 134.

And, of course, by the same token, the goal of the neurosciences is to reduce and translate secondary qualities (colors and sounds) and tertiary ones (beauty and goodness) to the primary ones of matter and motion as well. Colors really do not exist; what *really* exist are electromagnetic waves and/or photons of energy. But certainly the reductivist conviction into which Dr. Whybrow wishes to plunge us, by materializing the qualitatively *mental*, intellectual, aesthetic, and ethical into the quantitatively *physical*, chemical, biological, physiological, and neuroscientific requires a great deal more argumentation than he is able to provide for us. In brief, his materialistic reductionism follows our previously discussed elimination of the distinction between quantities and qualities. And clearly his sympathies are much more inclined toward Hobbes rather than Locke as evidenced in the following passage in which he criticizes the non-mechanistic outlook of the proponents of qualitative levels and distinctions. Thus he cites with approval the following defining Hobbesian principle.

> One of the marks of Hobbes' modernist metaphysics is his denial that there are degrees of being. For him, all beings are on the same level. In contrast, Plato, Aristotle, and almost all the scholastic philosophers distinguished between levels or grades of being. For them, some things were more real than others (18–19).

But this admission appears to contradict his earlier claim that we are evolving into kinder folk. For Dr. Whybrow, the above quotation clearly testifies to the fact that moral distinctions are not real despite his previous assurances to the contrary that we are evolving into nicer, gentler people. What happened to the dinosaur egg metamorphosing into mammalian maternalism? In reality, according to the neurosciences there is no genuine difference between good and evil, between beauty and plainness. Theoretically the neurosciences are committed to physical determinism and evaluative (both moral and aesthetic) relativism. So what are we to make of his so-called commitment to evolutionary "moral neuroplasticity"?

Moreover, it also seems rather odd for Dr. Whybrow to imply that in terms of the ethical evolution of the human brain that it was morally (quantitavely or qualitatively?) worse in the seventeenth-century than it is now in the twenty-first century. How? More than a hundred billion brain cells today and more to come? The bigger the brain the better? Is that *why* we are so morally improved today? If one initially rejects qualitative differences, how does on manage to later re-introduce qualitative distinctions of "better" and "worse," and "prettier" and "plainer" as they pertain to ethical and aesthetic valuations? When you eliminate quality, you extinguish morality and beauty from the world. There is no quantitative and objective *science* of virtue and art based on brain quantity. We recall that Bentham's utilitarian hedonistic calculus is based on a criterion of quantitative measures of physical pleasure and pain alone; and when John Stuart Mill tries to improve upon it by introducing the quality of happiness instead, it founders because happiness is essentially subjective and evaluative rather than objective and quantitative. Ethics deals with theories of value. If Dr. Whybrow is correct, the *real* distinction between primary qualities (matter and motion) and those that are subjective and mind-dependent (colors and sounds) also vanishes along with all the tertiary qualities, which include ethical and aesthetic valuations.

Dr. Whybrow has Darwinized the seventeenth- and eighteenth century philosophers in an anachronistic attempt to recruit them to his version of neuroplasticity, the doctrine that our neuronal cells are able to self-adjust and to create humanly desirable options and "advances" as his title suggests. But there is no conclusive *empirical* evidence of any such connection between improved intelligence and ethical ennoblement. The history of mankind is a history of conflicts and global colonization, wars committed toward the goal of narcissistic racial, religious, and national self-aggrandizement, power, and profit. Not infrequently the world displays a spectacular theater for the expression of man's inhumanity to man. Dr. Whybrow has unrealistically committed himself to misreading history; by securing himself in his laboratory populated by unreflecting electric computers, he has shut out the human world and its truly formative intellectual ages.

All this is not to deny the obvious scientific fact of evolution but it is intended *to challenge that simply because humans are becoming more intelligent—which may be challenged—it necessarily follows that they are getting kinder.* This is the same sort of illicit and naïve assumption made by Stephen Pinker in his aforementioned study. Dr. Whybrow's claim that as we evolve the brain undergoes a beneficial and ethical improvement needs to be supported by much stronger empirical evidence than he is able to provide. How this could be done, I am not sure.

More to the point, however, if the alleged precision serving in the neurosciences holds true, then presumably it should be possible that brain scans could *predict* a murderer and a terrorist as well as a philanthropist and a saint according to their brain scans. Thus by imprisoning the first and rewarding the second we could both qualitatively and quantitavely improve the lot of humankind. Remember the defining mark of any genuine science theoretically depends on its predictive value. Without the mantle of prediction, "science" is mere guesswork. The statistical measure that a "certain" percentage of individuals will successfully commit suicide in a society is hardly a useful tool in performing therapy on individuals.

At a single stroke, Dr. Whybrow dismisses out of hand—simply on the grounds of the last thirty years of neurological research!—well over 2,500 years of philosophy, literature, art, science, and religion when he dismisses (a) the mental dominion of the soul, mind, and ego; and (b) reduces the spontaneous, reflexive, and intentional acts of the mind to mechanical stimulus-response re-actions and the electrical chartings of the brain on a machine.

Dr. Whybrow also has something to say about "empathy"—"the capacity to feel what others feel." Obviously empathy can serve as both a psychological concept as well as an ethical one.

> Empathetic understanding is principally a *learned behavior* shaped by cultural norms and indeed recent findings in neuroscience reveal that there is a set of brain cells—appropriately called mirror neurons—that are delegated to this activity. Mirror neurons have the interesting property of firing both when an action is taken (for example, raising food to one's mouth) *and* when an action is merely observed being undertaken by another individual (8; italics mine).

How do we vault from conditioned and "learned behaviors" to ethical principles? This sounds more like the imprinting undergone by ducklings. Also if it is a learned behavior, then inevitably it will be restricted to merely expounding relativistic theories of morality and all his assurances to the contrary that we are *genuinely* improving all fall to the wayside as irrelevant. Recall as well that early on we distinguished the Is and the Ought in Hume and Kant. If this is the case, then evolution cannot bridge the gap. When Dr. Whybrow describes "empathy" as a learned behavior, he has forfeited any jurisdiction regarding a universal ethical standard or criterion.

But the very metaphor of a "mirror" seems especially unfortunate. Mirrors essentially provide two-dimensional images, while even the human *body* displays three dimensions. By contrast, the soul, mind, self, or ego exhibits a startling multi-dimensionality, an overwhelming multiplicity of active aspects, boundless complexity, and intimate intricacy. Nevertheless, Dr. Whybrow goes on to expand beyond empathy to account for the ultimate origin of "kinship behavior," which according to him, basically resides in the evolving mammalian brain of the female and the mother's nurturance of her young. But then it would seem to follow that mainly females would be endowed with this nurturing gene but males much less. Perhaps this is why Aristotle quipped that women love their offspring more than their male counterparts because at least they know they are theirs.

Finally, what does Dr. Whybrow have to say about Freud in relation to all of the foregoing spectacular advances in the neurosciences?

So you may be asking yourself what about Sigmund Freud?...In all honesty, I must tell you that Freud's contribution to behavioral science made almost a century ago are discussed more frequently today in literature than in neuroscientific circles (17).

According to Dr. Whybrow, the cause of Freud's shortcomings are his misguided psychological views of man, which misled him to be overly critical of the sexually repressive tendencies prevalent in the Victorian Age in which he lived as well as his pessimistic attitude fostered after the First World War and the advent of the second global conflict. In his passing criticism of Freud, he of course says nothing about "the better nature of our angels" during the Great Depression of the 1930s; the rise of Hitler, the atrocities committed in the networks of concentration camps, and the genocides of the Second World War and its aftermath. He remains silent about Communism and the betrayals of Hungary, Romania, Poland, Czechoslovakia, Bulgaria, and Yugoslavia and the internment of European nations behind the Iron Curtain; Stalin and the Russian pogroms and purges (Alexandre Solzhenetsin), and the internment of European nations behind the Iron Curtain. Perhaps we can at least conclude that today the brains of the ISIS combatants and suicide bombers are woefully lacking in neuroplasticity when they crucify priests, burn families in cages, and behead individuals in public. Surely their moral plasticity will improve in time as they continue to evolve.

In an article aptly titled *Neurotrash*, Raymond Tallis, himself a well-known neuroscientist, is dismayed by the extravagant claims of many of his colleagues and critical of all the exaggerated promises proposed regarding anticipated breakthroughs in neuro-economics, neuro-jurisprudence, neuro-ethics, neuro-aesthetics, neuro-theology, neuro-philosophy, and neuro-neuro (higher order "neuros"), and especially of the use of brain scans in an effort to scientifically pinpoint the neuronal location for *ethical* behaviors and all else for that matter. Although in this particular book review article, he does not discuss "neuroplasticity," nevertheless the claim that the brain self-evolves, that it can modify itself, is a common boast of other researchers as we have just seen, all of whom have gone on to claim that we can at least theoretically identify and point toward certain clusters of "bad" or "aggressive" cells, thus opening up the possibility of altering "human nature" and improving our ethics by surgery, radiation, and other invasive procedures. All that needs to be done is to isolate the "evil" neurons. But to the neuroscientists' rallying cry that "We are our brains" and the conviction that we can connect human functions to specific isolated cells, Tallis offers the following observation:

But this is not the only reason why neuroscience does not tell us what human beings "really" are: it does not even tell us how the brain works, how bits of brain work (or even if you could accept that dubious assumption that human living could be parceled up into a number of discrete functions), which bit of the brain is responsible for which function. The rationale for thinking of the kind—"this bit of the brain houses that bit of us" is mind-numbingly simplistic.[3]

The assumption is that neurophysiology can specifically locate all of our important cerebral functions so that whenever a new one is discovered, tested, and examined, it can be located in a *particular* cluster of activated neurons. It is like discovering, locating, and charting the motion of a new star in the firmament of the brain. A crucial difficulty, however, as Tallis conceives it, is that even *before* the brain reacts to *specific* stimuli, it is *already* actively "functioning," i.e., responding on a number of different fronts and levels; it is *already* collectively re-acting to *general* physical stimuli generated by the external environment and therefore we should not unrealistically entertain any hopes of pinpointing and observing the new or additional *neuronal* activities triggered by the novel stimuli. Neuroscience naively assumes that we can separate a tiny cluster of cells from the mass of "more than one hundred billion nerve cells." To do so, however, requires an endless and futile series of repetitious and fallible procedures in order to try to ferret out *exactly, precisely* which stimuli cause which particular "thoughts"; and accomplishing all that without taking into account the changing moods of the subject as repeated investigations are performed during the lengthy examination procedures.

Even more daunting is the fact that the neuronal investigations would be vulnerable to Heisenberg's principle of uncertainty as well as the distorting intrusions of the examiner and the unnatural experience of being hooked up to a machine.

In reviewing two other related neuroscientific studies, Tallis asks us first to consider the thesis of Drs. Zeki and Andreas in regard to the emotion of "love" as it is signaled by its own specific signature of neuronal activity "in the medial insula and the anterior cingulated cortex and, subcortically, in the caudate nucleus and the putamen, all bilaterally." Why won't this work? Let us read Tallis' objection.

> Finally and most importantly, the experiments look at the response to very simple stimuli—for example, a picture of the face of a loved one

---

[3] Raymond Tallis, "Neurotrash," *New Humanist*, 124:6 (2009), n.p.

compared with the face of one who is not loved. But romantic love is not like a response to a stimulus. It is not even a single enduring state, like being cold. It encompasses many things, including not feeling in love at that moment; hunger, indifference, delight; wanting to be kind, wanting to impress, worrying about the logistics of a meeting; lust, awe, surprise, imagining conversations, events; speculating what the loved one is doing when one is not there; and so on. The most sophisticated neural image, by the way, cannot even distinguish between physical pain and the pain of social rejection: they seem to "light up" the same areas!

But notice the Bergsonian catalogue of complications and complexities in the passage above as it points to *affective and evaluative qualities*—both secondary and tertiary. Recording the reaction of the brain to sensory stimuli, e.g., reaction to a bright light, is very different than plotting the response to emotionally laden "stimuli," which is never "simple." Being "in love" is qualitatively different than eating your favorite chocolates. Further imagine that the neuro scientist is searching to determine the brain cells, neurons, and synapses in order to *isolate* the *emotion* of loneliness, the *meaning* of loneliness in a subject's life at a particular moment in time, for example when she was ten-years-old. The quality of her loneliness presumably would be very different now that she is a divorced single mother with several children living in poverty. How does the neuroscientist "parcel out" the difference, the nuances of past memories from the present "tainted" recollections? Moreover, the *present feeling* of loneliness, like the emotion of love (above), is not a "simple" emotion; it is encrusted with feelings of abandonment, betrayal, isolation, jealousy, anxiety, anger, etc. These intimate and irreproducible feelings and many others are the complex and multi-dimensional aspects of loneliness. Like love loneliness is not "one thing" nor can the intertwined synthetic *a priori* "components" be separated? Loneliness is essentially a conglomeration of (1) *affective* and (2) corresponding *cognitive* states including *meanings* that are embedded and interwoven with *emotional feelings* of past regrets as well as future expectations of intimacy; and even further (3) *evaluative judgments* such as "Is all this really worth it?" The point is that powerful emotions, like love or hate or loneliness or intimacy, occur within the context of "lived" experiences with a multiplicity of nuances, fringes, and horizons of feelings, meanings, and relations within consciousness. Presumably the electroencephalograph machine is unable to distinguish the *quality* of my loneliness in grieving the death of a friend from my loneliness following a rejection by a friend. Also the *reflexive feeling* of the emotion is one "thing"; the *intentional nature* of the emotion is quite another issue. No provisions are made for differentiating the *reflexive* from the *intentional* qualities attached to objects, moods, and situations; or in distinguishing the quality of temporality involved in feelings and thoughts that are *intended* to refer to the past, present, or future. The loneliness of regretting the past is qualitatively different than the pain of experiencing the loneliness of the present and the anticipatory anxiety of loneliness in the future. Fortunately, of course, for the neuroscientist there are over one hundred billion brain cells in the human skull so presumably s/he should be able to find *some* close matches among so many interminable possibilities. And once more exactly how many brain cells are required to form a sensation as opposed to a feeling and a feeling as opposed to a meaning and a meaning as opposed to a thought and a thought as opposed to a proposition and a proposition as opposed to an inference? Tallis refers to all these misguided efforts as forms of "neo-phrenology" and "neuromania."

By following Tallis' trenchant criticisms and playing off all of the foregoing overly optimistic neuroscientific promises of success while comparing and contrasting them with the models of consciousness advocated by philosophical dualism, rationalism, idealism, phenomenology, and existentialism, we shall discover the following difficulties:

> The problems begin at a very basic level. The brain as understood by neuroscience is a piece of matter tingling with electrochemical activity. There is nothing in this activity that would make the stand-alone brain capable of making the material objects around it have the *appearance* to it or able to have the [self-conscious, reflexive] sense of itself as the subject to whom these objects appear. Consider something as elementary as seeing something in front of you. While it is easy to understand how the brain, understood as a material object, would respond with nerve impulses to light falling upon it, it is not possible to explain how those nerve impulses then become a *representation* [i.e., the representative theory of perception] of the source of that light; how the effects of the light in the brain reach back in a counter-causal way [i.e., in a reflexive, self-conscious way] to the object from which the light originated.

What remains unexplained is how a neuronal sensation is different from a neuronal reflexive "thought." Material causation, in short, explains or is able to describe a path to *how* the light gets into the brain and impacts it but not *how* the human gaze is able to *actively* "boomerang" the visual look back to itself; to recapture the arc; to return it to *self*-consciousness; how to *both* look out *and* return the look to its original source; to both *see* and *mean* an illuminated world. In short, self-consciousness with its power to reflexively view its own "representations" remains unaccounted for in neuroscience. Self-consciousness is *both* immediately aware of its present activity but also temporally aware of having done so, of having acted. Can the electroencephalograph distinguish between a present sensation and the memory of a sensation? These secondary questions involve the *temporal* aspect, the *temporal* dimension of the neurons themselves. And what about dreams? Can the neuroscientist distinguish waking states from dreams and dreams from fantasies? For a phenomenologist the difference resides in intentionality.

And yet Tallis declares there are still more formidable difficulties ahead as well:

> However, there are other aspects of human consciousness—the unity of the self [Kant], the formulation of intentions [Husserl], the performance of voluntary actions—that are even further out of reach of the neuroscientific explanation. So although the brain is a necessary condition of consciousness, it does not follow from this that it is a sufficient condition of consciousness or that its workings are identical with consciousness.

Moreover, arguing by extrapolation, neuroscientists, like Patricia and Paul Churchland and John Cacioppo, simply assume on *evolutionary grounds* that by extension the individual brain is able to metamorphise into a social brain because the same dynamics that apply to the person will also work as well when applied to the group. This premise is terribly presumptuous.

> The notion of "the social brain" is an attempt to have the brain as an evolved organ, and as a participant in a social sphere that an unprejudiced view would see as being remote from organic life, though of course requiring it. This both having-and-eating is not on. Firstly, the brain *qua* brain is a piece of matter which, though it may be wired into the larger environment, including other brains, is essentially solitary. That is precisely why it is possible to look at it in isolation in the lab and, indeed, to examine animal brains in the same way we examine human brains and find very similar things going on—including the activity of those mirror neurons I referred to earlier, which have been touted as the basis of human empathy and solidarity. The brain is a solitary organ within a solitary organism (Tallis).

In addition, human societies are not comparable or even remotely analogous to animal nervous systems and groups. As Aristotle tells us in his *Politics*, there are some creatures such as ants and bees that are by their very nature and instinct "social" but there is no indication that they are still significantly evolving as far as we can tell from individual instincts to a "communal consciousnesses."

Generally animal species evolve because of environmental conditions. Humans evolve because of intellectual challenges. In short:

> There is a huge gap between the community of minds of animal quasi-societies. The vast landscape that is the human world has been shaped by the activity of explicit [self-conscious] individuals who do things deliberately [i.e., self-consciously, intentionally, and purposefully]. Uniquely, the denizens of that world entertain theories about their own nature and about the world; they systematically inquire into the order of things and the patterns of causation and physical laws that seem to underpin that order; create cities, laws, institutions, frame their individual lives within a shared history; justify and excuse their behavior according to general, *abstract principles*. Neuro-evolutionary theorists try to ignore all this evidence of difference.

Consistently Tallis appeals to reflexive self-consciousness and purposeful intentionality. There is an enormous difference between the animal instincts of neuroscience and the human intellect. As Kant suggested long ago, if the only goal for human beings was some version of utilitarian pleasure or happiness, then we would all have been better served by being endowed by nature with instincts instead of reason (*Foundations of the Metaphysics of Morals,* Section 393). Note also Tallis' references to "abstract principles" and "laws" as *meanings* as opposed to neurons and synapses.

But what if the neuroscientist's assumption that evolution necessarily impels us toward an increasing social existence can be questioned and challenged? What if each of us realizes we are getting more and more crowded by a humanity of strangers and each of us begins to evolve toward a more aggressive sense of self-preservation, an internally generated "neuroplastic" independence and self-reliance? Could not our socioplasticity evolve into monoplasticity? And then what follows for "morality"? Will that make us more or less moral? Evolution is a double-edged sword.

In a companion review, Tallis proceeds to criticize two other recent works from within the perspective of the neurosciences and specifically ones in which the issue of the *origin* of self-consciousness is at stake.[4] The mistake that both of the reviewed books commit is in trying to "explain" self-consciousness in neurological terms. Basically they assume it while attempting to explain it away. First Tallis criticizes Nicholas Humphrey's *Soul Dust: The Magic of*

---

4  Raymond Tallis, "A Mind of One's Own: The Metaphysical Limitations of Neuroscience," *New Statesman,* February 24, 2011, n.p.

*Consciousness,* in which the author argues how a piece of matter, such as a human brain, can have conscious experiences, an awareness of certain (mental) items that do not seem to be of such a nature that they can be conjured up from matter alone. Humphrey's "explanation" is that consciousness is "a magical mystery show that you lay on yourself"; "a self-created entertainment for the mind" staged by one part of the brain to entertain another part of the brain. According to Tallis, the critical point in Humphrey is the mistaken goal of trying to discredit the Lockean and Humean "representational theory of perception"—that ideas are images or copies of something other than themselves, namely the external world—by eliminating the dualism inherent in those particular forms of metaphysical and epistemological thinking. In attempting to do so, Humphrey appeals to "higher" and "second order" intelligences by reducing and degrading consciousness to lower more basic modes of physical sensations and thus eliminating the imputation of primacy to representational consciousness. Tallis' response to this strategy follows:

> You cannot get to representation, however, without prior conscious, first order representation, so the latter cannot explain the former. Neuroscientists of consciousness try to elude this obvious objection by asserting that representations are not necessarily conscious. In fact, all sorts of aspects are not conscious at all. According to Humphrey, "before consciousness ever arose, animals were engaged in some kind of internal monitoring system of their own responses to sensory "stimulation." What is "inner" about unconscious processes, material events in the material brain? And how can they account in monitoring? These questions are not silenced by the author's reasoning that consciousness is "the product of some kind of illusion chamber, a charade." Nor does Humphrey tell us how he awoke from his consciousness to discover that it is an illusion.

The next work Tallis reviews is Antonio Damasio's *Self Comes to Mind: Constructing the Conscious Brain* and finds it even more puzzling and evasive than the previous study. Once more, consciousness is "constructed" from certain prior evolutionary advances in biological and cerebral transformations, which supposedly build on animal "feedback loops" designed to secure an interior path to the "self." Allegedly this will account for the activity of *reflexive* self-consciousness. So-called "feedback loops," however, are simply a very naïve and crude way to avoid twenty-five hundred years of dualist, rationalist, and idealist philosophical principles and insights by simply dubbing them "feedback loops." But when, like Humphrey, Damasio simply ascribes a crucial but unaccounted for role to the endless human evolutionary generations of selfhood by merely invoking biological "feedback loops" in the brain, this strategy completely fails to account for the "character" of *reflexion* when consciousness actively turns back on itself and *knows* that it has done so *self*-consciously, while in the very same moment *unifying* various sensations, feelings, and thoughts *within* and *to* the *same* self. Simply appealing to lower animal "feedback loops" fails to capture the *spontaneous* binding, unifying, synthesizing acts that Kant establishes as a bedrock principle for his theory of *apperceptive* self-consciousness. Remember that perception and apperception are not the same. Empiricists perceive; dualists, rationalists, and idealists apperceive. Passive perception, i.e., sensation according to the empirical account is not only a lower order of cognitive awareness in comparison with self-consciousness but indeed a terminal one as well. It goes no farther than the sensations themselves. The activity of thought is essentially a *beyondness* whereas sensation is a *thereness* and *a nowness* (Hegel's Sense-Certainty Section).

Feedback loops are at best u-turns; they are not circles, not reflexive acts. They cannot make us self-aware that we exist completely alone in our own intimate temporal-frames. Also feedback loops cannot *create* new "orders of reality" for our selves and others. Biting into a brown apple and realizing that it is rotten may be a biological "feedback loop" we share with chipmunks but thinking about planting an apple orchard is a very different and higher order of qualitative self-conscious activity. There is a "world of difference" between animal "feedback-loops" and human creativity and it cannot be explained away simply on the basis of Darwinian and biological evolution.

In addition, Tallis assures us that "feedback loops" are evident throughout the biosphere, even at the level of single cells—and he further informs us that they are even present in the meanest pocket calculator. But do pocket computers possess not only (a) "feedback loops" but indulge in (b) "mirroring" capacities as well? Can we hold them ethically accountable? And as Tallis continues, such "feedback loops" could deliver a real *self only if* consciousness had *already* been achieved in the loops that are feeding back on themselves, which he denies.

As Tallis informs us, other micro-neurologists and micro-neo-phrenologists have erroneously and quixotically promoted notions of "higher order" paradigms of consciousness all supposedly replete with increasingly complex and novel technicalities sanctioned by such impressive adjectival subtitles as "actualist neuroscience," "dispositional neuroscience," "self-representational neuroscience," "perceptual neuroscience," and so on *ad nauseum*.

But I shall argue in the last chapter that loneliness, *both* as a psychological feeling *and* a cognitive meaning, is constituted in consciousness as an "umbrella concept," a genus to species relationship, which includes the feelings and the meanings of hostility, anxiety, abandonment, betrayal, shame, guilt, depression, and so on. This will lead to two problems for the neuroscientist. First, it would be prohibitively time-consuming and self-defeating to attempt to trace back all the cells, neurons, and synaptic firings in these multiple *nuanced* synthetic *a priori* feelings, meanings, associations, and relations back to the original more than one hundred billion brain cells. In other words, I am contending that when a person both emotionally feels and cognitively knows they are lonely, it is a dynamic flowing state of consciousness that indicates a constituted *multiplicity of emotions in a unity;* a complex of *shifting* feelings and meanings (Bergson). Loneliness is a foundational psychological principle and it is not at all like experiencing thirst, which is relatively simple by comparison and so is its cure. One drinks a glass of water and the situation is resolved. By contrast, the feelings, meanings, nuances, and relations involved in loneliness *often* entail the self's sense of rejection by another self, who has her or his own unique "aura" that also has to be taken into consideration. Simply (a) feeling lonely and alone by my self and (b) feeling *both* rejected by an other self *and* alone are very different experiences. That difference without considering anything beyond it, testifies to the utter complexity of loneliness. The dynamics of loneliness and its relation to other multiple selves is complicated and its alleviation even more so. This is where intentionality enters in. My loneliness is different when I am rejected by my wife, child, friend, neighbor, employer, etc. All these *meaningful* considerations need to be taken into account.

In his own extended study, *Aping Mankind,* Tallis systematically continues to challenge the exaggerated claims of his colleagues on a number of central points. In quoting Daniel Dennett's *Materialism and Behaviorism,* Tallis makes clear the position he wishes to attack by citing Dennett's *Consciousness Explained.*

> There is only one sort of stuff, namely *matter*—the physical stuff of physics, chemistry, and physiology—and the mind is somehow nothing but a physical phenomenon. [But is the "phenomenon" physical or mental?] In short, the mind is the brain...We can (in principle) account for every mental [physical?] phenomenon using the same physical principle, laws, and raw materials that suffice to explain radioactivity, continental drift, photosynthesis, reproduction and growth.[5]

The term *phenomenon* derives from the Greek meaning appearance. The distinction is between appearance *versus* reality and the related claim that things

---

5  Raymond Tallis, *Aping Mankind: Neuromania, Darwinitis, and the Misrepresentation of Humanity* (London: Routledge, 2011); 41; cf. 138. hereafter cited as Tallis, *AM.*

are not always what they seem. It's probably the original and the oldest philosophical distinction. It means there are *two* "entities" and not "only one sort of stuff." Between this dualistic chasm lies a world of meaningful differences with (presumably) reality on one side and the multiplicity of appearances on the other side; the One and the Many; a material realm and a plurality of monadic mental spheres. And that is why philosophers since Plato have distinguished the two into what is real and what *appears* to be real but is not. Therefore Dennett's careless and interchangeable use of the terms matter, mind, and phenomenon only produces serious confusions. The obvious conclusion for Dennett is what he eventually blurts out: "You are your brain." And then the words "mind," "mental," and "phenomena" should simply drop out. It does not make any sense to talk about "the chemistry of the mind" or the "physics of phenomena" in materialism.

Tallis' philosophical perspective proposes four criticisms against neuroscience: (1) the extravagant claims of the neurosciences; (2) the adoption of strict determinism with the consequent rejection of freedom; (3) the erroneous comparison of human thought with animal behavior on the basis of evolutionary Darwinian principles; and (4) the analogy of the human brain to a computer. Beyond this quartet of disagreements, he tentatively *seems* to suggest a fifth challenge to neuroscience by defending metaphysical dualism and freedom. He puts his thesis quite suggestively in the following terms: "The truth is no theory of matter will explain why material entities (e.g., human beings) are conscious and others are not" (Tallis, *AM*, 119). Referring to "the lunacy of behaviorism," he goes on to state:

> Behaviorism denied that there was anything of much interest to scientific psychology in human beings between their perceptual input and their behavioral output, between stimulus and response.
>
> TALLIS, *AM*, 119

Gilbert Ryle, in his behaviorally slanted study, *The Concept of Mind*, allows for "dispositional attributes," which is essentially a means of explaining away thinking based on a modified way of extending the stimulus-response mechanism. For example, glass is dispositionally liable to break should it be struck sharply. It is dispositionally brittle. Analogously, an automobile driver's body is dispositionally conditioned to stop at a red light. One does not need to appeal to a Cartesian "ghost in the machine" in order to account for the driver's bodily responses. No appeal to self-consciousness is necessary; by the principle of Occam's razor, there is no need to involve an immaterial mind in order to account for a motorist suddenly stopping at an unexpected red light while he is driving.

He is not performing two things at once; *both* physically driving *and* thinking ahead about possibly having to stop suddenly. That would be a "category mistake." Rather, he is dispositionally *conditioned* to react behaviorally to the sudden stimulus of an unanticipated red traffic light.

Further behaviorism denies not only "introspection" or self-consciousness but also the existence of the mind itself. It cuts through this bifurcation by analogizing the brain to a computer (Tallis, *AM,* 191 ff.). The scientific "beginning and end" of this equation identifies the brain as just another piece of the cosmos distributed in an infinite chain of causes and effects leading back to the Big Bang (*AM,* 52, 251, 257) . Not only can senseless matter think but "consciousness" is merely a certain kind of physiological brain motion demonstrating a single homogeneous material quality consonant with the original formation of the universe. There is no "qualitative" difference between turning on a table lamp and someone waking up in the morning; no real difference between a supernova exploding and someone raging in anger. In fact, we can simply eliminate the term "quality" altogether and confine ourselves in describing reality in quantitative terms of matter and motion alone.

As stated, Tallis himself appears to suggest a dualist metaphysical stance by bluntly maintaining that the brain is a necessary condition but *not* a sufficient one for consciousness to exist (*AM,* 90). If this is indeed Tallis' position, I would fully agree with it but much more has to be said by Tallis in its qualified defense.

In any event, the philosophical tenor and strength of his book lies in demonstrating that we are very different from both computers and lower animals. On both counts, he challenges the claims of the neurosciences as leading to an extreme form of reductive materialism, which rejects any semblance of human freedom. Both neuroscience and behaviorism offer a paradigm of mankind accompanied by a strict determinism; both eliminate the reality of the mind and its mental, non-physical activities and adopt a system of causal explanation readily translating human conduct into stimulus-response mechanisms and overt, publicly observable behaviors.

Reports of subjective experiences and introspection are dismissed by neuroscientists as metaphysical, irrelevant, and basically either non-existent or illusionary. The brain is interpreted as the passive recipient of external motions striking the senses. In turn, this mechanistic theory leads to a physical determinism, which in effect is able inexorably to trace causally the lineage of each and every event in reverse back to the Big Bang as previously intimated, which Tallis categorically rejects as he champions a form of undefined human freedom. In the following we shall see that many of his criticisms are in line with dualist and/or idealist assumptions. I am not suggesting that Tallis himself is a dualist or an idealist—although a strong case can be made for that interpretation—but rather that he clearly sees that the neurosciences are incapable of answering what dualists and idealists assume to be the theoretical strengths of their anti-determinist doctrines.

> For humans [mental] perception is not simply a means by which, as organisms, we are wired into the world; it is also the basis for the *distance* that is opened up between ourselves as self-conscious agents and the world we can operate on as if from an outside: a virtual outside that is built up into a real, but *non-physical* outside that is the human world. Our perception yields objects that transcend our awareness; we are explicitly aware that the object is more than our perceptions—it is not exhausted by our perceptions—and that it is other than our self. This transcendent object, which is seen as something only partly revealed, is related to a transcendent self that is other than it. There is no room for this kind of [dualistic?] thing in a causally hard-wired universe of material things (*AM*,109; cf. 105, 119, 172, 229; italics mine).

That "distance," that "non-physical space" strongly suggests metaphysical dualism.

In addition he insists:

> You cannot be a materialist and ascribe to the brain the capacity of making the material world [self-consciously] present to itself. More specifically you cannot deal with the two features of consciousness [i.e., world and self-consciousness] that are connected and to make other items appear.
> *AM*, 103–104

Systematically Tallis separates his criticisms of neuroscience under several headings. His comments concerning the subsection titled "Self-Consciousness and the Unity of Consciousness" presents a discussion of consciousness that clearly recalls Kant's theory of transcendental apperception and the *unity of consciousness* principle, wherein *the concept of the self is mutually constituted by the concept of the object within the mind itself* as it is borne out throughout Tallis' text. Thus, according to Tallis, "There is another problem encountered facing the neurosciences at the most basic level of consciousness: awareness itself" (*AM*, 99–100; cf. 118), which deals with the "unity of consciousness being one over time" and the question "what knits together a multidimensional lace of moments" (*AM*, 121). (We recall Plotinus' telling phrase that it is self-consciousness alone that can "knit time together.")

Commenting on *Intentionality,* Tallis also supports Husserl's principle of transcendence as well when he next turns to a discussion of intentionality as the other defining attribute of consciousness presented in Brentano's *Psychology from an Empirical Standpoint.* Although not mentioning Husserl by name (possibly because he regards him as an idealist and isn't familiar with his writings), Tallis describes mental items as possessing the essential activity of *intentionality,* the active property of consciousness to go beyond itself, to be engaged with the "aboutness" of meanings and things; that our thoughts are directed toward meaningful-"things"; consciousness targets meanings that are constituted as *transcendent* to the self; "on things other than the subject." In fact, Tallis sets no limit to the power of intentional acts as they are

> directed on objects or parts of the world that are real or virtual entities or clusters of possibilities that are felt to be other than the subject. But they are also present in all knowledge and, indeed, all perception....There is nothing elsewhere in [material] nature comparable to intentionality. It will prove to be the key to our known human differences: our subjectivity; our sustained self-consciousness; our sense of others as selves like us; first- and second-person beings; our ability to form intentions [i.e., goals, purposes, plans]; our freedom and our collective creation of a human world offset from nature.
> TALLIS, *AM,* 104–105 cf., 103–104, 109 and Chart, 252

Again:

> Even neuromaniacs should appreciate...their basic claim that consciousness is located in the brain still requires the brain to transcend, to get outside [to go beyond] itself, beginning with the full-blown intentionality of human perception.
> TALLIS, *AM,* 237

Clearly in these passages Tallis is convinced that neurophysiology and neuroscience are in principle completely incapable of accounting for the *acts* and *activities* of intentional consciousness.

At this point in his text, Tallis offers a diagram highlighting the difference between the neuroscientific account of what he describes as (1) the linear "Direction of causal relation" traveling *from* his Red Hat *to* the "Neural activity" of the brain resulting in "Perception" as opposed to (2) the linear "Direction of intentionality" directed *at* the meaning of his "Red Hat" as it travels *from* his "perception" *to* the external world (Tallis, *AP,* 106). In a similar diagram in my article, "The Simplicity Argument versus a Materialist Theory of Mind" (1976) and in my study, *Contingent Immaterialism* (1984), I offer the same illustration but I also add a third principle and paradigm. Both of our diagrams show the causal arrow of materialism as shooting from the Red Hat (to use his example) to strike the brain in contradistinction to the intentional arrow projecting from consciousness outwardly to *mean* the Red Hat as an object in the world. Both our arrows "move" unidirectionally, linearly with the first moving from the external world to the brain and the second as a trajectory of intentionality moving from consciousness to *mean* the Red Hat as an intentional object in the world. The first is empirically passive, while the second is intentionally active. But the problem is that there is also a third distinguishable movement: reflexive circularity, the self actively returning upon its self and carrying the projected *meaning* of the object both reflexively and *temporally* "back" to itself. This model is circular. And Tallis acknowledges this. Consciousness *retrieves* itself. That is why I maintain that there are two motions depicted in idealism and phenomenology, an intentional as well as a reflexive one. The first is unilinear and the second is circular. But both are actively, i.e., spontaneously necessary and together they constitute consciousness. Because both are complementary acts of consciousness they constitute a synthetic *a priori* relation.

As Tallis continues, it is important to emphasize that this "mysterious" *attribute* of intentionality represents a challenging puzzle that the brain alone is incapable of addressing let alone resolving because brains are like sponges, which merely absorb certain *aspects* or *ingredients* from their immediate sensory environments but are incapable of exuding anything beyond their own composition. According to Tallis, "Intentionality highlights the mystery of what brains are, ultimately, supposed to do; namely, *to make other* [meaning-intending] *items, indeed worlds, appear to someone*" (*AM,* 111). All intentionalities are transcendent acts that culminate in *"meant meanings"* open to self-conscious explorations, investigation, and the creation of further and richer meanings (*AM,* 231; cf. 237).

Tallis repeatedly confirms that the *act* of transcendence is an *act* of freedom, a freedom which (at times) breaks the bonds of causal determinism. It is the essential ability of consciousness to circumvent the "Laws of Nature" by exploiting and transcending them for its own purposes. It is futile for man to circularly repeat the same thoughts forever insularly. Man is only truly free when he knows not only his own thoughts but transcends them, travels *beyond* them as well. "We *utilize* the laws of nature by aligning ourselves with the one that leads [beyond our selves] to our goal and we do so from a virtual outside-of nature that is the world opened up by intentionality" (*AM,* 259).

Tallis throughout his work assumes both self-consciousness and personal identity without necessarily realizing the *reflexive* nature of what he has unsuspectingly incorporated within his epistemological and ontological scheme. On the other hand, perhaps he *is* self-aware of his "accommodation." In any case, throughout the book, he makes it manifestly clear that the neurosciences are unable in any serious fashion either to *causally explain* the unity of consciousness; its reflexive nature; its immanent temporality; its intentional acts; or its freedom. For the neuroscientist, "There is no model of *merging* activity in the nervous system that would not lead to *mushing* of the merged components and a loss of their individual identity" (*AM*, 116). Further, "This, then, is the heart of the problem: consciousness is manifestly a unified one but at the same moment it is also explicitly multiple" (*AM*, 117). And accordingly Tallis rather unknowingly aligns his own positive concept of "merging"—as opposed to "mushing"—with Leibniz's and Kant's "unity in multiplicity" and Hegel's "identity in difference" principles.

In his discussion of *Immanent Time-Consciousness,* Tallis is perspicacious enough to bring forward the self's capacity for creating an immanent time-consciousness of the Kantian and Husserlian varieties without, however, apparently being aware of their many implications all of which are deeply committed to an idealist and immaterialist paradigm of consciousness. Thus, he describes how we, as human beings, exhibit a unity of consciousness "over time" (*AM*, 121). He criticizes Hume's "bundle theory of the self" as consisting of a succession of impressions without realizing that Kant uses Hume's admission of succession as a refutation of the latter's skepticism regarding the substantial and continuous unity of the self. In any case, for my purposes, the important thing is his acknowledgment that neuroscience is systematically unable to "explain" internal time-consciousness as opposed to the neuroscientific account of time as a perception of the motion of objects through space.

> Our discussion has led us to think about the nature of time; more particularly about the physics of time. It is important to appreciate that, in the absence of an observer, time has no tenses [i.e., no meaning]; not only does the physical world not have past and future in which events are located, but it doesn't have the present. For an event to count as being present, there has to be someone for whom it is present, for whom it is "now" as opposed to "then" and "not yet" (*AM*, 132).

Under the subtitle of *The Representational Theory of Perception and Its Qualia,* Tallis introduces another critical factor that reinforces the distinction—and the complication—between the physical and the mental. It is grounded in the ability, the power of mental acts to somehow "elicit" a sphere of appearances—the mysterious "veil of perception"—from the material world thereby problematically separating three *distinct* "elements" from each other: (a) matter; (b) representational phenomena or mental appearances; and (c) active mind(s). But if the neurosciences reduce and transform *everything, all existence* into permutations of matter and motion, to primary and objective quantities *alone,* as they claim, then it is impossible (a) to distinguish thinking selves from each other or (b) to account for the difference between primary versus subjective secondary and tertiary qualities. In brief, it is impossible to show how matter *alone* can *cause* such entirely different *kinds* and *levels* of experiences: sensory, affective, primary, mental, secondary and tertiary qualities, as well as evaluative. Indeed, Tallis proceeds to subtitle another section in the chapter as "Material objects do not have (phenomenal) appearances when viewed through the eyes of physics" and he adds that according to neuroscience "The material world has only primary qualities such as solidity, extension, motion, number and shape" and consequently that "These by themselves would not, however, amount to a full-blown appearance" (*AM,* 140 ff.; 183 ff.). "Nothing in appearance-less nerve impulses suggests that they have the ability to make appearance-less material things acquire (phenomenal) appearances" (*AM,* 143).

In *The Primacy of Consciousness over Language* section, Tallis disparages the contortionist attempts of linguistic meta-theorists as they attempt to translate and solve philosophical issues by determining a precise form of linguistic "meaningfulness." He points out that there is an obvious difficulty because of the mediating factor that consciousness has *already* interposed between itself and matter. In other words, language is twice removed from reality. This, of course, prevents any and all efforts to reach reality "in itself." Language and words pervert how we "see" and "talk" about the world and ourselves in it (Wittgenstein). The use of language is highly relativistic and subjectivist. It not only varies from culture to culture but also its "meanings" vary from person to person. It is when we transfer epithets and misuse language by applying words inappropriately through the use of metaphors and analogies that our difficulties begin; when we endow inanimate objects with the qualities of human consciousness and slip from nominal definitions and descriptions into using illicit adventitious explanations in the manner of Dr. Whybrow that we go astray. Language is thrice removed from what is real, first by material things; second by the interposition, the mediation of representational consciousness, ideas as phenomenal images; and third by its *symbolic* re-re-presentations provided through and by the mediation of words *qua signs and symbols.* Consider in what sense or manner a mathematical system functioning as a "language" *corresponds* to reality. At best, it can only serve as a "descriptive" language that merely measures and weighs spaces and the distance between events. But it tells us absolutely nothing about the qualities prevalent in the world (Bergson, Husserl). Consciousness and language are worlds apart. Words are restricted and confined to their definitions while meanings are liberated by their nuances. Think of the brain as composed of Lego blocks. Then think of the mind as a flowing river at times turbulent and at other times forming quiet pools; think of playing scrabble and then think of creating a poem. The first sets are quantitative and the second group is qualitative.

Tallis also criticizes Wittgenstein and his "picture theory" of language for holding us captive and urging us "to look and see" how words are used (Tallis, *AM*, 183–184). At the start of the *Philosophical Investigations,* following St. Augustine, Wittgenstein describes how words are used to communicate between a builder and his assistant and that "individual words in a language name objects." This leads to an assumption that words and things exhibit a natural affinity; the Aristotelian notion that language reflects reality; that words accurately capture the world. But *before* we can use words, before the functional use of words can assist us as human beings, there is *already* consciousness *without* words. Consciousness and meanings flow, while words remain static instruments. They are intended to be precise as opposed to nuanced. But words are far removed from Husserl's *eidetic* desideratum, which is to move beyond words and go directly "to the things themselves," i.e., to intuit essential meanings before, beneath, and/or beyond language. Accordingly, Tallis invites us to turn to *essences* that are intentionally meaningful modes of consciousnesses *independently* of language:

> Neuromania demands of its adepts that they should ascribe human characteristics to physical processes taking place in the brain. This depends on a cavalier way with words that is now so universal as to have been almost invisible, making it quite difficult to see the unbridgeable gap between what happens in the brain and what people do [and say]. It illustrates the force of Wittgenstein's observation that we are held captive by a picture of ourselves from which we cannot escape because it is written into the very language in which we think about our nature. The linguistic habit that has kept so many in thrall to Neuromania is referring to the brain and bits of the brain in ways that would be appropriate only if we were referring to whole human beings.
> TALLIS, *AM,* 183–184

There are minds and there are things; there are pictures of things and names of things; and names in different languages can refer to the "same" things because they are *indirect* symbols and only *by proxy* signs of realities that are *not* symbols and signs. And thus we are seduced into thinking that the words *are* the reality; that words give us power over nature. This is the Fortress of the Linguists.

Consider this. Both James Joyce and Ernest Hemingway are English-speaking writers. But when one reads their novels there is a glaring difference in what *we as the readers* feel and think when we read them because of their very different *styles of expression*, how *they* experience the world, how *they* experience time, how *they* feel and think, and how *differently* they may use the *same* words. Each human consciousness expresses a unique existential style of existence. This radical difference can only be present in consciousness but never in words. It is this very difference that neuroscience is unable to account for because it effaces the difference between radically different spheres of consciousness as well as between our selves.

The neurosciences are erected on two incompatible pillars: (1) Darwin's undeniable theory of evolution; and (2) the paradigm of the brain with its *quantitative* mappings and measurements leading us to analogizing it to a computer. But Tallis forges a powerful distinction between the living functions of higher order animals and the intentional, teleological plannings of human beings (Tallis, *AM,* 163). Humans, as he frequently reiterates, are intimately self-conscious not only of their own selves *but also of their surrounding world and other selves.* They enjoy a singularly high degree of social other-awareness not given to our neighboring mammalian species. It is exactly this dual unity of the self, its own assurance of an intimate and personal identity within itself, while simultaneously buttressed by a conscious awareness of our juxtaposition with other selves in a social context as well as a correspondingly-shared geographic setting that places humans in the unique position to be *trebly* self-aware of: the self'; the world; and other selves (*AM,* 267–274).

Not unexpectedly, after Tallis' dismantling of neuromanic texts and aspirations, we find him seeking comfort in man's inherent freedom. Indeed, in his Seventh Chapter, "Reaffirming Our Humanity," he seeks to "welcome us back to our original freedom," while at the same time declaring that our "freedom is the first blessing of our nature" (*AM,* 243). His sustaining conviction is that he has been able to re-establish freedom simply through his thoroughly devastating critique of the neurosciences as if in itself it is sufficient to establish the positive reality of human freedom. By a simple strategy of elimination, he seems to be saying, either neuroscientific determinism *or* human freedom; *not* neuroscience; *therefore* freedom. But alas, Tallis offers a rather weak "argument" for freedom by essentially suggesting that the burden of proof is on the adherents of neuroscience to refute freedom, as if it were something obvious.

> Anyone who doubts that we can individually deflect the course of events should consider what we have achieved in building up a human world so extensive as virtually at times to conceal the natural one...This should be enough to satisfy everyone that we are capable of truly free actions. There will be still some who are dogmatically opposed to the idea of our being free because it doesn't fit with what they believe to be the scientific world picture. To them we offer this question: if freedom really is an illusion, where on earth did the illusion come from? And it is a tenuous illusion.
> AM, 261

This will hardly do! The freedom-determinism controversy has gone on since ancient times. By simply claiming that the mind is capable of "freely" constructing buildings and bridges as well as creating illusions is hardly a proof of freedom. The battlewagon of science will hardly be untracked by such personal and subjective appeals. It is not enough to simply point out what is wrong with the neurosciences. Beyond that it is necessary to replace it with a more plausible and truer theory of self-consciousness, intentionality, and spontaneous freedom.

Nevertheless, Raymond Tallis' work offers a strong indictment of why materialism, determinism, and the neurosciences cannot provide the necessary and sufficient conditions to account for our humanity (AM, 30, 90); and that correlation and causation are not identical. Consequently neuroscience cannot offer sufficient proofs that the brain is the sole foundation of human reality controlling our existence (AM, 85, 95). Behaviorism is a naïve and reductivist attempt to eliminate human consciousness (AM, 41). But what remains as a central challenge for both the neurosciences and psychoanalysis is their flagrant inability to *predict* human emotions, thoughts, and actions. And even more importantly their inability to provide a convincing theory in accounting for how we are capable of *creating* theoretical, artistic, and ethical *systems* as well as their *evaluations*.

Neuroscience and psychiatric medications unfortunately seem naturally to go together. In the early 1960's, the American Psychiatric Association misleadingly assured the Kennedy Administration, state governments, and county public mental health clinics that all mental disorders are due to chemical imbalances in the brain and that institutionalized mental patients in all the state psychiatric hospitals could be safely discharged and successfully treated at county mental health clinics and facilities or in small board-and-care residences. Today millions of Americans in countless walks and situations of life wander around helplessly and hopelessly on their "meds." As stated previously, certain medications are highly addictive: opioids, pain, sleep, anxiety medications, etc. Anti-psychotic meds may improve a "patient's" public behavior but not necessarily his thought processes. I recall doing a "reading group" with psychotic clients and starting out with the novel *I Never Promised You a Rose Garden* by Joanna Greenberg. After a number of sessions, I realized the participants read well enough mechanically but later they could not recall the narrative they had read. Soon after I turned to reading O. Henry's short three-page stories, but they had difficulty processing the irony. When one is medicated both the memory and their thought processes are appreciably affected.

Interestingly Kant in his Table of Categories of relation in the *Critique* distinguishes between agent and patient. Whenever one has classified the other as a patient it implies that something is being done to them rather than by them. It implies dependence as opposed to freedom (think Thomas Szasz).

My own experience, after thirty years of working in numerous county social services offices, medical hospitals, mental health clinics, a state institution for the developmentally delayed, and acute and long-term psychiatric hospitals have led to a conviction confirming that much is amiss. I have worked in out-patient, acute, and long-term locked psychiatric facilities with children, adolescents, and adults; with Child and Adult Protective Services; and with literally hundreds of psychiatrists whose misplaced faith in psychiatric medications has resulted in compounding the limitations of their treatment efforts. Frequently not only is the medication ineffective but often, all too often, it is downright harmful. I recall numerous times when I worked with children, who were prescribed Ritalin, Cylert, and Aderall. Invariably the precipitating conditions exhibited a familiar dynamic pattern. An overwrought teacher forced to travel 50 miles through LA traffic in order to get to her school and her class of 40-plus first graders only to be confronted by some energetic little boys "horsing" around. She would grab the most active child by the arm and usher him into the principal's office, while the mother was called and advised to place her child on psychiatric medication as a condition for his return to class. And in other settings I have worked endlessly with adults suffering from depression and anxiety while our therapy sessions were limited to offering only six visits before we discharged them to their medical doctor for ongoing medication. The underlying reality is that America has sold its collective soul to the Faustian god of Medication. America's fanatical faith in science and technology has destroyed its common sense.[6]

---

6 James Ridgeway, "Mass Psychosis in The US: How Big Pharma Got Americans Hooked on Anti-Psychotics," *Al Jazeera*, July 12, 2011, https://www.aljazeera.com/indepth/opinion/2011/07/20117313948379987.html

**PART 2**

CHAPTER 7

# The Simplicity Argument versus a Materialist Theory of Mind

> Each man is like a nautilus who lives in a house of his own making and carries it around on his back.
> BRAND BLANSHARD, *The Nature of Thought*

∴

One of the problems in dealing with theories of consciousness is how to distinguish them from each other so that they can be dealt with as clearly and distinctly as possible. The following classifications are vulnerable to various interpretations. In *Loneliness in Philosophy, Psychology, and Literature* (1979, 2012), I distinguish what I consider to be five mutually exclusive paradigms of human *consciousness*: (1) immaterial, active, and *reflexive self-consciousness,* which includes both (1a) subjective idealism (Plato, St. Augustine, Descartes, Leibniz, Kant, Fichte) and also (1b) objective idealism (Parmenides, Hegel, Royce); (2) passive, empirical, and "reflective" consciousness, with the emphasis on *phenomenal perceptions* (Locke, Hume, and the empiricist tradition in general); (3) active *transcendent intentionality* (Husserl, Sartre); (4) the double aspect theory wherein matter and mind, body and soul are simply two sides of the same coin (Spinoza) and the closely related theory of neutral monism (James, Russell, Ayer); and (5) reductive materialism and behaviorism with its denial of the existence of the soul or mind (Democritus, Epicurus, Hobbes, Armstrong, Ryle, Skinner, Dennett). The fifth classification presents special problems. I suppose we can cite the Epicureans with certainty as materialists but interpretational difficulties arise when materialism seeps into invoking mental and perceptual terms when in fact all the while its exponents are absolutely convinced that *all* that exists is matter plus motion. For example, Hobbes is regarded as a classical materialist but he still asserts there are perceptual subjective "phantasms" in experience and he distinguishes primary from secondary qualities. Phantasms are secondary distortions, appearances, which are in turn dependent on material causal realities. More importantly, he regards space as a perceived "phantasm of something existing without the mind." Because of this uncertainty, strictly speaking, it is difficult to read him simply as a strict materialist or behaviorist. We will see a similar problem with D.M.

Armstrong, namely the strain between claiming that all reality consists of matter and motion and yet being seduced into talking about *mental* perceptions.

But as far as *classical* metaphysical materialism is concerned, it seems exceedingly peculiar to assume and claim a doctrine of naïve realism, that the world would "exist" independently of any mind, that even in the event of an absolute absence of all sentient life in the universe following a cosmic holocaust, it still makes sense, it is *meaningful* to maintain that matter and motion would exist and still continue as before. For many scientists, the overwhelming plausibility of the physicalist doctrine of reality derives from the Epicurean-Lucretian dictum that nothing comes from nothing; that all existence can be reduced to material motions; that the universe is eternal and so is matter; and that it is a meaningful statement to assert that matter and motion would continue to exist even in the absence of any conscious life in the universe.

In *Feeling Lonesome: The Philosophy and Psychology of Loneliness* (2015), I changed my perspective from my earlier studies grounding loneliness in self-consciousness alone and I currently maintain that both (1) and (3), reflexive self-consciousness and transcendent intentionality—the first circular and the second unilinear—are mutually necessary to account for our consciousness of emotional and cognitive isolation. Moreover, the connection between self-consciousness and intentionality, I now submit, constitutes a synthetic *a priori* relation; that they are mutually implicative, necessary, universal, and supportive. I also maintain that although Husserl emphasizes intentionality, he also frequently allows for genuinely reflexive acts of consciousness, which further confirms their theoretical compatibility and congruence.

I now wish to sharpen my criticisms against (5), materialism, which essentially illustrates a "family resemblance" between the unified movements of materialism, mechanism, determinism, the empiricist theory of perception (or phenomenalism), behaviorism, and the neurosciences. In pursuing this goal, I have elected to concentrate on D.M. Armstrong's definitive work, *A Materialist Theory of the Mind*. As I suggest above, a key difficulty in materialist and empiricist theories is the failure to clearly distinguish brains from minds; physical attributes from mental predicates; and therefore perception from apperception or self-consciousness.

Historically the simplicity argument continues to serve as a controlling premise as well as a paradigm for a substantive theory of the self, a philosophy of mind, which challenges the materialist theory limiting the "mind" to the corpuscular, molecular workings of the brain as proposed in a highly influential work by D.M. Armstrong.[1] In the preceding chapters, I advocated for an

---

[1] David Malet Armstrong, *A Materialist Theory of Mind* (London: Routledge and Kegan Paul, 1968); hereafter cited as MTM. I take Gilbert Ryle's *Concept of the Mind* (New York: Barnes & Noble, Inc., 1949) and B.F. Skinner's *Walden Two* (Cambridge: Hackett Publishing, 1976)

immaterialist and active paradigm of self-consciousness and intentionality as more adequately corresponding to our idealist, phenomenological, and existential experiences of the self and that these philosophical tendencies more plausibly account for certain realities a great segment of mankind, both religious and humanistic, continue to insist upon. Accordingly, I argue that materialism and empiricism entail the denial of the self as well as the reflexive and intentional acts of consciousness and further that the tenets of both dualism and idealism, each in their different ways, reject the assertion that the brain-"mind" is analogous to a computer.

In regard to human *cognition,* materialism contends that when atoms collide and strike bodily organs, sensations result causing "perceptions," *apparently* consisting of a peculiar and special form of quasi-material compositions of minute, singly insensible particles of matter impinging on sense organs resulting in brain-traces. These trace-entities are in turn "observable" by an electroencephalograph device. A perception is then defined as an *indirect* "re-presentation" of an independent object, a "corresponding"—but not identical—copy of something existing separately from the perceived object.

Now as I conceive it, the most critical points of attack against materialism lie in its vulnerable alliance with (a) the cognitive theory of *perception,* its re-presentational theory of ideas; (b) its denial of self-consciousness; and therefore (c) the reality of the self. In Armstrong's central-state materialism, this is expressed by an identification of "thought" with the material motions in the brain. According to Armstrong, the mind is essentially the brain as it functions in coordination with "the physico-chemical workings of the brain in concert with the central nervous system" (*MTM,* 89 ff.). "Inner processes" and "mental states" are not denied. Rather they are re-interpreted as "purely [i.e., as reductive] physical states of the central nervous system" (*MTM,* 273, 337, 355–356). As we previously outlined, the "mind" (actually the brain) is similar to a computer (*MTM,* 344), with certain "dispositional responses" built into the paradigm (Gilbert Ryle); reactions that can be externally triggered causally and then unrolled like trains upon a track.

According to Armstrong, causes can be either "mental" or physical (*MTM,* 349). For materialists and phenomenalists the "dual" vocabulary is simply an inconsequential issue regarding semantic choices and the words "brain" and "mind" or sensation and perception can be used interchangeably. The overt behaviors of the body are invariably causally determined, and indeed the "future is predictable" (*MTM,* 49); and one must assume, I suppose, controllable

---

to be based on fundamentally similar theses as Armstrong's (*MTM,* 10, 54–56) and therefore vulnerable to the same arguments I wish to propose against Professor Armstrong. Cf. Ben Mijuskovic, "The Simplicity Argument versus a Materialist Theory of Mind," *Philosophy Today,* XX:4 (1976), 292–306.

as well. On this interpretation, then, there is no freedom in human consciousness; "freedom" is merely an ignorance of the underlying causes involved. As Spinoza expresses it, "We are aware of our desires but not their causes" (*Ethics*).

By the same token, the neuroscientific causal *explanation* for all human behavior is assumed to be the result of previous "mental" events, which can be readily "translated" into prior sets of physiological responses stretched out in a sequential chain of inflexible cause-effect-cause-effect...patterns running forward (and theoretically backward) showing the events as arranged like links in a chain. Raymond Tallis, we recall, in *Aping Mankind* describes this unbreakable chain as theoretically receding all the way back to the original Big Bang. Again, a physical stimulus elicits a physiological response, which can be assigned both a position and a measurable force, triggering a "mental" or inner cause in the brain and central nervous system. The brain has the capacity to "self-scan" both (a) "its" internal sensations and thoughts, which then (b) determine certain external, publicly-observable, behavioral responses. These repetitive "mental causes" are then interpreted as mediating between—and linking—the stimulus with the response (*MTM*, 162 ff., 349–350). The "mental" or inner cause itself is, of course, a physical occurrence in the brain as minute physical particles impinge upon receptive sensory neurons and cells thus causing sensations and stimulating the brain and central nervous system. Sensations are *material* collisional events related to the five senses and *quantitatively* measurable, distinguishable into separate and thus distinct parts located in different areas of the brain, which are then in turn traceable back to specific stimuli and their determinable responses.

But the problem centers on the meaning of Armstrong's "inner *self*-scanning process." First, it is intended to substitute for the role of *reflexive* self-consciousness in the dualist, rationalist, and idealist traditions, while at the same time denying that the self is *reflexively* self-conscious or able "to catch itself." Often the terms "introspection" and "reflection" (*n.b.* not=reflexion) are used. Secondly, it denies that there is a *substantial* self exhibiting the essential capacity to *continue* as the *same* self throughout a series of temporal sequences. (So Hume in the *Treatise* but again he is not so sure in the Appendix.) We recall that he admits to a *succession* of atomistic simple impressions but then puzzles about *both* (a) their distinctness *and* (b) how they can be unified in the *same* consciousness.

> In short there are two principles, which I cannot render consistent; nor is it in my power to renounce either of them, viz. *that all our impressions are distinct existences, and that the mind never perceives any real connexion among distinct existences.* Did our perceptions inhere in something simple and individual, or did the mind perceive some real connexion

among them, there wou'd be no difficulty in the case. For my part, I must plead the privilege of a sceptic, and confess that this difficulty is too hard for my understanding.
*Treatise,* 626; italics his

First, each impression is unique, separate, distinct and transiently *existent*. Actually, each impression is an individual substance as long as it lasts, which is only for a moment. *But the mind first notices, observes, perceives, takes note; and only then in psychological anticipation feels the forthcoming temporally succeeding set of distinct impressions.* It could not do so unless it was the *same* continuous self which takes notice of the passage, anticipates the change, the difference between a temporal "earlier" and a "later" subsequent "now" set of impressions. Hume's difficulty lies in his determination to hold on to his theory that consciousness is composed, constructed from simple parts, simple impressions. This is the same problem Hume confronts when he attempts to supplant the rationalist principle of *a priori* causal relations dictating a temporal chain of interconnected links in which causes and effects sequentially follow each other with Hume's contrasting psychological *feeling* of anticipation. But once more for Hume, if impressions are distinct and therefore separate, this cannot actually occur. It follows for Hume that the "rationalist's principle" is only something we psychologically *feel* and *believe* rather than know. Thus Hume fails on both counts because when he attempts to "partition" the flow of *consciousness* by breaking it up into single impressions, distinct parts, and separate events, while treating them as *belonging* to the same identifiable temporal "bundle," these paradoxes inevitably occur. The reason is that consciousness is not "constructed" from separate parts or simple impressions distinct from each other but rather that consciousness is both a *reflexive* temporal flow and a self-contained unity.

For Armstrong, when external physical motions impact the brain, the ensuing sequence of motions, of cerebral events in the brain exhibit a clear stimulus-response pattern. Roughly, the model can be schematized in the following *unidirectional* manner:

**An initiating physical stimulus external to the human body>causes the five sensory organs>to relay an impact to the brain>in turn transmitting impulses to the central nervous system>causing a bodily reaction>ending in an overt publicly-observable behavior**

Or more simply the following:

**physical world>>motion>>passive re-"active," responsive brain>>>overt behavior**

As the diagram demonstrates the initial physical motion, the stimulus, to which the responding brain and body reacts, is *external* to the brain; the brain basically serves as its *passive* recipient. The brain functions as a physical conduit between the external environment and the sensations caused and *passively* "registered" by the brain and the central nervous system (*MTM,* 40, 120, 144, 262–265). The model presents a reductivist view of the "mind" and provides a "purely physicalist view of man" (*MTM,* 269). It has certain scientific advantages and certain philosophical disadvantages obvious to everyone. But as it stands, it depends on a particular paradigm of what I have called elsewhere the "unidirectional" conception of a passive-reactive brain. This view is already adequately represented by the materialism of Democritus and Epicurus and the phenomenalisms of Hobbes, Locke, and Hume. As a theoretical system, it is essentially collectively shared by materialists, empiricists, phenomenalists, behaviorists, and neuroscientists (*MTM,* 11). As mentioned, it readily lends itself to analogizing the brain to an electrochemical computer; a mechanical, registering, purposeless device, instrument, or tool.

As illustrated above, according to the behavioral theory, the cognitive response can be represented as an arrow projected from the external world and directed toward the brain (obviously the brain as a physical object in the external world). *Ideas,* as immediate modes of "consciousness," or *perceptions* are then caused by atomistic particles in motion striking the sensory organs. It is critical to notice that Locke defines a *mental* idea as "an immediate mode of consciousness," a perception but then quickly proceeds to hold that "*bodies* produce [i.e., cause] *ideas* in us; …and that is manifestly by [physical] *impulse* the only way which we can conceive bodies to operate in us" (Locke, *An Essay Concerning Human Understanding,* II, viii, 8 and 11). The problem, of course, is that Locke's dualism simply leaves the issue of interaction between mind and body simply unaccounted for, just as Armstrong does.

The result is that clusters of *phenomenal* re-presentations or appearances are assumed to be caused by material motions. If one defines phenomenalism as a piecemeal "construction" of *mental* sensations (Locke) or impressions (Hume), the result is a manufacturing *of images into the appearance* of (a) objects and the external world; (b) the causal "association" of ideas; as well as (c) the fiction of the "self."

In Chapter 1, I discussed the critical difference in principle between (A) empirical *perception* and *reflection* versus (B) *apperception* and *reflexion* by challenging the claim that the former can replace the duties and functions of the latter. In short, perception is not the same as self-consciousness. In the French language, the phrase "moi-meme," me-myself, more properly captures this subject-object reflexive self-relation.

According to Hume, the initial first-order *impressions,* when they are no longer present to consciousness in their *immediate* form, are "replaced" by less vivacious and forceful *perceptions,* i.e., *ideas.* Impressions are transmuted into perceptions, they become diluted, weakened, and acquire a second-order status called *ideas* but both impressions and ideas remain truly mental for Hume and there is no real distinction between immediacy and mediacy, between impressions and ideas, except one of vivacity with impressions being more forceful than ideas. A similar difference is attributable to Hobbes, who defines the imagination as "decaying sensations." Next Hume describes a contingent recurrent *association* between impressions and their consequent ideas as *connected* by resemblance and contiguity thus forming our experience of the causal sequence resulting in a psychological *feeling* of a "constant conjunction," a "necessary connection" between "earlier" and "later" impressions despite the fact that impressions can only be immediate.[2] This is what is generally described in the literature as Hume's "associationist psychology" and it suffices to account for our *imagined* idea of causal sequences, i.e., our *feeling, sentiment* of causal "inference." At this juncture in consciousness, we are *psychologically* prepared to anticipate further events and we imagine that the future will resemble the past, that the "the uniformity of nature principle" will hold. Psychologically we come *to expect, to anticipate* predictable events to repeat the same patterns. In effect, this entire empirical sequence produces a psychological *feeling* of expectation, i.e., a *belief* in contrast to a rational certainty,

Both empiricists and phenomenalists assume that *after* the mind is stimulated to observe external events, *perceiving* a tree for example as a *patchwork* of visual sensory "parts," as well as "reflectively," "inwardly," "introspectively," observing or re-imagining a *previously perceived* tree as a set of decaying after-images, *reflectively perceiving* the tree as no longer visually present, as a "mental" state of visual configurations, it is then able to experience a *feeling*

---

[2] For example, Hume's *idea—not* relation—of resemblance is a good case in point. Impressions, Hume tells us, are associated when they *resemble* each other (*Treatise,* I, i, 4). But the problem is that we have no impression of *resemblance;* it is itself not an impression or even a fainter copy of one, i.e., an idea. Yet, according to Hume, all our perceptions are said to be reducible to simple (as opposed to compound) impressions. In this case, however, Hume rather obviously begs the entire issue, since he assumes a principle of connection or relation, which is neither an impression nor an idea but quite unlike either. Further, in order to affirm a resemblance between two or more things or ideas I have to be able to compare and contrast them. But resemblance, comparison, and contrast are all three relations as opposed to impressions; cf. Norman Kemp Smith, *The Philosophy of David Hume* (London: St Martin's 1964), 260–261; Brand Blanshard, *The Nature of Thought* (Humanities, 1955), I, 267–268. One is reminded of Russell's remark in this regard, namely, that presupposing has all the advantages over demonstrating that theft has over honest labor.

of *having seen, i.e., perceived* a tree. It is a less vivacious memory-idea, which was originally "given" as a set of immediate direct impressions "caused" by an independent and distinct material object. This sequence of mental events will then *explain* and fulfill all the requirements necessary and sufficient in accounting for "internal" *reflection*. Empirically memory is the attempt to reconstruct the order, the original sequence of images, whereas imagination is the relatively "free" re-arrangement of original impressions according to Hume. Again, Hume causes himself some difficulty when he confesses the possibility that under certain circumstances an impression can be less forceful and vivacious than an idea as for example walking in a fog as opposed to having a nightmare.

We must remember, however, that the *original* sensations (Locke) or impressions (Hume) were *initially* mere sets of *immediate states of consciousness;* and secondly they consisted of sets of divisible, distinct *simple* impressions or ideas. The idea of "white" for Locke or Hume is at first a simple sensation or impression; the idea of "sugar" is a complex or compound idea consisting of both color and sweetness. So what one initially observes or perceives are Locke's "ideas," i.e., immediate simple sensations; or Hume's immediate simple impressions *but not the self. Perception is not self-conscious.* It is to be noted that Locke and Hume's *passive "reflection"* is a mere configuration of sensory "parts"—what was originally an observation of something *other* than the self. Reflection is *not* identical to *self-conscious reflexion* in the dualist, rationalist, or idealist epistemological systems. The problematic nature of self-consciousness is exhibited to perfection in the following passage from Locke, while at the same time it betrays his uncertainty about his own account.

> Since it is the *understanding* [but obviously not reason] that sets man above the rest of sensible beings, and gives him all the advantage and dominion which he has over them; it is certainly a subject…worth our labor to inquire into. The understanding, like the eye, whilst it makes us see and perceive [i.e., observe] all other things, *takes no notice of itself;* and it requires art and pains *to set it at a distance* and make it its own object. But whatever be the difficulties that lie in the way of this inquiry, *whatever it be that keeps us so much in the dark to ourselves;* sure I am that all the light we can let in upon our minds, all the acquaintance we can make with our own understandings, will not only be very pleasant, but bring us great advantage, in directing our thoughts in the search of other things.
> 
> *An Essay Concerning Human Understanding,* I, i, first paragraph; italics mine

The analogy of the eye to the understanding is that although the eye is able to see *other* things it cannot see itself. Correspondingly, although the understanding can know *other* things it cannot know *its self.* Here Locke clearly shows the problem of self-consciousness still remains unresolved. Similarly Hume describes the process of *observing* impressions and ideas that are *not* the self.

> The mind [in passively] *receiving* the ideas mentioned in the foregoing chapters from without when it turns its view inward upon itself and [passively] *observes* its own actions about those ideas it has, takes from thence other ideas which are capable to be the *objects of its contemplation* as any of those it *received* from foreign things.
> Book I, *Chapter VI; Of Simple Ideas of Reflection;* italics mine

"Receiving" and "observing" sensations from an *outward* source is not the same as *reflexively* capturing, binding, and synthesizing its unity *within the self.* Simply put, *perception* is not *apperception;* consciousness is not *self*-consciousness; observation is not reflexion. There is no comparable reflexive *act* as a self-perception or introspection for Hume. Perception is a cognitive, passive experience of something *other* than the self. Basically perception is completely unrelated to a "self." Perceptions simply float unmoored and untethered to a self. By simply invoking the term "reflection," one has muddled an important and genuine distinction. Thus in reference to the alleged "internal" observations of "reflection," e.g., feeling hungry, there is a serious difficulty, which we may title "the paradox of the unobserved observer." According to Locke and Hume, ideas of reflection (Hume, *Treatise,* 7) are interpreted, e.g., as painful "internal" observations focused on an "inner" mental impression of discomfort. As there are sensations or impressions of "external" objects, correspondingly there are sensations of "internal" objects but not the *self* for Hume. Hence, there is a contradiction lurking in Hume's account of reflection and it is dramatically brought into prominence by him. It involves the same passage we have analyzed previously in the section *Of personal identity* in the *Treatise* when Hume compares the mind to a theater before which impressions appear and vanish like players on a stage. Thus he intimates that the mind *passively* views the performers on the stage; it merely *observes* the players *as if* they are completely independent of any accompanying *impression* or *idea* of the self during this entire operation. But that is precisely the problem. Hume assumes the spectator, the audience of one but denies any possibility of an active *participator.* But "who" (or "what") is (reflexively?) watching the play? By describing consciousness as the observation of entities, which have no reference to the self, Hume has effectively denied its existence. To be sure we may have an abiding *belief, a natural fiction, a product of the imagination* inclining us to believe in the existence of the "self" but not an intimate or reflexive *knowledge* of it.

By contrast, for any dualist, rationalist, or idealist there *always* must be a self present *to unify the impressions* in the same mind (Kant); otherwise the mind would be like a box of loose marbles without a box; a puppet theater without a puppeteer. Unattached impressions, disunified aggregates of perceptual impressions cannot occur without an intermediary, a unifying agent binding the contents within a possessing self.

Let us now turn back to Professor Armstrong's account of the "self-scanning" process, which presumably describes how the handicapped mind *reflectively* inspects its "self," while it is (a) passively restricted *solely* to observational perceptions; and (b) completely deprived of any and all acts of self-unification, self-awareness, and therefore a substantial self.

> In the case of perception, we must distinguish between the perceiving, which is a mental event, from the thing perceived which is something physical. In the case of introspection, we must similarly distinguish between the introspecting and the thing introspected. Confusion is all the more easy in the latter case because both are mental states of the same mind. Nevertheless, although they are both mental states, it is impossible that the introspecting and the thing introspected should be one and the same mental state. A mental state cannot be aware of itself, any more than a man can eat himself up. The introspection [the observational perception] may itself be the object of a further introspective awareness, and so on, but, since the capacity of the mind is finite, the chain of introspective awareness, of introspections must terminate in an introspection that is not an object of introspective awareness. If we make the materialist identification of mental states with material states of the brain, we can say that introspection is a self-scanning process in the brain. The scanning operation may itself be scanned, and so on, but we must in the end reach an unscanned scanner.
> 
> MTM, 324; also consult pages 94 and 333–334

This passage not only concludes in: (1) a denial of a genuine self but it also ends in (2) a rejection of any possible act of reflexive self-consciousness as well. In effect, the radical nominalisms of Hobbes, Hume, and Armstrong, by denying the reality of both the self and the act of genuinely self-conscious reflexions, are unable to account for any real meaning concerning man's sense of self-intimacy, of subjective self-identity. Armstrong's "unscanned scanner" is reduced to passive observations without an active observer. There are passive observations but no active observer.

Also notice that according to Armstrong's explanation the mind's "capacity is finite" and therefore its only conceivable beginning point is to be discovered in a backward trek, which must inevitably stop at a certain *"first* observational perceptual cause," presumably birth. There can be no infinite regress. The passive principle of perception must originate with a *specific* set of *first* sensations or impressions—but in its reversible journey and backward trek, it can never encounter its own self. It is like searching everywhere else for something that you already possess. It's like the eye again. You are looking everywhere for the source of sight when it's already in your head. By contrast, self-conscious reflexion is *circular*; it already *has* its self; it is self-contained, as Plato long ago speculated and Descartes, Leibniz, Kant, Fichte, Schopenhauer, Hegel, Schelling, Royce, Bergson, and Husserl all confirmed.

In contrast to Armstrong's theory of empirical consciousness as a unidirectional scanning observation, the rationalist reflexive principle conceives of cognition as inherently relational, i.e., *judgmental* in Kant's terminology, because it is constituted through synthetic *a priori* acts of connection actively binding the subject and object within its self, while in the same moment distinguishing its self in opposition to a realm of independent objects (Kant); or between the self and an alien realm of other selves (Hegel's Lordship and Bondage dialectic). To thetically posit the principle that "All consciousness is self-consciousness" is to assert that the subject and the object (Kant) or the self and the other-self (Hegel) *universally stand in a mutual oppositional but inseparable relation* to *each other*. For Hegel, to be self-consciously reflexive is to struggle both to master nature and subdue others. These embattled separations as they transpire throughout life will turn out to be the ultimate sources of human loneliness. (Think Robinson Crusoe.)

Unlike the assumption of an empirical passive *tabula rasa* in accounting for perceptions, by contrast the activity of the mind in reflexion is independent of any *specific* sensory beginnings, since it spontaneously initiates a "movement" from within itself whenever it is self-consciously and intentionally activated. Whether in waking states, dreams, or fantasies, the mind is always thinking at some level until death finally captures the soul forever.

As Hegel conceives it, the self is *universally* present, whether implicitly or explicitly, in all our feeling and cognitive acts and states. It is an underlying *substance,* a constant presence unifying sensory, affective, and conceptual predicates, whether that self is primitive or advanced; whether consciousness is prenatal, subconscious, unconscious, self-conscious, and intentional and whenever it knows itself or the entire cosmos.

Against Armstrong's theory of introspection, we can also cite Auguste Comte's criticism of introspective psychology when he critically indicates that the object of introspection and the instrument of introspection cannot be one and the same. The passive recipient of the observation (the brain) and the active tool for inspecting the observation (the brain) cannot be the same. One cannot forge a hammer with only a hammer as the tool for making it; the eye cannot see itself (Locke); and viewing the eye in a mirror is not a functional eye; it is a mere flat, two-dimensional appearance of an eye. This criticism also applies to the neuroscientific fiction that there are "mirror neurons" that "empathetically" feel what others feel. Empathy requires a mutual affirmation and participation between two selves. One cannot be empathic with one's own self.

So what is the "self" for Armstrong and how do we know "it"? He maintains that "a group of happenings constitute a single mind because they are all states, processes, or events in a single [material] substance" (*MTM*, 137). He also displays a willingness to consider *memory* as a possible criterion for personal identity: "So perhaps memory is the uniting principle that the 'Bundle' Dualist' [Hume] seeks." (We have already addressed Leibniz's criticism of Locke's postulation of memory as a criterion for personal identity on the grounds of both forgetfulness and the unconscious.) Nevertheless for Armstrong memory still remains to be translated into something much more substantial, to wit, the brain and its coupling with central state materialism (*MTM*, 17).

Armstrong also goes on to suggest that perhaps the self or "personal identity" is simply a "theoretical concept."

> I suggest that the solution [to the problem of personal identity] is that that the notion of 'a mind' is a *theoretical* concept: something that is *postulated* to link together all the individual happenings of which introspection makes us aware.
> *MTM*, 337; cf. 54–56, 67

Presumably for Armstrong "a *theoretical* concept" is a way to avoid positing a metaphysical one. If so, then the mind or self cannot be a substance. It is only at best a nominal fiction, even more ephemeral than Hume's "natural fiction," which at least commands some psychological "belief." Armstrong also discusses Wittgenstein in a number of passages suggesting that the "self" may be similar to Wittgenstein's linguistic analogy of a rope consisting of a crisscrossing, overlapping, and interweaving of fibers rather than being "held together" or unified by a single *essential* thread running throughout the entire length of the cord (*Philosophical Investigations,* Section 67). Or perhaps we can compare the "concept" of the self to the operational ability of special words to serve as elements in a "language game" as they display various *uses* throughout different verbal contexts and situations. "Don't think but look and see" then sanctifies the notion of the "self" simply through our ordinary language discourse. But this paradigm switch from materialism to a linguistic and nominalist model still fails to provide for a *continuous, temporal, unified and substantial self*. It reduces the self by likening it to a roll of separate film prints on a reel, which is readily susceptible to endless splicing.

In Armstrong's central-state materialism, the elimination of the self directly results from the radical transformation of "thought" and consciousness into matter, since he is convinced that matter alone can both sense and think. The brain is grossly material, whereas "sensations" are converted into insensible minute physical particles, something that can be "indirectly" observable on an electroencephalograph machine. "Ah, there it is; did you see that thought!" For Armstrong, materialism (what exists) is coupled with mechanism (how things happen). By contrast, I wish to contend that although sensations, emotions, and thoughts are contingently dependent on material conditions or circumstances, they are nevertheless *not* reducible to, identical with, or explainable by their material conditions *alone*. Once more, as stated in the first chapter, I agree with Hume that it is not only conceivable but actually the case that matter not only can but really does produce an *existent* "entity" that is *both* immaterial *and* active and yet separate, distinct from the originating matter: "when apply'd to the operations of matter, we may certainly conclude, that [matter and] motion may be, and actually is, the cause of thought and perception" (Hume, *Treatise,* 248); so Malebranche and Schopenhauer.

Recently I gave a talk at a university. Imagine that at the same time in another room, my speech was being transcribed and "scanned" or "reproduced" on an electroencephalograph machine recording my brain motions. How effective might that be? Maybe if one had a transcribing machine that translated the gyrations on the graph back to my words. Is that possible?

If we compare the neuroscientific stimulation of neuronal cells in the brain as analogous to the collision of billiard balls on a pool table, and then contrast it with the self-conscious *succession* of temporal moments present within the mind, the comparison falls significantly short. Material collisions apart from any reflexive consciousness of temporal succession are *qualitatively* different precisely because the latter is *self*-aware that it *is* a succession, whereas the billiard balls remain unaware of any sustained continuity between and among the colliding spheres. On the materialist account, the only possible "awareness" of time-motion *must* be *immediately* restricted between only *two* colliding balls but never capable of *passing beyond* that *specific* immediate contact to "form" a *continuous succession*. The collision could never extend *beyond* the "instant point" of contact, the *immediate* physical impact of the balls. We recall in Chapter 4 Husserl and Bergson's phenomenological description of the "flowing" constitution of *listening* to a melody. In a real sense we anticipate the actual notes even if we have never heard the song before. The point is that immanent time-consciousness cannot be causally explained in terms of colliding neurons. The activity is very different from the meaningful intentionality of unifying the notes as constituting a song.

In Chapter 3, prior to his neutral monism phase, I discussed William James' description of "the stream of thought," while emphasizing its essential *qualities* by stressing that every thought (1) expresses an essential relation to a *personal* consciousness; (2) it exhibits a constancy of change that is continuous with other thoughts; (3) it deals with objects other than its self; and (4) it chooses, intentionally selects some objects and rejects others as its concern thus concluding that "The only thing which psychology has a right to postulate at the outset is the fact of thinking itself." We remember that in this context James refers to Kant's Third Paralogism, *Of Personality,* which, of course, is concerned with the issue of personal identity. But the point once more is that neuroscience is perfectly incapable of causally explaining subjective time-consciousness.[3]

Similarly, if we compare and contrast Armstrong's materialist and mechanist construct of the "unscanned scanner" to Husserl's principle of intentionality, we find Husserl combining several inter-related traditional concepts that are historically allied within rationalism and idealism: immanent time-consciousness; the reflexive nature of consciousness; and the intentional purposiveness of consciousness to his advantage:

> We pass now to a particularity distinctive of experiences, which we may definitely refer to as the general theme of "objectively" oriented phenomenology, namely Intentionality. It is to this extent an essential peculiarity of the sphere of experience in general, since all experiences, in one way or another participate in intentionality, though we cannot in one and the same way say of *every* experience that it has intentionality [e.g., sensations and feelings *per se* do not], as we can say for instance of every experience which enters as object into the focus of possible reflexion... that it has a temporal character. It is intentionality which characterizes *consciousness,* in the pregnant sense of the term, and justifies us in

---

3   William James, *The Principles of Psychology* (New York: Dover, 1950), I, 224–225; cf. also "The Stream of Thought," I, 339; and Norman Kemp Smith, *Commentary to Kant's 'Critique of Pure Reason'* (New York: Humanities Press, 1962), 461.

describing the whole stream of experience as at once a stream of consciousness and a *unity* of *one* consciousness.[4]

And Husserl proceeds to explicitly connect spontaneity to Cartesian and Kantian modes of thought.

> We reply: "conceptual construction" certainly takes place spontaneously, and free fancy likewise, and what is spontaneously produced is of course a product of mind.
> *Ideas,* Section 23

The "free fancy" alluded to is the method of "free imaginative variation," which is so critical in discovering the full range of *eidetic* meanings:

> It is then to this world, *the world in which I find myself and which is also my world-about-me,* that the complex forms of my manifold and shifting *spontaneities* stand related…All these together with acts of the Ego, in which I become acquainted with the world as *immediately* given me through spontaneous tendencies to turn toward it and to grasp it, are included under the one Cartesian expression: *Cogito.*
> *Ideas,* Section 28

Spontaneity (or creativity), however, is not some sort of mysterious or miraculous event. Indeed, it lies at the very heart of our intentional acts and their reflexive acknowledgment. And further, on the same page, Husserl proceeds to connect all these acts with a "pervading unity of the synthetic consciousness." But again, it is important to reinforce Husserl's conceptual allegiance to these interrelated modes of Cartesian, Leibnizian, and Kantian thought: spontaneity, synthesis, immanent temporality, and the unity of consciousness:

> The thesis or synthesis becomes in so far as the pure Ego actually advances step by step; itself lives [temporally] in the step and "steps on" with it. Its *free spontaneity and activity* consists in positing on the strength of this or that, positing as an antecedent or consequent, it does not live within the theses as a passive indweller: the theses radiate from it as a primary source of generation…But *each act* of whatever kind can start off in this

---

4 Edmund Husserl, *Ideas: General Introduction to Pure Phenomenology,* translated by W.R. Boyce Gibson (New York: Collier Books, 1962), Section 84 (p. 222); hereafter cited as Husserl, *Ideas.*

*spontaneity modus of a so-to-speak creative beginning,* in which the pure Ego steps on the scene as subject of the *spontaneity.*
                *Ideas,* Section 122

Perhaps we can compare and contrast the *active* unilinearity of Husserl's intentionality with the *passive* linearity of Armstrong's empirical perceptions in the following way.

**Husserl: [bracketed ego?] -> consciousness -> active intentionality -> meaning**
or:
ego -> active spontaneity -> noetic act -> noema=transcendent "object" meant
*versus*
**Armstrong: perception <- receptive brain <- active material world**

The arrows of consciousness point in different directions. Nevertheless, in terms of self-conscious reflexion, there is a considerable confusion in Husserl, as we have indicated. At times, intentionality clearly leaks into reflexive circularity or self-consciousness. For example, in the *Paris Lectures* and *Cartesian Meditations,* Husserl frequently abandons his own model by rather paradoxically appealing to a reflexive principle of consciousness (to be further discussed below). Hence, he refers to a transcendental ego or subject as a "center of consciousness," a *monad* from which radiating arrows emanate while failing to realize that in Leibniz and Kant this special defining dynamic is the most essential and characteristic property of self-consciousness (above). Thus at times, Husserl opposes intentionality to reflexion, while in other instances he espouses it. But in *Ideas* (1913), the transcendental subject is given its due and in the *Cartesian Meditations* it dominates his thinking.

Thus, sometimes "phenomenological seeing" means *reflecting on,* or an intentional *seeing of* a non-reflexive experience; at other times, however, he states that to think *means* we can reflexively re-experience our ideas (*Cartesian Meditations,* Section 48; p. 105). This has been challenged by certain analytic critics who question whether reading "without thinking about it" and reading in order to *directly, immediately* "see" what is happening is the *same* experience.[5]

---

5 Paul Feyerabend, "Wittgenstein's *Philosophical Investigations,*" reprinted in *The Philosophical Investigations,* edited by George Pitcher (New York: Doubleday, 1966), 112–128; cf. Emmanuel Levinas, *The Theory of Intuition in Husserl's Phenomenology* (Evanston, IL: Northwestern University Press, 1973) 136–137; hereafter cited as Husserl, *TIHP*; and Edmund Husserl, *The*

In the reading cases, the "outward-bound," transcendently oriented intentional act is conceived as one which is paired with *both* a reflexive *and* a temporal mode of awareness. An *act* can be spontaneous and immediate, in which case it is an intuition (e.g., Descartes' cogito). But *acts* can also be both immediate and repetitiously spontaneous when they constitute a "train of thoughts" as in inferential thinking. Certain continuous acts display a beginning, middle, and end. Because this is the case, we are justified in combining these mutually implicative activities—intentionality and temporality—with self-consciousness as together constituting a synthetic *a priori* relation within the *same* consciousness. Moreover, acts are *essentially* and *ideally intentional, purposeful.* Thus, Husserl's "intentionality principle" is already *historically* and *conceptually* contained and implied within classical rationalism. It *means*, it *intends* a teleological purpose; it intrinsically includes the meaning of freedom or transcendence directed *at a goal, it targets an end.* Husserl's notion of intentionality, like the classic notion of reason, essentially involves purposiveness because all rational thought is a purposeful activity (Aristotle); it is aimed at an end. This critical feature is a universal and necessary constituent of rational thought; reason *only* acts outwardly, beyond itself, and toward an *end, aiming at a goal transcendent to the self.* For example, the ultimate purpose of the causal maxim is to order the cosmos, to emulate God. Correspondingly, human motives, unlike physical and mechanical causes, incorporate rational intentions, i.e., human purposes (whether they are successful or not). Reason in its guise of having *already* attained knowledge may be reflexive but when it transcendently and intentionally seeks knowledge, it is teleological and outwardly directional. Take the Aristotelian syllogism as an example. The major and minor premise correspond to the intentional acts and the conclusion is the teleological end.

I am suggesting that when rationalists and idealists invoke the term "purposiveness," they mean or intend what Husserl signifies by intentionality. An instructive discussion combining the aspects of intentionality, reflexion, and purposiveness occurs in Royce's *The World and the Individual.* Consequently,

---

*Crisis of European Sciences and Transcendental Phenomenology* (Evanston, IL: Northwestern University Press, 1970), 251. Again, there is confusion in Husserl. At times "phenomenological seeing" means reflecting on a non-reflexive experience; at other times, he seems to think we can reflexively, i.e., *self-* consciously re-experience our ideas. Cf. *Cartesian Meditations* (The Hague: Martinus Nijhoff, 1960), Sections 48, 105. This has been challenged by certain critics, who question whether reading "without thinking about it" and reading in order to "see" what is happening is the same experience? One appears to be "reflective," while the other is "reflexive." Cf. also: Husserl, *The Crisis of European Sciences and Transcendental Phenomenology* (Evanston, IL: Northwestern University Press, 1970), 251.

Royce invokes the intentionality principle of consciousness when he discusses the "external meaning" of an idea as that which refers *beyond* its self; it points toward a realm of transcendent "otherness," toward objectively oriented ideas=meanings.

> All these not merely have their obvious internal [reflexive] meaning, as meeting a conscious purpose by their very presence, but also they at least appear to have that other sort of meaning, that reference beyond themselves to objects, that cognitive relation to outer facts, that attempted correspondence with outer facts, which many accounts of our ideas regard as their primary, inexplicable, and ultimate character.[6]

Whereas Husserl is bracketing consciousness, Royce by contrast is relating meanings to corresponding "outer facts" by positing externally oriented meanings as *intended* to *"correspond"* to something *independent* of the self; they have an *external* reference, which transcends, goes beyond, and surpasses the corelative internal meaning of an idea (Royce, *WI,* 27); while Husserl's intentions are bracketed *within* consciousness Royce's transcend beyond. In this respect, Royce's concept of an external meaning appears as if it were essentially a sort of imitation or image of a being, and this being, the external object of our thoughtful imitation, appears to be, in so far as possible, quite separate from these our ideas that seeks to imitate its characters or that attempts to correspond to them (*WI,* 27–28; see also 271, 272, 281, 325). Nevertheless, according to both Royce and Husserl, in conformity with the intentionality archetype, a meaning functions as a directional target referring *beyond* itself, toward something external or outer in Royce's "corresponding" description but immanently contained within consciousness in Husserl's bracketing procedure. Also Royce, significantly enough in this passage refers to Brentano's *Psychology from an*

---

[6] Josiah Royce, *The World as Will and Individual* (New York: Dover, 1959), I, 26; see also: 24–25, 34, 35, 222, 293, 396–397, 417; hereafter cited as *WI*. According to Royce, meanings, as nonextended "realities," or existences, directly imply idealism (pages 396–397); and reality itself is thus first and foremost a *system of meanings* (*WI,* 42, 418, 454). Again, for Royce, ideas, as meanings, can be imageless (*WI,* 307, 309–311). Consequently, Royce explicitly insists that the unity of consciousness is actually a unity of meaning (*WI,* 424–426, 437, 442, 464–469). Following Kant, Royce also endorses the spontaneity of consciousness as the act of unification. "Intelligent ideas then, belong, so to speak, to the [intentional, purposive] motor side of your life rather than to the merely sensitive. This is what Kant meant by the spontaneity of the understanding" (*WI,* 22). The ultimate first principle in all idealism is *spontaneity.* Cf. John Dewey, "Voluntarism in the Roycean Philosophy," 79–88, in *John Dewey: The Middle Works, 1899–1924,* edited by Jo Ann Boydston (Carbondale, IL: Southern Illinois University Press, 2008).

*Empirical Standpoint* at this point in his discussion in a footnote on page 282 in an effort to validate his alliance with the most recent trends of thought in philosophy. In other passages, Royce continues to confirm the inseparable connection between reason, purposiveness, and intentionality.

> The idea, I have said, *seeks its own. It can be judged by nothing but what it intends*. Whether I think of God or of yesterday's events, of my own death, or of the destiny of mankind, of mathematical truths, or of physical facts, or of Being itself, it is first of all what I mean…Moreover, my idea is a cognitive process only in so far as it is, at the same time, a voluntary process, an act, the partial fulfillment, so far as the idea consciously extends, of a purpose.
> *WI*, 325

Once more:

> In seeking its object, any idea whatever seeks absolutely nothing but its own explicit, and, in the end, complete determination as this conscious purpose. The complete content of the idea's own purpose is the only object of which the idea can ever take note.
> *WI*, 329; italics his

Machines do not have purposes; a goal can only "reside" in an intentional and self-conscious subject. What would it mean to say that a computer is reflexive and intentional and that it has purposes? Purposes have two elements: purposive intentionality and reflexive self-acknowledgment. I conceive of a goal and I intend to enact it. When my purpose fails, I pout. Do computers pout?

And finally Royce affirms:

> My idea imperfectly expresses, in my present consciousness, an intention, a meaning, a purpose; and just this specific meaning is carried out, is fulfilled, is expressed by my object.
> *WI*, 353; cf., pages 433–434

An internal meaning, by contrast, is clearly self-sufficient, for it fulfills the purpose for which it is intended; it is complete, self-contained, and self-sufficient within itself; it does not refer to something beyond itself (Royce, *WI*, 23, 25, 35, 38). Royce gives the example of someone humming a tune; this is a self-contained continuous filament of temporal meanings completely devoid of any external reference. And, roughly it would correspond to my model of reflexive thought. But then Royce proceeds to emphasize that we cannot leave matters this way. We cannot close with a separation between the external meanings—implying an act of intentional reference to knowing the world—and the internal meanings entailing the self-referential act of knowing the world, securing the world. Consequently, fortified by the claim that he is following Kant in this regard, Royce invokes Kant's notion of the *spontaneity* of thought. "This is what Kant meant by the spontaneity of the understanding" (*WI,* 22 ff.); it serves as the means of overcoming, of unifying the initial transcending separation between knowing and willing through an activity of the mind. "This spontaneity unifies that which is external with the internal through synthetic *a priori* 'meaningfulness.'" In fact, all ideas—both self-referential and purposively intentional—are fundamentally *meanings*: "An idea is any state of mind that has a conscious meaning" (*WI,* 24). So in the last analysis, the two principles, to wit (1) the intentional, outwardly directional and (2) the reflexive or circularly self-enclosed are comprehensively and synthetically integrated by Royce, a fairly Hegelian move.

The above relational descriptions are universal in all forms of thought that are inimical to materialism and mechanism but supportive of rationalism and idealism as exhibited in this defining passage from Hegel.

> What has just been said can also be expressed by saying that Reason is *purposeful activity.* The exaltation of a supposed [mechanistic] Nature over a misconceived thinking, and especially the rejection of external teleology, has brought the form of purpose into general discredit. Still, in the sense that Aristotle, too, defines Nature as purposive activity, purpose is what is immediate and at rest, the unmoved which is also *self-moving,* and as such is [the reflexive] Subject. Its power to move, taken abstractly, is *being-for-self* or pure negativity [think Spinoza, Sartre]. The result is the same as the beginning, only because the *beginning* is the *purpose* [i.e., the spontaneous active force]; in other words, the actual is the same as its Notion only because the immediate, as purpose, contains the self or *pure actuality* within itself. The realized purpose, or the existent actuality, is movement and unfolded becoming; but it is just this unrest that is the self; and the self is like that immediacy and simplicity of the beginning because it is the result, that which has returned into itself, the latter being similarly just the self. And the self is the sameness and simplicity that relates itself to itself.[7]

---

[7] G.W.F. Hegel, *Phenomenology of Spirit,* translated by A.V. Miller (Oxford: Oxford University Press, 1977), Section 22, italics mine.

The *pure actuality,* referred to above, is a force without antecedent conditions; it is always the same "pure" simplicity of spontaneity that is the essence of consciousness in all idealism. We have already commented on Hegel's dialectical transformations of Consciousnesss moving from Sense-Certainty, Perception, and Understanding as each former stage is overcome, transcended, and carried forward toward becoming a full-blown self-conscious self and his explicit reference to "the two moments, which in their appearing merely *occur,* and come into being: one being the movement of [intentional] pointing-out or the *act of perceiving,* the other being the same movement as a simple event or the *object* [internally and reflexively] *perceived*" (*Phenomenology,* Section 111). Again, it is precisely this act which is spontaneous. It accounts for both intentionality and reflexivity or vice versa. On my view, Hegel's "dialectic" is none other than Kant's synthetic *a priori* movement of thought as it develops through his categories in the *Phenomenology* and the greater *Logic.* I am aware of his efforts to distinguish his mode of conscious activity as different from that of Kant, but their essential mutual agreement arises from their shared commitment to the innate spontaneous activities of consciousness and ultimately their dual commitment to the Achilles premise.

The recurrent motif of spontaneity and purposiveness, which repeatedly surface in Leibniz, Kant, Fichte, Hegel, Husserl, and Royce, is a critical assumption in all these writers, a defining premise, a first principle that cannot itself be proved but serves as the assumed basis for all that follows. Whether it is termed freedom or spontaneity or transcendence or ek-stasis, it denotes an act that is purely self-generating. It has only one opposite: determinism. As it develops, it can be expressed rationally or arbitrarily but its inception is always *sui generis.* Anything else would be an absolute violation of idealism. Of course, Kant in words rejects the notion of a metaphysical noumenal freedom in the Dialectic (Third Antinomy), but in the guise of spontaneity and his formulation of the creative "productive imagination," he has opened a back door to it within his system. His deepest thought is admittedly expressed in the following passage in the Dialectic.

> We must then assume a causality through which something takes place, the cause of which is not itself determined in this spontaneity, but that the very determination of this spontaneity to originate the series, that is to say, the causality itself, will have an absolute beginning; there will be no antecedent through which this act, in taking place, is determined in accordance to fixed laws.
>
> A 446=B 474

Although this passage occurs in the Dialectic, I submit that it presents Kant's deepest conviction concerning the most essential *quality* of consciousness: its spontaneity. This thetic metaphysical positing is actually at the root of the productive imagination, time-consciousness, and the unity of consciousness. In this respect it is identical to Fichte's self-positing Ego. And this is why virtually at the very beginning of the Analytic he strategically credits spontaneity with the production of the categories, time-consciousness (A 97), and the unity of consciousness (B 132). It is the agency, the act of spontaneity that invests "the mind's power of producing representations from itself, the spontaneity of knowledge, itself called [the faculty of] the understanding" (*Critique,* A 50=B 74; cf. A 51=B 75 and A 68=B 93). We need to realize that over half of the *Critique* is dedicated to discussing the metaphysics of Western rationalism.

But what remains important in all these philosophical reflections is that it highlights a number of common themes that are central in Leibniz, Kant, Fichte, Hegel, and Schopenhauer as well as Husserl and Royce: Consciousness is spontaneous, reflexive, intentional, and purposive. Machines and computers are not. These positive themes collectively eventuate by contributing to a commitment toward a structured, comprehensive, coherent, synthetic *a priori system,* which we can indifferently describe as idealistic, phenomenological, and/or existential.

Spontaneity in Sartre notably appears in his conviction that each of us—*absolutely alone*—is "condemned to freedom." But Sartre, as we have shown, is also quite clear about rejecting the Cartesian, Leibnizian, and Kantian principle of self-reflexion as well as Husserl's limping concessions to reflexivity in *The Transcendence of the Ego.* Accordingly, he categorically denies that a *substantial* ego exists and that it is reflexively self-conscious.

> But this spontaneity must not be confused with the spontaneity of consciousness. Indeed, the ego, being an object is *passive*....Genuine spontaneity must be perfectly clear; it *is* what it [intentionally] produces and can be nothing else. If it were tied synthetically to something other than itself, it would in fact embrace an obscurity.[8]

---

8 The dualists and idealists claim that the reflexivity of consciousness is only possible if it is immaterial, active, and therefore circular. Instead, Sartre contends it is immaterial (a nothingness, "a hole in being," "un *neant*") *but* non-reflexive. And he struggles to distinguish his own paradigm of consciousness against Bergson's theory expressed in the *Essai sur les données immédiates de la conscience* by citing his own conceptions of spontaneity, transcendence, creation *ex nihilo, intentional relations,* emanation, etc. Jean-Paul Sartre, *The Transcendence of the Ego,* translated by Forest Williams and Robert Kirkpatrick (New York: Noonday Press, 1962), 76–82, where Sartre struggles to distinguish his conception of spontaneous freedom

For Sartre, if spontaneity were tied to an ego, it could not be free by definition. It would be tethered to something other than itself and therefore dependent.

> Consciousnesses are given as emanating [intentionally] from states, and states as produced by the ego. It follows that consciousness projects its own spontaneity into the ego-subject to confer on the ego the creative power which is absolutely necessary to it [to transcend itself].
> Sartre *TOE*, 81; cf. 76–82

But it is a spontaneity that emanates or explodes, virtually self-propelled despite the complete absence of a *substantial* ego. Often, Sartre avails himself in using the term *ek-stasis,* meaning standing beyond itself or transcendent to itself as synonymous with spontaneity. It is interesting to notice how Husserl, Bergson, and Sartre judiciously avoid referring to causal relations between the self and world when describing consciousness. In connection with constitutive acts, spontaneity, ek-stasis, transcendence, freedom, and emanation are the preferred descriptions. Basically, the derivation of the term is Plotinian meaning "standing beyond its self."

For Sartre, it is because consciousness is an immaterial translucent purity, an essential nothingness, a negation of the Hegelian in-itself that it cannot be self-conscious within itself. At first there is "nothing," neither intuitions, categories, nor structures—just pure translucent activity, spontaneity. When I run to catch the streetcar, for example, I am said to be pre-reflectively conscious. My whole consciousness is immersed and consumed by the object, the departing vehicle. But later when I "reflect" on the event, I remember "me" as an object in the world chasing the streetcar. But then I am simply narrating a third-person story to someone who happens to be "me." I am then properly reflective (not=reflexive); but I do not, nor can I ever, possess reflexive knowledge of my *pure* self or ego. If I did, then "I" could not be free. My "ego" as a transcendent object would get in the way and impede my freedom. It would be tantamount to having something in my eye distorting my field of vision

---

against Bergson's view. Bergson posits a plenum of qualitative presences in consciousness, whereas Sartre assumes it to be empty. According to Marjorie Grene, however, "The pre-reflective cogito, then, is the condition of the Cartesian cogito as of every [intentional or transcendent] cogitation [of a cogitatum]. But it is precisely here that Sartre has foundered. He has cut off the bridge from the thinker to thought that Husserl's method had established and has insulated the empty self against any impact except through negativity from the world," *Sartre* (New York: New Viewpoints, 1973), 122. With this trenchant criticism I would totally agree.

thereby limiting my freedom, my access to infinite possibilities of choosing. What I can do in relation to my existence is describe my solitary human condition in terms of the existential categories of despair, anxiety, and forlornness.

Thus Sartre is convinced that a requirement for absolute freedom is that consciousness is perfectly empty, a nothingness. But the sort of spontaneity to which he subscribes can only exist on the condition that the soul, mind, or consciousness is an immaterial, an *existential* "nothingness." In this regard, Sartre's dualism shares the same simplicity principle as the idealists.

Beyond these considerations, one also needs to realize that Descartes' cogito is itself an *existential* declaration. One may wish to criticize it as a "pure," i.e., as an empty, formal concept but the reality is that it could not be thought unless "something" active exists. Ayer, in *Language, Truth, and Logic,* criticizes it as simply tantamount to the statement "There is a thought *now*."[9] Perhaps so but as Ayer neglects to realize and as we saw in a previous chapter dealing with Hegel's brand of objective idealism, this simple qualitative Parmenidean Nothing, this pure *intuition* is spontaneously active and encompasses the entire history of Western thought within its implicit Notion. And significantly enough the same incontrovertible admission that "There is a thought now" was sufficient in and of itself to get Hegel started on the "ontological argument" as the gestational birth not only of Being and Consciousness but of the entire history of philosophy (again, *Science of Logic,* first four Observations, 95–118). Thought comes from nothing and from nowhere *except from within itself.* That is what it means to be an intuition.

> Being, pure Being—without any further determination. In its indeterminate immediacy it is similar to itself alone, and also not dissimilar from any other; it has no differentiation either within itself or relatively to anything external.

This we recall is the opening sentence in the *Science of Logic. Something* exists—Being/Consciousness. It isn't God who creates the universe of thought and consciousness but man (Ludwig Feuerbach). Again, this is precisely the point, namely that "Something exists"; and whatever the "Something" is, it can only be grasped as consciousness *qua* consciousness. For Hegel, this is actually the basis of the ontological intuition/"argument." To expound on precisely

---

9 Alfred Jules Ayer, *Language, Truth and Logic* (New York: Dover, 1936), 46. Significantly enough, this simple admission regarding the "nothingness" of consciousness is sufficient to get Hegel started in the opening triad of Being-Nothing-Becoming and the ontological argument as discussed in the previous chapter.

what *this* "Something" is remains the monumental task of philosophy, what David Chalmers has christened "*the* problem of consciousness," i.e., philosophy.

Whatever Descartes accomplished, he certainly topically shifted the focus from metaphysics to epistemology, from discussing Substance, e.g., God, immortality, and free will to Consciousness, e.g., what is it and how does it work, and that is why Leibniz, Kant, Fichte, Hegel, and Schopenhauer as well as their empiricist counterparts, each in their own and very different way, seek to resolve the issue of Substance by doubling back through the openings affirmed by Consciousness. That is the whole thrust of the Epistemological Age so it must be recognized that it is one thing to move "past" or "beyond" the Metaphysical Age but it is quite another matter to delude one's self into believing its questions have been solved or even adequately addressed. They have simply been put aside for a while just as if a woman were to divorce one husband and take another. The problems remain.

Beyond that, even a cursory glance at the history of ideas and consciousness exhibits a long-standing commitment to the immaterial and active nature of the soul or mind. Certainly beginning with Plato's *Phaedo* and *Republic* and just as importantly through Aristotle's *Metaphysics*, extending through Augustine, Aquinas, Descartes, Leibniz, and on into German idealism, many prominent philosophers have posited the immaterial nature of consciousness as a grounding principle. But to repeat, it should be noted—a situation generally avoided—that the great empiricist thinkers, Locke and Hume, were themselves infected with dualistic tendencies, and Berkeley, in his empiricist disguise, was an avowed *immaterialist*. And even when we get to Husserl, he can overwhelm us with his five variant forms of the epoche, he can "bracket," "put out of gear," and "suspend" all of our naïve, scientific, and metaphysical concerns and attitudes regarding the external world and our protean selves as much as he desires—but after all is said and done what remains is an *ideal, conscious* "something" that is simply and stubbornly resistant. His phenomenological tasks, methods, descriptions, and all his various analyses of consciousness remain irrevocably immaterialist and idealist.

If we go back to the central theme of this treatise, namely, the Battle between the Gods and the Giants, between materialism and idealism, the critical stumbling block remains: the "notion" that consciousness, immateriality, and "nothingness" exhibit identical meanings, essences. It represents Hegel's paradoxical challenge that Being *is* Nothing. So now once again at this point in our discussion, we stand confronted by the frequent refrain concerning the mysterious Parmenidean status of the "Nothingness of Consciousness" as reushered into the mainstream of philosophy by Hegel and forcefully revived by Sartre. In its most profound *meaning*, it stands for the active immateriality of consciousness, the antithesis to Matter. The metaphysical choice is simply this: senseless physical motion or the spontaneity of consciousness! What is implicit in the statement that "Consciousness is a nothingness" is that (1) it functions as an existent immaterial medium for the appearance of phenomena; (2) it provides the potentiality for active self-conscious reflexion; and (3) it offers the possibility for an explosive intentionality, a transcendence beyond its own nothingness.

Descartes defines the soul in two quite different ways. First as an immaterial, active, intuitive substance (*Synopsis* to the *Meditations*) and secondly as a translucent, diaphanous medium in Sartre's version, similar perhaps to light, empty in itself but allowing objects to appear luminiscently "within" it while at the same time conditioning the possibility of cognition; a substance through which objects appear and disappear, pass and repass.[10] Subsequently pressed to respond to Princess Elizabeth's insistent questions regarding how a material *and* an immaterial substance, which share no attribute in common, can possibly interact, Descartes rather guilelessly confesses to her that "it is a problem best solved by thinking least about it." But the problem remains. Our ideas are *meaningful,* and meanings cannot be reduced to just sensations, impressions, and mere images or simply explained or analyzed into constituent sense-data and qualia. A catalogue of separate sensations is not a meaning. Sense-data do not come carrying their own consciousnesses within themselves; *per se,* they are meaningless. Sensations alone cannot mean anything.

But then where does meaning come from? Seeing a chair is a *judgmental* process. Judgment is intentional and unifying. It can also be expanded to unify different sets of judgments about multiple "collections of sensations" or *hyletic* data. Cognitive acts intend and reflexively grasp an object *as a constellation of meanings.* The chair signifies, means, intends a transcendent thing: it is made by human hands; it is placed on a surface; off the floor; it is an object/concept to be sat upon; a chair on which no one could conceivably sit is not a chair; it is constructed with legs and a seat; materially able to support some minimal weight; it cannot be constructed from water, etc. But a chair in order to be *fully*

---

10   Rene Descartes, "Synopsis" to the *Meditations;* see also the *Philosophical Works of Descartes,* edited by E. Haldane and G.R.T. Ross (New York: Dover, 1931), 196. The Synopsis was composed a year later after the six Objections to the *Meditations* were circulated by Father Mersenne; see also: Norman Kemp Smith's discussion of Descartes' "diaphanous medium" in his *Commentary on Kant's 'Critique of Pure Reason'* xl. It is probably from Descartes that Sartre borrows his concept of "nothingness" as a transparent and translucent medium from Descartes. For a thorough discussion of this topic, cf. Norman Kemp Smith, *New Studies in the Philosophy of Descartes* (Russell & Russell, 1963), 143–148, 153–154, 158, 215, 230; and S.V. Keeling, *Descartes* (Oxford: Oxford University Press, 155–156).

meaningful must be placed in a larger context with relations to other objects of furniture, within the larger context of a culture (Hegel, Husserl). This is the difficulty the empiricists, phenomenalists, nominalists, and linguists have failed to grasp. Locke, Berkeley, Hume, Mill, along with Russell and Ayer, are all afflicted with the same myopic epistemological shortcomings because of their insistence that all external things are only meaningful as separate objects and moreover as collections or constructions of sense qualia. But a meaning always *exceeds, transcends* its definition.

J.S. Mill metaphorically described sensations as onions threaded through the string of consciousness until F.H. Bradley pointed out that consciousness is *aware* of the onions, whereas strings are not. In a famous argument between Mill, an empiricist, and William Whewell, a Kantian, Mill contends that Kepler's discovery of the elliptical orbit of the planets was simply a matter of connecting the observed nocturnal dots to each other, while Whewell pointed out that astronomers had been gazing at the heavens for millennia without arriving at that conclusion. And by its self the concept of the ellipse offered no obvious relation to Newton's law of gravity. But once more what does it mean to maintain that the law of gravity is an *empirical* construction of sensory data or that empirical laws are completely reducible to simple and compound sensations without any appeal to relations or conceptions?

The critical issue is the relation between sensation and meaning. An interesting argument on the immaterial nature of meaning is proposed by C.E.M. Joad. He imagines writing a book on his reasoning in regard to a geometrical proposition expressed in a formula, and he writes the book outlining his reasoning. The book is read and understood by A. It is translated into French and read and understood by B. He gives a lecture on it and it is heard and understood by C. The reasoning process produces the *same* meaning throughout all four presentations although the sensory stimuli are very different in the four cases: "Therefore it seems incredible that all these different stimuli should have been able to produce the same meaning if their respective reactions to them were confined to physical responses which were different in the four cases."[11]

Whether all meanings entail images is a critical question upon which we have already touched. In the dualist, rationalist, and idealist traditions, certainly relations as meanings are imageless. This is an integral heritage from our Platonic past and continues in the later idealisms of Leibniz, Kant, Hegel, Royce, Blanshard, and even Husserl. In phenomenology, for instance, there are meanings which refer to essences—as opposed to relations—that are meaningfully intended but do not present or display any *hyletic* data, as for example

---

11  C.E.M Joad, *How Our Minds Work* (London: Westhouse, 1946), 62–63.

the meaning of a "square circle" or a "regular decahedron" or even paradoxes such as "Epimonides the Cretan says, 'All Cretans are liars.'"[12]

Hobbes' materialism no less than Armstrong's physicalism both directly entail nominalism, the thesis that only particulars exist; and the co-relative thesis that all "ideas" are only patchworks of sensory images. But meanings, whatever they are, seem to be a great deal more than simply momentary firings in the skull confined to single instants in time. Kant's theory of apperception requires continuity along with unity. The mind constantly *relationally* compares and contrasts meanings and judgments with and against each other and these *relations* cannot be accomplished unless the mind transcends imagery and particularity and temporally *holds* both concepts and judgments within the mind. For dual or multiple objects to be present to the mind in order to compare and contrast them in relation to their "resemblances" or "differences," to and from each other, we simultaneously need to "hold" them together in our minds so we can consider the similarities and dissimilarities.

A rather nice way of formulating this Platonic principle against nominalism can be found in a commentary by G.L. Vander Veer on F.H. Bradley, which is similar to Royce's point (above).

> Bradley's criticism of the [nominalist thesis] of images-as-thoughts is summed up by saying that such a view ignores the fact of meaning. Everything that exists has two aspects—existence and concept. Things exist with a certain character, and this is true of images as of anything else. But an idea must "mean" something other than itself and it is hard to see how it can do this while remaining an individual thing. Only universals can mean; only that taken apart from its existence can stand for something other than itself.[13]

If "ideas" were identical to mechanical motions in the brain, then we should be able to know precisely what idea is present or firing in the cerebral cortex by reading off the trace patterns on an electroencephalograph machine. After all, since the spikes on the graph are minutely precise, why should not the thoughts be as well? But I submit that we cannot match them. *That* a person is thinking may be inferred from a machine; but *what* he is thinking cannot.

---

12   Emmanuel Levinas, *The Theory of Intuition in Husserl's Phenomenology*, (Evanston, IL: Northwestern University Press, 1973): "We may have concepts which refer to essences that are 'merely meant' but do not exist," 105.

13   G.L. Vander Veer, *Bradley's Metaphysics and the Self* (New Haven: Yale, 1970), 21. Cf. Henri Bergson, *Matter and Memory* (London: George Allen & Unwin, 1970), xvii–xviii; and Brand Blanshard, *The Nature of Thought*, I, 337, 371.

Thought may be inferred from the spiked lines traced by an appendage to a machine but the jagged movement of the arm is not the thought. Nor is fear identical to sweating palms, the faster beating of the heart, or the trembling of the body, although all these bodily motions may and actually do accompany the fear. Rather fear is a meaning, an intention; fear is always *of* or *about* some meaningful object or situation or event. It is an objective meaning that is recognized and can be shared as a meaning but not as a set or collection of random sensations.

Meanings unlike definitions can continue to "accrue" novel and essential *qualitative* features and adumbrations that remain consistent with its nuclear meaning or essence. Meanings are *legitimately* nuanced. Meanings and experiences can be enriched by what Husserl calls fringes and horizons as they are experienced, developed, and connected to the same noematic nucleus. For example, the *essential* theory of diseases can be expanded to cover ever new findings and maladies and configurations. But they do not do so in the manner of material quantitative changes.

There is an important conceptual shift, which occurs when philosophers decide to discuss meanings rather than ideas. The credit for the transition is once more to be attributed to Kant, who stresses the judgmental nature of consciousness. Again, for Kant, all consciousness is judgmental just as for Hegel all consciousness is dialectical. Thus a judgment is a larger "unit" of meaning as opposed to an empirical idea as a complex of visual, auditory, etc., sensations. A simple idea or a simple impression alone, in the fashion of Locke or Hume, cannot be either true of false; e.g., simply saying "blue" as an utterance versus a judgment or a proposition is incorrigible and therefore non-assertive.

The traditional principle of the "unity of consciousness," as it is classically formulated by Plato and Plotinus and moving forward to Leibniz and Kant, becomes reinterpreted in more contemporary times as a "unity of meaning," especially in Husserl. The arguments for it, as well as the claims in its behalf, remain fundamentally the same. Husserl is a good example of this reinterpretation and readjustment. Similarly, in Royce, meanings are able to "increase" because they are immaterial animations and not just dead facts. As Royce argues, in *The World and the Individual,* the doctrine of meanings as immaterial intrinsically implies idealism (Royce, *WI,* 396–397). Reality is thus first and foremost a *system of meanings* (*WI,* 42, 418, 454) frequently composed of imageless realities as well (*WI,* 307, 309–311). The unity of consciousness is a unity of meaning (*WI,* 424–426, 437, 442, 464–469). Whether we agree with Kant's contention that meanings are discursively relational or with Husserl's claim that they are directly, immediately constituted, apprehended, and accessible to "intuitive seeing" is relatively unimportant. The salient consideration is that both philosophers concur that meanings are first attributable to spontaneous acts of consciousness and only subsequently open to empirical confirmation. Knowing and testing are different acts or procedures.

But what does it mean to say that there is a "unity of consciousness" and/or a "unity of meaning" in awareness. Perhaps we may illustrate it by an example borrowed from T.H. Green. When we speak a sentence, we utter the sounds successively; in this sense, the proposition advances in time and our listener grasps the significance of our propositional statements successively. But we ourselves are conscious of the *whole* meaning *before* expressing it in words, its entirety, all at once before we pronounce it aloud. And if we were not, then we could not proceed; or if we could, then we would be constantly surprised at what we said next; and beyond that when we eventually arrived at the end of our sentence. By the same token, when we read, it is a condition, a presupposition of understanding a sentence that it will have a "unity of meaning," an intrinsic relation of meaningful "parts" to a greater meaningful whole constituted as a unified web of meanings.

> In reading the sentence we see the words successively, we attend to them successively, we recall their meaning successively. But throughout the succession there must be present continuously the consciousness that the sentence has a meaning as a whole; otherwise the successive vision, attention and recollection would not end in a comprehension of what the meaning is.[14]

---

14　T.H. Green, *Prolegomena to Ethics* (Oxford: Clarendon Press, 1906, 5th edition), Chapter 2, Section 71 (page 81). Notice how in Green's comment, the unity of consciousness, meaning, and the temporal structure of time are interwoven. Similarly we recall that in Husserl's *Phenomenology of Internal Time-Consciousness*, he describes "immanent time as the flow of consciousness" as directly "open" to "intuitive seeing" (§ § 1–3, 6–8, 16). We recall his example of hearing a melody, with its merging, blending, and interpenetration of "separate" notes into the temporal unity we *mean, intend* when we are conscious of listening to a song. In this example, we could say that when we hear the melody it is given to us in "intuitive hearing." And if we consider Green's example of reading a sentence, it further underscores the inextricability of our sensuous experiences through the thread of time, "that the perception of duration itself presupposes duration of perception" (42–43; cf. Bergson as well). Indeed, Husserl believed that if he could discover the key to temporal constitutive acts, this would serve as the universal passkey to all constitutive meanings. Cf., Robert Sokolowski, *The Formation of Husserl's Concept of Constitution* (The Hague: Martinus Nijhoff. 1970), 82–86; and *Husserlian Meditations* (Evanston, IL: Northwestern University Press, 1974), 143 ff.: "The flow of inner time-consciousness allows an inner object to be constituted as a unity within a manifold of temporal phases. It also allows my self to be constituted as the one to whom these inner objects appear" (page 136).

The priority of consciousness over language is a first principle for Husserl. In order to phenomenologically "see," intuit meanings or essences, we must "look" at consciousness itself *before* we can apply language in our descriptions. Prior to our ability to observe *how* we use language, we must first investigate the meanings of our words prior their implementation. Words are symbols substituting for but not equivalent to meanings and thoughts. This is where the linguists and analytic philosophers go wrong beginning with Hobbes.[15]

All consciousness involves temporality; not of course in the trivial sense that awareness always takes time, but rather in the important sense that consciousness *is* time. Hence, philosophers have denied the existence of an independent world of external objects (Descartes); they have even questioned the existence of the self (Hume) but none has been so skeptical as to deny consciousness of time, as Kemp Smith has cogently argued (NKS, *Commentary,* 241–244). In terms of the subject matter of this study—the nature of consciousness—Kemp Smith's interpretations are critical. It means that Kant's *ultimate* premise of the entire Transcendental Analytic in the first edition Deduction is incontrovertible. And to Husserl's credit, this is also why, in the *Phenomenology of Internal-Time Consciousness,* he views temporality or time-consciousness as the formative key to *all* constitutive acts and essences. In addition, the temporal nature of our awarenesses is forcefully pressed forward by numerous tendencies in both the idealist and phenomenological traditions according to which (paradoxically) time appears *both* as immediate *and* mediate, *both* reflexive and transcendent at once. We recall that in Kant's Aesthetic, the intuition of time is passively "given," directly, immediately, while in the Analytic it is identified with consciousness itself; relationally, synthetically, mediately, discursively structured and ordered. It is this second description that bears study despite the fact that he retained the flawed intuitive version promoted in the Aesthetic.

Husserl, in *Ideas* credits Kant as having *almost* entered the truly phenomenological field in his description of temporal consciousness and he was convinced that if he could uncover the key to temporal constitutive acts this would serve as his Kantian "transcendental clue" to all constitutive meanings (*Ideas,* Section, 62). In distinguishing the immediate/direct from the mediate/relational activities involved in temporal awareness—intuition/apprehension-spontaneity/imagination-reflexive/cognition (A 99–104), Kant sets the stage for their reintegration. These passages are related to Kant's allusion to

---

15  Edmund Husserl, *The Idea of Phenomenology,* translated by George Nakhinian (The Hague: Martinus Nijhoff, 1964), xxi–xxii, 24, 41; and *Cartesian Meditations* (The Hague: Martinus Nijhoff, 1973), Section 5.

the *hypothetical* nature of the subconscious (A xxvii). Between intuition and conception, between receptivity and spontaneity lie the synthetic activities of the imagination, the latter involving processes which are at once sensuous and free, spontaneous, transcending, and reflexive. What Kant accomplishes is a philosophical revolution, which switches from simply assuming the principle of clarity involved in Cartesian self-consciousness to investigating the mystery and depths of temporal consciousness. The transcendental unity of apperception thus becomes a self-conscious unity through time, within the individual ego. How is consciousness itself possible? Its activity not just its conditions. These series of acts are also replicated in Husserl's account of the transcendental subject as well, his "wonder of wonders." Once more, we recall Paton's critical remark, that "our minds seem to last through time, as they do not seem to extend through space," as well as Findlay's equally pregnant remark that "In the conscious constitution of objects, athwart the flux of time, we have the necessary foundation for the constitution of a consciousness of consciousness, a point remade latterly and hammered home by Husserl."

Husserl's description of temporal constitution as it permeates and absorbs all intentional acts and *eidetic* meanings was not lost on Sartre.

> Temporality is evidently an organized structure [or synthesis]. The three so-called 'elements' of time, past, present, and future, should not be considered as a collection of [inactive] 'givens' for us to sum up—for example, as an infinite series of [immediate] 'nows' in which some are not yet and others no longer are—but rather as the structured moments of an original synthesis. Otherwise we will immediately meet with this paradox: the past is no longer; the future is not yet; and as for the instantaneous present, everyone knows that this does not exist at all but is the limit of an infinite division, like a point without dimension....The only possible method by which to study [i.e., describe] temporality is to approach it as a totality which dominates its secondary structures and which confers on them their meanings.[16]

---

16   Jean-Paul Sartre, *Being and Nothingness: An Essay on Phenomenological Ontology*, translated by Hazel Barnes (New York: Washington Square Press, 1966), 128–129, 225–226; hereafter cited as *B & N*. These discussions, logically enough, occur in the section on "Transcendence." Transcendence is frequently used by Sartre as meaning or intending "spontaneity," a non-reflexive act that explodes beyond reflexive consciousness. Thus, according to Sartre, man is always beyond himself in projects, he transcends himself toward the future by positing tasks, external to himself. Man lives in the future in the sense that he projects meanings or goals ahead of himself, beyond his immediate present experience.

It is because of this unique virtually paradoxical difficulty that philosophers like Bergson and Husserl have discovered themselves constrained to describe *duration,* or *internal time-consciousness* as an immediate flow, a seeming contradiction.

Described in different terms, both the past and the future are mediately relational but the present is an *immediate,* presumably non-temporal point. The common goal toward which both Bergson and Husserl strive is an overthrow of the psychologistic and empiricist formulation of time as a disconnected series of *instantaneous* "events," as the measurement of *distinct* points traversing and alternating in space. Thus, for example, Hume's atomistic psychology serves as an attempt to *explain* time in terms of *causal* contiguity and impressions replacing each other one after another. But phenomenological, experienced, personal time—as opposed to scientific, objective, impersonal time—is not a series of snapshots like a film screen. Years ago during a controversy about whether a racing horse's hoofs were completely off the ground a film clip "determined" they were. That's science. Science abstracts and separates "reality." But for Bergson the *human* flow of inner-time is both *meant* and *felt* as an absolutely *intimate, personal, possession,* which denies any possibility of sharing it with another self. It is always subjective but never inter-subjective. We can share clock and calendar times with others but not the *quality* of immanent time-consciousness. It is because of their rejection of the scientific explanatory principle of temporal contiguity that Bergson and Husserl both seek to replace the naive psychological model of objective time by instead indicating its "immediate continuity," its continuous stream—for not only is consciousness a unity but it is a continuity as well. Consequently, there are no gaps in consciousness. Otherwise, consciousness would be impossible.

There can be no doubt that there are cognitive ideas in consciousness, that we are constantly aware of meanings even in dreams—no one challenges that! But there may be more of a difficulty in acknowledging that there are also *innate* relational structures. Sartre, of course, denies this possibility for it would make consciousness opaque and not luminous or translucent as it must be if intentional freedom is to occur. But I believe, on the contrary, that there must be spontaneously engendered imageless relational forms to hold meanings together, otherwise our states of consciousness could never be unified and meanings would disintegrate into the confusing and disordered buzzing, blooming confusion and chaos of James' beleaguered infant (*Principles of Psychology,* 1, 488). In any case, if such immediate relations exist in awareness—and perhaps they can only exist as a matrix of pure possibilities—they must function as meaning-endowing acts. Simply put, consciousness must be directly constituted by at least *some* order or set of rules, *some* relational structures, some lawful principles, which are not reducible to sensations alone or to the accidental material collisions amongst the brain's neuronal cells and synapses. The least minimal order at least involves the distinction within consciousness between "subject" and "object," "ego and non-ego" or "self" and "other self." And this in turn constitutes the ultimate source of each self's feeling and meaning of alienation from the world and others; it constitutes our individual sense of loneliness, separation, apartness, and estrangement.

Again, it is not my intention, nor do I regard it as my task, to judge whether Bergson's principle, argument, or description of freedom is truer to the mark than Sartre's. That issue, once more, is relatively insignificant. What is worth noticing, however, is that both philosophers base their proofs of the freedom of consciousness upon the Achilles premise that consciousness is *both* immaterial *and* spontaneous. For Bergson, the simplicity argument points toward the conclusion that self-consciousness—at privileged moments of *duration* at least—is self-contained, completely unified, hence constituted as a "whole self," *le moi profond,* and therefore independent of external causes. In Sartre's early work, *The Transcendence of the Ego,* the simplicity argument grounds an explosive, outward-directed spontaneous act of freedom. In both cases, their principles can be conceptually compared to Kant's emphasis on the *spontaneity* of thought, on the mind's inherent ability to produce "something out of nothing" by way of its own internal resources. In the *Critique of Judgment,* his treatise on aesthetics, he declares: "Now, if in the judgment of taste the imagination must be considered in its freedom, it is in the first place not regarded as reproductive, as it is subject to the [empirical] laws of association, but as productive and spontaneous" (§ 22); again, "the imagination (as a productive faculty of cognition) is very powerful in creating another nature, as it were, out of the material that actual nature gives it" (§ 49). The third *Critique* was published in 1790 thirteen years after the second edition of the first *Critique* and clearly Kant remains prepared to credit spontaneity with a defining role. After Kant, as we saw, this self-transcending force of consciousness becomes of paramount importance in the theories of freedom as it plays out in Fichte, Hegel, and Schopenhauer where it retreats and appears underground. With Sartre, however, the ek-static freedom of consciousness starts to break away from its cognitive role of unification and it emerges instead as a radically creative force, one which explicitly assumes the function of creating and re-creating meanings and values for the "self" alone. Sartre's intentionally is concerned with a commitment, an engagement, an investiture of meaning dedicated solely to the value of one's own existence. Each of us has the freedom to create and re-create meaning for ourselves alone at each moment of time. Whenever the nothingness, the emptiness of consciousness has lost its meaning, it is poised to create anew. Sartre's "bad faith" is the avoidance of assuming personal responsibility for our choices and falsely blaming others or our environments, circumstances, or the Freudian unconscious. Whenever our insular awareness confronts its own radical freedom, then consciousness recognizes its absolute power to spontaneously create and reconstitute reality, especially in terms of moral values. These declarations naturally enough occur in the section on Transcendence in *Being and Nothingness*. Thus man is always potentially beyond himself in projects, ek-statically in his decisions toward the future by positing tasks beyond himself. Unlike a paper-cutter that has a pre-defined essence man must create himself absolutely alone (Sartre, *B & N*, 218–219, 225–226). Sartre's existentialism is a full-blown frontal attack on psychoanalytic determinism.

A year after the publication of Armstrong's study, H.D. Lewis' book appeared in print. It was directed not at Armstrong's views but rather at preceding works, such as Ryle's *Concept of Mind*, which presents a system in many ways similar to Armstrong's as far as fundamental assumptions and an accompanying paradigm of consciousness are concerned. Consequently, it seems worthwhile to come full circle and return briefly and discuss Lewis' views from Chapter 1 vis-a-vis Armstrong's materialist model of consciousness we have just considered and underscore Lewis' own debt to the simplicity argument and its major implications. Although Lewis' metaphysical dualism posits the probable locus of conscious interaction is the brain, he does not feel constrained to conclude that it follows that thoughts are reducible to physiological processes.[17]

As far as personal identity is concerned, Lewis is convinced that it consists in self-consciousness, in a reflexive consciousness of continuity during which "we have direct cognizance of our own minds" (Lewis, *EM*, 31); "one knows oneself as one ultimate indivisible being in the course of having any experience whatsoever" (*EM*, 237–239). As far as mental substances and thoughts are concerned, Lewis adopts a thoroughly immaterialist position. Thus, he concludes that "there is an inner, non-material character to all [mental] experience" (*EM*, 25). And "We are all the time aware of being aware; self-awareness is the obverse of our awareness of things" (*EM*, 164–165). Disagreeing with Ryle's

---

17   H.D. Lewis, *The Elusive Mind* (London: George Allen & Unwin, 1969), 28–29, 43, 52–53; cf. 164–165. Lewis frankly declares his metaphysical dualism on pages 166, 168, 187, 205–206, 232–233, 270, 274, 295, and 308, while admitting that the probable locus of interaction is the brain but does not feel constrained to conclude that therefore thoughts can be reduced to physiological processes. In fact, he insists that experience assures us of their distinct existence. Often the immaterial nature of the soul has been used to demonstrate its immortality. On my view, although the active mind depends on material conditions, once the physical conditions expire, consciousness ceases.

assertion that we can provide a completely behavioral account of the feigned trippings and stumblings of a clown, without any appeal to hidden and in principle unobservable thought processes going through the entertainer's "private" mind, Lewis challenges Ryle's behavioral analysis with his own counterclaim. Instead Lewis holds that there is *something more* involved in a *pretended* physical act of tripping or stumbling beyond the skill of the overt performance of the clown and this something more concerns the *intentional* immaterial meaning of feigning, the purposeful intention of simulation, which is not identical or reducible to the mere external movements of the clown's body; it is an immaterial, non-extended intention hidden from the sensory observation of others. In other word, there is a critical difference between a circus clown *pretending* to stumble and someone *actually* tripping and that critical difference is an unobservable mental *intention, i.e., a pretending to trip that is designed to fool the children.* What is missing from the behavioral account of the feigning tumbler is the *intentional,* the *purposive* goal to entertain the audience *beyond* and *separate* from his outward physical behavior; basically his intention to deceive (*EM,* 52–53). Intentionality it can be said is thus the difference between appearance and reality.

Lewis announces his commitment to substance dualism in the following terms.

> If there are radically distinct sorts of things in the world—and why should there not be?—they have to be recognized in their distinctness without dogmatically seeking to find terms common to both or reduce one to the other. By material standards mental activities are odd, for although they consume time, they are not in space or spatially extended at all. This is what makes them so elusive when, accustomed as we are to be outward looking and coping with the world around us...there is the aggravated temptation to suppose that mental realities, like external ones, must have some kind of quasi-tangible or solid character.
> LEWIS, *EM,* 19

But rather:

> The truth seems to be that we do not strictly ascribe corporeal characteristics and mental characteristics to the same thing...My mind has neither height nor length nor breadth. It would be absurd, except in a thoroughly figurative sense, to ask how big is my mind. To speak of a "small mind" is sheer metaphor. Minds are neither big nor small. If anyone denies this let him give me the approximate length of his mind, or any other, and say

how he measures it. Is it six inches, or a foot, or a mile, or what? Clearly it is none of these...The much maligned Descartes was obviously right in maintaining that it was distinctive of minds not to be extended.
ibid., 148–149

It follows that all existences with an "internal" ontological status should be classified as non-physical (Lewis, *EM,* 104); so are smells, noises, heat, and cold, since they are non-spatial (*EM,* 206). But what about physical objects? Are they not extended and, if so, how are we to know them at all if in truth our minds are *substantively* different? As Lewis himself puts it: "How can the spatial characteristics of physical things be reproduced in the unextended non-spatial mind?" (*EM,* 173). To this query, Lewis' answer is as brief as it is sufficient.

The dualistic view of mind and body ... does not imply in the least that spatial characteristics are "reproduced" in the mind. They are known by the mind, but the mind does not have to become in some way spatial in order to accommodate spatial reality in the sense of knowing it. Knowledge of space or matter need not be itself spatial or material in any sense.
ibid., 173–174

There is *both* matter *and* mind and once again, on Humean principles, it is cogently arguable that the inter-action between the two is inexplicable and apparently promises to remain so. Mind and matter are "distinct," even if it is the case—which it *actually* is—that thought somehow "indirectly" depends on matter. But neither reason nor experience can prove that they cannot coexist any more than reason can demonstrate that both colors and sounds cannot coexist in consciousness despite their radically different functions, i.e., *essences.* Similarly, both matter and life exist but it doesn't thereby follow that all mater is hylozoic (an issue that Cudworth criticizes at great length in *The True Intellectual System of the Universe*).

Mind would still remain distinct from body in its own nature, even though it could not be conceived to function without the body. Mental processes do not become physical processes by being dependent upon them in a peculiar way.... I do not become my body by not being able to function without it.
*EM,* 225

And should it eventually transpire that there is some correlation between certain physiological states and their corresponding or parallel mental dispositions, still it would not follow that our states of consciousness are reducible to, identical with, or solely explained by their material conditions because correlation does not necessarily imply causation (*EM,* 178). Matter "supports" thought but thoughts are not simply matter. Humans do require the brain for consciousness to exist but reciprocally brains need consciousness to be known.

Much of all of this depends on the recurring issue that has followed us throughout the text, namely the legitimacy of the claimed distinction between (1) passive and active consciousness and (2) quantitative and qualitative categories and existences.

In the foregoing, I have tried to argue that although individual, monadic consciousnesses are an immaterial presence in the world, nevertheless they are somehow chock-full of ***spontaneous acts,*** meanings, and relations. And I expect that for most of my readers, there must be something problematic, even paradoxical in such a view. But I do not know how else to go about describing the powers of the mind except in the fashion which I have undertaken in this study. It seems clear to me that the idealist tradition has credibly emphasized the existence of relational activities as internally active within the mind, whereas the materialist, empiricist, and positivist camps have neglected it, if not simply outright denied it. At times the difference is no more than this, namely, that the former group recognizes the importance of relations and the latter does not. But in other instances, the idealist tradition has valiantly struggled to say something significant about the relational contents and powers of the mind. In this case, it is not so much a matter of "explaining" the relations, or their origins, for this would be obviously circular and self-defeating, but rather in giving them their due, so to speak. To explain and describe are very different operations. To explain is already to relate entities, usually in a cause and effect sequence. But that is just the question at issue: how are relations at all possible, or as Kant suggests, "how is the faculty of thought itself possible?" (*Critique Reason,* A xvii). In the process of undertaking a descriptive investigation of the relational structures permeating consciousness, we soon discover that cause and effect relations are obviously not the only connections possible and that there are innumerable others—notably "self" and "other"— as well. Matter exists and so does consciousness. They are co-dependent. But to depend on something, as Lewis suggests, is not the same as *being* that something.

In general, we create our decisions and values in a restricted environment, one which is in a great measure conditioned by our natural and social surroundings, our training and education, and especially by our habits. To this extent and this respect, our conduct is (roughly) determinable. However, we need not always remain imprisoned in this fashion. And whenever we reflexively think on our situation, we shall realize our absolute freedom to forge very different meanings and decisions as different situations and contexts arise.

A final question arises: how to reconcile spontaneity with rationalism. Spontaneity itself is intrinsically uncaused, radically volitional, whereas rationality is inherently structured and circumscribed by definition with all the elements fitting smoothly internally together. Basically, acts of spontaneity initiate the mind's journey. Spontaneity gives us the initial "direction," either in terms of desire, cognition, or both. But "reason" is only conditionally "true," i.e., consistent within a selected prescribed system. For example, rational systems like mathematics are only descriptive within themselves.

The mind can create alternate systems that in their own way are (presumably) internally consistent and coherent (universal, necessary), e.g., Euclidean, Riemannian, or Lobachevskian geometries. But in terms of their application to certain astronomical systems, one is deemed to be "true" and the other two are not; or one is true to Newtonian physics but not to sidereal space. Hence Einstein comments that our freely created concepts and systems may "miraculously" (his word) end up in "applying" either to an independently existing universe of three- or four- or more dimensions of space and time.

Let me finish on a positive note. Human beings are incredibly creative because of the spontaneous "agency" of Kant's "productive imagination." They can conceptualize all sorts of possibilities as long it does not imply a contradiction (Leibniz). For example, mathematicians can create all sorts of "scientific" theories, paradigms, models, and systems. As Einstein mused when he suggested that our free, arbitrarily created concepts and systems often miraculously "apply" to an independent world.[18] Or as Kant puts it in applauding Francis Bacon, we must legislate to nature (*Critique,* B xii). Human beings, as I have argued are "conditionally rational." By that I mean what Aristotle meant. They can make connected inferences as in the 264 forms of the syllogism, some will be "valid" and most not. They can create multiple mathematical and geometric systems, some "applicable" and others not. And most importantly, two of the greatest realms open for human activity, for creation, imagination, and reason are the fields of aesthetics and ethics.

---

18   Albert Einstein, "Physik und Realitat," *Journal of the Franklin Institute*, Volume 331, 36.

**PART 3**

CHAPTER 8

# The Bicameral Mind, the Abyss, and Underworlds

> And when the messenger had spoken, he who had the first choice came forward and in a moment chose the greatest tyranny; his mind having been darkened by madness and sensuality had not thought out the whole matter before he chose; and did not at first sight foresee that he was fated, among other evils, to devour his own children.
> 
> PLATO, *Republic*, 'Myth of Er'

∴

The chapter treats two different topics but in a closely related context. First I discuss consciousness with special attention to the collapse of the distinction between its immediate and mediate aspects, and secondly I address the province of the subconscious mind with a concentration on its darker elements, since they are the primary ones that come into play in the dynamics of loneliness and aggression. Throughout the text I have mainly—but not completely—focused on the negative and violent expressions of consciousness simply because those are the dangerous ones that hold humanity in hostage. Accordingly, in what follows, I wish to clarify my frequent appeal to two principles and their roles in the various thinkers I have discussed: (a) spontaneity as a *causa sui* comparable to Schopenhauer's irrational Will as it surfaces in Julius Jaynes' depiction of the bicameral mind; and (b) the difference between a retrievable unconscious, as in Freud, and the subconscious as irretrievable in Kant and especially in Schopenhauer. Although Kant suggestively promises the reader to explore a deeper *cognitive* role for it, his assurance remains unfulfilled (*Critique*, xvi–xvii), while in Schopenhauer it assumes a powerful *affective* function in the guise of his noumenal irrational Will.

    I intend to enlist four studies by three authors, Julius Jaynes, Jon Mills, and very briefly Berthold Bonds, respectively, in an attempt to offer some degree of insight into the wide spectrum of aggressive fantasies and behaviors initiated by individuals. And I want to begin with Julius Jaynes, who collapses the distinction between affective immediacy and the mediacy of thought along with the apparent separation between feeling and thinking.

Julius Jaynes was a psychologist, who was educated at Harvard, taught at Princeton, and initiated his quite unusual study of consciousness with this singularly dramatic but highly memorable opening passage:

> O' what a world of unseen visions and heard silences, this unsubstantial country of the mind! What ineffable essences, these touchless rememberings and unknowable reveries! And the privacy of it all! A secret theater of speechless monologue and prevenient counsel, an invisible mansion of all moods, musings, and mysteries, an infinite resort of disappointments and discoveries. A whole kingdom where each of us reigns reclusively alone, greeting what we will, commanding what we can. A hidden hermitage where we may study out the troubled book of what we have done and yet what we may do. An introcosm that is more myself than anything I can find in a mirror. This consciousness that is my self of selves, that is everything and yet nothing at all—what is it? ...How do these ephemeral existences of our lonely experience fit into the ordering array of nature that somehow surrounds and engulfs this core of knowing?[1]

In what follows I intend to explore Jaynes' thesis that originally there was a wide range of motivational acts that were spontaneously triggered, which displayed a paradoxical *dual aspect* of feeling/thought as immediately experienced acts. In pursuing this theme, I will turn to his novel theory of the "bicameral mind," a mind with two "chambers" that expresses itself in unmediated "synthetic" acts.

According to Jaynes, three-thousand years ago, the dichotomy between acting *and* thinking or thinking *and* acting did not exist; there was no bifurcation, no separation between being told to do something and doing it; hearing and acting were indistinguishable. Today, generally speaking, when we are given a command (hearing), we have the option to think about it, to consider complying or not; we deliberate about the possible outcome before we act. But Jaynes describes an earlier state of a more original form of human consciousness in which Iliadic man heard and acted at once, immediately. To hear *and* to act were the same; affect and thought were identical; the mind did not separate the act from the thought or the thought from the act because man had *internalized* the commanding voice as that of a god *within* his consciousness. Thus in the pre-Hellenic Age, there was no possibility—no temporal "space" in between—allowing for a deliberation about the command and its implementation. If Jaynes is right, such an act in our contemporary age would appear to

---

[1] Julius Jaynes, *The Origins of Consciousness in the Breakdown of the Bicameral Mind* (Boston: Houghton-Mifflin, 1990), 1–2; hereafter cited as Jaynes, *BM*.

an external observer as "motiveless," "meaningless," and thus defying any possible rational explanation or moral justification. However, in ancient times the mediacy of thought in such acts was completely nullified. There was no temporal "space" to judge whether an act was good or bad; wise or stupid; beautiful or ugly; elegant or clumsy.

We recall that Plato in the *Sophist* and *Theaetetus* defined thinking as the soul's internal dialogue with itself as a preparation for forming a correct judgment. Jaynes, however, is alluding to an age before Plato's time during which the ability to formulate reflexive judgments had as yet not evolved.

The concept of the bicameral mind offered a unique paradigm of consciousness because it collapsed the difference between the immediacy and the mediacy of consciousness in the context of human actions. It posited a mind exhibiting two chambers that act in unison as one, simultaneously. There was no temporal "space" between the "two" modes of consciousness. In this context, we recall Bergson's criticism of the "spatialization" of time. What Jaynes is describing is something akin to an intuitive act.

Basically Jaynes also appears to be suggesting some sort of "animistic" connection between the human and the divine. In such a universe, there could be no individual sense of *moral* responsibility because the act was determined by a god's voice. In turn, Jaynes also describes these identities as psychotic episodes: hallucinatory and delusional. In effect what he is intimating is that originally man's consciousness was directly "wired" (his term) to his subconscious. His command hallucinations were deeply engrained within the "self" and operated well below and apart from both human thought and language or what we now consider as our "normal" way of thinking, speaking, and doing. These long-ago highly charged emotional acts were impulsively and intrinsically unpredictable by their very nature because men lacked the ability to distinguish causal or motivational antecedents and consequents. Only the listener was exposed to the command. Only the hearer could see and hear the god, goddess, or the apparitions. These were acts "unto themselves," *sui generis*. They exhibited an essential non-temporal quality. It was not possible to provide either a causal explanation or a moral justification for what someone did beyond simply saying, "I was commanded by my god or daemon." The act itself was self-explanatory and *causa sui*. The question, "*Why* did *you* do it?" was meaningless. "The god directed me"; or "It was not I; it was the god" sufficed. In effect, the two factors of immediacy and mediacy within consciousness were collapsed into one. As Jaynes describes it, "Preceding our contemporary concept of consciousness there was a very different mentality based on verbal/auditory hallucinations." It follows, then, that before man learned to distinguish his own self-consciousness from both an independent natural world and other separate selves, the bicameral mind consisted of a single agency displaying twin aspects. The god or goddess spoke directly, immediately and therefore could not be "disobeyed," since (a) *both* listening *and* acting imply a *temporal separation*; and (b) disobedience implies a further *spatial separation* between the god and a distinct self, both of which did not exist at that time; it did not entail two "poles" of consciousness. Rather the bicameral mind presented two chambers but one act. Introspection was not possible. In Jaynes' paradigm of consciousness, inevitably the lines between being awake and experiencing dreams, hallucinations, delusions, and fantasies became blurred; in fact there was but one consciousness with two distinguishable aspects functioning within a single dimension of awareness. Although we are currently "[self-]conscious human beings...at one time human nature was split into two, an executive part called a god and a follower part called a man." One part was the speaker and the other the doer but bicameral man regarded the speaker as a god whose commanding voice was identical with the act itself.

> The characters of the Iliad do not sit down and think what to do. They do not have conscious minds such as we say we have and certainly no introspection. It is impossible for us with our subjectivity to appreciate what it was like. When Agamemnon robs Achilles of his mistress [Breisis], it is a god that grabs Achilles by his yellow hair and warns him not to strike Agamemnon. It is a god who arises from the sea and consoles him in his tears of wrath...a god who whispers low to Helen to sweep her heart with homesick longing, a god who hides Paris in a mist in front of the attacking Menelaus, a god who tells Glaucus to take bronze for gold, a god who leads the armies into battle, who speaks to each soldier...who debates and teaches Hector what he must do, who urges the soldiers on or defeats them...It is the gods who start quarrels among men that really cause the war. It is one god who makes Achilles promise not to go into battle, another who urges him to go, and another who then clothes him in golden fire and screams through his throat at the Trojans rousing in them panic. *In fact, the gods take the place of consciousness.*
> JAYNES, 72; italics mine

Consequently for Jaynes, reflexive self-consciousness was non-existent; individuals did not meditate or deliberate on *what* should or should not be done; *why* or why not; or *how* it should be done. These problematic issues were later developments in human evolutionary thought. But in the beginning, the commanding voice *and* its simultaneous discharge were but one and the same act.

Unpacked what Jaynes is describing is virtually a solipsistic self that has created another self, a god or goddess, perhaps for the purpose of companionship just as children often do, within its self in order to account for what the self desires and does. In the privacy of its own soul, it has fabricated plausible "reasons" or "motives," i.e., commands to and for its self and what it does. Such a "self" is immune from the ethical judgments of others. It has its own intimate, private "desires/motives/reasons" sufficient unto its self and it is able to disregard all external authority. It is completely self-insulated. Obviously such a depiction of human consciousness on Jayne's terms is, as he indicates, essentially and inevitably a lonely one.

Thus commences one of the most unusual doctrines of consciousness I have ever pondered but it suggests a fruitful connection in regard to the evolution of subjectivity and self-consciousness. As we proceed, we will draw on Jayne's speculations, since they offer valuable insights into the internal dynamics of what transpires in the minds of many individuals who commit violent, seemingly inexplicable acts, irrational acts of violence and self-destruction. We shall discover that there are myriads of situations during our earthly existence, which involve spontaneous and unpredictable acts emanating from forces "below" or "underneath" reflexive consciousness and thus preventing any conceivable insight or understanding into *why*. They consist in actions that completely mystify strangers as well as intimates. The origin and force of these actions, their true source lies irretrievably hidden in a personal subconscious, in obscure desires submerged within intricate but fragile webs of feelings, urges, and impulses; nestled within the lonely labyrinthine vessels of the soul to which we are unknowingly responsive and in the presence of which we are completely unable to assign any determinable, meaningful, or relational structures or plausible motives, reasons, or justifications. "Normally" our everyday behaviors display an obvious connection, a relation holding between intentions and goals; they portray a quality of purposiveness between our originating desires, our deliberations concerning implementations, the means available, and the ends intended, which basically correspond to Aristotle's concept of human actions as having a distinguishable beginning, middle, and end. This, however, was—and perhaps is— not the case if Jaynes is correct and so in a great number of instances of wanton destruction, when the act is embedded in immediate affective impulses, consciousness spontaneously *acts*. As "rational" creatures, we naively assume we can always theoretically in principle understand everything if only we search and look for causes and motives long enough; that we can either mechanically reconstruct an event in terms of natural causes or in terms of psychological motivations; that there is always some "meaningful" answer for everything we feel, think, and do. Jaynes' paradigm, however, dismisses all these assumptions by collapsing the distinction between immediacy and mediacy, act and thought, and in a word reducing consciousness to pure spontaneity, to two very different *functions* but a single act. It's not that the subject does not know what s/he is doing but that the option to "think through," "judge," or to do otherwise does not exist. In short, *obsessions* admit of no countervailing influences. The essence, the nature of an obsession is to act and not to think. It is as the French say, *"une idée fixe."* Mediate thinking is not only irrelevant but indeed non-existent. The act is sufficient unto itself whether in fantasy or implementation. Obsessions are intrinsically desiderative and not contemplative.

Not until much later and only after the Homeric and Hesiodic myths had run their course, did this original twofold-feeling/act become split into distinguishable functions. It was not until the time of Plato and Aristotle that eventually the conception of this uniquely singular act evolved into conceptual divisions between (a) hearing a command; (b) deliberatively attending to it; (c) coming to a conclusion; and only then (d) acting or not acting.

In fleshing out his theory, Jaynes asks us to start with the physical bifurcation of the brain into a right and left hemisphere. Next we are to follow him along an evolutionary path as feelings and thoughts are transformed into words and language. And thirdly, we are solicited to agree that each mind displays a multitude of "schizophrenic" (his term) tendencies and more specifically "symptoms" that we still currently classify today as command hallucinations and delusions, which have been present in mankind since the dawn of human (?) consciousness. These three assumptions are designed to provide for our understanding of his theory of the evolution of "introspection." Introspection is Jaynes' term for "diremptive" self-consciousness, a bifurcation of the self into an 'I' or 'me' as separate from an external world of objects and an interpersonal realm of other selves. As an aside, having "interacted" with psychotic patients for over twenty years as a therapist, I can testify to the sense of *my* own feelings of "disconnectedness" from the "other" and my *inference* that the "other" feels the same alienation during our "exchanges."

In acknowledging this unusual bicameral unification, this primitive indistinct "unity of consciousness," virtually a synthetic identification of two selves within the one, Jaynes refers to an ancient Sumerian admonition to support his thesis: "Act promptly, make your god happy," which he interprets for us as: "Don't think: let there be no time-space between hearing your bicameral voice and doing what it tells you" (Jaynes, *BM,* 204). Notice again the reference to a Bergsonian "time-space" suggesting how the temporalization of space becomes implicated and actually intrudes between inner immediate intuition versus causal and conceptual abstractions. Men—presumably women as well—simply respond to their interior divine voices, their god. Much of this is reminiscent of Schopenhauer's irrational Will. It is as if affective impulses are either personified: "it was the god who did it"; or dissociated; "a god made me do it."

> The beginnings of actions are not in conscious plans, reasons, and motives; they are in the actions and speeches of gods. To another, a man seems to be the cause of his own behavior. But not to the man himself. When Achilles...reminds Agamemnon of how he robbed him of his mistress, the king declares, "Not I was the cause of this act, but Zeus, and my portion and the Erinyes who walk in darkness; they it was in the assembly put wild *ate* upon me when I arbitrarily took Achilles' prize from him, so what could I do?"...Scholars who in commenting on this passage say that Agamemnon's behavior became "alien to his ego" do not go nearly far enough. For indeed the question is what is the psychology of the Iliadic hero? And I am saying he did not have any ego whatever.
> JAYNES, *BM*, 72–73

There is a passage in Hegel's *Anthropology* which corresponds to Jaynes' completely self-enclosed "I."

> But the reason why such an *idée fixe* irreconcilable with my concrete actual world, *can* arise in me is that I am in the first instance, a wholly abstract, completely indeterminate 'I' and therefore open to any arbitrary content....Man alone has the capacity of grasping himself in this complete *abstraction of the 'I.'* This why he has, so to speak, the privilege of folly and madness.
> *Hegel's Philosophy of Mind*, Section 408, Note

I would further venture to connect these psychological reflections with Schopenhauer's irrational Will.

What Jaynes' theory offers is a much more primitive account of consciousness, one which ascribes *certain* human actions to subconscious forces. What his theory does *not* allow is any possibility of predicting what his subjects will do because the entire transaction is spontaneously confined *within, inside* the (human?) soul.

As further proof of his thesis, Jaynes emphasizes that scholars are unable to discover any written texts confirming a separation of the self from the world and other selves in any of the earlier writings of mankind.

> Iliadic man did not have subjectivity as we do; he had no awareness of his awareness of the world, *no internal mind-space to introspect upon.* In distinction to our own subjective conscious minds, we can call the mentality of the Myceneans a *bicameral mind.* Volition, planning, initiative is organized with no [external purposive] consciousness whatever and 'told' to the individual in his familiar [persona] language, sometimes with the visual aura of a familiar friend or authority figure or 'god' or sometimes a voice alone. The individual obeyed these hallucinate voices because he could not [conceptually] 'see' [i.e., distinguish] what to do by himself.
> JAYNES, *BM,* 75; italics mine

Again notice once more the tendency in several of the authors we previously discussed in our text to interpose a temporal "space" between our immediate *internal* thoughts and the "spatialization of time." The bicameral mind was not invested with or privy to an "internal mind-space."

According to Jaynes, in the "pre-reflexive age," there was no *clear* separation between "states of mind" and a distinct realm in regard to "objects of knowledge" prior to Plato's Divided Line passage. To Jaynes' point, to the best of my knowledge, it is indeed true that the soul's ability to reflexively, circularly think its own thoughts is not described and isolated as "an internal dialogue with itself" *until* Plato's *Theaetetus* (189e) and *Sophist* (263e) and Aristotle's *Metaphysics* (1075a), as previously discussed. In other words, there is more than a kernel of truth in Jaynes' conviction that self-conscious reflexivity is an outcome of evolutionary thinking, i.e., philosophical thinking. Similarly clearly and later in Thucydides' speech the dialogue form of discursive consciousness presents the mind from the interiors of consciousness as reflexive as well as personally declaratory.

Jaynes further maintains that as words and language evolved, they became transformed into visual and temporal "analogs" and "metaphors" mimicking the external world of space and time, a realm of existence beyond and apart from consciousness. Language pragmatically evolved in order to serve as an internal "mechanism," a device enabling the mind to intervene as a communicative "medium" inserted between the voice of the god and the actions of men; between the original command and its obeisance; between word and deed. Consequently, after "the breakdown of the bicameral mind," language begins to serve as an instrument for *separating* the soul or self as it is situated within the locus of an Aristotelian "ensouled" substance and also as *distinct, separate* from the world and other conscious beings (Jaynes, *BM,* 55, 63, 65–67, 72–75, and 79). "The spatializing of time occurred because one of the essential properties of consciousness was the metaphor of time as space that could be regionalized such that events and persons could be located therein, giving that sense of past, present, and future which made narratization possible" (Jaynes, 250). Without a spatialized time, science and objectivity cannot operate. Consequently, as Jaynes conceives it, "Consciousness is based on language" (Jaynes, 447) and language of course is mediate and pragmatically representational.

Interestingly in a lecture on Egyptian art many years ago, Kenneth Clark made the insightful observation that the Egyptians, who as long as they communicated their ideas by visual cuneiforms, ideographs, and hieroglyphs were unable to develop either a philosophy or a conception of abstract thinking. The Greeks, by contrast, using syllables to stand for sounds achieved a predominantly symbolic and imageless form of communication. I take this to imply that the Greeks attained the ability to think in terms of imageless universal concepts, pure concepts without the encumbrances of distorting, limiting, or confining iconic cuneiform "scratches." As the net of human cognition is cast wider and wider in human thought, the lesser and lesser is imagery required (Jaynes, 176–177). Recall Plato's qualitative levels in the Divided Line, the lower world of sensations and objects against the upper realm of imageless mathematical symbols, Universal Forms, and the comprehensive unification of the Good, which of course is not an image or a visual experience.

It's also speculatively interesting to wonder whether Jaynes believes Iliadic man was closer to reality than we are. In any case, Jaynes' thesis is that "history is impossible without the spatialization of time, which is characteristic of [contemporary] consciousness" (Jaynes, 251). This implies that the breakdown of the bicameral mind had something to do with the temporal spatialization of consciousness. But in any event, the sequence seems to be the following. First there were men with bicameral minds and something akin to command hallucinations but they did not "possess" self-consciousness. And only later were there men, who were reflexively self-conscious, i.e., "introspective" following the implementation of a more precise form of an "objectifying" language, which allowed them to distinguish themselves clearly from the world of nature and other selves. Accordingly the evolution of language served the purpose of distinguishing the self from the other self in order to develop a conscience and the moral imputability of responsibility.

Thus according to Jaynes, the reason humans evolved toward forging a conception of the self as a distinct person, separate from other selves, was so that ethically they could assume the mantle of a private conscience as well as an intimate sense of personal responsibility. Only then could men and women deliberate about their proposed acts and judge not only the intentions of others but their own as well. For Jaynes, developing the distinction between the self and other selves is a prerequisite for the possibility of (a) introspection;

(b) making moral distinctions based on the possession of a conscience; and therefore (c) the imputation of moral responsibility, first in order to egotistically blame other selves and only later to holding one's own self to account.

In our contemporary world, the actual realities and diagnoses of psychotic disorders and more specifically schizophrenia of course still persist and are generally considered as "irrational" and sometimes dangerous aberrations. Obviously in terms of mental health, we consider two of the most disorienting "symptoms" to be command hallucinations and megalomanic and paranoid delusions. Paired with Jaynes' "inner voices of the gods," these internal stimuli are considered delusions, which foster directive feelings, thoughts, and commands—"the voices told me"—and acts that often lead to long-standing obsessions and monomanias. The nucleus, the command can be present for an extended period of time; it can "incubate" and remain transfixed in its intent for prolonged periods. The feeling, the impulse, the urge can fester and germinate over lengthy spans of time while retaining the same urgency; or it may also *qualitatively* intensify or diminish over time becoming stronger or weaker. These intentional, obsessive, and commanding *feelings* serve as fuses ready to explode at any moment. They function as dynamic forces but not causes or motivations in our sense of those terms. As the cumulative incidents of conflicted feelings surface within the self brought on by the ravages and stress of loneliness, explosions of anger and anxiety are turned against both others and/or the self (Jaynes, 93–94). The spectrum of aggressive intensity in human beings spans a wide arc extending all the way from mild to violent, from consuming daydreams of revenge to murderous outbursts. Thus, although the actual physical implementation of the act itself may take place days or even years later, it is the obsessional goal, the desired/act that guides the ultimate discharge; not the lapse of time. Feelings—like sensations—are immediate, direct, non-relational, and qualitatively simple. But the fixation on the same goal can continue over time. By contrast, "hows" and "whys" are mediate, discursive, and relational reconstructions of spatio-temporal thought processes and deliberations before they turn into public events. But the *act of* spontaneity remains by its very nature unpredictable and unexpected. It is an existential "decision"; an absolutely free "choice" more akin to an impulse than a deliberation.

And so we ask ourselves if Professor Jayne's theory has any plausibility or usefulness in our account of consciousness? We remember that Socrates in the *Apology* refers to his Daemon, who frequently cautions him about going too far or speaking too much. St. Augustine, in his *Confessions,* credits his conversion to Christianity as a response to a child's directive voice instructing him to read a specific passage in the Christian Bible. It is interesting that Jaynes does not cite Kierkegaard's *Fear and Trembling* with its example of Abraham hearing God's commanding voice to kill/sacrifice his only son, Isaac. In the story, Abraham is unable to tell anyone, including Sarah, what he has been directed to do. This seems to qualify as an auditory hallucination in Jayne's sense of the term: God directing, commanding Abraham. His internalized conflict is beyond words; beyond language; it is incommunicable. It cannot be conveyed or shared with anyone beyond his private sphere of consciousness. Pointless to try to tell Sarah his irresolvable conflict: *either* sacrifice Isaac *or* disobey God. Abraham is absolutely alone with his Deity. It is beyond understanding, mediation, or communicative language. For Abraham, the conceptual *mediacy* of language is intrinsically opposed to the *immediacy* of the hallucinatory voice/command given by God. Abraham's command is uniquely existential and individual. His Lord dwells inside him.

By contrast we can mediately understand Agamemnon's sacrifice of Iphegenia; it expresses a terrible but considered *ethical* choice; it conforms to a universal *moral* criterion and therefore commands a meditated decision: without the sacrifice of his daughter to the goddess, Artemis, the Greek fleet cannot sail to Troy. And the king's judgment to commit infanticide sets in motion his own murder by Clytemnestra because of maternal grief and in turn her own death by her vengeful son, Orestes. These however are deliberative acts we understand.

Jaynes' theory I believe has considerable plausibility. It readily applies to many, all too many, situations. There are serious limits in gaining insight and understanding into the deep intensity of human desires; when the soul feels assaulted and is under great stress and siege and when all hope has vanished. Often the "motives" cannot be found by searching from the outside; they lie spontaneously within. All that exists is a desire to narcissistically impose one's unique existence against the balance of everyone else and the world at large. During these subconscious feelings, our desires, fantasies, illusions, and thoughts remain completely hidden from others and even indecipherable to the self.

Narcissism actually represents a very much unrecognized and underappreciated dynamic. Consider for a moment the seemingly annoying practice of someone writing graffiti on public places. It is actually motivated by anger, an insistence that one's own unique existence be recognized against those of others. Consider also the homicidal-suicidal motivation to express one's existence at the expense of a society of strangers even at the cost of one's life. The dynamic is the same. "I exist and you better acknowledge it at your peril." It's not very different form the child who would rather be disobedient than ignored.

Thus Jayne's relevance in the present study lies in offering a theory of consciousness that is able to metaphysically "account" for *why* so many violent acts preclude the possibility of providing behavioral, psychodynamic, or neuroscientific *causal* explanations or moral justifications for violent and destructive acts either toward others and/or the self. On Jaynes' account, the feeling/act is completely independent of causal explanations or motivational justifications and therefore it is *sui generis* and unpredictable. Jaynes' account of the bicameral mind plausibly describes a multitude of feeling/acts as spontaneous; as deriving from the roots of the subconscious mind. Spontaneous acts display a deep *human* origin precisely because, unlike instincts, the acts are both free and self-conscious without any thought of consequences beyond the desire to have one's existence recognized, acknowledged.

The chronically lonely individual simply acts. They care not a whit about explaining or justifying themselves to others, although various rationalizations may be offered in order to "excuse" the self and project guilt on others. The individual frequently offers *de facto* fabricated *rationalizations* alleging fictitious precipitating conditions, political ideals, or prejudices cynically expressed out of anger, shame, and guilt in a final effort to enhance their wounded vanity. But how can someone rationalize an obsession?

Finally, in defending his paradigm, Jaynes criticizes a wide variety of metaphysical and psychological theories of consciousness, including materialism (pages 4–5); classical Epicureanism (page 14); Cartesian dualism (pages 291, 335); Locke's empirical paradigm of the *tabula rasa* paradigm (page 27); Hegelian idealism (page 437); doctrines of "emergent evolution" and "critical naturalism" propounded by Samuel Alexander and Bertrand Russell (pages 11–12); contemporary behaviorism (page 442); as well as the current movements promoting "medical materialism," psychopharmacology, and indeed all "scientisms" in general (*passim*).

Jon Mills' first study, *The Unconscious Abyss,* undertakes to describe how Hegel's philosophical thought anticipated the Freudian unconscious. Mills' treatment is quite insightful as it pursues several goals. First, he assumes a comparative approach; he is not arguing that Hegel influenced Freud but simply that there are strong similarities between the two thinkers. Second, he shows how the unconscious processes, which are described in Hegel's "nocturnal abyss" of consciousness, serves as a foundation for the higher forms of intelligence and *subjective* Spirit as Hegel makes it clear that unconscious activities underlie all dimensions of human awareness. And third he provides valuable insights how Hegel's theory of a "dark unconscious" was informed by his historical predecessors, including the influence of Neo-Platonism, theosophic Christianity, and early German idealism, which Mills identifies with passages from Hegel's *Encyclopaedia of the Philosophical Sciences.*[2]

---

[2] Jon Mills, *The Unconscious Abyss: Hegel's Anticipation of Psychoanalysis* (Albany, New York: State of New York Press, 2002), 2. 23, 29; hereafter cited as Mills, *UA*.

When the censors of sleep relax and the doors of the unconscious are breached, a Pandora's box of pervasive visions, dark fantasies, narcissistic desires, and delusional anxieties are liberated and invade the soul; when wandering nocturnal reveries and violent emotions seize the sanctuary of consciousness and gain access, they are capable of capturing the beleaguered self throughout the more turbulent episodes of our lives. Trapped in the vice of tensions wrought upon the soul and fueled by sinister thoughts and nightly terrors, Hegel's "feeling soul" often erupts in angry recriminations toward the self as well as others.

Hegel begins his discussion of the "feeling soul" with the declaration "that everything called matter, no matter how much it conveys to ordinary thinking the illusory appearance of independence, is known to have no independence relatively to mind" (Section 389). And he goes on to liberally sprinkle his discussion with references to the soul's diremptive internal divisions, to mental illness, insanity, *idée fixe,* madness, etc.

But Mills primary emphasis is on the demonic, the frightening sources and contents of the unconscious, which he traces back to Jacob Boehme as anticipating—but not influencing—Freud. Consequently, for my purposes, Mills' descriptions of the Hegelian abyss prove to be a fertile background to my conception of the subconscious.

According to Mills, Hegel's abyss first finds expression in Plotinus and later Neo-Platonic thought as it influenced Boehme. It is important in this context, to realize that Plotinus, Proclus, and especially Boehme describe the One or God as the sole Reality, as extending from the lowest to the highest levels and realms of Being, from lowly matter and sensuousness as evil to a continuous span to pure unadulterated goodness; all of reality is *already* contained within the one Being. The original dialectical sources for the Proclean ontology consist of the varying levels of being and knowledge, which derive from Plato's doctrine of the Divided Line in the *Republic* and his cosmological myth presented in the *Timaeus.*[3]

In Plotinus and Neo-Platonism in general, evil is identified with matter, sensuousness, and lust in man; it is an "emanation" and not the result of God's creation of man and his subsequent sinful Fall. Evil is *already* in the world, in sensuousness, in the very nature of man. Given this paradigm of graded levels of Being and Consciousness, as initially instituted in the Platonic

---

3   A.O. Lovejoy, *The Great Chain of Being* (New York: Harper Torchbooks, 1961), 46 ff.; cf. 179 and 181. Lovejoy also connects "the great chain of being," beginning with Plato's *Tmaeus* and Plotinus' *Enneads* to the metaphysical thought of Leibniz and credits Schelling, Hegel, and Bergson with their contributions.

dialogues, if we start from the very first inception of life and consciousness, we find a *continuous* gradation of awarenesses emanating from a primordial abyss ascending toward the fullest stages of explicit self-consciousness. Lovejoy's interpretation of the "great chain of Being," as it applies to the continuity of Being or Nature, is grounded in the premise that God, Who is omnibenevolent, would have allowed for as much reality as compossible; He would have brought into being as many levels and intricacies, complexities of reality as metaphysically compatible. Because of Leibniz's idealism—he calls himself the "first idealist"—the same principle of continuity is also applicable to human monadic consciousness as it is to the entire rational order of the universe. Leibniz's guiding principle of continuity rules both reality and consciousness; knowledge and truth. As Leibniz declares, "Nature makes no leaps" and neither does consciousness. This testifies to the twin Leibnizian principles of unity and continuity as they are passed on to illuminate Kant's subjective idealism and subsequently Hegel's objective version. For Hegel, this principle and model of plenitude, continuity, and unity is as applicable to the gradations inherent *within* the individual soul as it is to the entire outer macrocosm of Nature. Consciousness is every bit as continuous, complex, variegated, and rich as "the great chain of Being" itself precisely because it is Spirit that formulates all that exists as well as all that is known. It encompasses the various forms and permutations of immanent Consciousness as well as the ontological levels of Being in both the *Phenomenology* and the *Logic.*

It follows from this point of view that all modes of intelligence are to be conceived as emanating from the unconscious mind, from the existing unmediated *simplicity* of the *feeling soul* as it moves toward higher levels of consciousness. Ultimately it is from this germinating potentiality, from this pregnancy of universal Spirit that the first forms of consciousness become impregnated with all the *qualities* of existence and progressively come into being as an ascension to higher forms. In Hegel's version of objective idealism, both Consciousness and Being develop in step but both their beginnings are steeped in the immaterial *qualitative* simplicity of thought. In the following passage we notice the Aristotelian principle of potentiality at work in Hegel's description.

> To grasp intelligence as this night-like mine or pit in which is stored a world of infinitely many images and representations, yet without being [explicitly] in consciousness, is from the one point of view the universal postulate which bids us treat the notion as concrete, in the way we treat the germ as affirmatively containing in virtual possibility all the *qualities* that come into existence in the subsequent development of the tree. It

is the inability to grasp a universal like this, which, though, intrinsically concrete, still continues *simple*.[4]

We recall Schopenhauer's allusion to the metaphor of the tree in offering insight into understanding consciousness but it is the emphasis on the universality of *qualities* that is of paramount importance in the citation. Feelings—"the feeling soul"—offer the foundational qualities that first and foremost animate human existence. Brooding fantasies, demanding needs, and conflicted desires constantly erupt within the soul as different elements fight to reach the surface, to attain fuller consciousness and expression (Schopenhauer).

According to Mills, the concept of the "dark abyss" begins with Plotinus, continues in Neo-Platonism, and then enters through the mystical and theosophic reflections of Jacob Boehme until it finally influences the thought of Hegel. Mills accordingly undertakes to demonstrate how, in the passage quoted above, this "night-like abyss within which a world of infinitely numerous images and representations is significantly preserved without being in consciousness" plays out and is developed in Hegel's *Anthropology*. The abyss, this unknown but powerful fount of distorted feelings and impulses dominates the unconscious mind. For Hegel, at this level of consciousness, every desire, thought, and action is "unconsciously busy." Thus there is a disturbing tension within this deepest of all feeling-levels of consciousness occurring in what Hegel describes as "the unthought." It is insidiously hidden "behind the back of consciousness" as it formatively forges the primordial ground of Spirit. The abyss, the *Ungrund* is "the unthought thought"; its essence consists of feelings and thoughts, which are "a riddle to itself." For how can one think "the unthought"?

And so Mills dramatically begins his first study of the Freudian unconscious by ushering in what he describes as the most deep-seated question of mankind:

> Thought lives underground. What is the ground of human consciousness—of subjectivity—the very essence that makes thought, hence spirit possible? Does such a ground exist, and if so, to whom does it belong—to the I or to an It as Nietzsche suggests ["Not 'I think,' but 'it thinks in me'"] or perhaps nothing at all?.... Before thought appears, it lives underground. For Hegel, as for psychoanalysis, the unconscious is the

---

4  G.W.F. Hegel, *Hegel's Philosophy of Mind,* translated by William Wallace (Oxford: Clarendon Press, 1971), Part 3 of the *Philosophical Sciences,* Section 453; italic his.

> primordial ground of consciousness—an underground abyss that inhabits the psychic space between reason and desire, intuition and thought, between I and the It. And it is such that this abyss within the psychic space is itself a space, a pit [a black hole] that divides consciousness from what it is not, the known from the unknown. It is precisely this pit, this unknown that organizes [i.e., orders and unifies] thought and defines its operations, and yet it is itself beyond [or below] thought. But the unthought that dwells underground hibernates in its pit, an eternal slumber. Such hibernation, however, is not the passive peacefulness of sleep, rather it is an activity, an unrest of the soul.
> 
> MILLS, *UA*, 21–22

It is this *qualitative* restlessness, this activity that Boehme will introduce as the source of all consciousness and existence; this will be what gets the whole qualitative "something" of Being energized. In the Note to Sections 402 and 408 in the *Anthropology*, Hegel connects primitive consciousness to "insanity," to estrangement, to the alienation of the self in its profound subjectivity, "which means the soul is divided against itself, is on the one hand already master of itself, and on the other hand not yet master of itself, in an isolated particularity in which it has its actuality" (Hegel, *PM*, Section 402; cf., 402 Note). Clearly in the first developmental stages of human consciousness, hallucinatory and delusional feelings and thoughts will predominate. Obviously at this level, they are not recognized as fictions belonging to the self. The real issue is: to what extent and how will these feeling/thoughts prevail in subsequent stages of life? It is worth recalling here once again Kant's appeal to the spontaneous, creative, dynamic imagination. Again the difference is that Kant is speculating on how *cognitive* immanent time-consciousness and the unity of consciousness itself are possible, whereas Hegel is clearly concerned with the *affective* forces seething under the surface of insanity, of "a soul divided against itself."

The original "feeling soul" is not yet capable of cognitive judgments or formulating explicit states or levels of reflexive self-consciousness. It has no cognizance of relations providing for the unity and identity of the self. At first this incipient awareness is only expressed through the "animalistic feeling soul," which Hegel describes in the *Anthropology*. Before explicit self-consciousness is attained,

> Spirit is aware of itself unconsciously as an agent that intuits and feels itself before it posits itself in consciousness, which is its next shape. Self-consciousness constituted through intersubjectivity, therefore, becomes

> more fully actualized as spirit progresses toward self-understanding. While self-consciousness becomes more elaborate and refined in relation to the other [self], it is already pre-established—its unfolding is already unconsciously prepared.
> MILLS, *UA*, 139

But as the soul develops from feeling states and through various levels, stages, or moments of awareness in order to reach cognitive self-consciousness, it is forced to retain all it has gained and undergone as well as all it has desired and suffered during its secretive autobiographical journey and history. All the feelings and primitive thoughts are navigated through the dark channels, tides, shoals, and eddies of the soul. The soul carries its earliest defeats and victories within itself; all its accumulated possessions; everything from whence it all began is carried forward to whither everything is going. All that once was is now *always, forever* here on the inside and possessively retained for better or for worse.

The journey of the soul dialectically moves from within itself through sense-certainty, to perception, to understanding, and toward a critical self-defining interpersonal conflict with an other self only to return to its self—vanquished and enslaved or victorious and lordly. Like Odysseus, the soul searches without only to discover that the truth dwells within.

> We may see the logical consistency of Hegel's method, which he applies from within the dynamic progression of spirit itself: unconscious spirit emerges from (a) an undifferentiated unity to (b) sensation then to (c) consciousness while conscious spirit moves from (a) undifferentiated sense-certainty to (b) differentiated perceptions to (c) understanding.
> MILLS, *UA*, 85

At this point, it is helpful to elaborate on Hegel's description of the conflicting principles and philosophies of materialism and idealism exemplified by the thought of Francis Bacon and Jacob Boehme in *Hegel's Lectures on the History of Philosophy* as they touch upon Mills' study because this is where Hegel's own discussion of Mills' unconscious abyss is most fully grounded. It is also in these passages that Hegel offers his own version of the Battle between the Giants and the Gods as it initiates a truly Modern Philosophy, which begins with the opposition between the philosophical utterances of Lord Bacon on the one hand and Jacob Boehme on the other hand, between empiricism and spiritualism. For Hegel, it is Bacon and Boehme, who first set the stage for the eventual resolution of the contradictions inherent in Cartesian dualism through his own philosophical thought.[5] According to Hegel, already in Plato we have the seed of the idealist philosophy planted, namely "that ultimate reality lies in consciousness, since all reality is Thought, which embraces in an absolute unity all reality as well as thinking" (Hegel, *LHP*, II, 1). Philosophically the principle of the unity of consciousness first clearly appears in Aristotle's *Metaphysics*, although it is already present in incipient form in Plato. All reality is potentially self-consciousness because it is the product, the work of the mind. In Plotinus and Neo-Platonism these strategies are systematically carried forward and eventually enter into the thinking of Jacob Boehme: "the nature of thought is to think itself [and thus] the universe is produced from thought" (Hegel, *LHP*, II, 419). Further, "thought is the originating activity and at the same time the object" of its own thought (Hegel, *LHP*, II, 412). Consciousness is reflexively *self*-conscious and in the same moment dynamically unfolding; it develops *dialectically* from within itself (Proclus). Within the unity of the one Reality, the Plotinian One, there is already both Spirit and Matter; light and darkness; good and evil; as well as the unconscious, the self-consciousness, and the rational. This line of thought is later incorporated in the Christian theosophical writings of Jacob Boehme. As Hegel conceives it, modern philosophy importantly begins with the dialectical conflict generated between the finite natural standpoint of inductive empiricism promoted by Francis Bacon on the one side as it is set against the challenge poised against it by "the inward, the mystical, and the godly Christian life dedicated to God and the pantheism of the Trinity" advocated by Jacob Boehme on the other side (Hegel, *LHP*, III, 194). But what is critical in this interpretation is that it is Boehme who most profoundly instantiates the conception of the "dark abyss," "the ground without a ground." Boehme's most significant contributions to philosophical thought is that he is the first to begin with the Category of Quality as *intrinsically active* thus undercutting the doctrines of materialism and external motion, the twin pillars of natural science, and the presuppositions of empiricism and phenomenalism. According to Boehme, "The quality posits itself…and signifies in general the internal unrest of quality by which it produces and preserves itself only in conflict." In the *Science of Logic*, Hegel specifically cites Boehme's contribution to the conception of Quality just before launching into the *qualitative* essence of

---

5   G.W.F. Hegel, *Lectures on the History of Philosophy*, translated by E.S. Haldane and F.H. Simson (London: Routledge & Kegan Paul, 1968), III, 161, 188–216. It is Francis Bacon and Jacob Boehme who first usher in the age of truly Modern Philosophy and set the stage for resolving the contradiction inherent in Cartesian dualism.

the "Something" of Being *qua* Consciousness. *Something qualitatively determinate exists.* That is the indubitable beginning of both Consciousness and Being.

> "Qualation" or "Inqualation"—an expression belonging to Jacob Boehme's philosophy, a philosophy which goes deep but into a murky depth—means the *movement* of a quality in itself, in so far as it posits and confirms itself in its negative nature (*quale*) as opposed to another and is its own restlessness, so that it is only by means of a struggle that it produces and maintains itself (*SL,* I, 127; italics mine). (Consciousness, thought "moves" itself. Matter is moved by the external natural force of gravity).

This distinction is critical. Materialism and empiricism *assume* matter and motion. By contrast, idealism *assumes* consciousness *qua quality,* which is intrinsically self-moving, "restless" and "struggling" and eventually dialectical. It is further to be noted that this restlessness is "spontaneous" (*SL,* I, 108). Both consciousness and Being "emanate" through restlessness and conflict. This is the animating soul of the dialectic. As in Fichte, consciousness is spontaneously self-positing but beyond Fichte's first principle Quality is not only movement, an "internal unrest" but it unfolds itself dialectically through conflict. This is the true beginning of modern philosophy, whose goal for Hegel is to overcome, to transcend Kantian subjectivism as well as his mistaken version of metaphysical dualism, which bifurcates the phenomena and the noumena.

It is also worth mentioning that for Hegel although "the rational is real and the real is rational," nevertheless he respects mystical veins of thought because they offer a common cause with idealism. Again, the definition of idealism is that all reality is mental, mind-dependent or spiritual (G.E. Moore).

Thus Hegel credits Boehme as truly the first German (or "Teutonic") philosopher, while also praising him for ushering in the New Age of modern thought. As we have already intimated, essentially Boehme's conception of God is based on Neo-Platonic and mystical forms of an all-inclusive knowledge. His "fundamental idea," according to Hegel, "is the effort to comprise everything in an absolute unity, for he desires to demonstrate the absolute union of all opposites in [the one] God" (*LHP,* III, 196). He further shows "how evil is present in the good" (Hegel, III, *LHP.* 194). This necessarily follows, since "consciousness alone is capable of unity so both elements must be already contained within it" (III, 193). Further, Boehme combines the *quality* of the unconscious with the conscious; darkness with light; the negative with the positive; and evil with goodness thus affirming the *qualitative* unity of all Being.

Again, it is critical to realize that we are here dealing solely with qualities and not empirical quantities. For Hegel, only qualities can be unified; quantitative matter is essentially divisible, abstract, and disunified. For both Plotinus and Boehme, evil and imperfection are *already* there in matter, in sensuousness, in human lust and greed and therefore in mankind. Both God and the Devil co-exist; the Good and the Evil together, side by side. Further, the Abyss is God considered as the Ungrund, the source of all subsequent grounding. Like Plotinus, it is a doctrine of emanation as opposed to creation, which was much more congenial to the dialectical thought of Hegel.

> [M]ore especially the highest moments—good and evil, or God and the Devil [exist]. God is, and the Devil likewise; both exist for themselves. But if God is absolute existence, the question may be asked, What absolute existence is this which has not all actuality, and more particularly evil within it?...Boehme's great struggle has been—since to him God is everything—to grasp the negative, evil, the devil, in and from God, to grasp God as absolute.
> 
> LHP, III, 194

This is not only Boehme's "torturous struggle" but Hegel's as well. The *Phenomenology* and *Logic* will be his pantheistic response, his theodicy.

According to Hegel, then, what he admires about Boehme is that he acknowledges that evil is already in the world and in its most profound intimations it is already manifest in man's "feeling soul" as discussed and described in the *Anthropology*. Given this sympathetic reading of Boehme, it follows for Hegel that the source of evil lies in man's *nature* and not in the Christian doctrine of the freedom of the will; it arises within the primitive "feeling soul"; the *potential* for evil is *already* there in human nature (*EP*, Section 396; Aristotle). Importantly, Hegel also emphasizes that Boehme maintains that the "body of God embraces all qualities" (*LHP*, III, 199). This agrees with Hegel's own thesis that in terms of his conceptual categories, Being is essentially determinate quality; it precedes quantitative magnitudes (*Logic*).

Eventually out of the Abyss of Darkness will shine the light of the individual soul as it gains ascendance toward absolute knowledge. Boehme's doctrine of the Trinity also anticipates the Hegelian dialectic and the inward turn toward the Protestant conception of an inner personal freedom and conscience, which serves as a powerful counterfoil to the Papal authoritarianism of Catholicism. But the salient point in Plotinus, Proclus, and Boehme remains clear, namely that the unconscious, the darkness, and the evil in man are *already* and *eternally* there from the beginning. So unlike traditional Christianity, which presents God as immutable and perfect, omnipotent, omniscient, and omnibenevolent, theistically separate from the world of man. Boehme's theosophical perspective is an all-inclusive form of pantheistic and mystical idealism and thus especially congenial to the thought of Hegel. God is not transcendent to the world as Plato portrays the Good; He is not distinct and "beyond" the sublunar sphere as Aristotle conceives the Unmoved Mover; and He does not create the universe and each individual soul *ex nihilo* in time as Christian and Cartesian dualism maintain. Rather as Spirit, He is immanent to the world. It is both Proclus' dialectic, Plotinus emanation, and Boehme's theosophic immanence that Hegel has in mind in his interpretational exegesis of Boehme's all-embracing inclusive unity. This line of thought, I believe, resonates with Hegel's own brand of pantheistic idealism. (Confer Hegel's discussion of Spinoza's "idealism" in the *Lectures on the History of Philosophy,* III, 257.)

Mills describes the *Ungrund* as "unfathomable," "inconceivable," "ineffable" (Mills, *UA,* 25). In mysticism and theosophy, we are in *direct, intuitional* contact with God and His inherent, immanent *qualities*. However like Boehme, Hegel is also paradoxically intent on showing the "knowability of the unknown." It is Boehme who, according to Hegel in the *Lectures on the History of Philosophy,* begins his discussion of Being with the category of Quality rather than as Kant had previously with the category of Quantity. Similarly, as we have shown, both Hegel's *Phenomenology of Spirit* and more importantly his *Science of Logic* also respectively start with the category of Quality and intensity as well as with the spontaneous animation of feeling before proceeding to Quantity and extensity. In Hegel's version of idealism, the *quality* of consciousness cannot be conceived in any such terms as quantitative parts may imply. This is Boehme's great insight as well.

Again, qualities by their very nature are intrinsic to both Consciousness and Being, and Boehme has captured this conception by declaring that "God's essence [which proceeds from the eternal deep of the World Soul] is thus not something far away which possesses a particular position or place, for essence is the abyss of nature and creation, is God himself" (Hegel, *LHP,* III, 212). In sum, "The fundamental idea, in Jacob Boehme, is the effort to comprise everything in an absolute unity...and the union of all opposites in God," (Hegel, III, LHP, 196). Basically, Hegel uses Boehme as a disguise for his own pantheistic convictions. In support of this interpretation, we recall that Kant got into a considerable difficulty with his treatise on *Religion within the Bounds of Reason Alone* and was forbidden to write further on the topic by Fredrick the Great.

Mills also offers an extended discussion of Fichte's conceptualization of the unconscious abyss as the province of primitive feeling-drives and feeling/thoughts as deriving from Fichte's concept of the will as absolutely unconditioned, spontaneous, and essentially identical to an uncaused cause. This conception of the will can only be grasped as an "intellectual intuition," which allows neither presuppositions nor inferences for its establishment. It is absolutely self-sufficient and free. "It is only through this act [of will], and first by means of it, by an act upon an act itself, which specific act is preceded by no other act whatever, that the self *originally* comes to exist for itself."[6]

> [Self-consciousness] is then obliged to think of this self-reversion as preceding and constituting all other acts of consciousness, or—what comes to the same—must think of it as the most primordial act of the subject... as for *him* a wholly unconditioned and thus absolute act.
> FICHTE, *SK,* 37; italics his

Once more:

> The self's own positing of itself is thus its own pure [non-empirical] activity. *The self posits itself,* and by virtue of this mere self-assertion it *exists;* and conversely, the self *exists* and *posits* its own existence by virtue of merely existing. It is at once the agent and the product of the action; the active, and what the activity brings about; action and deed are one and the same; and hence 'I am' expresses an Act, the only one possible, as will inevitably appear from the *Science of Knowledge.*
> FICHTE, *SK,* 97; italics his

For Mills, the significance of this in relation to the unconscious is that it ties in with Kant's conception of the unconscious as expressed by his transcendental unity of apperception.

According to Mills, prior to Fichte, Kant introduces an unconscious force as the common ground for the transcendental unity of apperception. By contrast, Fichte relies on an absolutely *simple, productive, creative* act of spontaneous volition again metaphorically akin both to God's creation of the world and a plurality of monadic souls. Fichte specifically mentions Leibniz, spontaneity, and freedom as "something absolutely indemonstrable" (*SK,* 82–83 and *passim*). For Fichte, it is the *will* alone that is the *free, unmediated, voluntary* act/source for the positing of its own self-consciousness. It is its own principle of self-declaration without any conceivable antecedent. It is pure spontaneity. Characterized in these terms, the will is an absolute, unrelational, intuitive *feeling/act.* And as such it is completely self-validating because it demands

---

[6] Johann Gottlieb Fichte, *Science of Knowledge* (New York: Appleton-Century Crofts, 1970), 34–35; italics his; hereafter cited as Fichte, *SK.*

nothing before or beyond itself except its own act. Fichte, like Hegel, believes that Kant's dependence on the transcendental unity of apperception, on self-conscious reflexion, exposes him to positing an illicit presupposition, an unproven assumption, and that it could not stand on its own.

I believe that this is an unfair criticism of Kant. Kant's "spontaneous act" improves on Leibniz's version because he forges an explicit connection between spontaneity and the created structures of consciousness, i.e., the categories of the faculty of the Understanding, while promising in the future to "show elsewhere that it is not really hypothetical" (*Critique,* xvii); how it creates time-consciousness and the unity of consciousness; how the faculty of thought itself is possible. Accordingly, for Kant spontaneity creates the structures of consciousness. For Fichte it *merely* creates the Ego and he offers an insufficient "deduction" for his further "creation" of the non-egos, i.e., objects and other selves.

But to return to Fichte, he claims that Kant's apperception is unable to "demonstrate," "deduce," or "justify" its own activity because this would entail a circular begging of the question. Thus the self must posit itself intuitively as an act and not as a cognitive judgment and therefore Fichte seeks to avoid all epistemological presuppositions. Again, Fichte's 'I' or Ego is a spontaneous act of the self, which escapes the charge of circularity basically by simply unsubstantially undercutting it (Mills, *UA*, 137). The self-positing is without prior conditions or causes; it is "the ground without a ground." This is presumably his presuppositionless beginning.

I think it is helpful to compare and contrast the foregoing philosophers in order to gain clarity not so much on the differences between their thought but because it illuminates the various forms the Achilles premise is able to assume. For all these thinkers, the crucial point remains that consciousness is conceived as immaterial and active—technically spontaneous—and even in Hegel as "unconsciously conscious" but active in its immediacy.

Whereas Parmenides, Leibniz, Schopenhauer, James, and Heidegger all metaphysically inquire "Why is there something rather than nothing?" Fichte provides the answer: The willing act is its own self-grounding. Thus Fichte is the first thinker, according to Mills, to make active subjectivity and self-consciousness possible without taking reflexion as its presupposition as Descartes, Leibniz, and Kant had done. But Mills also holds that "Fichte's absolute self may be compared to the unconscious functions of Kant's transcendental unity of apperception—the impersonal unifying agent of all mental activity that *directly knows but cannot be known directly*" (Mills, *UA*, 35; italics mine). Perhaps it can be "compared" but only if one involves and inserts Kant's *subconscious, creative* "productive imagination" into the discussion, which Mills does not. Otherwise Kant's version of spontaneity extends no further than the formal transcendental self while Fichte's absolute Ego "posits" the Non-Ego and the entire world and its objects as well as other egos as a realm of opposition in order to create an operational ethical field in which to morally act. But the other critical point for Mills is how does this relate to Freud's unconscious? Freud's unconscious does not seem to be in any manner "spontaneous." The Id does not seem to be in any significant sense spontaneous. Granted it is dangerous, hidden, sinister, and lustful but not creative. Again, I would venture that spontaneity and Freudian determinism are polar opposites.

In any case, these considerations are crucial for idealists because their major criticisms directed at materialism and empiricism is that both presupposes: (1) the independent existence of a material world; (2) physical objects *cause* "representations"—the "representational theory of ideas"—eventuating in some sort of inexplicable "correspondence" between the physical world of material extension and phenomenal images in "the mind," i.e., brain; and (3) the assumption that the physical universe would continue to exist in the absence of any and all sentient life. Clearly (3) is absolutely unverifiable and therefore a violation of the criterion of empirical positivism.

One last word on Mills' *Unconscious Abyss*. On page 3, Mills refers to a "distinct usage for unconsciousness" in relation to "that which was once conscious but became concealed from self-awareness as in repression." The relation between the abyss and repression suggests that the abyss can be retrieved by psychoanalysis possibly through free association, the interpretation of dreams, etc. That is not possible given Kant's allusion to *subconscious* activities as we have previously described or Schopenhauer's noumenal hidden and obscured irrational Will. The subconscious roots and activities and how they *influence—not cause*—consciousness are as unknowable as they are subterranean; they spontaneously underlie Kant's conception of time-consciousness and the unity of consciousness; Fichte's spontaneous creative act; Schopenhauer's metaphysical Will; and Hegel's internal "spontaneous generation of universal concepts" (Hegel, *PM*, Sections 456, Note and 457). This is precisely why in the last analysis human passions, thoughts, and actions are unpredictable. There is an indeterminate *qualitative* force within consciousness that uncompromisingly "grounds" the absolute freedom of the subconscious. Hence, Mills' conception of the unconscious is essentially Freudian and structured while Hegel's I would argue is not. Repression means and implies a traumatic experience; something that was consciously experienced but pushed into the unconscious but theoretically re-accessible. Even in Leibniz, the unconscious *petites perceptions* are retrievable. But it is *spontaneity* that is productive, creative and unpredictable in terms of its acts.

Freud incorporates a therapeutic agenda; Hegel does not. It is not possible to enter Hegel's dark abyss with a revealing flashlight. Similarly, my notion of the subconscious is indebted to Kant, Hegel, and Schopenhauer. The originating hidden opaque forces and dynamism of the subconscious can be indifferently described as creative, productive, and spontaneous but they are also ultimately *irretrievable and consequently so are their alleged "causes" for their expressions.* By contrast, Freud's unconscious derives in association to a clearly identifiable past, connected to painful traumatic experiences that are repressed in a desperate and often failed attempt to "defuse" them. But theoretically the original *causes* can be recovered in principle through the method of "free association" and the interpretation of dreams when they become sufficiently "uncensored." This is not conceivable on my account of the subconscious any more than it is possible to penetrate into the ultimate *acts* and *workings* of Kant's "productive imagination"; or to plunge into the depths of Schopenhauer's metaphysical Will; or to access Hegel's "ground without a ground." Basically my interpretation of the subconscious shares a fundamental similarity with that of Schopenhauer's (affective?) Will but with the critical difference that his Will is metaphysical, while mine, like Kant's, is monadic and self-initiated within each of us and therefore uniquely subjective and intimately personal. It is a monadic cavern of darkness, which forbids any luminous trespassing by the self and which will never see the light of day. When we try to gain access to it, at best all we can do is *feel*—but not know—our surroundings as we fearfully stumble deeper. This is the dominion of the subconscious.

Before proceeding to Mills' second book, let me comment on the conception of spontaneity through an example. Spontaneity implies the positive *malleability* of consciousness, while at the same time denying strict predictability. Malleability means the potentiality for human adaptation and adjustment, i.e., freedom in Raymond Tallis' sense. But it also means much more than that. Let me offer an example. I have read the *Brothers Karamazov* a dozen times. Each time I was exposed to the same stimuli of printed words on the same pages. But each time I discovered new and different *meanings, relations, and interpretations*. I have forgotten some, changed others, found new ones, and gained ascending levels of interpretation and so on. Hegel's *Phenomenology* and *Science of Logic* are similar in the sense that they are clearly intended to be malleable, nuanced, and open to insight as opposed to offering tools for future predictions. His categories reflexively and intentionally both create and discover the intricacies and the richness of Consciousness/Being and Being/Consciousness.

In his second study of the unconscious, *Underworlds,* Mills unfolds various mythologies and metaphysical theories starting with the ancient Egyptian descriptions of the soul's travel to the nether world and once again he extends his discussion into German idealism, Hegel, and continues on to Whitehead's metaphysics and contemporary existentialism.[7] His guiding purpose is to show through a history of consciousness methodology how the conception of the unconscious has been influential from the very earliest times of recorded history to the present. Hence he begins with the mythical writings of the ancient Egyptians. In his treatment of their mythology, he describes an Underground realm of sinister drives and desires as found within the textual descriptions of the earliest documented expressions of mankind's fears and terrors as recorded in *The Egyptian Book of the Dead*. In order to prepare the dead for their journey to their final destination, the Egyptian privileged class mummified the deceased, while various sorts of provisions were supplied to aid them toward their transitional path to their new world. This elaborate preparation for entombment implies for Mills that the Egyptian conception of the afterlife clearly assumed some sort of identifiable bodily and psychic continuance into the next life as well (Mills, *Underworlds,* 11).

> Few have imagined a more convoluted and horrific afterlife than the ancient Egyptians. Death marked the beginning of a treacherous journey through the underworld, where kings and mortals alike battled a series of creatures, ghosts, and dark forces for the resurrections of their souls... This battle for resurrection transpired in the Egyptian version of hell, a nightmarish netherworld envisioned before the birth of Christ and 3,700 years before Dante's *Inferno* (*Underworlds,* 1).

And:

> The *ba*-form appears at death and signifies the soul in an afterlife plain, which could be reunited with the earthly (material) body of the departed. This imagery also suggests that the soul is the substance of what lives on beyond the grave and can recognize its previous terrestrial form as a human mummification, itself a qualitative function of self-consciousness that is attributed to the transcendent powers of the soul (*Underworlds,* 4).

Hegel's *Anthropology* once again assigns the unconscious abyss to the animalistic "natural soul," to the "feeling soul." For Hegel, through a dialectical and

---

7 Jon Mills, *Underworlds: Philosophies of the Unconscious from Psychoanalysis to Metaphysics* (London and New York: Routledge, 2014), 21–22, 27; hereafter cited as Mills, *Underworlds*.

developmental process of thought, we can retrace the path from a subjective self-conscious back to the unconscious "feeling soul." Nevertheless, the salient point is, as Mills affirms, that within the individual soul, and before self-consciousness, "unconsciousness lives underground" (Mills, *Underworlds*, 21). All this is intended to demonstrate in his study that the unconscious was a viable conception from the very first ages of recorded history and that it now continues unchallenged in the epistemology of Lacan, the metaphysics of Jung, the cosmology of Whitehead, and the existentialism of Kierkegaard, Nietzsche, and Sartre, three obvious masters regarding the poignancy of loneliness as the essential human condition.

In his brief discussion of the ancient Greek contribution regarding the soul, interestingly Mills seems to make a special point of favoring Aristotle's peripatetic paradigm of the self as an "embodied soul," while curiously leaving aside any allusions to Greek mythology, which Freud emphasized so much as the universal key to human nature. Mills' thesis succinctly follows.

> Aristotle concludes that in order to act or be acted upon, soul has to possess a body as a prerequisite of its existence and that therefore any study of the soul must fall within the 'science of nature' as a composite of embodied events. This is the making of modern psychological [psychoanalytic?] science.
> MILLS, *Underworlds*, 10.

This unexpected emphasis seems to be motivated by Mills' wish to explicitly connect himself with Hegel's version of "embodied" idealism by adopting Aristotle's model, thereby enabling him to also connect it to Freudian psychoanalysis. Of course, Mills is correct; Hegel's "feeling soul" is indeed correspondingly "embodied" as is that of Aristotle. But Hegel is an idealist; Aristotle is not; at best he is a dualist. But Mills specifically cites these bodily endowments as the single most important "prerequisite of [the soul's] existence," namely mummified Egyptians and Aristotelian embodied souls. His conclusion then follows that "embodiment" is the connecting link in relating Aristotle to Hegel as well as to Freud and so this connection seems eminently important to him. I believe it is his way of linking Hegel's idealism with Freud's empiricism and phenomenalism and thereby establishing an internal conceptual and theoretical connection as well as a historical continuity for the concept of the unconscious while it "spans" from the Egyptians; briefly through the Greeks; missing the Christians; and then on into our more contemporary psychoanalysts; metaphysicians; and existentialists. But the difficulty persists. Both Kant and Hegel despite their differences are both idealists and committed to the spontaneous character of the mind whereas Freud's "dynamic" psychiatry is phenomenalist and determinist.

Next Mills vaults from his discussion of the ancient Egyptians (and Greeks) in the first chapter to Hegel in the second chapter. But what lies in between, of course, and noticeably unmentioned are the Christian Middle Ages, a period during which the soul is conceived as immaterial, spiritual, active *but unbodily.* And so there is virtually no mention of the unconscious. Lots of free willing and sinning, but nary a word about the unconscious until Fichte and Hegel. And I think this is significant. The third chapter is titled "Freud's Unconscious Ontology," which connects the unconscious to the "person." This is why I believe Mills wishes to connect Aristotle directly with Hegel, while bypassing the Middle Ages and then proceed on to Freud and contemporary psychoanalytic theory. Hence the subtitle of the book: "philosophies of the unconscious from psychoanalysis to metaphysics."

In any case, it is the Egyptian description of the terrifying journey to the afterlife and the ensuing battle to reach the Underworld safely that is the important textual subject matter of the *Egyptian Book of the Dead.* Thus dark myths and frightening legends are the original innermost expressions of mankind's earliest fears and desires. In order to understand the darker and more insistent urges of the mind that lie embedded in universal human nature itself, we must dwell on our dreams and fantasies; they serve us as the entryway into our hidden desires, anxieties, hostilities, and sexual lusts embedded in all of us since the dawn of human consciousness. There is something seductively tempting about inviting the soul into gloomy forbidding woods; into the recesses of caves and the nether regions of the earth where our primitive feelings and unlicensed thoughts indulge in the clandestine explorations of the imagination as it meanders through the uncharted fields of consciousness.

Thus in the second chapter, Mills returns once again to Hegel's conception of the dark forces attributable to the "feeling soul" reminding us of Hegel's previous descriptions in the *Unconscious Abyss* of the netherworld as a terrifying realm of horrors, obstacles, dangers, and portraying the unconscious as a "nocturnal mine or pit" underlying human intelligence. He repeats that "For Hegel, the abyss is the ultimate ground from which consciousness emerges" (Mills, *Underworlds,* 26) and goes on to explain that this "night-like pit is a necessary presupposition not only for the imagination but also for the higher forms of intelligence." In other words, the unconscious once more remains as the *necessary* foundation for all human consciousness; it not only serves as the inescapable portal into the sphere of self-consciousness itself but it also continues as our constant companion throughout the rest of our lives as well. In Hegel as we recall it is because of the dialectic that all of our phenomenological stages or moments of consciousness are carried forward as they are transcended into richer intricacies and unities.

In both the *Abyss* and *Underworlds* Mills presents the unconscious as the original ground from which all consciousness emerges or emanates as he expends considerable energy in connecting this horrific Realm of the Dead by relating it to the Freudian unconscious. Quoting Hegel, Mills repeats the explanatory Note for Section 453: "No one knows what an infinite host of images of the past slumbers within him; now and then they do indeed accidentally awaken, but one cannot, as it is said, call them to mind" (*Anthropology*). Mills stake in all this is to show how these dark dreams and fantasies are indelibly interwoven throughout the intimate fabric of our human, all-too human secret lives.

As in his previous study, Mills turns once more to the Gnostic writings of Jacob Boehme.

> The concept of the abyss (*Ungrund*), however, derives from the theosophic Christianity of Jacob Boehme who (introduced by Plotinus) radically reconceptualized God, "the being whose essence is to reveal itself." Boehme developed an elementary form of dialectic [indebted to Proclus] consisting of positive and negative polarities [e.g., good and evil] as emerging out of the Godhead's undifferentiated non-being (*das Nichts*) which unfolded through orderly stages of manifestation toward absolute self-consciousness (*Underworlds,* 26–27).

It seems clear why Mills once more returns to Boehme. It is because of his importance to Hegel (again see *Hegel's Lectures on the History of* Philosophy, III, 188–216) and one can sense again Boehme's imposing shadow looming over Hegel's discussion of the category of Quality in the *Science of Logic* (I, 127). But I am not sure why Mills seeks to connect with the *Egyptian Book of the Dead* rather than forging a stronger alliance with the Homeric and Hesiodic myths and legends, especially the Greek dramas and the tragedies that consume the House of Atreus, all of which so strongly impressed Freud. Nevertheless both Freud's and Mills' points are valid. Mythology provides a valuable insight into the darker regions of the soul. It provides a seemingly entertaining "excuse" to concentrate on the darkest feelings and thoughts of mankind. The Brother Grimms' "fairy tales" similarly take advantage of the same excuse for entertaining children. But both inform us of our true human (inhuman?) nature under the guise of sublimation.

From our current vantage point we can survey the ancient panorama of myths from the perspectives of Freud and Julian Jaynes. The Hellenic and Roman myths are much more explicit in their portraits of human nature as they are permeated by disturbing, frightening, and illicit sexual allusions drawn from the tales of the Titanic and Olympian gods and goddesses, the plays of Sophocles regarding the darker aspects of human nature, and the dynamic of tragic fates. They provide a deeply disturbing insight into the darkest recesses of human consciousness with stories of the father devouring his sons and the son castrating the father (Saturn and Kronos); Prometheus as the martyred benefactor of mankind chained to the lonely cliffs of the Caucuses where a ravenous eagle daily tears out his bowels (Jung); the son killing the father and incestuously sleeping with the mother and impregnating her (Oedipus, Laius, and Jocasta); the father sacrificing his daughter so the Greek fleet could sail to Troy (Agamemnon and Iphegenia); the vengeful murder of a wife slaying her husband (Clytemnestra and Agamemnon); the act of matricide (Clytemnestra and Orestes); the seeress Cassandra whose declared apocalyptic warnings go unheeded; the abduction of Persephone by Pluto; the distress of Demeter losing her daughter (Persephone); the dutiful sister sentenced to be entombed alive for burying her brother (Antigone and Kreon); the madness of Dionysius; Zeus' marital indiscretions; his rape of Europa and Leda; Hera's jealousy and punishment of the maidens he seduced; the loneliness of Pyrrha and Deucalion as sole survivors of the deluge; the avenging Erinyes and Furies; Orpheus' loss of Eurydice in the underworld; and so on. In Homer's *Odyssey,* Hades is described as a "Realm of Shades" where the dead appear as ghost-like apparitions bemoaning the misery of their eternal lot. Although they are immaterial specters, nevertheless they visually appear as two-dimensional beings allowing for personal individuation. When Odysseus visits the House of the Dead, he is able to converse with Achilles, who tells him what a miserable place it is. In Hesiod's *Theogony,* Uranus (the Sky) buries his sons in their mother's earthen flesh so they cannot depose him; and his son, Cronus, castrates him, while Cronus himself in turn devours his own sons for fear they will usurp him. In Plato's Myth of Er, one of the first souls to pick his future lot in life chooses precipitously only to discover that he is fated to unknowingly eat his own children as a meal, a favorite menu served to special enemies; and finally our lustful heritage of incestuous Electral and Oedipal desires. Many of these myths, of course, later play out in Freud's depictions of our deepest hidden sexual desires and anxieties that universally permeate our shared human nature. And most importantly, let us not forget the myth of Narcissus, the original source of all our human conceits, egoistic demands, and destructive entitlement issues. Collectively these desires and anxieties all powerfully testify to the darker motives and machinations of humanity. In all this Freud's insights were clearly right. Perhaps man is evolving intellectually but his basic and deepest human nature, what sort of an animal he is, remains indelibly Schopenhauerian and unchanged.

In an interesting article, R.K. Gupta identifies Schopenhauer's irrational Will with Freud's Id. But this is a difficult equation. Schopenhauer's metaphysical Will is universal and not individual. It unknowingly lies beneath consciousness whereas Freud's Id invades the surface of consciousness through sexual impulses, aggression, and anxiety. Although I suppose it could be argued that both lend themselves to sublimation as Gupta contends.[8]

My interest in Mills' two studies stems from my agreement that there are irrepressible forces emanating from the subconscious (Mijuskovic) or unconscious (Mills) mind that routinely influence our passions and deeds. The critical difference on the issue, however, is that for me their ultimate dynamics are irrecoverable, whereas for Mills the Freudian unconscious is in principle recoverable. The problem for me is that psychoanalysis, as Mills intimates, pretends to be a science and therefore it is based on an "unconscious" causal structure that claims traumatic causes determine (the old) neurotic effects. These psychodynamic events are protectively "repressed" as they are driven into the unconscious (Freud's metaphor of the unconscious as the submerged force of an iceberg). But they can be retrieved. Two momentous implications follow: (1) psychological causes and effects are *completely* determined and predictable as they course from the present back to the past and from the past to the present. And therefore it is theoretically possible to gain therapeutic and curative "insight" in alleviating dysfunctional anxieties. This is not possible if the subconscious is irretrievable. Absolute, *sui generis* spontaneities are both irretrievable and "incurable" just as human breath is incurable.

Mills, however, appears to be on the right track when he introduces a discussion in regard to Hegel's concept of the "reproductive imagination" and alludes to it (*Philosophy of Mind,* sections 455–457; *Underworlds,* 30). But Hegel's description, which significantly includes the concepts of spontaneity, creativity, *and significantly the production of intelligence* (Leibniz), needs to be read in conjunction with Kant's own discussions on the spontaneity and creativity of consciousness (again, *Critique,* A 50-B 74, A 51-B 75, A 68-B 93). We remember, it first appears in A 97 in conjunction with the threefold syntheses generating immanent time-consciousness and it is connected to *the pure, creative, synthetic imagination* (*Critique,* A 118), which serves as the gateway to Kant's equally pure categories and the unity of consciousness. It is spontaneity that triggers and produces the *structures,* which synthetically mediate between our imaged sense contents and the unification of consciousness. The imagination is both sensuous and free at once. But Kant clearly distinguishes between the

---

[8] R.K. Gupta, "Freud and Schopenhauer," in *Schopenhauer: His Achievement,* edited by Michael Fox (Sussex, England: Harvester Press, 1980), 226–235.

*pro*-ductive imagination, which is spontaneous, creative, and generative, and therefore clearly *functionally* distinguishable, from Mills' interpretation of the *re*-productive imagination (above), which is empirical, repetitive, and associative. But Hegel in these three sections is actually criticizing the *empirical* "so-called law of the association of ideas, which was contemporaneous with the decline of philosophy" (Hegel, *PM,* Sections 455–457). And as he proceeds, he goes on to induct "the spontaneity, creativity, and intelligence of consciousness," which clearly implies that he is thinking of Kant's discussion in A xvi–xvii. Then the problem becomes: Does Hegel believe—as Kant suggests—that the unconscious is irretrievable; or does he in principle think—as Freud does—that it is potentially completely recoverable? If the first, then therapy is impossible. If the second, then therapy is possible but it hardly reaches beyond the title of a mnemonic science.

In the critical passages under discussion, Mills reports that "Hegel acknowledges the activity of the unconscious abyss, as limitless and infinite, to be *inaccessible* to the conscious will" (*Underworlds,* 30; italic mine). Thus according to Mills, in Thesis 1, Hegel (seemingly) concludes that "the abyss of 'inwardness' remains unavailable to immediate self-reflection." It is *in principle* "irretrievable" (*Underworlds,* 30). But if this is Hegel's position—which I believe it is—then it directly conflicts with the causal and deterministic schematism of Freudian psychoanalytic theory. Differently put, if the *deepest* levels of the Hegelian *subconscious*—versus Freud's unconscious—remain inviolable in the manner of Kant's allusions to an impermeable "subjective deduction" or to Schopenhauer's irrational Will, psychoanalytic treatments must inevitably fail. *But* if in opposition, Mills' alternate Thesis 2 allows for a reconstruction of the empirical "re-productive associative imagination," which is merely based on contingent, empirical connections is correct, then it follows that Freudian psychology can be saved. Only if Hegel's "dark abyss," his "black pit" is recoverable can it function as an appropriate resource and connecting link for successful psychoanalytic therapy. But if it is knowable, then it cannot be "unavailable to self-reflection" (Mills' Thesis 1) and therefore implemented in therapy. So for Mills, the critical question becomes: are the Hegelian *acts* and *contents* of the unconscious abyss *irretrievable* as Hegel proposes (Thesis 1); or are they *retrievable* in principle (Thesis 2)? If the former, Thesis 1, then this obviously raises serious implications not only for Freud's "therapeutic insights" but also for *any* possibility of psychologically implementing (a) predictive and/or (b) curative principles and methods as well.

Accordingly, the problem is that Mills wishes to compare the Kantian-Fichtean-Hegelian-Schopenhauerian subconscious to Freud's unconscious. My resistance to this line of thought is that Freud's theory of the unconscious is basically committed to science via psychological determinism for only then could it be applied in promoting therapeutic interventions. In Freud, the dynamic activity of the unconscious is psychologically determined by prior traumatic experiences, which *cause* distressful feelings and thoughts to be *repressed,* i.e., temporarily "put out of mind," and protectively driven into the unconscious. As repressed *memories,* they continue to emotionally *affect* the subject through unresolved—but in principle resolvable—anxieties. Through the therapeutic strategy of free association, gentle and supportive prodding, these underlying traumas can be mnemonically retrieved and thus (presumably) aligned into causal structures and when penetrated further resolved into liberating "rational insights." Freud's assumption is that the mind never forgets a psychic *injury.* But all that is dramatically undercut if the subterranean powers, the subconscious forces of the mind are absolutely unreachable.

But in terms of interpreting Hegel's "pathology of the mind," Mills himself also seems to concur that "There is an aggressivity to madness and the disordered mind" that is inherent to such states as melancholia, i.e., loneliness (Mills, *UA,* 159). In madness and schizophrenia "consciousness is withdrawn inwardly into a state of solipsism, what Hegel refers to as a 'monad' degraded to a state of feeling alone" (*PM,* Section 406; Mills, *UA,* 166, 172). It is precisely this state of loneliness, of feeling abandoned, betrayed, and rejected by "significant selves" in particular or the world in general that impels the mind to retreat to its darkest corners and take refuge in acts of rebellious anger and destruction.

Finally, according to Berthold-Bond, Hegel views madness as a disruption within the soul itself, an internal alienation, during which the mind is separated from the shared world of others, the world of intimacy. This characterization is clearly manifest in the section in the *Phenomenology* entitled "The Unhappy Consciousness" but it is also more thoroughly discussed in the *Philosophy of Mind,* Section 408, Note. In Berthold-Bond's study and his treatment of Hegel's conception of melancholy—his word for loneliness—loneliness assumes a form of "madness proper as the individual is imprisoned in a 'fixed idea' of the loathsomeness of life" and "constantly broods over its unhappy idea to the exclusion of all else" (ibid.). In particular, the movement of withdrawal from social contacts and society in general is a direct response to the pain and distress of loneliness following the self's unsuccessful and painful encounters with other selves thus causing it to further retreat within itself (*PM,* 40). Imprisoned within its self, the soul is trapped in a dream state: Madness becomes a *"dreaming while awake"* (ibid., 27; Section 408, Note). In this condition, the individual acts out his fantasies of destruction against the self and others.

> Like Freud's "primary narcissism," the soul for Hegel does not distinguish between inner and outer at all; the soul is a "differenceless unity" prior to any opposition between interior and external realities (*Philosophy of Mind,* Section 398 note)...Hegel's theory of madness thus relates mental illness within the soul, and relies heavily on a psychology of the unconscious. Anticipating Freud, Hegel sees madness as a regressive turn backward into archaic states of the mind, a "reversion" or "sinking back" of the developed, rational consciousness into the more primitive world of instincts and drives, or what Hegel calls "the life of feeling." In insanity, the "reversion" to mere nature displaces the normal principles of rational consciousness—what Freud calls "the laws of the ego" and "the reality principle"—and liberates the feelings, passions, and instincts of the soul: "the earthly elements are set free" and "the natural self...gains mastery over the objective, rational...consciousness" (*PM,* 408, Note). The most general characteristic of madness is this motion of withdrawal into the soul, or the unconscious life of feeling, and the corresponding displacement of the usual relationship with reality. The "sinking of the soul into its inwardness ... of consciousness from its connection with the outside world," so that the soul "contemplates its individual world not *outside,* but *within* itself" (*PM,* 406, note). Or, as Freud says, "material reality" is replaced by "psychical reality." In this state of "communing merely with its interior states the opposition between itself"—the soul—"and that which is for it"—the world or reality—"remains shut up within in it" (*PM* 402, note). Reality thus becomes a projected image of the "earthly elements" or passions and drives of the soul, "a shadow cast by the mind's own light—a show or illusion which the mind imposes as a barrier" (*PM,* Section 386) between itself and the external world from which it has withdrawn in an attempt to escape some experience of pain and alienation [i.e., loneliness].[9]

Freud early on both believed that (a) our personalities are already set by age 5 and (b) we are universally neurotic in varying degrees. I would rather suggest that in varying degrees each of us carries a kernel of psychosis, hallucinatory, and delusional symptoms beneath our surface consciousnesses (Schopenhauer), which makes us all vulnerable to the duress of extreme loneliness.

In psychology, the concept of an obsessional or "fixed idea" is constituted as an overpowering feeling that is empowered to last indefinitely through time. In

---

9 Daniel Berthold-Bond, *Hegel's Theory of Madness* (Albany, New York: State of New York Press, 1995), 26.

older times, the term "monomania" was frequently used. Its qualitative essence and power can be immediately, directly, or intuitively present to consciousness for extended periods of time and that is why it can be discharged "at a moments notice" as an "uncaused," spontaneous, motiveless act at *any* unspecified future moment. Such affective feeling states have a timeless quality; they do not change but rather impatiently wait for an occasion to explode. In such cases, the individual is unaware of what they are going to do next or even why they are doing it. They frequently declare some fictitious "motive" that is basically intended to hurt others as if others were at fault for their misery. Recently the many atrocities of suicidal individuals, who suddenly claim "political radicalization" are in reality the acts of disenfranchised, alienated, estranged individuals. Their anger has reached such a boiling point that they narcissistically rationalize a "moral" justification for their acts when in reality the impending force, the Schopenhauerian Will—not cause—is loneliness, their dissatisfaction with their lives, and their resentment real or feigned regarding how others have treated them. The horrors perpetrated by ISIS members, the acts of crucifying priests, beheading prisoners, and burning families alive in iron cages manifestly testifies to the underlying loneliness and retaliatory inhumanity of these deranged tormentors.

Finally, Kant confesses in the *Preface* to the first edition of the *Critique* how much difficulty it cost him, indeed "the greatest labor" for him to think through the first Deduction of the Categories presumably *because it involved two separate issues:* (1) subjectively "how…the faculty of thought itself [is] possible?" and this difficulty is because "it seeks to investigate the pure understanding itself, its possibility, and the cognitive faculties upon which it rests; and so deals with it in its subjective aspect." This speculative task, Kant informs us, "is, as it were, the search for the cause of a given effect, and to that extent is somewhat hypothetical in character…and I would appear to be taking the liberty simply of expressing an *opinion,* in which case the reader would be free to express a different opinion" (A xvi–xvii). Why, then, is it so problematic? And the answer we now know is because the underlying activities of the *subjective* subconscious must first exist and be put into play *before* self-consciousness can appear and be acknowledged. For Kant, these *subjective* acts of spontaneity are ultimately and intrinsically unknowable and he suggests that

> only the *productive* synthesis of the imagination can take place *a priori:* the reproductive rests on empirical conditions. Thus the principle of the necessary unity of pure (productive) [i.e., creative] synthesis of the imagination, prior to apperception, is the ground for the possibility of all knowledge, especially experience (A 118).

His promise to provide a subjective Deduction for the "productive imagination" is never fulfilled. My guess is that Schopenhauer picked up on this theme and ran with it. Kemp Smith, as we saw, declares his puzzlement why Kant was unwilling to dig deeper into the "psychological"—as opposed to the transcendental—activities of the subconscious (*Commentary,* 261–262). Although he stresses that Kant nevertheless incorporated it into his argumentation throughout the entire *Critique* and I agree. But reciprocally (2), Kant turned more securely to delineating, providing, and describing the transcendental, logical, and objective synthetic *a priori* conditions required for our ordinary and scientific human experiences.

The role and activity of the productive imagination *precedes* the *structures* of the Understanding in Kant. There are more than ample "clues" throughout the *Critique* clearly indicating that he is convinced there are underlying *subconscious*—as opposed to unconscious—forces and activities that are due to the *spontaneous* acts of the creative imagination as consciousness struggles both to *further* synthesize, mediate, bind, and *unify* as well as to coherently *order* consciousness according to *rules required for empirical knowledge, for both our ordinary and scientific experiences.* The volcanic forces of the subconscious, however and in contradistinction, boil from below, while only the surface layers of phenomenal lava reach an exposure to the world above. Thus Kant concludes that the productive imagination "is an art concealed in the depths of the human soul, whose real modes of activity nature is hardly likely ever to allow us to discover and have open to our gaze" (A 141=B 180). These *subjective* speculative thoughts must have produced a strong effect on Fichte, Hegel, and Schopenhauer as they sought to translate them for their own purposes, to transform how subconscious processes are able to spontaneously *create* Being and Consciousness; the Ego and the non-Ego; and the irrational Will.

But again (2) the second goal for the Deduction was *objectively* to "determine the rules and limits of [the understanding's] employments" (A xvi). This second purpose he finds himself satisfied in succeeding, by achieving, by instituting the categories within his Transcendental Logic as the synthetic *a priori* conditions for both science and human experience. *But my focus in the present text has been on the first issue: How is consciousness itself possible?*

We are strangers to our selves because there are unchartable currents coursing through our souls. Their suspected presence is only indirectly signaled by intermittent acts of *purely* theoretical creations, artistic expressions, ethical principles as well as tragic and violent interruptions on the surface waters of human existence, while below there remains a seething and turbulent current of fear and anger. How else account for man's malicious and gratuitous acts of inhumanity toward others along with his myriad forms and expressions of violence and destruction?

Materialists, mechanists, empiricists, behaviorists, neuroscientists, and neo-phrenologists, by reducing the brain to separate, disunified cells, of course, have no way of accommodating the unconscious let alone the subconscious or the foundational reality of a genuine personal identity. There are no subconscious or unconscious neurons; they won't show up on an electroencephalograph. As we have seen previously, in the eighteenth-century, anatomists knew that within seven years the entire body replenishes all its cells. If so, then it is impossible for memory cells to be retained past seven years? For how could a past and former memory cell be physically transmitted to a "newborn" memory cell? These problems are the destructive shoals of neurophysiology and neo-phrenology.

The conceited overblown claims of psychoanalysis and the neurosciences to predict, to control, and to cure loneliness simply dismiss the human factor: immediate feelings, emotions, and mediate causes that are essentially antithetical. The advertised mandates of these alleged sciences seek to place events and behaviors in the familiar causal matrix of psychological and physical determinism. But this is to dismiss the reality of human freedom and spontaneity.

The reality of the subconscious mind is the only possible answer to the events that transpired in Europe from 1933 to 1945, which obviously includes the advent of Nazism and the Second World War with all its atrocities and its concentration camps: Buchenwald, Auschwitz, Treblinka, Dachau, Jasenovac, the Nazi and the Fascist occupations of conquered countries. Today those same forces and horrors are carried forward individually and militarily, sporadically and systematically throughout the Middle East as well as globally by suicide bombers, terrorists, as well as armed forces worldwide.

*Why* is it that individuals, groups, and nations have systematically practiced wanton destruction, racial prejudice, cruelties, atrocities, and even genocides? *How* is it that men have been motivated to erect their terrifying monuments dedicated to pain and torture, the network of concentration camps, testimonial monuments that still stand empty today as reminders for what humans are *truly* capable of?

Beyond that, for three decades, in my capacity as a social worker and licensed therapist I witnessed some of the direst examples of the loneliness of the human soul in various settings, including the Department of Public Aid, the War on Poverty, numerous Mental Health Clinics, locked acute facilities, long term mental health hospitals, "institutions for mental disease," and a state institution. Throughout all these experiences, I was exposed daily to the multi-faceted images of human loneliness, drug addiction, depression, bipolar disorders, and psychosis. As far consciousness, philosophy, and psychology are concerned, it is my firm conviction that loneliness is our universal and common human fate and that it is more stressful than the fear of death.

The terrain of the subconscious mind is a province that can generate profound and elaborate intellectual systems; empathic ethical principles; and expressive artistic beauty but it can also result in the manifestations of terror, anxiety, and anger, while the injured shadowy self wanders alone aimlessly until it eventually erupts into acts of uncontrollable sadness, misery, rage, aggression, violence, malice, and thoughts of self-harm; when it reflexively turns the pain toward its self. The thesis I am defending is that when human beings suffer intense or prolonged periods of loneliness, disenfranchisement, alienation, estrangement, betrayal, or call it what you will, their generally controllable feelings of narcissism, entitlement, and egoism become so insurmountably frustrating that it provokes fantasies of murderous cruelty toward others or thoughts of suicide. Every depression is fused with anger at others or the self and as such it is highly vulnerable to the discharge of primitive instincts, including regressive reversions to our reptilian heritage as announced by Dr. Whybrow in a previous chapter. These irrational dark forces lie deeply embedded in the first tiers of the subconscious mind; in hallucinatory feeling-states, raw impulses, and seething tendencies that defy any and all "human" explanations or justifications. There are many shades of anger in the human soul from prejudice to bullying to spite to revenge and every shade in between but the brush that paints them all with the same hue is loneliness and human neglect.

CHAPTER 9

# Loneliness: In Harm's Way

> We are lonely from the cradle to the grave—and perhaps beyond.
> JOSEPH CONRAD, *An Outcaste of the Islands*

∴

> Naked and alone we came into exile. In her dark womb we did not know our mother's face; from the prison of her flesh have we come into that unspeakable and incommunicable prison of the earth. Which of us has known his brother? Which of us has looked into his father's heart? Which of us has not remained prison-pent? Which of us is not forever a stranger and alone?
> THOMAS WOLFE, *Look Homeward, Angel*

∴

After the biological drives for air, water, nourishment, sleep—and *before* sex—are met, the most insistent psychological need and motivational drive in human beings is to escape loneliness and secure an intimate relationship to and with another self-conscious creature beyond one's self, whether animal, human, or divine. The twin principles I propose to defend are that all we feel, think, say, and do occur between the dual emotional and cognitive poles in human consciousness, between the solipsistic insularity of loneliness and the intentional desire to transcend it by attaining intimate attachments with a *mutually* responding self-conscious being beyond our selves. In effect, I wish to replace Freud's primary principle of libidinal energy with the anxiety of isolation and the drive for intimacy. From the beginning of life and consciousness, I view the solitary self as emotionally seeking a *mutual* affective and cognitive unification, an attachment with and to another reflexive being through intimacy. Loneliness is first fueled by a desire, a motivation to be intimately related to another sentient creature psychologically, cognitively, and usually socially. When this fails, the consequences can be disastrous.[1]

---

[1] Ben Mijuskovic, "Loneliness: An Interdisciplinary Approach," *Psychiatry: A Journal for Interpersonal Processes*, 40:2 (1977), 213–232; reprinted in *The Anatomy of Loneliness*, edited by

But first I want to consider two compelling reasons in support of my dually pronged first principle concerning the universal fear of loneliness and its consequent desire to avoid it by securing intimacy. The first reason I will treat rather briefly but the second will consume some length. The first deals with the end of life and the second with its beginning.

The centrality of loneliness in human existence is grounded in the simple psychological fact that no human being would ever wish to be immortal at the expense of being the only self-conscious creature in a lifeless universe, condemned to exist eternally alone in the infinite expanses of space and time. Kant, quoting at length from an article in the *Bremen Magazine* (Kant seldom quotes at all let alone from a magazine), recounts the story of a miserly merchant, who cared for no one but himself and as he was nearing the termination of his life due to his advanced age, he wished to come to an account concerning his prospects for gaining admission to heaven. That night, in a dream, he was visited by the Angel of Death, who informed him that because of his lifelong disdain for his fellow man, he was doomed to be transported to the farthest and darkest corners of the universe there to dwell throughout all eternity alone without any intercourse human or divine or even an acknowledgment of his existence by another conscious being.

---

Joseph Hartog, Ralph Audi, and Yehudi Cohen (New York: International Universities Press, 1980), 65–94; "Loneliness and a Theory of Consciousness," *Review of Existential Psychiatry and Psychology*, XVI:1 (1977), 19–31; reprinted in *Counseling and Therapy*, edited by E. Cohen and S.W. Zinaich (Cambridge Scholars Press, 2013); "Loneliness and the Reflexivity of Consciousness," *Psychocultural Review*, 1:2 (1977), 202–215; "Loneliness and Personal Identity," *Psychology: A Journal of Human Behavior*,16:3 (1979), 11–20; "Loneliness and Suicide," *Journal of Social Philosophy*, XI:1 (1980), 11–18; reprinted in *Geriatrics and Thanatology*, edited by Elizabeth Pritchard (Praeger, 1984); "Loneliness and Human Nature," *Psychological Perspectives: A Review of Jungian Thought*, 12:1 (1981), 69–78; "Loneliness and Adolescence," *Adolescence*, XXI:84 (1986), 941–951; "Loneliness , Anxiety, Hostility, and Communication," *Child Study Journal*, 16:3 (1986), 227–240; "Loneliness and Sexual Dysfunctions," *Psychology: A Journal of Human Behavior*,24:4 (1987), 15–22; "Reflexivity and Intentionality: The Self-Contained Patient," *The Psychotherapy Patient*, 4:3/4 (1988), 39–50; "Loneliness and Adolescent Alcoholism," *Adolescence*, XXIII:92 (1988), 503–516; "Child Abuse, Neglect, and Dependent Personalities," *Psychology: A Journal of Human Behavior*, 25:3 (1990); "Loneliness and Intimacy," *Journal of Couples Therapy*, 1:3/4 (1991), 39–48; reprinted in *Intimate Autonomy: Autonomous Intimacy*, edited by Barbara Jo Brothers (Praeger, 1991); "The Phenomenology and Dynamics of Loneliness," *Psychology: A Journal of Human Behavior*, 33:2 (1996), 41–51; *Loneliness in Philosophy, Psychology, and Literature* (Bloomington, IN: iUniverse, 2012, 3rd edition; originally published in 1979 by Van Gorcum); *Feeling Lonesome: The Philosophy and Psychology of Loneliness* (Santa Barbara, CA, Praeger, 2015); and "Cognitive and Motivational Roots of Loneliness," in *Addressing Loneliness: Coping, Prevention, and Clinical Interventions*, edited by Ami Sha'ked and Ami Rokach (New York: Routledge, 2015), 20–34.

> Carazan, you have closed your heart to the love of humankind and held on to your treasures with an iron hand. You have only lived for yourself. And hence in the future you shall also live alone and excluded from all communion with the entirety of creation for all eternity.[2]

Such a fate would be tantamount to being buried alive, except in this case Carazan's tomb would be the most inaccessible region of the universe, one absolutely devoid of any possibility of either human or divine contact. I recall a client at our clinic suffering intensely from anxiety, whose wife would have to bring him in because he couldn't drive and during the entire session he would huddle in a corner on the floor of my office. Suffering from extreme anxiety and panic attacks, he would tell me that he felt he was buried alive and the fear was so severe that he felt he couldn't breathe. But it wasn't the lack of oxygen that terrified him but rather the thought that no one could reach him, that he would never escape his entombment. The source of his suffocating fear was a feeling of endless and utter abandonment without hope or consolation.

The second argument regarding the primacy of loneliness, which will be treated rather extensively, involves the many writings on early childhood disorders by Margaret Ribble, Donald Winnicott, John Bowlby, Rene Spitz, Anna Freud, Dorothy Burlingham, Margaret Mahler, and Harry Harlow's experiments with young Rhesus monkeys, researchers who collectively demonstrate that without sufficient emotional nurturance from the mother, or a caring surrogate, infants regress toward the womb and even death. Over half of the deaths of institutionalized children under the age of one in England during the First World War died. The original "diagnoses" for the disorder were indiscriminately called *marasmus, hospitalism, anaclitic depression* (Rene Spitz), etc. Today it is more aptly described as "failure to thrive" or possibly a more adequate description would be the loss of the *desire* to thrive or even to live. Clinically, it is often currently diagnosed as Reactive Attachment Disorder of Infancy and Early Childhood (*DSM-IV*, 313.89).

I remember initially reading about it in a general psychology textbook during my first year in college. Psychologists dramatically became aware of the disorder in England during the First World War when mothers were asked to voluntarily institutionalize their very young children in hospitals so they could be free to aid in the war effort by working in factories making armaments and so on. The infants were physically tended to but left emotionally neglected although their basic biological needs were adequately met. The alarming result

---

2   Immanuel Kant, *Observations on the Feeling of the Beautiful and Sublime and Other Writings* (Cambridge: Cambridge University Press, 2011), "Carazan's Dream," 16–17.

was that half the infants under the age of one year died. The textbook showed remarkable contrasts between early onset and recovery in "before and after" photographs first taken during the early stages of the child's hospitalization and separation from the mother and then after the reunion with her. The visual impact struck me quite forcibly.[3] The caption under one of several photographs gives the following warning.

> Losing the mother during the first year of life without adequate substitution severely limits the child's emotional and neuromuscular development. Even if a later attempt is made to correct the loss, lasting damage can only be avoided if the emotional deprivation is held within narrow time limits.
> PL, Ruch, 135

In these cases it would be important to learn precisely which children died—whether it was the ones who were nurtured for an extended period of time before hospitalization; or those who were removed from maternal care immediately after birth. This could provide critical information about the severity of the emotional damage relative to the varying lengths of institutionalization and separation from the mother thus allowing for some anticipation—not prediction—of later problems for the surviving children.

Several still photos of a documentary film of the time, *Grief: A Peril in Infancy,* are included in the book, which also provides the appended text.

> At first these infants become weepy, showing a conflict between disappointment at the approach of a stranger and the craving for human contact. Later they become withdrawn and reject any approach. Toward the end of the third month the facial expression becomes rigid; screaming subsides, weeping also; and the child often presents eating and sleep disturbances, lies mostly prone in its cot...The periods of separation varied from five to twelve months and the children showed progressive degrees of physical and mental deterioration.
> RUCH, PL, 136

---

3 *Psychology and Life,* edited by Floyd R. Ruch (Chicago: Scott, Foresman, 1953), 134–136; hereafter cited as *Ruch*. Cf. Ben Mijuskovic, "Loneliness and Intimacy," *Journal of Couples Therapy,* I:3/4 (1991), 39–49; reprinted in *Intimate Autonomy: Autonomous Intimacy,* edited by Barbara Jo Brothers (Haworth Press, 1991), 39–49. For two excellent studies on the biological risks to the heart from prolonged loneliness, consult James Lynch, *The Broken Heart: The Medical Consequences of Loneliness* (New York: Basic Books, 1977) and *A Cry Unheard: New Insights into the Medical Consequences of Loneliness* (Baltimore: Bancroft Books, 2000), which latter focuses on children and adolescents.

If we analyze the dynamics of infant consciousness at these early stages of childhood, we note a number of things that we discussed in previous chapters. Kant and Freud both maintain, although on different grounds, Kant on transcendental and Freud on empirical principles, that *self*-consciousness requires *both* a distinction *and* a connective relation between the (concept of the) self and (the concept of) an object. Kant designates this as a synthetic *a priori* relation (Kant, *Critique,* A 107–110). More precisely, self-consciousness requires triadic interplay between the conceptions of (a) the self; (b) objects; plus (c) a cognitive relation between the two.

Freud, however, in *The Ego and the Id* as well as in *Civilization and Its Discontents,* provides a further four-fold elaboration as he moves from (a) the anxiety state of birth when the fetus is evicted from the womb; (b) the resultant "oceanic feeling" of conscious indeterminacy; (c) the reality of the *separation* of its *self* from an independent realm of objects, while centering on the mother's breast as an inanimate *object* of *desire* requiring some exertion on its part to achieve fulfillment; and (d) the recognition of the mother's ego as set against its own. Certain objects are desired and others are not. So we have two epistemic poles: subject and object and the cathetic relation of desiderative cognition between them. Andrew Brook argues, for example, that Kant and Freud agree in these cases that the relation is an actively synthetic one.[4] Further, what is important for both Kant and Freud is that self-consciousness initially depends upon a cognitively constituted (Kant) or empirically cathected (Freud) connection between the self and objects. By contrast, Hegel's paradigm of self-consciousness is grounded in a *mutual* dialectical relation between two equal self-conscious beings in a conflictful relationship. This dynamic relation is the seed for both loneliness and intimacy. The first obvious instantiation of conflict is between mother and child. Generally speaking, Hegel's dialectic is triadic; the prior moments are "superseded," transcended, carried over, synthesized into a third unifying category. But this is not the case in the prevailing Lordship and Bondage stage; it is a qualitative dyadic connection expressed in a struggle for ego supremacy and dominance. First narcissistic assertion before reconciliation.

In order to appreciate the difference between Kant and Freud's positions on self-consciousness and both vis-à-vis Hegel's, which we will treat next, it may be helpful to interject the virtual case of a "feral child" discovered in Florida in 2005. It highlights the psychological reality that the initial "sense" of selfhood *first* occurs as a result of an acknowledged *separation* between the self

---

4  Andrew Brook, "Freud and Kant," in *Psychoanalytic Knowledge,* edited by M. Cheung and Colin Feltman (Palgrave, 2002), 20–39.

against a background of distinct, i.e., separate objects rather than the Hegelian relation of the self to an other self, i.e., in the context of the infant-mother relation. It should also be noted, that psychologically as the infant's desires begin to concentrate on the recalcitrant nature of physical objects, it sets up a relation of *separation/opposition* anxiety and anger between the self and an inhospitable world of things. A fearful sense of deprivation is the constant companion to desire. The child's sense of desired appropriation and possession of objects—a sense of "mineness"— and its narcissistic first efforts to control desired objects and situations is unceasingly sought for against an unfeeling world of unresponsive things and thus initially within the context of a physical struggle between and against inanimate objects, their possession and their control. Later these "conflicts of desire" arise between the mother, siblings, and other children ("the terrible two"s).

Second, in order to highlight the difference between Kant and Freud's theories of the origin of the self and Hegel's, I will turn to a newspaper story reporting an incident that appears for all intents and purposes as an encounter with a feral child. It starts with a neighbor passing by a house one day and seeing the emaciated face of a young girl staring blankly out of a window through panes of broken glass; a child with hollow, vacant eyes gazing well past the observing woman; a child either unwilling or unable to make any eye contact with the observer. It was the sort of longing faraway look that one often sees in animals at the zoo, both a stare of disengagement, of emotional disconnection and yet also a yearning gaze for something beyond its self; a search for something undefined. The neighbor had never seen the child before, and so the concerned woman reported the incident to Child Protective Services and two police officers investigated. They found a six-year-old girl, Danielle or Dani, living with her mother and two much older male siblings. She was extremely thin, weighing only forty-six pounds, seriously undernourished, covered with sores, wearing filthy diapers, and couldn't speak. Fecal matter was dispersed throughout her tiny bedroom. She appeared to have been confined to a single unfurnished room and slept on the floor and had apparently spent her entire existence within that impoverished environment. Her inexpressive eyes looked beyond people.

The incident was reported to Child Protective Services and she was removed by police officers from her mother's custody, transported to a hospital, treated, and then transferred to a "temporary" shelter. She continued to decline to engage in eye contact, never cried, and was unable to chew solid food. Brain scans showed no abnormalities. There were no clinical indications of autism or other familiar childhood mental or developmental disorders. She did not appear to be depressed in any normal sense of the word and exhibited a consistently "flat affect." She was not interested in human contact or in interacting with people. Eventually she was placed for adoption and finally two years later adopted by an unusually devoted couple, who were warned that it could be a disastrous placement. A decade later, in 2015, she still could not talk; she persisted in having severe problems in relating to people; and she only tentatively responded to her adoptive male parent, which seemed significant in light of her mother's neglect. The refrigerator in the home had to be locked for otherwise she would voraciously eat everything in it. She remained seriously and emotionally impaired and unable to engage in any social activity but frequently experienced severe fits of uncontrollable anger, and quite significantly preferred to relate to objects instead of people (Kant's subject-object relation).[5] This last remark is important because it indicates that developmentally the subject-object relation fully qualifies in providing the necessary and sufficient conditions for *cognitive* reflexive self-consciousness, e.g., she could recognize the distinction between her self and food-objects but she remained uninterested in human contact. It is pure speculation to conclude she was "lonely" because she could not self-report and she showed no signs of human "clinginess." Nevertheless, Dani's unfortunate developmental difficulties, her stunted and unresponsive affect toward people, and her truncated behavioral responses all seemed to point to an unfulfilled emotional *need or desire* for human contact. Her inability to speak, of course, directly interfered with her capacity to communicate, to ask for things, or express her feelings, and therefore she expressed no reason to reach out. Any hope of reaching other selves had long ago been extinguished and severed. In phenomenological terms, she was unable to "intentionally" transcend her loneliness. She was reflexively self-enclosed and self-insulated. Without the use of speech she was incapable of asking to be with others. It was only a speculation to "label" her lonely, since she could not self-disclose her own feelings verbally, Nevertheless one naturally presumes that after birth she had normal needs and desires but that they were extinguished by the unresponsiveness of the mother.

Her sad situation and restrictive behaviors allow us to reach an important insight regarding the consequences of social withdrawal. Dani's obsession with certain objects, primarily food, to the exclusion of seeking more satisfactory and lasting human relationships resulted in grossly limited cognitive states. Her innate desire for human warmth had been long ago extinguished through her many disappointments. At her attained arrested stage of development, her sense of control was literally and primitively "incorporative"; she

---

5 Lane DeGregory, "The Girl in the Window," *Tampa Bay Times*, August 3, 2008, http://www.tampabay.com/project/the-girl-in-the-window/danielle.

internalized the *desired* significant objects bodily; she ate and consumed them. Once consumed, they could not be taken away from her. Whereas a normal child might become emotionally dependent on her teddy bear or doll, while investing it with an aspect of personalized significance, this consolation was not possible for Dani. Dani's adaptive struggles and psychic adjustments were all essentially *intra-psychic*. Unlike a normal child, she was unable *intentionally* "to reach out beyond" herself. She was completely object-dependent but the objects became physically internalized, appropriated. The "other" belonged to her only in so far and to the extent that she could consume it. If we contrast the dynamics of apperception and intentionality, she had confined herself within a cocoon of self-consciousness.

Incidentally, this may also provide us with a clue in regard to elderly hoarders, who anxiously fear being separated from their valued objects. They are unable to discard things. Their relation is to objects as opposed to persons. The existential *meaning* of their individual human existence is defined in terms of their possessed objects with which they have surrounded themselves and with their related memories, i.e., feelings and meanings that those objects—mementos—entail for them. Their identity, their existence is vicariously sought through the memories the possessed objects have for them. Their personal identity becomes transferred and communicated through emotionally charged *objects*. But, again, my main point is that self-consciousness is first achieved through and within the subject-object distinction. Subsequently and ideally we seek for a reciprocating other-self to mutually engage us in acknowledging the relationship. Failing that, anger and sadness result.

To the best of my knowledge, the earliest study to treat loneliness as a subject matter in its own right appears in a magazine article authored by Gregory Zilbborg, a psychoanalyst. In the essay, Zilboorg argues that when the child is first born, it is lavished with admiration, devoted care, and nurturance; its every need is quickly fulfilled; it is coddled, adored, cooed, and essentially spoiled. It is made to feel that it has absolute value. And during that early stage, it is not required to respond or to reciprocate in kind. It consumes care and affection without being forced to reciprocate. Consequently the ego develops a strong narcissistic sense of overweening entitlement issues. But when inevitably the indulgences and the attentiveness become more curtailed, when maternal restrictions become instituted, and behavioral limits imposed, the infant develops an increasing *sense of separation anxiety* fueling a mixture of feelings of anger, resentment, lost advantages, and the collective frustration accompanied by fears of separation, loneliness, abandonment, and betrayal issues. Originally and basically, the twin emotions of anger and anxiety are the result of the infant's sense of *separation* from the mother. On this account, Freud was clearly correct.

If these negative *relational* discordances between mother and child fail to be adequately addressed, or they are insufficiently redirected, the child's hostility and frustration become directed at the mother and/or the self, which leads either to blaming others for not being adequately loved or blaming the self for being insufficiently loveable. Sibling rivalries don't help. In children and adults and under difficult circumstances and unresolved issues, according to Zilboorg, *because of the dynamics of loneliness,* aggressive reactions can become so severe that they can lead to feelings and thoughts of murder/and or suicide. In effect, Zilboorg proposes an intrinsic synthetic *a priori* relation between a triad of psychodynamic concepts: narcissism, loneliness, and hostility. The narcissistic self represents the core, the subjective ego. Thus the experience of an enforced sense of separation from states of desired intimacy engender feelings of frustration and a corresponding sense of loss. There can be no loneliness without anger; it's not possible and therapists should take note of this important implication. In Zilboorg's article, extreme cases of narcissistic and pathological loneliness directly lead to powerful feelings of megalomania, delusions of grandeur, irrational entitlement issues, and destructive impulses. Imagine for instance a world leader whose narcissism demands unconditional adulation; who sees the public as a mirror to his greatness; whose desires require constant capitulation to his whims and instant gratifications, someone who psychopathically insists on absolute loyalty from others but cannot return the virtue and bristles at the slightest questioning of his wishes. This is the portrait of undiluted narcissism.

For Zilboorg, when feelings of loneliness are intensified or unduly prolonged, they not infrequently lead to feelings of jealousy leading to murder and suicide. One may recall the cases of the Columbine High School massacre killings on April 20, 1999 as a result of two teenagers responding to bullying by their peers; Adam Lanza and the killings of young pupils at the Sandy Hook Elementary School on December 14, 2012; Andreas Lubitz, the Lufthansa pilot who, on March 24, 2015, found it necessary to kill 149 perfect strangers by crashing his plane into the Swiss Alps after telling his estranged girlfriend that someday he would do something the world would always remember; and Omar Mateen, a "disgruntled loner," who on June 12, 2016 systematically murdered four dozen human beings during a standoff with police. The most instructive of all these tragedies is the case of Elliot Rodger, a student at a community college in Santa Barbara, California, who on May 23, 2014, murdered five students because coeds would not date him. His anger at being ignored by young women and remaining a virgin at the age of 20 convinced him he had to destroy as many female students as possible and so he formulated a plan to penetrate a sorority house and kill everyone inside; he wanted others to suffer because he was lonely. In his highly revealing 140-page detailed, single-spaced autobiography, he outlines the entire story of his life from early childhood on while documenting the impact of loneliness on his life, which directly led him to the killings (google: Elliot Rodger Manifesto: "My Twisted World"; https://www.documentcloud.org/documents/1173808-elliot-rodger-manifesto.html). More recently, Stephen Paddock, despite all the external appearances of a normal and successful man, systematically assassinated 58 people and wounded almost five hundred others at a Las Vegas nightly concert on October 10, 2017. Authorities have been unable to discover any credible motive. I suggest the "motive" of extreme narcissism, self-hatred, hatred of others, alienation, and estrangement as a "compensation" for suffering loneliness.

Why do some human beings feel impelled to kill others, themselves, or both? In a word, it is because of a sense of irreparable *separation* from those they desire to be closest to. They either blame others or the self for their loneliness and they are unable to forgive both. The defense mechanisms of displacement, projection, rationalization, etc., all become insufficient in absolving them from their consuming guilt, shame, and the pain of isolation. Indiscriminately they direct their anger at the world at large. Someone else is to blame and has to pay for their disappointments. The malice is a direct derivative of their loneliness. This is generally the case with the current rash of "suicide bombers." It is a direct consequence of their hatred and anger brought to a boil in the crucible of loneliness. The universal grounding "motive" will generally be loneliness.

Usually we tend to think of lonely individuals as depressed and sad. And they undoubtedly are. But because of the dynamics of narcissism and its related entitlement issues, they are also angry. Further, according to Zilboorg, this destructive dynamic is not only true of individuals but also of groups and nations as well and when these larger units perceive themselves as alienated, estranged, and unappreciated by their surrounding social communities, or the world at large, horrific and catastrophic results can occur. This is what transpired in the aftermath of the First World War, for example, when Germans felt humiliated, shamed, and resented their harsh punishment after losing the war. It directly led to their espousal of Nazism with all its destructiveness, atrocities, holocausts, and concentration camps; it was also encouraged by their narcissistic compulsion and conviction to view themselves as the "master race." What else could possibly justify the course they embarked upon?[6] We recall that

---

6  Gregory Zilboorg, "Loneliness," *The Atlantic Monthly* (January 1938). 45–54. Cf. Ben Mijuskovic, "Loneliness and Narcissism," *Psychoanalytic Review,* 66:4 (1979–80), 479–492; "Loneli-

Zilboorg is expressing these concerns in 1938, a year before the Germans invaded the Czechoslovakian Sudentland and pretty much all the rest of Europe.

This same theme is repeated more at length in Hannah Arendt's powerful study, *The Origins of Totalitarianism,* in which she similarly blames the dynamics of national loneliness, ethnic disenfranchisement, societal and economic alienation, and a sense of cultural estrangement as responsible for the terrors of German Nazism, Italian Fascism, and subsequently Russian Communism after the Second World War.[7] Today we sadly and anxiously witness in alarm throughout the world nations who feel so extremely demeaned and ignored from the rest of humanity, shunned by those they most desire to impress, that their dominant motivation is obssessionaly determined by their motive to hurt and destroy others in horrific gestures designed not only to massively annihilate others but themselves as well.

The struggle for Hegel's narcissistic unilateral Recognition is a fight to the death.

> This presentation is a twofold action; action on the part of the other; and action on its own part. In so far as it is the action of the *other,* each seeks the death of the other. But in doing so, the second kind of action, action on its own part, is also involved; for the former involves the staking of its own life. Thus the relation of the two self-conscious individuals is such that they prove themselves and each other through a life-and-death struggle.
> HEGEL, "Lordship and Bondage," *Phenomenology*

The second article dedicated solely to the subject matter of loneliness presents an interdisciplinary perspective and once more treats it as a topic in its own right. It is authored by another psychoanalyst, Frieda Fromm-Reichmann. While working in a state mental institution, she experienced an encounter with a catatonic schizophrenic woman. After repeated efforts to communicate and engage her, she finally held up a single finger and uttered the words, "That lonely?" and suddenly the doors of communication flooded open. Thus, in her groundbreaking article, she concludes by identifying two additional dynamics in relation to Zilboorg's core narcissism and projected hostility concepts by proposing that loneliness essentially derives from two related sources.

---

ness and Hostility," *Psychology: A Journal of Human Behavior,* 20:3/4 (1983), 9–19; "Loneliness and Adolescence," *Adolescence,* XXI:84 (1986), 941–951; "Loneliness, Anxiety, Hostility, and Communication," *Child Study Journaql,*16:3 (1986), 227–240; and "Loneliness and Adolescent Alcoholism," *Adolescence,* XXIII:92 (1988), 503–516. A classic novel depicting the cruelty and hostility generated by loneliness is Jerzy Kosinski's *The Painted Bird.*

7 Hannah Arendt, *The Origins of Totalitarianism* (New York: Harcourt & Brace, 1976; first published in 1948), 474–475.

First from a feeling of failed communication (Virginia Satir); from the subject's sense that no one is listening to them, that no one understands them, and even worse that no one cares. Second, this feeling of incommunicability directly results in a state of anxiety and a fear of abandonment. Indeed, she concludes her article by *identifying* loneliness and anxiety.[8] This is significant because in Freud the dominant and identifying feature of neurosis is anxiety. In his turn, Erich Fromm adds depression, guilt, and shame.[9]

Now when we combine these various meanings, relations, and insights together into the mix of loneliness, we begin to realize that it all begins with narcissism (recall Schopenhauer's focus on "egoism") as the initial *subjective* source that provides the powerful centripetal unifying agency, which connects the feelings of loneliness—and entitlement—with the meanings of hostility, anxiety, incommunicability, depression, grief, shame, and so on in the ego. *But their common source is the narcissistic ego.* When we tie all these threads together, we begin to realize that loneliness constitutes a unifying knot of seemingly different threads. Or, to change the metaphor, it is an "umbrella concept" and under its extended spokes it includes a variety of constitutive emotions and inter-related meanings all *a priori* synthetically covered together. Loneliness is the genus; its variants are its emotional species.

Phenomenologically the meanings, relations, and the dynamics of loneliness, I believe, can be fruitfully studied and expanded and developed into a full-blown system supplanting Freud's vision of psychoanalysis. Not to be studied or promoted as a causally structured "science" but to gain *insight* into human consciousness. This is the true meaning of the Socratic dictum: "Know thyself." It would consist of a coherent system constituted by synthetic *a priori* meanings, relations, structures, laws, and principles that are readily identifiable. These *eidetic* essences are not only open to intuitive "seeing" and organization but they also form a system of *both* affective *and* cognitive relations. Consequently, it is important to explore not only *what* human beings can know (Kant) but also more critically *why* they act, what motivates them, what energizes them, what we can expect, and what we cannot expect from them (Schopenhauer). Precisely because the meaning of loneliness is a universal *theoretical* concept, its "fullness" transcends any simple classification and hence it does not appear—nor is it even mentioned—in the *Diagnostic and Statistical Manual of Psychiatric Disorders,* which basically consists of what

---

8 Frieda Fromm-Reichmann, "Loneliness," *Psychiatry: A Journal for the Study of Interpersonal Processes,* 22:1 (1959), 1–15. I used her article as a model for my own, which also appeared in *Psychiatry.* Cf. Ben Mijuskovic, "Loneliness and Communication," in *Man and His Conduct,* edited by Jorge Gracia (Rio Piedras, Puerto Rico: University of Puerto Rico Press, 1980), 250–260.

9 Erich Fromm, *The Art of Loving* (New York: Harper & Row, 1970), 6–7.

Bergson would criticize as abstract, artificial, definitional constructs. In other words, loneliness is not a definable symptom like Intermittent Explosive Disorder (*DSM,* 312.34).

Importantly, one cannot understand loneliness without gaining insight into the dynamics of intimacy. Loneliness is the reflexive pole while intimacy is the intentional pole. Loneliness is discovered within; intimacy is searched for without.

More specifically, the dynamics of loneliness consist in a sense of being *separated* from others with whom we most wish to *belong to* and to *be with*. It arises from a desperate sense of failure in not achieving intimacy. Indeed, *belonging* is the deepest meaning of intimacy, while emptiness is the deepest meaning of loneliness. There are no introverts, only discouraged extroverts (Jung). Whenever the bonds of belonging and intimacy are threatened or violated, whenever we are confronted with loneliness, whenever mistrust looms, there are basically two self-defeating recourses: either (a) withdrawing within the self and retreating into submerged levels of depression; or (b) exploding beyond the confines of the self by indulging in exaggerated expressions of manic activity. These two dysfunctional responses mimic the dual activities of consciousness we have been tracing throughout the length of this treatise: (c) reflexive self-consciousness and internalization and (d) transcendent intentionality and externalization.

In psychiatric terms, depression is essentially reflexive; it expresses an internalization; a retreat into the self, while mania is primarily intentional, an externalization, an attempt to escape the sense of isolation by uncontrolled activity; by running so fast one cannot stop to face their misery. The first is inner-directed and the second outer-directed. Often, when the pressures of loneliness assume overwhelming proportions, the soul in desperation takes on the twin symptoms of a "bipolar disorder"; of alternating cycles of depression and mania (*DSM,* 296, with or without psychotic features). Both are flawed strategies for coping with loneliness.

In an insightful study on loneliness, *The Flesh-Colored Cage,* James Howard begins by assuming as his premise a quasi-Cartesian principle.

> We read our sensations, presuming to know by inference the things those mere sensations cannot demonstrate—that things and creatures outside our selves actually exist.[10]

---

10   James Howard, *The Flesh-Colored Cage: The Impact of Man's Essential Aloneness on His Attitudes and Behaviors* (New York: Hawthorn Books, 1975), ix. Howard contends that the cage is a bodily one rather than a mental "enclosure," which of course is unsustainable

This premise commands the further realization of our utter loneliness because of our separation from other caged selves.

> I am here contending that the fact of being separated provides man with an unremitting tension state that is the basic motivational force in all human existence. Further I believe it is behavioral alterations accumulating as the sum of our attempts to relieve this continual tension that can account for all the superstructures we call personality, civilization, and culture (ibid, page x).

Thus, Howard wants to use the principle of loneliness as a *base,* a *foundation* for erecting his edifice of a psychological and sociological superstructure, which is comparable to Marx, who enlists economics as the base for his elaboration of a system in *A Contribution to the Critique of Political Economy* (1859). The base is economics and the pyramidal superstructure consists in a gradation of superimposed levels: first law; then politics; philosophy; religion; art; manners; etc. Just so for Howard, starting from the base of human loneliness (as opposed to Marx's base of economics), Howard is convinced we can build a graduated psychological and sociological superstructure grounded on loneliness as the foundation. The foundation would start with maternal nurturing, Maslow's hierarchy of needs, and then progressively proceed to other metalevel needs, like ethics, politics, education, philosophy, literature, art, and so on, all dedicated in an effort to understand—not cure—the deleterious effects of loneliness and possibly enhance intimacy.

> Psychologists and philosophers have compiled many lists of drives and motives of men. These overlook the obvious fact of separateness of individual creatures. I contend that this is a grave oversight filled with consequences for those who would seek to understand or deal with human behaviors. The "primary drives" or "absolutely dependable motives" and their elaborations are more understandable or predictable if seen as the logistic or tactical situations of a creature responding to some more fundamental strategy of dealing with loneliness (ibid., page xi).

Howard further insightfully underscores two desperate psychological strategies in trying to overcome loneliness, which he defines as "incorporation" and "decapsulation." In the first endeavor, one unrealistically tries to force the other within their own sphere of consciousness by demanding they sacrifice their

---

as a paradigm for the simple reason that physiologically our bodies are continually changing.

own interests and values in order "to engulf them within themselves," as for example the domineering husband. In the second strategy, one abandons their own interests and sacrifices their values in order to masochistically please the other self; "to give until it hurts," as in the case of the abused spouse. Although Howard's paradigm rests on a mistaken assumption that we are physiologically trapped "within our own skin," within our cages of flesh, rather than within our own sphere of consciousness, nevertheless his theory insightfully captures and reflects the dynamics of reflexion and intentionality, incorporation and decapsulation, as well as the dynamics of depression and mania. Howard's study is liberally peppered with impressive and persuasive case studies. Well worth reading for insights into the "mechanics" and the failed strategies for dealing with loneliness that are ineffective and even dangerous. To be forewarned is to be forearmed.

Within a psychological context, because loneliness is essentially insular and readily recedes into disintegrative depression, a retreat back toward the womb or death, being "stoned" by the use of drugs and medication, in search of an oblivious non-existence, it is vital to struggle by using intentionality as the means to reach out to creatures beyond the self. One of the best remedies in forestalling loneliness is to help others because it "gets you out of yourself." It encourages a mutual sense of *a priori* synthetic unification between two kindred souls for a while at least; to feel and think as one. Aristotle it is said defined friendship as one soul in two bodies.

I remember a middle-aged woman in our Day Treatment program benefiting significantly from volunteering to care for pelicans and other sea birds by cleaning their wings after a major oil spill on the seacoast for several weeks. Then one day, she didn't come to the program, and we learned she had gone to court and the judge finalized her divorce from her husband and later that night she hung herself. How infinitely sad. The pelicans and I will miss her. She fought her loneliness until she could struggle no longer. It's difficult for me to see the pelicans fly by my home and not think of her.

In the following, I wish to show four things: (a) *that* all human beings are innately lonely; (b) *why* this is so; (c) its *consequences*; and (d) *what* can be done about it, its *remedies*.

Before getting into the specific dynamics of loneliness, it may be worthwhile to distinguish several meanings of the term that are often confused with each other. Loneliness is always negative. As such, it indicates a strong desire not only to avoid it but much more importantly to *do* something about it in so far as that is possible. The *fear* of loneliness elicits powerful motivational forces all of which are designed to escape it. The term *isolation,* however, is usually a neutral one and it is intended as merely descriptive, although quite often it is also considered negatively. Sometimes the word *alone* is intended as a synonym for isolation, as merely descriptive signifying for instance that I am separated but not distressed by the fact of separation. For instance, I am isolated and separated from millions of strangers that I shall never personally meet but I am not distressed or anxious by the fact. By contrast, *solitude* generally implies a positive, pleasant, and peaceful experience; an indication of being "comfortable" within one's own self so to speak. Spiritual meditation is often tendered as an example of that particular form of satisfying tranquility. Therefore solitude is often sought for its therapeutic advantages. But, of course, no one would wish to undergo the state of "solitude" forever. It would no longer be solitude because it would eventually turn into a sense of isolation and finally loneliness. Even hermits and Trappist monks need God for companionship. In any case, all these meanings are essentially related—as essences—to each other through their shared implications referring to a *single, subjective* state of mind. But obviously they display different but related meanings, since they intend a subjective state of consciousness. Although it is seldom mentioned in the same context as loneliness, actually boredom is a species, a minor form of loneliness *meaning* one feels separated from important activities or values. Schopenhauer attributes the high rate of frequent suicides in Philadelphia's penal system to prolonged boredom and observes that frequently the prisoners simply preferred death to endless boredom. Often people are able—up to a point—to substitute values in place of persons. But like loneliness, it can be deadly when unduly prolonged.

In addition, there are certain Hegelian technical terms, like *alienation,* exemplified in the Lordship and Bondage passage, which anticipates a Marxist treatment; and *estrangement,* in the Unhappy Consciousness section, which foreshadows Kierkegaard's emphasis on a sense of separation from God. Both are grounded in the Hegelian roots of reflexive consciousness. In Kierkegaard's case, it rests on his extreme individualistic Protestant bias, as we previously noticed in *Fear and Trembling.* Originally, Hegel conceived the Jewish consciousness as exemplifying the Unhappy Consciousness but later switched it to connect it to Catholicism. In any case, all these distinctions and various meanings rest on a simple psychological foundation: the feeling and meaning of a *separate* existence from other selves or from the Lord but they also represent attitudes of thought from which we seek relief and recovery, which can only occur in so far as the self is able to secure a sustaining relationship with other beings or a privileged Being.

Interestingly—and wisely—the Neo-Freudians later went on to replace Freud's over-emphasis on individual libidinal sexual energy in order to include "object relations" and *interpersonal* attachments as *dynamic* forces as well.[11] Essentially the terms "dynamic energy" and "dynamic psychiatry" imply a constellation of meanings, including Malebranche's psychic energy attributed to his conception of imagery; Leibniz's concept of psychic activity or power as distinguished from physical causality; and functionality as opposed to organicity.[12]

Until now we have learned that loneliness is essentially constituted by a constellation of feelings and meanings surrounding the fear of separation from other selves and the consequent yearning to be intimately connected to other sentient beings and often most importantly to and through their *values*. This qualitative relation is something neuroscience fails to take into account. Negatively the terms forlornness or loneliness consist in a desire to avoid separation and thus follows the ensuing commitment to prevent, struggle, and avoid it. The opposite of separation, then, is a sense of intimacy, belonging, or togetherness with another active agent, a self-conscious subject, who is both distinct from our self but yet at the same moment related *meaningfully, emotionally, and cognitively* to a special other conscious creature, "a significant other." Fish do not qualify but dogs do.

## 1 Five Developmental Sources of Human Separation

First source: *object-object separation*. This is the initial biological separation, the ejection of the fetus from the womb (physically painful and distressful object-object separation). It represents Freud's first state of separation anxiety: "the first great anxiety-state of birth and the infantile anxiety of longing—the anxiety due to the *bodily* separation from the protecting mother" (*The Ego and the Id,* italic mine). During these brief moments, there is the painful distress of consciousness without any sense of an ego.

Second source: *self or ego-object separation*. We have already treated this stage in our discussion of the "oceanic feeling" as an "undifferentiated oneness." During this stage and level of consciousness, there is only consciousness without any sense of the ego in its relation to an independent object. Originally,

---

11  Mary D. Salter, "Object Relations, Dependency, and Attachment: A Theoretical Review of the Infant-Mother Relationship," *Child Development,* 40:4 (1969), 969–1025. Harry Stack Sullivan and Frieda Fromm-Reichman are integral members of this movement. The use of the terms "object relations" to substitute for "other egos" clearly lends itself to a phenomenalist interpretation of Freud.
12  Henri Ellenberger, *The Discovery of the Unconscious: The History and Evolution of Dynamic Psychiatry* (New York: Basic Books, 1970), 289–291.

this amorphous feeling of oneness corresponds to Hegel's phenomenological description of Sense-Certainty. Self-consciousness exhibits two functions, separation and unification, which are *a priori* synthetically related. Thus the second stage of separation is only consummated when the conscious subject emotionally and cognitively separates its self from the external world by becoming *self*-conscious as it distinguishes itself from a realm of *inanimate* things. At this stage of child development, the sense of separation is essentially *intra-psychic*. It is a state of consciousness negatively *defined* by the loss of the previous symbiotic relationship.

Third source of separation: *Self-other-self separation*. It is classically signaled by ambivalence and anxiety over the trauma of the realized separation from the mother's sphere of consciousness. It is constituted by emotional and cognitive uncertainty and alternating states of conflict and rapprochement; it also introduces a state of incipient co-dependency and pre-intimacy.

> Individuation proceeds very rapidly and the child exercises it to the limit; he also becomes more and more aware of his separateness and employs all kinds of mechanisms in order to resist and undo his actual separateness from the mother. The fact is, however, that no matter how insistently the toddler tries to coerce the mother, he can no longer function effectively as a dual unit—that it is to say, the child can no longer maintain his delusion of parental omnipotence, which he still at times expects will restore the symbiotic status quo.[13]

Although initially infants are able to cognitively orient themselves among objects and things in developmental terms (Dani), they next require to relate *emotionally* to another self; to relate *communicatively* to another *responding* self, primarily to the mother through cooing, smiling, touching, feeding, etc. (child-mother relation). But this comes at a price. The child has its own *desires* and *demands* but reciprocally the mother also has her own quite *different* agenda. This places the opposing consciousnesses in situational conflicts: the needy child against the dominant parent, which directly leads to self-other-self separation inevitably generating feelings of loneliness, anger, and anxiety in the infant as the mother increasingly enforces feeding and toileting strictures with the consequence that each separate self strives to have its own insistent desires recognized. At this stage, the separation is dynamically *inter-personal* as opposed to *intra-psychic*.

---

[13] *The Psychological Birth of the Human Infant,* edited by Margaret Mahler, Fred Pine, and Anni Bergman (New York: Basic Books, 1970), 78–79.

But during this mental level and developmental stage of increasing cognitive acuity there are several readily distinguishable meanings of separation of the self from the "other-self" as they become displayed in various contexts of loneliness: personal; estranged; alienated; existential, and social in name as the major divisions.

*Personal.* The loneliness is interpersonal when the narcissistic self initially generates conflicts of resistance, assertion, hostility, and anxiety between the ego and the other self, at first usually the mother. It begins when the breast is something the mother can offer or withhold at will from the child thus engendering an inter-personal struggle and generating vacillating feelings of fear and anger versus security and intimacy. The mother demands compliance and the infant resists in seeking its own independence. It is readily noticed in the "play" of young children seeking a "dominant" relation over desired objects in the nursery and playground but it is a dynamic that will follow us throughout our lives. St. Augustine in the *Confessions* describes two siblings at their mother's breast and although the first is sufficiently satiated, it still nevertheless strives to prevent the other child from sharing.

But personal loneliness can also be tragically punctuated by loss of the significant other. One of the saddest periods in American history involves the black "family" in the United States before, during, and even after the Civil War:

> Enslaved people lived with the perpetual fear of separation through the sale of one or more family members. Slaves were considered as private property. A father could be sold by his owner while the mother and the children could be sold separately. The fear of separation haunted adults who knew how likely it was to happen. Young children innocently unaware of the possibilities quickly learned of the pain such separations could cost.[14]

In 1965 I began my career in social services at the welfare office on the South Side of Chicago on 63rd St. I was assigned to the Midway Office, which was situated a few blocks south from the University of Chicago, and assigned to an ADC (Aid to Dependent Children) caseload consisting of some five hundred minors confined to a single block of substandard housing on 63rd St. The living quarters, originally erected in the 1920s and 1930s, consisted of old "railroad" apartments with each featuring six or seven bedrooms. The seventh and last

---

[14] Heather Andrea Williams, "How Slavery Affected African American Families," Natural Humanities Center, http://nationalhumanitiescenter.org/tserve/freedom/1609-1865/essays/aafamilies.htm.

bedroom was originally reserved for the live-in maid and/or cook. My block ran parallel to the elevated train track (the El) and when I visited the apartments on the second floor I could look into the cars as they noisly ran along the tracks. The street was littered with bars and often stragglers urinated and even defecated in the vestibules to the unlocked and unprotected hallways. The "port of entry" for Southern Blacks migrating north to a "better way of life" was the Greyhound depot on 63rd St. and Stony Island. Six or seven blocks down the street from my office was the Southern District Office, located at 63rd and Cottage Grove locally known as "Sin Corner." Basically welfare was predominantly the only "way of life." Poverty and unemployment ran throughout the Woodlawn area. Ironically most of the slum housing was owned by the University of Chicago, which was desperately trying to move the Blacks out of the neighborhood by eviction in order to redevelop the area and restore it to its "original glory" of the 1920's when it flourished after the construction of the famous 1893 Columbian World's Fair. In alarm and self-defense, the Black community hired a well-known labor organizer, Saul Alinsky, to slow down the evictions and improve the housing. (A youthful Hilary Clinton composed her Bachelor's thesis at Wellesley addressing the Black community's self-survival strategies implemented by Alinsky and TWO The Woodlawn Organization). Because of the multiple-bedroom units, the mothers lived with their numerous children, often accommodating as many as 8–10 offspring, and just as often sired by an equal number of fathers. The fathers were not allowed to live in the home with the mothers and the children; it was considered as a case of fraud, since the men were unemployed. (A few years later, ADC was renamed AFDC, Aid to Families with Dependent Children, thus demonstrating the tolerance of the new liberalism and *under certain circumstances* a father was permitted to live with his child(ren) and to be subsidized by the State). Work for Blacks was non-existent and yet young people continued to pour in by the busload from the South.

The tragic legacy of the destruction of the Black family perpetuated by American slavery has persisted till today and it is only within the last few generations that it has begun to improve economically and sociologically. However, in the slum pockets of many cities, as for example the cities of Chicago and New Orleans, with which I am most familiar, the murder and suicide rate among blacks is absolutely alarming. Many of the young men will tell you, if you care to ask, that they do not expect to live beyond their twenty-fifth year of life. Robbed of "acceptable" opportunities, forced to assert themselves in the only ways at their disposal because of economic restrictions and surrounded by street drugs, they turn to self-destructive modes of expression. And why should they not given the desperate loneliness of their living conditions, the restrictions on their future, and the circumstances to which they have been subjected and confined.

A few years previously to my tenure in 1965 as a Caseworker, a very influential book appeared by Michael Harrington, *The Other America: Poverty in the United States* (New York: Macmillan, 1962), and it impressed both John Kennedy and his successor, Lyndon Johnson, to the extent that the War on Poverty was launched with the novel concept of helping the poor by investing them with the power to help themselves. They would be hired to work with and to aid those whom they understood best, those like themselves. It was structured as a comprehensive simultaneous approach in addressing the problems of the glaring inadequate resources for employment, housing, education, health, economic outlets, discrimination, legal services, and child development issues and so on. A year later (1966), I was hired as a Headstart worker and assigned to an Urban Progress office on 63rd St. across from my old workplace at the Midway District Office. The educational program for children was designed to recruit young preschoolers as well as their mothers to help as aides. Virtually all of the Headstart schools were housed in neighborhood Black churches. The War on Poverty was envisioned to be a massive comprehensive and coherent frontal assault on all the ills perpetuated on the Black "community" since the American Age of Slavery.

Alas another war intervened: The Viet Nam War and all the funding collapsed and all the ideals along with the funding. Headstart, however, continued to prove itself and as the years have transpired, it was discovered that the high school dropout rate of the Headstart graduates was dramatically lower. Given this early advantage, the children persevered to finish high school.

The extremes of loneliness play a significant role in Post Traumatic Stress Disorder diagnoses as well (309.81). Three decades later in Oceanside, California, I worked at the San Diego County Mental health Clinic near Camp Pendleton Marine Corps base with a few servicemen diagnosed with PTSD. This contact was forbidden and when the Corps discovered it, the soldiers were confined to the base. Generally, clinical professionals at the time followed the *DSM* guidelines and related the disorder to anxiety. Anxiety is often successfully treated *behaviorally* by using desensitization techniques. For example, a person experiencing a fear of closed spaces can be helped by gently and gradually exposing them to riding repeatedly in an elevator with a trusted friend. On the assumption that PTSD is simply a form of severe anxiety, the VA Hospitals promoted a strategy of "flooding," of repeatedly exposing the subjects to battle scenes from movies like *Forest Gump* and eliciting extremely poor results. Anxiety medications seemed to make matters even worse, since they are highly addictive. In brief, both therapeutic "interventions" seemed to be essentially worthless at best.

My "reading" of the situation is that the most defining characteristic of PTSD is that it is directly related to a complete breakdown of *trust* in human beings, their agencies, and their institutions—a loss of trust so profound it cannot be resurrected. In fact, a psychiatrist in Germany, Michael Linden, has proposed renaming it PTED, Post Traumatic Embitterment Disorder because of the loss of *all* trust in humanity, which can never be restored. An example of its severity can be most clearly found in holocaust victims as well as children subjected to the extremes of child abuse and incest.

While working as a clinical therapist for the Department of Mental Health in Los Angeles, I assessed a twenty-year-old Hispanic female. She had never been treated or "diagnosed" previously. She sporadically lived with her mother and her younger sister, who was her junior by four years, amidst continual family rows. At other times, she lived in her car before it was impounded. And during other periods she intermittently stayed with a physically abusive boyfriend. I saw her for three years. She had had numerous problems as a juvenile, in and out of juvenile court, and intermittently interned in group homes. She had at best only "completed" the ninth grade and she sold cosmetics on a street corner in downtown LA in order to financially survive. During the initial assessment, she was emotionally overwrought, crying hysterically, and sobbing, but the thing that startled me was her verbal ability to express herself between her tears, to articulate what was bothering her, her issues and her distress, and most of all her anger about what had happened to her, as well as her hopes and ambitions for her future life. She was the victim of a three-year history of incest by her father from the ages of six through eight. It was inadvertently discovered by the mother, who worked, which accounted for her absence from the home during the day, and the mother reported "the incident" to Child Protective Services. The father was arrested and because of the severity of the case—semen was discovered—he was sentenced to eight years in prison. The dynamics of exploitation, complete betrayal by her father, and the inability of the mother to realize what had transpired had become deep-seated and severe in the child. It involved not only an absolute loss of trust for what he had done but also the mother's "failure to protect." What the young woman wanted more than anything was for the father to acknowledge what he had done; to "own" the violation of his daughter. To make matters worse, the father had been recently released from prison and he returned to Mexico and started a second family. He never apologized to his daughter for what he had done and never acknowledged the outrage.

During the assessment, I confess I was struck by her vehemence and anger at the father's complete betrayal, the mother's "neglect," and the violation of parental trust but at the same time fascinated and intrigued by her articulate verbal skills and her obvious intelligence. She clearly was very bright. Obviously, since she was a young woman, I hesitated but asked her if, under the circumstances, she would prefer a female therapist. For whatever reason, she informed me she preferred to stay with me. (Possibly because she was unwilling to have to tell this story all over again to someone else.) In order to provide clinical services, we are required for insurance purposes to venture a diagnosis. I gave her a Post Traumatic Stress Disorder diagnosis. In the "treatment plan objective," the agreed upon goal was that she would finish high school. My own treatment plan for her was to try to instill some sense of trust in me. That was the main advantage I had over a female therapist.

She declined medication, which was encouraging from my viewpoint. I was able to get her SSI funding quickly and even subsidized federal housing after only a few months. I supervised social work interns twice a week from UCLA and USC, who were but slightly older than she, and I thought that it would make for a positive "fit." Subsidiary plans were to have her volunteer at the clinic and then apply as a Peer Advocate, which would pay her $3,000 monthly as a County employee with health insurance and pension benefits. "Our" hope, our long-term "objective" goal was that she would graduate high school and then go on to social work school. I was teaching part-time at a California State University campus that had an MSW program.

After the three years, in retrospect I realized that I had been oblivious to the fact that those were my goals and not necessarily hers although she seemed to espouse them and graduating from high school seemed a doable "treatment plan." It seemed to have the advantage of a clear "objective" *quantifiable* goal. As time and therapy went on, she often missed her appointments, both for individual and group therapy. She avoided the interns and never followed through on the volunteering or the Peer Advocacy opportunities and after several weeks of sporadic and failed efforts to continue school, she pretty much lived her life as she had previously. At one point, she was involuntarily hospitalized after a fight with her mother. Without trust in either parent, she had no one to turn to who could provide her sufficiently with the support and confidence she so desperately needed, which included my best but failed efforts.[15] The entire situation reminded me of a title of a book by child psychoanalyst, Bruno Bettelheim, *Love Is Not Enough,* my neighbor in Chicago.

In 2014, I retired from County service and I have never looked back. Today reflecting on my interactions with her, in the end I came to believe that her forced sexual experiences and what I imagined to be her father's progressive

---

15   Ben Mijuskovic, "Loneliness, Self-Consciousness, and PTSD," *Psychology Journal,* 11:1 (2014), 44–54.

sexual expectations—which I did not explore with her, were never described to me, and were not a focus of treatment—had resulted in a "fear of failure" in her, an anxiety concerning her ability to please others or to perform adequately, which I believe is what destroyed her. Shame and guilt prevented her from trying (Fromm) and she developed a strategy of avoidance behaviors (DSM, 309.81, C, 1–7). Rather than fail, don't try.

In any case, I remain convinced that in my twenty years as a clinician, I never "cured" anyone. People cure themselves through their own insight, through their own determination.

*Estrangement.* Although medieval and contemporary man draws great strength from the consoling solace of a faith secure in the knowledge that God intimately knows their every thought and deed, nevertheless, there is always the constant terror that one may have disobeyed or displeased the Lord through insufficiency or subtle disobediences and was therefore threatened by an utter abandonment and condemned to dwell in Dante's ninth circle of Hell forever in incommunicable agony and alone. The *"Fear of the Lord is the beginning of wisdom"* (*Proverbs,* 9:10). To be estranged from God is the ultimate terror. Consider St. Augustine's Prayer to the Lord:

> Who will give me help so that I may rest in You? Who will give me help... so that I may forget my evils and embrace You, my one good? Have pity on me, so that I may speak. What am I myself to You, that You command me to love You, and grow angry and threaten me with mighty woes unless I do?[16]

This is Kierkegaard's "sickness unto death," the despair and anxiety, the existential *angst* over the possibility of displeasing and disobeying the Lord. The terror of eternal separation spawns the desire to placate the divine Other at any cost as in Abraham's decision to sacrifice his only son. Before the ages of the great existential philosophers, Kierkegaard and Nietzsche, loneliness and melancholy were primarily the province of poets and novelists rather than philosophers.[17]

*Alienation.* Marx borrows heavily from Hegel's Lordship and Bondage dialectic and Hegel in turn borrows heavily from Hobbes' political description

---

16   St. Augustine, *The Confessions of St. Augustine* (New York: Doubleday, 1960), Chapter 5, 45.
17   Josiah Thompson, *The Lonely Labyrinth: Kierkegaard's Pseudonymous Works* (Carbondale. IL: Southern Illinois University Press, 1967), 15, 43–49. Throughout Thompson's study, he emphasizes Kierkegaard's ruling principle of the subjective reflexive nature of self-consciousness.

concerning "the monster of the deep," "the fear of death," and "the great artificial man," which we recognize as civil society (*Leviathan*). Historically, Hobbes' particular "dialectic" is nestled within three interrelated concepts: the State of Nature or the condition of man before the institution of moral and legal laws (Conrad's *Heart of Darkness,* Golding's *Lord of the Flies*); Human Nature and the critical issue regarding the real nature of man, and what man is really capable of; and the artificial conditions of an original Social Contract. Nevertheless, it all begins with the *Republic* of Plato and Glaucon's recounting of the Myth of Gyges with the shepherd's discovery of a magical ring empowering him to become invisible. What is human nature really like? What if a man had complete power to do as he pleased rather than to do as he should? As Glaucon proposes perhaps the best thing in the world is to injure others with impunity and the worst is to suffer injury without recourse. Throughout the seventeenth-, eighteenth-, and nineteenth-centuries, the viability and the ethical foundation of the social contract and its variations was a hotly contested issue embroiling philosophers as diverse as Hobbes, Spinoza, Rousseau, Kant, Fichte, Hegel and eventually Marx to name but a few.[18] But Hegel's treatment is especially congenial to Marx's interpretation as it serves to illustrate the special dyadic conflict between the capitalist and proletarian classes. Alienation is grounded in economic, racial, and national inequality, which begins in Marx with an original exploitation based on a distinction between intellectual labor as opposed to physical labor starting as early as Egyptian times in pitting the priestly class against the slaves (*The German Ideology*). It is an alienation which is defined by the worker's sense of separation from nature; his labor; the product of his labor; and his fellow man through competition for a living wage. As Marx describes it, alienated man becomes stunted and deformed, dehumanized by a ruling economic system as well as machines that enslave him; by a system that systematically exploits him.

*Existentialism.* Matching Kierkegaard's extreme religious individualism, Nietzsche poetically forges his own brand of atheistic loneliness.

> No one talks to me other than myself and my voice comes to me as the voice of a dying man. With you, beloved voice, with you as the last vaporous remembrance of all human happiness, let me tarry an hour longer. With your help I shall deceive my way back into society and love. For my

---

18   Plato, *The Republic of Plato,* translated with an Introduction and running commentary by F.M. Cornford (London: Oxford University Press, 1968), II, 357a-267e: and J.W. Gough, *The Social Contract: A Critical Study of Its Development* (Oxford, Clarendon Press, 1957), *passim.*

heart refuses to believe that love is dead, it cannot bear the terror of the loneliest loneliness. It compels me to talk as if were two (unidentified prose fragment).

*Social separation.* In *The Lonely Crowd,* the authors distinguish three forms of societal organization and therefore three types of social loneliness. The study thus depicts the loneliness of the individual in relation to the prevailing and surrounding societal masses. In the tradition-oriented society, India for example, under the caste system, the lower castes and especially the "untouchables" suffer extreme loneliness and separation through both economic and social discrimination. In the inner-directed society, Victorian America for example, dominated by Protestant values and subjective conscience, individual man prevails and prospers, but as Max Weber convincingly argues, in *The Protestant Ethic and the Spirit of Capitalism,* so does the Calvinist doctrine of "the elect," wherein the wealthy individual prospers and although he may be secure in his riches and his conviction that he is one of the chosen few privileged to anticipate eternal salvation, nevertheless "it's lonely at the top." Meanwhile, in the outer-directed society of America in the 1960's and apparently continuing on, the fear of being unpopular and suffering "loneliness in a crowd," of being shunned among one's peers drives individuals to adopt any fad that provides a greater opportunity to gain approval from others. The need to be liked by the reigning mass becomes the guiding principle of conduct. Moral values are unimportant. What is important is to please others as confirmed on Facebook. In these three different types of societal organization, the avoidance of loneliness is predicated by the organizational structure of the social order.[19] Social loneliness can also be meted out by the punishment of enforced isolation promoted by certain religious sects, notably Catholics, Jews (Spinoza was excommunicated), Mormons, and Amish, who practice formal excommunication and social and economic "shunning" of (allegedly) rebellious members.

Fourth source of separation: *self-enclosed "self" separation.* Psychosis is an internal schism during which the self separates its self from itself in an attempt to completely internalize its loneliness and thereby control it from within generally by falsely attributing one's difficulties to hostile forces as external to the self; by denying the source of its loneliness within itself and instead projecting it outwardly as due to the existence of malevolent forces outside its self; to external sources or conditions so that the mind can control the loneliness

---

19    David Riesman, Reuel Denney, and Nathan Glazer, *The Lonely Crowd;* and cf. Ben Mijuskovic, "Organic Communities, Atomistic Societies, and Loneliness," *Journal of Sociology and Social Welfare,* XIX:2 (1992), 147–163.

from within. Insight into this destructive dynamic of loneliness is powerfully expressed in certain classic novels, such as Arthur Machen's *The Hill of Dreams* and William Golding's *Pincher Martin.*

Interestingly, Hegel, we recall, insists that we must *first* understand madness *before* we can comprehend sanity wherein psychosis is simply a stage of psychic development (*Philosophy of Mind,* Section 408). Freud, by contrast, basically avoided treating psychotics. He also tended to avoid dealing with loneliness and preferred to concentrate on sexual repression, the misuse of libidinal energy, and traumatic incidents, while obviously regarding neurotic symptoms as curable but perhaps realized that the "symptoms" of loneliness were not of the same order.

Fifth source of separation: *death.* We are born alone and we die alone. Each human being must face her or his own terminal separation from the rest of humanity by herself or himself. For Freud, death signals the natural cycle of an ultimate "separation" and the return of the organic to the inorganic, the re-entry into the lifeless womb of matter from whence we all came; the return to the inanimate.

> The fear of death in melancholia [i.e., loneliness] only admits of one explanation… [The ego] sees itself deserted by all protective forces and lets itself die. Here, moreover it is once again the same situation as that which first underlay the great anxiety-state of birth and the infantile anxiety-state of longing [i.e., loneliness] due to separation from the protective mother.
>
> FREUD, *Ego and the Id,* 48

So we have come full circle. We are born alone and we die alone, a favorite existential theme (Leo Tolstoy, "The Death of Ivan Ilyich").

We may conclude, then, that it is these painful separations that we need to address and circumvent in so far as we can. This is the work of intelligence, acceptance, and Stoic understanding. Loneliness like death is inevitable.

Most current researchers—materialists, mechanists, determinists, empiricists, phenomenalists, behaviorists, and neuroscientists—contend that loneliness is externally *caused* by hereditary, environmental, cultural, situational conditions, and even by chemical imbalances in the brain and therefore temporary, transient, and avoidable. Indeed, the American Psychiatric Association christened the 1990s as "the decade of the brain." By contrast, I argue that loneliness is internally *constituted*—not externally caused—*within* consciousness by the *innate* activities and structures of Kantian self-consciousness and Husserlian intentionality and therefore universal, necessary, permanent, and unavoidable. I suggested (above) that loneliness is an "umbrella concept," that it connects—or subsumes—a constellation of emotions, including anger, anxiety, depression, guilt, shame, abandonment, betrayal, jealousy, etc. under its all-inclusive canopy. When we put all these elements together, loneliness functions as the nucleus around which our lives ceaselessly revolve. On a more abstract level, theoretically loneliness constitutes a system consisting of synthetic *a priori* meanings, relations, and laws forming a coherent system.

CHAPTER 10

# Metaphysical Dualism, Subjective Idealism, and Existentialism

> But surely you and everybody have a notion that there is, or should be an existence of yours beyond you. What were the use of my creation if I were entirely contained here? If all else perished and he remained, I should continue to be, and if all remained and he were annihilated, the universe would turn into a mighty stranger.
>
> EMILY BRÖNTE, *Wuthering Heights*

∴

There is *both* an active immaterial self *and* there is an opposing material world and other bodily selves to match against it. That is the definition of metaphysical dualism.

Closely related to this assertion is the scientific challenge to metaphysical idealism by the ancient atomists, which persists from the time of Parmenides and into the neurosciences of today. It declares that if we start from the mind, what assurance do we have that an external world of matter and other selves exists beyond or apart from the self? In Chapter 1, I defend dualism and subjective idealism on the basis of Hume's *empirical* argument that anything can produce anything, "Creation, annihilation, motion, reason, volition; all these may arise from one another or from any other object we can imagine," which principle is later repeated by Schopenhauer citing Malebranche. Both are founded on a conception of the radical contingency of nature, namely that anything can spontaneously metamorphose, arise, evolve, erupt, or emanate *sui generis* by turning into its opposite; that quantitative material extensities can spontaneously be transformed into qualitative mental intensities with the obvious result that both matter and mind co-exist. All of which leads us to skeptically ask along with Hume "why a cause is always necessary?" (*Treatise,* 78). Imagine if forthwith all caterpillars died before they turned into butterflies, we would never know what beautiful winged creatures they could have become. Or if after death bones were immediately turned into water, then we would never know dinosaurs had once existed. It's not God Who works in mysterious ways but Nature.

Subjective idealism and existentialism are actually closely related in the sense that the first is dedicated to a self-enclosed paradigm of temporal immanency and a unity of consciousness, while the second is committed to a phenomenological *description* of the human condition as both individualist and free. Together they sum up the nature of human existence. Subjective idealism seriously begins with Descartes and then continues with Leibniz and for the purposes of the present study progresses through Kant, Fichte, Hegel, Schopenhauer, Bergson, Royce, and Husserl, while at the same time promoting the dual principles of reflexive self-consciousness and transcendent intentionality, which together constitute a synthetic *a priori* relation grounding the self as an essentially insular and hermitic substance.

In earlier studies, I began by assuming the fear of loneliness as the most basic concern of humankind. In a manner similar to Kant, who essentially begins by asking how time-consciousness is possible and goes on to delineate its transcendental conditions, I assumed the primary universal force of loneliness in human existence and then sought to show not only how it is possible but indeed that it is inevitable because of the intrinsic nature of human self-consciousness. In the present work, I have reversed that approach, turned it upside down, and instead I have elected to start with consciousness in its most primitive form and go on to conclude with loneliness.

One of the considerations that especially piqued my interest is that during the Epistemological Age, starting with Descartes, relatively little is said about the *dynamics*, the *power* of our human emotions, although admittedly Descartes in the *Passions of the Soul*, Hobbes in the *Leviathan*, Spinoza in the *Ethics*, and Hume in Book II of the *Treatise* all offer fairly thorough *classifications* of the passions as the "springs of human conduct." But the aforementioned philosophers are more concerned with defining, classifying, and cataloguing the emotions in the interests of science as opposed to plumbing downward into their depths, exposing their roots, descending even more deeply and uncovering their strengths, and most importantly their expressions in human actions throughout the wide range of human feelings and thoughts. It was much more of a scientific enterprise designed to serve as a useful catalogue, an instrument for the purpose of discussion and clarity as it focused on separating and delineating the different emotions from each other. Often it seemed no more than a linguistic exercise rather than a serious enterprise aimed at penetrating the actual psychological nature of the human soul, self, mind, or ego. In that regard, Schopenhauer and to a lesser extent Hegel perform a much more credible job in addressing the force of the passions. Currently, the DSM manual serves as the definitional catalogue for both symptoms and personality disorders but refuses to dig deeper into their dynamics.

Thus, it occurred to me that collectively previous thinkers and currently contemporary psychiatric sources have failed to provide for a genuine sense of the underlying powerful dynamics of our emotions and I set out to explore their deeper origins within consciousness and especially their aberrant manifestations and consequences. It is not until the writings of the existentialists that one truly gets a sense of how dominating and forceful the passions can be in human life. The notable exceptions, of course, are Kierkegaard and Nietzsche but their "non-academic" approach made it difficult to understand *why* individuals are so lonely, so angry, and so anxious. To be sure, their constant theme is their *own* loneliness. But their testimony is more personal and descriptive as opposed to illuminating or revelatory in terms of our common human universality, which centers so much on human loneliness. Generally speaking, it is novelists, rather than philosophers and psychologists, who are able to successfully execute the best portrayals of loneliness and its effects, masters like Thomas Hardy, Joseph Conrad, James Joyce, Thomas Wolfe, William Faulkner, and others, and especially those writing in the stream of consciousness style. Basically the narrative style of the novel, whether composed in the first- or third-person, is simply a powerful conflation of the essays of Montaigne and the meditations of Descartes. The novel form only truly begins with works like Murasaki Shikibus' *Tales of Genji,* Cervantes' *Don Quixote,* and Defoe's *Robinson Crusoe* and with all three authors emphasizing human loneliness. Originally, it was the novel that led me to focus on literary writers in my previous study, *Loneliness in Philosophy, Psychology, and Literature.* Following those studies, I came to be convinced that I had not plunged deeply enough into the throes of loneliness and that my chances for a deeper understanding would be enhanced by returning once more to Kant's rich theory of reflexive self-consciousness, and so I recruited Kant again, but most significantly I also sought to understand loneliness by connecting it to Husserl's principle of intentionality and with what I interpreted as his subjective idealism, especially as declared in his *Cartesian Meditations.* Loneliness was the prison; intimacy was the escape. And so I concluded loneliness could not be understood without first considering consciousness itself.

It is to Kant's credit that his *intimation* that there are deeply hidden *subjective*—as opposed to transcendental—levels of consciousness, which can lead us to a speculative path below the surface of consciousness and downward toward a field of subconscious forces. And that this exploration may provide an insight into a fuller comprehension of man's true nature. No sooner was the path trod than it led to a region well below the surface and into the darker regions of the mind—the subconscious. But unfortunately having entered the threshold, Kant turned back believing that any further journey would be highly speculative, hypothetical, and insecurely "psychological" (*Critique,* xvii).

Freud's admiration for the ancient Greek myths, legends, and dramas pointed him to the correct path of descent, but he did not realize the ineradicable and tortuous nature of the subconscious. Although he respected the motivational forces of these powerful passions, he subordinated them to a causal structure. Basically, he sought to neuter them. The force of his libidinal desires was like an electrical charge but it was confined to specific conduits in the mind and he also assumed it could be disconnected, redirected, and safely sublimated. Although a case can be made for an underlying *theoretical* comparison between Fichte's spontaneous will and Schopenhauer's autonomous Will leading to Freud, the differences are much greater than the similarities:

> There is a striking similarity between Schopenhauer's view of the will and Freud's concept of the id. Both Schopenhauer and Freud reacted against the prevailing over-evaluation of reason and intellect in man and saw the real driving force behind his action in the dark depths of the unconscious...Fichte's doctrine that the will is the basic substance of the world, the whole will being differentiated into infinite forms of being. But whereas Fichte looks upon the will as a rational principle Schopenhauer regards it as blind, purposeless, and insatiable, a crying and raging in the darkness.[1]

But the problem with this comparison is that it fails to take into account that for both Fichte and Schopenhauer, consciousness is spontaneous. This is not the case for Freud, who remains essentially a determinist. Furthermore, for Schopenhauer the Will is metaphysical and much wider ranging in its "influence" than anything Freud imagines. It not only indirectly and transcendently "affects" the natural world but also the psychological, emotional, and intellectual sphere of the mind in completely opaque and indeterminate ways. By contrast, in Freud, the Id is primarily instinctual, sexual, aggressive, and readily recognizable by its surface expressions and sublimations. It is basically understood through its common emotional manifestations.

As we saw, Fichte sought to capitalize on Kant's conception of an *epistemic* spontaneity by transforming it into an *ethical* principle very differently from Kant. Fichte endowed it with the actional power of a self-creation of ethical values. The primitive act of spontaneity was credited not only in bringing forth the self but also an accompanying ethical world of other selves with

---

[1] R.K. Gupta, "Freud and Schopenhauer," in *Schopenhauer and his Philosophical Achievement*, edited by Michael Fox (Sussex: Harvester Press, 1980), 226.

which it could interact. However, the task of allowing this spontaneity to be implemented more widely and deeply was left for Schopenhauer to advocate under the penumbra of the irrational Will. Basically, what Schopenhauer did was turn Kant on his head by promoting the Will over Consciousness in a similar manner as Marx turned Hegel on his head by favoring Life over Consciousness. For Schopenhauer, not only do the passions spontaneously assume an initiating dynamic and a primary role in human awareness but indeed affective forces inaugurate and constitute the very first intimations of all human desire and hence existence: "The will to live." While the modern associationist psychologists were concerned with the task of distinguishing separate emotions as if they were lifeless objects viewed under a glass, thereby neglecting humanity's more tumultuous emotional dynamics, Schopenhauer was assiduously plunging onward—or more accurately below—to the darkest forces underlying consciousness. If there is within human consciousness a force that is both simultaneously subjectively hidden and yet outwardly explosive and intentional, it is his irrational Will. This is the justification for coupling spontaneity; subjectivity; passion; and existential freedom together.

In Sartre's essay, "Existentialism Is a Humanism," he explicitly connects subjectivism and existentialism when he states:

> The word subjectivism has two meanings, and our opponents play on the word. Subjectivism means two things. Subjectivism means, on the one hand, that an individual chooses and makes [i.e., spontaneously creates] himself, and, on the other, that it is impossible for man to transcend [his own lonely] subjectivity. The second of these is the essential meaning of existentialism. When we say that man chooses his own self, we mean that everyone of us does likewise but we also mean by that in making his choice he also chooses for all men.

I gather that what Sartre is objecting to is that the opponents of existentialism had criticized it as a species of moral relativism. And I concur that this is a false and misleading imputation. I agree with him "that it is impossible for man to transcend his subjectivity," his loneliness. But his third claim, that when one makes a choice "he chooses for all men" is clearly at odds with his own radical principle of freedom. Nevertheless, I wish to use his definition in order to formulate my own position. What Sartre means in the passage are two things: first that man is radically individualistic; monadic; subjective; he exists absolutely alone, separate from all other beings. In this regard and to this extent, subjective idealism and existentialism are perfectly compatible. Secondly, that he is absolutely free precisely because he exists completely severed from everyone else. He is free because—and only because—he is completely alone. Subjective idealism and existentialism both endorse loneliness and human freedom.

But what Sartre cannot say is "that in making his choice he also chooses for all men." That is simply a contradiction of his own commanding existentialist principle. Kant, of course, can say that when we choose the categorical imperative, we choose for all rational beings in any conceivable universe, but this cannot be true for Sartre. If *I* am condemned to an absolutely subjective freedom in Sartre's strong sense of the meaning, then when I choose my values, I choose for myself alone and not for anyone else let alone for all humanity. Also in the very next moment I can choose anew, so long as I assume moral responsibility for my spontaneous decisions. Clearly for Sartre the emphasis is both on the Cartesian insularity of consciousness—my subjective consciousness is absolutely distinct from yours—as well as a form of Husserlean intentionality. But from the above, it does not follow that man can be in any fashion *metaphysically* related to other men. Accordingly, I have argued in behalf of an image of man as both alone and free, which I believe is perfectly compatible with both *subjective* idealism—as opposed to objective—as well as existentialist themes. More than any other philosophical movement, ancient, modern, or contemporary, existentialism stresses human subjectivity, loneliness, temporality, freedom, and the centrality of a *personal*—as opposed to a universal—moral commitment. But whereas Sartre restricts consciousness to intentionality alone and rejects the Cartesian-Leibnizian-Kantian principle of reflexivity, by contrast, I welcome both as necessary and universal, i.e., synthetic *a priori* constitutive structures of human consciousness.

Beyond that, let me mention a number of other themes I share with existentialists in general. Professor Irving Yalom helpfully alerts us to the four iconic watchwords signaled in a manifesto, which appeared in the fledgling periodical, *Journal of Humanistic Psychology,* as it first announced its publishing debut in 1963.

1. *Man as man supersedes the sum of his parts,* that is, man cannot be understood from a scientific study of part-functions.
2. *Man has his being in a human context* [as opposed to a scientific one], that is, man cannot be understood by ignoring interpersonal experiences. But he is not the sum total of his interpersonal experiences. He stands alone and apart.
3. *Man is self-aware* and cannot be understood by a psychology which fails to recognize man's continuous many-layered self-awarenesses.
4. *Man has choice, i.e., freedom;* he creates the meaning of his own experiences and his values.

And obviously I would repeat that consciousness is both self-conscious and intentional. Further, man is morally responsible for his choices. He can even change the meaning of his own past and its values as long as he is alive (Sartre, *Nausea*). He can at a moment's notice completely re-evaluate the *meaning* of his unique existence for better or for worse (Sartre's *St. Genet*). He can pivot from sinner to saint and back again. Although perhaps God cannot change the past, man can choose its *meaning* for himself alone as long as he exists.[2]

Professor Yalom's study also goes on to offer four centering concerns that essentially define existential thought as they are expressed in the writings of philosophers, novelists, and dramatists. (1) The *meaninglessness* of human existence, its essential absurdity; its radical contingency; and the inexplicable nature of human suffering and death (Sartre, Camus); (2) the extreme sense of anxiety (*angst*) brought on by our absolutely solitary freedom and its consequent personal moral responsibility (Kierkegaard, Nietzsche); the realization that our choices and decisions are untethered either to (a) God's divine commands; (b) an unchanging universal human nature; or (c) the relative and conventional dictates of our surrounding society; that "God is dead" and that we have killed him as Zarathustra announces from his lonely mountain hilltop; that we are each of us alone "condemned to freedom" in Sartre's telling evocative phrase; (3) that the intimate nature of our own impending death defies sharing with others no matter how close they are to us and we to them; that we live and die as we breathe—absolutely alone; and finally (4) the fact of our irredeemable loneliness that permeates each human existence "from the cradle to the grave." This portrait of human existence expresses the ultimate nothingness and utter meaninglessness of human existence; of a world bereft of God with each human being contingently thrown into the cauldron of Being and Nature sans purpose or defining reason to justify her or his own existence, since ultimately we are each of us left all alone to flail in the wind and toss in the sea.

> The concerns of "nothingness" and of self-creation have another deep and unsettling implication: loneliness, as an existential loneliness, which extends far beyond ordinary social loneliness; it is the loneliness of being *separated* not only from people but from the world, as one ordinarily experiences it, as well. The responsibility for the "for-itself" (that is individual consciousness) is overwhelming, since it is to the "for itself" that it happens there is a world.
> 
> YALOM, *EP,* 221, italic mine

---

2 Irvin Yalom, *Existential Psychotherapy* (New York: Basic Books, 1980), 18–19; hereafter cited as Yalom, *EP.*

There is an uncanny and eerie feeling about our own human existence; a disturbing feeling of "why am I here and what am I expected *to be, to do?*"; there is a sense of indefinable vulnerability surrounding the *quality* of our own loneliness; a feeling of being lonely even in a crowd; that we are each of us a stranger in this land of strangers; and above all there is an indeterminate, affective *quality* to our loneliness that is unshareable. In many cases, I am surer of the *meaning* of *your* existence than I am of my own; I have defined "you" as an object but I cannot define my self. Like Sartre's paper-cutter, you are an object to me while I am a mystery to my self. Generally I know what you are going to do but not myself. My mind is abuzz with dizzying possibilities.

> The process of deepest inquiry that Heidegger refers to as "unconcealment" leads us to recognize that we are finite, that we must die, that we are free, and that we cannot escape our freedom. We also learn that the individual is inexorably alone.
> *EP,* 353

This sense of reflexive isolation is metaphysical; it has nothing to do with empirical or scientific causes, psychological determinants, or neuro-physiological brain cells.

> Individuals are often isolated from others and from parts of themselves, but underlying these *separations* is an even more basic isolation that belongs to existence—an isolation that persists despite the most gratifying engagement with other individuals and despite consummate self-knowledge and integration. Existential isolation refers to an unbridgeable gulf between oneself and any other being. It refers, too, to an isolation even more fundamental—a *separation* between the individual and the world.
> *EP,* 355, italics mine

And finally:

> There is of course no solution to irredeemable isolation. It is the essential part of our existence...Communion with others is our major available resource to temper the dread of isolation. We are lonely ships on a dark sea. We see the lights of other ships—ships that we cannot reach but whose presence and similar situation affords us much solace. We are aware of our utter loneliness and helplessness. But if we can break out

of our windowless monad, we become aware of the others who face the same lonely dread.

*EP,* 398

Given this condemning portrait of *spiritual* marooning, is there any conceivable path toward *human* salvation? And hopefully there is. The solution to the problem of monadic solipsism lies in the assurance that human *intimacy* is possible and there is before us a world of other selves beyond our own circumscribed self and the "proof" is found in our affective natures rather than in our intellectual capacities. The following is the only proof possible that although we are all intrinsically alone nevertheless there is *some* psychological *affective* evidence that there are other lonely souls inhabiting our universe with whom we can *meaningfully* connect and interact.

Empathy and intimacy are intrinsically, i.e., synthetically *a priori* connected. The opposite of loneliness is intimacy, a sense of belonging with those to whom we wish to be *intimately* attached and with whom we yearn *to share* a relation of *mutual* trust, *mutual* affection, *mutual* age-appropriate respect, as well as physically sharing a common "lived world" of phenomenal time and space together. The most essential requirement in an *intimate* relationship is trust. As Aristotle declares, the essence of friendship is living intimately together through friendship (*Nicomachean Ethics,* Book VIII). Indeed two of the ten Books of his treatise on ethics are dedicated to the intimate values of shared friendship. This highest and noblest sentiment is also echoed by the Hellenistic Epicureans. It is grounded in the consistency of a constant companionship; in a *positive* co-dependence; in a mutual *participation, a sharing* of feelings, meanings, and values with another self-conscious creature. Friendship accordingly depends on the continual interplay of a *moral* commitment to the other person, a constant loyalty along with positive, successful, and frequent inter-communication. Again a guiding principle is offered by Kant's second formulation of the categorical imperative: "Always treat other selves as ends in themselves possessing infinite worth, dignity, and value and never as a means to your own egoistic or utilitarian ends." Although Kant applies this principle universally to *all* rational beings in the universe, I would restrict it to a select few. His maxim is more demanding than the Golden Rule. Kant's imperative counsels and commands us to place the interests of the other person above our own, even to sacrifice our selves for the sake of the other self. When that directive is shared and instituted by *both* parties in the relationship toward each other, with an abiding *intentional* care and concern for one another, then both will have reached true intimacy. Often this *commitment* is seen in the one-sided investment of a mother's love for her child, but by definition it cannot be reciprocal because of the infant's emotional and cognitive limitations but it nevertheless serves as one-half of the ideal for the fully secure principle for intimacy. Whenever fortune and devotion secures this relation between two (or possibly more individuals) toward each other, then they will have reached intimacy.

Thus the most powerful *positive* affective bond soldering one soul to another is constituted through *empathy*. It is the exact opposite of hatred of the other self, which is signaled by the desire to separate the other self from his existence (Aristotle). Empathy has two powerful virtues: (a) It is the only possible *affective—versus cognitive—*assurance that we possess that effectively assures us that we are not alone; and (b) it serves as the best means in achieving the *feeling* and *meaning* of intimacy.

Theodor Lipps first defines and recruits it as an aesthetic concept, whereas Husserl summons it as a phenomenological meaning. But both fail because they misinterpret it as *one-sided*. Lipps argues that the observer has the ability to "feel into" (*Einfuhlung*) the aesthetic object. In appreciating a beautiful object, the subject projects his or her own feelings and expressions "into" the object, their own emotions of freedom, harmony, pride, enjoyment, proportion, balance, beauty, etc., are projected ecstatically into the contemplated object. In effect, it's a form of intentionality.

> Lipps' version begins by defining the "esthetic object." It consists of "the sensuous appearance," not the bare physical object, but the image as remodeled in the imagination and charged with vital meaning. It is the beautiful thing contemplated, and is therefore to be distinguished from the act of contemplation. Attention is not [reflexively] aware of itself, it is directed outward [projected intentionally] in the object and absorbed therein. Nevertheless, what gives esthetic import to the object, and what constitutes the *ground* of its enjoyment, is this very act of consciousness. The mind unconsciously enlivens the outward form by fusing [Bergson?] into it the modes of its own activity—its striving and willing, its sense of freedom and power, etc. The moods thus transported into the object do not spring from the practical [i.e., moral] ego but only from the ego so far as contemplative. First there is the inner activity, the motion of pride, the feeling of vigor and freedom; second, there is the external sensuous as bare physical stimulus. The esthetic object *spontaneously* springs into existence as a result of the *fusion* of these two factors. The ego unconsciously supposes itself at one with its object and there is no longer any duality. Empathy simply means the disappearance of the twofold consciousness

of self and object. So completely is the self transposed into the object that the contemplator of a statue may unconsciously imitate its posture and movements...In empathy, the mind lends to the object its own spirit and feels at one with it. Empathy involves a transference of vital feelings from the subject into the object.[3]

I have quoted this passage at length because it touches upon so many essential connections that we have explored in the preceding and it is often directly applicable to the innumerable contexts I have discussed throughout the text. My main "objection" to Lipps' conception is that his account is one-sided. The object of the empathic fusion is unidirectional; it is obviously not reciprocated by the aesthetic object. The statue does not in turn mimic the observer. Both intimacy and empathy must occur, transpire between two mutually engaged subjects *with each other*. I am suggesting that *both* parties must be equally, mutually involved and committed in the empathetic relation; both need to be *reciprocally involved in the same emotions and meanings and values*. Indeed, there are frequent experiences in our lives when the empathy *is* mutual and it runs both ways. When this happens, the two selves *feel* as one; the feeling forms or constitutes a dual but indivisible unity of two consciousnesses as one. As Montaigne mused,

> In the friendship I speak of, our souls mingle and blend with each other, so completely that they efface the seam that joined them, and cannot find it again. If you press me to tell you why I loved him, I feel that this cannot be expressed, except by answering: Because it was he, because it was I (*Of Friendship*).[4]

Husserl also picks up on the concept of empathy in his Fifth *Cartesian Meditation,* in his search for a solution to the critical problem of epistemic solipsism, as he struggles to describe the projection of one's own body into the body of another through acts of "emanation," "mirroring," by the *mediacy* of "appresentation" and by "analogical apperception" in an effort to (*eidetically?*) phenomenologically "see" and describe the bodily "pairing" of the self as it empathically places itself in the body of the "other."

---

[3] Theodor Lipps, "Empathy, Inner Imitation, and Sense Feelings," in *A Modern Reader of Esthetics,* edited by Melvin Rader (New York: Holt, Rinehart, and Winston, 1979), 5th edition, 371–377.

[4] Michel de Montaigne, *The Complete Essays of Michel de Montaigne,* translated by Donald Frame (Palo Alto, CA: Stanford University Press, 1968), 139.

> Now in case there presents itself, as outstanding in my primordial sphere, a body "similar" to mine—that is to say a body with determinations such that it must enter into the phenomenal *pairing* with mine—it *seems* clear without more ado, that with the transfer of sense, this body must forthwith appropriate from mine the sense [or meaning]: animate organism.[5]

But this will never do. First of all, both "appresentation" and "analogical apperception" are modes of *mediate* meanings, essences, relations, or judgments and therefore fail the test of being genuine *eidetic intuitions*. And second what is needed in *genuine* empathy is a "meeting of the twin hearts and minds" and not the mediate—virtually inferential—"transposition" of one body (mine) into the imagined (?) body of the "other."

Empathy has to be constituted by an *immediate inseparable duality; a directly shared feeling* and *meaning*. It is a unified passional and cognitive communication between two resonant selves participating in the same feeling/meaning act(s). Empathy has to be grounded in mutual feelings, meanings, reflexions, and intentionalities *and recognized, acknowledged as such* between two (or possibly more) individuals, who are at those moments in time and in temporal succession both self-consciously aware of what each is reflexively feeling, meaning, and intending. It cannot be one-sided; otherwise it is merely sympathy or pity.

Throughout a shared life with another sentient being, empathic interludes and episodes regularly occur and should be constantly acknowledged, communicated, and thoroughly enjoyed, and even celebrated. These empathic couplings, however, can be either joyous or tragic and everything in between. Intimacy has a special unique *quality* that cannot be reduced to quantitative neuronal motions. Perhaps a couple of illustrations may help. Consider a young couple experiencing the sudden tragic death of their only child. Their *shared* mutual grief and sense of permanent, irreplaceable loss is an example of genuine empathy; it is a profound feeling of *one's* own as well as the *other's* sense of irreparable loss as the same, as identical, as a single unity of two consciousnesses. Or imagine an older devoted couple, who have shared a long and loving life together learning that one of them has terminal cancer. That shared consuming anxiety and sorrow is what empathy means. No other animal except a human one can intend, mean, and reflexively share it with another being. That is both our human salvation and our redemption from all the horrors of life. That is the compensation for our human existence.

---

5   Edmund Husserl, *Cartesian Meditations* (The Hague: Martinus Nijhoff, 1973), Meditation v.

The bridge between loneliness and intimacy is either as strong or as weak as the bonds of trust between two souls. One of my favorite authors is Graham Greene. He treats the issues of mistrust and betrayal as the most dangerous impediment to friendship and shared values. But if one digs the foundations of trust deep enough between selves, the structure of the relationship should be sufficiently strong to endure and maintain the alliance indefinitely. Without it, one has built one's hope on a house erected on shifting sands.

The problem of loneliness is closely related to the classic "problem of evil" (*Book of Job,* St. Augustine). When the self is painfully subjected over time to prolonged and/or intensive feelings of loneliness, it lashes out in three rather distinct ways. Either it seeks relief in (a) reflexive thoughts of suicide, dependence on alcohol, street drugs, or prescribed medications; (b) Stoic or existential resignation or acceptance; or (c) intentionally self-destructive and murderous fantasies and acts of violence toward other human beings or the self. In respect to the third dynamic, it has profound and important *moral* implications.

Ethical values can be distinguished into two classes reflecting meaningful principles and criteria. *Relativism*: (a) empirically based and relative to certain societies, customs, and periods; (b) subjectively varying from person to person with both (a) and (b) and therefore (c) resulting in moral skepticism. Both psychoanalysis and the neurosciences fit into this classification. *Absolutism*: universally valid, objectively determinable, and knowable. There are four sets of principles and criteria establishing absolute goodness from evil and they can be further resolved into (a) immediate and (b) mediate relations. *Rationalism*: (1a) intuitionism (Plato, Cudworth); and (1b) rational (Kant). *Empiricism or human nature*: (2a) sentiment (Aristotle, Hume); (2b) utilitarianism (Hume, Bentham, Mill); (3) *Fideism or faith:* (St. Augustine). These are based in universal criteria. By contrast *existentialism* is absolute but the criterion is grounded in the individual; it is not universal but neither is it relative (Sartre). Any of these four principles claim the moral right to judge those who injure and/or destroy others as a response to their own loneliness.[6]

---

6  Ben Mijuskovic, "Ethical Principles, Criteria, and the Meaning of Life," *The Journal of Thought: An Interdisciplinary Journal,* 40:4 (2005), 67–88 and "Virtue Ethics," *Philosophy and Literature,* 31:1 (2007), 133–141.

# By Way of an Epilogue

*Is loneliness conquerable during the finite length of time that is allotted to us? Yes but only if the God of Chance smiles on you. I met my wife in a South Side bar in Chicago on a freezing night in the winter of 1965. We drank heavily for those first four memorable nights, at the same bar, and talked and talked and talked.... On the fourth night, sufficiently drunk, I mustered the courage and asked her if she would marry me and she said "yes." I would have asked her on the first night but I was afraid that she might think I was rushing it. That was more than half a century ago.*

# Bibliography

Aaron, Richard. *John Locke.* Oxford: Clarendon Press, 1955.

Al-Azm, Sadik. *The Origins of Kant's Arguments in the Antinomies.* London: Oxford University Press, 1972.

Alexander, H.G., ed. *The Leibniz-Clarke Correspondence.* Manchester, England: Manchester University Press, 1965; first published by Samuel Clarke himself (1717) and then by Pierre Desmaizeauz (1720).

Alexander, Ian. *Bergson: Philosopher of Reflection.* London: Bowes & Bowes, 1957.

Arendt, Hannah. *The Origins of Totalitarianism.* New York: Harcourt & Brace, 1976; first published in 1948.

Aristotle. *Nicomachean Ethics, The Basic Works of Aristotle,* edited by McKeon, Richard New York; Random House 1941.

Armstrong, David Malet. *A Materialist Theory of Mind.* London: Routledge & Kegan Paul, 1968.

Augustine. *The Confessions of St. Augustine.* New York: Doubleday, 1960.

Ayer, Alfred Jules. *Language, Truth and Logic.* New York: Dover, 1936.

Barrett, William. *Irrational Man: A Study in Existential Philosophy.* New York: Random House, 1990.

Beck, Lewis White. *A Commentary to Kant's Critique of Practical Reason.* Chicago: University of Chicago Press, 1960.

Berger, Gaston. *The Cogito in Husserl's Philosophy.* Evanston, IL: Northwestern University Press, 1972.

Bergson, Henri. *Essai sur les données immédiates de la conscience.* Paris, 1889.

Bergson, Henri. *Creative Evolution.* New York: Holt, 1928.

Bergson, Henri. *An Introduction to Metaphysics.* Translated by T.E. Hulme. Indianapolis: Bobbs Merrill, 1955.

Bergson, Henri. *Time and Free Will: An Essay on the Immediate Data of Consciousness.* Translated by F.L. Pogson. New York: Harper & Row, 1960.

Bergson, Henri. *Matter and Memory.* London: George Allen & Unwin, 1970.

Bergson, Henri. *A Study in Metaphysics: The Creative Mind.* Translated by Mabelle Andison. Totowa, NJ: Littlefield Adams, 1970.

Bermudez, J.L. "Locke, Metaphysical Dualism and Property Dualism." *British Journal for the History of Philosophy* 4, no. (1996), 223–245.

Berthold-Bond, Daniel. *Hegel's Theory of Madness.* Albany, NY: State of New York Press, 1995.

Bjelland, Andrew. "Bergson's Dualism in *Time and Free Will.*" *Process Studies* 4, no. 2 (1974): 83–106.

Blanshard, Brand. *The Nature of Thought.* George Allen & Unwin, 1969.

Block, Ned, Owen Flanagan, and Guven Guzeldere, eds. *The Nature of Consciousness: Philosophical Debates.* Cambridge, MA: MIT Press, 2007.

Boas, George. *The History of Ideas.* New York: Charles Scriber's Sons, 1969, 3–23.

Brentano, Franz. *Psychologie vom empirischen Standpunkt.* Leipzig: Verlag von Duncker & Humboldt, 1874.

Broad, C.D. *The Mind and Its Place in Nature.* London: Routledge & Kegan Paul, 1925.

Brook, Andrew. "Freud and Kant." In *Psychoanalytic Knowledge,* edited by M. Cheung and Colin Feltman, 20–39. London: Palgrave Press, 2002.

Camus, Albert. *The Plague.* New York: Alfred Knopf, 1948.

Catalano, J. *A Commentary on Jean-Paul Sartre's Being and Nothingness.* New York: Harper & Row, 1974.

Chomsky, Noam. *New Horizons in the Study of Mind and Language,* Cambridge, MA: MIT Press, 2000.

Chomsky, Noam. *Chomsky Notebooks.* New York: Columbia University Press, 2007.

Chomsky, Noam. "The Mysteries of Nature: How Well Hidden?" *The Journal of Philosophy* 106, no. 4 (2009): 167–200.

Chomsky, Noam. "What Kind of Creatures Are We?" New York: Columbia University Press, 2013.

Copleston, Fredrick. *Arthur Schopenhauer: Philosopher of Pessimism.* Oxon, England: Heythrop College, 1947.

Cornford, Francis Macdonald. *Plato's Theory of Knowledge.* London: Routledge & Kegan Paul, 1964.

Cousin, Victor. *Introduction to the History of Philosophy.* Boston: Hilliard, Gray, Little, 1832.

Cudworth, Ralph. *The True Intellectual System of the Universe.* Stuttgart-Bad Cannstatt, 1964.

Cudworth, Ralph. *A Treatise Concerning Eternal and Immutable Morality.* Cambridge: Cambridge University Press, 1996.

Cummins, Phillip. "Hume as Dualist and Anti-Dualist." *Hume Studies* 21, no. 1 (1995), 47–56.

DeGregory, Lane. "The Girl in the Window." *Tampa Bay Times*, August 3, 2008. http://www.tampabay.com/projects/girl-in-the-window/danielle.

Desan, Wilfrid. *The Tragic Finale.* New York: Harper Torchbook, 1960.

Descartes, Rene. *Philosophical Works of Descartes.* Edited by E. Haldane and G.R.T. Ross. New York: Dover, 1931, 1967.

Dewey, John. *John Dewey: The Middle Works, 1899–1924.* Edited by Jo Ann Boydston. Carbondale, IL: Southern Illinois University Press, 2008.

Einstein, Albert. "Physik und Realitat." *Journal of the Franklin Institute,* 331 (March 1936), 313–347.

Ellenberger, Henri. *The Discovery of the Unconscious: The History and Evolution of Dynamic Psychiatry*. New York: Basic Books, 1970.

Emerson, Ralph Waldo. *The Complete Works of Ralph Waldo Emerson*. Edited by E.W. Emerson, 12 vols. Boston: Houghton Mifflin, 1903–1904.

Emerson, Ralph Waldo. *The Letters of Ralph Waldo Emerson*. Edited by R.L. Rusk. New York: Columbia University Press, 1939.

Emerson, Ralph Waldo. *The Early Lectures of Ralph Waldo Emerson, 1833–1836*. Cambridge, MA: Harvard, 1959.

Emerson, Ralph Waldo. *The Journals of Ralph Waldo Emerson, 1819–1822*. Cambridge, MA: Belknap, 1960.

Ewing, A.C. *A Short Commentary on Kant's Critique of Pure Reason*. Chicago: University of Chicago Press, 1967.

Ewing, A.C. *Idealism: A Critical Survey*. Boston, MA: Methuen, 1974, 68.

Feyerabend, Paul. "Wittgenstein's *Philosophical Investigations*." Reprinted in *The Philosophical Investigations*, edited by George Pitcher, 112–128. New York: Doubleday, 1966.

Fichte, Johann Gottlieb. *The Vocation of Man*. La Salle, IL: Open Court, 1955.

Fichte, Johann Gottlieb. *Science of Knowledge*. New York: Appleton-Century-Crofts, 1970.

Ford, Lewis E. "Boethius and Whitehead on Time and Eternity." *Philosophical Quarterly* 7, no. 1 (1968): 39–53.

Ford, Lewis E. "Boethius and Whitehead on Time and Eternity." *Philosophical Quarterly* 8, no. 1 (1968): 39–42, 49–53.

Forster, Michael. *Hegel's Idea of a Phenomenology of Spirit*. Chicago: University of Chicago Press 1998.

Freud, Sigmund. *Civilization and Its Discontents*. New York: W.W. Norton, 1961.

Fromm, Erich. *The Art of Loving*. New York: Harper & Row, 1970.

Fromm-Reichmann, Frieda. "Loneliness." *Psychiatry: A Journal for the Study of Interpersonal Processes* 22, no. 1 (1959): 1–15.

Gallagher, Kenneth. "Kant on the Synthetic A Priori." *Kant-Studien* 63, no. 3 (1972): 341–342.

Gibson, John. *Locke's Theory of Knowledge and Its Historical Relations*. Cambridge: Cambridge University Press, 1968.

Gilson, Etienne. *History of Christian Philosophy in the Middle Ages*. New York: Random House, 1955.

Gomez, A.M. "Descartes on the Intellectual Nature of Human Perception: From the Innermost Self to the Material World." *Análisis. Revista de investigación filosófica* 2, no. 3 (2015), 163–193.

Gough, J.W. *The Social Contract: A Critical Study of Its Development*. Oxford: Clarendon Press, 1957.

Green, T.H. *Prolegomena to Ethics*. 5th ed. Oxford: Clarendon Press, 1906.

# BIBLIOGRAPHY

Grene, Marjorie. *Sartre.* New York: New Viewpoints, 1973.
Gross, David. Review of George Boas' "The History of Ideas." *Telos* 6 (1970): 211–212.
Gupta, R.K. "Freud and Schopenhauer." In *Schopenhauer: His Achievement,* edited by Michael Fox, 226–235. Sussex, England: Harvester Press, 1980.
Gupta, R.K. *Schopenhauer and His Philosophical Achievement.* Edited by Michael Fox. Sussex: Harvester Press, 1980.
Hamlin, D.M. "Schopenhauer: On the Principle of Sufficient Reason.", in *Schopenhauer: His Achievement,* edited by Michael Fox, 79–80, 85–86, 92–93. Sussex, England: Harvester Press, 1980.
Hegel, G.W.F. *Science of Logic.* Translated by W.H. Johnston and L.G. Struthers. London: George Allen & Unwin, 1951.
Hegel, G.W.F. *The Philosophy of History.* Translated by J. Sibree. New York: Dover, 1956.
Hegel, G.W.F. *The Logic of Hegel: The Encyclopedia of the Philosophical Sciences.* Translated by William Wallace. Oxford: Oxford University Press, 1959.
Hegel, G.W.F. *Lectures on the History of Philosophy.* Translated by E.S. Haldane and F.H. Simson. London: Routledge & Kegan Paul, 1968.
Hegel, G.W.F. *The Philosophy of Right.* Translated by T.M. Knox. London: Oxford University Press, 1969.
Hegel, G.W.F. *Hegel's Philosophy of Mind: Being Part Three of the Encyclopaedia of the Philosophical Sciences,* translated by William Wallace and the *Zusatz* by A.V. Miller and Introduction by J.N. Findlay. Oxford: Clarendon Press, 1971.
Hegel, G.W.F. *Phenomenology of Spirit.* Translated by A.V. Miller. Oxford: Oxford University Press, 1977.
Heidegger, Martin. *An Introduction to Metaphysics.* Translated by Ralph Manheim. New Haven, CT: Yale University Press, 1959.
Heinamaa, Sara, Vili Lahteenmaki, and Paulina Remes, eds. *Consciousness: From Perception to Reflection in the History of Philosophy.* New York: Springer, 2007.
Holman, C. Hugh. *The Loneliness at the Core: Studies in Thomas Wolfe.* Baton Rouge, LA: Louisiana State University Press, 1975.
Hopkins, Burt. *The Philosophy of Husserl.* Montreal: McGill-Queens University Press, 2010.
Hospers, John. "The Range of Human Freedom." In *Problems of Moral Philosophy,* edited by Paul Taylor, 317–329. Belmont, CA: Wadsworth, 1978.
Howard, James. *The Flesh-Colored Cage: The Impact of Man's Essential Aloneness on His Attitudes and Behaviors.* New York: Hawthorn Books, 1975.
Hume, David. *An Enquiry Concerning Human Understanding.* Oxford: Clarendon Press, 1972.
Hume, David. *A Treatise of Human Nature.* Oxford: Clarendon Press, 1955, 1973.
Husserl, Edmund. *Ideas: General Introduction to Phenomenology.* Translated by W.R. Boyce Gibson. New York: Collier Books, 1962.

Husserl, Edmund. *The Idea of Phenomenology.* Translated by George Nakhinian. The Hague: Martinus Nijhoff, 1964.

Husserl, Edmund. *The Paris Lectures.* Translated by Peter Koestenbaum. The Hague: Martinus Nijhoff, 1964.

Husserl, Edmund. "Philosophy and the Crisis of European Man." in *Phenomenology and the Crisis of Philosophy.* New York: Harper Torchbook, 1965, 149–192.

Husserl, Edmund. *The Phenomenology of Internal Time-Consciousness.* Bloomington, IN: Indiana University Press, 1966.

Husserl, Edmund. *Formal and Transcendental Logic.* Translated by Dorion Cairns. The Hague: Martinus Nijhoff, 1969.

Husserl, Edmund. *The Crisis of European Sciences and Transcendental Phenomenology: An Introduction to Phenomenological Philosophy.* Translated by David Carr. Evanston, IL: Northwestern University Press, 1970.

Husserl, Edmund. *Cartesian Meditations.* The Hague: Martinus Nijhoff, 1973.

Husserl, Edmund. *Experience and Judgment: Investigations in the Genealogy of Logic.* Translated by James Churchill and Karl Ameriks. Evanston, IL: Northwestern University Press, 1973.

Hyppolite, Jean. *Genesis and Structure of Hegel's Phenomenology of Spirit.* Evanston: IL: Northwestern University Press, 1974.

Inge, William. *The Philosophy of Plotinus.* New York Greenwood Press, 1968.

James, William. *Principles of Psychology.* New York: Dover, 1950.

Jaynes, Julius. *The Origins of Consciousness in the Breakdown of the Bicameral Mind.* Boston: Houghton-Mifflin, 1990.

Joad, C.E.M. *How Our Minds Work.* London: Westhouse, 1946.

Kant, Immanuel. *Critique of Judgment.* Translated by J.H. Bernard, New York: Hafner Publishing, 1951.

Kant, Immanuel. *Critique of Pure Reason.* Translated by Norman Kemp Smith. London: Macmillan & Co., 1962.

Kant, Immanuel. *Observations on the Feeling of the Beautiful and Sublime and Other Writings.* Cambridge: Cambridge University Press, 2011.

Keeling, S.V. *Descartes.* Oxford: Oxford University Press, 1968.

Klein, Jacob. *A Commentary on Plato's Meno.* Chapel Hill, NC: University of North Carolina Press, 1965.

Kockelmanns, Joseph. *Edmund Husserl's Phenomenological Psychology.* Pittsburgh: Duquesne University Press, 1967.

Kojeve, Alexandre. *Introduction to the Reading of Hegel.* New York: Basic Books, 1969.

Koyre, Alexandre. *From the Closed World to the Infinite Universe.* Baltimore: Johns Hopkins University Press, 1968.

Laing, B.M. *David Hume.* New York: Russell and Russell, 1968.

Laird, John. *Hume's Philosophy of Human Nature.* New York: Methuen, 1967.

Lauer, Quentin. *Phenomenology: Its Genesis and Prospects.* New York: Harper Torchbook, 1965.

Leclerc, Ivor. *The Philosophy of Nature.* New York: Humanities, 1971.

Leibniz, Gottfried Wilhelm. *The Monadology and Other Philosophic Writings.* Translated and with an Introduction by Robert Latta. Oxford: Oxford University Press, 1968.

Leibniz, Gottfried Wilhelm. "The Principles of Nature and Grace." In *Philosophical Essays*, edited by Roger Ariew and David Garber. Cambridge: Hachette Publishers, 1989.

Lennon, Thomas, and Edward Stainton, eds. *The Achilles of Rationalist Psychology.* New York: Springer, 2008.

Levinas, Emmanuel. *The Theory of Intuition in Husserl's Phenomenology.* Evanston, IL: Northwestern University Press, 1973.

Lewis, H.D. *The Elusive Mind.* London: George Allen & Unwin, 1969.

Lewis, Wyndham. *Time and Western Man* Boston: Beacon Hill, 1957.

Lipps, Theodor. "Empathy, Inner Imitation, and Sense Feelings." In *A Modern Reader of Esthetics*, 5th ed., edited by Melvin Rader, 371–377. New York: Holt, Rinehart, and Winston, 1979.

Locke, John. *An Essay Concerning Human Understanding.* Edited by John Yolton, New York: Dutton, 1967.

Loewenberg, Jacob. *Hegel's Phenomenology: Dialogues on the Life of Mind.* La Salle, IL: Open Court, 1965.

Lovejoy, A.O. *Essays Philosophical and Psychological in Honor of William James by His Colleagues at Columbia University.* Edited by "His Colleagues at Columbia University." New York: Longmans, Green, 1909.

Lovejoy, A.O. *The Great Chain of Being: A Study of the History of an Idea.* New York: Harper & Row, 1953.

Lovejoy, A.O. *The Reason, the Understanding and Time.* Baltimore: Johns Hopkins University Press, 1961.

Lukács, Georg. "The Bourgeois Irrationalism of Schopenhauer's Metaphysics." In *Schopenhauer: His Philosophical Achievement,* edited by Michael Fox. Sussex: Harvester Press, 1980.

Lynch, James. *The Broken Heart: The Medical Consequences of Loneliness.* New York: Basic Books, 1977.

Lynch, James. *A Cry Unheard: New Insights into the Medical Consequences of Loneliness.* Baltimore: Bancroft Books, 2000.

Mackie, J.L. *Problems from Locke.* Oxford: Clarendon Press, 1976.

Mahler, Margaret, Fred Pine, and Anni Bergman, eds. *The Psychological Birth of the Human Infant.* New York: Basic Books, 1975.

Malebranche, Nicolas. *De la Recherche de la verité*, 1674–1675.

Mandelbaum, Maurice. *The Phenomenology of Moral Experience.* Baltimore: Johns Hopkins University, 1969.
Martin, Raymond and John Barresi. *The Rise and Fall of Soul and Self: An Intellectual History of Personal Identity.* New York: Columbia University Press, 1995.
Martinich, A.P. *A Hobbes Dictionary.* Cambridge, MA: Blackwell, 1995.
Martinich, A.P. *Hobbes: A Biography.* Cambridge: Cambridge University Press, 1999.
McTaggart, Ellis. "Hegel's Treatment of the Categories of the Mind." *Mind* 11, no. 44 (1902): 503–526.
McTaggart, John and Ellis McTaggart. *A Commentary on Hegel's Logic.* New York: Russell and Russell, 1964.
Mijuskovic, Ben. "A Reinterpretation of Being in Hegel's *Science of Logic*." *Telos* 6 (1970): 286–294.
Mijuskovic, Ben. "The Synthetic *A Priori* in Plato." *Dialogue* 12, no. 1 (1970): 13–23.
Mijuskovic, Ben. "Descartes's Bridge to the External World: The Piece of Wax," *Studi Internazionali di Filosofia* 3, no. 3 (1971): 65–81; reprinted in *Rene Descartes: Critical Assessments,* edited by Georges Moyal, II, 312–328. London: Routledge, 1996.
Mijuskovic, Ben. "Hume and Shaftesbury on the Self." *The Philosophical Quarterly* 21, no. 85 (1971): 324–336.
Mijuskovic, Ben. "The Premise of Kant's Transcendental Analytic." *The Philosophical Quarterly* 23, no. 91 (1973): 155–161.
Mijuskovic, Ben. "Spinoza's Version of the Ontological Argument." *Sophia* 12, no. 1 (1973): 16–24.
Mijuskovic, Ben. *The Achilles of Rationalist Arguments: The Simplicity, Unity and Identity of Thought and Soul from the Cambridge Platonists to Kant: A Study in the History of an Argument.* The Hague: Martinus Nijhoff, 1974.
Mijuskovic, Ben. "The General Structure of Kant's Argument in the Analytic." *The Southern Journal of Philosophy* 12, no. 3 (1974), 357–365.
Mijuskovic, Ben. "Marx and Engels on Materialism and Idealism." *Journal of Thought* 9, no. 3 (1974): 157–168.
Mijuskovic, Ben. "Locke and Leibniz on Personal Identity." *Southern Journal of Philosophy* 13, no. 2 (1975), 205–214.
Mijuskovic, Ben. "The Simplicity Argument and Absolute Morality." *Journal of Thought* 10, no. 2 (1975): 123–135.
Mijuskovic, Ben. "The Problem of Evil in Camus's *The Plague*." *Sophia* 15, no. 1 (1976): 11–19.
Mijuskovic, Ben. "The Simplicity Argument and Meaning in Wittgenstein and Russell." *Critica* 8, no. 4 (1976): 85–103.
Mijuskovic, Ben. "The Simplicity Argument versus a Materialist Theory of Mind." *Philosophy Today* 20, no. 4 (1976): 292–306.

Mijuskovic, Ben. "Hume on Space (and Time)." *Journal of the History of Philosophy* 15, no. 4 (1977): 387–394; reprinted in *David Hume: Critical Assessments,* edited by Stanley Tweyman, 167–175. London: Routledge & Kegan Paul, 1994. 167–175.

Mijuskovic, Ben. "Loneliness: An Interdisciplinary Approach." *Psychiatry: A Journal for Interpersonal Processes* 40, no. 2 (1977): 213–232; reprinted in *The Anatomy of Loneliness,* edited by Joseph Hartog, Ralph Audi, and Yehudi Cohen, 65–94. New York: International Universities Press, 1980.

Mijuskovic, Ben. "Loneliness and a Theory of Consciousness." *Review of Existential Psychiatry and Psychology* 16, no. 1 (1977): 19–31; reprinted in *Counseling and Therapy,* edited by E. Cohen and S.W. Zinaich. Newcastle-upon-Tyne: Cambridge Scholars Press, 2013.

Mijuskovic, Ben. "Loneliness and the Reflexivity of Consciousness." *Psychocultural Review* 1, no. 2 (1977): 202–215.

Mijuskovic, Ben. "The Simplicity Argument and Time in Schopenhauer and Bergson." *Schopenhauer Jahrbuch* 58, (1977): 43–58.

Mijuskovic, Ben. "Brentano's Theory of Consciousness." *Philosophy and Phenomenological Research* 38, no. 3 (1978): 315–325.

Mijuskovic, Ben. "Loneliness and the Possibility of a 'Private Language.'" *Journal of Thought* 13, no. 1 (1978): 14–22.

Mijuskovic, Ben. "Loneliness and Time-Consciousness." *Philosophy Today* 22, no. 4 (1978): 276–286.

Mijuskovic, Ben. "The Simplicity Argument and the Freedom of Self-Consciousness." *Idealistic Studies* 8, no. 1 (1978): 62–74.

Mijuskovic, Ben. "Loneliness and Narcissism." *Psychoanalytic Review* 66, no. 4 (1979–80): 479–492.

Mijuskovic, Ben. "Loneliness and Personal Identity." *Psychology: A Journal of Human Behavior* 16, no. 3 (1979): 11–20.

Mijuskovic, Ben. "Loneliness and Communication." In *Man and His Conduct,* edited by Jorge Gracia, 250–260. Rio Piedras, PR: University of Puerto Rico Press, 1980.

Mijuskovic, Ben. "Loneliness and Suicide." *Journal of Social Philosophy* 9 no. 1 (1980), 11–18; reprinted in *Geriatrics and Thanatology,* edited by Elizabeth Pritchard. Santa Barbara, CA: Praeger, 1984.

Mijuskovic, Ben. "Loneliness and Human Nature." *Psychological Perspectives: A Review of Jungian Thought* 12, no. 1 (1981): 69–78.

Mijuskovic, Ben. "Loneliness and Hostility." *Psychology: A Journal of Human Behavior* 20, no. 3–4 (1983): 9–19.

Mijuskovic, Ben. *Contingent Immaterialism: Meaning, Freedom, Time, and Mind.* Amsterdam: Gruner, 1984.

Mijuskovic, Ben. "Loneliness and Adolescence." *Adolescence* 21, no. 84 (1986): 941–951.

Mijuskovic, Ben. "Loneliness, Anxiety, Hostility, and Communication." *Child Study Journal* 16, no. 3 (1986): 227–240.

Mijuskovic, Ben. "Loneliness and Sexual Dysfunctions." *Psychology: A Journal of Human Behavior* 24, no. 4 (1987): 15–22.

Mijuskovic, Ben. "Loneliness and Adolescent Alcoholism." *Adolescence* 23, no. 92 (1988): 503–516.

Mijuskovic, Ben. "Reflexivity and Intentionality: The Self-Contained Patient." *The Psychotherapy Patient* 4, no. 3/4 (1988): 39–50.

Mijuskovic, Ben. "Child Abuse, Neglect, and Dependent Personalities." *Psychology: A Journal of Human Behavior* 25, no. 3 (1990) 1–10.

Mijuskovic, Ben. "Loneliness and Intimacy." *Journal of Couples Therapy* 1, no. 3–4 (1991): 39–48; reprinted in *Intimate Autonomy: Autonomous Intimacy,* edited by Barbara Jo Brothers. Santa Barbara, CA: Praeger, 1992, 39–48.

Mijuskovic, Ben. "Loneliness and Intimacy." *Journal of Couples Therapy* 1, no. 3–4 (1991): 39–49; reprinted in *Intimate Autonomy: Autonomous Intimacy,* edited by Barbara Jo Brothers. Philadelphia, PA: Haworth Press, 1991, 39–49.

Mijuskovic, Ben. "Organic Communities, Atomistic Societies, and Loneliness." *Journal of Sociology and Social Welfare* 19, no. 2 (1992): 147–163.

Mijuskovic, Ben. "The Phenomenology and Dynamics of Loneliness." *Psychology: A Journal of Human Behavior* 33, no. 2 (1996): 41–51.

Mijuskovic, Ben. "Ethical Principles, Criteria, and the Meaning of Life." *The Journal of Thought: An Interdisciplinary Journal* 40, no. 4 (2005): 67–88.

Mijuskovic, Ben. "Virtue Ethics." *Philosophy and Literature* 31, no. 1 (2007): 133–141.

Mijuskovic, Ben. "The Simplicity Argument and the Unconscious: Plotinus, Cudworth, Leibniz, and Kant." *Philosophy and Theology* 20, no. 1–2 (2008–09): 53–83.

Mijuskovic, Ben. "The Argument from Simplicity: A Study in the History of an Idea and Consciousness." *Philotheos* 9 (2009): 228–252.

Mijuskovic, Ben. "The Simplicity Argument: A Study in the History of an Argument," *Philotheos,* 9 (2009): 228–252.

Mijuskovic, Ben. "Kant's Reflections on the Unity of Consciousness, Time-Consciousness, and the Unconscious." *Kritike* 4, no. 2 (2010), 105–132.

Mijuskovic, Ben. *Loneliness in Philosophy, Psychology, and Literature.* 3rd edition. Bloomington, IN: iUniverse, 2012; originally published in 1979 by Van Gorcum.

Mijuskovic, Ben. "Loneliness, Self-Consciousness, and PTSD." *Psychology Journal* 11, no. 1 (2014): 44–54.

Mijuskovic, Ben. "Cognitive and Motivational Roots of Loneliness." In *Addressing Loneliness: Coping, Prevention, and Clinical Interventions,* edited by Ami Sha'ked and Ami Rokach, 20–34. New York: Routledge, 2015.

Mijuskovic, Ben. *Feeling Lonesome: The Philosophy and Psychology of Loneliness.* Santa Barbara, CA: Praeger, 2015.

Mills, Jon. *The Unconscious Abyss: Hegel's Anticipation of Psychoanalysis.* Albany, New York: State of New York Press, 2002.

Mills, Jon. *Underworlds: Philosophies of the Unconscious from Psychoanalysis to Metaphysics.* London and New York: Routledge, 2014.

Mohanty, J.N. *Edmund Husserl's Theory of Meaning.* The Hague: Martinus Nijhoff, 1969.

Montaigne, Michel de. *The Complete Essays of Michel de Montaigne,* translated by Donald Frame. Palo Alto, CA: Stanford University Press, 1968.

Moore, G.E. "The Refutation of Idealism." In *Philosophy of the Twentieth-Century*, edited by William Barrett and Henry Aiken, 543–560. New York: Random House, 1962.

Mure, G.R.G. *A Study of Hegel's Logic.* London: Oxford University Press, 1950.

Nettleship, Robert L. *Lectures on the Republic of Plato.* New York: St. Martin's, 1967.

Novakovic, Andrea, "Hegel's Anthropology." In *The Oxford Handbook of Hegel,* edited by Dean Moyar, Chapter 18. Oxford: Oxford University Press, 2017.

Odegard, Douglas. "Locke and Mind-Body Dualism." *Philosophy* 45, no. 172 (1970): 87–105.

Paton, H.J. *Kant's Metaphysic of Experience: A Commentary on the First Half of the 'Kritik der reinen Vernunft'.* London: George Allen & Unwin, 1965.

Peirce, C.S. "How to Make Our Ideas Clear." In *Essays in the Philosophy of Science,* edited by Vincent Tomas, New York: Liberal Arts Press, 1957.

Peursen, C.A. van *Leibniz: A Guide to his Philosophy.* New York: Dutton, 1970.

Pippin, Robert. "Kant on the Spontaneity of the Mind." *Canadian Journal of Philosophy* 17, no. 2 (1987): 449–475.

Plato, *Sophist, Plato's Theory of Knowledge: The Theaetetus and the Sophist,* translated with a running commentary by F.M. Cornford. London: Routledge & Kegan Paul, 1964.

Plato, *Phaedo.* In *The Collected Dialogues,* edited by Edith Hamilton and Huntington Cairns. New York: Pantheon Books, 1966.

Plato. *The Republic of Plato.* Translated with an Introduction and running commentary by F.M. Cornford. London: Oxford University Press, 1968.

Plotinus. *The Enneads,.* Translated by Stephen MacKenna New York: Pantheon, 1969.

Popkin, Richard. *The History of Scepticism: From Erasmus to Descartes.* New York: Harper & Row, 1964.

Ricoeur, Paul. "Kant and Husserl." *Philosophy Today* 10, no. 3 (1966): 147–168.

Ricoeur, Paul. *Husserl: An Analysis of His Phenomenology.* Translated by G.E. Ballard. Evanston, IL: Northwestern University Press, 1967.

Ridgeway, James. "Mass Psychosis in the US: How Big Pharma Got Americans Hooked on Anti-Psychotics." *Al Jazeera.* July 12, 2011. https://www.aljazeera.com/indepth/opinion/2011/07/20117313948379987.html.

Riesman, David, Reuel Denney, and Nathan Glazer. *The Lonely Crowd.* New Haven: Yale University Press, 1989.

Robinet, Andre. *Bergson et les métamorphose de la durée.* Paris: Seghers, 1965.

Rockmore, Tom. *Kant and Idealism.* New Haven, CT: Yale University Press, 2007.

Rohlf, M. "Immanuel Kant." *Stanford Encyclopedia of Philosophy.* (2010). https://plato.stanford.edu/entries/kant.

Royce, Josiah. *The World as Will and Individual.* New York: Dover, 1959.

Ruch, Floyd R. *Psychology and Life.* Edited by Floyd R. Ruch. Chicago: Scott, Foresman, 1953.

Russell, Bertrand. *A Critical Exposition of the Philosophy of Leibniz.* London: George Allen & Unwin, 1958.

Rutherford, Donald. "Laws and Power on Leibniz." In *God, Man and the Order of Nature: Historical Perspectives,* edited by Eric Watkins. Oxford University Press, forthcoming.

Ryle, Gilbert. *Concept of the Mind.* Barnes & Noble, 1949.

Salter, Mary D. "Object Relations, Dependency, and Attachment: A Theoretical Review of the Infant-Mother Relationship." *Child Development* 40, no. 4 (1969): 969–1025.

Sartre, Jean-Paul. *The Age of Reason,* translated by E. Sutton. St. James Ward, England: Hamilton/Penguin Publishers, 1947.

Sartre, Jean-Paul. *The Flies.* Translated by Stuart Gilbert. New York: Alfred Knopf, 1947.

Sartre, Jean-Paul. *The Transcendence of the Ego: An Existentialist Theory of Consciousness.* Translated by Forrest Williams and Robert Kirkpatrick. New York: Noonday, 1962.

Sartre, Jean-Paul. *Being and Nothingness: An Essay on Phenomenological Ontology.* Translated by Hazel Barnes. New York: Washington Square Press, 1966.

Scheler, Max. *Formalism in Ethics and Non-Formal Ethics of Values.* Evanston, IL: Northwestern University Press, 1973.

Schopenhauer, Arthur. *Essays on the Freedom of the Will.* Translated by K. Kolenda. Indianapolis, IN: Bobbs-Merrill, 1960.

Schopenhauer, Arthur. *The World as Will and Representation.* Translated by E.F.J. Payne. New York: Dover, 1969.

Skinner, B.F. *Walden Two.* Cambridge: Hackett Publishing, 1976.

Smith, David Woodruff. *Husserl.* New York: Routledge, 2013.

Smith, John. *Select Discourses.* by Oxford: Oxford University Press, 1979.

Smith, Norman Kemp. *A Commentary to Kant's 'Critique of Pure Reason'.* New York: Humanities Press, 1962.

Smith, Norman Kemp. *New Studies in the Philosophy of Descartes.* New York: Russell & Russell, 1963.

Smith, Norman Kemp. *The Philosophy of David Hume.* London: Macmillan & Co., 1964.

Sokolowski, Robert. *The Formation of Husserl's Concept of Constitution.* The Hague: Martinus Nijhoff. 1970.

Sokolowski, Robert. *Husserlian Meditations.* Evanston, IL: Northwestern University Press, 1974.

Sorley, W.R. *A History of British Philosophy to 1900.* Cambridge: Cambridge University Press, 1965.

Spiegelberg, Herbert. *The Phenomenological Movement.* The Hague: Martinus Nijhoff, 1965.

Stace, W.T. *The Philosophy of Hegel.* New York: Dover, 1955.

Tallis, Raymond. "Neurotrash." *New Humanist* 124, no. 6 (2009). https://newhumanist.org.uk/articles/2172/neurotrash. n.p.

Tallis, Raymond. *Aping Mankind: Neuromania, Darwinitis, and the Misrepresentation of Humanity.* London: Routledge, 2011.

Tallis, Raymond. "A Mind of One's Own: The Metaphysical Limitations of Neuroscience." *New Statesman,* February 24, 2011.

Thompson, Josiah. *The Lonely Labyrinth: Kierkegaard's Pseudonymous Works.* Carbondale, IL: Southern Illinois University Press, 1967.

Todd, Dennis. *Imagining Monsters: Miscreations of the Self in Eighteenth-Century England.* Chicago: University of Chicago Press, 1995.

Vander Veer, G.L. *Bradley's Metaphysics and the Self.* New Haven: Yale, 1970.

Welsh, E. Parl. *The Philosophy of Edmond Husserl.* New York: Octagon Press, 1965.

Whitehead, Alfred North. *Science and the Modern World.* New York: Macmillan, 1926.

Whybrow, Peter. "After Freud, What Do Neuroscience Advances Have to Tell about Human Nature?" Paper presented at the Mount Perlin Society Annual Meeting in Sydney, Australia (2010). https://elbertcounty.net/blog/wp-content/uploads/2010/11/after-freud-what-do-neuroscience-advances-tell-us-about-human-nature-dr-peter-whybrow.pdf.

Williams, Heather Andrew. "How Slavery Affected African American Families." National Humanities Center. http://nationalhumanitiescenter.org/tserve/freedom/1609-1865/essays/aafamilies.htm.

Wolfe, Charles T. "Elements for a Materialist Theory of the Self." HAL ID 01238149, December 4, 2015.

Wolfe, Thomas. *Look Homeward, Angel.* New York: Scribners, 1957.

Wolfe, Thomas. *Of Time and the River.* New York: Schusters, 1963.

Wolfe, Thomas. *You Can't Go Home Again.* New York: Simon & Schuster, 1968.

Wolff, Robert Paul. "Hume's Theory of Mental Activity." *The Philosophical Review* 69, no. 3 (1960): 289–310.

Wolff, Robert Paul. *Kant's Theory of Mental Activity; A Commentary on the Transcendental Analytic of the Critique of Pure Reason.* Cambridge, MA: Harvard University Press, 1963.

Wolfson, Harry Austryn. *The Philosophy of Spinoza.* Cambridge, MA: Harvard University, 1934.

Yalom, Irvin. *Existential Psychotherapy.* New York: Basic Books, 1980.

Yolton, John. *John Locke and the Way of Ideas.* Oxford: Clarendon Press, 1968.

Yolton, John. Review of Ben Mijuskovic, *The Achilles of Rationalist Arguments: The Simplicity, Unity and Identity of Thought and Soul from the Cambridge Platonists to Kant: A Study in the History of an Argument. Philosophical Books,* 16, no. 2 (1974): 17–19.

Yolton, John. *Thinking Matter: Materialism in Eighteenth-Century Britain.* Minneapolis: University of Minnesota Press, 1983.

Zilboorg, Gregory. "Loneliness." *The Atlantic Monthly,* January 1938, 45–54.

# Name Index

Agrippa of Nettesheim  58
Alexander, Ian  234–235, 235n12, 237
Alexander, Samuel  376
Anaxagoras  284
Aquinas, Thomas  66, 281, 347
Arendt, Hannah, *The Origins of Totalitarianism*  413
Aristotle  14, 32, 37, 42n23, 56, 58, 61, 66, 76, 92, 100, 139, 145n4, 150, 152–153n8, 247, 281, 299, 361, 369–370, 392, 440, 443
  change and  113
  choice and  137
  consciousness and  38, 45–46, 81, 265, 382
  *De Anima*  14, 46, 250, 293
  duty and  100n22
  embodiment and  391
  free will and  139
  friendship and  439
  on intelligence  54
  *Metaphysics*  74, 203, 347, 372, 382
  motion and  113
  *Nicomachean Ethics*  60, 100n22, 104
  peripatetic paradigm of self as "embodied soul"  391
  *Politics*  304
  purposeful activity and  339
  quantity-quality distinction and  283
  reflexive conception of Unmoved Mover  8
  reflexive self-consciousness and  41
  reflexivity principle and  151
  *tabula rasa* paradigm of consciousness  38, 81
  ten categories of  111
  time and  113
  unity of consciousness and  265, 382
  Unmoved Mover and  32, 76, 133, 229, 385
Armstrong, D.M.  9, 323, 324, 325–328, 332–333, 334, 335–336, 338, 350, 357
  the brain and  324–325
  *A Materialist Theory of the Mind*  324
Arnauld, Antoine  80
  "Fourth Set of Objections"  13
Ashley-Cooper, Anthony, 3rd Earl of Shaftesbury  85

Augustine  9, 55, 65–66, 84, 347, 426
  *Confessions*  205, 205n2, 374, 421
  consciousness and  323
  free will and  137, 139, 139n2, 146
  on original sin  169
  predestination and  71
  self-consciousness and  41
  subjective idealism and  323
  time and  113
Ayer, A.J.  10
  consciousness and  323
  *Language, Truth, and Logic*  346
  meanings and  349
  neutral monism and  323

Bacon, Francis  62, 361, 381–383, 382n5
Bain, Alexander  124, 182
Balguy, John  78
Barrett, William  241–242
Bayle, Pierre  83
Beck, Lewis White  101, 101–102n23, 102
Bennett, Jonathan  264
Bentham, Jeremy  298, 443
Bergson, Henri  36, 47–48, 54, 124, 142, 191–192, 198, 268, 280, 308
  "acetylene flame" and  218
  Achilles argument and  228n8
  Battle between the Gods and the Giants and  238
  causality and  345
  consciousness and  172–179, 188–189, 234–235, 265, 344–345n8, 356
  *Creative Evolution*  181, 190–191, 233
  dualism and  191n18, 239–240
  *durée*/duration and  172–173, 173n13, 174–182, 183–187, 189, 191n17, 228n8, 234–238, 236n13, 241, 355, 356
  *Essai sur les données immédiates de la conscience*  140, 344–345n8
  experience and  234
  extensity vs. intensity in  269
  freedom and  171–192, 233
  free will vs. determinism and  186–187
  idealism and  207

Bergson, Henri (cont.)
    immediacy and   191n17
    indetermininacy and   190–191
    intuition and   184–186, 234–235, 238, 241
    on language   47
    materialism and   191n17
    *Matter and Memory*   191, 191n18, 240
    meaning and   82, 237–238
    memory and   191n18, 240
    "nothingness" and   191
    perceptions and   238, 240
    physiological psychology and   240
    psychologism and   182
    relations and   82
    the self and   241
    self-consciousness and   179, 186–187, 191n17, 333
    sensations and   233
    simplicity argument and   183, 233, 356
    simplicity premise and   140, 171
    on song as analogy for consciousness   232–233, 336
    space and   236, 370
    "spatialization" of time and   367
    spontaneity and   181, 183, 191–192, 233, 234–235, 246
    stream of consciousness and   172, 177
    subjective idealism and   432
    "successive immediacies" and   183
    synthesis and   234
    time and   171–173, 173n13, 183–187, 189, 191n17, 206, 223–241, 228n8, 232–238, 236n13, 241–242, 355, 356, 370
    *Time and Free Will*   50, 240
    time-consciousness and   206, 223–241, 241–242, 355
    time-space and   370
    unity of consciousness and   179, 191n17, 238–239
    unpredictability and   190–191
    words vs. meaning distinction   178–179
Berkeley, George   18n12, 21–22, 22n15, 25, 51n27, 53, 86, 119
    empiricism and   347
    God and   83
    idealism and   82
    immaterialism of   112, 115, 347
    language and   47
    meanings and   349

*minima sensibilia* and   122, 122n30, 206
*A New Theory of Vision*   122, 122n30
*Principles*   83
space and   122
Berlin, Isaiah, *The Hedgehog and the Fox*   154
Berthold-Bond, Daniel   397–398
Bettelheim, Bruno, *Love Is Not Enough*   425
Blanshard, Brand   29, 71, 323, 349
Boas, George   3, 63
    *The History of Ideas*   58
Boehme, Jacob   281, 285, 377, 379, 380–385, 382n5, 393
Bonds, Berthold   365
Bowlby, John   405
Bradley, F.H.   9, 116, 349, 350
Brahe, Tycho   151
Brentano, Franz   231–232n10
    *Psychology from an Empirical Standpoint*   312, 340–341
Brönte, Emily   431–444
Brook, Andrew   407
Bruno, Giordano   214
Buridan, Jean   137–138
Burlinghame, Dorothy   405

Cacioppo, John   251, 304
Camus, Albert   437
    *The Plague*   139n2
    *The Stranger*   180
Carnap, Rudolph   138
Cervantes, Miguel de, *Don Quixote*   433
Chalmers, David   37, 347
Chomsky, Noam   51–52, 52n28, 191
Churchland, Patricia   251
Churchland, Paul   251, 304
Cicero   57
Clark, Kenneth   373
Clarke, Samuel   78, 114–119, 120n29, 121
Coleridge, Samuel Taylor   64, 207
Columbine High School, shootings at   411
Comte, Auguste   334
Conrad, Joseph   220, 276, 403, 433
    *Heart of Darkness*   171
Copleston, Frederick   158, 213–214, 217, 264
    *Schopenhauer: Philosopher of Pessimism*   210–211
Cornford, Francis Macdonald   9n3
Cousins, Victor   83n10
Cratylus   203

NAME INDEX 461

Cudworth, Ralph   12, 15, 64, 69n2, 73n7, 84, 91, 93, 94, 95, 104, 136, 291
  concepts and   87
  Copernican Revolution and   79
  essences and   78
  *Eternal and Immutable Morality*   84
  as Ethical Intuitionist   104
  ethical philosophy and   68–79
  Forms and   86
  idealism and   78
  immaterial nature of consciousness and   68, 68–79, 82, 104
  intuitionism and   78, 443
  intuitive method of   101
  knowledge and   78
  meaning and   71n6, 73n7, 87
  moral intuitionism and   69
  passive-active dualism within the mind and   75
  perceptions and   74–75
  Platonism and   72–73, 73n7, 76, 77, 78, 87, 104
  rationalism and   68–79, 82, 104
  self-consciousness and   41, 73–74, 76
  simplicity argument and   86
  simplicity premise and   140
  synthetic *a priori* relations and   78
  *A Treatise Concerning Eternal and Immutable Morality*   69, 82
  *The True Intellectual System of the Universe*   68–69, 82, 359
Cummins, Phillip   24–25

Damasio, Antonio, *Self Comes to Mind: Constructing the Conscious Brain*   306–307
Defoe, Daniel, *Robinson Crusoe*   433
Democritus   9, 44, 65, 68, 73, 113, 138, 155, 282, 323, 328
Dennett, Daniel   9
  consciousness and   323
  *Consciousness Explained*   308–309
  *Materialism and Behaviorism*   308–309
  reductive materialism and   323
Denney, Reuel, *The Lonely Crowd*   428
Descartes, René   8–9, 13, 21–23, 48, 52, 66, 75–76, 92n17, 98, 109, 118, 142, 187–188, 236, 337, 347
  animals as automatons and   251

  Christian doctrine of free will and   144
  cogito and   34, 90, 277, 346
  consciousness and   144–145, 323
  dualism and   112, 163, 207
  emotions and   432
  epistemology and   144–145
  error and   39–40, 146
  free will and   39–40, 139, 144–145
  God and   83, 207
  infinity and   120
  intuition(s) and   93
  matter and   76, 113–114, 143
  mechanical materialism and   71–72
  mechanism and   251
  *Meditations*   13, 18n12, 31–32, 32–33n20, 39–40, 80, 83, 145, 156, 348, 433
    Synopsis   348n10
  nothingness and   348, 348n10
  *Passions of the Soul*   156, 432
  "pure" self in   32–33
  self-consciousness and   41, 333
  solipsism and   112, 145
  the soul and   348
  space and   112, 113–114, 120, 125, 207
  spontaneity and   144, 145, 146
  subjective idealism and   323, 432
  substance and   347
  temporality and   111
Dewey, John   247
Dilthey, Wilhelm   9–10
Dostoyevsky, Fyodor
  *The Brothers Karamazov*   170
  *Crime and Punishment*   170, 218, 220
  Grand Inquisitor passage in   197

Einstein, Albert   361
Elizabeth, Princess   113–114, 348
Emerson, Ralph Waldo   83n10, 91, 93–95, 104, 207
  Achilles argument and   82
  Cambridge Platonists and   82, 86
  "Circles"   84
  concepts and   87
  empiricism and   85–86
  epistemological idealism and   82–83
  as Ethical Intuitionist   104
  Forms and   86
  German idealism and   86
  ideal and eternal values and   85

Emerson, Ralph Waldo (cont.)
   idealism and   68, 82–87, 104
   "Ideal Theory"   82–83
   immaterial nature of consciousness and   68, 82–87, 104
   inconsistencies in   86
   intuitive and rationalist ethics of   86
   intuitive method of   101
   Kantian transcendentalism and   84, 86, 104
   materialism and   85–86
   meanings and   86, 87
   Neo-Platonism and   85, 86
   "Nominalist and Realist in Plato"   84–85
   "The Over-Soul"   85, 86
   phenomenalism and   85–86
   Platonism and   84, 86, 87
   "Plato; or, the Philsopher"   85
   sentiment and   85
   simplicity argument and   82, 83–84, 86
   "spiritual doctrine" of   84
   "Spiritual Laws"   86
   "The Transcendentalist"   84, 85–86
Epicurus   7n2, 9, 65, 138, 201, 282, 323, 324, 328
Ewing, A.C.   131–132, 131–132n32, 264

Faulkner, William   242, 433
Feuerbach, Ludwig   346
Fichte, Johann Gottlieb   42, 52, 53, 54, 154–155n9, 198, 227, 282, 383, 392
   Achilles premise and   222
   actional ego and   223
   "act of self-creation" and   140
   Christian doctrine of free will and   144
   consciousness and   148–149, 265, 323, 344
   on contradictory first principles   240
   Ego and   104, 146, 148, 149, 167, 192n19, 223, 264–265, 344, 387, 388
   freedom and   150, 356
   free will and   144, 148–149
   idealism and   148
   immediacy and   148
   intentionality and   344
   intuition and   149
   meanings and   82
   *minima sensibilia* and   150, 206
   Non-Ego and   167
   purposiveness and   343, 344
   relations and   82
   *Science of Kowledge*   148
   self-consciousness and   41, 148–149, 333
   simplicity argument and   148, 150
   social contract and   427
   spontaneity and   144, 146, 148–150, 246, 343, 344, 386–387, 434–435
   subconscious and   396, 400
   subjective idealism and   258, 323, 432
   substance and   347
   synthesis and   149
   unconscious abyss and   385–386
   unity of consciousness and   222
   *Vocation of Man*   150
   will and   385–387
Ficino, Marsilio   9, 66
Findlay, J.N.   42–43, 44, 264–265, 354
Foucher, Simon   22n15
Freud, Anna   405
Freud, Sigmund   15, 42, 285, 299–300, 376–388, 389, 396, 398, 414, 419n11
   *Civilization and Its Discontents*   199, 407
   consciousness and   273–276
   determinism and   65, 199–201, 392, 434
   *The Ego and the Id*   407, 429
   ego vs. other and   273–274, 273n8
   empiricism and   391
   as Epicurean   201
   Greek mythology and   391, 393, 394, 434
   Id and   201, 395, 434
   infant consciousness and   273–276
   mythology and   393
   neurosis and   398
   "oceanic feeling" and   273–274
   over-emphasis on libidinal sexual energy   418
   phenomenalism and   391, 392
   primary principle of libidinous energy   403
   psychosis and   429
   self-consciousness and   407–408
   separation anxiety and   410, 419
   the subconscious and   434
   the unconscious and   199, 209n5, 276–277, 365
Fromm, Erich   414
Fromm-Reichmann, Frieda   413–414, 419n11

NAME INDEX 463

Gallagher, Kenneth  97–98
Gassendi, Pierre  66
Genet, Jean  196n21, 197
Gibson, John  203–204
Gide, André  180
Gilson, Etienne  60, 80
Glazer, Nathan  428
Godefroy of St. Victor  58
Golding, William  171, 220, 429
Green, T.H.  352, 352n14
Greenberg, Joanna  318
Greene, Graham  443
Grene, Marjorie  344–345n8
Gross, David  58–61
Gupta, R.K.  395

Hardy, Thomas  433
Harlow, Harry  405
Harrington, Michael  423
Hegel, G.W.F.  9, 12–13n8, 18n12, 29, 54, 81, 96, 100, 142, 179, 191n17, 198, 227, 435
　Absolute Spirit and  257
　the abyss and  379–380, 381–382, 384–385, 389–393, 396–397
　Achilles premise and  222, 343
　actuality and  181
　affective qualities and  286
　*Anthropology*  256, 258, 271, 276, 371, 379, 380, 384, 390–391, 393
　"association of ideas" and  396
　Being and  257, 258, 263, 269–270, 278–286, 346–348, 384–385
　Being-Nothing-Becoming and  281–282, 346, 346n9
　categories of  258
　Civil Society phase and  285
　cognition and  333
　coherence theory of truth and  29–30n19, 151
　consciousness and  15–16, 144, 152, 155–157, 255–286, 323, 333, 343–344, 346–348, 351, 376, 378–379, 385
　desire and  261, 267, 277–278, 277n9
　desire for recognition and  277n9
　dialectic and  146, 154–155, 263, 277, 343, 392–393, 407–408
　dualism and  163, 257
　egoism and  285
　embodiment and  391
　emphasis on interpersonal relations  277
　empiricism and  142
　*Encyclopedia of the Philosophical Sciences*  376
　extensity vs. intensity and  271
　feelings and  261–262
　"feeling soul" and  13, 256, 260–261, 271, 377, 380, 384, 390–393
　freedom and  150–152, 152–153n8, 158, 356
　free will and  144
　Freudian unconscious and  376–389, 396, 398
　*Geist* and  264–265
　*The German Ideology*  59
　gravity and  161–164
　*Hegel's Lectures on the History of History*  385
　*Hegel's Lectures on the History of Philosophy*  146, 282, 381–382
　*Hegel's Philosophy of Mind*  371
　human awareness and  258
　idealism and  155, 279, 282, 383, 385, 391–392
　"identity in difference" principle and  314
　infant consciousness and  258–261, 263, 266–267, 272–276, 272n7
　intentionality and  343, 344
　intuition and  346–347
　James and  272n7
　*Lectures*  152–153n8
　levels and structures of consciousness and  15–16
　levels of consciousness and  378–381, 392–393
　levels of soul in  276
　"Lordship and Bondage"  413
　madness and  397, 429
　master-slave dialectic and  258, 259, 267, 277–278, 277n9, 333, 413, 426
　materialism and  142, 155, 156, 342
　matter and  76–77, 143, 161
　meaning and  82, 349
　mechanism and  342
　metaphysics and  282–283
　modern philosophy and  382, 383
　nothingness of consciousness and  347–348
　objective idealism and  151, 245, 258, 323, 346, 378

Hegel, G.W.F. (cont.)
    "ontological argument" and   346
    pantheistic idealism and   279, 385
    passions and   432
    perception and   267, 271–272, 343
    personal identity and   285
    phenomena-noumena distinction
        and   211, 257
    *Phenomenology of Spirit*   28–30, 146,
        154–155, 157, 246, 255–278, 280–281, 283,
        286–287, 342–343, 378, 384–385, 389
        "Lordship and Bondage"   413
        "The Unhappy Consciousness,"   397
    philosophical evolution and   257–258
    *Philosophy of History*   155
    *Philosophy of Mind*   42–43, 146,
        152–153n8, 246, 260, 271, 397–398
    phrenology and   257, 287
    physiology and   257
    "presuppositionless" philosophy and   98
    primacy of sensory and affective qualities
        and   258–259
    purposiveness and   342, 343, 344
    quantity/quality and   157, 255–258,
        262–271, 278–286, 383–384, 385, 393
    rationalism and   152–153n8
    Recognition and   413
    reflexivity and   41, 143, 151, 343
    relations and   82
    "reproductive imagination" and   395–396
    *Science of Logic*   28–29, 30, 154, 157, 245,
        258, 269–270, 276–286, 343, 346, 378,
        382–385, 389
        "Immaterialism of the Soul"   282–283
        Quality and   255–256
        Quality of Being and   263, 278–286
        spontaneity and   146
    the self and   333, 342, 343
    self-consciousness and   41, 74, 150, 152,
        152–153n8, 161, 267, 277–278, 277n9, 333,
        343, 380–381, 407–408
    Sense-Certainty and   255–256, 258,
        260–263, 265–266, 269, 271–272, 343,
        419–420
    sensory and affective qualities and
        261–262
    simplicity and   138n1, 284–285
    simplicity argument and   255–278
    social contract and   427
    soul and   276
    speculative metaphysics and   281–282
    Spirit and   152–153, 286
    spontaneity and   144, 146, 246, 279–280,
        343–344, 391–392
    the subconscious and   286, 389, 396, 400
    subjective idealism and   432
    on subjective mind   257
    substance and   347
    synthesis and   153
    synthetic *a priori* and   28–29, 30, 153,
        153–154, 258
    thinking and   151
    triadic categories in   154
    truth and   141
    the unconscious and   376–388, 389,
        390–393, 396–398
    understanding and   343
    *Ungrund*   389
    the Unhappy Consciousness and   397,
        418
    unity of consciousness and   265–266
    "way of ideas" argument and   83
Heidegger, Martin   92, 387, 438
    *aletheia*   99
    *Da-sein/Mit-sein* of   91
    *Introduction to Metaphysics*   52–53
Hemingway, Ernest   317
Heraclitus   73, 137, 173n13, 191n17, 203, 282
Herbart, Johann Friedrich   124, 231–232n10
Herbert of Cherbury   55
Herbert of Cherbury, Sir   55
Hesiod, *Theogony*   394
Hobbes, Thomas   9, 43, 65, 66–69, 79–80,
    144, 182, 295–297, 353, 426–427
    alternative politics of   60
    atomistic Epicureanism of   76
    consciousness and   323
    denial of existence of the self and   332
    egoism and   294
    ethical relativism of   69
    human nature and   294, 427
    imagination and   329
    language and   47
    *Leviathan*   71, 156, 286, 295, 432
    materialism and   66, 71–72, 323, 350
    moral relativism and   68, 71, 72
    nominalist thesis of   71, 72
    Objections to Descartes's *Meditations*   80

NAME INDEX

"phantasms" and   82, 323
phenomenalism and   328
reductive materialism and   323
sensations and   71, 329
social contract and   427
space and   135–136, 207
State of Nature and   427
*tabula rasa* paradigm of consciousness and   81
Homer
  *Iliad*   137
  *Odyssey*   70, 394
Hospers, John   200
Howard, James, *The Flesh-Colored Cage*   415–416n10, 415–417
Hume, David   9, 13–14, 14n9, 17, 22–25, 30, 32, 41, 52n29, 53, 56, 63, 79, 85, 132, 162–163, 182, 191, 224, 235, 295–296, 431
  "associationist psychology" of   128, 140, 329
  "association of ideas" principle and   156, 246–247
  atomistic psychology of   355
  belief and   45
  on Berkeley's extreme immaterialism   112
  "bundle theory" of the self and   34, 259, 293, 314, 327, 334
  causality and   327
  collapses distinction between immediacy of impressions and mediacy of relations   246–247
  "compositional" theory of knowledge and   203–204
  consciousness and   33–34, 44, 48–50, 128–130, 323, 326–327, 330–332
  contiguity and   126–127
  denial of existence of the self and   332
  distinction between contents and activities of the mind   128
  distinction between "relations of ideas" and "matters of fact"   94
  distinction between the Is and the Ought   66–67, 88, 98, 299
  dualism and   48–51, 142–143n3, 226, 347
  emotions and   246–247
  empiricism and   33–34, 50, 443
  epistemology and   80–81
  *An Essay Concerning Human Understanding*   49–50, 49n25
  on extension   114–115
  extension and   121–122, 127–130
  human nature and   443
  idea of space and   127–130
  ideas and   115, 116, 329, 329n2, 331
  imagination and   45, 330
  impressions and   33–34, 48, 86, 121–122, 126–127, 130, 134, 328–329, 329n2, 330–332
  inability to separate the self from the external world   247
  language and   47
  *Leibniz-Clarke Correspondence* and   114–115, 117, 121
  Malebranche and   51n27, 226
  materialism and   50, 51–52
  matter and   164
  "matters of fact" and   140
  meanings and   349
  metaphysical dualism of   24–25
  *minima sensibilia* and   122, 122n30, 206
  Newton and   246
  observing and   331–332
  perceptions and   34, 43–44, 48–50, 86, 113, 126–127, 129, 306, 323, 329, 331–332
  personal identity and   128–129
  phenomenalism and   93, 112, 116, 121, 328
  principle of radical empirical contingency   48–50
  rationalism and   126, 327
  reflection and   330, 331–332
  relational acts and   127
  relational theory of space and   127–130
  relations and   87–88
  resemblance and   329, 329n2
  the self and   33–34, 44, 331–332
  self-consciousness and   128, 331–332
  sensations and   34
  space and   112–117, 121–123, 125–130, 133, 134, 135
  spontaneity and   142
  succession of impressions and   314, 326–327
  theory of radical contingency between ideas and things   48–50
  *A Treatise of Human Nature*   14n9, 24, 45, 48–49, 114–115, 126–128, 140, 156, 326–327, 335, 432
    *Of ideas of space and time*   123
    *Of personal identity*   33–34, 293, 331

Hume, David (cont.)
   trespassing prohibition and   98
   turns to empirical sentiments grounded in human nature   68
   "uniformity of nature" principle and   141
Humphrey, Nicholas, *Soul Dust: The Magic of Consciousness*   305–306
Husserl, Edmund   9, 36, 42–43, 48, 54, 71, 86, 90–91n15, 104–105, 109, 198, 344–345n8
   Achilles premise and   222
   analogy of song and   230–233, 231–232n10
   *Cartesian Meditations*   89–90n13, 89–92, 92n17, 102–105, 112, 192, 338, 433, 441–442
   categorical imperative and   103–104
   causality and   345
   commitment to essences   92–93
   commitment to phenomenology   88
   concepts and   87
   consciousness and   68, 87–101, 104, 105–107, 135, 192, 265, 323, 336–341, 344
   *Crisis of European Man and Transcendental Phenomenology*   91, 135
   disengagement from "psychologistic phase"   106
   distinction between the Is and the Ought and   88
   duration and   232
   duty and   102
   ego and   89–90n13, 90, 92, 277, 337–338
   *eidetic* intution and   94, 98
   *eidetic* meaning and   106, 135, 237, 316, 337, 441–442
   empathy and   91, 440, 441–442
   essences and   91, 93, 96, 98, 105
   as Ethical Intuitionist   104
   ethical theory and   68, 87–101, 104, 105–107
   *Experience and Judgment*   94
   flux of time and   42–43
   freedom and   102
   "free imaginative variation" and   94
   free will and   144
   hyletic data and   93
   idealism and   68, 78, 87–101, 89n12, 92n17, 104, 105–107, 336–337, 347
   idealist theory of consciousness and   104–105
   *Ideas: General Introduction to Pure Phenomenology*   337–338, 353
   imageless concepts and   95
   immaterialism of   347
   intentionality and   45, 64, 89–90, 93, 98–100, 102–105, 107, 113, 195, 252, 323, 324, 336–340, 339, 344, 429, 433, 436
   intuition and   93, 98–99, 99, 101, 237
   on language   47
   meaning and   78, 82, 87, 88–90, 93, 100–101, 349, 351
   necessity and   96–98
   non-spatiality of meanings and ideas and   89–90, 89n12
   *The Paris Lectures*   89–90n13, 92, 338
   perception and   271–272
   "phenomenological seeing" and   338–339n5
   phenomenology and   68, 102–103, 104, 112, 116
   *Phenomenology of Internal Time-Consciousness*   352n14, 353
   Platonism and   87, 93, 106
   "presuppositionless" philosophy and   98
   *a priori* synthetic acts and   94
   *a priori* synthetic relations and   105–106
   priority of consciousness over language and   353
   psychologism and   182
   purposiveness and   343, 344
   rationalism and   87–88, 100, 336–337, 339
   rationality and   89n12
   reflexion and   337–338
   reflexivity and   41, 100, 344
   rejection of Platonic realism   87
   relations and   82, 87–90
   Sartre and   194–195
   self-consciousness and   41, 333, 338, 338–339n5
   simplicity argument and   88–89
   simplicity paradigm of consciousness and   88–89
   simplicity premise and   91–92
   solipsism and   91, 102–104, 112
   on song as analogy for consciousness   336
   space and   112–113, 116, 135
   spontaneity and   105, 246, 337–338, 339, 343, 344
   subjective idealism and   432

NAME INDEX

synthesis and 337–338
synthetic *a priori* in 27–28, 27–28n18, 30
synthetic *a priori* judgments and 95, 96–98, 133
synthetic *a priori* relations and 94, 100
synthetic *a priori* relations and meanings and 104
system of ethics and 100–101
temporal constitution and 265
temporality and 230–231, 231–232n10, 232, 337–338, 339
time-consciousness and 99–100, 230–231, 231–232n10, 237, 336–337, 352n14, 353–355
transcendence and 64, 252, 312, 323
trespassing prohibition and 98
truth and 141
unity and 237
unity of consciousness and 89–90, 100, 237, 337–338
unity of meaning and 91, 92
universality and 96–98
words vs. meaning distinction 178–179
Hutcheson, Francis 67, 85, 246

Jacobi, Friedrich Heinrich 207
James, William 10, 52, 53, 78, 124, 189–190, 219, 355, 387
  consciousness and 323
  on contradictory first principles 240
  empiricism and 105–106
  Hegel and 272n7
  infant consciousness and 275–276
  Kant and 272n7
  "Mysticism" 161
  neutral monism and 323
  personal identity and 336
  *The Principles of Psychology* 26, 272, 272n7
  radical empiricism of 105–106
  "stream of thought" and 336
  "A World of Pure Experience" 105–106, 247
Jaynes, Julius 365, 365–376, 393
Joad, C.E.M. 349
Johnson, Lyndon 423
Joyce, James 317, 433
  *Ulysses* 242–243
Jung, Carl 220, 391

Kant, Immanuel 9–10, 12, 14–15, 19, 29, 36, 54, 81, 92n17, 100–104, 117, 128, 191n17, 198, 227, 238, 272n7, 282, 305, 333, 337, 361, 400, 404–405
  Achilles argument and 26
  Achilles premise and 343
  Aesthetic of 86, 110, 120n29, 122, 131–132, 206, 213, 260–262, 268, 270, 353
  Analytic of 131, 132, 206, 213, 261–262
  Analytic of Principles and 206, 260–261
  Anticipations of Perception and 260–262, 269
  apperception and 26, 89, 89–90n13, 92, 149, 153, 221–222, 307, 311, 350, 386–387
  Axioms of Intuition and 260–261, 268
  "bundle theory" of the self 259
  categorical imperative and 78, 84, 101, 103–104, 436, 439–440
  categories of 131–132, 257, 258, 344
  categories of Logical Judgments 260–261
  categories of relations 81
  Christian doctrine of free will and 144
  cognition and 212, 333
  consciousness and 89–90n13, 91, 100, 110, 132, 149, 192, 208–210, 221–223, 231–232n10, 259–261, 263–265, 268–273, 323, 333, 340–341n6, 343–344, 351, 395, 433
  "creative imagination" and 146
  creativity and 149
  *Critique of Judgment* 101–102n23, 102, 145–146, 271, 356
  *Critique of Practical Reason* 101–102, 104, 145–146, 271
  *Critique of Pure Reason* 4–6, 26, 35, 78–80, 86, 102, 104, 145–146, 148–149, 208–210, 255–256, 259, 271–272, 344
    Aesthetic of 191n17, 208, 266
    Analytic of 266
    Deduction 26, 27, 191n17, 208, 210, 353, 399–401
    Dialectic (Third Antimony) 343–344
    First Argument of the Metaphysical Exposition of Space 120
    First Deduction 208
    first edition of 26–27, 110, 157, 191n17, 208, 353, 356
    First Paralogism 8

Kant, Immanuel (cont.)
    Fourth Paralogism, *Of Ideality*   8, 20,
       21, 25–26, 26–27
    Introduction   133
    Metaphysical Exposition   130
    Paralogisms in   5–8, 7n2, 20, 21, 25–27,
       95, 138n1, 171, 189, 190n16, 208, 221,
       261, 336
    as "patch-work"   136
    *Prologomena*   133
    quartet of proofs as metaphysical
       fallacies in   5–6, 8
    Second Antimony   7n2, 12n7
    Second Deduction   171, 208
    second edition of   25–27, 157, 261
    Second Paralogism, "Of Simplicity"
       5–7, 7n2, 8, 25–27, 26, 138n1, 208, 221
    Subjective Deduction   157
    Table of Categories   318
    Third Paralogism, *Of Personality*   8,
       189, 190n16, 336
    Transcendental Analytic   353
    Transcendental Deduction   27
  determinism and   270–271
  discursive synthetic *a priori* categorical
     imperative of   64
  distinction between the Is and the Ought
     and   67–68, 88, 98, 299
  dualism and   166, 383
  duty and   101–102
  dyadic categories in   154
  ethical philosophy and   6
  experience and   260
  extensity vs. intensity in   268–269,
     270–271
  faculty of Understanding and   268
  as first "professional" philosopher   80
  "forms of intuition" and   121
  *Foundation of the Metaphysics of*
     *Morals*   103–104
  freedom and   101–102, 101–102n23, 104,
     263, 270–271, 343, 356
  free will and   144, 148
  "given *forms* of sensibility"   37
  as "hard" determinist   262, 263
  Hume and   164
  idealism and   391–392
  Ideals of Pure Reason   279
  imageless categories/concepts and   41,
     95–96
  imageless relations and   81
  imagination and   99–100, 101–102n23, 134,
     147, 147n5
  infant consciousness and   273–275
  influence on Schopenhauer   157
  "inner sense" and   99–100, 149, 259
  institution of space over time
     by   260–261
  intentionality and   92, 100, 344
  intuition and   113, 115, 116, 130–136, 185,
     261–262
  judgment and   351
  knowledge and   131
  Leibniz and   269
  *Leibniz-Clarke Correspondence* and   115,
     120n29
  levels of consciousness and   433
  meaning and   82, 349, 351
  metaphysics and   282–283
  *minima sensibilia* and   122, 122n30,
     124–125, 206
  modes of awareness and   269
  necessity and   96–98
  neglect of affective qualities   286
  Newtonian science and   258, 260
  noumenal-phenomenal distinction
     and   158, 160–161, 166, 211, 212, 257
  perception and   260–261, 262, 271
  personal identity and   336
  phenomenology and   102–103, 104
  Platonism and   78–80
  principle of autonomy and   197
  productive imagination and   13, 140,
     146–147, 147n5, 157, 209–210, 213,
     231–232n10, 245, 257, 263, 265, 343–344,
     361, 380, 387–389, 395–396, 399–400
  *Prolegomena to Any Future Metaphysics*   4
  purposiveness and   343, 344
  quantity/quality and   206–207, 255–258,
     260–261, 264, 268, 270–271, 283, 286
  rationalism and   344, 443
  reflexivity and   41, 100
  Regulative Principle of   29
  relational conception of space
     and   121–122
  relations and   82, 90

NAME INDEX 469

Schopenhauer and   212–213, 221–222
scientific approach of   262, 268–271
Scientific Revolution and   206
the self and   44–45, 90
self-consciousness and   41, 45, 213, 221–222, 259, 264–265, 277–278, 285, 307, 333, 338, 386–387, 407–408, 429, 433
sensations and   93, 116, 119, 262, 314
sensibility and   115, 130, 133, 134
sensory and affective qualities and   262
social contract and   427
space and   70, 110, 112–113, 115–117, 119–124, 130–136, 131–132n32, 206, 261–262, 270
spontaneity and   101–102n23, 102, 105, 133–134, 144–146, 157, 209, 213, 220, 246, 252, 257, 270–271, 307, 340–341n6, 340–344, 356, 380, 387, 388, 391–392, 399–400, 434–435
the subconscious and   147, 209n5, 365, 387–388, 389, 396, 399–400, 433
subjective idealism and   64, 245, 258, 323, 378, 432
subjectivism and   383
subject-object dichotomy and   42, 259, 273–274
substance and   347
synthesis and   130–134, 146, 153, 187, 208–209, 213, 259, 263, 270, 272, 399–400
synthetic *a priori* and   27–28n18, 27–31, 35, 44, 90–91n15, 94–97, 100–102, 105–106, 125, 130–135, 153–154, 208–209, 258, 272, 343, 407
synthetic temporal mediacy and   184
systems of relations and   94–95
Table of Categories   283, 318
Table of Judgments   260
time and   91, 110, 206, 261–262, 265, 270
time-consciousness and   99–100, 125, 146, 206–210, 212–213, 215, 220–223, 259, 344, 353–354, 380, 388, 432
transcendental analytic of   36, 255–278
transcendentalism and   26–27, 36–37, 78–80, 81, 90, 112–113, 115, 116, 257, 401
transcendent pure concepts and   81
trespassing prohibition and   98
twelve categories of thought   211, 246
the Unconditioned and   96
the unconscious and   147n5, 386, 396

Understanding and   84, 105, 146, 257, 387
"unity in multiplicity" and   314
Kemp Smith, Norman   4, 26, 130, 131, 136, 147n5, 206, 209–210, 353, 400
   *Commentary*   29, 116, 201, 209–210, 263–264, 348n10
   distinction between Kant's subconscious and Freud's unconscious   209n5
   extension and   121–122, 124–125
   relational theory of space and   127–128
   sensations and   123–125
Kennedy, John F.   423
Kepler, Johannes   151, 349
Kierkegaard, Søren   179, 181, 198, 219, 391, 418, 426n17, 427, 433, 437
   *either/or*   276
   *Fear and Trembling*   374–375, 418
   "sickness unto death"   426
Kojeve, Alexandre   267, 277–278, 277n9
Korner, Stephen   264
Koyre, Alexandre   70, 117, 118

Lacan, Jacques   391
Laing, B.M.   121
Laird, John   121
La Mettrie, Julien   144
Lanza, Adam   411
Latta, Robert   42n23, 145n4
Leclerc, Ivor   117
Leibniz, Gottfried Wilhelm   7–9, 7n2, 12, 15, 18–21, 29, 36, 51n27, 52–54, 91, 104, 169, 191n17, 198, 201, 246, 258, 269, 278–279, 292, 296, 337, 347, 361, 378, 387
   Christian doctrine of free will and   144
   coherence theory of truth and   29–30n19
   confused conceptions and   113, 114, 116, 119, 122
   consciousness and   105, 129, 132, 140, 145, 154–155n9, 278, 323, 344, 351
   continuity and   378
   epistemological theory of knowledge of   119
   extension and   119–120
   free will and   143
   God and   83, 120
   idealism and   378
   intelligence and   145
   intentionality and   344

Leibniz, Gottfried Wilhelm (cont.)
   *Leibniz-Clarke Correspondence*   114–115,
      116–119, 120n29, 121
   meaning and   349
   memory and   334
   *minima sensibilia* and   122, 122n30, 206
   monadological metaphysics of   8, 42n23,
      54, 80, 89–90n13, 92, 102–103n24, 112,
      114–116, 118–121, 132, 145–147, 154–155n9,
      189, 198, 277–278
   *Monadology*   36, 154
   "multiplicity in unity" and   153
   Newton and   260
   "principle of individuation" and   174
   psychic activity and   419
   purposiveness and   343, 344
   self-consciousness and   41, 154–155n9,
      333, 338
   sensations and   119
   space and   112–123, 120n29, 135
   spontaneity and   42n23, 54, 72, 76,
      144–146, 145n4, 234, 246, 343–344
   subjective idealism and   112, 116, 145, 258,
      323, 432
   substance and   347
   synthetic *a priori* in   28–29
   *Theodicy*   145
   theory of knowledge of   119
   time and   118–119, 120
   unconscious and   388
   "unity in multiplicity" and   314
Lennon, Thomas   12n7
Le Roy, Edouard   207
Leucippus   9, 44, 65, 68, 138, 155
Lewis, H.D.   9, 51, 51n27, 56, 357–358,
   357–359, 357n17, 360
Lewis, Wyndham   236–237, 236n13
Linden, Michael   424
Lipps, Theodor   91, 440–441
Locke, John   7n2, 9, 13–14, 22–23, 22n15, 41,
   52, 52n29, 69, 182, 294–295, 297
   alternative politics of   60
   "compositional" theory of knowledge
      and   203–204
   consciousness and   23, 86, 323, 330
   dualism and   23–24, 328, 347
   empiricism and   77–78, 93
   epistemology and   80–81

   *An Essay Concerning Human
      Understanding*   18n12, 328, 330–331
   freedom and   293–294
   ideas and   328
   language and   47
   meanings and   349
   memory and   291–292, 334
   observation and   334
   perceptions and   23, 43–44, 262,
      306, 323
   phenomenalism and   328
   reflection and   330, 331
   on reflections   42–43
   self-consciousness and   330–331
   sensations and   330
   space and   207
   Stillingfleet and   51, 52n28, 292
   *tabula rasa* paradigm of consciousness
      and   81, 376
   theory of self and   292–293
   understanding and   330–331
   universal ideas and   77–78
Lotze, Hermann   124, 231–232n10
Lovejoy, A.O.   3, 29–30n19, 36, 55, 62–63,
   78–80, 117, 229, 236n13, 378
   *The Great Chain of Being*   58
Lubitz, Andreas   411
Lucretius   65, 324

Machen, Arthur   429
machine, metaphor of   251
Mahler, Margaret   405
Malebranche, Nicolas   18n12, 21, 25, 83,
   142–143n3, 162, 163, 335, 431
   *Eclaircissement*   50
   "occasional causes" and   142
   occasionalism and   173, 173n13, 207,
      225–226
   occasionalism of   53
   "occasionalist" doctrine   49, 50, 51n27
   psychic energy and   419
   spontaneity and   142
Mandelbaum, Maurice   100–101, 102
Marx, Karl   9, 59, 61, 261, 267, 294, 426–427,
   435
   alienation and   426–427
   *A Contribution to the Critique of Political
      Economy*   416

NAME INDEX

social contract and   427
*Theses on Feuerbach*   61
Masham, Lady   77
Maslow, Abraham, hierarchy of needs and   416
Mateen, Omar   411
"May I Take a Message, Please?" (*Newsweek*)   287–289, *288*, 290, 291
McTaggart, Ellis   284
Mendelssohn, Moses   25
  *Phaedon*   221
Mersenne, Marin   80
Mesmer, Anton   77, 142, 144
Mijuskovic, Ben Lazare   21–22, 22n15
  *The Achilles of Rationalist Arguments*   3, 10, 11, 12n7, 51–52, 52n28, 54, 63
  *Contingent Immaterialism*   3, 63, 313
  *Feeling Lonesome: The Philosophy and Psychology of Loneliness*   3, 26, 63, 245, 324
  "Hume on Space (and Time)"   122n30
  *Loneliness in Philosophy, Psychology, and Literature*   3, 63, 323, 433
  "The Simplicity Argument versus a Materialist Theory of Mind"   313
Mill, John Stuart   9, 124, 182, 248, 298, 349, 381–382, 443
  *System of Logic*   106
Mills, Jon   281, 365, 379–388
  Freudian psychoanalysis and   391
  *The Unconscious Abyss*   376–388, 392–393, 395, 397
  *Underworlds*   389–397
Milton, John   69
Montaigne, Michel de   17–18, 18n12, 86, 433, 441
Moore, G.E.   12–13n8
More, Henry   70, 78, 82, 112, 114, 117, 118
Muller, Johann   124
Mure, G.R.G.   264

Neurath, Otto   138
Newton, Isaac   51, 52, 80, 107–108, 114–119, 120n29, 121, 142, 155, 246
  law of gravity and   81–82, 138, 142, 143, 144, 151–152, 152–153n8, 156, 248, 349
  mechanical and deterministic principle   156

  space and   70, 111, 114, 117, 135, 260
  time and   111, 114, 117, 260
Nietzsche, Friedrich   150, 198, 220, 227, 379, 391, 426, 433, 437
  loneliness and   427–428
  will-to-power and   212, 276
Norris, John   82
Novakovic, Andrea   138n1
Novalis (Georg Philipp Friedrich Freiherr von Hardenberg)   207

Orwell, George   250
Overton, Richard   69

Paddock, Stephen   412
Parmenides   52, 258, 282, 323, 346, 387, 431
Pascal, Blaise   18, 53, 240
Paton, H.   20, 35, 100, 130, 130–131, 209, 264, 268, 270, 354
Peirce, C.S.   229–230, 232–233
Philo Judaens   58
Pinker, Stephen   298
  *The Better Nature of Our Angels*   295–296
Pippin, Robert   264
Plato   3, 6, 7, 7n2, 9, 29, 37, 45, 86, 92, 100, 136, 139, 309, 370
  Allegory of the Cave   15, 220, 223
  *Apology*   225, 374
  Battle between the Gods and the Giants   71, 108, 125, 141, 259
  consciousness and   38, 45–46, 73–74, 323, 377–378
  *Cratylus*   46–47, 203
  dialogues of   40–41
  doctrine of innate ideas and reminiscence   14
  dualism and   163
  *Euthyphro*   72
  free will and   138–139
  idealism and   382
  impressions in   38–39
  intuitionism and   443
  on knowledge   46–47
  on language   46–47
  meanings and   349
  *Meno*   14, 27–28, 27–28n18
    *a priori* synthetic relations in   90–91n15

472                                                                                          NAME INDEX

Plato (cont.)
   metaphor of soul as mind's eye   93
   metaphysical dualism and   8–9, 40, 48
   Myth of Er   137
   *Parmenides*   40, 282
   *Phaedo*   8–9, 25, 40–41, 347
   *Phaedrus*   250
   *Philebus*   58
   *Republic*   8–9, 15, 41, 61, 78, 250, 347, 427
      Divided Line passage in   29, 29–30n19, 31, 46, 80, 81, 372, 373, 377
      'Myth of Er'   365, 394
      Ring of Gyges myth   60–61
   self-consciousness and   37–38, 41, 333
   sensations in   38–39
   *Sophist*   9, 10, 37–38, 46, 108, 293, 367, 372
   as source of most ideas   58
   space and   113
   subjective idealism and   323
   synthetic *a priori* in   27–28, 27–28n18, 90–91n15, 94–95
   *Theaetetus*   37–39, 46, 367, 372
   *Timaeus*   40, 113, 117, 118, 212–213, 377
   unity of consciousness and   351
   wax metaphor for mind   38–39
Plotinus   7, 9, 12, 36, 83, 85, 107, 150, 152–153n8, 181, 212–214, 311, 345, 377–379, 384–385, 393
   circle-consciousness analogy   89–90n13, 92, 154–155n9
   circle-consciousness analogy and   224–225
   *The Enneads*   14–15, 73n7, 152–153n8, 215
   metaphor of self-consciousness as circle   73, 76
   "multiplicity in unity" and   153
   reflexive self-consciousness and   41
   unity of consciousness and   191n17, 351
Pomponazzi, Pietro   66
Porphyry   58
Price, Richard   78
Priestley, Joseph   182
Proclus   152–153n8, 377, 384, 385
Protagoras   68
Proust, Marcel   174
Pyrrho of Elis   83, 112

Ribble, Margaret   405
Ricoeur, Paul   92, 92n17
   "Kant and Husserl"   102–103n24, 102–104, 105
Riesman, David, *The Lonely Crowd*   428
Rodger, Elliot   411–412
Rosen, Stanley   264
Rosenfield, Leonora Cohen   251
Ross, W.D.   45
Rousseau, Jean-Jacques   48
   alternative politics of   60
   *Emile*   61
   social contract and   427
Royce, Josiah   54, 350
   consciousness and   265, 323, 339–342, 340–341n6, 344
   ideas and   340–341n6, 340–342
   intentionality and   339–342, 344
   meaning and   82, 340–341n6, 340–342, 349, 351
   objective idealism and   323
   purposiveness and   339–341, 343, 344
   reason and   340–341
   reflexion and   41, 339–340
   relations and   82
   self-consciousness and   41, 333
   spontaneity and   246, 340–341n6, 340–344
   subjective idealism and   432
   *The World and the Individual*   339–340, 351
Russell, Bertrand   10, 125, 329n2, 376
   consciousness and   323
   meaning and   349
   neutral monism and   323
Ryle, Gilbert   9, 251, 324–325n1, 325, 357–358
   *The Concept of Mind*   309–310, 324–325n1, 357
   consciousness and   323
   reductive materialism and   323

Sartre, Jean-Paul   9, 54, 56, 110–111, 150, 157, 180, 198, 391, 437–438
   *The Age of Reason*   195–197, 196n21
   "bad faith" and   357
   Being and   192–195
   *Being and Nothingness*   357

causality and   345
cogito and   344–345n8
consciousness and   192–195, 192–198, 192n19, 193n20, 265, 323, 344–345n8, 344–348, 355–356
denial of existence of ego   344
dualism and   346
ego and   344–345, 345–346
existentialism and   435
*Existentialism Is a Humanism*   197, 435
freedom and   192–193, 195–197, 344–345n8, 345–346, 356–357, 435–436
freedom of consciousness and   171–172, 192–198
free will and   144
Husserl, Edmund and   194–195
insularity and   436
intentionality and   195, 197–198, 344, 436
"The Look"   278
meaning and   356–357
*Nausea*   180, 437
nothingness and   192, 344–345n8, 345–348, 348n10
*a priori* synthetic relations and   193–194
reflexion and   197, 344
reflexivity and   344, 436
the self and   192–195
self-consciousness and   192–193, 344
simplicity argument and   192, 197
spontaneity and   246, 344, 344–345n8, 344–346
spontaneous consciousness of freedom and   195
*St. Genet*   437
subjectivism and   435
synthesis and   194–195
synthetic *a priori* in   27–28, 27–28n18, 96–97
time-consciousness and   354
transcendence and   344–345, 344–345n8, 354n16, 357
*The Transcendence of the Ego*   192, 192n19, 344, 356
transcendent intentionality and   323
Satir, Virginia   414
Scheler, Max   90–91n15, 142
Schelling, Friedrich Wilhelm Joseph   42, 214
  Achilles argument and   228n8

Ego and   227–229, 228n8
idealism and   206–207
self-consciousness and   241, 333
simplicity and   228n8
subjective idealism and   227–228
temporality and   232
time-consciousness and   228–229
Schlick, Moritz   138
Schopenhauer, Arthur   12, 15, 27, 50, 52, 96, 112, 142, 144, 150, 157, 198, 220, 296, 335, 379, 387, 400, 431
Achilles premise and   222
analogy of tree and   226
Buddhism and   159–160n10, 164, 224
causality and   159, 160
circle-consciousness analogy and   224–225
consciousness and   157, 159–160n10, 159–164, 222–225, 256, 265, 344
death and   225
desire and   165, 212
determinism and   161
"double aspect theory" and   157–158, 166
dualism and   166, 222–223
ego and   223
egoism and   256, 294
emotions and   212
eternity and   212, 213, 221, 224
evil and   169–171
extension and   162–164
"extensionless point" and   219
freedom and   356
freedom of consciousness and   157–171, 158
free will and   144, 159–160n10, 160–161, 169
gravity and   161–164
Hinduism and   164, 224
idealism and   206–207
as idealist   158
imagination and   165
immaterialism and   165–166
immaterialist premise of   166–167
immateriality argument and   216
immediacy and   216–217
immortality and   220–221
intentionality and   344
Kant and   212–213, 221–222, 223

Schopenhauer, Arthur (cont.)
    magic latern analogy for the self   223–224
    matter and   76–77, 161–164
    meanings and   82
    mechanism and   161
    mysticism and   161, 214
    narcissism and   256
    Oriental thought and   214, 216
    passions and   165, 432, 435
    Platonic Forms and   216
    purposiveness and   344
    relations and   82
    salvation and   211–227
    the self and   223–224
    self-consciousness and   158–159, 161–168, 246, 333
    sexuality and   165
    simplicity argument and   220
    simplicity premise and   211–227
    simplicity principle and   165–166
    the soul and   220–221
    spontaneity and   142, 144, 146, 158, 246, 344
    the subconscious and   165, 365, 389, 396, 400
    subjective idealism and   157–158, 159–160n10, 214, 432
    substance and   347
    theory of the self's intercession with Will   241
    time-consciousness and   157, 206, 210–227
    transcendence of phenomena-noumena distinction and   210–211, 212–213
    transcendental idealism and   210–211
    Will and   146, 157–168, 171, 201, 209–212, 216–227, 241, 246, 249, 365, 371, 388–389, 395, 399–400, 434–435
    *The World as Will and Representation*   50, 142–143n3, 211
Scruton, Roger   264
Segond, Joseph   207
Seneca   58
Seurat, Georges   33–34
Shikibus, Murasaki, *Tales of Genji*   433
significant others, loss of   421–423
Skinner, B.F.   9, 294
    consciousness and   323
    reductive materialism and   323
Smith, Adam, *Wealth of Nations*   294
Smith, John   73n7, 82, 85
Socrates   40, 46–47, 220, 225, 374
Spinoza, Baruch   12–13n8, 18, 29, 55, 80, 169, 188, 278–279, 282
    causality and   326
    coherence theory of truth and   29–30n19
    consciousness and   323
    "double aspect theory" and   10, 157–158, 323
    *Ethics*   154, 156, 432
    social contract and   427
    Substance   278–279
Spitz, Rene   405
Stace, W.T.   264, 285–286
Stainton, Edward   12n7
Stillingfleet, Edward   51, 52n28, 292
Strawson, P.F.   264
Stumpf, Carl   90–91n15
Sullivan, Harry Stack   419n11
Sumner, William Graham   295
Swinburne, Richard   9
Szasz, Thomas   318

Taine, Hippolyte   182
Tallis, Raymond
    *Aping Mankind: Neuromania, Darwinitis, and the Misrepresentation of Humanity*   308–310, 311–314, 315–318, 326
    dualism and   310–311
    four criticisms against neuroscience   309
    freedom and   310–311, 317–318
    idealism and   310–311
    intentionality and   312–313
    linguistic meta-theory and   315–316
    "A Mind of One's Own"   305–307
    *Neurotrash*   300–305
    physical vs. mental and   314–315
    *The Representational Theory of Perception and Its Qualia*   314–316
    self-consciousness and   317
    time-consciousness and   314
    transcendence and   313–314
Taylor, Charles   264
Tertullian   65
Thompson, Josiah   426n17
Thucydides   372
Todd, Dennis   11n4

NAME INDEX

Vaihinger, Hans 136
Valla, Lorenzo 9, 66
Vanderbilt, William 294
Vander Veer, G.L. 350
Voltaire, *Ignorant Philosopher* 201

Ward, James 240
Weber, Max, *The Protestant Ethic and the Spirit of Capitalism* 428
Weldon, T.D. 264
Whewell, William 349
Whitehead, Alfred North 3, 109, 390, 391
Whybrow, Peter 315, 402
　"After Freud: What Do Neuroscience Advances Tell Us About Human Nature?" 289–300
William of Ockham 66–67n1, 72, 309

Winnicott, Donald 405
Withers, George 69
Wittgenstein, Ludwig 88, 98, 315, 316
　*Philosophical Investigations* 47, 316, 334–335
Wolfe, Thomas 403, 433
　*Of Time and the River* 242–244, 244n18
Wolff, Robert Paul 128–130, 132, 134, 208, 209
Wolfson, Harry Austryn 29–30n19
Wundt, Wilhelm 124

Yalom, Irving 436, 437–439
Yolton, John 11n4

Zeki, Dr. 301–302
Zilbborg, Gregory 410–413

# Subject Index

*Note: Locators in italics indicate figures.*

abandonment, fear of   414
"Absolute Being"   241
absolute equality, concept of   41
absolute morality, doctrine of   68–79
Absolute Spirit, Hegel and   257
absolutism   443
abstractions   215
the abyss   365–402
   Hegel and   381–382, 389, 390–393, 396–397
   repression and   388
abyss, Hegel and   384–385
Achilles argument   5–6, 24–25, 55, 57, 63, 70, 113, 142, 214, 238, 244
   Bergson and   228n8
   Emerson and   82
   epistemic theories of consciousness   245
   vs. immateriality principle   221
   Kant and   26, 27
   Schelling and   228n8
   subjective idealism and   245
Achilles conclusion   214
Achilles premise   64, 116, 191, 214, 222, 387
   as bridge connecting Platonism with contemporary conceptions of consciousness   68
   Fichte and   222
   freedom and   185
   freedom of consciousness and   356
   Hegel and   222, 343
   Husserl and   222
   Kant and   343
   revival of   80
   Schopenhauer and   222
   time-consciousness and   185
Achilles principle   56
actional ego, Fichte and   223
actions   255–256, 376, 388, 395
aesthetic empathy (*Einfühlung*)   91, 440–441
aestheticism   217
aesthetics   16, 61, 65, 298, 361, 440–441
affective qualities   255–256, 261, 262, 272–273, 272n7, 276, 285, 286

affects   248, 249, 250, 267, 286. *See also* emotions
afterlife   56, 65, 69, 70
Age of Imagination   247
agency   344
aggression   256, 365, 374, 411. *See also* violence
alienation   256, 285, 397, 412, 413, 418, 426–427
Allegory of the Cave   15
aloneness   437. *See also* loneliness
American Psychiatric Association   250–251, 318
   "The Decade of the Brain" and   287, 429
analytic philosophers   6, 47, 203–204, 353
anger   256, 397, 402, 410, 412
angst. *See* anxiety
"animal magnetism"   144
Anticipations of Perception   260–261, 262, 269
anxiety   199–201, 256, 346, 394, 395, 397, 405, 410, 414, 423–424, 437
*apatheia*   217
apperception   89, 307, 328, 350
   vs. perceptions   324
   transcendental   311
   unity of   89–90n13, 92, 132, 149, 153, 221–222, 245, 386–387
apprehension   147n5
Aristotelian syllogism   339
Aristotelianism   67
art   61
asceticism   216–217
"association of ideas" principle   156, 245, 246–247, 396
associationist theory of psychology   140, 187, 329, 435
atheism   65, 66, 68
Atheists   9
atman   224

atomic theory   44, 65, 68, 73, 76, 138, 138n1, 155, 431
  atomistic psychology   355
  Greek   138
attachment   403, 418–419
aversion   156
avoidance behavior strategy   426
awareness   255–256, 266
Axioms of Intuition   260–262, 268

Battle between the Gods and the Giants   9, 9n3, 10, 29, 47, 65, 68, 71, 77, 108, 125, 141, 142, 163, 238, 259, 347–348, 381–382
Becoming   281
behavior   245
  determinism and   156
  evolution and   294–295
  predictabililty and   250
  stimulus-response model of   45
behavioral sciences   56
behaviorism   4, 9, 19, 46, 54, 57, 58, 113, 287, 309–310, 324, 401
  alternative to   136
  causality and   328
  cognition and   328
  consciousness and   323
  freedom of consciousness and   182
  ideas and   328
  loneliness and   429
  neurosciences and   318
  perceptions and   328
  quality of consciousness and   247, 251
  sensations and   328
Being   258, 281–282, 283, 378, 383, 400
  Being Itself   269–270
  Being-in-Itself   218–219, 278–279
  graded levels of   377–378
  Hegel and   346–347, 384, 385
  Quality and   280–282, 284
belief   16, 45, 246–247, 329, 334
bicameral mind   365, 366–376
black families, separations of   421–423
the body
  community of soul and body   18n12
  the soul and   10, 13, 142, 225–226, 323
the brain   9, 40, 45, 56, 57, 214–215, 251, 257, 287–291, 324–325, 327

analogy between brains and computers   317
analogy to computers   309
bifurcation into right and left hemispheres   370
brain-computer metaphor   251–252, 309, 317, 325, 328
brain-traces   325
  as computer   251–252, 325, 328
  experience and   259
  materiality of   335
  mind and   325–326
  vs. minds   324–325
  "neuroplasticity" of   251–252
  neurosciences and   287–319
  observation and   332–334
  passive-reactive   328
  reductivism and   401
  stimulus-response pattern and   327–328
British Romanticism   236n13
Buddhism   159–160n10, 164, 224, 282
"bundle theory" of the self   259, 293, 314, 327, 334

Calvinism   71
  Calvinist predestination   68, 71
  doctrine of "the elect"   428
Cambridge Platonists   7, 10, 12, 15, 64, 66–68, 85, 117–118, 136
  Emerson and   82, 86
  idealism and   71
  immaterial nature of consciousness and   68–79, 82, 104
  rationalism and   68–79, 82, 104
  reflexive self-consciousness and   41
capitalism   293–294, 427
Cartesian dualism   109, 191n18, 382–383, 382n5, 385
Cartesian metaphysics   207
categorical imperative   78, 101, 103–104, 436, 439–440
causality   9, 67, 138, 140, 175, 185, 211, 251, 330
  Armstrong and   325–326
  behaviorism and   328
  Bergson and   345
  Hume and   327
  Husserl and   345
  imagination and   329

causality (cont.)
    neurosciences and   326
    perceptions and   329
    psychoanalysis and   200–201, 247
    relation of   45
    Sartre and   345
    Schopenhauer and   159, 160
    Spinoza and   326
chance   138, 140
change   113, 229
child abuse   424–426
choice   45, 137, 345–346, 436, 437. *See also* decisions
Christianity   10, 65–66, 282, 384, 391, 392
    Christian fideism   48
    Christian soul   4
    Christian theism   66
    dualism and   163
    free will and   139–140, 142, 144, 146, 198, 384
    spontaneity and   146
    theosophic   376
circle-consciousness analogy   89–90n13
class-consciousness, self-consciousness and   59
classification, science and   248
cogito   4, 31, 32, 54, 66, 93, 337, 344–345n8, 346
cognition   16
    Armstrong and   333
    behaviorism and   328
    Hegel and   333
    as inherently relational   333
    Kant and   212, 333
    materialism and   325
    rationalism and   333
    states of in Plato's *Republic*   15
    synthetic *a priori* relations and   333
    two ways of addressing   4–5
cognitive behavioral sciences   46
cognitive theory of perception, materialism and   325
coherence theory of truth   29, 29–30n19, 37, 94, 141, 151
Coleridge, Samuel Taylor   64, 207
colonialism   298
color, extension and   90–91n15, 96, 125–126, 127, 136, 206
colors   172–173
Columbine High School, shootings at   411

"communal consciousness"   304
communication, failed   414
communion   438–439
community of soul and body   18n12
companionship   439
confused conceptions   113, 114, 116, 119, 122
consciousness   8, 16, 22–23, 63, 158, 226, 280–281, 347–348. *See also* the mind
    as active and immaterial   150
    active models of   37
    active nature of   246
    activity of   4, 84
    affective qualities of   276
    Aristotle and   45–46
    Armstrong and   323
    Augustine and   323
    Ayer and   323
    behaviorism and   323
    Being and   269–270, 281–282, 283, 383, 400
    Bergson and   172–179, 188–189, 234–235, 265, 344–345n8, 356
    bicameral mind and   366–376
    as circular   89–90n13, 92, 154–155n9, 224–225, 344–345n8
    classification of elements within   32
    "communal"   304
    concept of primitive power within   140
    constituted from within   42–43, 44
    continuity of   34–35, 36, 37, 105
    creativity of   87
    Democritus and   323
    Dennett and   323
    Descartes and   144–145, 323
    doctrine of "absolute" meanings and relations in   54
    dormant   14
    double aspect theory and   323
    dualism and   259, 267–268
    duration and   174–177, 189
    elimination of   251
    empiricism and   43, 46, 47–48, 174, 323
    Epicurus and   323
    epistemic theories of consciousness and   245
    Fichte and   148–149, 265, 323, 344
    five paradigms of   323
    fluidity of   16–17
    freedom and   54, 87, 137–202, 143, 147, 233, 241, 244, 326, 356

SUBJECT INDEX 479

Freud and   273
German idealism and   80
graded levels of   377–380, 392–393
Hegel and   144, 152, 155–157, 263, 265, 267–269, 271–273, 278–286, 343, 346–348, 351, 376, 378–379, 385
Hegel's approach vs. Kant's approach   266–267
hierarchy of thoughts and   15
Hobbes and   323
Hume and   33–34, 44, 48–50, 128–130, 323, 326–327, 330, 331–332
Husserl and   106, 135, 192, 265, 323, 336–337, 338, 339–340, 344
idealism and   21, 259, 267–268
ideas and   328
identity of   37, 105
immanent nature of   89–90n13, 241
immanent temporality of   23
as immaterial and active   64, 214, 255, 283, 344–345n8
immaterialist paradigm of   64, 87
immateriality of   15, 21, 56, 68, 104–105, 115, 347–348
implicit, uninterrupted   13
impressions and   330
infant   258, 259, 260, 261, 263, 266–267, 272–273, 272n7, 407
insularity and   436
intensity of   176, 182
intentionality and   90–91, 98–99, 105, 143–144, 195, 325, 344, 437
intentionality of   27–28
intuitions and   185
irrational vs. rational   265
James and   323
as kaleidoscope   256
Kant and   41, 110, 132, 149, 192, 259–265, 268–273, 323, 333, 340–341n6, 343–344, 351, 433
language and   46–48, 315–317, 353, 372–373
Leibniz and   129, 140, 145, 323, 344
levels of   15–16, 433
limitations of   86
Locke and   23, 323, 330
loneliness and   4, 57, 259, 429–430, 433
as "magic lantern"   256
malleability of   389

as material and active   3, 5–6
materialism and   43, 323–324, 335–336
matter and   335, 347–348, 360
as mechanical   46
mediate vs. immediate aspects of   217–218, 365
metaphors for   38
*minima sensibilia* and   125
monadic model of   4, 7n2, 20, 42n23, 54, 89–90n13, 91–92, 112–116, 118–121, 145–147, 154–155n9, 189, 198, 277–279 (*see also* ego)
moral   100–101
movement of   285
as "multiplicity in unity"   129, 132
neo-phrenology vs.   287–319
neuromania vs.   287–319
neurons and   335–336
neurosciences and   335–336
neutral monism and   323
nothingness and   192–196, 345–346, 346n9, 347–348, 356–357
observation and   331–332
paradox of   128–129
Parmenides and   323
as passive, empirical, and "reflective"   323
passive contents of   245
passive models of   37, 39, 323
perceptions and   48–50, 323
as phenomenal and eternal at once   217–218
phenomenal perceptions and   323
phenomenalism and   223
phenomenological   90
phenomenology and   106
Plato and   38, 45–46, 323, 377–378
Platonism and   45, 68
Plato's states of   15
Plato's wax metaphor for   38–39
powers of   86
predictabililty and   389
primitive   380
problem of   29, 347
purposiveness and   45–46, 344
qualitative differences within   15–16
qualitative elements of   252
qualitative primacy of subjective sensory and affective features   255

consciousness (cont.)
    qualitative states of  116
    qualitative-quantitative distinction
        and  55, 174–176, 247, 249–250,
        252–254, 255, 256–278
    qualities of  65
    quality and  245–286
    quantitative differences within  15–16
    rationalism and  47–48, 89–90n13,
        267–268
    reality and  20–21
    reductive materialism and  323
    reflective mnemonic  14
    reflexive  47, 73–74, 167–168, 324,
        336–337, 344, 344–345n8
    as reflexive self-consciousness  272
    reflexivity and  27–28, 313, 325
    relational acts and  245
    relational structures of  96–97
    representational  306
    Royce and  265, 323, 339–342, 340–341n6,
        344
    Russell and  323
    Ryle and  323
    Sartre and  192–198, 192n19, 193n20, 265,
        323, 344–345n8, 344–346, 355–356
    Schopenhauer and  159–160, 159–160n10,
        161–164, 265, 344
    self-consciousness and  333, 437
    sensations and  44–45, 233, 330
    sensory and affective qualities and  276
    simplicity paradigm of  88–89
    Skinner and  323
    solipsism and  32–33n20
    song as analogy for  184, 230–233,
        231–232n10, 336, 352n14
    space and  115, 117, 206–207
    Spinoza and  323
    Spirit and  279–280 (see also Spirit)
    spontaneity and  9, 29, 54, 87, 140,
        143–144, 146–149, 153–155, 198, 206, 241,
        245–246, 270–271, 340–341n6, 343–344,
        348, 383, 434
    states of  15–16
    subject-object reciprocity and  265
    synthetic *a priori* and  324, 436
    *tabula rasa* paradigm of  38, 39, 46, 293
    theory of  3
    time and  36, 109, 110, 185, 239, 259, 266,
        353 (see also time-consciousness)
    transcendence and  54, 87, 143
    transcendent intentionality and  323
    transformation into matter  335
    two elements of  32, 245
    as two-fold activity  45–46
    unconscious and  392–393
    unity of  8–10, 23, 26, 35–37, 73–74,
        84, 89–90n13, 89–91, 100, 105, 128–129,
        136, 156–157, 179, 191n17, 208–210,
        221–224, 231–232n10, 233, 237–239,
        265–266, 337–338, 344, 351–352,
        352n14, 382, 395
    world views (*Weltanschauungen*)
        and  9–10
consequences, unpredictability and
    255–256
continuity  12–13n8, 36, 105, 378
Copernican Revolution  8, 20, 26, 36, 79, 80,
    95, 212, 257
correspondence  340
correspondence theory of belief  16, 37
correspondence theory of truth  63, 140–141
Cousins, Victor  83n10
"creative imagination"  146
creativity  102, 144, 149, 361, 395
"critical naturalism"  125, 376

Darwinian evolution  251–252, 283, 284,
    295–296, 298, 307, 309, 317
Day of Judgment  69
death  225, 429, 437, 438
decapsulation  416–417
decisions  179–180, 183, 219, 360, 374,
    436, 437
deduction  257
deism  55
delusions of grandeur  411
depression  414, 415, 417
deprivation  408–409
desire  45, 141, 156, 195, 199, 220, 224, 227, 261,
    267, 274, 278, 285, 394, 403
    conflicts of  408
    elimination of  224
    Hegel and  277–278, 277n9
    vs. intellect  247
    for recognition  277, 277n9, 278
    Schopenhauer and  165, 212
    unpredictability and  255–256
despair  346
Destiny (*moira*)  137

destructive impulses   397, 400–401, 411–412.
    *See also* violence
determinism   4, 19, 54, 63, 65, 68, 111, 144, 156,
    181, 195, 234, 251, 324, 343, 401
  alternative to   136
  behavior and   156
  empiricism and   138
  existentialism and   357
  freedom and   67, 137–202, 313–314, 318
  Freud and   199–201, 388, 392, 434
  Freudian unconscious and   397
  "hard" vs. "soft"   199–201
  Kant and   262, 263, 270–271
  loneliness and   429
  mechanistic   73
  neurosciences and   309, 310, 318
  psychoanalysis and   199–201, 357
  psychological   65, 199–201, 202
  Schopenhauer and   161
  of science   9
*Diagnostic and Statistical Manual of
    Psychiatric Disorders*   248, 414–415,
    432
dialectic   286
  Hegel and   146, 263, 277, 343, 392–393,
    407–408
  self-consciousness and   278, 407–408
  synthetic *a priori* movement and   343
dialectical transcendence, Hegel, and   146
*dianoia*   15
directionality   339
discontinuity   13–14
distress   201
doctrine of self-sustaining "internal
    relations"   81
double aspect theory   166, 323
dualism   4–6, 14–16, 18n12, 52–58, 65,
    76–77, 125, 142–144, 163, 191, 244,
    247, 287, 303, 307–309, 344–345n8,
    385
  Bergson and   191n18, 239–240
  Cartesian   109, 112, 115, 191n18, 207,
    382–383, 382n5, 385
  consciousness and   259, 267–268
  dependency on God's interventions   83
  empiricism and   347
  Hegel and   163, 257
  Hume and   50–51, 142–143n3, 226, 347
  Jaynes and   376
  Kant and   166, 383

Lewis and   357–359
Locke and   328, 347
matter and   76, 143
meanings and   349
metaphysical   3, 8–10, 21–26, 40, 48–50,
    57, 66, 431–444
neurosciences and   309, 311
ontological   115
reflexive self-consciousness and   41
rejection of brain-as-computer and   325
Sartre and   346
Schopenhauer and   166, 222–223
the self and   332
self-consciousness and   44, 326
solipsism and   112
space and   112
spontaneity and   143, 182
substance   64
Tallis and   310–311
duration   181–182. See also *durée*
  Bergson and   172–187, 189, 191n17,
    234–238, 236n13, 241, 355–356
  consciousness and   174–177, 189
  Husserl and   232
  immediacy of   187
  meaning and   237–238
*durée*, Bergson and   236, 236n13
duty   101–102
"dynamic energy"   419
"dynamic psychiatry"   419
*dynamis*   7

ego   167, 223, 224, 227–229, 277, 299, 400
  absolute   42
  activity of   54
  denial of existence of   344
  Fichte and   104, 146, 148, 223, 264–265,
    344, 387, 388
  freedom and   227–228
  Husserl and   89–90n13, 90, 92
  identity of   92
  immersion within timeless Will   216–217
  infant   273–274, 273n8
  Leibnizian   91
  narcissism and   273–274, 273n8, 414 (see
    also narcissism)
  reflexivity and   154
  Sartre and   344–346
  Schelling and   227–229, 228n8
  Schopenhauer and   223

ego (cont.)
   separation from other and   273–274, 273n8
   spontaneity and   144, 154
   transcendental   105
   unity of   92
egoism   217, 256, 267, 275–276, 285, 294, 394, 402, 414. *See also* narcissism
*The Egyptian Book of the Dead*   390, 392, 393
Egyptian mythology   390, 392, 393
Egyptians   390
*eidetic* insights   47, 94, 98, 101, 106
*eidetic* meaning(s)   30, 92, 106, 135, 237, 316, 337, 441–442
*eidos*   87
*eikasia*   15
*Einfühlung*   91, 440–441
*ek-stasis*   193–195, 344–345, 356
"elanguescence"   221, 261
Eleatics   282
Electra complex   394
electrochemical reactions   251, 257
electroencephalograph devices   325, 335, 350–351, 401
electromagnetic forces   143, 144
emanation, doctrine of   384
embodiment   391
emotions   116, 156, 206, 226, 248, 255–256, 260, 266–267, 273–276, 286, 302–303, 374, 376. *See also* passions
   classification of   432
   as conglomeration of states   302–303, 308
   control of   401
   Descartes and   432
   dynamics of   432–433
   Hegel and   261–262
   intentional qualities of   302–303
   materiality and   335
   primacy of   261
   reflexive feelings of   302–303
   Schopenhauer and   212
   suppressed   275
   thinking and   365
   unpredictability and   255–256
empathy   299, 439, 440
   as aesthetic concept   91, 440–441

Husserl and   91–92, 440, 441–442
neurosciences and   334
empiricism   4–6, 9, 14–16, 19, 23, 30–32, 39–41, 48–54, 57–58, 109, 111–113, 287, 360, 382–383, 388, 396, 401, 443
   alternative to   136
   belief and   45
   Berkeley and   347
   classical   46
   conceptual impoverishment of   80–81
   consciousness and   43, 46, 47–48, 174, 323
   denial of the self and   325
   determinism and   138
   dualism and   347
   Emerson and   85–86
   freedom of consciousness and   142–144
   Freud and   391
   Hume and   33–34, 50
   idealism and   81, 86
   imagination and   45
   impressions and   44
   intentionality and   440
   James and   105–106
   Jaynes and   376
   limitations of   52
   linearity and   44
   Locke and   77–78, 93
   loneliness and   429
   meaningful statements and   94
   meanings and   80–82, 349
   methods of   268
   neurosciences and   182, 251
   perception and   42–43, 96, 307, 323, 329–330
   quality of consciousness and   258, 267–268, 284–286
   radical   247
   vs. rationalism   67–68, 71n6
   reflection and   42–43
   relations and   81
   self and   44
   self-consciousness and   44
   sensations and   44, 73n7, 96
   spiritualism and   381–382
   synthetic *a priori* and   97
   theory of perception   324

SUBJECT INDEX 483

English Platonism  78–80, 82, 112. *See also* Cambridge Platonists
English Renaissance  10, 66
entitlement  256, 273–274, 273n8, 278, 394, 402, 410, 411, 412, 414
Epicureanism  44, 46, 47, 48, 66, 68, 73, 76, 376
Epicureans
  ancient  139, 439
  language and  178–179
  modern  7, 69, 71n6, 76, 77
*episteme*  15
epistemology  80–81, 144–145
*epoché*  90
equality, concept of  41
error  38–40, 146
essences  64, 87, 91, 93, 104. *See also* Forms
  Cudworth and  78
  Husserl and  92–93, 96, 98, 105
  ideality of meaning and  99
  as intentional acts  93
  as "multiplicity in unity"  105
estrangement  256, 412, 418, 426
Eternal Recurrence  111, 227
eternity  188, 215, 216
  Achilles argument and  214
  immediacy and  216–219
  present and  216
  Schopenhauer and  212, 213, 221, 224
  self-consciousness and  212–213, 241
ethics  61, 298, 361
  Ethical Intuitions  104
  ethical philosophy  78
  ethical relativism  4, 68, 69
  ethical theory  68, 87–101, 104, 105–107
  ethical values  16, 65, 443
  humanistic values of  61
  qualitative values of  56
  vs. science  66–68
  theory of  64
events  140
evil  139, 139n2, 169–171, 219–220, 224, 227, 377, 383, 384, 443
evolution  251–252, 283, 284, 294–300, 304, 306–307, 309, 317
excommunication  428
existential freedom  192–198, 202

"existential nothingness," Sartre's definition of consciousness as  192
existentialism  4, 9, 55, 58, 141, 198, 241–242, 244, 303, 344, 391, 427–428, 431–444
  determinism and  357
  freedom and  435–436
  loneliness and  435–436
  passions and  433
  problem of evil and  139n2
  self-consciousness and  325
  spontaneity and  142
  subjective idealism and  432
  subjectivism and  435
expectation  329
experience  43, 259, 260, 267
extension  90–91n15, 96, 112–115, 117–122, 124–127, 136, 162–164, 214, 236, 260–261
extensity  260–261, 268–269, 270–271, 286. *See also* extension
external reality  8, 21, 32, 113. *See also* phenomenal realm

facts  66–68, 140, 141
faith  443
family separations  421–423
Fascism  401, 413
Fate (*moira*)  137
fear, meaning of  107
"feedback loops"  306–307
"feeling soul"  256, 260, 261, 271, 377, 378–380, 384, 391–393
feelings. *See* emotions
"feral child"  407–410
fideism  443
first principles, contradictory  240–241
fixed ideas  370, 371, 377, 398
for-itself (Self-Consciousness as Being)  192–194, 257
forlornness  346, 419
Forms  7, 15, 29, 41, 46, 64, 65, 67, 212, 216
  Cudworth and  86
  Emerson and  86
  immateriality of  70–71
  Plato and  40–41
  of Virtue  29

free will   6, 67, 68, 374
   Aristotle and   139
   Augustine and   137, 139, 139n2, 146
   Christian doctrine and   139–140, 142, 144, 146, 198, 384
   Descartes and   39–40, 139, 144–145
   vs. determinism   186–187
   determinism and   175–176
   Fichte and   144, 148–149
   German idealism and   146
   Hegel and   144
   Husserl and   144
   idealism and   146, 148
   Kant and   144, 148
   Leibniz and   144
   Plato and   138–139
   Sartre and   144
   Schopenhauer and   144, 159–160n10, 160–161, 169
   spontaneity and   139
freedom   63, 87, 102, 259, 318, 343, 401, 436. *See also* free will
   Achilles premise and   185
   Bergson and   233
   consciousness and   143, 326, 356
   vs. determinism   67, 137–202
   determinism and   313–314, 318
   ego and   227–228
   existential   192–198, 202
   existentialism and   435–436
   Fichte and   150, 356
   Hegel and   152–153n8, 356
   intuitions and   180–181
   irrational   195
   Kant and   101–102, 101–102n23, 104, 263, 270–271, 343–344, 356
   Locke and   293–294
   loneliness and   197, 435–436
   neurosciences' rejection of   309
   philosophy of   9–10
   reflexivity and   153
   Sartre and   192–193, 195–197, 344–345n8, 345–346, 356–357, 435–436
   Schopenhauer and   356
   self-consciousness and   42n23, 54, 150, 152–153
   of Spirit   151–152
   spontaneity and   142–143, 144
   subjective idealism and   435–436
   Tallis and   310–311, 317–318
   transcendence and   67, 142
freedom of consciousness   241, 244
   Achilles premise and   356
   Bergson and   171–192, 233
   four arguments for   147
   Hegel and   150, 158
   neurosciences and   198
   psychoanalysis and   198
   Sartre and   171–172, 192–198
   Schopenhauer and   157–171
   simplicity argument and   137–202
   spontaneity and   147
   time-consciousness and   140
freedom of will. *See* free will
the Freudian unconscious   14, 146, 248, 249, 388, 395, 396–397
   determinism and   397
   Hegel and   376–388, 389, 396, 398
friendship   417, 439
functionality   419
future   204–205

*Geist. See* Spirit
genius   218
German idealism   4, 71, 76, 80, 86, 142, 144, 146, 347, 376, 390
German Romanticism   214, 227–228, 236n13
"ghost in the machine"   251
Gnosticism   393
God   18n12, 19, 32–33n20, 48–49, 51n27, 52n28, 52n29, 55, 69, 78, 117–118, 187–188, 377, 384–385, 437
   conceivability of existence of   6
   dependency on interventions of   83
   Descartes and   83, 207
   estrangement from   426
   as first mover   207
   Leibniz and   120
   Power of   139
   sensoria of   72, 114, 118
   Will of   139
the good   15, 29, 118, 139, 139n2, 224, 227, 383, 384, 385
goodness   15, 220
grace   139n2
gravitation   142–144, 151–156, 152–153n8, 158, 161, 246, 263
   Hegel and   161–164

SUBJECT INDEX        485

Schopenhauer and   161–164
self-consciousness and   161–164
as self-destructive   151, 152–153n8, 155
"great chain of Being"   36, 378
Greek mythology   391, 393–394, 434
Greek philosophy   10, 391
*Grief: A Peril in Infancy*   406
Grimms' fairy tales   393
growth   284
guilt   414

habit   252
hatred   412
Heisenberg's principle of uncertainty   138, 301
hierarchy of needs   416
Hinduism   164, 224
history of ideas and consciousness   18n12, 55, 61–63, 81, 134, 136, 141, 347, 390
   criticism of   58–61
   interdisciplinarity and   57–58
   methodology   201–202
   value of   57
hoarders   410
Holocaust   401
hostility   411, 413
human condition, existential description of   57
human loneliness. *See* loneliness
human nature   294, 427, 437, 443
human sciences   175
humanism   9, 16, 61, 66, 87
humanity
   man as machine   251
   paradigms of   251–252
"hylozoism"   68

Id   201, 388, 395, 434
idealism   4, 6, 8–9, 9n3, 14, 16, 21, 32, 32–33n20, 53, 55, 57–58, 65, 104–105, 111, 113, 125, 303, 307, 313, 344, 344–345n8, 383
   Bergson and   207
   Berkeley and   82
   Cambridge Platonists and   71
   consciousness and   104–105, 259, 267–268
   Cudworth and   78
   definition of   12–13n8

dependency on God's interventions   83
"embodied"   391
Emerson and   68, 82–87, 104
empiricism and   81, 86
epistemological   10, 54, 57, 82–83
ethical   41, 100
Fichte and   148
free will and   146, 148
freedom of consciousness and   141, 144, 158, 198
German   4, 71, 76, 80, 86, 142, 144, 146, 347, 376, 390
Hegel and   155, 282, 383, 385, 391–392
Husserl and   68, 78, 87–101, 89n12, 92n17, 104, 105–107, 336–337, 347
intentionality and   339–340
Jaynes and   376
Kant and   391–392
Leibniz and   378
materialism and   259, 280, 347–348, 381–382
matter and   76, 143
meanings and   77, 81, 349
metaphysical   41
*minima sensibilia* and   125
moral   54, 66
motion and   114
mystical   385
neurosciences and   311
objective   9–10, 21, 41, 151, 157, 245, 258, 323, 346, 378
objects and   114
ontological   10
pantheistic   385
phenomenalism and   85–86
Plato and   382
purposiveness and   339–340
reflexive self-consciousness and   41
relations and   81
Schelling and   206–207
Schopenhauer and   206–207
science and   163
the self and   332
self-consciousness and   44, 325, 326
simplicity premise and   91
space and   64–65, 109, 112, 114, 115, 116
spontaneity and   42n23, 142–143, 182, 234, 235n12, 343
subjective   3, 9–10, 20–21, 32–33n20, 41, 54, 64, 100, 135, 150, 157–158, 159–160n10,

idealism (cont.)
214, 227–228, 244–245, 258–259, 287,
323, 378, 431–444
  Tallis and  310–311
  three themes  91
  transcendentalism  26–27
  truth and  107
  unity of consciousness and  154–155n9
  universals and  77
ideas  64, 267–268. *See also* Forms
  as active and immaterial  150
  associated  140
  behaviorism and  328
  consciousness and  328
  doctrine of innate ideas and
    reminiscence  14
  Hume and  115, 116, 329, 329n2, 331
  Husserl and  89–90, 89n12
  immateriality of  104
  Locke and  328
  Royce and  340–341n6, 340–342
  sensations and  350–351
*idée fixe. See* fixed ideas
identity  31, 36, 41, 129
  of consciousness  105
  "identity in difference" principle  314
  of the self  91
  unity of  90
imageless categories  41
imageless concepts  71n6, 87, 95–96
imageless meaning(s)  92
imageless thoughts  71
imagery  146, 349–351
imagination  45, 330, 361
  causality and  329
  creative  146, 147
  Hobbes and  329
  Hume and  330
  Kant and  99–100, 134, 147, 147n5
  productive  146, 231–232n10, 245
  Schopenhauer and  165
  spontaneity and  81
  synthetic  395
immanent temporality, Husserl
  and  337–338
immanent time-consciousness, simplicity
  argument and  203–244
immaterialism  22n15, 55–57, 64, 68, 112, 115,
  165–167, 347

immateriality  7, 8, 70–71, 104–105, 125, 216,
  221, 347–348
immediacy  63, 183, 184–185, 204–205, 213,
  215, 217, 230
  Bergson and  191n17
  of duration  187
  eternity and  216–219
  Fichte and  148
  of impressions  246–247
  of intuition  234
  mediacy and  184, 185, 365, 370
  Schopenhauer and  216–217
  self-consciousness and  215
  of sensations  246–247
  sensations and  232
immediate sensations  230
immediate succession  205
immortality  220–221
impressions  43, 125–126, 140, 156, 246–247,
  267–268, 328, 330, 333, 351. *See also*
  sensations
  consciousness and  330
  empiricism and  44
  Hume and  33–34, 48, 86, 121–122,
    126–127, 130, 134, 328–329, 329n2, 330,
    331–332
  immediacy of  246–247
  in Plato  38–39
  the self and  332
  succession of  34–35, 259, 314,
    326–327
impulse  275
incest  424–426
incorporation  416–417
indeterminacy  190–191
indeterminism  138, 144
indirect approach  101
individual vs. species experiences  257
individuality, loss of  217
individuation  373–374, 420, 437
Industrial Revolution  294
infant consciousness  260, 261, 266–267,
  273–274, 273n8, 275–276, 407
  Hegel and  258, 259, 263, 272–273,
    272n7
  self-consciousness and  266
  sensory and affective qualities
    and  272–273
  time-consciousness and  266

SUBJECT INDEX 487

infant-mother relation   407–411, 419, 420, 421, 440
infants, narcissism and   273–274, 273n8
inference   32, 63, 75
inferences   215
infinite divisibility   112
infinity   120, 133
inhumanity   400–401
in-itself (Being as Consciousness)   192–194, 257, 345
"inner sense"   99–100, 149, 259
insight   253–254
insularity   256, 436
intellect   220, 234, 247
intelligence   223
   Aristotle on   54
   intuitions and   177
   Leibniz and   145
   pictorial   146
   spontaneity and   145, 145n4, 146
   unconscious mind and   378
Intelligibles   15, 64, 70–71. See also Forms; meanings
intensity   176, 182, 236, 260–261, 286
intention, unity of   90
intentionality   32, 57, 90–91, 93, 198, 246, 302–304, 305, 348, 358, 417
   active models of   45–46
   avoidance of by science   56
   consciousness and   27–28, 98–99, 105, 143–144, 195, 325, 344, 437
   empiricism and   440
   Hegel and   343, 344
   Husserl and   89–90, 98–99, 100, 102–103, 104–105, 107, 113, 195, 324, 336–340, 429, 433, 436
   idealism and   339–340
   Kant and   92, 100
   loneliness and   308, 429
   purposive   3
   rationalism and   339–340
   reflexion and   338
   Royce and   339–342
   Sartre and   195, 197–198, 344, 436
   self-consciousness and   142, 167, 324, 325
   solipsism and   102–103
   spontaneity and   125, 143–144, 167–168
   Tallis and   312–313
   transcendent   9, 16, 136, 195, 241, 252, 259, 432
intentionality principle   339
interdisciplinarity   3–4, 57–58, 62–63
interiority   182
"internal accidents"   7, 7n2
internalization   415
intimacy   63, 258, 259, 397, 411, 419, 439, 440
   desire for   4
   drive for   403–404
   dynamics of   415
   as escape   433
   loneliness and   416, 443
introspection   326, 332–334, 336, 370, 373–374
intuitionism   64, 69, 78, 86, 104, 443
intuition(s)   32, 63, 75, 78, 86, 93, 176–177, 179, 188, 208, 370
   as active and immaterial   31
   Bergson and   184–186, 234–235, 238, 241
   consciousness and   185
   Descartes and   93
   Fichte and   149
   freedom and   180–181
   Hegel and   346–347
   Husserl and   93, 237
   immediacy of   47, 234
   intelligence and   177
   intuitive insight   98–99
   intuitive method   101–102
   intuitive "seeings"   99
   Kant and   113, 115, 116, 132, 133–134, 135, 136, 185, 261–262
   non-sensory   64
   passive   130–133
   rational   66–67
   vs. relations   204–205
   spontaneity and   149, 235
irrationality   201, 226–227
isolation   4, 256, 275, 403–404, 417–418, 428, 438–439
Italian Renaissance   10, 66

jealousy   411
Johns Hopkins University   3
judgment   348–349, 350, 351, 367, 373–374

Kant-Hegel controversy 255–278
knowledge 19–20, 21–23, 29–30, 45, 46–47, 56, 246–247. *See also* epistemology
    Cudworth and 78
    Kant and 131
    language and 46–48
    Leibniz and 119
    of other minds 31–32
    transcendental epistemic 6

*laissez faire* doctrine 294
language 63
    consciousness and 46–48, 315–317, 353, 372–373
    Epicureans and 178–179
    knowledge and 46–48
    language games 334–335
    Leibnizian 103
    meanings and 353
    Plato on 46–47
    vs. reason 47
    the self and 334–335
    value of 47
Las Vegas, mass shooting in 254
laws, loneliness and 430
Leibniz, Gottfried Wilhelm, monadological metaphysics of 4
*Leibniz-Clarke Correspondence* 114–115, 116–117, 118–119, 120n29, 121
linguistics 113, 315–316, 335, 349, 353
literature 61, 433
    neuroscience and 317
    stream of consciousness and 242–243
    time-consciousness in 242–244
logical positivism 6
loneliness 23, 32, 32–33n20, 44, 63, 247, 252–254, 285, 365, 391, 397–402, 415–416n10, 437
    anger and 410, 412
    behaviorism and 429
    as conglomeration of states 302–303, 414, 430
    consciousness and 57, 259, 429–430, 433
    in a crowd 428, 438
    determinism and 429
    dynamics of 414–415
    empiricism and 429
    escape from 403–404, 433

    evil and 443
    existentialism and 435–436
    fear of 4, 417, 432
    freedom and 197, 435–436
    in harm's way 403–430
    inevitability of 259
    innate quality of 3, 5
    intentionality and 308, 429
    interpersonal 421
    intimacy and 415, 416, 443
    laws and 430
    materialism and 429
    meaning and 438
    meanings of 414–415
    meanings of the term 417–418
    mechanism and 429
    murder and 411–412
    narcissism and 414
    negative connotations of 417
    neurosciences and 419, 429
    Nietzsche and 427–428
    phenomenalism and 429
    Post Traumatic Stress Disorder and 423–425
    primacy of 405
    as prison 433
    qualitative vs. quantitative approach to 256–278
    reflexive self-consciousness and 259
    relations and 430
    relations of 414–415
    scientific, empirical perspective vs. subjective idealist approach 259
    self-consciousness and 5, 259, 324, 429–430
    separation from other and 333
    social 428
    sources of 413–414
    strategies to overcome 416–417
    subjective 27
    subjective idealism and 259, 435–436
    subject-object dichotomy and 259
    synthetic *a priori* meanings and 430
    as a system 430
    transcendent intentionality and 259
    as umbrella concept 307–308, 414, 430
    as unavoidable 429–430

SUBJECT INDEX 489

machine, metaphor of  251
madness  218, 397, 429
magnetism  142, 143, 144
mania  415, 417
master-slave dialectic  267, 277–278, 277n9, 333, 407, 413, 426–427
material compounds  7n2
material objects, epistemological status of  113
materialism  4–7, 9n3, 16–19, 45, 54, 57–58, 65–68, 109–113, 270, 280–281, 284–287, 296–297, 313, 360, 383, 388, 401
  alternative to  136
  Armstrong and  325, 335, 336
  atomistic  9, 73
  Bergson and  191n17
  central-state materialism  325, 335
  classical metaphysics  324
  cognition and  325
  cognitive theory of perception and  325
  consciousness and  43, 323–324, 335–336
  criticism of  324–325
  Democritus and  328
  denial of the self and  325
  Descartes and  71–72
  Emerson and  85–86
  Epicurus and  328
  experience and  259
  freedom of consciousness and  142–144
  Hegel and  155, 156, 342
  Hobbes and  71–72, 323, 350
  Hume and  50, 51–52
  idealism and  259, 280, 347–348, 381–382
  Jaynes and  376
  loneliness and  429
  materialist theory of mind  323–364
  as metaphysical worldview  53
  mind-brain distinction and  324, 325–326
  neurosciences and  68, 71, 198, 297, 310, 318
  perceptions and  325
  quality of consciousness and  251–252
  reductive  323
  rejection of brain-as-computer and  325
  relations and  81
  science and  156
mathematics  111–112, 207
matter  16, 18n12, 23, 111–113, 118–119, 308–309, 323–324, 382–384

  concept of  111, 112
  consciousness and  347–348, 360
  defined by quantities  156–157
  Descartes and  113–114, 143
  extension and  214
  freedom of consciousness and  144, 151–157, 152–153n8
  Hegel and  143, 161
  Hume and  164
  inability to think and  7, 9, 29, 55, 57, 58, 74, 113, 214, 222–223
  inactive  74
  as inactive and unconscious  76
  inert  142
  the mind and  10, 13, 142, 225–226, 323, 359–360
  as passive and inert  75, 76
  quality of  65
  quality of consciousness and  280–281, 284–285
  Schopenhauer and  161–164
  science and  111–112
  self-consciousness and  161
  as self-destructive  151, 155, 156
  space and  111, 118
  spontaneity and  142–143
  three aspects of  143
  time-consciousness and  207
  transformation of thoughts and consciousness into  335
"May I Take a Message, Please," *Newsweek*  287–289, *288*, 290, 291
meaninglessness  437
meaning(s)  41, 46, 54, 64, 73n7, 136, 246, 259, 348, 350, 352n14
  Ayer and  349
  Bergson and  82, 237–238
  Berkeley and  349
  Blanshard and  349
  Cudworth and  71n6, 73n7, 87
  dualism and  349
  duration and  237–238
  *eidetic*  91, 92
  Emerson and  86, 87
  empiricism and  80–82, 349
  ethical  86
  Fichte and  82
  Hegel and  82, 349

meaning(s) (cont.)
   Hume and   349
   Husserl and   78, 82, 87, 88–90, 89n12, 93, 349, 351
   hyletic   349–350
   idealism and   77, 81, 349
   imageless   41
   images and   349–350
   immaterialist paradigm of consciousness and   87
   immateriality of   349
   Kant and   82, 349, 351
   language and   353
   Leibniz and   349
   linguistics and   349
   Locke and   349
   loneliness and   438
   Mill and   349
   nominalism and   349
   origins of   348–349
   phenomenalism and   81–82, 349
   phenomenology and   349–350
   Plato and   349
   rationalism and   77, 349
   Royce and   82, 340–341n6, 340–342, 349, 351
   Russell and   349
   Sartre and   356–357
   Schopenhauer and   82
   sensations and   348, 349–350
   unity of   90, 91, 92, 351–352
   vs. words   178–179
   world as a system of   351
mechanism   4, 19, 44, 46, 52, 54, 111, 144, 195, 251, 285, 324, 401
   alternative to   136
   Armstrong and   335, 336
   Hegel and   342
   loneliness and   429
   mechanistic determinism   73
   Schopenhauer and   161
mediacy   63, 184–185, 204–205, 217, 230, 267
   immediacy and   184, 185, 365, 370
   of intellect   234
   mediate-deductive approach   101
   of relations   246–247
   of thoughts   230, 246–247
"medical materialism"   376

medication, psychiatric   318–319, 376, 423
meditation, spiritual   418
megalomania   411
melancholy   397, 426
memory   180, 191, 240, 330, 401
   Armstrong and   334
   Bergson and   191n18
   Leibniz and   334
   Locke and   291–292, 334
   memory-images   240
   personal identity and   292
   sensations and   43
mental predicates, physical attributes of   324
metaphysical dualism   3, 8–10, 21–26, 40, 48–50, 57, 66, 431, 431–444
metaphysical flux theory   73
metaphysical premises   12
metaphysical worldviews   53–54
microcosm   58
Middle Ages   392
Middle East   227
the mind   15–16, 18n12, 36–37, 287, 299, 308–309. See also consciousness; mind-body duality; mind-brain distinction
   as active and immaterial   87, 150
   activity of   54
   Armstrong and   332–333, 334–335
   brain and   325–326
   channels of   16–17
   continuity of   36–37
   denial of existence of   323
   distinction between contents and activities of   128
   elimination of   251
   as fiction   334–335
   identity of   36–37
   as immaterial and active   55, 57, 64, 74, 347
   immateriality of   117, 122
   Leibniz's monadological paradigm of   80
   as material and active   5–6
   matter and   10, 13, 142, 225–226, 323, 359–360
   as metaphysical fiction   251
   minds of others   22–23
   perceptions and   328–330
   philosophy of   324–325
   plasticity and   75–76

SUBJECT INDEX 491

"problem of error" and   38–39
reality and   20–21
reduction to brain   40
reductivism and   328
reflection and   332–333
reflexion and   333
reflexivity and   87, 151, 154
"self-scanning" process and   326, 332–333
simplicity of   122
space and   113, 116–117, 118
spontaneity and   154, 333
states of   15–16
subconscious   14
subjective   257
*tabula rasa* and   293
as "theoretical concept"   334–335
thinking and   12–13n8, 13
unity of   36–37
mind-body duality   10, 22–23, 328
mind-brain distinction   324–326
*minima sensibilia*   115–116, 118–119, 122, 130, 173, 206, 229, 241, 260
   Berkeley and   122n30
   consciousness   125
   doctrine of   115–116
   Fichte and   150
   Hume and   122n30
   idealism   125
   Kant and   122n30, 124–125
   Leibniz and   122n30
*minima tangibilia*   116, 119, 121
*minima visibilia*   116, 119, 121, 125–126
mirror neurons   334
modern philosophy   382, 382n5, 383
modes of awareness   269
monadic consciousness   4, 7n2, 20, 42n23, 54, 91, 92, 112–121, 145–147, 154–155n9, 189, 198, 277–279. *See also* ego
monism, neutral   323
monomania   399
mood   256
moral commitment   439–440
moral idealism   54, 66
moral identity   10, 12–13n8
moral intuitionism   69
moral meaning(s)   100–101, 109
moral relativism   71, 72
moral responsibility   138, 139, 199, 373–374, 436, 437

moral sense, criterion of   67
moral sense theory   67
moral values   428
mother
   "object loss" of   273–274, 273n8
   separation from   410
motion   16, 111–112, 118, 144, 207, 280–281, 284, 285, 323–324, 383
   Aristotle and   113
   idealism and   114
   phenomenalism and   114
   science and   111–112
motivation   4, 199, 256
Mount Perlin Society Conference   289
"multiplicity in unity"   105, 132, 153, 154–155n9
murder   411–412
mutuality   439
mysticism   161, 214, 281, 379, 383, 384–385, 393
Myth of Gyges   427
mythology   390, 392, 393
   Egyptian   390, 392, 393
   Greek   391, 393–394, 434
   Roman   393–394

narcissism   217, 267, 273–276, 278, 285, 375, 394, 402, 407, 410–413
   capitalism and   294
   ego and   273–274, 273n8
   infants and   273–274, 273n8
   loneliness and   414
   Schopenhauer and   256
natural sciences   19, 56, 140–141, 262
naturalism   9
nature   157, 378, 431
Nazism   227, 249, 401, 412, 413
necessity   96–98
needs, hierarchy of   416
negation   192–195, 192n19
negative solitude   100
neglect   402, 408–409
Neo-Freudians   418–419
neo-phrenology   251, 287–319
Neo-Platonism   6, 8, 14, 66, 82, 85, 86, 139n2, 376, 377–379, 382, 383. *See also* Cambridge Platonists
the nervous system   9
Neurath, Otto   138

neuromania 287–319
neurons 250, 287–291, 301, 302–303, 307–308, 401
    consciousness and 335–336
    mirror 334
"neuroplasticity" 251–252, 294, 300, 305
neurosciences 4, 9, 19, 44–46, 54–58, 65, 113, 123–125, 135–136, 287–319, 324, 328, 350–351, 401, 431, 443
    alternative to 136
    analogy between brains and computers 309
    atomic theory and 138n1
    causality and 326
    collapse of 289
    consciousness and 335–336
    Darwinian evolution and 317
    determinism and 309
    dualism and 309, 311
    empathy and 334
    Epicurean materialism and 68
    erroneous comparison of human thought and animal behavior based on Darwinian evolution 309
    extravagant claims of 309
    four criticisms against 309
    freedom of consciousness and 141–143, 156, 175, 182, 198, 202
    idealism and 311
    limitations of 230, 238, 250
    literary style and 317
    loneliness and 419, 429
    materialism and 71, 198
    mirror neurons and 334
    predictability and 250
    psychiatric medication and 318–319
    quality of consciousness and 245–247, 251, 254, 257, 270, 284
    quantitative approaches of 256
    rejection of freedom 309
    self-consciousness and 303–304
neurosis 398, 414
neutral monism 10, 323, 336
Newtonian science 260
Newtonians 117
*noesis* 15
nominalism 71, 72, 332, 335, 349, 350
non-egos 167, 387, 388, 400

nothing 324
nothingness 192–195, 192n19, 282, 347–348, 437
    Bergson and 191
    consciousness and 192–196, 345–348, 346n9, 356–357
    Descartes and 348, 348n10
    Hegel and 347–348
    Sartre and 344–345n8, 345–348, 348, 348n10
noumenal realm 8, 19, 20, 36–37, 67, 79–80, 158, 159–161, 166, 226
*nous* 264–265, 284–285
nuclear arms 227

objective idealism 9–10, 21, 157, 323
    Hegel and 151, 258, 323, 346, 378
    Parmenides and 323
    reflexive self-consciousness and 41
    Royce and 323
    synthetic *a priori* relations and 258
objective "science" 36
objects 112–113, 118, 140
    concept of object 215
    epistemological status of 113
    hyletic 113
    idealism and 114
    "object loss" of the mother 273–274, 273n8
    object relations 418–419, 419n11
    object-object separation 419
    phenomenalism and 114
    self and 407
    space and 110

observation
    consciousness and 331–334
    Locke and 334
    passive 332–333, 334
occasionalism 49, 50, 51n27, 53, 142, 173, 173n13, 207, 225–226
"oceanic feeling" 273–274, 419–420
Oedipal complex 394
Oneness 15
ontological argument 346, 346n9
ontological idealism 10
Oriental thought, Schopenhauer and 214, 216

SUBJECT INDEX 493

original sin   169
other minds, knowledge of   32

pain   156, 201, 255
pantheism   55, 385
pantheistic idealism   279, 385
"paradox of the unobserved observer"   43–44
passions   74, 156, 159, 220, 256, 395. *See also* emotions
    classification of   432
    existentialism and   433
    Hegel and   432
    Schopenhauer and   165, 432, 435
    unpredictability of   388
passive-reactive brain, "unidirectional" conception of   328
past   204–205
Pelagianism   68, 169
perception(s)   17–18, 22–25, 43, 116, 156, 174–176, 215, 266–267, 307, 325–326. *See also* observation; sensations
    vs. apperception   324
    Armstrong and   324, 332, 338
    behaviorism and   328
    Bergson and   238, 240
    causality and   329
    cognitive theory of   325
    consciousness and   48–50, 323
    Cudworth and   74–75
    discontinuity and   13–14
    empirical   338
    empiricism and   42–43, 96, 323, 324, 329–330
    Hegel and   271–272, 343
    Hume and   34, 43–44, 48–50, 86, 113, 126–127, 129, 323, 329, 331–332
    Husserl and   271–272
    interrupted   13
    Kant and   260–261, 262, 271
    Locke and   43–44, 262, 323
    materialism and   325
    as mental entities   43–44
    mind and   328–330
    passive   307, 332–333 (*see also* impressions; sensations)
    phenomenalism and   329–330
    reflection and   328
    representational theory of   306
    self-consciousness and   324, 328
    sensory   13–14, 16
    space and   117
    time and   117
personal identity   10, 14, 285. *See also* the self
    Armstrong and   334–335
    continuity of   12–13n8
    Hume and   128–129
    James and   336
    Kant and   336
    memory and   292
    self-consciousness and   357–358
personal separation   421–426
"phantasms"   43, 323
phenomenal appearances, knowledge of   19
phenomenal perception(s), consciousness and   323
phenomenal realm   158, 166, 226, 308–309
phenomenalism   4, 9, 23, 50, 54, 328, 382. *See also* empiricism
    alternative to   136
    Emerson and   85–86
    Freud and   391, 392
    Hobbes and   328
    Hume and   93, 112, 116, 121, 328
    idealism and   85–86
    Locke and   328
    loneliness and   429
    meanings and   81–82, 349
    mind-brain distinction and   325–326
    motion and   114
    objects and   114
    perceptions and   329–330
    sensations and   328
    space and   64–65, 109, 114, 115, 116
phenomenology   9
phenomena-noumena distinction   308–309
    Hegel's rejection of   257
    Kant and   212
    transcendence of   210–211, 212–213
"phenomenological seeing"   338, 338–339n5
phenomenology   4, 55, 58, 90, 92–93, 141, 198, 271–272, 303, 313, 344
    consciousness and   106

phenomenology (cont.)
   Husserl and   4, 68, 102–103, 104, 112, 116
   Kant and   102–103, 104
   limitations of   253–254
   meanings and   349–350
   as methodology   88
   self-consciousness and   325
   spontaneity and   142
   synthetic *a priori* judgments and   96–98
philosophy   61. *See also specific philosophies*
   modern   382, 382n5, 383
   vs. science   57
   valuative theories of   57
phrenology   257, 287, 401
physical things, Plato and   40–41
physicalism   324, 328, 350
physics   19, 111–112, 238
physiological psychology   240
physiology   58, 257
pictorial intelligence   146
*pistis*   15
plasticity, the mind and   75–76
Platonic Forms. *See* Forms
Platonism   8, 14–16, 48, 67, 80–81. *See also*
    English Platonism; Forms
   consciousness and   45
   Cudworth and   72–73, 73n7, 76–78, 87, 104
   Emerson and   86, 87
   English   78–80 (*see also* Cambridge Platonists)
   Husserl and   87
   Platonic "Intelligibles"   106
pleasure   156, 201, 255
pointillism   34
positivism   6, 72, 360
possibility   181
Post Traumatic Embitterment Disorder   424
Post Traumatic Stress Disorder   423–425
potentiality   378
predictability   138, 200, 201, 202, 223, 225, 245, 255, 298, 329, 401
   behavior and   250
   consciousness and   389
   neurosciences and   250
   psychoanalysis and   248–250
   psychology and   252–254
   violence and   253–254

prediction   106–107, 141, 143, 175, 200. *See also* predictability
the present   204–205, 215, 216
Pre-Socratics   139
prime matter, Aristotelean formless   110–111
"principle of individuation"   174
"problem of divine attributes"   188
productive imagination
   Kant and   146–147, 147n5, 209–210, 213, 231–232n10, 257, 265, 343–344, 361, 380, 387–389, 395–396, 399–400
   spontaneity and   157, 209, 210, 245, 257, 263, 361
   time-consciousness and   245
pseudo-sciences   143, 249, 250, 254, 256
the psyche   4, 54
psychiatry   251
psychic energy   419
psychoanalysis   141–143, 175, 199–202, 245–278, 379–380, 388, 391–392, 396, 398, 401, 414, 443
   causality and   200–201
   determinism and   199–201, 357
   freedom of consciousness and   198
   limitations of   249–250
   Mills and   391
   obsessional or "fixed ideas" in   398–399
   predictability and   248–250
   quantitative approaches of   256
psychological determinism   65, 199–201, 202
psychologism   182
psychology   58, 61, 175, 182
   introspective   334
   limitations of   252–256
   predictability and   252–254
   as science   250–251
   unpredictability and   255–256
psychopharmacology   318–319, 376
psychosis   428–429
psychotic disorders   374
pure actuality   342–343
pure imageless relations   81
purposiveness   339. *See also* intentionality
   consciousness and   344
   Fichte and   343, 344
   Hegel and   342, 343, 344
   Husserl and   343, 344

SUBJECT INDEX

idealism and   339–340
Kant and   343, 344
Leibniz and   343, 344
rationalism and   339–341
Royce and   343, 344
Schopenhauer and   344
the self and   342 (*see also* intentionality)
spontaneity and   343
Pyrhonnien Skeptics   65–66

quality   245, 280, 282–283, 297–298, 382. *See also* quantity-quality distinction
Being and   280–282, 284
of consciousness   245–286
consciousness and   283–285
Hegel and   255–278, 282–285, 385
Kant and   260–261
as principle of the movement of consciousness   285
Quality of Being   258, 263, 278–286
quality of consciousness, simplicity argument and   245–286
*quanta*   250
quantity   245, 280, 282–283, 385. *See also* quantity-quality distinction
extensive   255–256
Hegel and   258, 262, 269–270
Kant and   257–258, 260–261
Quality and   263–264
quantity-quality distinction   65, 111–112, 153, 173, 247, 249–250, 252, 255–278, 280, 282–284, 286, 297
consciousness and   174–176, 260–261
Hegel and   157, 265–266, 269–270, 271, 383–384
individual vs. species experiences and   257
Kant and   206–207, 260–261, 268, 270–271
quantity-quality relation, in consciousness   258–259
quantum physics   138
quantum theory   250

radical contingency   437
radical empiricism   105–106, 247
rage   252–254
randomness   138
rational intuitionism   66–67

rationalism   4–10, 7n2, 12–13n8, 13–18, 29–30n19, 37, 46, 55–57, 86, 89–90n13, 119, 126, 142, 287, 303, 307, 443
cognition and   333
coherence theory of truth and   94
consciousness and   47–48, 267–268
Cudworth and   68–79, 82, 104
vs. empiricism   67–68, 71n6
Hegel and   152–153n8
Hume and   126, 327
Husserl and   87–88, 100, 336–337, 339
intentionality and   339–340
intentionality principle and   339
Kant and   344
Leibnizian   7
limitations of   52
matter and   76, 143
meanings and   77, 349
purposiveness and   339–340
reflexion and   42–43
reflexive self-consciousness and   41
the self and   332
self-consciousness and   42–43, 44, 326
spontaneity and   143, 235n12, 361
synthetic *a priori* judgments and relations and   94
truth and   107
universals and   77
rationality, Husserl and   89n12
Reactive Attachment Disorder of Infancy and Early Childhood (*DSM-IV*, 313.89)   405–406
reading   338–339
realism, naïve   324
reality   9–10, 16, 20–21, 214, 216, 281, 351
reason   45, 47, 64, 74, 139–140, 215, 339, 340–341, 361
reciprocity   278, 410
recognition   277, 413
reductive materialism   323
reductivism   4, 54, 57, 297, 310, 318, 328, 335
reflection(s)   42–43, 328, 330, 330–333, 338, 338–339n5
reflexion   43, 127, 215, 313, 330, 417
apperception and   328
Husserl and   337–338
intentionality and   338
mind and   333

reflexion (cont.)
   rationalism and   42–43
   vs. reflection   338–339n5
   Royce and   339–340
   Sartre and   197
   as self-referential   43
   spontaneity and   235
reflexive, Fichte and   149
reflexivity   143–144, 153
   consciousness and   27–28, 73–74, 313, 325
   ego and   154
   freedom and   153
   Hegel and   143, 343
   Husserl and   100, 344
   Kant and   100
   the mind and   154
   psychological determinism and   199–201
   reflexivity principle   151
   Sartre and   344, 436
   self and   154
   self-consciousness and   43
   the soul and   154
   spirit and   154
   spontaneity and   143–144
reincarnation   14
relational acts   127
relational theory of space   127–128, 127–130
relations   41, 44–45, 54, 63, 64, 126, 136, 246, 247, 259
   Bergson and   82
   empiricism and   81
   Fichte and   82
   Hegel and   82
   Hume and   87–88
   Husserl and   82, 87–90
   idealism and   81
   imageless   41
   immaterialist paradigm of consciousness and   87
   vs. intuitions   204–205
   Kant and   82, 90
   loneliness and   430
   materialism and   81
   mediacy of   246–247
   Royce and   82
   Schopenhauer and   82
relativism   443
   ethical   4
   subjective   73
religion   9, 16, 61. *See also specific religions*
   enforced isolation and   428
   simplicity premise in   12–13n8
reminiscence, doctrine of innate ideas and   14
representation(s)
   indirect   325
   self-consciousness and   303–304
repression   199, 276, 388, 395, 397
re-productive imagination   395–396
resemblance   127, 329, 329n2, 350
resentment   256, 399
retaliation   256
revenge   256
Roman mythology   393–394
Roman philosophy   10
Romanticism   236n13
   British   236n13
   German   214, 227–228, 236n13
   simplicity argument and   205–206
   "temporal" or "mystical"   205–206

salvation   439, 442
   Schopenhauer and   211–227
Sandy Hook Elementary School, shootings at   411
Sartrean existentialism   4
schizophrenia   374, 397, 413–414
school shootings   411
science   9, 16, 19, 56, 72, 111, 116–117, 201, 202, 223, 233, 235, 262. *See also specific fields*
   classification and   248
   correspondence theory of truth and   140–141
   determinism of   9
   vs. ethics   66–68
   idealism and   163
   Kant and   260
   materialism and   16, 156
   matter and   111–112
   motion and   111–112
   Newtonian objective   260
   objective   36
   vs. philosophy   57
   psychology as   250–251
   qualitative differences between sciences   57

SUBJECT INDEX                                                                 497

  space and    111–112
  time and    111–112
  truth and    141
scientific knowledge    5, 19
Scientific Revolution    64–65, 68, 108, 109,
    111, 113, 114, 115, 144, 156, 206, 259, 260,
    261
"seeing"
  intuitive    99
  phenomenological    338, 338–339n5
the self    13, 14, 17, 37, 226, 292–293
  alternate model of    4
  Armstrong and    334
  Bergson and    241
  as both immaterial and active    348
  "bundle theory" of the self    259
  continuity of    12–13n8
  continuous temporal identity of    8
  denial of existence of    325, 332–333, 335
  dualism and    332
  empirical theory of    23
  empiricism and    44
  as fiction    328, 332, 334–335
  Hegel and    333, 342, 343
  historical conceptions of    4
  Hume and    33–34, 44, 331–332
  Hume's "bundle theory" of    34
  idealism and    332
  identity of    91
  immateriality of    166
  impressions and    332
  interiority of    182
  as intuitive    348
  Kant and    44–45, 90
  language and    334–335
  Locke's theory of    292–293
  as magic lantern    223–224
  objects and    407
  phenomenal concept of    215
  "pure"    32–33
  purposiveness and    342 (see also
    intentionality)
  rationalism and    332
  reality of    4, 9, 325
  reflexivity and    154, 166, 226
  Sartre and    192–195
  Schopenhauer and    223–224
  spontaneity and    154

  substantive theory of    3, 4, 23–24,
    324–325
  thinking and    93
  time and    44
  transcendental    90
  as underlying substance    333
  as universally present    333
  Will and    241
self or ego-object separation    419–420
self-awareness    186–187, 436. See also
    self-consciousness
self-cognitive intuition    32
self-consciousness    3, 13, 57, 63, 74, 156, 267,
    275–278
  as active and immaterial    216, 324–325
  active models of    45, 54
  active reflexive    136
  avoidance of by science    56
  awareness and    266
  Bergson and    179, 191n17, 333
  as both immediate and mediate    184
  as a circle    73, 75–76
  class-consciousness and    59
  consciousness and    333, 437
  continuity of    37
  creative and transfiguring virtues of    201
  Cudworth and    73–74, 76
  denial of    325
  Descartes and    333
  dialectic and    278, 407–408
  dualism and    44, 326
  empiricism and    44
  eternity and    212–213, 241
  existentialism and    325
  Fichte and    333
  free will and    148–149
  freedom and    54, 150, 152–153
  Freud and    407–408
  gravity and    161–164
  Hegel and    74, 150, 152, 152–153n8, 161,
    267, 277, 277–278, 277n9, 333, 380–381,
    407–408
  Hume and    128, 331–332
  Husserl and    333, 338, 338–339n5
  idealism and    32, 44, 325, 326
  identity of    37
  as immaterial and active    323
  immateriality of    221

self-consciousness (cont.)
   immediacy and  215
   infant consciousness and  266
   intentionality and  142, 167, 324, 325
   as intra-psychic and pre-social  285
   intra-psychic vs. inter-psychic  277–278
   Kant and  41, 213, 221–222, 264–265, 277, 277–278, 285, 333, 338, 386–387, 407–408, 429, 433
   Leibniz and  154–155n9, 333, 338
   Locke and  330–331
   loneliness and  5, 259, 324, 429–430
   matter and  161
   monadic  132
   as multiplicity in unity  154–155n9
   neurosciences and  303–304
   origin of  305–306
   passive vs. active models of  44
   perceptions and  324, 328
   personal identity and  357–358
   phenomenal  216, 218–219
   phenomenology and  325
   Plato and  37–38, 333
   predictions and  175
   rationalism and  42–43, 44, 326
   reciprocity and  278
   reflexive  9, 16, 27, 40–43, 153, 155, 200–201, 241, 252, 259, 272, 305, 307, 323, 324, 326, 332–333, 338, 348, 415, 432, 433
   representations and  303–304
   Royce and  333
   Sartre and  192–193, 344
   Schelling and  241, 333
   Schopenhauer and  158–159, 161–168, 246, 333
   self-object distinction and  258
   separation and  420
   solipsism and  32–33n20
   spontaneity and  42n23, 44, 125, 252, 307
   subject-object dichotomy and  259
   subject-object distinction and  410
   succession and  335–336
   Tallis and  317
   transcendent intentionality and  324
   two functions of  420
   unification and  420
   unity of  7, 26, 37, 42, 43, 241
   Will and  216–219, 246

self-creation  437
self-determination  199
self-enclosed "self" separation  428–429
self-hatred  412
selfhood, "sense" of  407–408
self-other-self separation  420–428
self-reflexion  344
"self-scanning" process  326, 332–333, 336
self-self-conscious subjects  419
self-sufficiency, illusion of  256
sensations  16–19, 22–25, 32, 63, 73n7, 76, 116, 206, 226, 325–326, 328, 333, 335, 374
   behaviorism and  328
   Bergson and  233
   consciousness and  4–45, 233, 330
   empiricism and  44, 96
   freedom of consciousness and  140, 167, 174–176, 182
   Hobbes and  71, 329
   Hume and  34
   ideas and  350–351
   immediacy and  232
   immediacy of  246–247
   Kant and  93, 116, 119, 262
   Kemp Smith and  123–125
   Leibniz and  119
   Locke and  330
   materiality and  335
   meaning and  348, 349–350
   memory and  43
   Mill and  349
   as non-spatial  116
   passive  31, 32
   phenomenalism and  328
   in Plato  38–39
   primacy of  261
   quality of consciousness and  255–256, 260, 267–268, 274–276
   vs. thoughts  204–205, 246–247
sense organs  214–215
Sense-Certainty  255–256, 258, 260–262, 263, 265–266, 269, 271–272, 343, 419–420
senseless matter, inability to think and  7, 9, 29, 55, 57, 58, 74, 113, 214, 222–223
senses  17–18. See also perception(s); sensations
sensibility  130, 133, 134, 206
sensibles  121–122

SUBJECT INDEX 499

sensory qualities   255–256, 261, 262, 272–273, 272n7, 276, 285, 286
sentiment   85, 443
separation   258, 285, 410, 411, 415–416, 438–439
  alienation   426–427
  avoidance of   419
  death and   429
  estrangement   426
  existentialism and   427–428
  fear of   419
  five developmental sources of   419–430
  forced, of families   421–423
  intra-psychic vs. inter-psychic   420
  loneliness and   333
  object-object separation   419
  personal   421–426
  self or ego-object separation   419–420
  self-consciousness and   420
  self-enclosed "self" separation   428–429
  self-other-self separation   420–428
  social separation   428
separation anxiety   408, 410, 419
sexuality   165
shame   414
shunning   428
significant others, loss of   421–423
the simple, definition of   138n1
simplicity   129
  definition of   138n1
  Hegel and   284–285
  of the mind   122
  Schelling and   228n8
simplicity argument   3–63, 130, 154–155n9, 225, 259
  Bergson and   183, 233, 356
  as controlling premise and paradigm for a substantive theory of the self   324–325
  Cudworth and   86
  Emerson and   82, 83–84, 86
  Fichte and   148, 150
  freedom of consciousness and   137–202
  Husserl and   88–89
  immanent time-consciousness and   203–244
  Kant and   255–278
  vs. materialist theory of mind   323–364
  meanings, relations, and space   64–136

  philosophy of mind and   324–325
  quality of consciousness and   245–286
  role in epistemological and ontological context   245
  Sartre and   192, 197
  Schopenhauer and   220
  "temporal" or "mystical" romanticism and   205–206
simplicity premise   12–13n8, 56, 64, 113, 115, 119, 122, 136, 140, 214, 225, 259
  Bergson and   171
  freedom of consciousness and   137–202
  Husserl and   91–92
  "idea" of space and   64–65
  idealism and   91, 104–105
  Schopenhauer and   211–227
  time-consciousness and   140
simplicity principle   13, 105, 138n1, 165–166, 255–278, 283
simplicity proof   153–154
simplicity vs. compound issue   7n2
skepticism   66, 73, 117, 443
Skeptics   9, 17, 65–66, 73, 83
sleep   13, 14
"social brain"   304
social contract   427
social media   428
social sciences   141
social separation   428
social withdrawal   409–410, 415
social work, limitations of   252–254
sociology   58, 61, 141, 175
solipsism   18n12, 22–23, 31–32, 32–33n20, 100, 195, 256, 266, 369, 397, 441–442
  Descartes and   144
  dualism and   112
  Husserl and   91–92, 102–104, 112
  intentionality and   102–103
  subjective idealism and   32–33n20
  transcendental   102–103
solitude   100, 418
song   336
  consciousness and   184, 230–233, 231–232n10, 352n14
the soul   8, 299. *See also* "feeling soul"
  activity of   54
  ancient Greeks and   391
  the body and   10, 13, 142, 225–226, 323
  Christian   4

## SUBJECT INDEX

the soul (cont.)
    community of soul and body   18n12
    continuity of   36
    denial of existence of   323
    Descartes and   348
    Hegel and   276
    identity of   36
    as immaterial and active   7, 8, 10, 138n1, 347, 392 (*see also* simplicity argument)
    immateriality of   8–9, 85, 116
    immortality of   6, 10, 13, 56, 220–221
    as an independent substance   8
    levels of   276
    as mind's eye   93
    monadic   147
    Plato and   40–42, 250
    Platonic   41–42
    Plato's tripartite   250
    qualitative differences within   15
    reflexivity and   154
    reincarnation and   14
    Schopenhauer and   220–221
    as self-moving   7
    spontaneity and   154
    thinking and   14–15
    as translucent   348, 348n10
    transmigration and   14
    unity of   36
    unity of consciousness and   8
space   40, 108–136
    Bergson and   236
    Berkeley and   122
    concept of   112
    conceptual status of   111
    as "confused concept"   114, 116
    consciousness and   115, 117, 206–207
    continuity of   110
    Democritus and   113
    Descartes and   112, 113–114, 120, 125, 207
    dualism and   112
    epistemological status of   113
    Hobbes and   135–136, 207
    Hume and   112–117, 121–123, 125–130, 133–135
    Husserl and   112–113, 116, 135
    idealism and   54, 64–65, 68, 109, 112, 113, 114, 115, 116
    ideality of   259
    as intuition   86
    Kant and   70, 110, 112–113, 115–117, 119–124, 130–136, 131–132n32, 261–262, 270
    Leibniz and   112–123, 135
    *Leibniz-Clarke Correspondence* and   114–117
    Locke and   207
    materialism and   113
    mathematics and   207
    matter and   111, 118
    as mental rather than real   116
    metaphysical and epistemological status of   108–109
    the mind and   113, 116–117, 118
    More and   118
    negation of   120
    Newton and   70, 114, 117, 135
    objects and   110
    perceptions and   117
    phenomenalism and   54, 64–65, 68, 109, 114, 115, 116
    Plato and   113
    problem of   113, 123, 135
    relational conception of   121–122
    science and   64–65, 111–112
    as *sensoria* of God   70
    simplicity premise and   64–65
    space-in-itself   110
    "space-matter-extension"   260
    spatiality   117
    "spatialization" of time   36, 110, 367, 372–373
    temporalization of   370, 372
    time and   36, 205, 205n2, 206, 236, 260, 268, 370, 372
Spirit   42, 264–265, 285, 287, 378–382
    consciousness and   279–280
    defined by qualities   156–157
    Hegel and   152–153, 286
    as immanent   385
    spontaneity and   152–153
spirit
    reflexivity and   154
    spontaneity and   154
"spiritual atoms"   118
spiritualism   12–13n8, 381–382
spirituality   12–13n8
spontaneity   42n23, 44–45, 63, 76, 96, 102–103n24, 136, 235n12, 299, 307, 339, 360, 370, 374, 376, 388–389, 395, 401
    avoidance of by science   56

SUBJECT INDEX 501

Bergson and   181, 183, 191–192, 233, 234–235
Christian doctrine and   146
consciousness and   54, 87, 140, 143–149, 153–155, 198, 206, 241, 245–246, 270–271, 340–341n6, 343–344, 348, 383, 434
creative imagination and   147
Descartes and   145, 146
dualism and   143
ego and   154
epistemic   434–435
Fichte and   146, 148–150, 343, 344, 386–387, 434–435
free will and   139
freedom and   142–143, 144
freedom of consciousness and   140, 147, 181–182, 198
as grounding principle of idealism   42n23
Hegel and   146, 279–280, 343, 344, 391–392
Hume and   142
Husserl and   105, 337–338, 339, 343, 344
idealism and   142–143, 143, 234, 343
imagination and   81
intelligence and   145, 145n4, 146
intentionality and   125, 143–144, 167–168
intuition and   149, 235
Kant and   102, 105, 133–134, 145–146, 157, 209, 213, 220, 252, 257, 270–271, 307, 340–341n6, 340–344, 356, 380, 387–388, 391–392, 399–400, 434–435
Leibniz and   54, 72, 140, 144, 145, 145n4, 146, 234, 343, 344
Malebranche and   142
matter and   142–143
mind and   154, 333
productive imagination and   157, 209, 210, 245, 257, 263, 361
purposiveness and   343
quality of consciousness and   248, 259, 286
rationalism and   143, 361
reflexion and   235
reflexivity and   143–144
Royce and   340–341n6, 340–342, 343, 344
Sartre and   195, 344–345, 344–345n8
Schopenhauer and   142, 146, 158, 246, 344

self and   154
self-consciousness and   125, 252, 307
the soul and   154
Spirit and   152–154
the subconscious mind and   146–147, 248, 253–254, 271, 276
subject-object dichotomy and   265
thought and   258
time-consciousness and   99–100, 209–210, 234
State of Nature   427
stimulus-response pattern   327–328
Stoicism   217, 227
Stoics   139, 282
stream of consciousness   172, 177, 232–233, 242–243, 433
"stream of thought"   336
the subconscious mind   14, 63, 81, 201, 225–227, 248, 266, 275–276, 395, 402
avoidance of by science   56
evil and   227
Fichte and   396, 400
Freud and   434
Hegel and   286, 389, 396, 400
irretrievable   365
Kant and   147, 365, 387–389, 396, 399–400, 433
qualitative features and   255
Schopenhauer and   165, 365, 389, 396, 400
spontaneity and   15, 17, 19, 146–147, 248, 253–254, 276
vs. the unconscious   249
unpredictability and   276
Subject   278–279
subjective idealism   3, 9–10, 20–21, 54, 100, 135, 150, 157, 244, 287, 323, 431–444
Achilles argument and   245
Augustine and   323
Bergson and   432
Descartes and   323, 432
existentialism and   432
Fichte and   258, 323, 432
freedom and   435–436
Hegel and   432
Holocaust and   401
Husserl and   432
Kant and   64, 245, 258, 323, 378, 432

subjective idealism (cont.)
    Leibniz and   112, 116, 145, 258, 323, 432
    loneliness and   259, 435–436
    Plato and   323
    reflexive self-consciousness and   41
    Royce and   432
    Schelling and   227–228
    Schopenhauer and   157–158, 159–160n10, 214, 432
    solipsism and   32–33n20
subjective isolation   4
subjectivism   383, 435
subject-object dichotomy
    correlational connection between   42–43
    Kant and   259
    loneliness and   259
    spontaneity and   265
subject-object distinction, self-consciousness and   410
subject-object reciprocity
    consciousness and   265
    Kant and   273–274
sublimation   393, 395
substance   278–279
    Descartes and   347
    Fichte and   347
    Hegel and   347
    Kant and   347
    Leibniz and   347
    Schopenhauer and   347
substance dualism   64
succession   266, 335–336
suffering   224
suicide   411
symbolism   281
symbols   315, 316–317
synapses   250, 288–291, 302–303
synthesis   148
    Bergson and   234
    Fichte and   149
    Hegel and   153
    Husserl and   337–338
    Kant and   130–134, 146, 153, 187, 208–209, 213, 259, 263, 270, 272, 399–400
    Sartre and   194–195
synthetic *a priori*   5, 8, 27–28n18, 27–31, 63–64, 67–68, 90–91n15, 93–94, 101, 136, 302, 307–308, 313, 344, 417

    cognition and   333
    consciousness and   324, 436
    Cudworth and   78
    empiricism and   97
    freedom of consciousness and   166, 171
    Hegel and   153–154, 258
    Husserl and   94, 95, 96–98, 100, 104, 105–106, 133
    immanent time-consciousness and   209–210, 233, 241
    intentionalities and   90–91
    Kant and   44, 90–91n15, 94–97, 100–102, 105–106, 125, 130–135, 153–154, 208–209, 258, 343, 407
    loneliness and   430
    between narcissism, loneliness, and hostility   411
    objective idealism and   258
    phenomenology and   96–98
    quality of consciousness and   246, 263, 287
    Sartre and   96–97, 193–194
system-builders, vs. analytic philosophers   203–204

*tabula rasa* paradigm of consciousness   23, 38, 46, 81, 293, 333, 376
temporal constitution   265
temporality. *See* time
theism   55, 66
theosophy   384–385
therapy   199–201, 298, 395, 396, 397
thinking
    as circular and infinite   151
    feelings and   365
    Hegel and   151
    the mind and   12–13n8, 13
    the self and   93
    the soul and   14–15
"thinking matter," doctrine of   68
thought(s)   156–157, 226, 350–351. *See also* thinking
    as active and immaterial   150
    Armstrong and   325
    hierarchy of   15
    images and   350–351
    materiality and   335
    mediacy of   246–247
    pure acts of thought   151

## SUBJECT INDEX

quantitative measurements of   251
  vs. sensations   204–205, 246–247
  vs. sensibility   206
  spontaneity and   258
  transformation into matter   335
  unpredictability and   255–256, 388
time   102–103n24, 108, 259, 352n14. *See also* duration; *durée*; time-consciousness
  Aristotelian conception of   55
  Aristotle and   113
  Augustine and   113
  Bergson and   171–172, 232, 236
  consciousness and   109, 185, 239, 266, 353 (*see also* time-consciousness)
  Descartes and   111
  external vs. internal   205
  flux of   42–43
  Husserl and   230–232, 231–232n10, 339
  immediate vs. mediate temporal consciousness   204–205
  "inner" vs. "outer"   110
  as intuition   86
  Kant and   110, 261–262
  Leibniz and   118–119, 120
  *Leibniz-Clarke Correspondence* and   114–117
  negation of   120
  Newton and   55, 114, 117
  objective   63, 118
  objective vs. subjective   204–205, 235
  as passive form of intuition   208
  perceptions and   117
  reversal of   235
  Schelling and   232
  science and   111–112
  scientific and objective   63
  scientific vs. intimate   204–205
  self and   44
  as *sensoria* of God   70
  space and   36, 205, 205n2, 206, 236, 260, 268
  "spatialization" of   36, 110, 367, 372–373
  subjective   235
time-consciousness   5, 27, 34–35, 36, 65, 91, 168, 203–244, 344
  Achilles argument and   185, 214
  Bergson and   233, 234–235, 241–242, 355
  external   206

freedom of consciousness and   140
Husserl and   99–100, 230–231, 231–232n10, 237, 352n14, 353–355
immanent   23, 55, 64, 136, 156, 203–244, 259, 265, 314, 336–337, 395
immediate sensations and   230
infant consciousness and   266
internal   206, 229–230, 263
Kant and   99–100, 125, 146, 212–213, 259, 344, 353–354, 380, 388, 432
in literature   242–244
as mediate, synthetic, and relational   213
mediate thoughts and   230
Peirce and   229–230
personal and subjective   63
productive imagination and   245
Sartre and   354
Schelling and   228–229
Schopenhauer and   157, 210–227
simplicity argument and   140, 203–244
spontaneity and   26, 99–100, 209–210, 234
succession and   335–336
Tallis and   314
unity and   209–210, 233, 237
time-space   370
tranquility   217
transcendence   3, 6, 10, 98, 139, 312, 343, 348
  consciousness and   87, 143
  freedom and   142
  Sartre and   344–345, 344–345n8, 354n16, 357
  Tallis and   313–314
transcendent intentionality   16, 415, 432
  consciousness and   323
  Husserl and   64, 323
  Sartre and   323
  self-consciousness and   324
transcendentalism   26–27
  English Platonism and   78–80
  Kantian   78–80, 81, 84, 86, 90, 102–103, 104, 112–113, 116
  Schopenhauer and   210–211
transmigration   14
trauma   397
tree analogy   226
trespassing prohibition   98

trust, loss of  424
truth  87
    coherence theory of  29, 29–30n19, 37, 94, 141, 151
    correspondence theory of  63, 140–141
    rationalism and  107

*Umwelt*  91
the Unconditioned, Kant and  96
the unconscious  14, 15, 16, 63, 248, 249, 266, 384, 392, 395. *See also* "dark abyss," concept of
    consciousness and  392–393
    Fichte and  385–387
    Freudian  14, 199, 276–277, 388, 396–397
    Hegel and  376–388, 390–393, 396–397
    history of concept of  390
    intelligence and  378
    irretrievable  396
    Kant and  147n5, 386, 396
    Leibniz and  388
    retrievable  365
    vs. the subconscious  249
    theory of  12, 14–15
underground  390, 391
understanding  20, 225, 268
    categories of  93
    faculty of  41
    Hegel and  343
    Kant and  105, 146, 387
    Locke and  330–331
underworlds  365–402
*Ungrund*  379, 384, 385, 393. *See also* abyss
Unhappy Consciousness  418
"uniformity of nature" principle  141
unity  36, 259
    Husserl and  237
    Leibniz and  378
    self-consciousness and  43, 420
    time-consciousness and  237
"unity in multiplicity"  314
unity of apperception  245, 386–387
unity of consciousness  10, 105, 128–129, 156, 344, 351–352, 352n14, 395
    Aristotle and  265, 382
    Bergson and  179, 191n17, 238–239
    Fichte and  222
    Hegel and  265–266
    Husserl and  100, 237, 337–338
    idealism and  154–155n9
    Kant and  100, 208, 209–210, 221–222, 231–232n10, 344, 395
    Plotinus and  191n17
    Schopenhauer and  157, 222, 223, 224
    time-consciousness and  209–210, 233
    unity of meaning and  91
    Will and  224
unity of meaning, unity of consciousness and  91
universal essences  71n6
universal ideas  77–78
universality  96–98
universals  15, 64, 77, 87. *See also* Forms
University of California at San Diego  251
University of California at Santa Cruz  3
University of Chicago  3, 251
Unmoved Mover  8, 32, 133
unpredictability  190–191, 252–254, 255, 255–256, 276, 286, 388
utilitarianism  443

values
    Emerson and  85
    vs. facts  66–68
    world views (*Weltanschauungen*) and  9–10
Vienna Circle  138
Viet Nam War  423
violence  227, 248–249, 253–256, 275–277, 295–296, 298, 374, 375–376, 397, 400–401
volition. *See* free will; will, freedom of

War on Poverty  423
wax metaphor for mind  293
"way of ideas" argument  83, 86
will  215, 226
    autonomous  434
    circle-consciousness analogy and  224–225
    consciousness and  249
    creative spontaneity of  218
    eternal reality of  218–219
    Fichte and  385–386
    freedom of (see free will)
    as "intellectual intuition"  385–386

## SUBJECT INDEX

irrational   226–227, 365, 371, 395, 400
noumenal   216
phenomenal realm and   158–159
reason and   139–140
Schopenhauer and   146, 157–168,
    171, 201, 209–212, 216–223, 225–227, 241,
    246, 249, 365, 388–389, 399, 434, 435
the self and   241
self-consciousness and   216–219, 246

as thing-in-itself   216, 218, 224–225
unity of consciousness and   224
World and   222–223
withdrawal   397
words, vs. meanings   178–179
World, Will and   222–223
world views (*Weltanschauungen*)   9–10
World War I   412
World War II   227, 249, 401, 413

Printed in the United States
By Bookmasters